FreeCAD 1.1

Basics Tutorial

Tutorial Books

Send us an email to freecadtuts@gmail.com to get resource files

Contents

INTRODUCTION

FreeCAD, as a topic of learning, is very vast and has a broad scope. It is a package of many workbenches delivering exceptional value to enterprises. It offers a set of tools, which are easy-to-use to design, document, and simulate 3D models. Using this software, you can design your products free of cost.

This book provides a step-by-step approach for users to learn FreeCAD. It is aimed at those with no previous experience with FreeCAD. The user is guided by starting a FreeCAD session to creating parts, assemblies, and drawings. Each chapter has components explained with the help of real-world models.

Scope of this book

This book is written for students and engineers who are interested to learn FreeCAD for designing mechanical components and assemblies, and then create drawings.

This book provides a step-by-step approach to learning FreeCAD. The topics include Getting Started with FreeCAD, Basic Part Modeling, Creating Assemblies, Additional Modeling Tools, Creating Drawings, Sheet Metal parts, and CAM overview.

Chapter 1 introduces FreeCAD. The user interface and terminology are discussed in this chapter.

Chapter 2 takes you through the creation of your first FreeCAD model. You create simple parts.

Chapter 3 teaches you to create assemblies. It explains the Top-down and Bottom-up approaches for designing an assembly. You create an assembly using the Bottom-up approach.

Chapter 4: In this chapter, you learn the sketching tools.

Chapter 5: In this chapter, you learn additional modeling tools to create complex models.

Chapter 6 teaches you to create drawings of the models created in the earlier chapters.

Chapter 7 teaches you to create a sheet metal model.

Chapter 8 teaches you simulate manufacturing operations and generate toolpaths.

Chapter 9 teaches you add assembly joints between the components of an assembly.

Chapter 1: Getting Started with FreeCAD

This tutorial book brings in the most commonly used features of FreeCAD.

In this chapter, you will:

- Understand the FreeCAD terminology
- Start a new file
- Understand the User Interface
- Understand different workbenches in FreeCAD

In FreeCAD, you create 3D parts and use them to create 2D drawings and 3D assemblies.

FreeCAD is Feature Based. Features are shapes that are combined to build a part. You can modify these shapes individually.

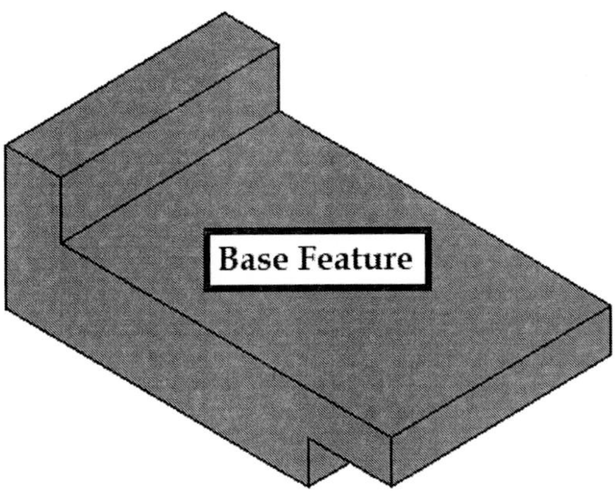

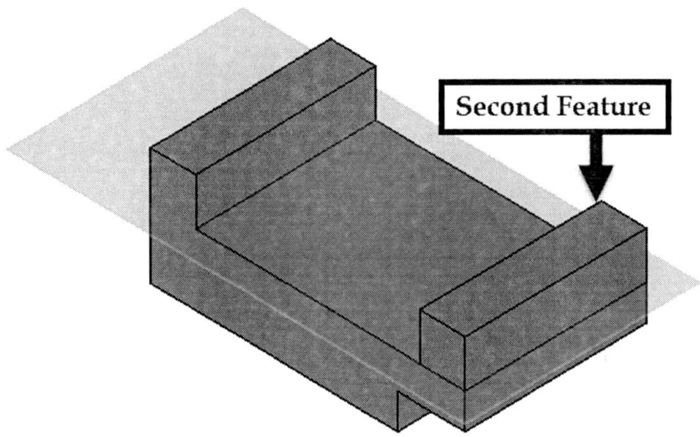

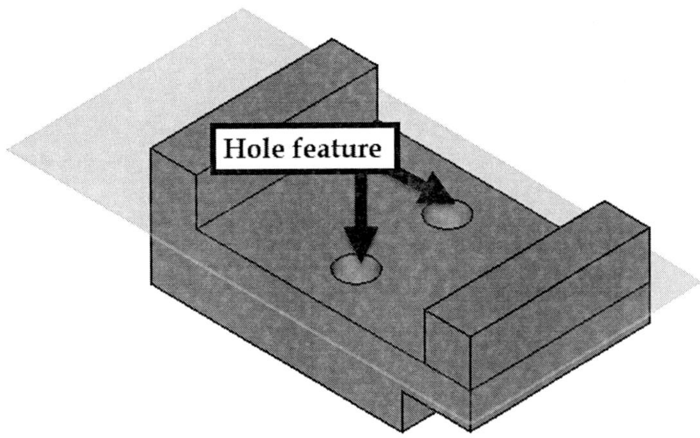

Most of the features are sketch-based. A sketch is a 2D profile and can be extruded, revolved, or swept along a path to create features.

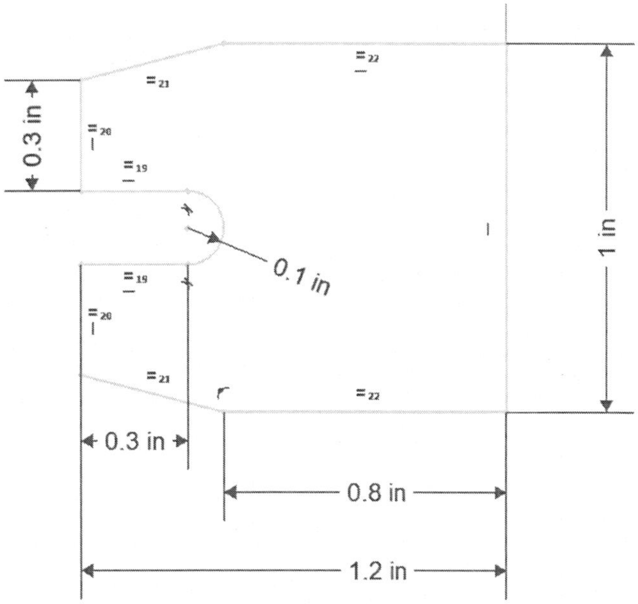

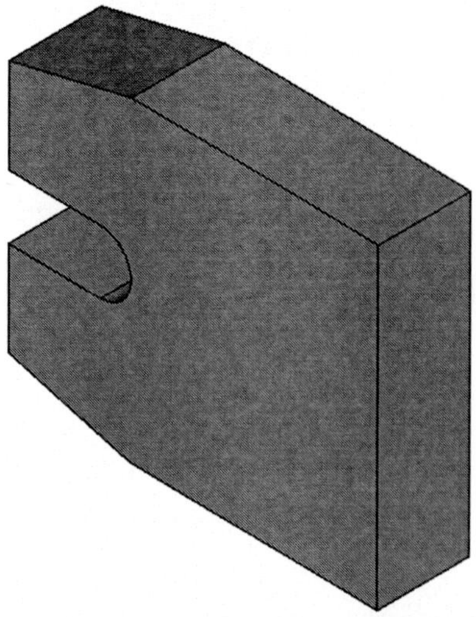

FreeCAD is parametric. You can specify standard parameters between the elements. Changing these parameters changes the size and shape of the part. For example, see the design of the body of a flange before and after modifying the parameters of its features.

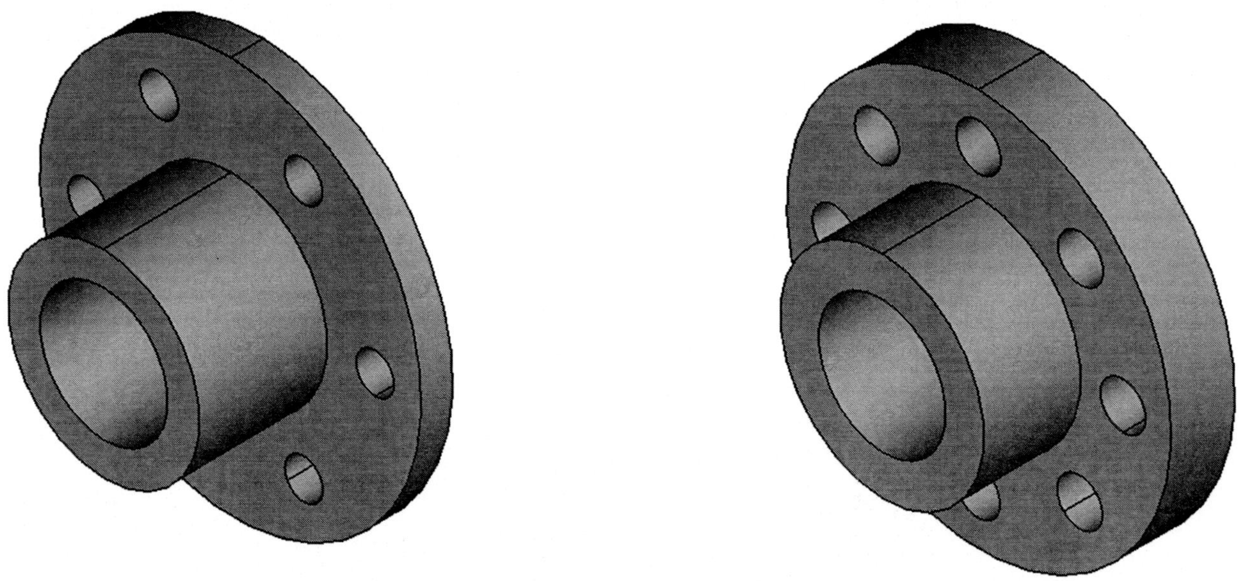

Downloading and Installing FreeCAD 1.1 on Windows

1. Go to the www.freecad.org
2. Click the **Download Now** button.
3. Double-click on the **x86_64 installer** button in the **Windows** section.
4. Specify the location of the downloaded file and click **Save** on the **Save As** dialog.
5. Double-click on the FreeCAD_1.1.1-Windows-x86_64-py311-installer file.
6. Click **Yes** on the **User Control** dialog.
7. Click **Next** on the **FreeCAD 1.1.1 Setup** dialog.

8. Click **Next** to accept the License agreement
9. Set the users for whom FreeCAD is to be installed. If you have no privilege to install for all users, select **Intall Just for me**.
10. Normally there is no need to change the settings. Click **Next** to go to the next settings
11. Click **Next** twice and then click **Install**.
12. After the installation has been completed and the dialog displayed **Completed FreeCAD 1.1 Setup**, click **Finish** to finish all installation process.

Downloading and Installing FreeCAD 1.1 on MacOS

1. Go to the www.freecad.org
2. Click the **Download Now** button.
3. Double-click on the desired disk image from the **Mac** section.

4. Once the download is complete, open the .dmg file.
5. Drag and drop the FreeCAD icon into the **Applications** folder.

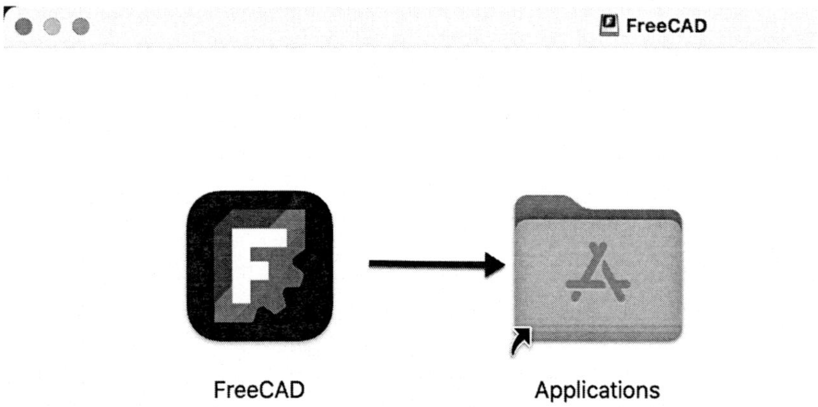

6. FreeCAD is now installed and ready to use.

Starting FreeCAD

- Click the Windows icon on the taskbar.
- Click **F > FreeCAD 1.1 > FreeCAD**.
- On the ribbon, click **File > New** to start a new part file.

If you are working in MacOS, click the **Lauchpad** button on the **Dock**. Next, click on the **FreeCAD** icon.

Notice these essential features of the FreeCAD window.

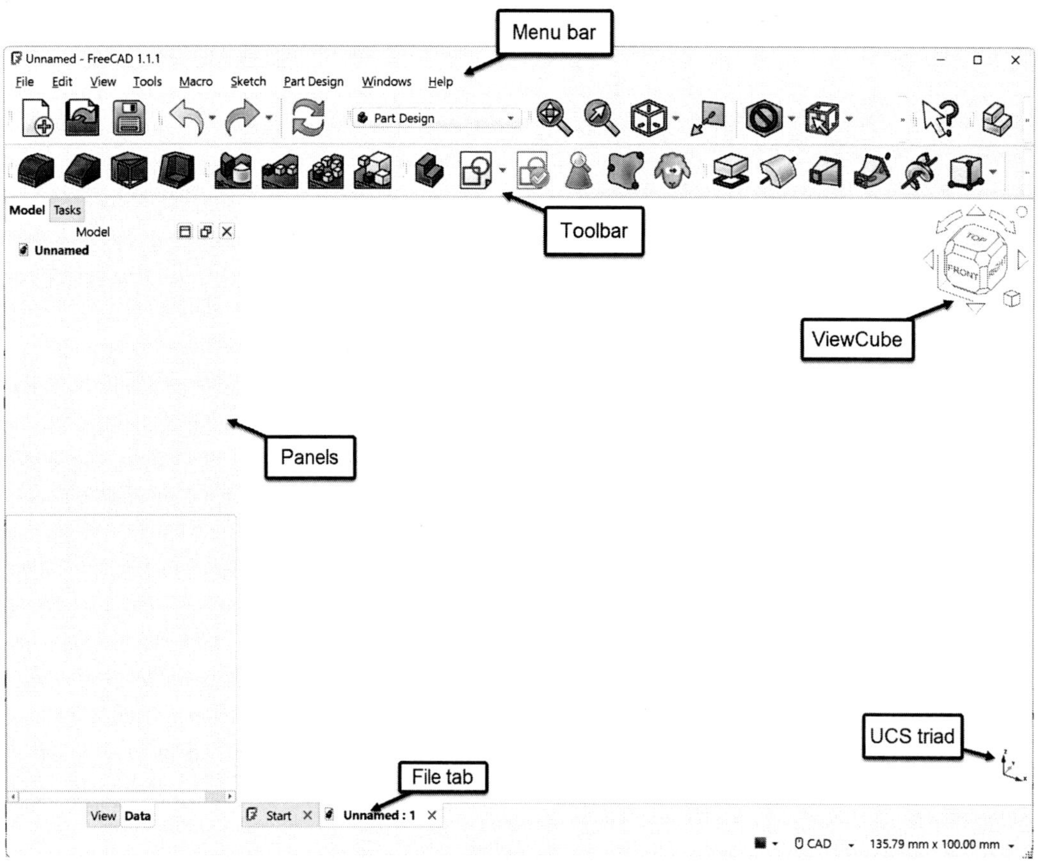

Workbenches in FreeCAD

A workbench is a set of tools and environments that can be used to create parts, assemblies, drawings, and so on. There are many workbenches available in FreeCAD. You can activate different workbenches by using the **Workbenches** drop-down located on the top-left corner.

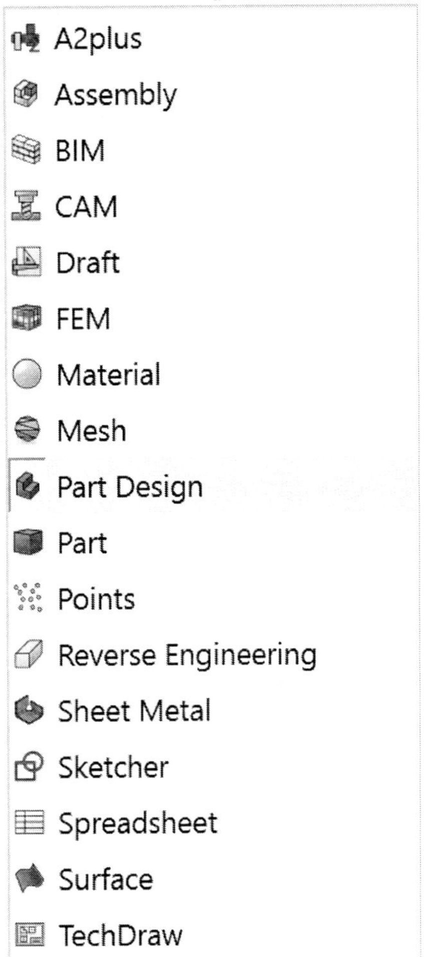

User Interface

Various components of the user interface are discussed next.

Menu bar

The menu bar is located at the top of the window. It has various options (menu titles). When you click on a menu title, a drop-down appears. Select an option from this drop-down.

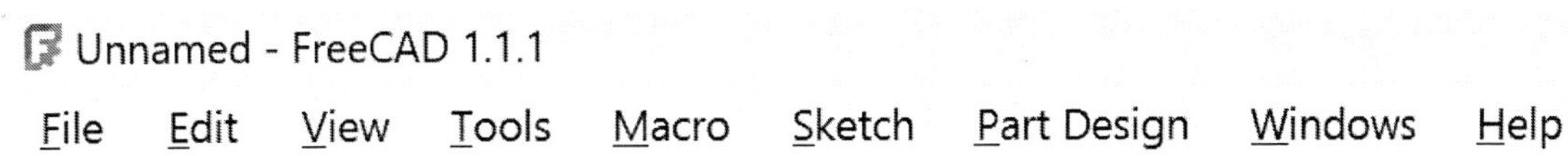

File Menu

The **File Menu** appears when you click on the **File** option located at the top left corner of the window. This menu contains the options to open, print, export, save, and close a file.

Toolbar

A toolbar is a set of tools, which help you to perform various operations. Various toolbars available in different workbenches are given next.

Start Toolbars

Workbench

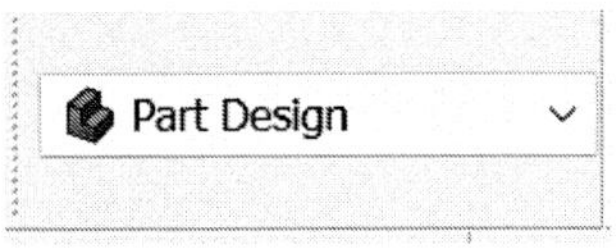

This toolbar has a drop-down to change the workbench.

Macro

This toolbar has tools to create and execute macros.

File

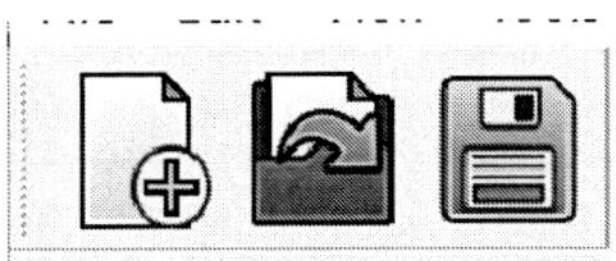

This toolbar has tools to create, open, and save files.

Edit

This toolbar has options to undo, redo, and recompute.

View

This toolbar has tools to manipulate the view of the model.

Structure 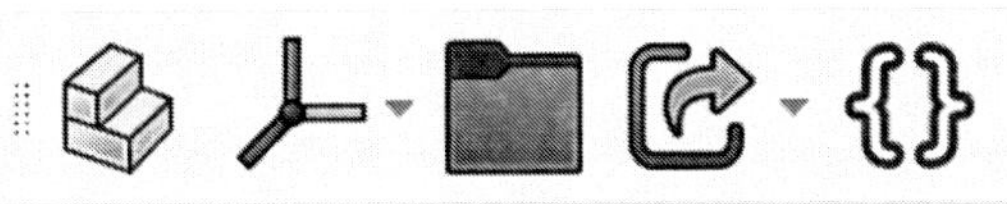 It has tools to create or open part files.
Sketcher Toolbars
Edit mode  This toolbar has tools to start or exit a sketch.
Geometries 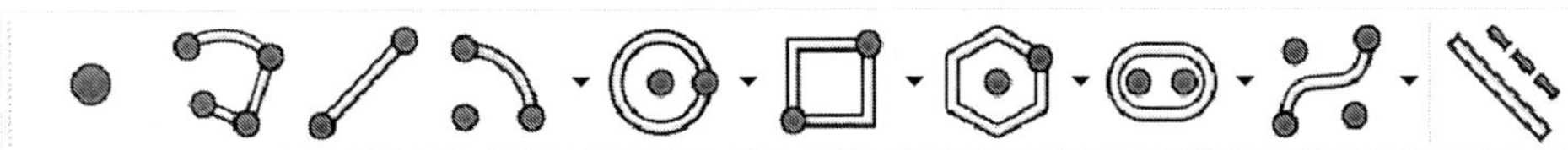 This toolbar has tools to New Sketch elements.
Constraints  This toolbar has tools to apply constraints between sketch elements.
Sketcher B-spline tools 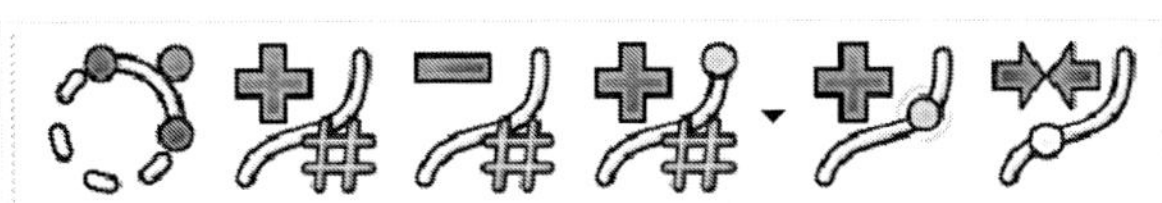 This toolbar has tools to create and edit B-splines.

<table>
<tr><td>

Visual Helpers

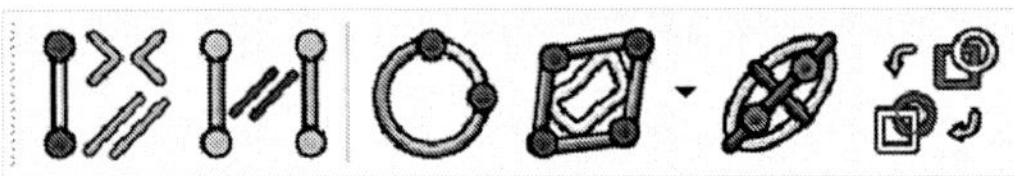

This toolbar has various selection tools and options that aid you in creating sketch elements very fast. It also has tool to hide or show constraints.

</td></tr>
<tr><td>

Sketcher tools

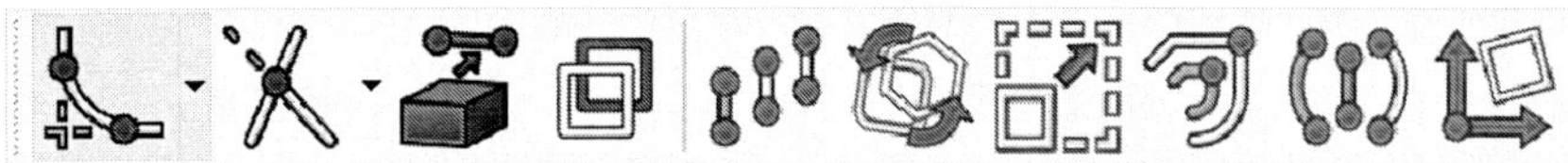

This toolbar has sketch editing tools

</td></tr>
<tr><td>

Part Design Toolbars

</td></tr>
</table>

Part Design Helper Features

This toolbar has tools to create new bodies, datum points, axis, datum planes, and clones. You can also create a new sketch.

Part Design Modeling Features

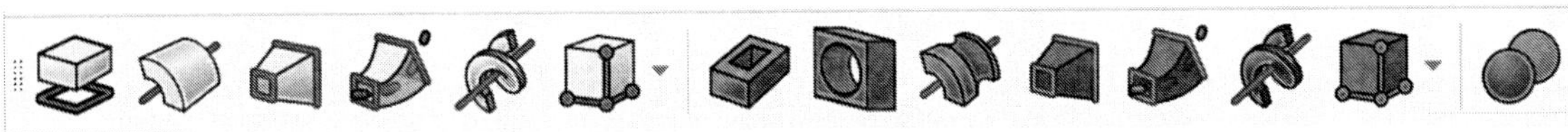

This toolbar has commands to create solid features based on the sketch geometry.

Part Design Dress-Up Features

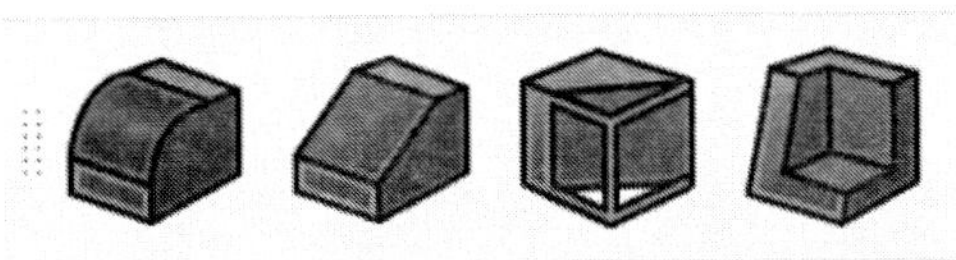

This toolbar has commands to add fillets, chamfers, drafts, and thickness to the existing solid features.

Part Design Transformation Features

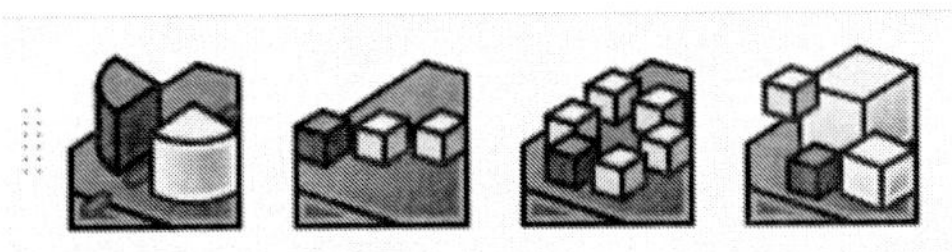

This toolbar has commands to mirror or pattern the existing solid features.

Assembly Toolbars

Assembly

This toolbar has tools to create components or insert existing components into an assembly.

Assembly Joints

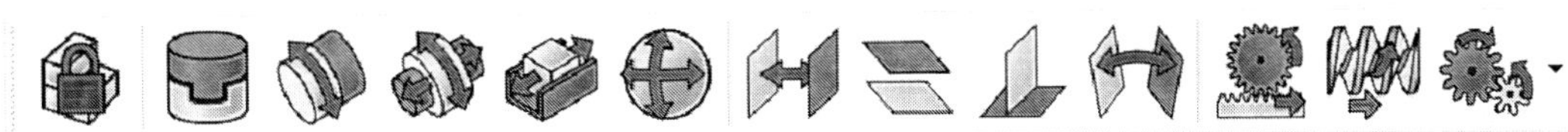

This toolbar also has tools to apply constraints between components.

Assembly

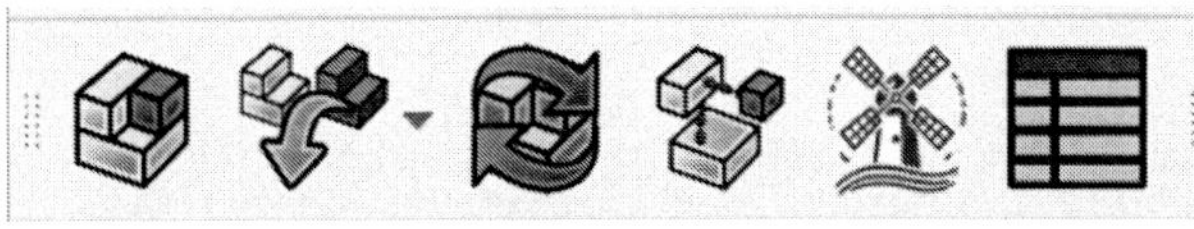

This toolbar also has tools to start an assembly, insert components, solve the assembly and view bill of materials.

TechDraw Toolbars

TechDraw Views

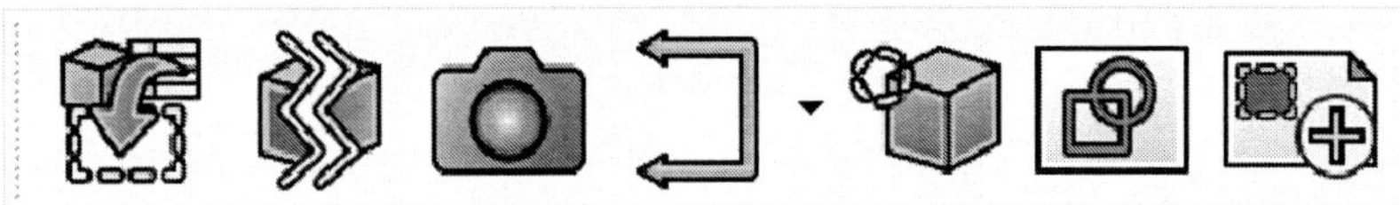

This toolbar has tools to generate standard views of a 3D geometry.

TechDraw Pages

The tools on this toolbar help you to add a new page.

TechDraw Dimensions

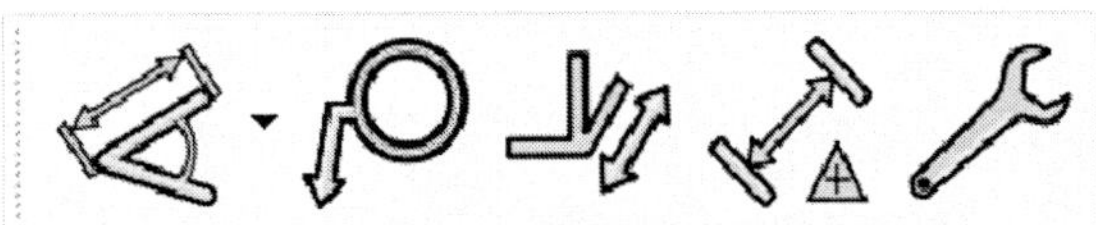

The tools on this toolbar help you to add dimensions to the drawing views.

TechDraw File Access

This toolbar helps you to export the drawing page to the SVG or DXF format.

TechDraw Decoration

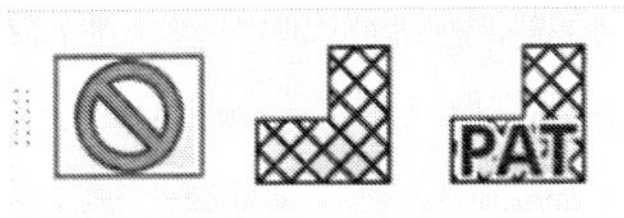

The tools on this toolbar help you to change the hatch patterns and insert images.

TechDraw Attributes

The tools on this toolbar help you to modify the attributes of the dimensions.

TechDraw Centerlines

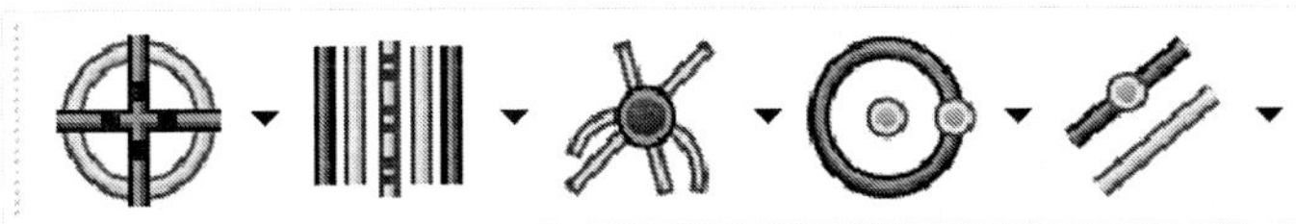

The tools on this toolbar help you to add centerlines and centermarks to the drawing views.

TechDraw Annotations

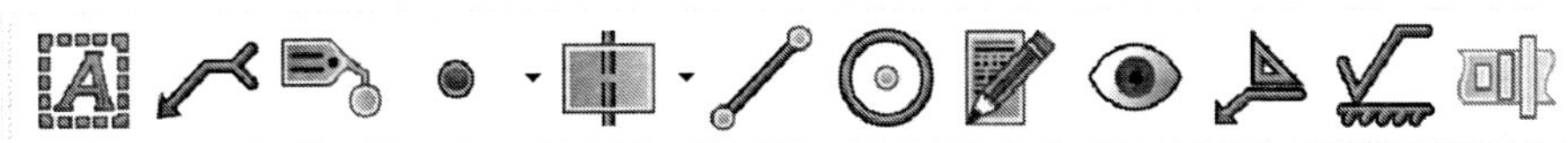

The tools on this toolbar help you to add annotations such as text, leaders, surface symbols, and so on.

TechDraw Extend Dimensions

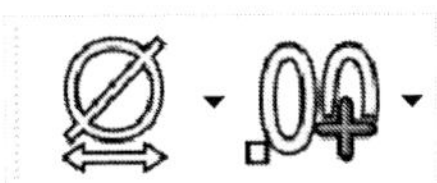

The tools on this toolbar help you to additional types of dimensions to the drawing view such as chain dimensions, coordinate dimensions, chamfer dimensions, and so on.

Sheet Metal Toolbars
Sheet Metal 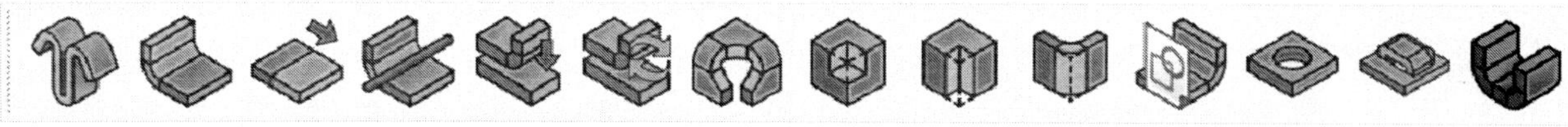 The tools on this toolbar help you to create a sheetmetal model.
FEM Toolbars
Model 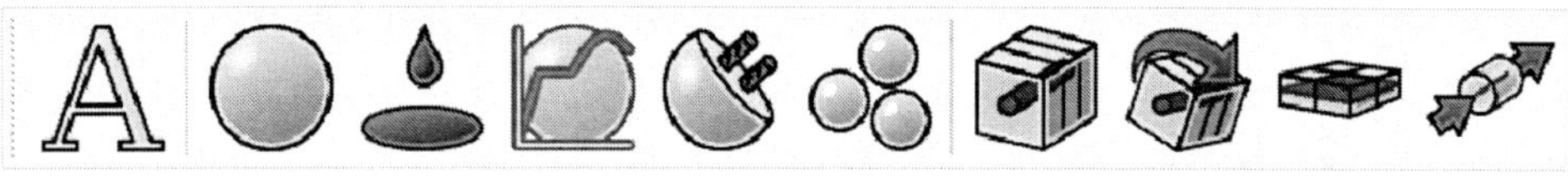 It has tools to define materials and element geometry of the model.

Mechanical boundary conditions and loads

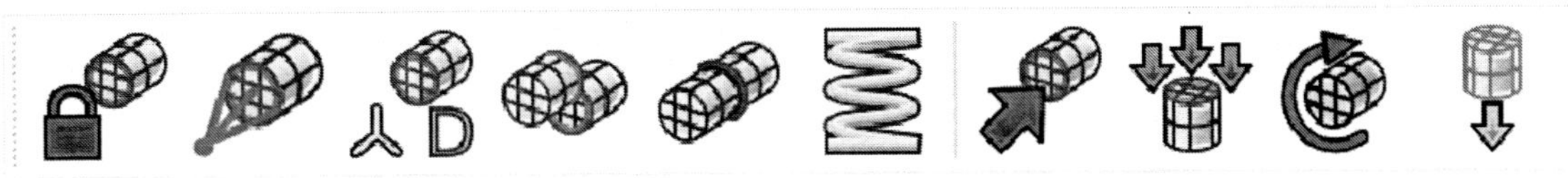

It has tools to define mechanical constriants.

Thermal boundary conditions and loads

It has tools to add thermal constraints.

Mesh

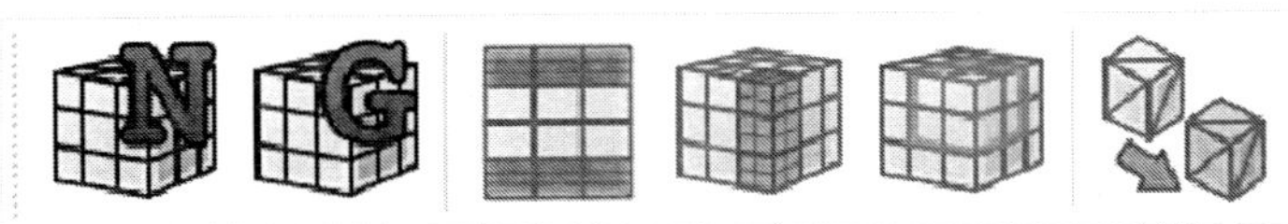

It has tools to mesh the model.

Fluid boundary conditions

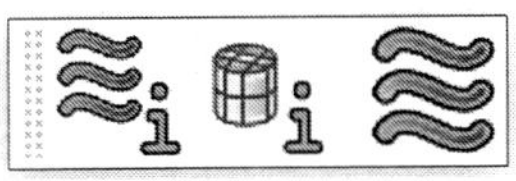

It has tools to add fluid constraints.

Electromagnetic boundary conditions

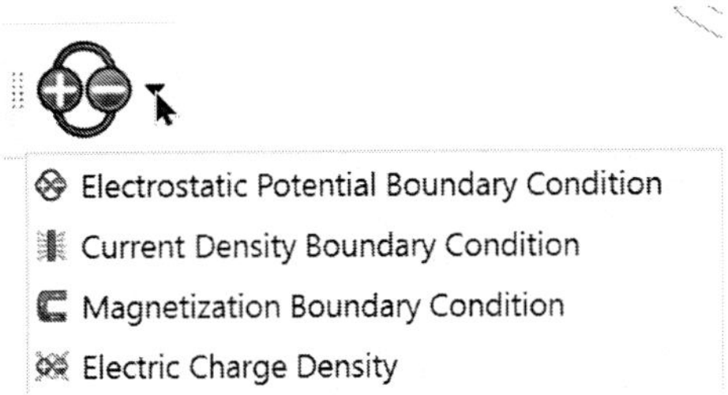

It has tools to add electrostatic constraints.

Solve

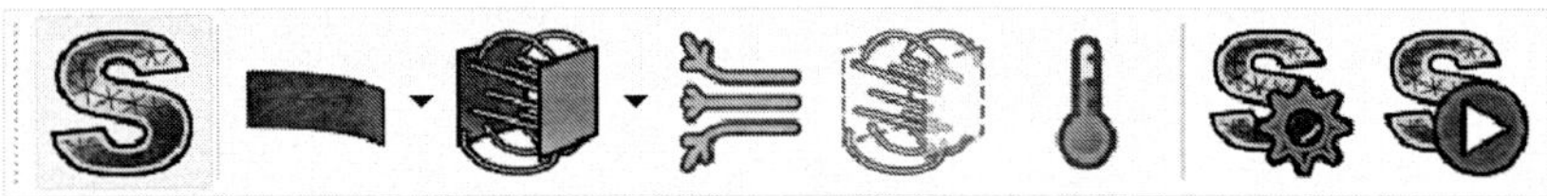

It has tools to perform the finite element analysis.

Results

It has tools display the results of finite element analysis.

Utilities

It has tools to clip and unclip faces.

CAM Toolbars

Project Setup

It has tools to create a job and export G-Code.

Tool Commands

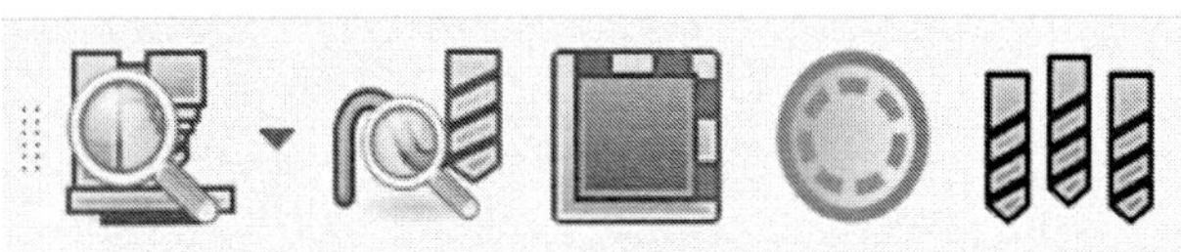

It has tools to create and manage tools.

New Operations

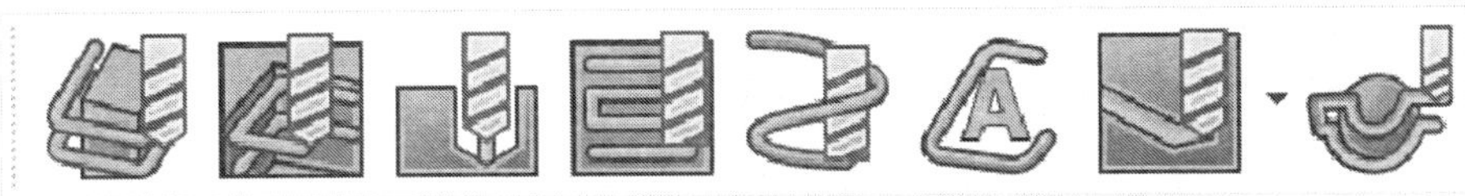

It has tools to create machining operations.

Path Modification

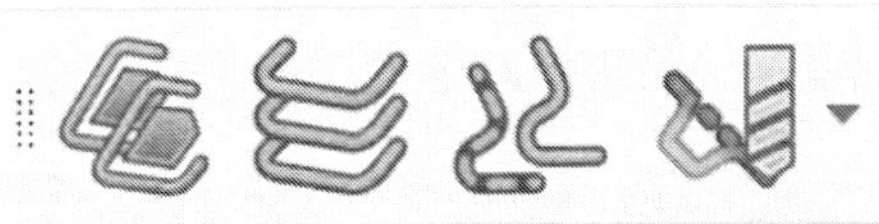

It has tools to modify tool paths.

You can hide or show toolbars in the application window. To do this, click **View > Toolbars**, and then select the toolbar name from the list displayed.

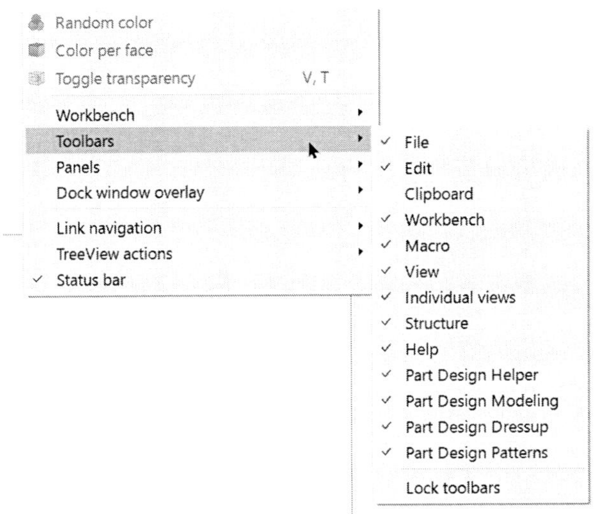

Status bar

The Status bar is available below the graphics window. It shows the action taken while using the commands.

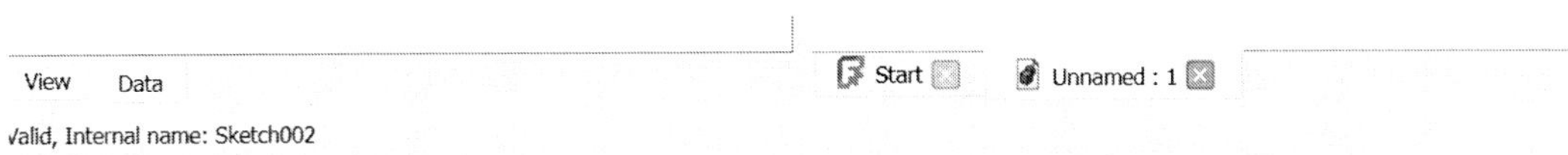

Model panel

It contains the list of operations carried while constructing a part.

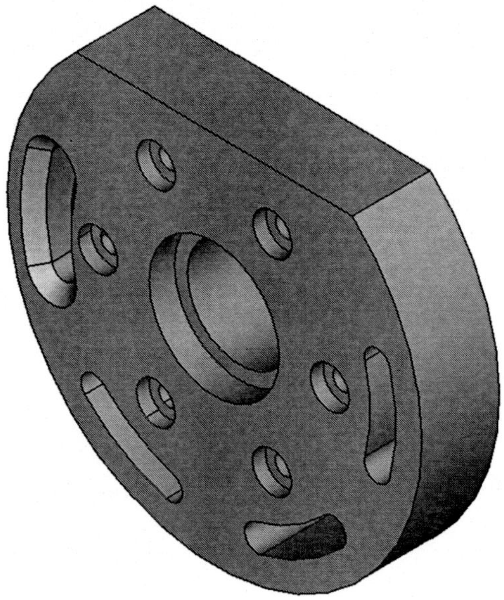

Dialog

When you click any tool in FreeCAD, the dialog related to it appears in the **Tasks** panel. A dialog has various options. The following figure shows various components of a dialog.

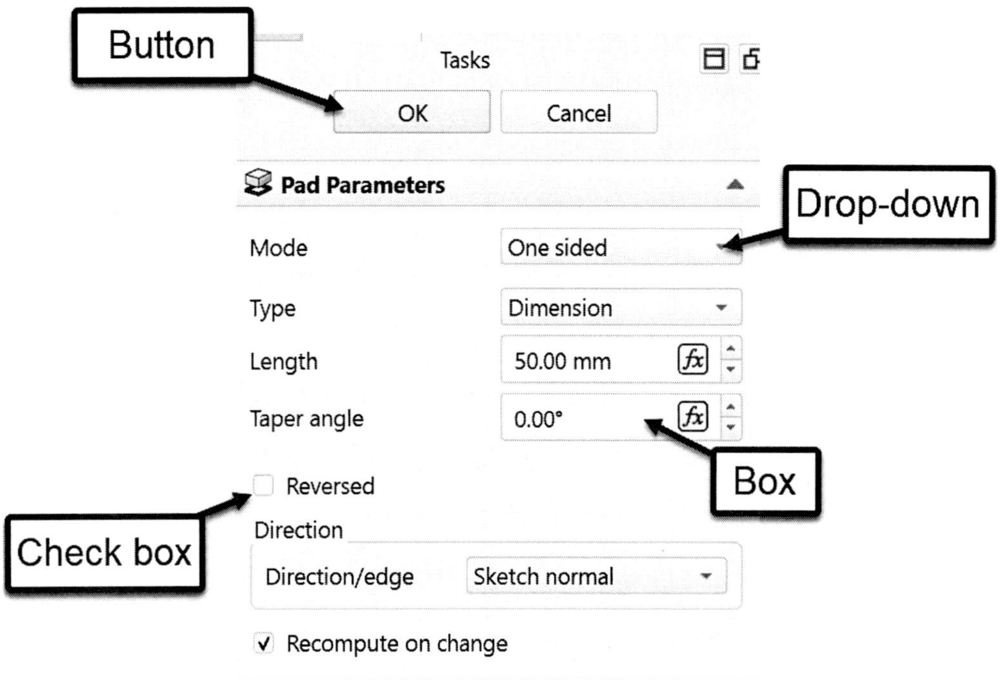

This book uses the default options on the dialog.

Navigation Styles

FreeCAD provides you with different types of mouse navigation styles: **OpenInventor**, **CAD**, **Revit**, **Blender**, **MayaGesture**, **TinkerCAD**, **Touchpad**, **Gesture**, and **OpenCascade**. You can select the desired navigation style from the drop-down located at the bottom right corner.

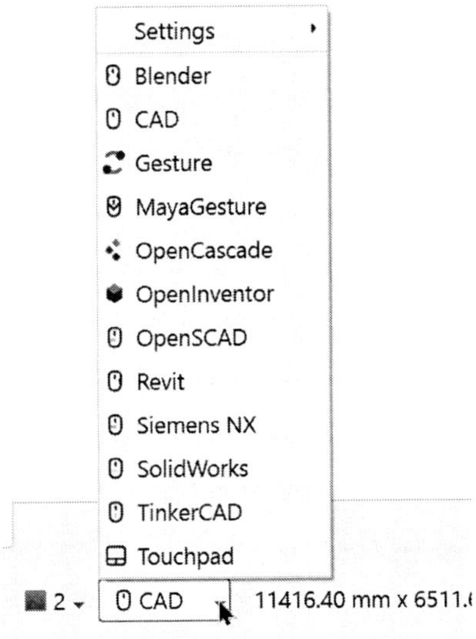

This book uses the CAD Navigation Style for your mouse. Select the **CAD** option from the **Navigation Styles** drop-down. Next, place the mouse cursor on the drop-down; the various mouse functions are displayed.

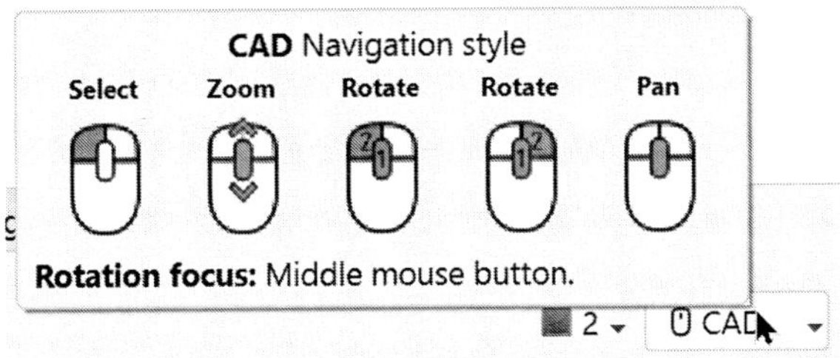

Background

To change the background color of the window, click **Edit > Preferences** on the Menu bar. On the **Preferences** dialog, click **Display > Colors** on the left side. Next, set the colors for various element types.

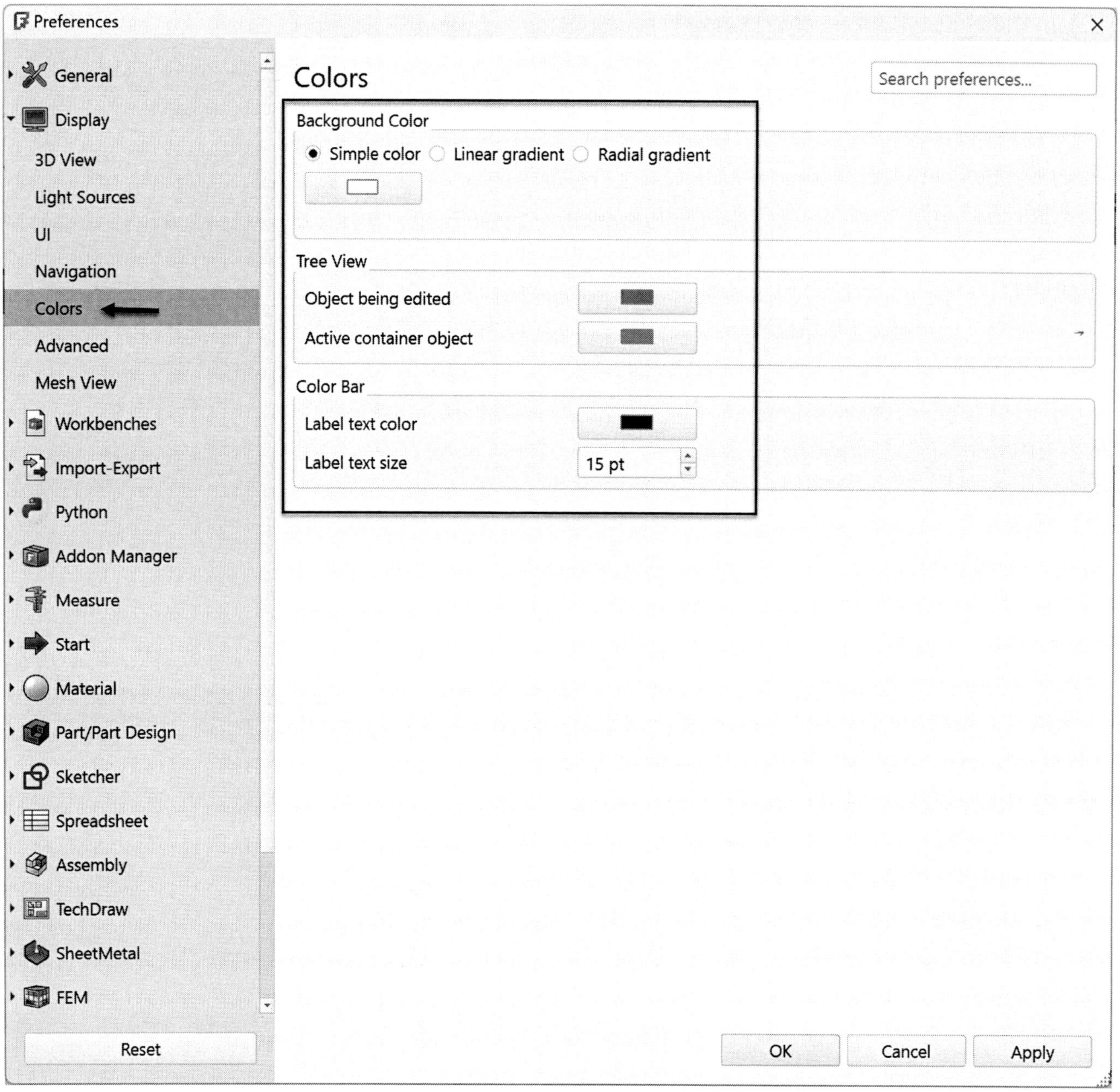

To change the color of sketch elements, click **Sketcher** > **Appearance** on the left side. Next, change the **Sketch colors**. Click **OK** to apply the changes.

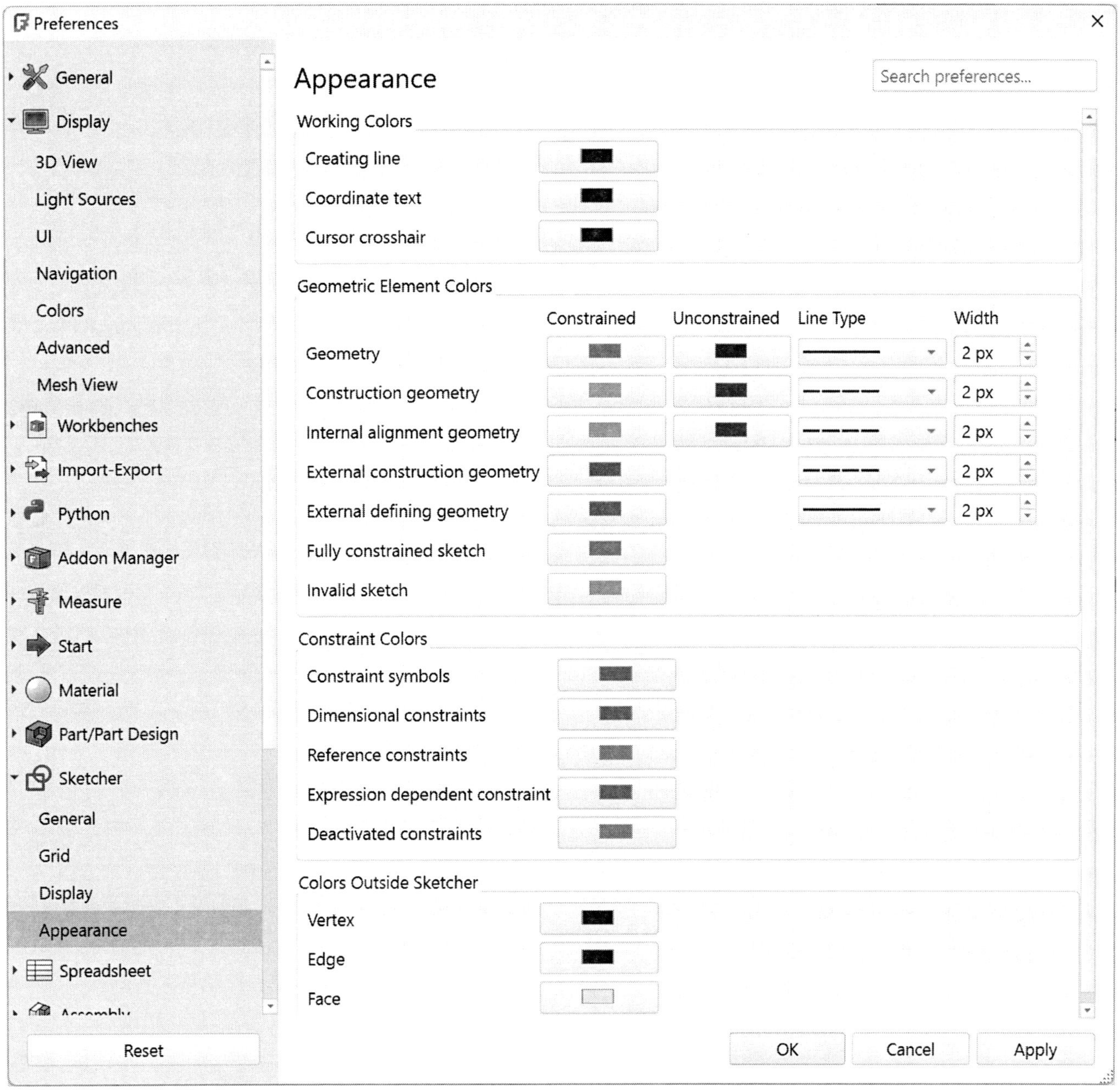
Preferences
General
Display
3D View
Light Sources
UI
Navigation
Colors
Advanced
Mesh View
Workbenches
Import-Export
Python
Addon Manager
Measure
Start
Material
Part/Part Design
Sketcher
General
Grid
Display
Appearance
Spreadsheet
Reset
Appearance
Search preferences...
Working Colors
Creating line
Coordinate text
Cursor crosshair
Geometric Element Colors
Constrained
Unconstrained
Line Type
Width
Geometry
Construction geometry
Internal alignment geometry
External construction geometry
External defining geometry
Fully constrained sketch
Invalid sketch
2 px
2 px
2 px
2 px
2 px
Constraint Colors
Constraint symbols
Dimensional constraints
Reference constraints
Expression dependent constraint
Deactivated constraints
Colors Outside Sketcher
Vertex
Edge
Face
OK
Cancel
Apply

Chapter 2: Part Modeling Basics

This chapter takes you through the creation of your first FreeCAD model. You create simple parts:

In this chapter, you will:

- New Sketches
- Create a base feature
- Add another feature to it
- Add fillets
- Shell the model
- Create Pocket features

TUTORIAL 1

This tutorial takes you through the creation of your first FreeCAD model.

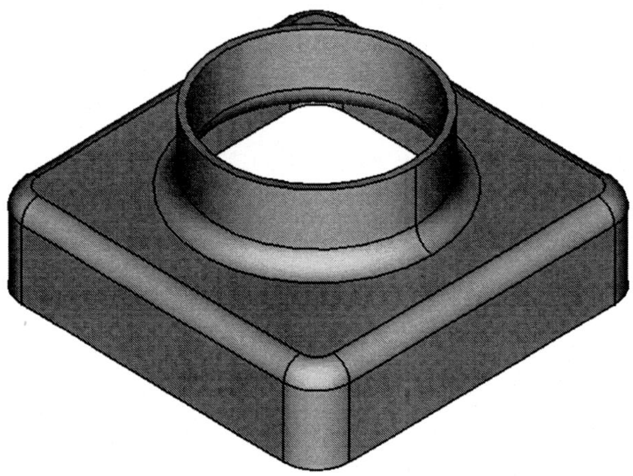

Starting a New Part File

1. To start a new part file, click **File > New Document** on the Menu Bar (or) click the **New Document** icon on the **File** toolbar.

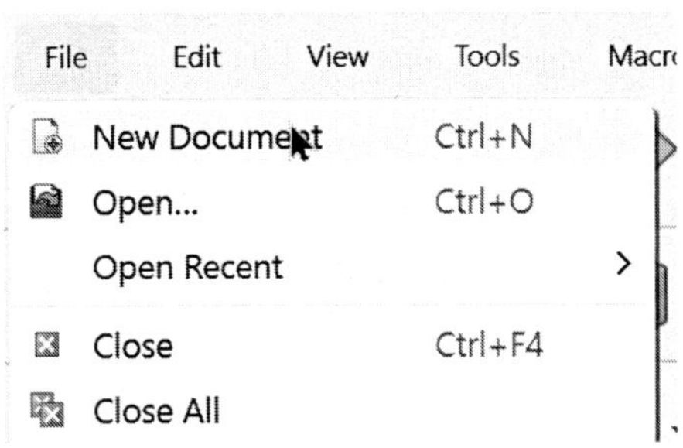

(or)

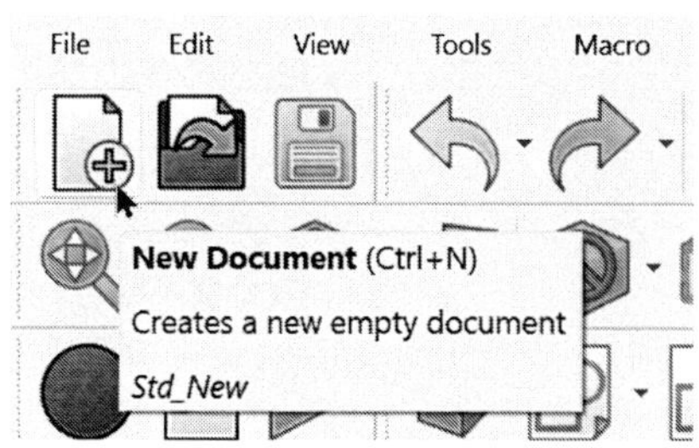

A new model window appears.

2. On the **Workbench** toolbar, select **Workbench** drop-down > **Part Design** (or) select **View > Workbench > Part Design** on the Menu bar.

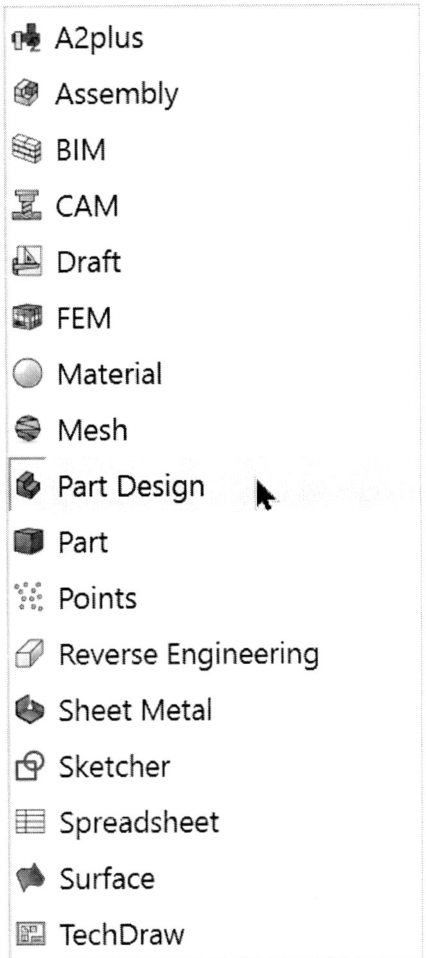

(or)

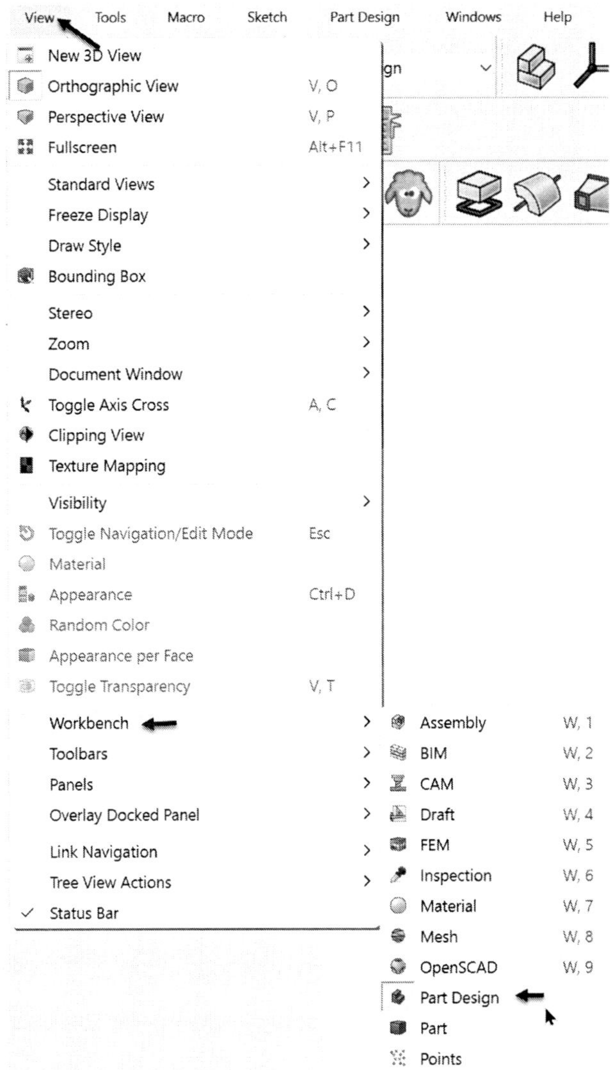

Starting a Sketch

Before you begin sketching, it is recommended to ensure that your FreeCAD settings match the settings used in this tutorial. Follow the next steps to adjust the settings.

1. Click **Edit > Preferences** on the Menu bar. If you are working on MacOS, then click **FreeCAD > Preferences** on the title bar. This will open the **Preferences** dialog box, where you can customize various settings for your FreeCAD workspace.
2. On the **Preferences** dialog box, click the **General** option at the left side to access the general settings for your FreeCAD workspace.

3. Select **Default unit system > Standard (mm/kg/s/degree)**. This setting ensures that your FreeCAD workspace uses the standard units of measurement (millimeters, kilograms, seconds, and degrees).
4. Type **2** in the **Number of decimals** box. This setting determines the number of decimal places displayed for measurements and dimensions in your FreeCAD workspace.
5. On the **Edit Preferences** dialog, click Sketcher > Grid. In the **Grid Settings** section, ensure the **Grid** checkbox is checked. This activates the grid display inside the Sketcher workspace, helping you align and position your sketch elements accurately.
6. Enable the **Grid auto spacing** checkbox directly below the **Grid** option. When this option is selected, the grid spacing adjusts automatically according to the current zoom level of your view, ensuring a consistent and readable grid at all times.
7. Set the Grid Spacing by confirming the value in the **Grid spacing** box reads 10.00 mm. This value defines the distance between two consecutive minor grid lines and serves as the base spacing unit when Grid auto spacing is active.
8. Click **OK** to save all settings and close the Preferences dialog box. These grid settings will help you work with accurate measurements and spatial alignment throughout your sketch.
9. To start a new sketch, click **Part Design Helper Features** toolbar **> New Sketch**  (or) click **Sketch > New Sketch** on the Menu bar. This step is done to initiate the sketching process and create a new workspace for your design.

10. Select the **XY-Plane**, and then click **OK** (or) select the XY plane from the graphics window. The sketch starts. This step is necessary to define the plane on which you will be sketching your design.

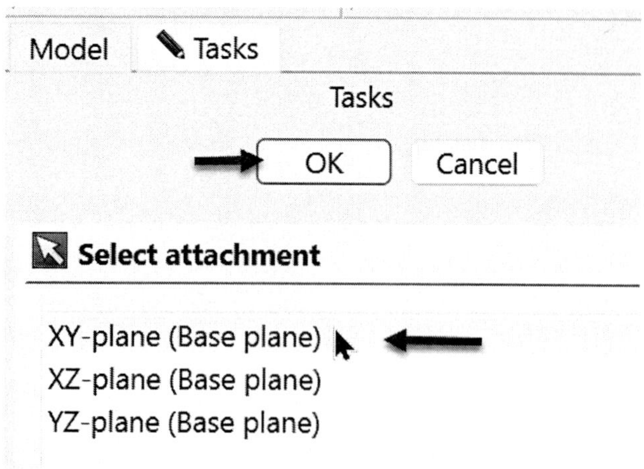

(or)

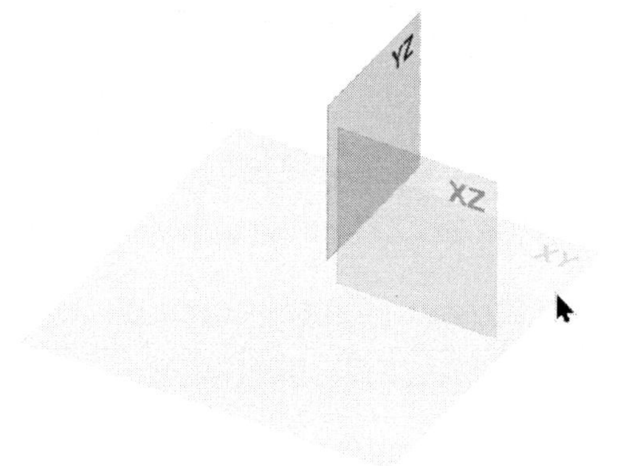

After completing these steps, you will notice the following:

- The sketch origin appears at the center. This indicates the reference point for your sketch and helps in positioning and aligning your design elements
- The **Edit mode, Geometries, Constraints, Sketcher tools, B-spline tools,** and **Sketcher visual** toolbars are displayed. These toolbars provide you with various options and tools for creating and editing your sketch.
- "**Empty Sketch**" appears in the **Sketch Edit** section in the **Tasks** panel. This message indicates that your sketch is currently empty and does not contain any geometries or constraints.

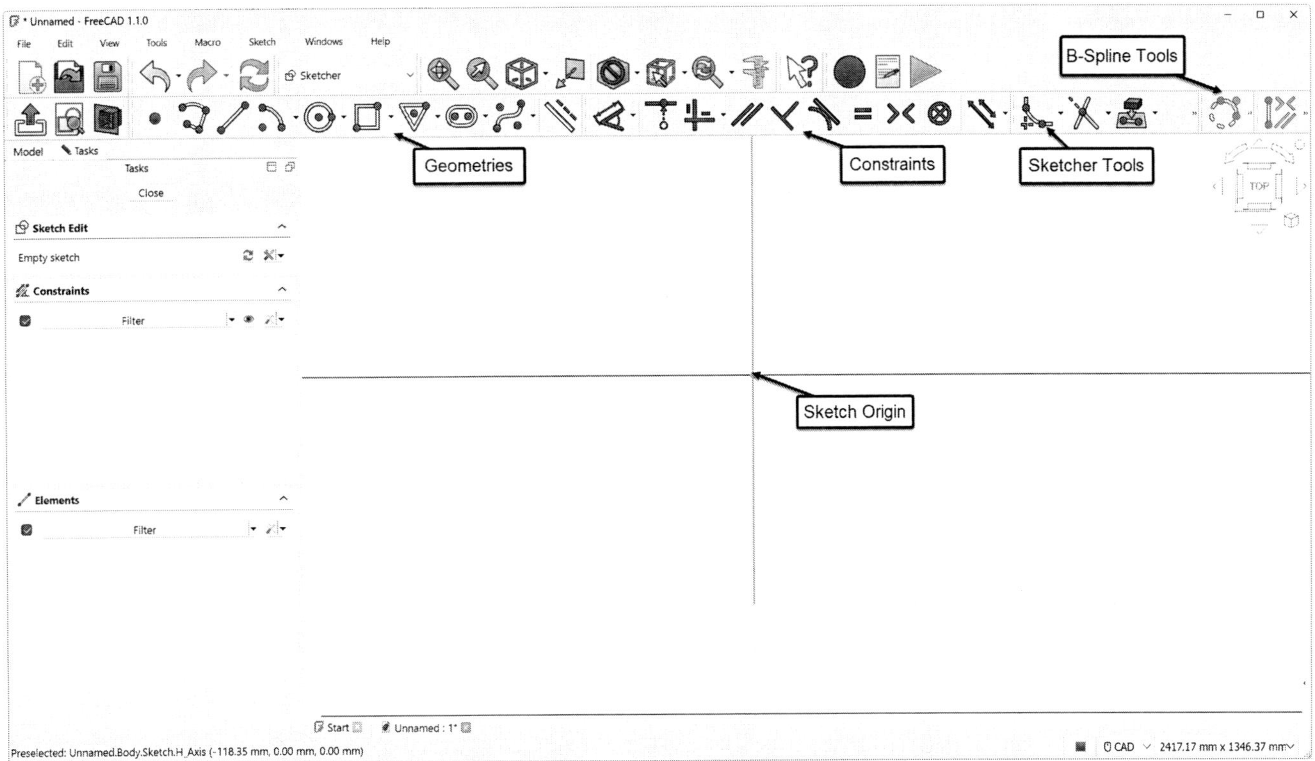

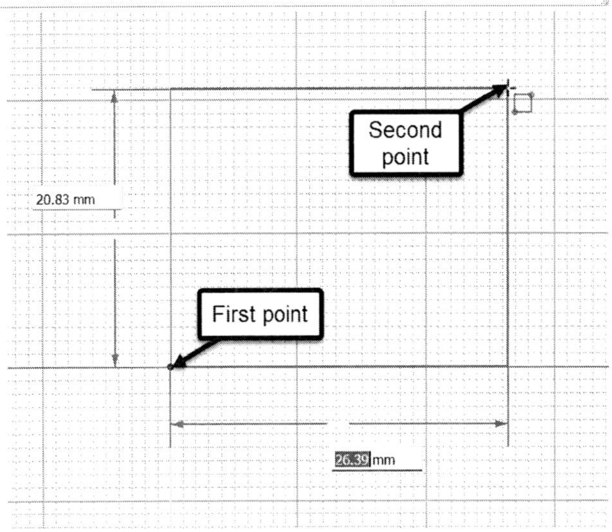

In this tutorial, the first feature is an extruded feature from a sketched rectangular profile. You begin by sketching the rectangle.

11. On the **Geometries** toolbar, click the **Rectangle** icon (or) click **Sketch > Geometries > Rectangle**.

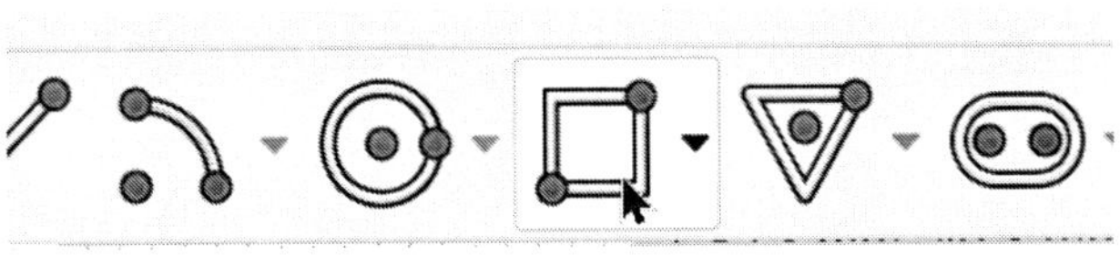

12. Move the cursor to the sketch origin located at the center of the graphics window, and then click on it.
13. Drag the cursor towards the top right corner, and then click to create a rectangle. This step creates a rectangle by dragging the cursor from the origin towards the top right corner and clicking to set the size of the rectangle.

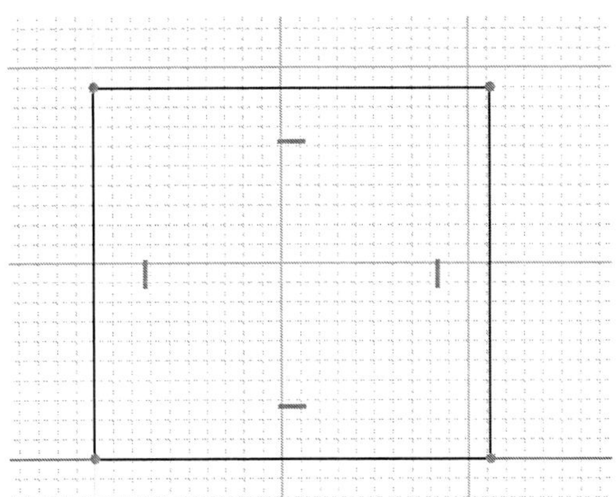

Adding Constraints

In this section, you specify the size of the sketched rectangle by adding constraints. As you add constraints, the sketch can attain any one of the following states:

Fully Constrained Sketch

- A fully constrained sketch has every element exactly defined. These definitions include dimensions, angles, distances, and relationships between lines.
- Applying enough rules and measurements leaves the drawing with zero degrees of freedom. The sketch becomes locked and retains its exact shape and size regardless of other design adjustments.
- FreeCAD highlights fully constrained entities in green. This visual cue confirms the geometry is locked in place and will only change if you edit the specific measurements.
- Fully defining a sketch guarantees design precision and prevents unexpected geometry shifts during later solid modeling steps.

Under Constrained Sketch

An under constrained sketch requires more measurements to define its exact geometry. The drawing retains degrees of freedom, allowing you to move or adjust certain elements manually.

FreeCAD displays entities with insufficient definitions in white or black, depending on your background color. This flexibility allows you to drag lines and experiment with the shape before locking it down.

Leaving a sketch under constrained can cause geometry to shift out of place when you alter other parts of the 3D model.

Redundant Constraints

Redundant constraints are duplicate rules added to a sketch that is already fully defined. FreeCAD includes an Auto remove redundants option to delete these duplicates. You can select this tool from the Settings menu located in the Constraints section of the Tasks panel. Once activated, the software automatically deletes any extra measurements you attempt to apply to a locked sketch.

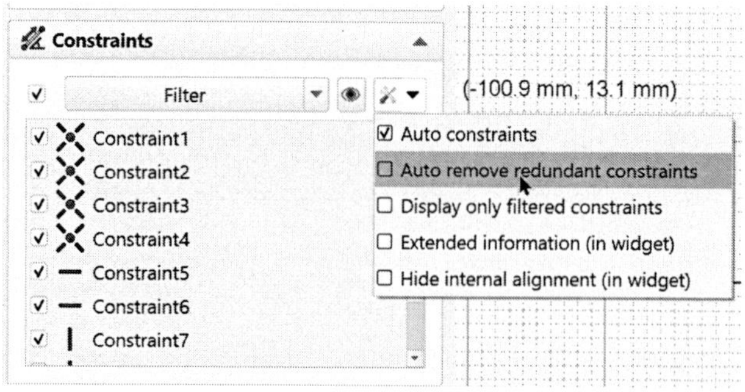

1. Click **Constraints** toolbar > **Dimension** drop-down > **Vertical Dimension** (or) click **Sketch > Constraints > Vertical Dimension** on the menu bar.
2. Select the right vertical line of the rectangle.
3. Enter **100** in the **Length** box of the **Insert Length** dialog and click **OK**. This step sets the length of the selected line.
4. Click **Constraints** toolbar toolbar > **Dimension** drop-down > **Horizontal Dimension** (or) click **Sketch > Constraints > Horizontal Dimension** on the menu bar.
5. Select the bottom horizontal line of the rectangle.
6. Enter **100** in the **Length** box of the **Insert Length** dialog and click the **OK** button. This step sets the length of the selected line.

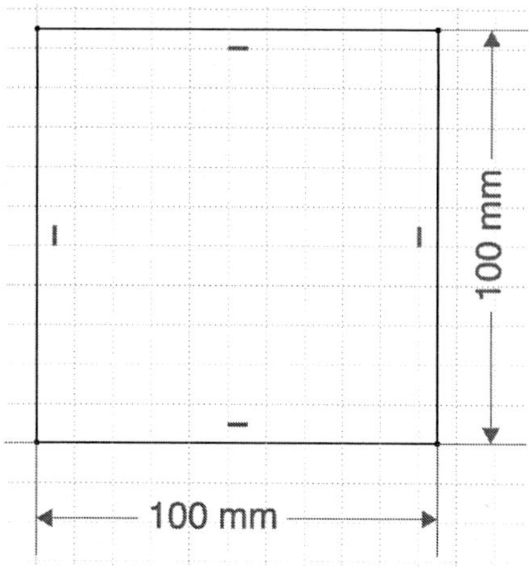

7. Press **Esc** to deactivate the **Horizontal Dimension** tool.
8. To display the entire rectangle at full size and to center it in the graphics area, use one of the following methods:

   - Click **Fit All** on the **View** toolbar.
   - Click **View > Standard Views > Fit All** on the Menu bar.

9. Click **Close** on the **Tasks** panel.

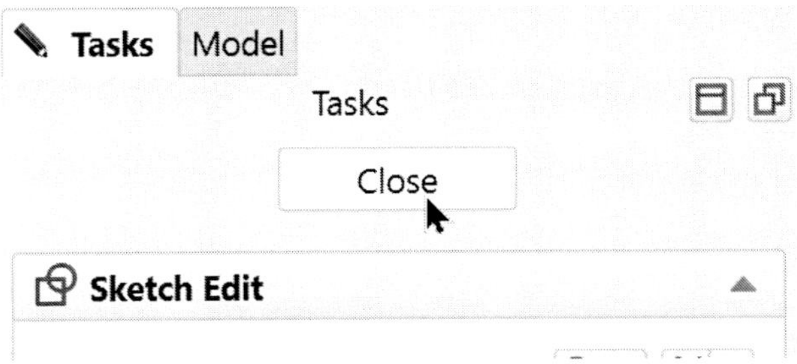

10. Again, click **Fit All** on the **View** toolbar.

Creating the Base Feature

The first feature in any part is called a base feature. You now create this feature by extruding the sketched rectangle.

1. Click **Part Design Modeling Features Features** toolbar **> Pad** (or) click **Part Design > Pad** on the Menu bar.
2. In the 3D view, a semi-transparent green preview of the extruded solid will appear. You will also see a red directional arrow in the center of the sketch. You can click and drag this red arrow to manually adjust the extrusion depth, or use the **Pad Parameters** dialog for exact measurements.

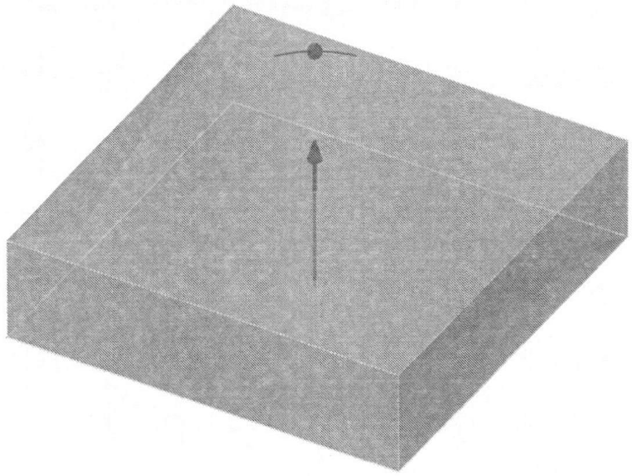

3. Type-in 25 in the **Length** box available on the **Pad parameters** dialog on the **Tasks** panel.
4. Click **OK** on the **Tasks** panel to create the pad feature.

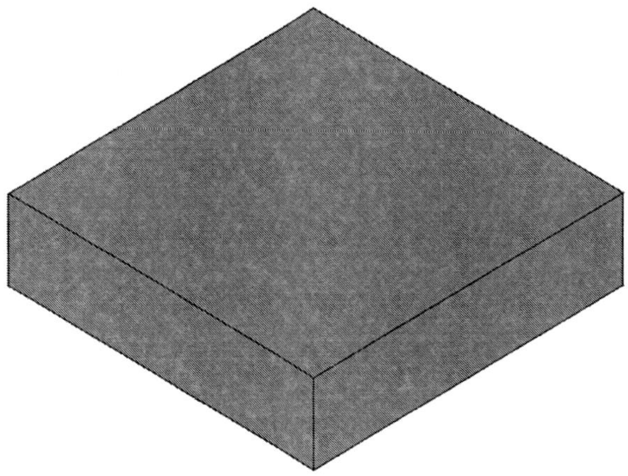

Notice the new feature, **Pad**, in the **Model** tab of the **Combo View** panel.

To magnify a model in the graphics area, you can use the zoom tools available on the **Zoom** submenu in the **View** menu of the Menu bar.

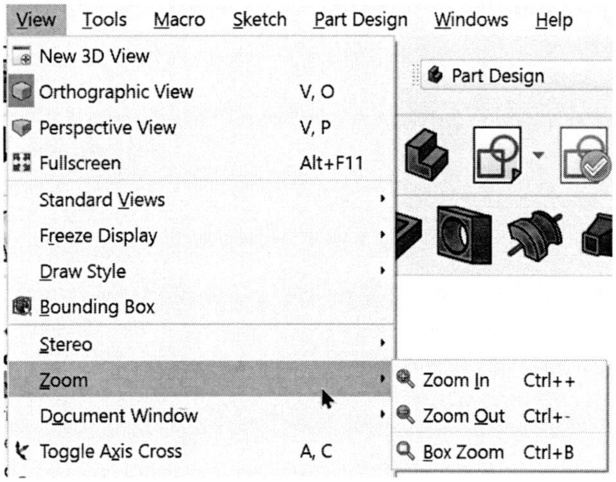

Click **Zoom In** to zoom into the model.

Click **Zoom Out** to zoom out of the model.

Click **Box Zoom**, and then drag the pointer to create a rectangle; the area in the rectangle zooms to fill the window.

The **View** toolbar has two more zoom tools: **Fit All** and **Fit Selection.**

Click **Fit All**  to display the full part size in the current window.

Click on a vertex, an edge, or a feature, and then click **Fit Selection** ; the selected item zooms to fill the window.

To display the part in different draw styles, select the options in the **Draw Style** drop-down on the **View** toolbar.

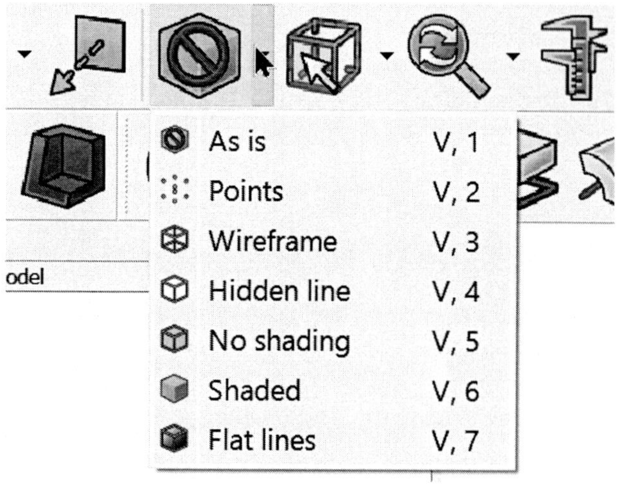

Normal Mode

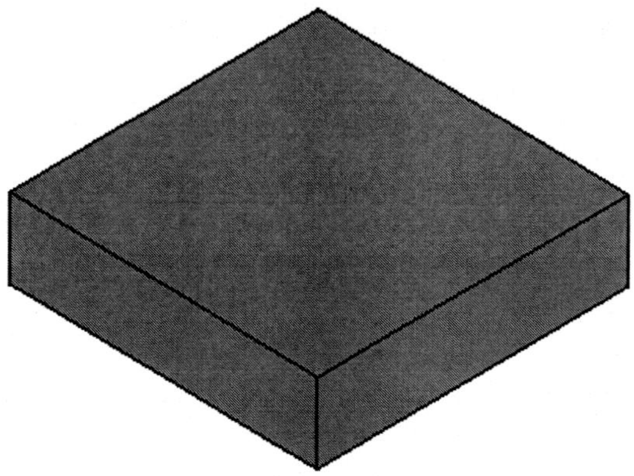

Flat lines

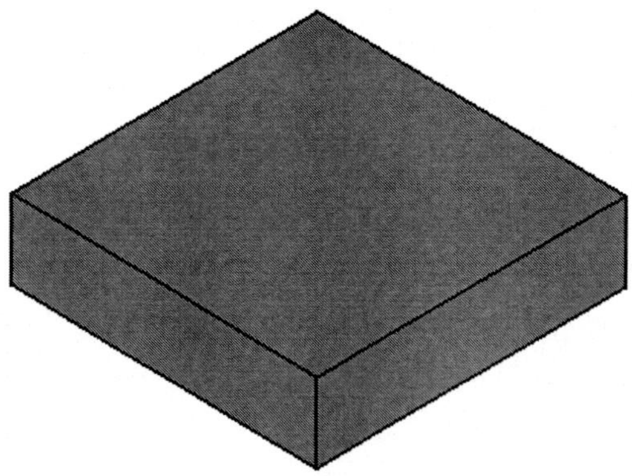

Shaded

Wireframe

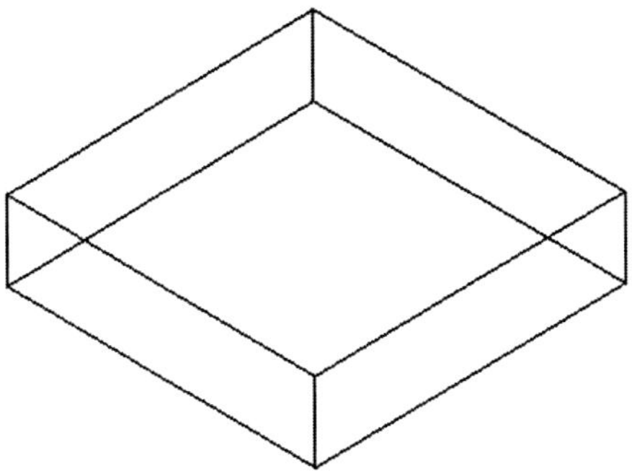

Points

Hidden Line

No Shading

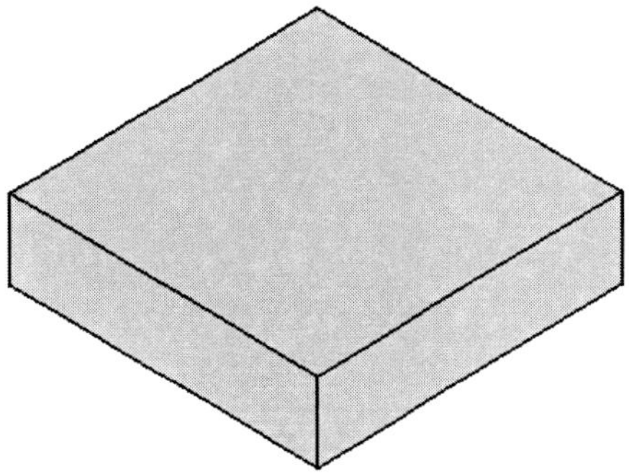

The default draw style for parts and assemblies is **Normal Mode**. You may change the draw style whenever you want.

Adding a Pad Feature

To create additional features on the part, you need to draw sketches on the model faces or planes, and then extrude them.

1. Click on the top face of the first feature.

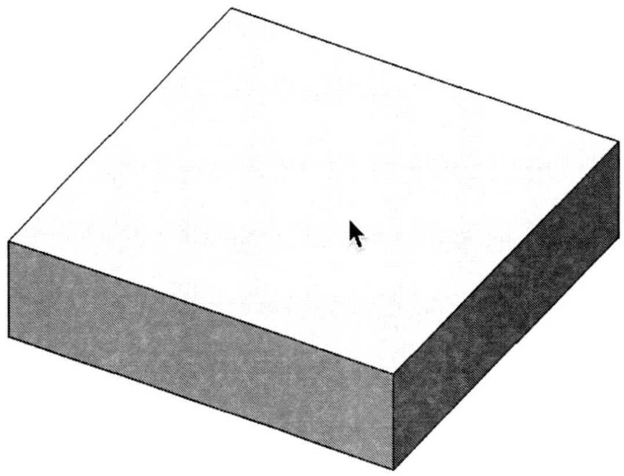

2. Click **New Sketch** on the **Face tools** section of the **Tasks** panel. A new sketch is started.

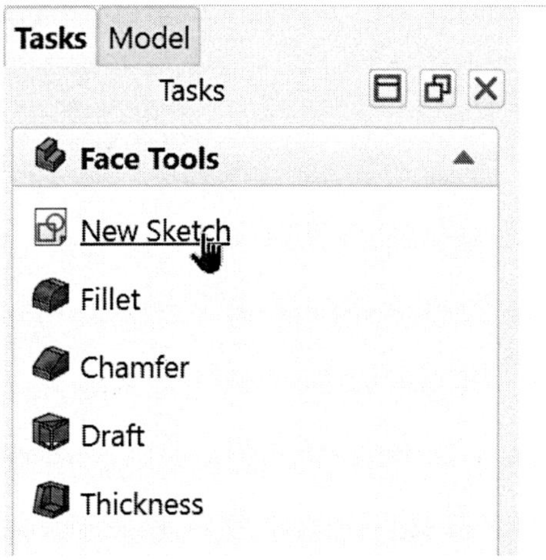

3. On the **Geometries** toolbar, click **Circle** drop-down > **Circle From Center.**

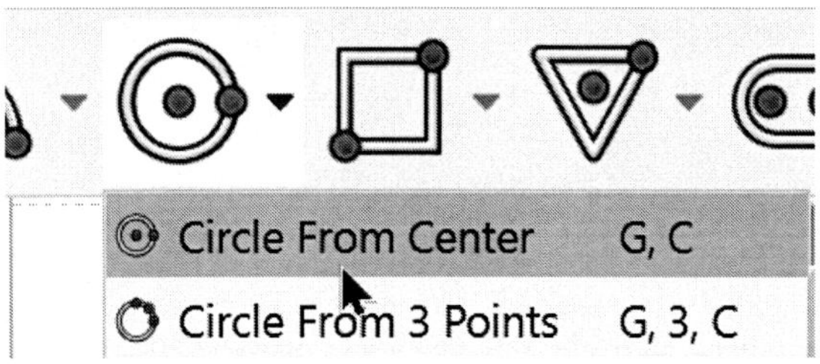

4. Click to specify the center point of the circle.
5. Move the pointer outward and click to create the circle.

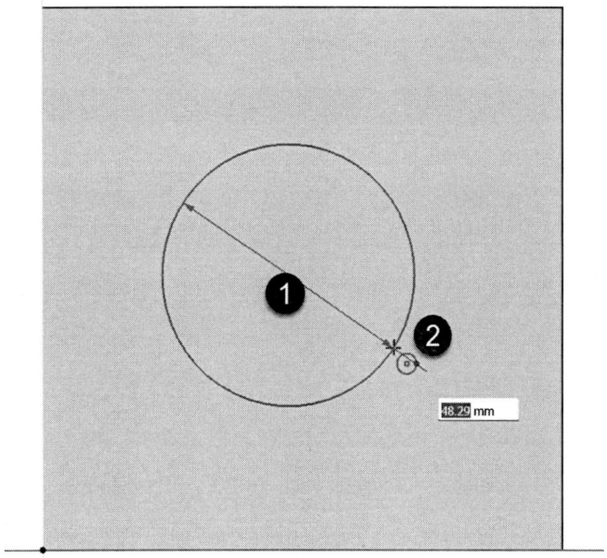

6. On the **Constraints** toolbar, click the **Dimension** drop-down > **Dimension** icon.

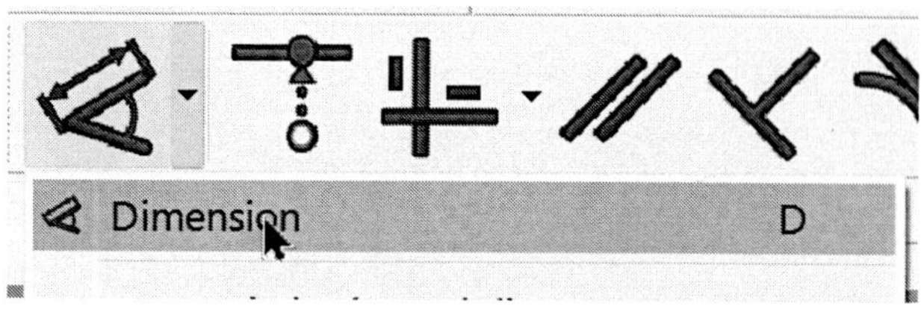

7. Select the center point of the circle.
8. Select the origin of the sketch if not already selected.
9. Move the pointer toward right and click.
10. Type **50** in the **Length** box of the **Insert Length** dialog.
11. Click **OK**.

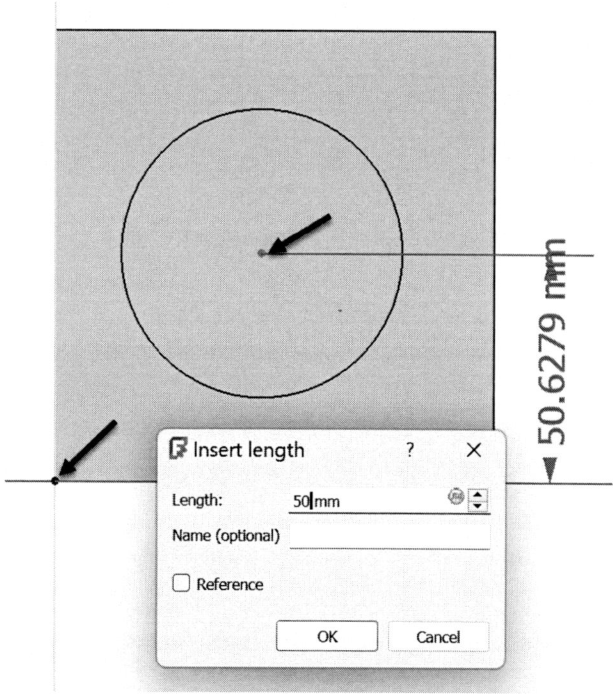

12. Select the center point of the circle
13. Select the origin of the sketch if not already selected.
14. Move the pointer toward up and click.
15. Type **50** in the **Length** box and click **OK**.

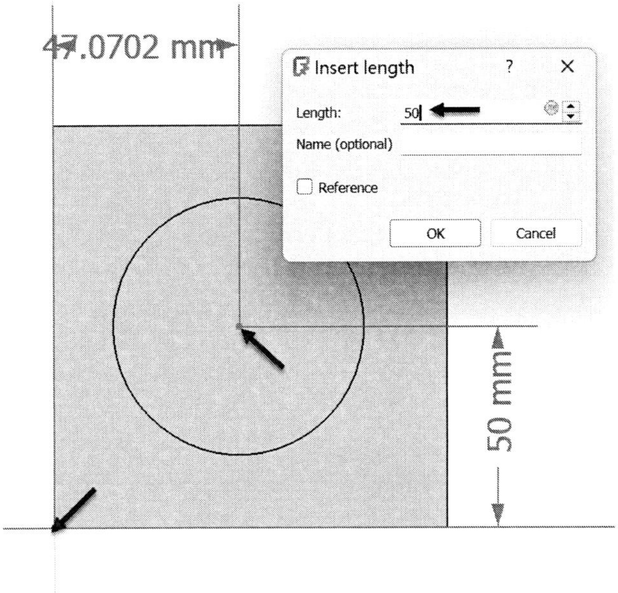

16. On the **Constraints** toolbar, click the **Dimension** drop-down > **Diameter Dimension**.

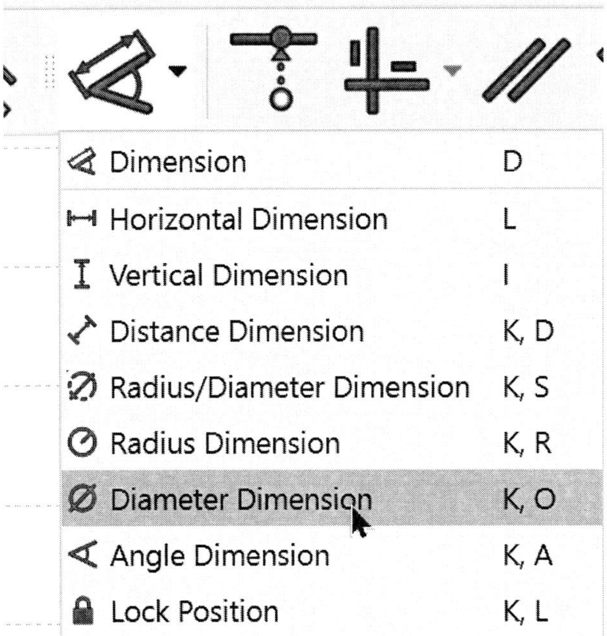

17. Select the circle and type **60** in the **Diameter** box of the **Insert diameter** dialog.

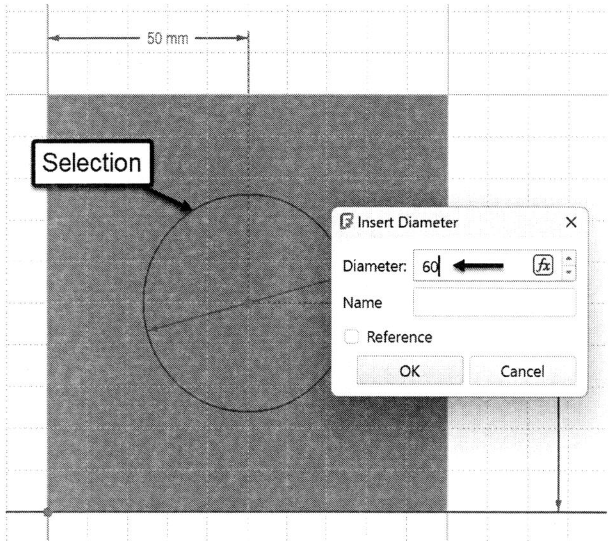

18. Click **OK**.
19. On the **Edit mode** toolbar, click the **Leave Sketch**  icon.
20. On the **Part Design Modeling Features Features** toolbar, click the **Pad** 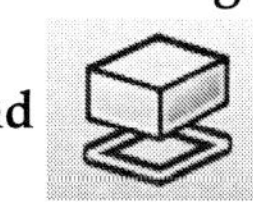 icon.
21. Type **20** in the **Length** box of the **Pad Parameters** dialog.
22. Click **OK**.

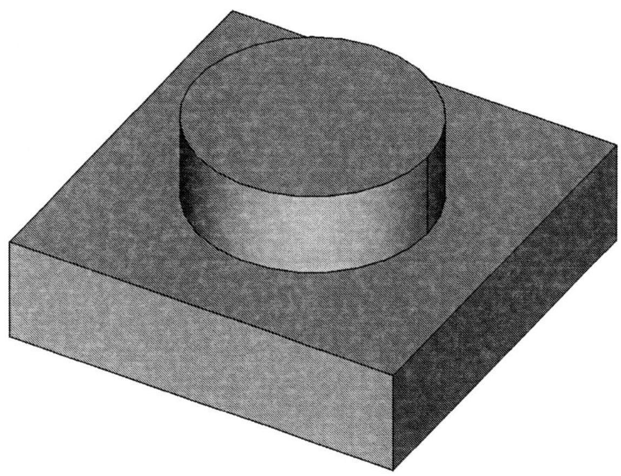

Filleting the Corners

The **Fillet** tool allows you to fillet the corners of the model.

1. On the **View** toolbar, select **Draw style > Wireframe**.

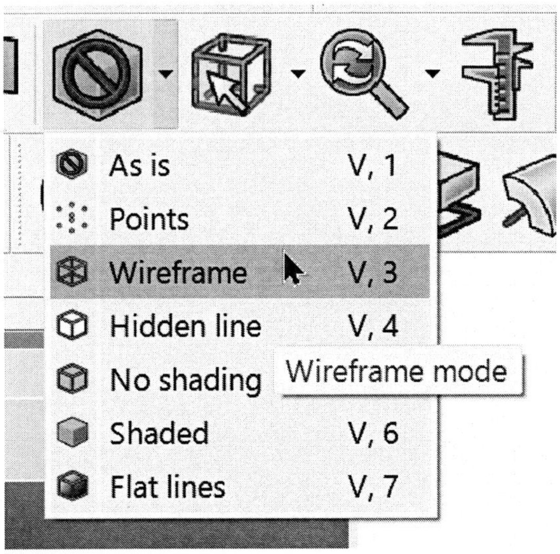

2. On the **Part Design Modeling Features Features** toolbar, click the **Fillet** icon.
3. Select the vertical edges of the model, as shown.

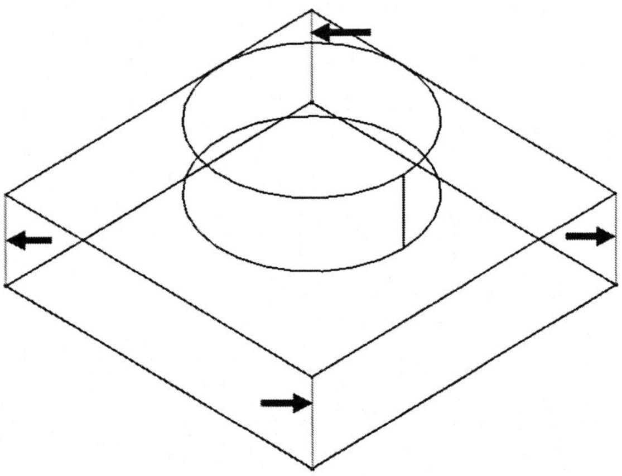

The selected edges will highlight in purple, as shown.

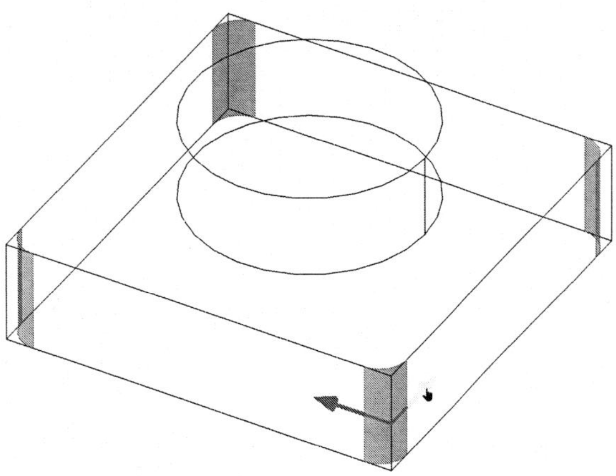

Notice the 3D manipulator handles (the red arrows) that appear on the active edge. You can click and drag the yellow arrow to visually push and pull the fillet radius directly in the 3D workspace.

4. Type **10** in the **Radius** box.
5. Click **OK**.
6. On the **View** toolbar, select **Draw style > Flat lines**.
7. Click on the horizontal face of the model, as shown.

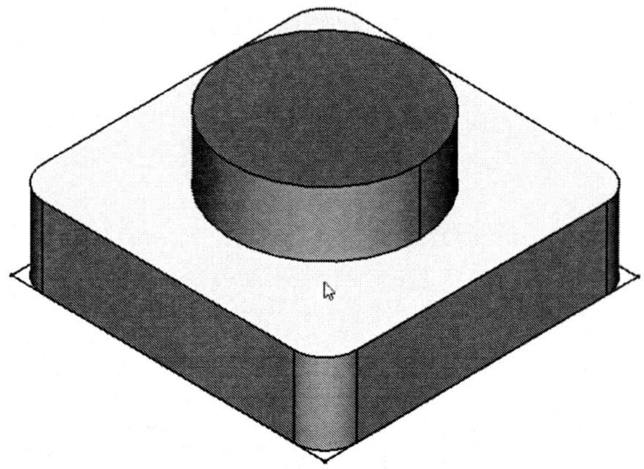

8. Click the **Fillet** icon on the **Part Design Modeling Features Features** toolbar.
9. Type **5** in the **Radius** box and click **OK**.

Changing the View Orientation

You can use the icons available on the **View** toolbar to change the view orientation of the sketch, part, or assembly.

Front

Top

Right

Rear

Bottom

Left

Isometric

The default planes of the part corresponding to the standard views are as follows:

- **XZ Plane - Front** or **Back**
- **YZ Plane - Top** or **Bottom**
- **XY Plane - Right** or **Left**

Rotating and Moving the Part

In addition to standard views, you can view the model from different angles by rotating them. By doing so, you can select the hidden faces and edges easily.

To rotate the part, use one of the following methods:

- On the Menu bar, click **View > Standard Views > Rotate Left** to rotate the model towards left.

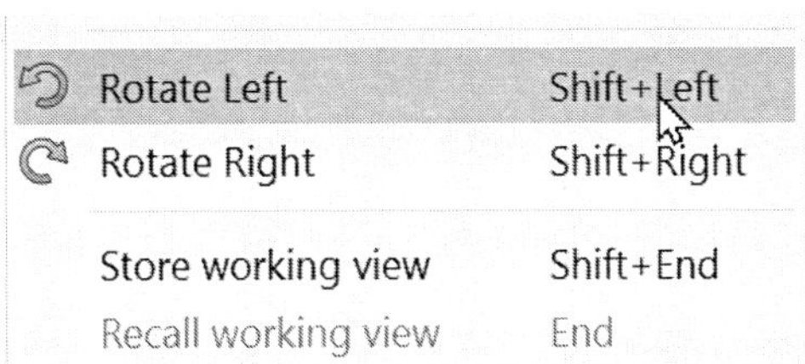

- On the Menu bar, click **Views > Standard Views > Rotate Right** to rotate the model towards the right.
- Press and hold the middle and the right mouse buttons. Next, drag the cursor to rotate the model.
- To rotate the part in 90° increments, press and hold the **Shift** key and use the arrow keys.

To move the part view, use one of the following methods:

- Press and hold the middle mouse button and drag the cursor.
- Press and hold the **Alt** or **Ctrl** key (**Command** key for Mac users) and use the arrow keys to move the view up, down, left, or right.

Shelling the model

The **Thickness** tool allows you to shell the model.

1. Press and hold the middle and right mouse buttons.
2. Drag the cursor upward to display the bottom face.
3. On the **Part Design Modeling Features Features** toolbar, click the **Thickness** icon.
4. Click on the bottom face.

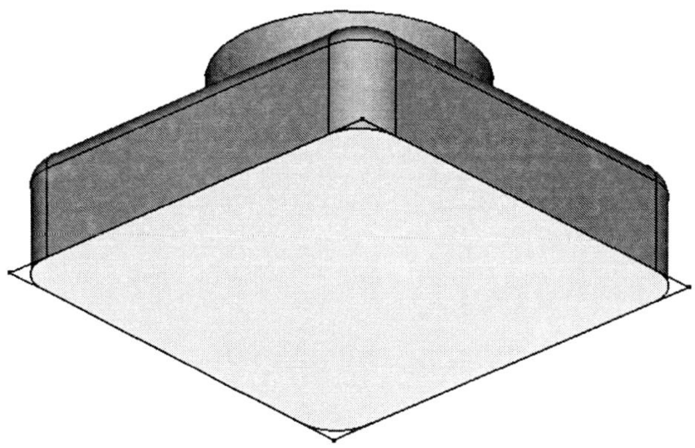

5. In the **Thickness Parameters** dialog, select **Mode > Skin.**
6. Select **Join Type > Intersection.**
7. Type **2** in the **Thickness** box.
8. Check the **Make thickness inwards** option.
9. On the **View** toolbar, click the **Isometric** icon.
10. On the **Thickness parameters** dialog, click the **Select** button.
11. Select the top face of the second feature.

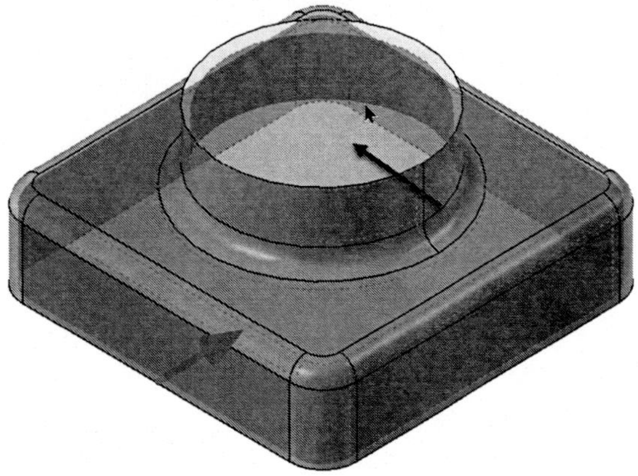

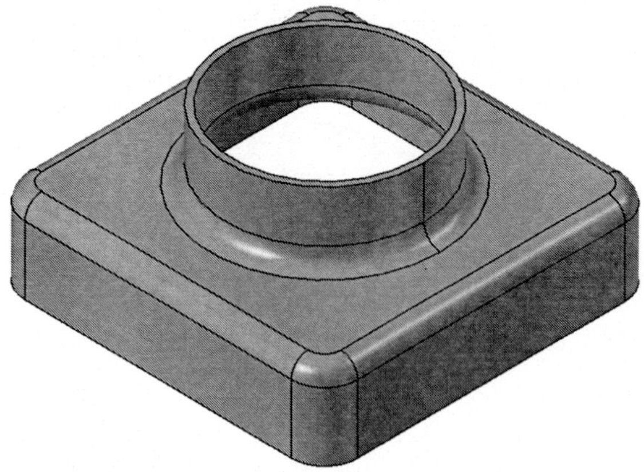

12. Click **OK**.

Saving the Part

1. Click **File > Save** on the Menu bar.
2. On the **Save As** dialog, type-in **Tutorial1** in the **File name** box.
3. Click **Save** to save the file.
4. Click **File > Close**.

Note:
*.FCStd is the file extension for all the files that you create in FreeCAD.

TUTORIAL 2

In this tutorial, you create the part shown below.

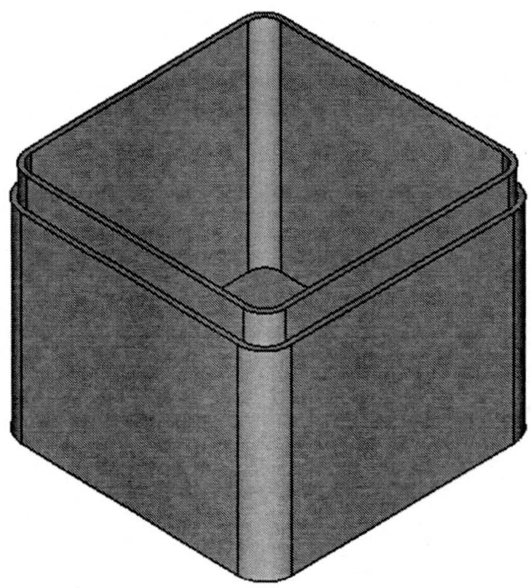

Starting a New File

1. On the Menu bar, click **File > New**.

2. Select **Part Design** from the **Workbench** drop-down.

Sketching for the Pad Feature

1. Click **New Sketch** icon on the **Part Design Helper Features** toolbar.
2. Select the XY-Plane from the graphics window.
3. Click **Rectangle** on the **Geometries** toolbar.
4. Create a rectangle, shown in the figure.

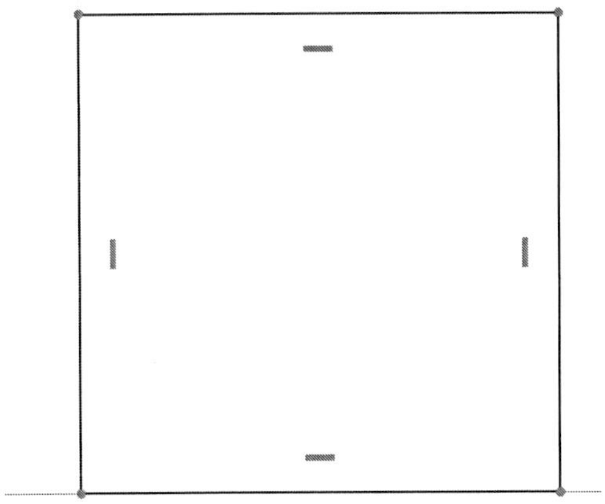

5. Add vertical and horizontal distance constraints to the rectangle, as shown.

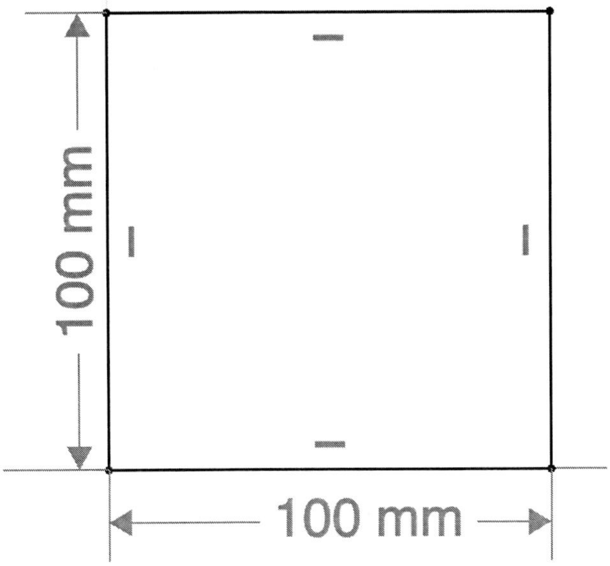

6. Click the **Leave Sketch** icon on the **Edit mode** toolbar.
7. Click **Pad** on the **Tasks** panel.

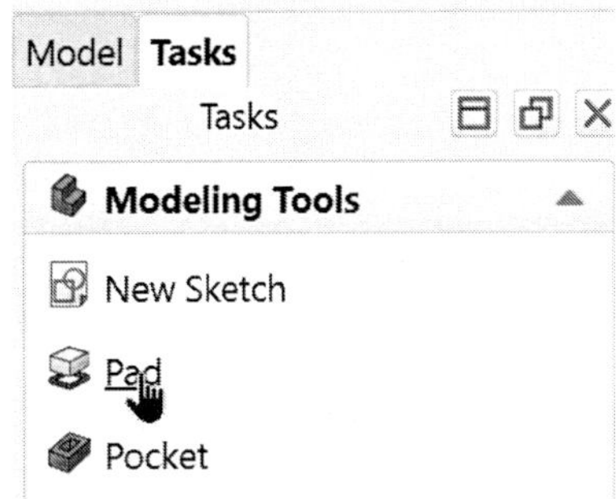

8. Type **70** in the **Length** box and click **OK**.

9. Select **Draw Style > Wireframe** on the **View** toolbar.
10. On the **Part Design Modeling Features Features** toolbar, click the **Fillet** icon.
11. Select the vertical edges.

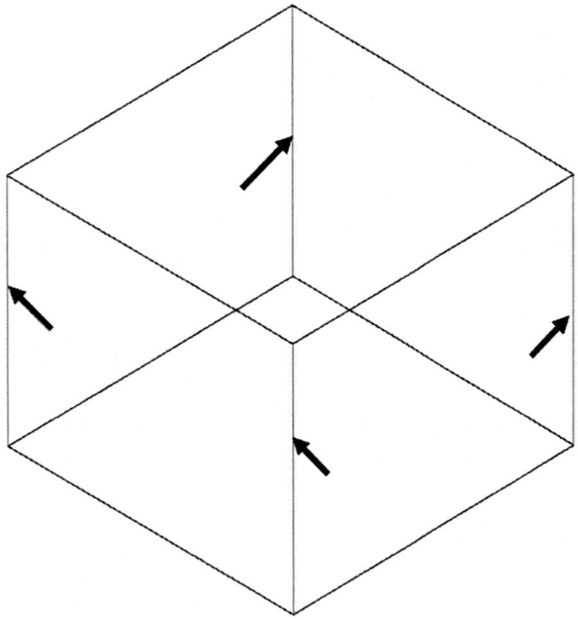

12. Type **10** in the **Radius** box.
13. Click **OK**.
14. On the **View** toolbar, select **Draw Style > Flat lines** .
15. Click on the top face of the model.
16. Click the **Thickness** icon on the **Part Design Modeling Features Features** toolbar.
17. Type 4 in the **Thickness** box.
18. Select **Join Type > Intersection**.
19. Check the **Make thickness inwards** option.
20. Click **OK**.

Creating the Cut Feature

1. Click on the top face of the first feature.

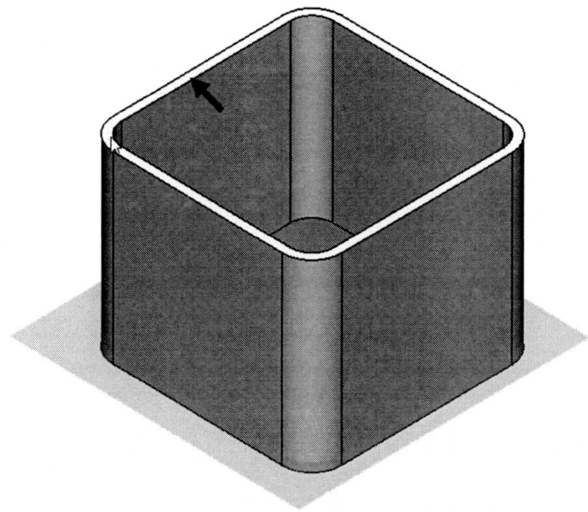

2. Click **New Sketch** on the **Face tools** section of the **Tasks** panel. A new sketch is started.

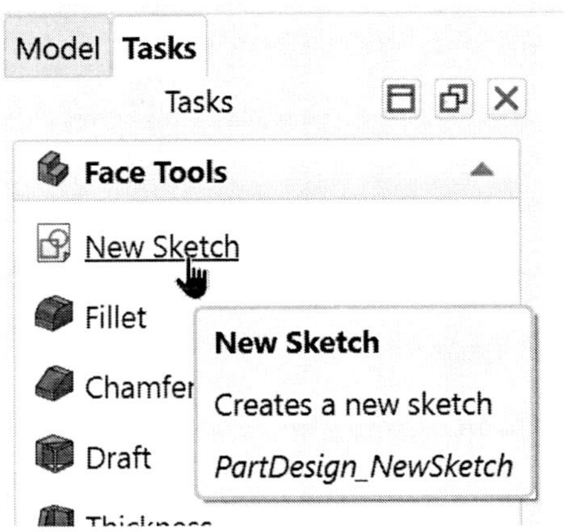

3. Click the **External Projection**  icon on the **Sketcher tools** toolbar.
4. Click on the inner edges of the model.

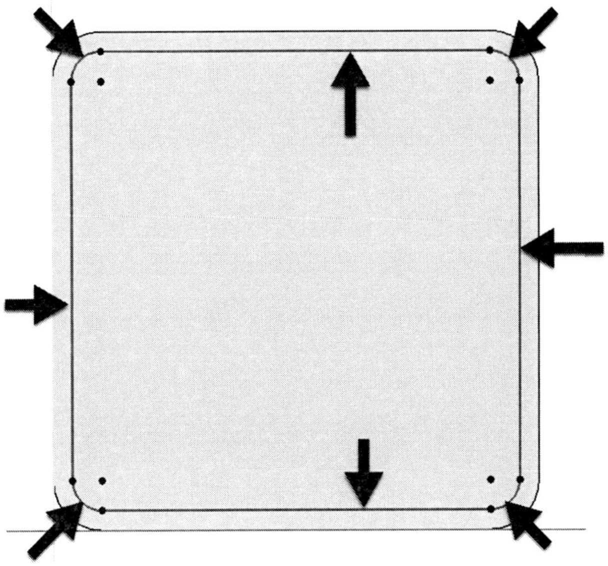

5. Create a selection window from left to right covering all the projected entities (or) Hold down the **Ctrl** key and click each of the four boundary lines of the existing square profile. The selected lines will turn green to confirm they are active.

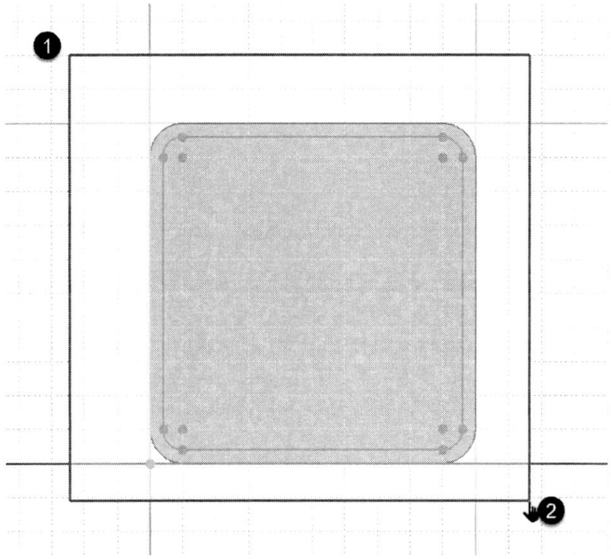

6. On the **Sketcher tools** toolbar, click the **Offset geometry** icon (the icon showing parallel curves with a directional arrow). Alternatively, you can use the keyboard shortcut by pressing **Z** then **T**.

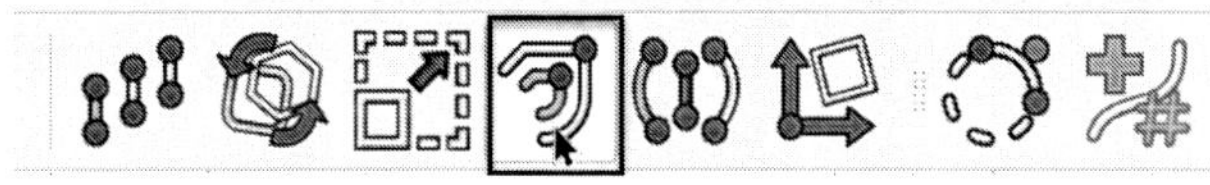

7. Once the tool is active, the **Offset Parameters** dialog will appear in the **Tasks** panel on the left side of the screen. Configure the following options:
   - **Delete original geometries (U):** Leave this checkbox unchecked so that both the original inner square and the new outer offset shape remain in the sketch.
   - **Add offset constraint (J):** Ensure this checkbox is checked. This automatically applies a dimensional constraint between the original geometry and the new offset line, allowing you to edit the exact distance later.

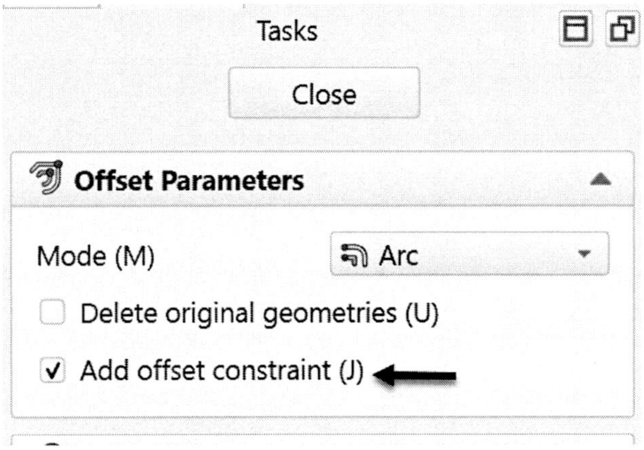

8. Move your cursor outward from the original shape in the 3D view. A live preview of the offset shape will follow your cursor, and an On-View Parameter (OVP) input box will appear.

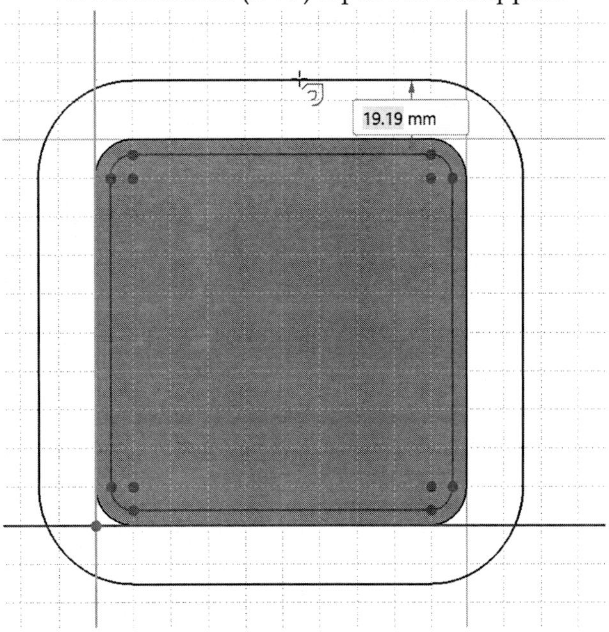

9. Without clicking the mouse, type **2** into the numerical input box on the screen and press **Enter**. This locks the offset outline at exactly 2mm outward from the original sketch geometry.

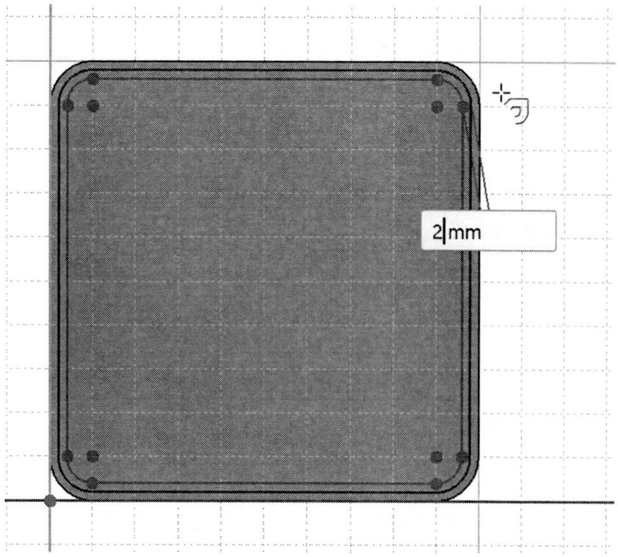

The new offset geometry is now created. You will notice a dimensional constraint of 2mm connecting the inner and outer profiles, and the outer corners will display arc points connecting the straight segments, confirming the Arc mode was successfully applied.

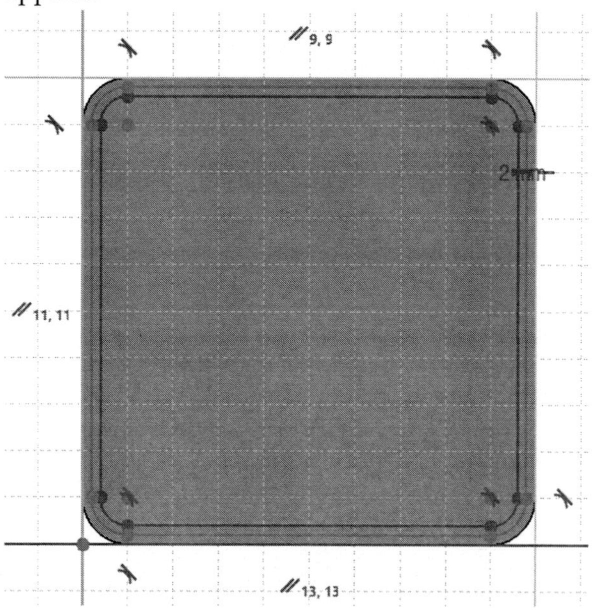

10. Click **Leave Sketch**  on the **Edit mode** toolbar.
11. Click the **Pad**  icon on the **Part Design Modeling Features Features** toolbar.
12. Type **10** in the **Length** box in the **Pocket parameters** dialog.
13. Click **OK**.

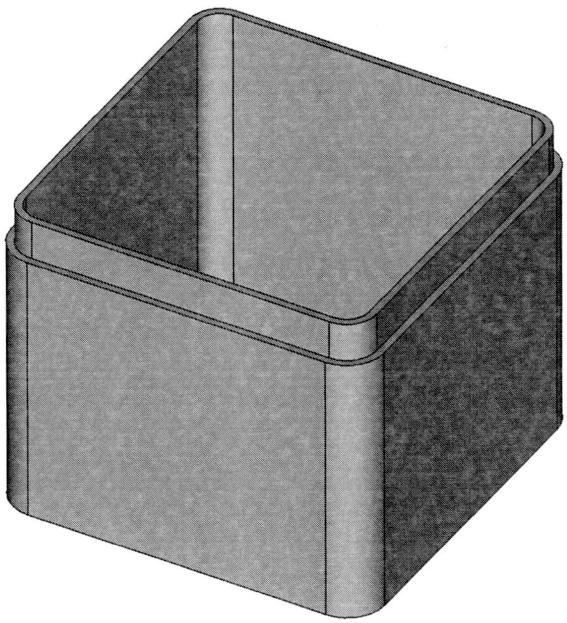

14. Save and close the file.

Chapter 3: Assembly Basics

In this chapter, you will:

- Add Components to assembly
- Apply constraints between components

TUTORIAL 1

This tutorial takes you through the creation of your first assembly.

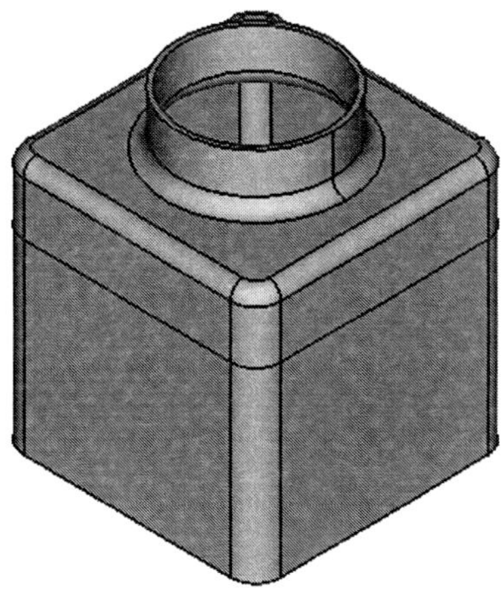

Starting a New Assembly File

1. Open the **FreeCAD** application.
2. On the **File** toolbar, click the **Save**  icon.
3. Type **Assembly_tutorial** in the **File Name** box on the **Save** dialog.
4. Click **Save**.
5. Click **Workbenches** drop-down menu and select the **Assembly** Workbench from the list.
6. Click the **New Assembly**  icon on the **Assembly** toolbar.

Inserting the Base Component

1. Click the **Insert Component**  icon on the **Assembly** toolbar (or) click **Assembly > Insert Component > Component** on the menu bar.
2. On the **Insert** section of the **Tasks** panel, click the **Open file** button.
3. Browse to the location of the **Tutorial 2** file of Chapter 1, and then double-click on it. The selected part is listed in the **Insert Component** section.
4. Select the **Body** under the Tutorial2 file from the **Insert Component** section; the selected body is inserted into the assembly.

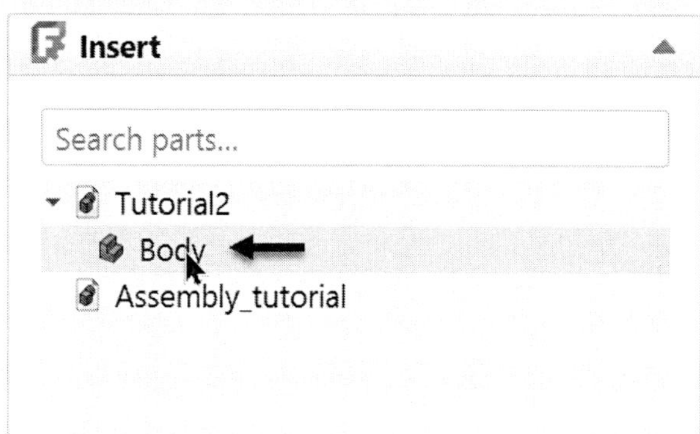

5. Click **Yes** on the **Ground Part** message box.

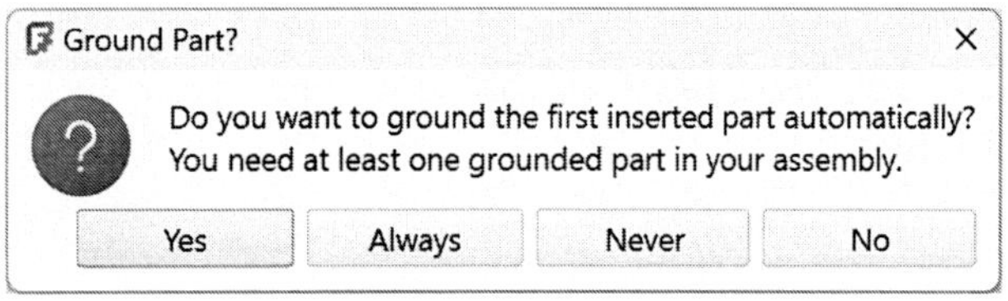

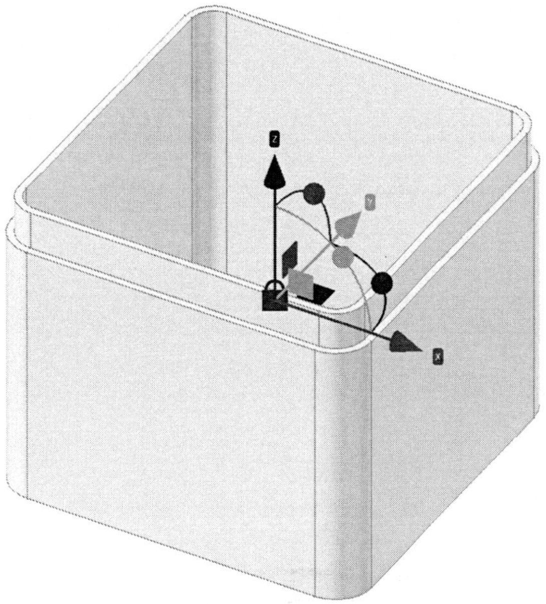

Adding the second component

1. On the **Insert** section of the **Tasks** panel, click the **Open file** button.
2. Browse to the location of the **Tutorial** 1 file of Chapter 1, and then double click on it.
3. Select the **Body** under the Tutorial1 file from the **Insert Component** section; the selected body is inserted into the assembly.
4. Click and drag the Z-axis of the triad in the upward direction and click; the component is moved.

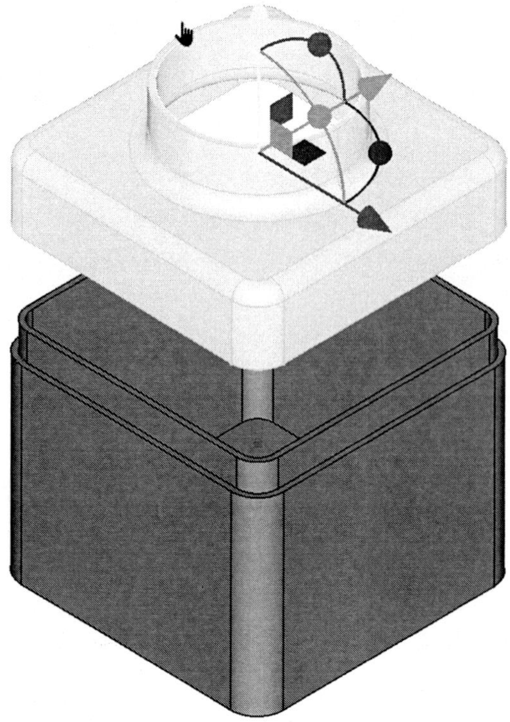

5. Click **OK** on the **Tasks** panel.

Creating Joints

After adding the components to the assembly environment, you need to create joints between them. By creating joints, you establish relationships between components.

The **Assembly Joints** toolbar has various tools to apply constraints between the components.

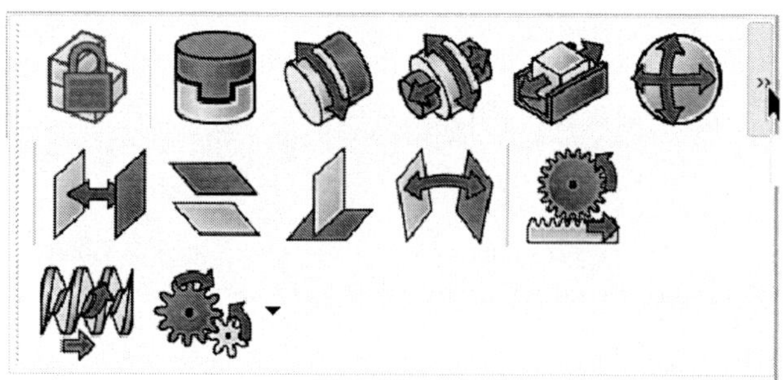

Different assembly joints that can be applied are given next.

 **Fixed Joint:** A Fixed joint fully constrains components, leaving zero degrees of freedom, effectively binding them into a single rigid body. You need select faces, edges, or points from the components to define this joint.

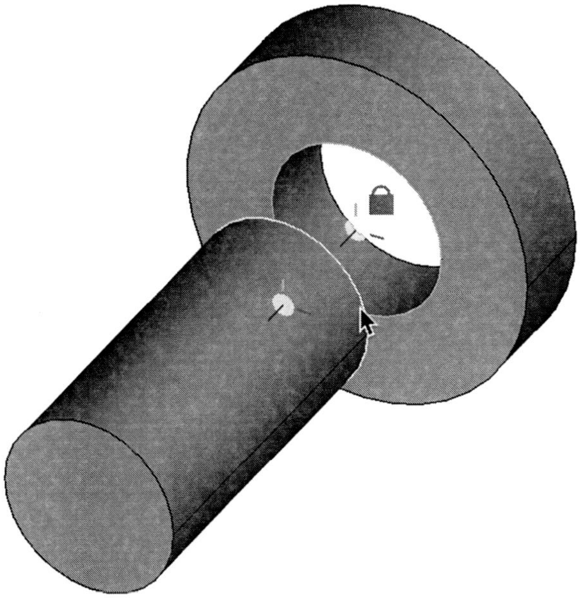

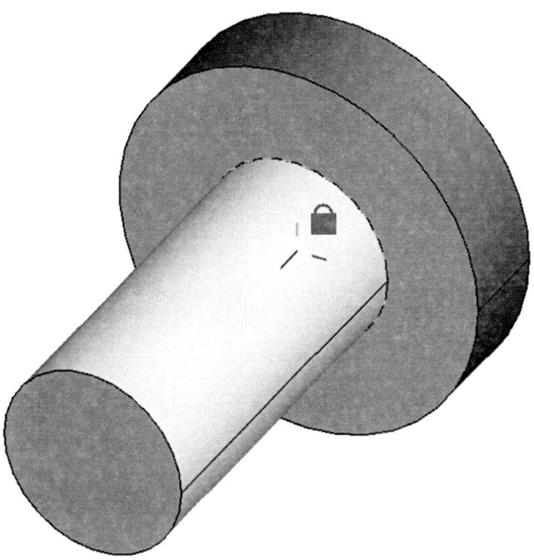

Addtionally, you can enter values in the **Offset** or **Rotation** boxes if components need precise positioning.

Click the **Reverse direction**  button on the **Create Joint** dialog to reverse the direction.

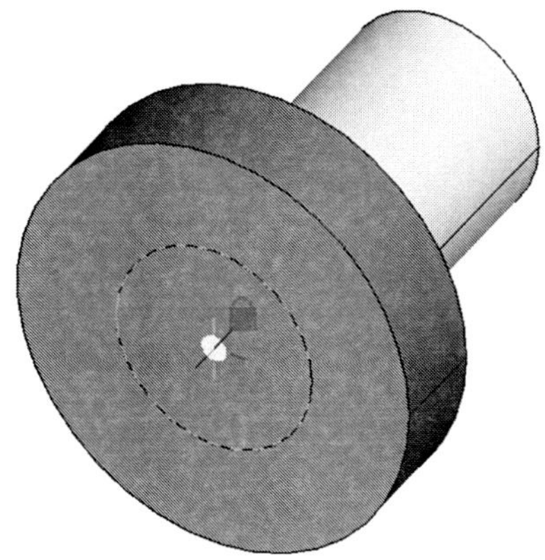

 **Parallel Joint:** The **Parallel Joint** constrains two components to maintain parallel alignment along a specified direction. It allows controlled movement while ensuring selected edges, axes, or planar faces remain parallel.

Activate the **Parallel Joint** command select faces, edges, or axes from two components; the two selections are made parallel to each other.

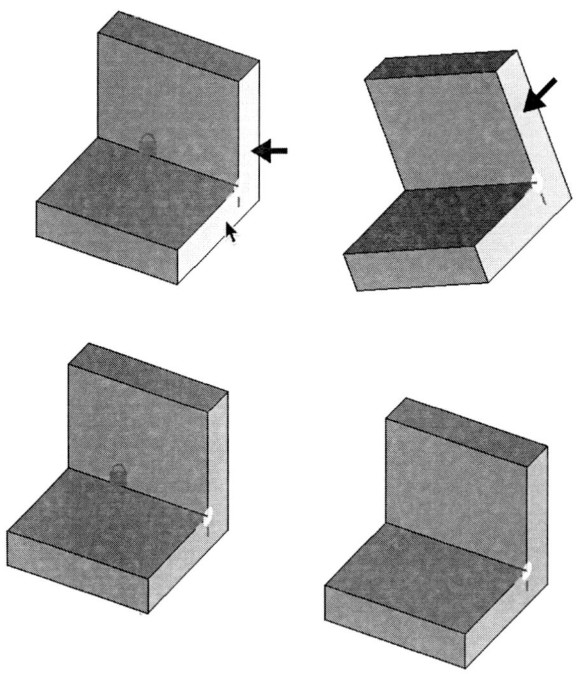

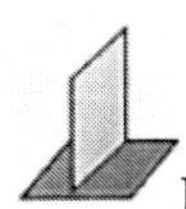 **Perpendicular Joint:** This joint forces the two components to stay at a 90-degree angle relative to each other.

Activate the **Perpendicular Joint** command select faces, edges, or axes from two components; the two selections are made parallel to each other.

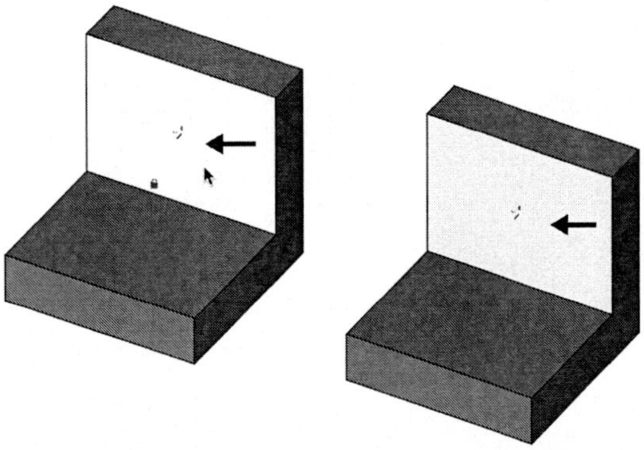

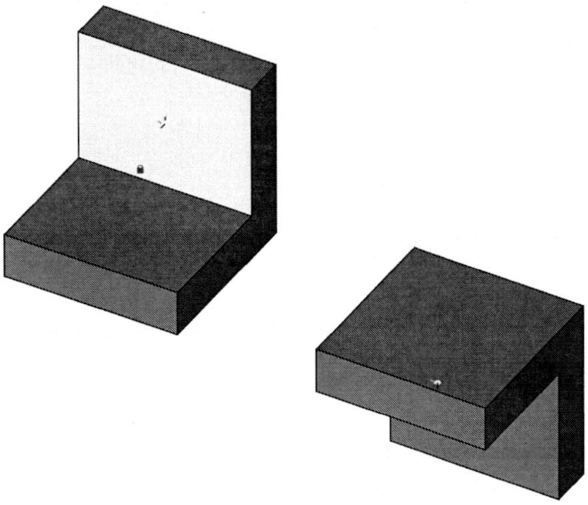

Distance Joint: The **Distance Joint** fixes the distance between two points, edges, or faces on components in an assembly. It ensures the selected geometry maintains a specific separation while allowing rotational movement around those points.

Activate the **Distance Joint** command and specify the joint origin on the first component by selecting a point, edge, or face. Next, specify the joint origin on the second component.

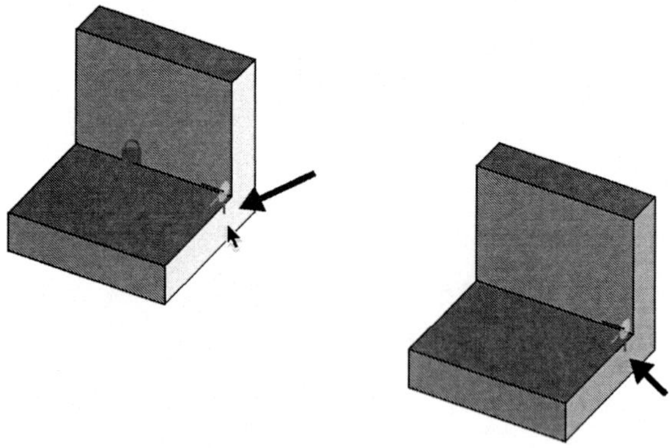

Type-in a value in the **Distance** box on **Create Joint** section of the **Tasks** panel. Use the **Reverse Direction** button, if you want to flip the side.

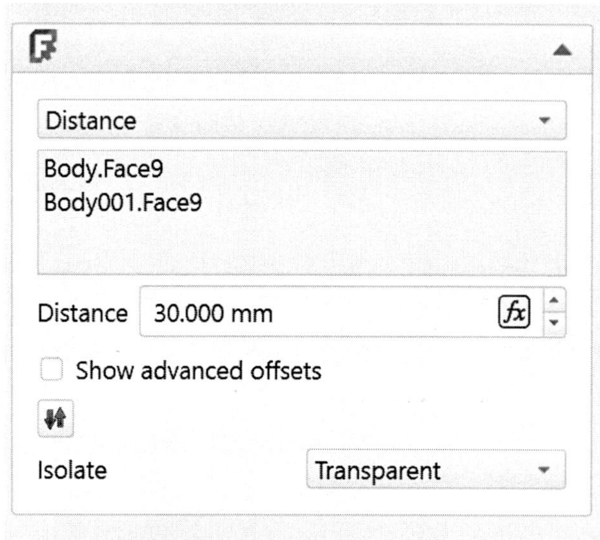

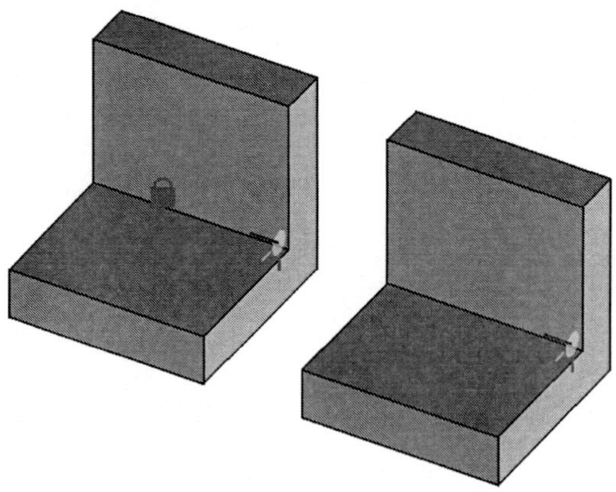

Next, click **OK**.

Cylindrical Joint: This joint allows two components to rotate and translate along a common axis. By integrating the rotational capability of a

Revolute Joint and the translational capability of a Slider Joint, this constraint enables simultaneous rotational and linear motion along a single axis.

Activate the **Cylindrical Joint** command and specify the joint origin by selecting a cylindrical edge on the first component. Next, specify the joint origin by selecting a cylindrical edge on the second component.

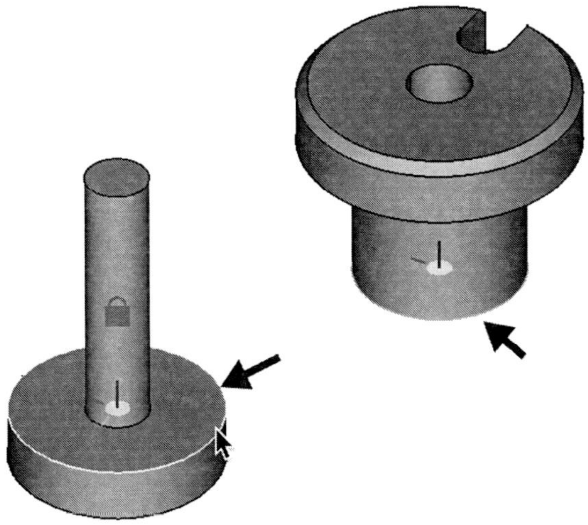

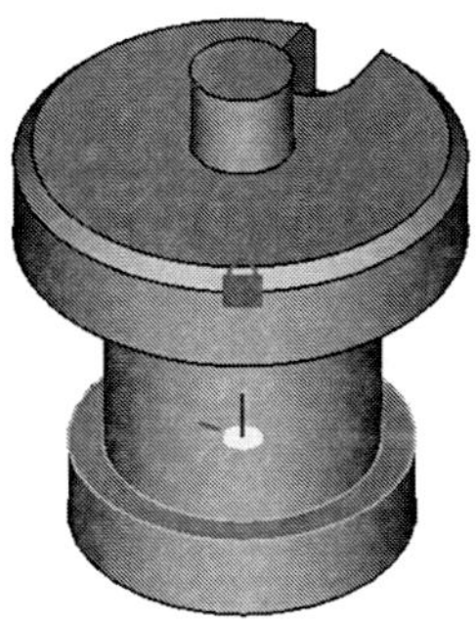

In the **Limits** section, check the **Min Length** and **Max Length** boxes and enter values in the respective boxes. This limits sliding distance.

Check the **Min angle** and **Max angle** boxes and enter values in the respective value box. This restrict rotational range.

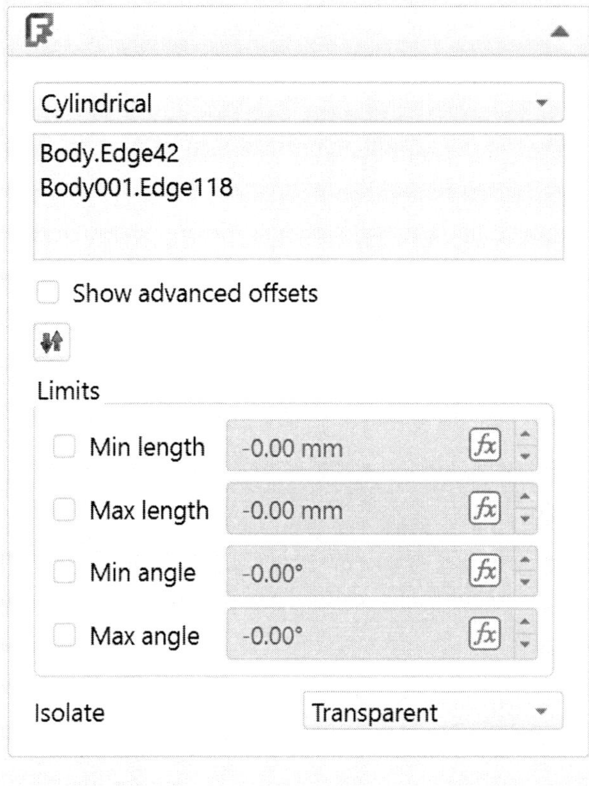

Note: Leaving values at 0 allows unrestricted motion.

Click **OK** to create the cylindrical joint. Click and drag anyone of the component and notice that it can rotate and slide along the shared axis.

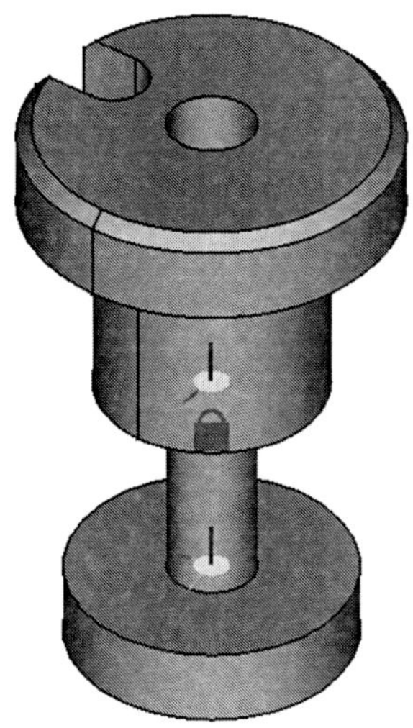

 **Revolute Joint:** A **Revolute Joint** restricts two components to rotate around a shared axis,

mimicking hinge-like motion. It allows 1 rotational degree of freedom (DOF) while preventing translation along or perpendicular to the axis.

Activate the **Revolute Joint** command and select a cylindrical face or edge on the first component to define the joint origin.

Select a corresponding cylindrical face or edge on the second component.

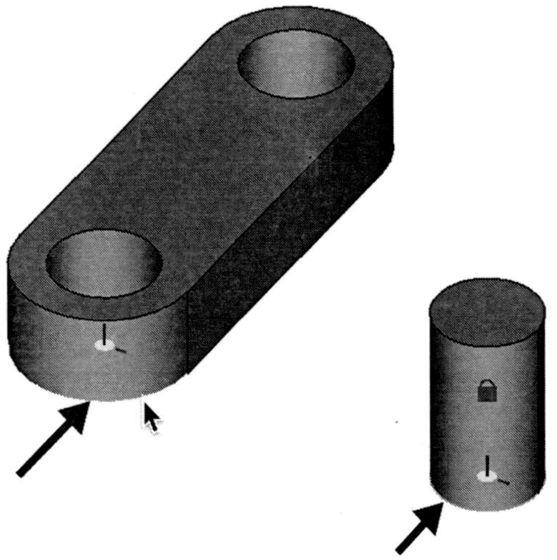

In the Limits section, enter values in the Min angle and Max angle boxes, to restrict rotational range.

Note that leaving both fields at 0.00° allows unrestricted 360° rotation.

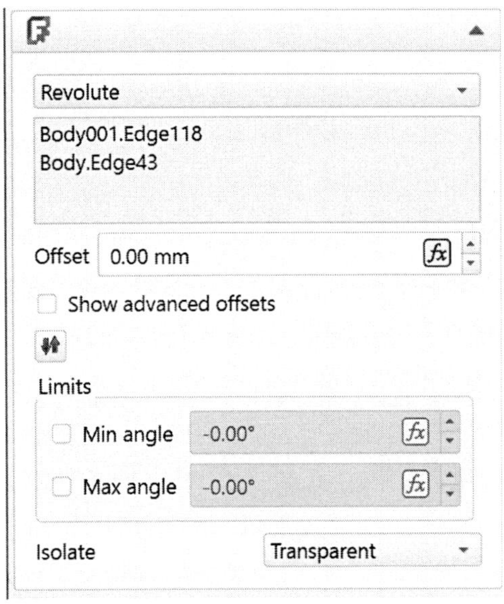

Click **OK** to apply the Revolute Joint.

The component can now rotate freely around the defined axis.

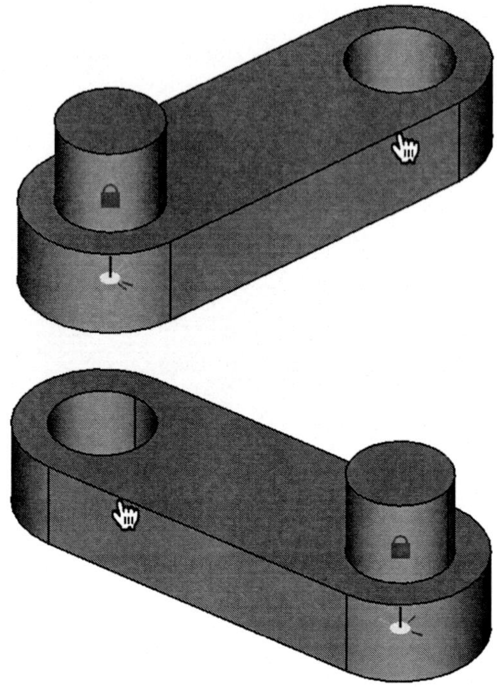

Angle Joint: Applies the angle constraint between two components. Activate the **Angle Joint** command and specify the angle value in the Angle box.

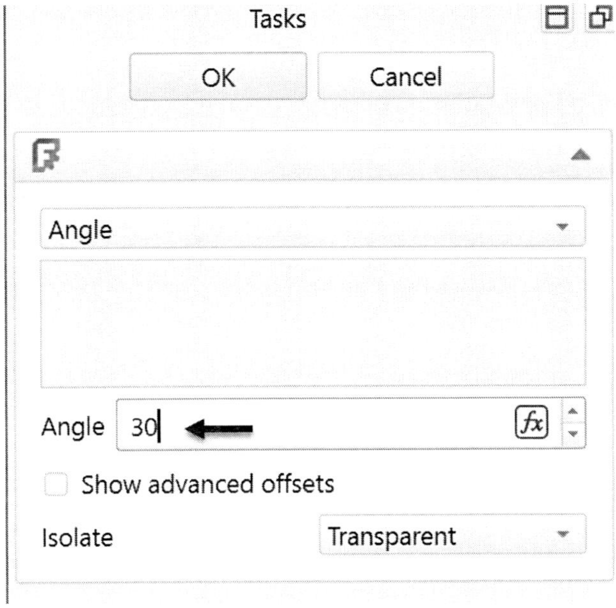

Select faces or edges on each component to define the joint origins (one selection per component).

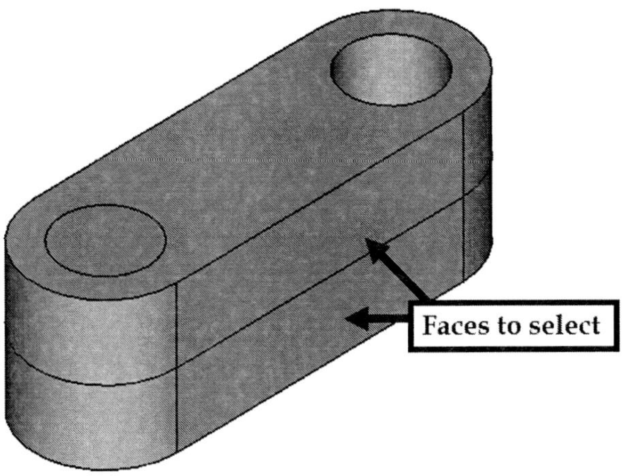

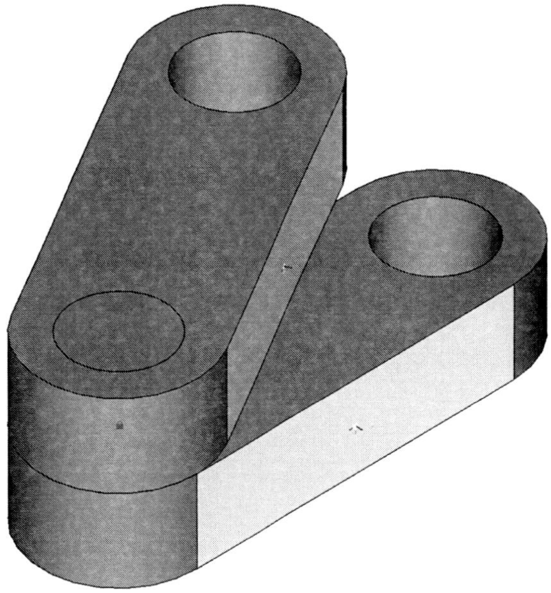

Click **OK** to create the angle joint.

Slider Joint: The slider joint allows the second component to move in a straight line along the direction defined by the selected faces/edges. It restricts rotation or sideways movement. Ensure the selected geometry aligns with the desired sliding path.

Activate the **Slider Joint** command. Next, specify the joint origin by selecting a face or edge on the first component (fixed part). For example, click on the middle portion of the edge, as shown to define the joint origin.

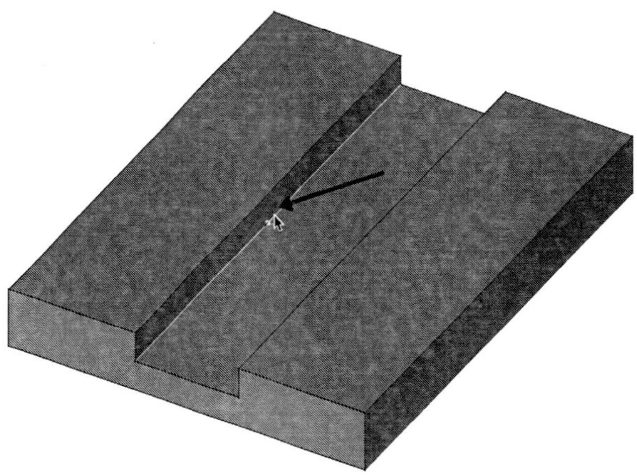

Likewise, click on the middle portion of the horizontal edge of the second component, as shown.

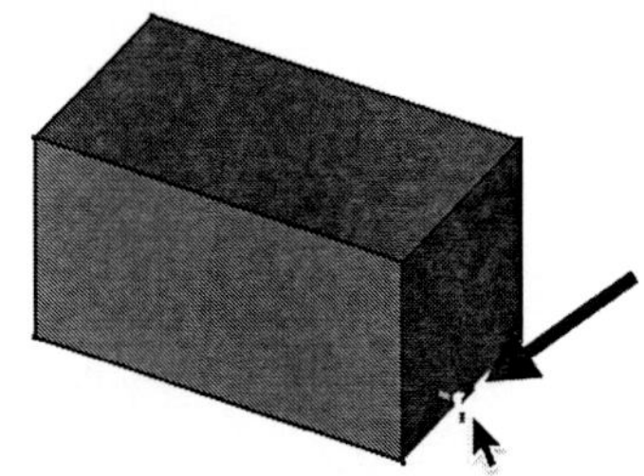

The selected edges are aligned together.

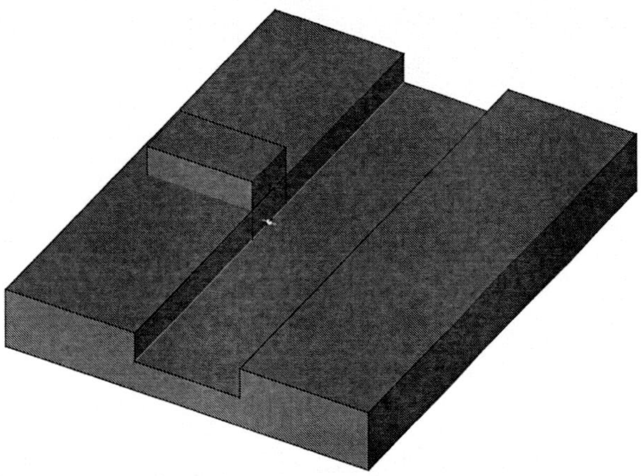

Click the **Reverse direction** icon to flip the movable part, if needed.

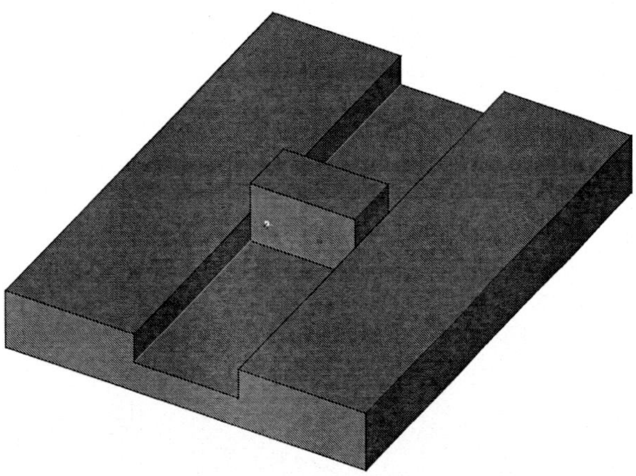

Check the **Min Length** and **Max Length** options and specify values in the respective value boxes. This restricts the sliding motion to the specified range. For example, with -30 to 30, the joint can move **30** units forward and **30** units backward from its starting position.

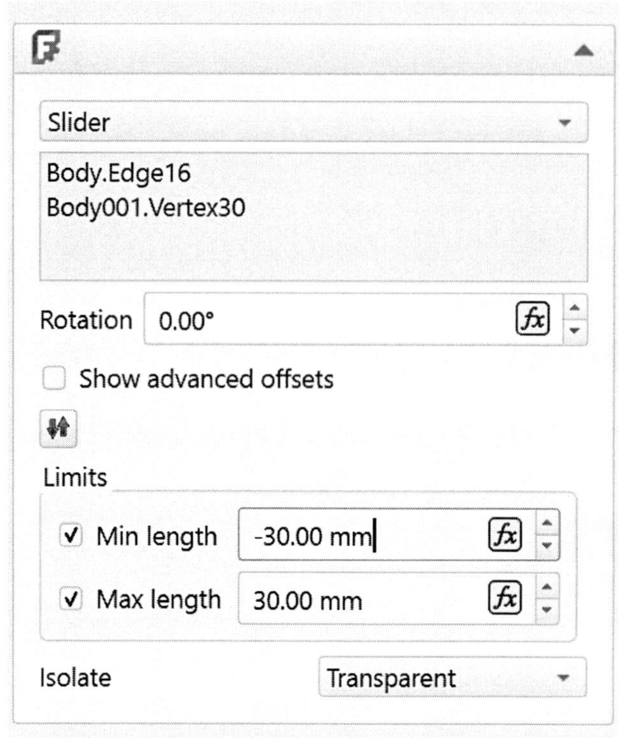

Click **OK** on the **Tasks** panel to create the slider joint. Next, click and drag the movable component and notice that it slides within the specified limits.

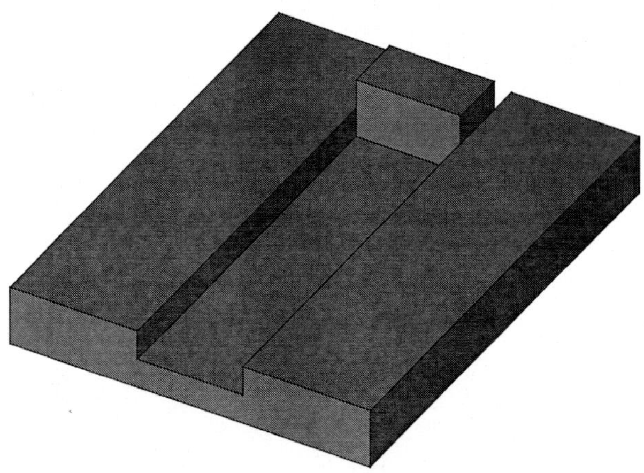

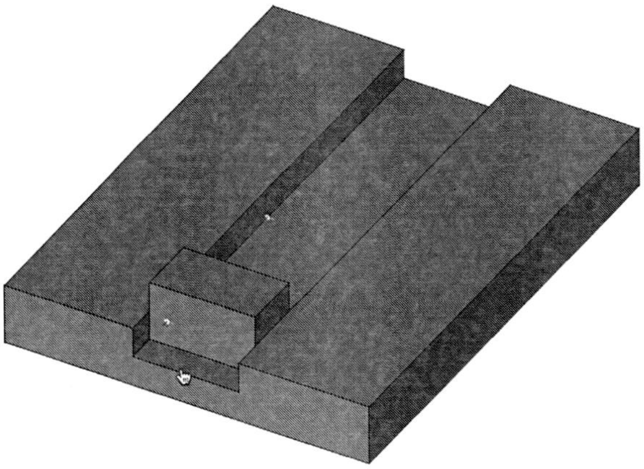

 **Ball Joint:** This Joint allows rotational movement in multiple axes. Activate the Ball Joint command and select the spherical face of the ball; the center point of the spherical face is snapped. Likewise, select the center of the socket cavity. Click **OK** on the **Tasks** panel.

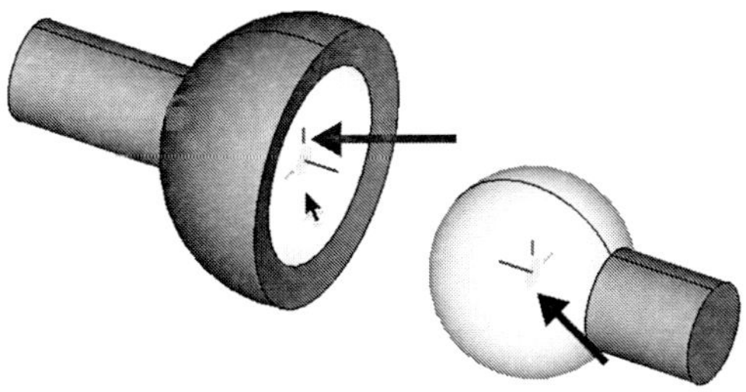

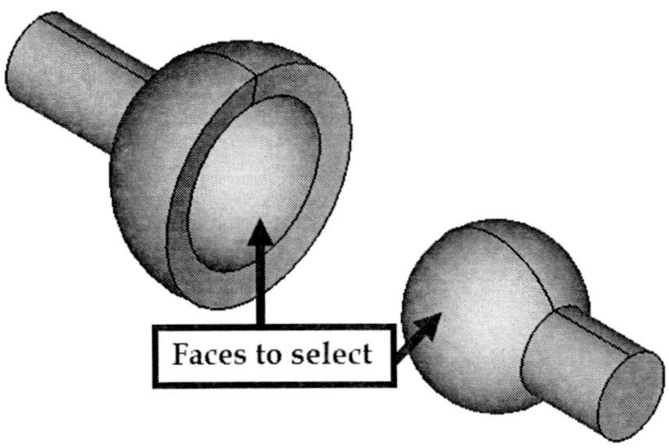

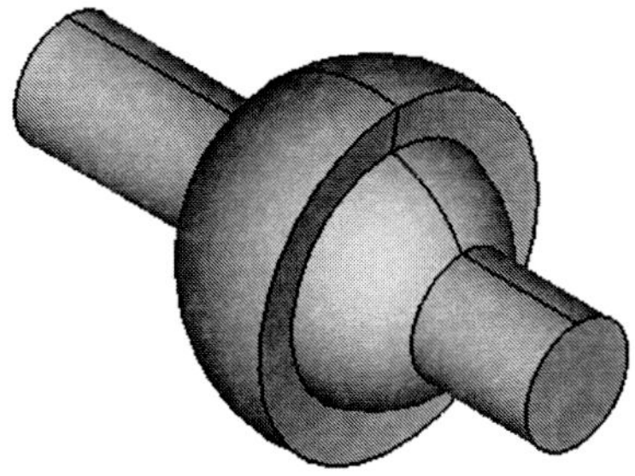

1. Click **Fixed Joint**  icon on the **Assembly Joints** toolbar.
2. Place the pointer on the midpoint of the lower horizontal edge of the Tutorial 1 component.
3. Make sure that the axes of the joint origin are oriented in the direction, as shown.

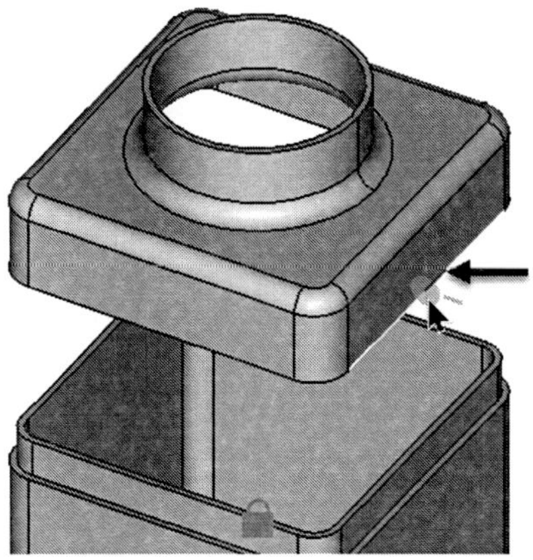

4. Click to define the joint origin.
5. Place the pointer on the midpoint of the horizontal edge of the Tutorial 2 component.
6. Make sure that the axes on the joint origin are oriented in the direction, as shown.

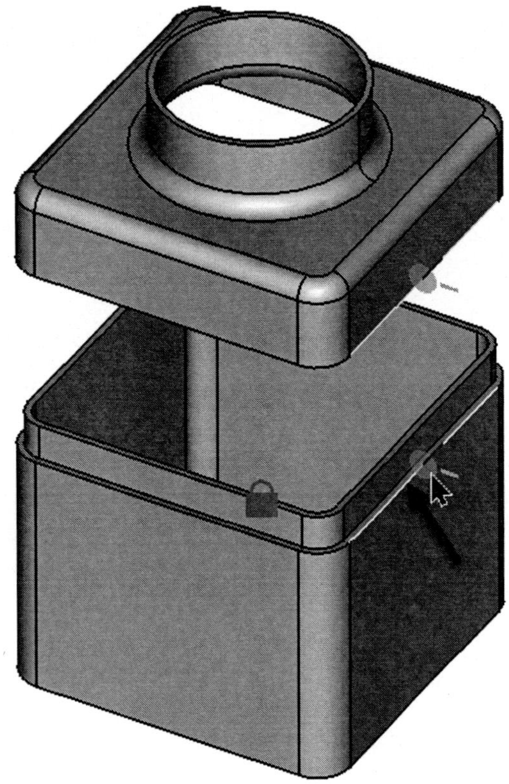

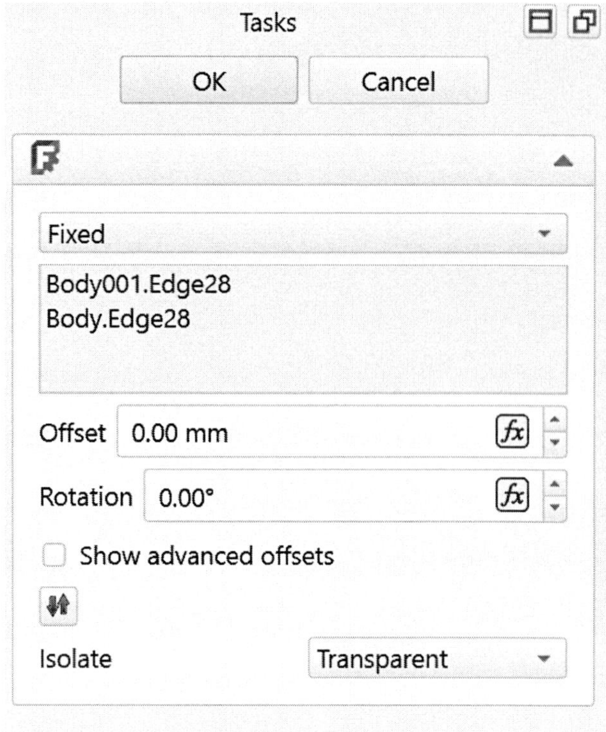

7. Click to define the joint origin.
8. Click **OK** on the **Tasks** panel to create the fixed joint.

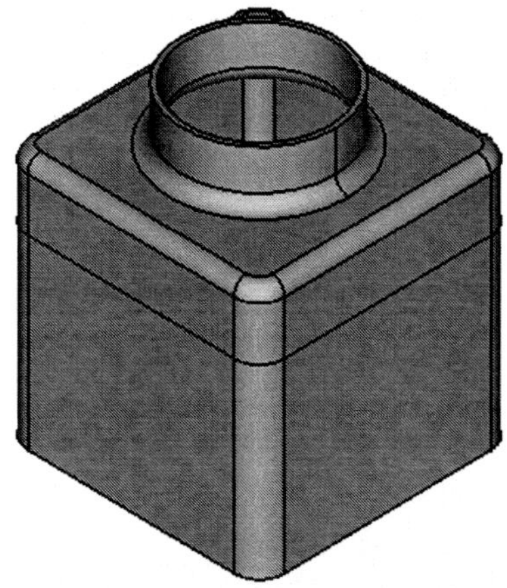

9. Click **File > Save** on the Menu bar.
10. Click **File > Close** on the Menu bar.

Chapter 4: Sketching

In this chapter, you learn the sketching tools. You learn to create:

- Polylines
- Polygons
- Slots
- Constraints
- B-Splines
- Ellipses
- Circles
- Trim
- Extend
- Toggle Construction geometry

Creating Polylines

The **Polyline** tool is the most commonly used while creating a sketch. It helps you to draw a continuous chain of connected line segments and arcs in one uninterrupted command. You can press M mid-command to toggle between straight segments and arc segments without restarting the tool. It is the preferred tool for drawing closed profiles like rectangular flanges, brackets, or any multi-segment outline efficiently.

1. To start a new part file, click **File > New** on the Menu Bar.
2. On the **Workbench** toolbar, select **Workbench** drop-down > **Part Design**.
3. Click **Sketch > New Sketch** on the Menu bar.
4. Select the **XY_Plane**. The sketch starts.
5. To activate this tool, you need to click the **Polyline** 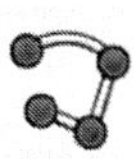 icon on the **Geometries** toolbar.
6. Click in the graphics window and move the pointer.
7. Click to create a line. Notice that another line is attached to the cursor.

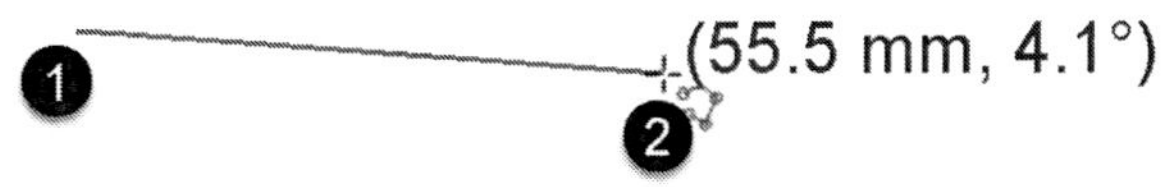

8. Move the pointer and click to create another line.

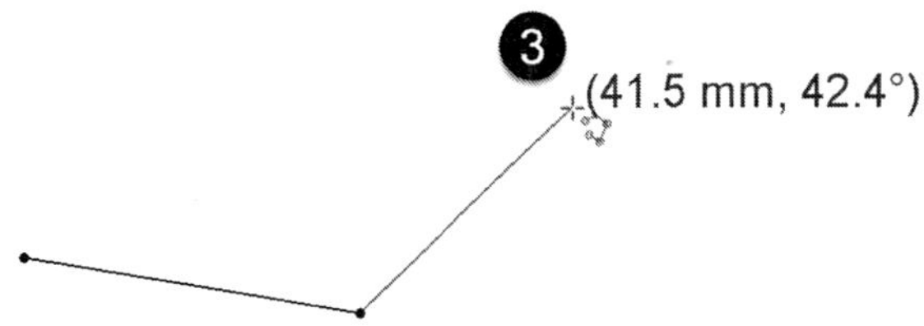

9. Press the **M** key on your keyboard.
10. Move the pointer and click to create a line perpendicular to the previous line.

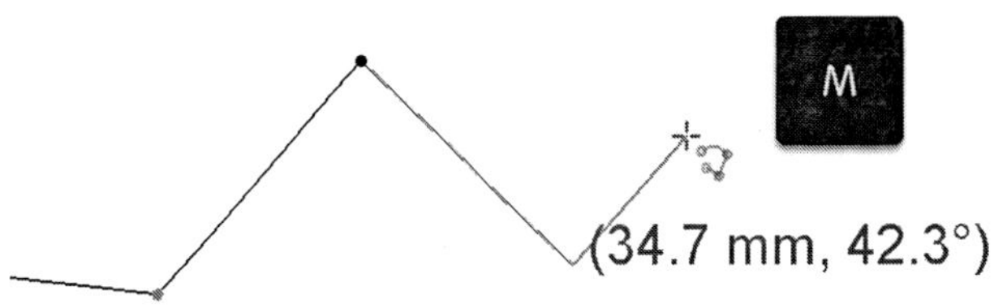

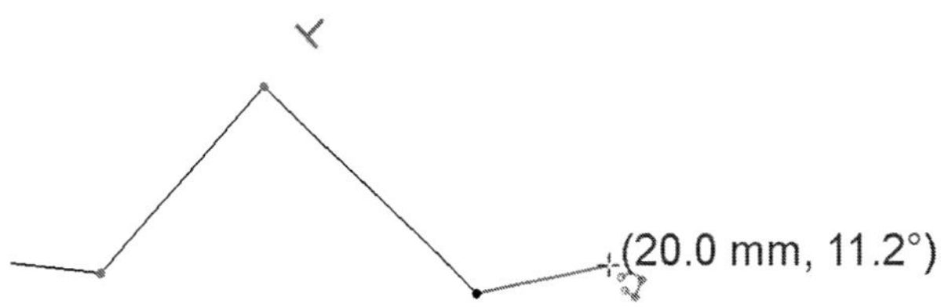

11. Press the **M** key twice on your keyboard.
12. Move the pointer and click to create a line colinear to the previous line.

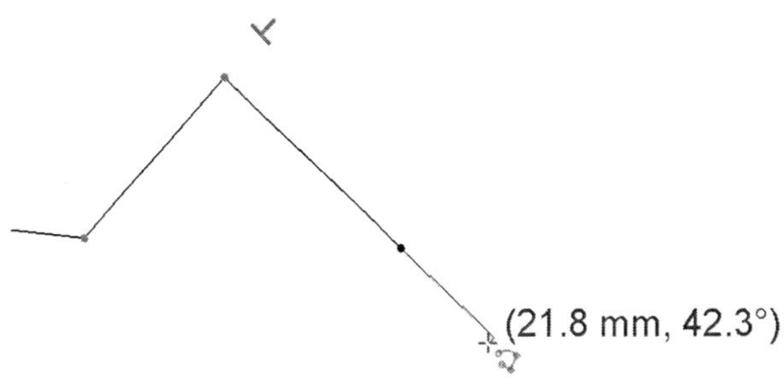

13. Press the **M** key thrice on your keyboard; a grey arc tangent to the previous line appears.

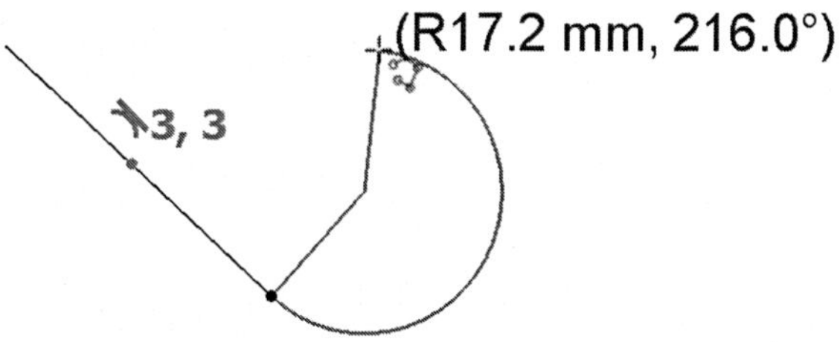

14. Move the pointer and click to create an arc tangent to the previous line.

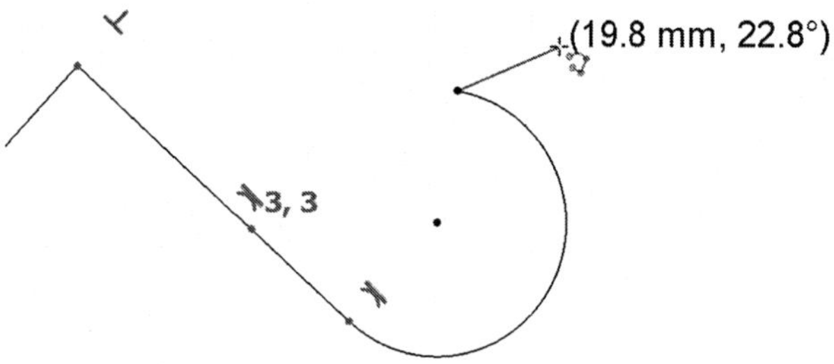

15. Press the **M** key four times to display an arc normal to the previous line.
16. Again, press the **M** key to change the direction of the normal arc.

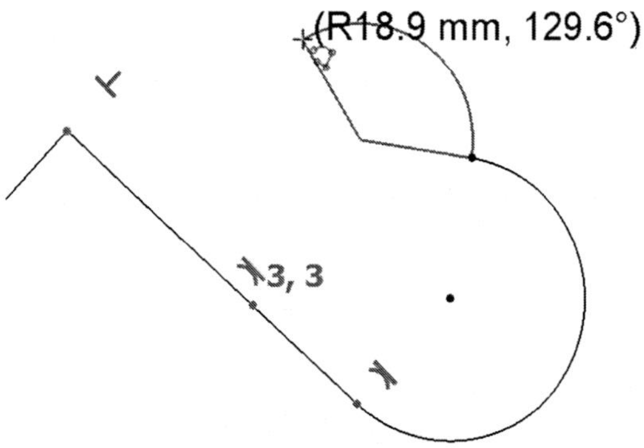

17. Click to create the normal arc.
18. Right click to end the line chain.
19. Again, right click to deactivate the **Polyline** tool.

Creating Polygons

A Polygon is a shape having many sides ranging from 3 to 1024. In FreeCAD, you can create regular polygons having sides with equal length. Follow the steps given next to create a polygon.

1. Click the **New Sketch** icon on the **Part Design Helper Features** toolbar.
2. Select the **XY_Plane**. The sketch starts.
3. On the **Geometries** toolbar, select **Polygon > Polygon** 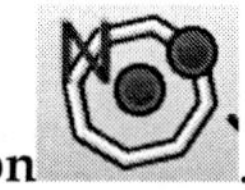.
4. On the **Create regular polygon** dialog, type **8** in the **Number of Sides** box.
5. Click **OK**.
6. Click to define the center of the polygon.
7. Move the pointer and click to define the size and angle of the polygon.

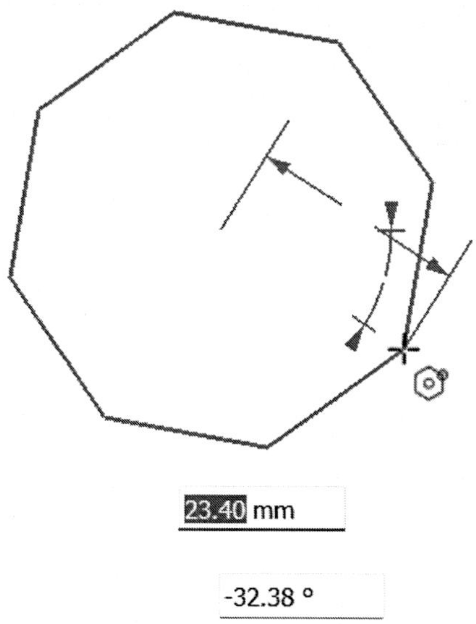

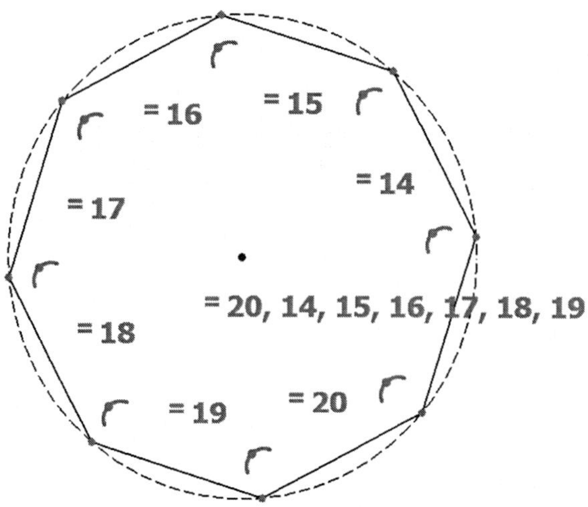

Creating a Slot

The **Create Slot** tool is used to create slots.

1. Click the **Slot**  icon on the **Geometries** toolbar.
2. Click to specify the centerpoint of the first semicircle.
3. Move the pointer and click to specify the centerpoint of the second semicircle.

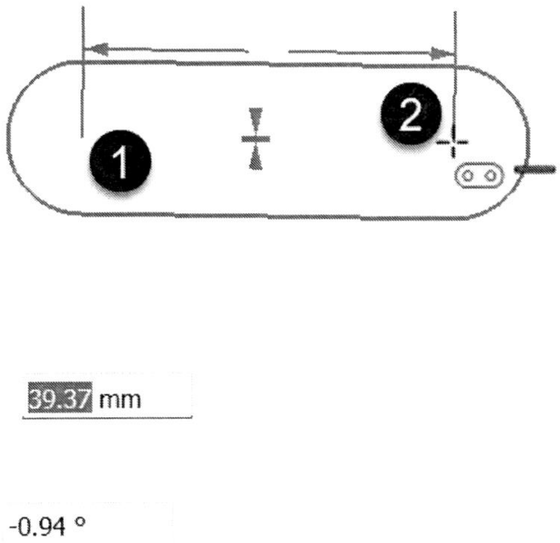

4. Move the pointer outward and click to specify the radius of the arc.

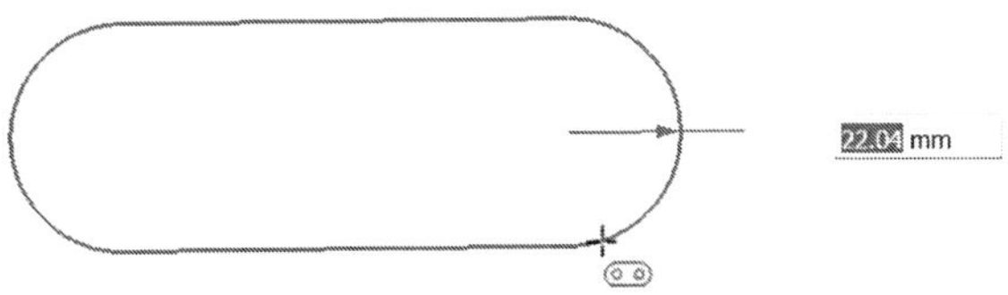

Constraints

Constraints are used to control the shape of a sketch by establishing relationships between the sketch elements. You can add constraints using the tools available on the **Constraints** toolbar.

Coincident Constraint

This constraint connects a point to another point.

1. On the **Constraints** toolbar, click **Coincident Constraint**  .
2. Select two points. The selected points are connected.

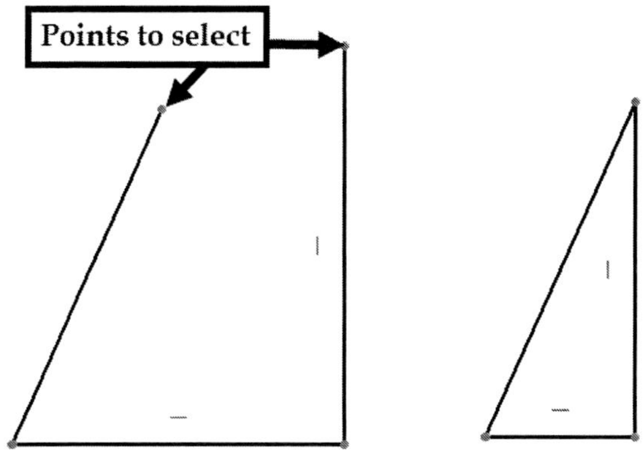

This constraint also makes a point coincident with a sketch element.

1. Click the **Coincident Constraint** icon on the **Constraints** toolbar.
2. Select the point and object, as shown.

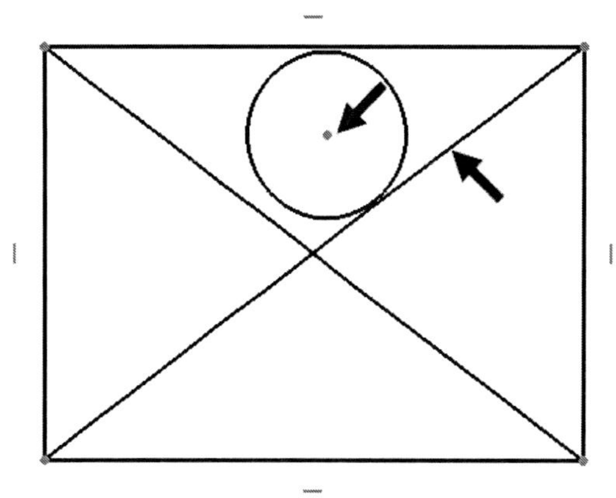

The point is made coincident with the object. Likewise, make the point coincident with another object, as shown.

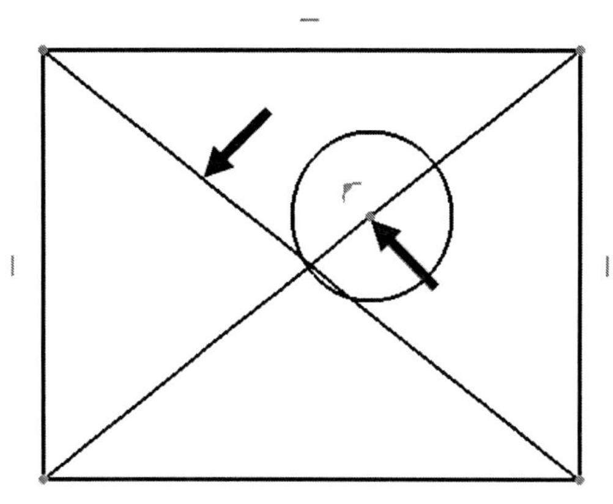

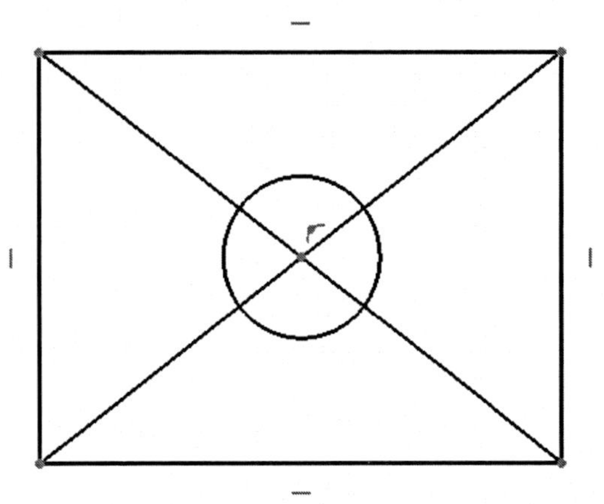

Horizontal Constraint

To apply the **Horizontal** constraint, click on a line and click the **Horizontal Constraint** icon on the **Constraints** toolbar.

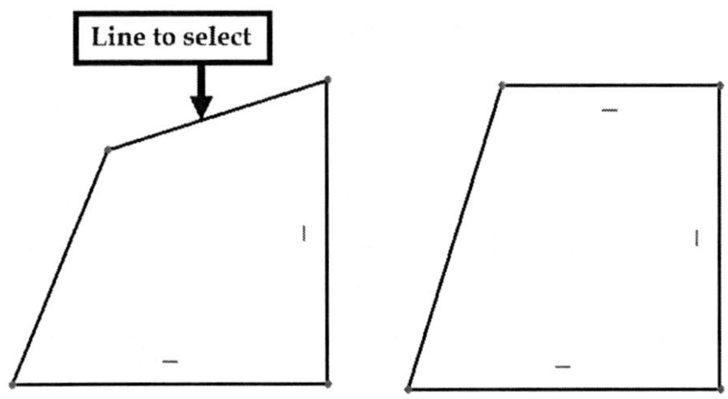

Vertical Constraint

Use the **Vertical Constraint** icon to make a line vertical.

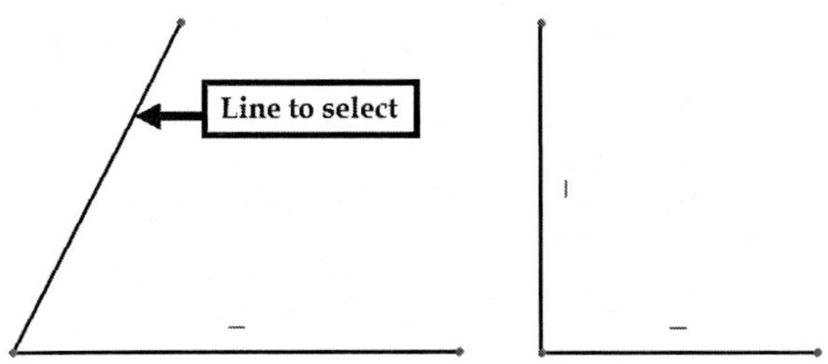

Tangent/Collinear Constraint

This constraint makes an arc, circle, or line tangent to another arc or circle. Click the **Tangent/Collinear Constraint** icon on the **Constraints** toolbar. Select a circle, arc, or line. Next, select another circle or arc; the two elements are tangent to each other.

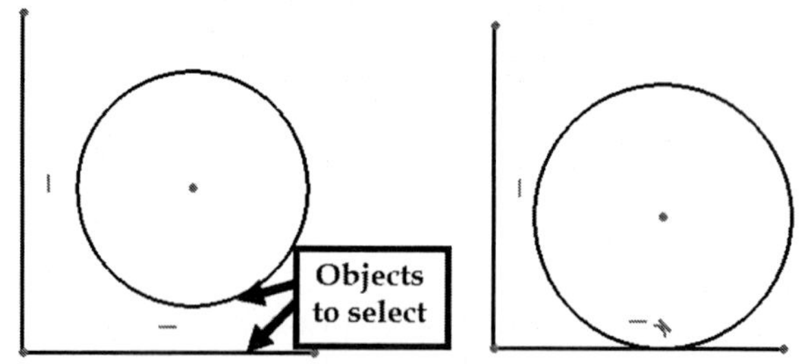

You can also make two lines collinear to each other using the Tangent/Collinear Constraint.

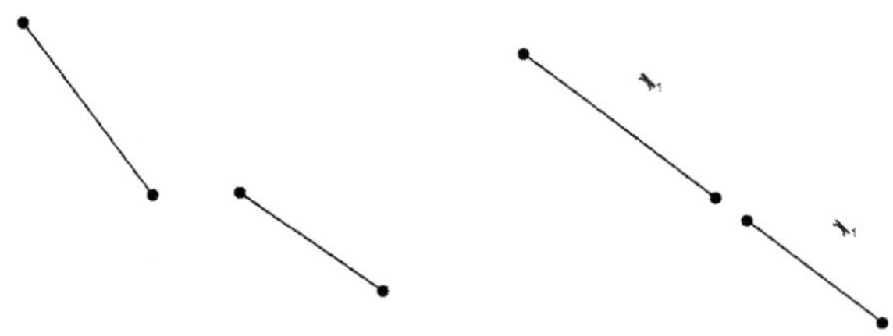

Parallel Constraint

Use the **Parallel Constraint** icon to make two lines parallel to each other. To do this, click the **Parallel Constraint** icon on the **Constraints** toolbar. Next, select the two lines to be parallel.

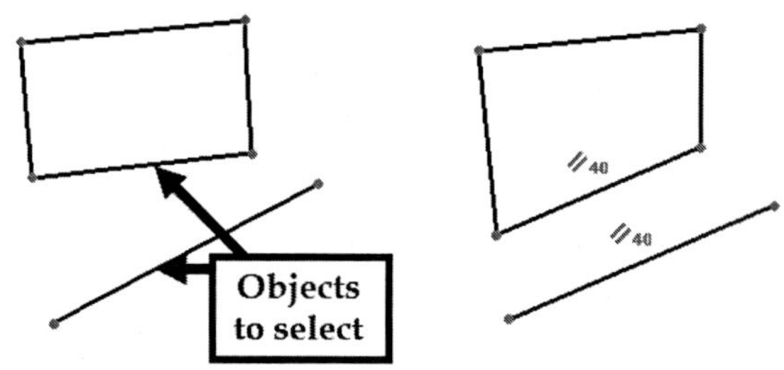

Perpendicular Constraint

Use the **Perpendicular Constraint** icon to make two entities perpendicular to each other.

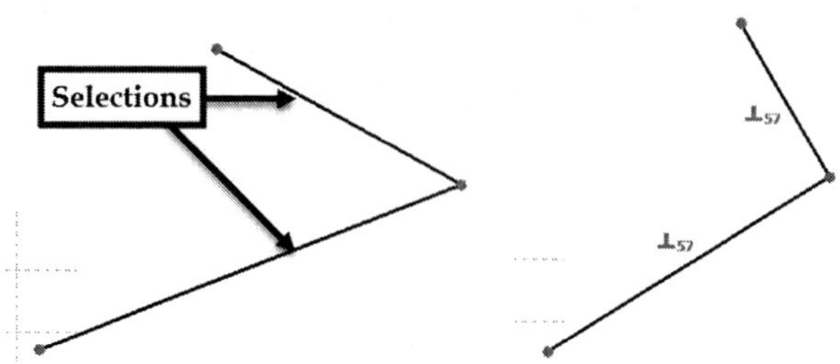

Auto Constraints

FreeCAD automatically adds constraints when you New Sketch elements.

1. Start a new sketch and activate the **Polyline** 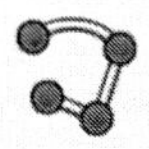 tool from the **Geometries** toolbar.
2. Click to specify the start point of the line.
3. Move the pointer in the horizontal direction.
4. Click to create a line with the **Horizontal** constraint.

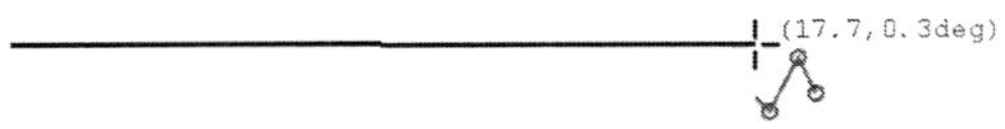

5. Move the pointer vertically in the upward direction .
6. Click to create a line with the **Vertical** constraint.

7. Create an inclined line, as shown.

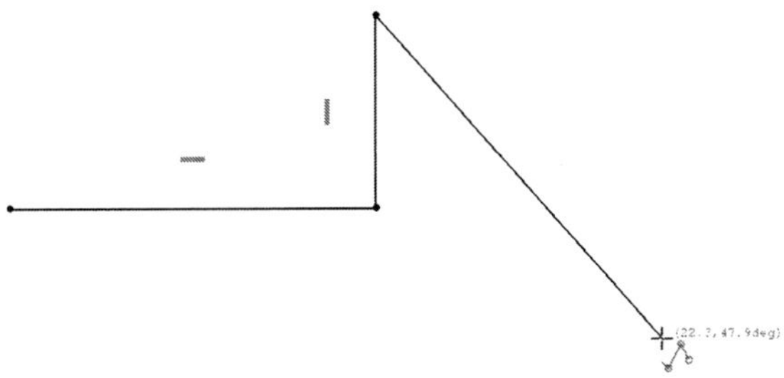

8. Right-click twice to deactivate the tool.

Deleting Constraints

Select the constraint and press **Delete** on your keyboard.

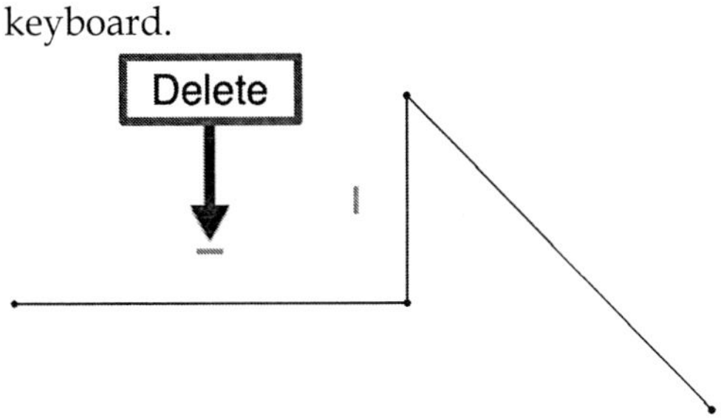

Symmetric Constraint

Use the **Symmetric Constraint** tool to make two sketch elements symmetric about a centerline.

1. Click on the elements to make symmetric.
2. Click on the symmetry line.
3. Click the **Symmetric Constraint** icon on the **Constraints** toolbar.

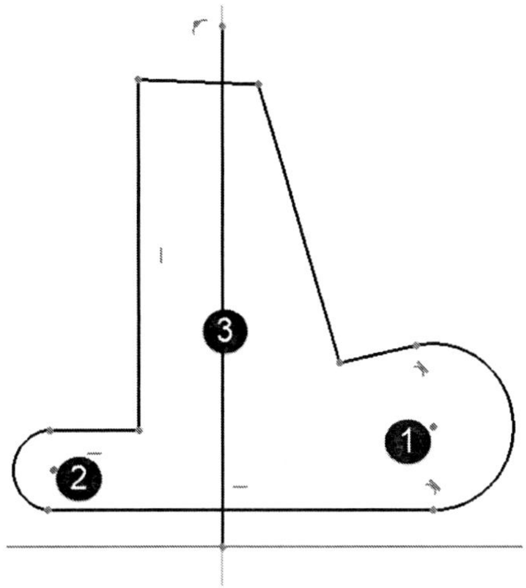

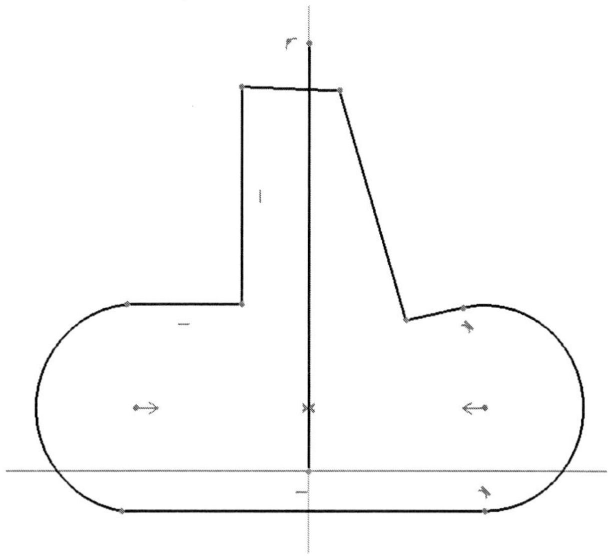

Lock Position

The **Lock Position** constraint locks a selected point by adding dimensions to it.

1. On the menu bar, click **Sketch > Constraints > Lock Position** icon.
2. Select a point from the sketch.

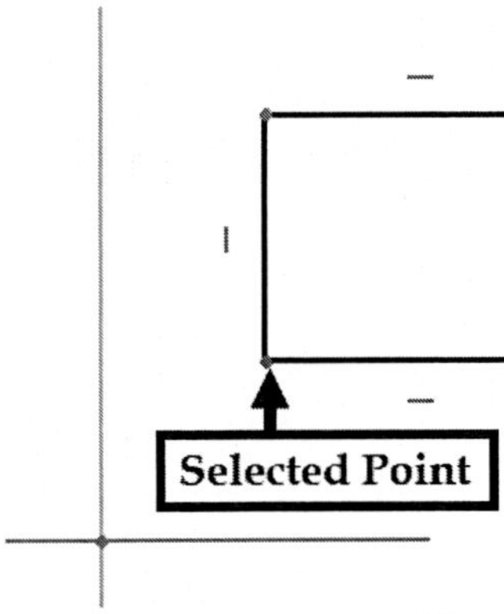

Dimensions are created between the selected point and the origin.

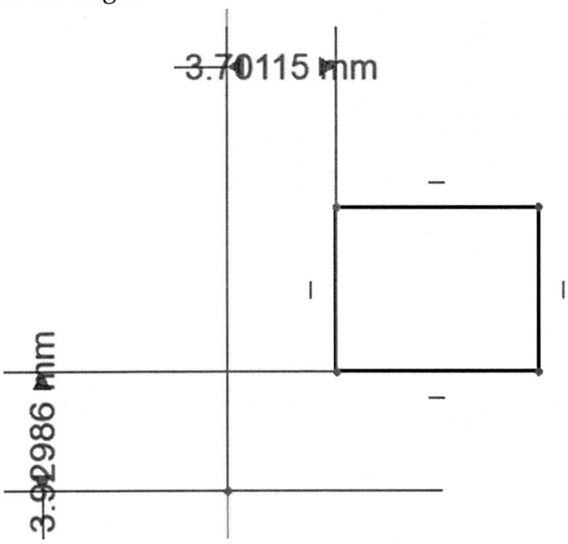

Block Constraint

This constraint fixes the sketch object at its location.

1. Click the **Block Constraint**  icon on the **Constraints** toolbar.
2. Select an object from the sketch.

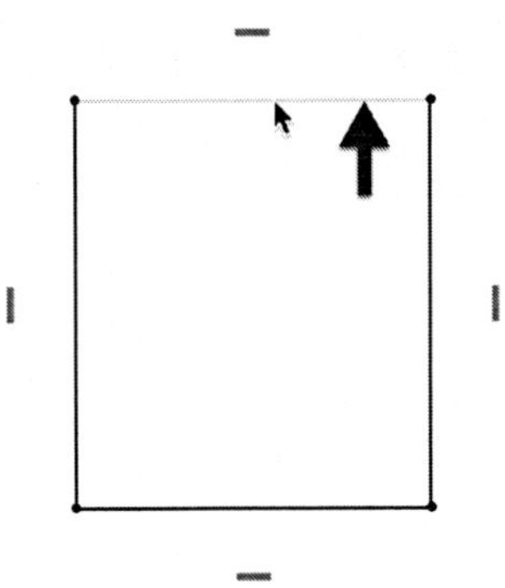

3. Click the object and drag; notice that it is fixed at its location.

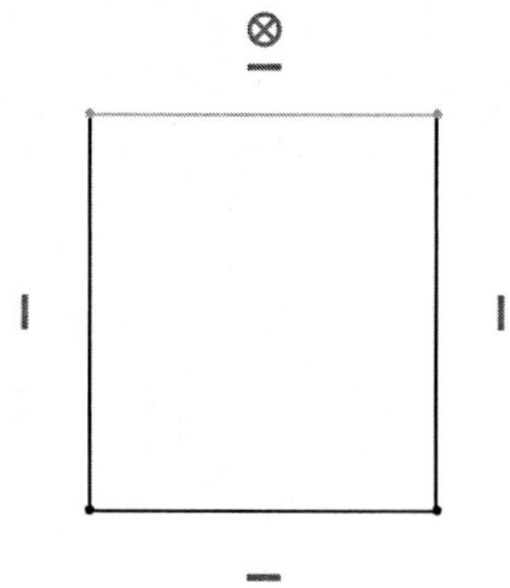

Hiding Constraints

To hide sketch constraints, uncheck the checkbox next to it in the **Constraints** section located in the **Tasks** panel.

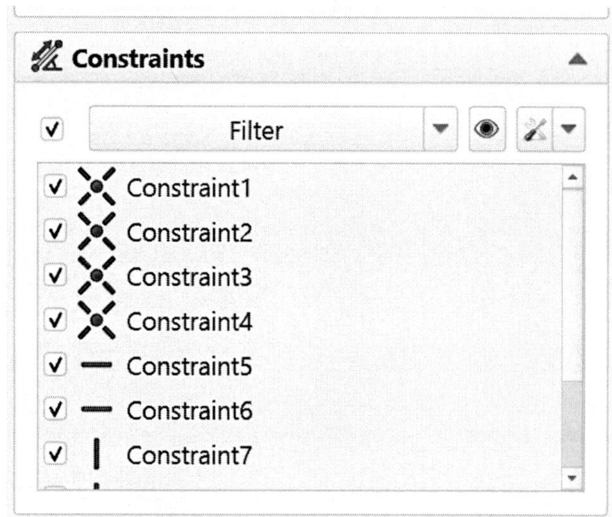

Create B-Spline

A B-spline curve, short for "Basis-spline curve," is a mathematical representation of a smooth curve defined by a series of control points. The fascinating aspect of B-splines is their ability to create curves that are not only smooth but also highly adaptable. The control points act as anchors, determining the general direction and shape of the curve.

1. On the **Geometries** toolbar, click **B-Spline** drop-down > **B-Spline** 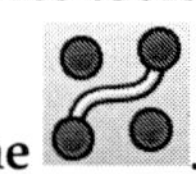.
2. Click to define points in the graphics window.

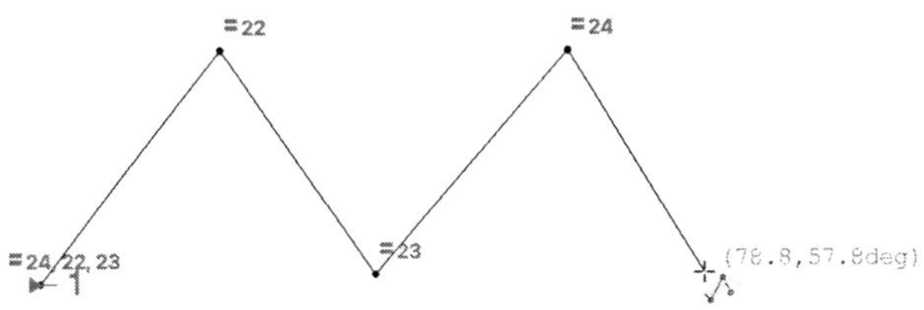

3. Right click to create a spline controlled by the selected points.
4. Press Esc to deactivate this command.

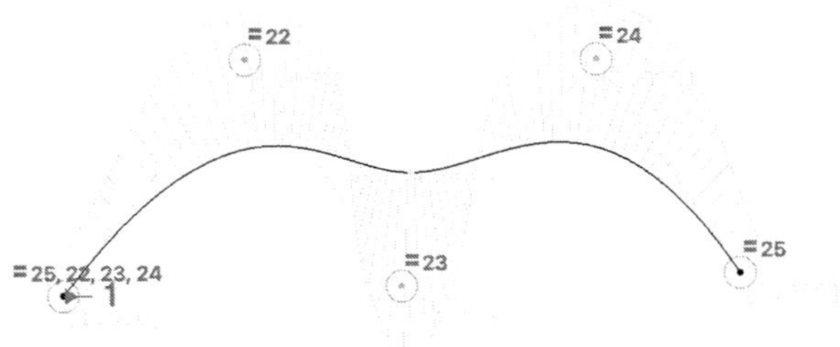

Create periodic B-spline

If you want to create a closed B-spline, then click the **B-spline** drop-down > **Periodic B-spline**  on the **Geometries** toolbar. Next, specify the control points. Right click to create a closed B-spline.

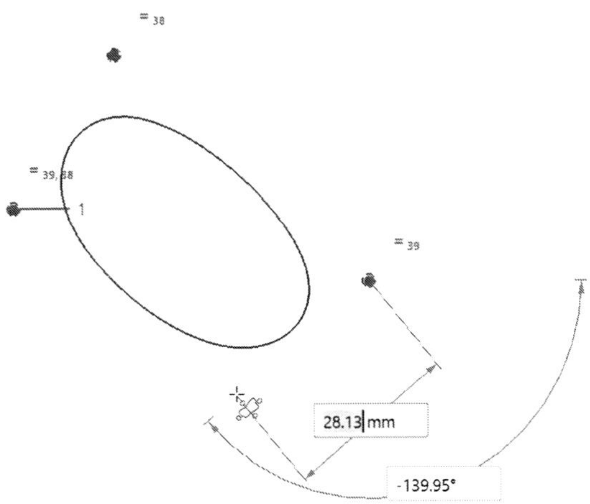

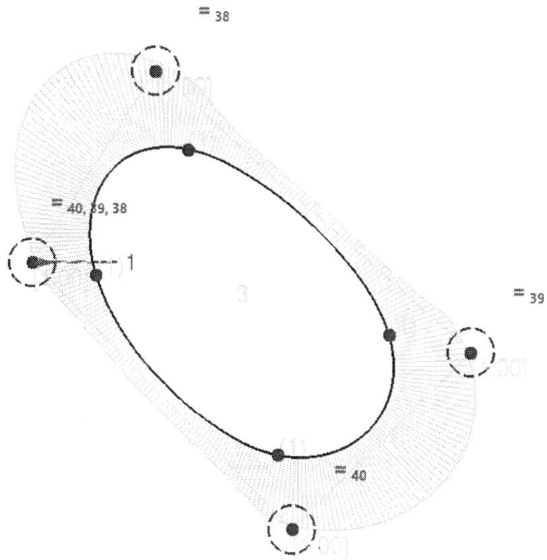

Create B-Spline From knots

The **B-spline From knots** tool is used to create a continuous and smooth spline that passes through specific control points. This tool is essential for generating precise and visually pleasing curves.

When you use the **B-spline From knots** tool, you define control points (knots) that influence the spline's shape. The algorithm calculates the curve so that it smoothly traverses these control points while maintaining smooth transitions between segments.

One key advantage of the B-spline is its flexibility. You can add or adjust control points to fine-tune the curve's shape to meet design requirements accurately. This adaptability makes it useful for various applications, from shaping product designs to creating organic forms.

1. On the **Geometries** toolbar, click **B-Spline** drop-down > **B-spline From knots** 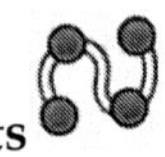.
2. Click to define points in the graphics window.

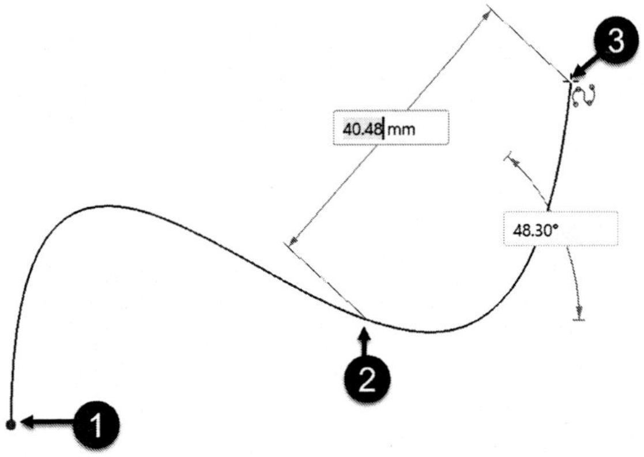

3. Right click to create a spline passing through the selected points.

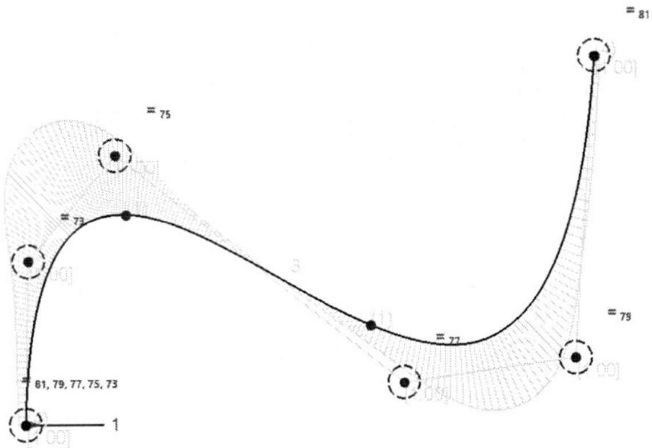

4. Press Esc to deactivate this command.

Ellipses

Ellipses belong to the category of non-uniform curves but have a uniform shape defined by their built-in symmetry. Unlike splines, which are created through control points and interpolation, ellipses are defined by precise mathematical equations. These equations produce a regular, closed shape that looks like an elongated circle.

Ellipses are closed shapes, meaning their boundaries form a continuous loop with no gaps or breaks. This sets them apart from open curves such as lines or arcs. In mathematical terms, the equation of an ellipse in a Cartesian coordinate system is:

$$\frac{x^2}{a^2} + \frac{y^2}{b^2} = 1$$

where a and b are the semi-major and semi-minor axes respectively. These axes define the size and proportions of the ellipse.

Ellipses are used across mathematics, engineering, astronomy, and art, where their consistent shape and well-defined mathematical properties make them practical and reliable.

1. Click the **New Sketch** icon on the **Part Design Helper Features** toolbar.
2. Select any one of the datum planes from the **Combo View** panel.
3. Click **OK**.
4. On the **Geometries** toolbar, click **Circle** drop-down > **Ellipse From Center** 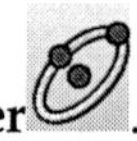.
5. Pick a point in the graphics window to define the center of the ellipse.
6. Move the pointer and click to define the radius and orientation of the first axis.

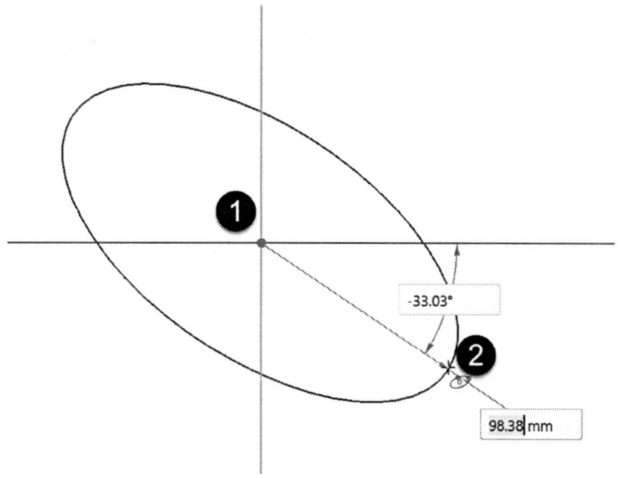

7. Move the pointer and click to define the radius of the second axis.

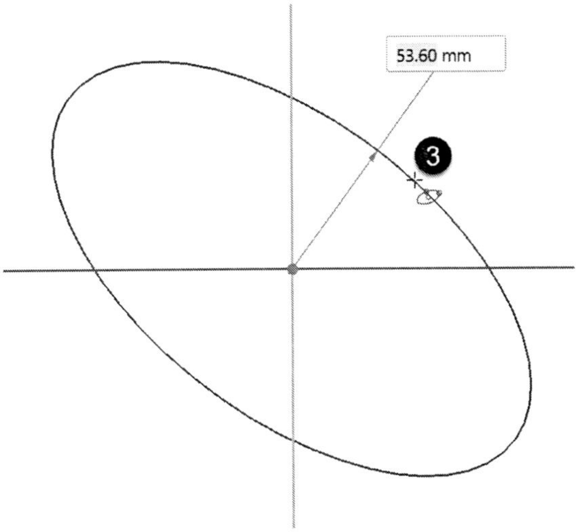

Click and drag the ellipse to notice that it is under-defined. You need to add dimensions and constraints to fully define the ellipse.

8. On the **Constraints** toolbar, click **Dimension** drop-down > **Angle Dimension** 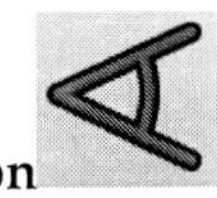.
9. Select the lines, as shown.

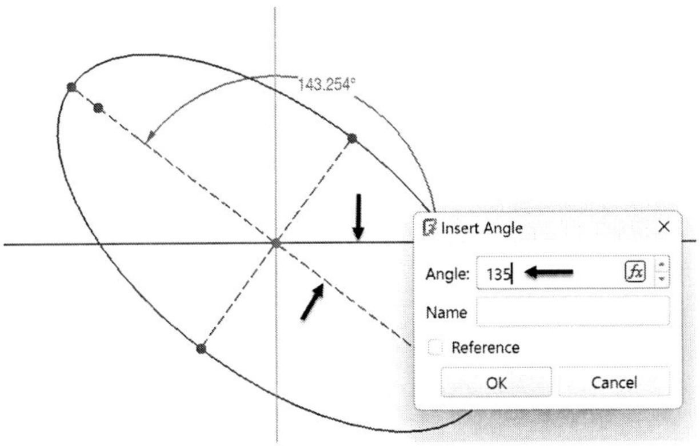

10. Type 135 in the **Angle** box and click **OK**.
11. Click the **Dimension** drop-down > **Distance Dimension** icon on the **Constraints** toolbar.
12. Select the major axis line.
13. Type 50 in the **Length** box and click the **OK** button.

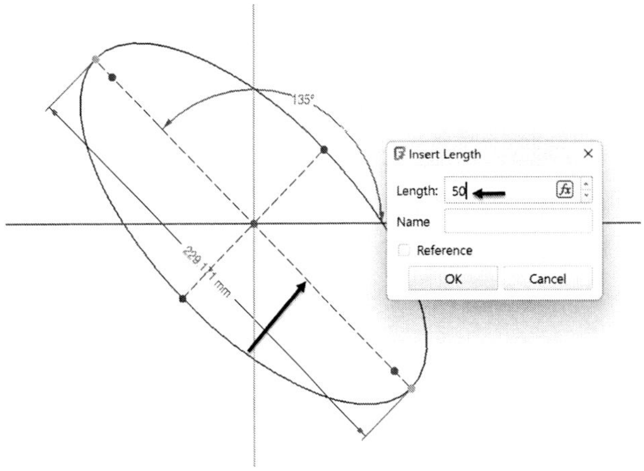

14. Likewise, add the distance constrain to the minor axis. The sketch is fully defined.

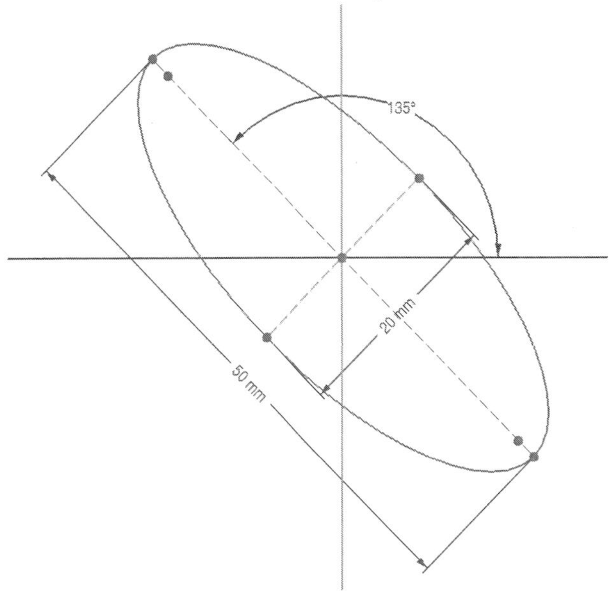

Extend Edge

The **Extend Edge** tool is used to extend lines, arcs, and other open entities to connect to other objects.

1. Create a sketch, as shown below.

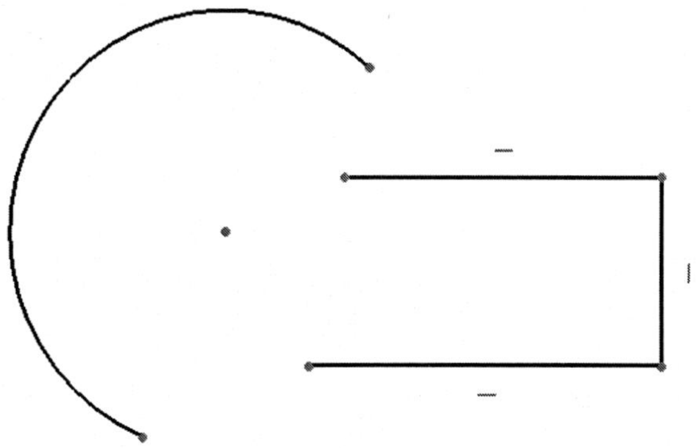

2. Click the **Trim Edge** drop-down **> Extend edge** icon on the **Sketcher Tools** toolbar.

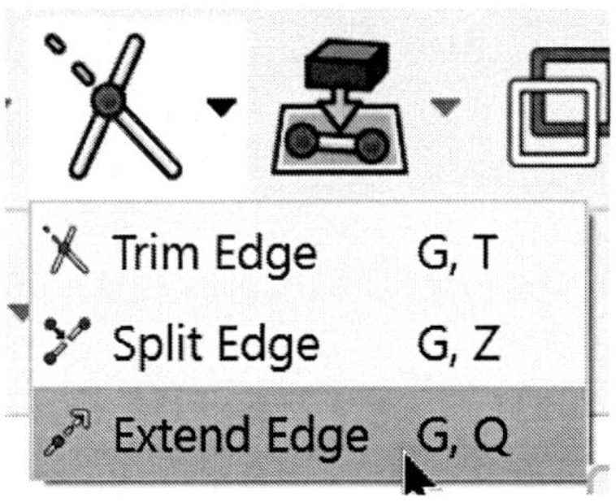

3. Select the horizontal open line.
4. Select the arc; the line is extended up to the arc.

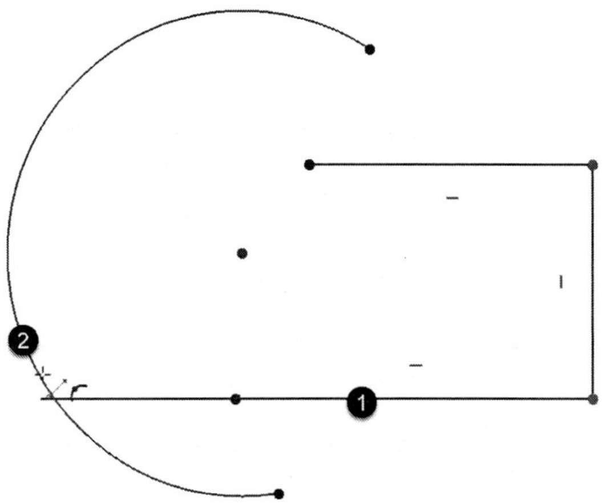

Likewise, extend the other elements, as shown.

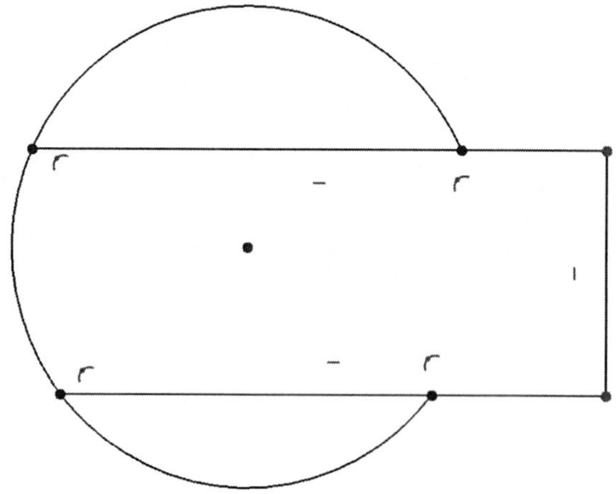

Trim Edge

The **Trim Edge** tool is used to trim the unwanted portions of the sketch using an intersecting edge.

1. Click the **Trim Edge** icon on the **Sketcher Tools** toolbar.
2. Click on the edges to trim.

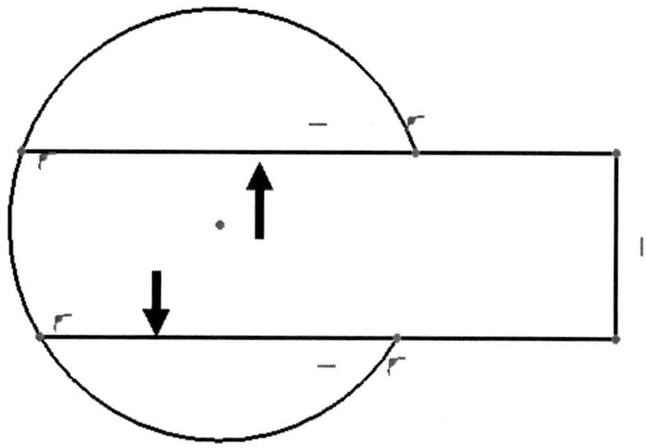

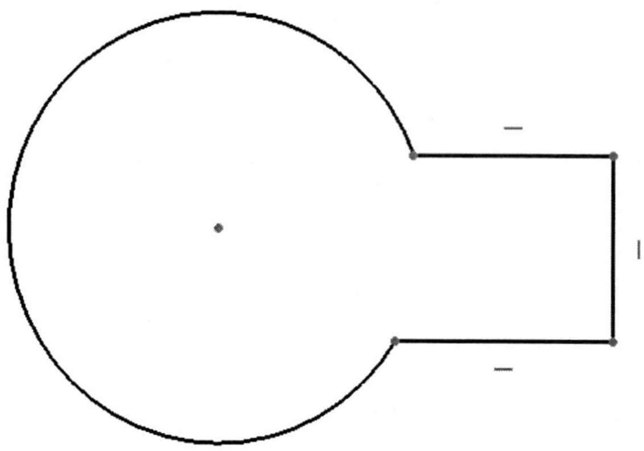

Toggle Construction geometry

This command converts a standard sketch element into a construction element. Construction elements support you to create a sketch of a desired shape and size. To convert a standard sketch element to construction element, click on it and select **Toggle Construction geometry** on the **Geometries** toolbar.

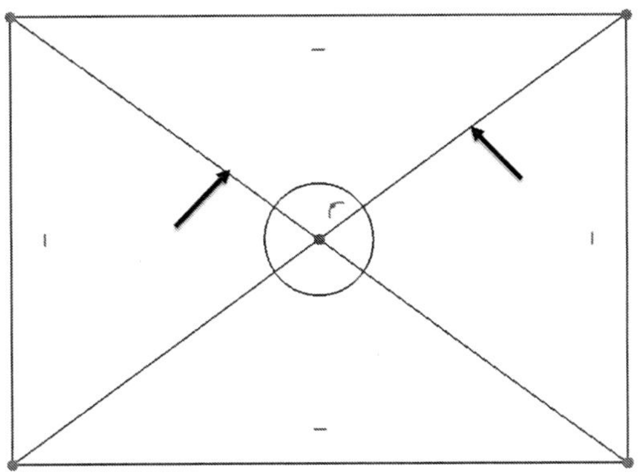

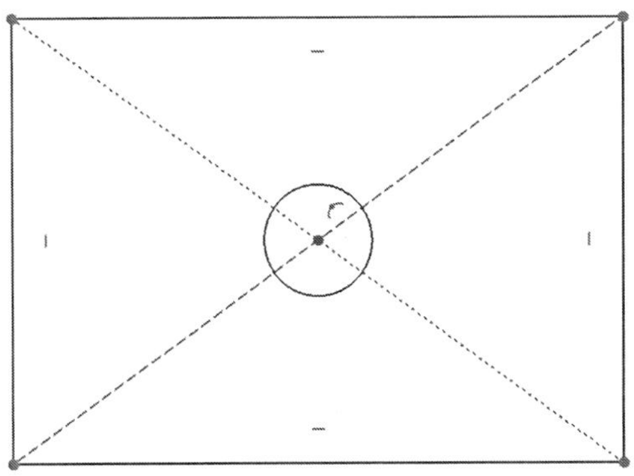

You can also convert it back to a standard sketch element by clicking on it and selecting the **Toggle Construction geometry** icon on the **Geometries** toolbar.

TUTORIAL 1

In this tutorial, you create the sketch shown in the figure.

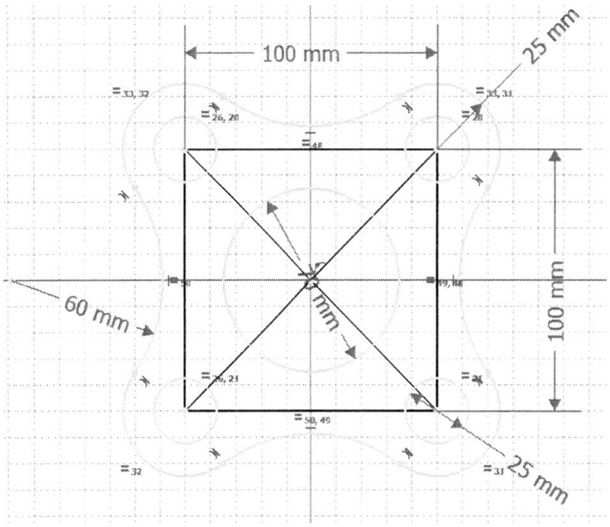

1. Open the FreeCAD application.
2. Click **File > New** on the Menu bar.
3. Select the **Part Design** option from the **Workbenches** drop-down.
4. Click the **New Sketch** icon on the **Part Design Helper Features** toolbar, and then select the XY Plane.
5. Click **OK** to start the sketch.
6. Click the **Circle** drop-down **> Circle From Center** icon on the **Geometries** toolbar.
7. Select the origin point of the sketch.
8. Move the pointer outward and click to create a circle.
9. On the **Geometries** toolbar, click the **Rectangle** drop-down > **Centered Rectangle** (or) click **Sketch > Geometries > Create centered rectangle**.

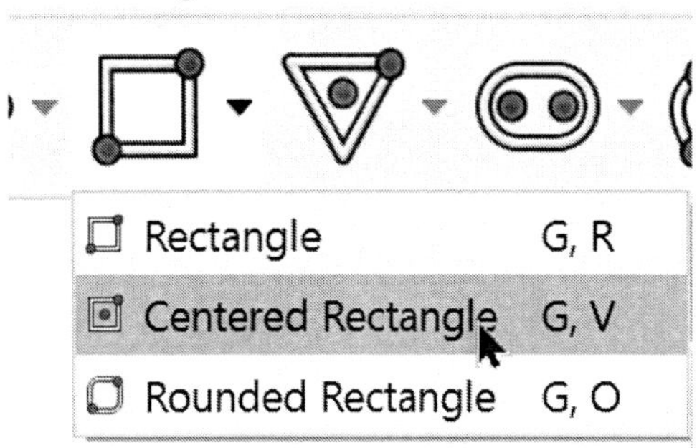

10. Select the origin point of the sketch.
11. Drag the cursor towards the top right corner, and then click to create a rectangle.

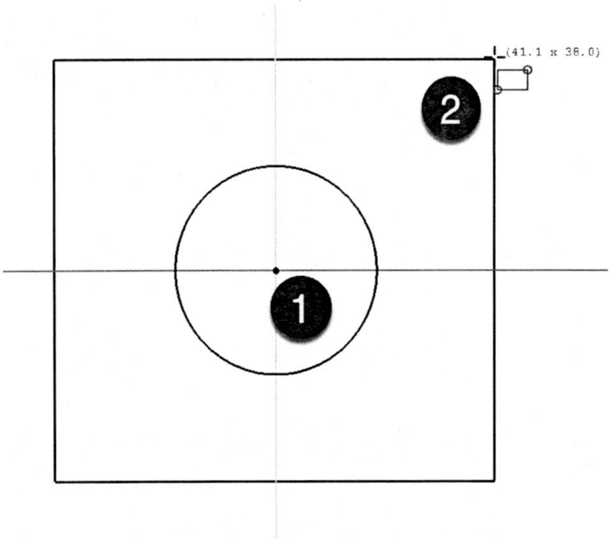

12. Click the **Circle** drop-down **> Circle From Center**  icon on the **Geometries** toolbar.
13. Select the top-left corner point of the rectangle.
14. Move the pointer outward and click to create a circle.

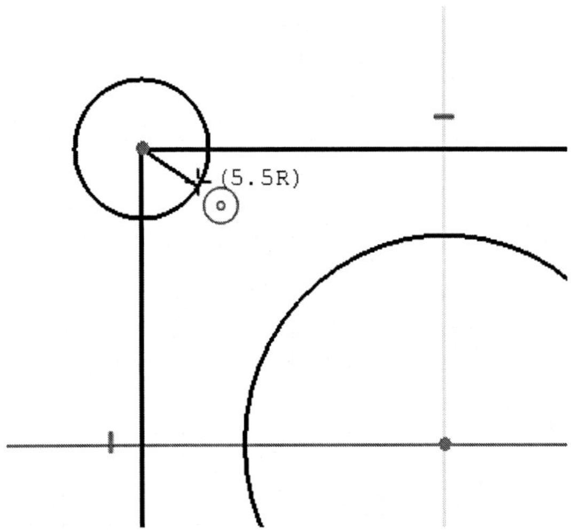

15. Likewise, create three more circles on the remaining corners. Next, press ESC.

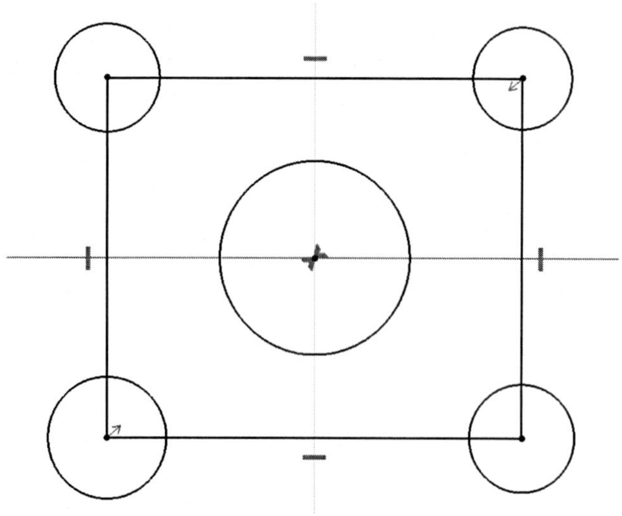

16. Select the edges of the rectangle.
17. Click **Toggle Construction geometry** 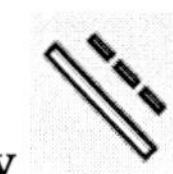 on the **Geometries** toolbar.

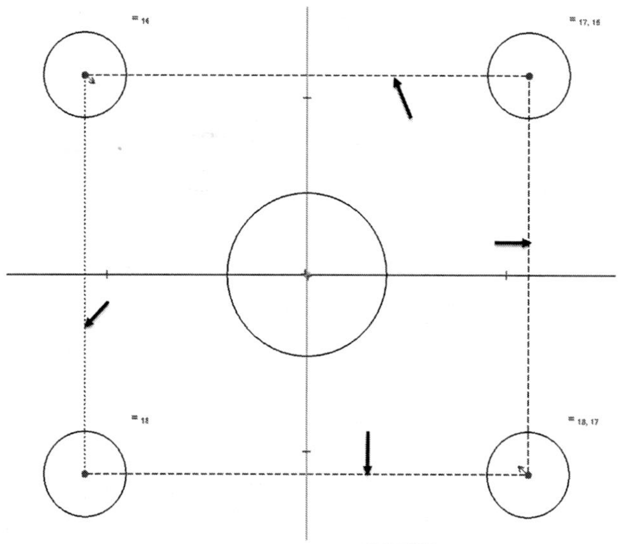

18. Click the **Equal Constraint**  icon on the **Constraints** toolbar.
19. Select the circles located on the corner points of the rectangle (start from the top-left corner circle).
20. Select the bottom-left and top-left circles; the diameters of the circles are made equal.

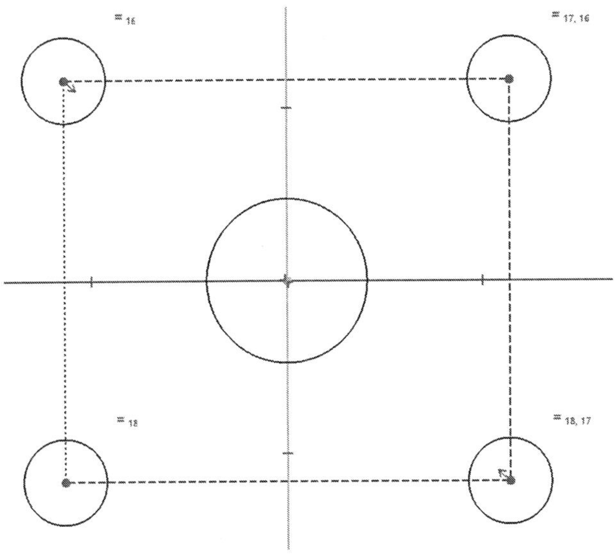

21. Click **Dimension** drop-down > **Distance Dimension** on the **Constraints** toolbar.
22. Select the vertical line of the rectangle.
23. Type 100 in the **Length** box, and then click **OK**.
24. Select the horizontal line of the rectangle.
25. Type 100 in the **Length** box, and then click **OK**.

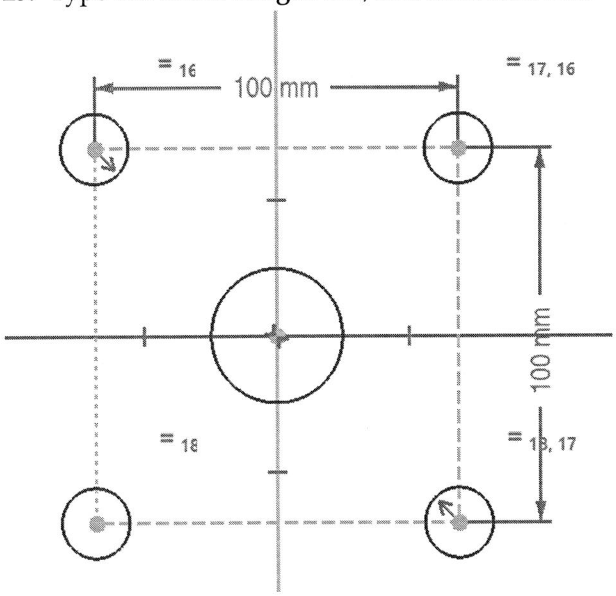

26. Click the **Dimension** drop-down > **Diameter Dimension** on the **Constraints** toolbar.

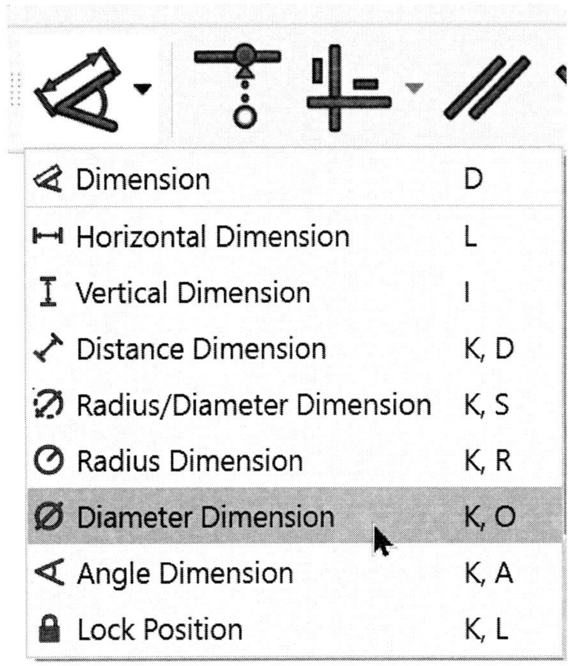

27. Select the circle located at the center.
28. Type **70** in the **Diameter** box and click **OK**.

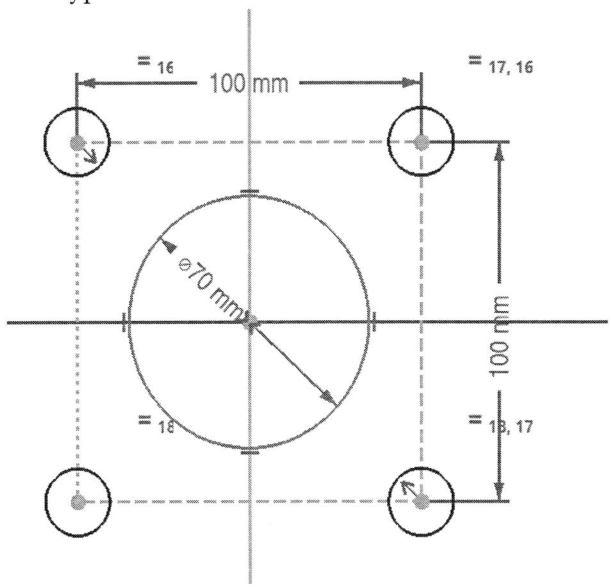

29. Select any one of the circles located on the corner points of the rectangle.
30. Type **25** in the **Diameter** box, and click **OK**.

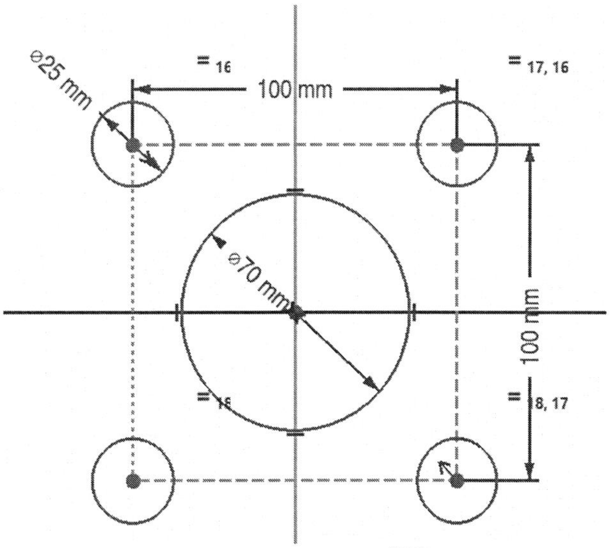

31. Click the **Circle From Center** icon on the **Geometries** toolbar.
32. Circle From Center from centers on the corner points of the rectangle, as shown.

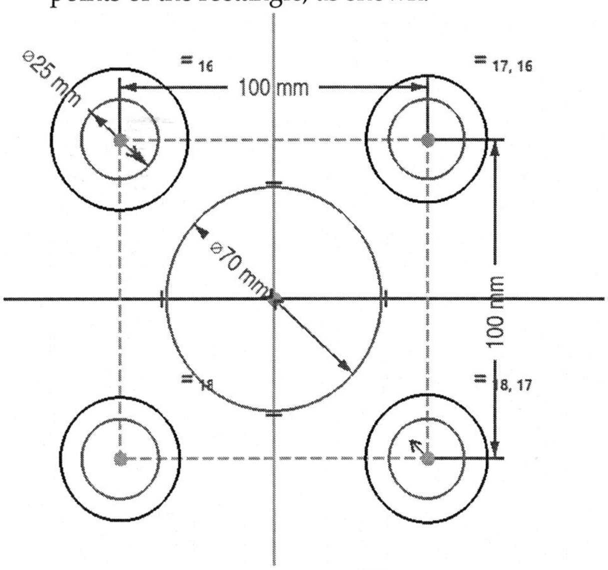

33. Click the **Equal Constraint** icon on the **Constraints** toolbar.
34. Select the newly created circles.
35. Select the bottom-left and top-left circles; the diameters of the circles are made equal.

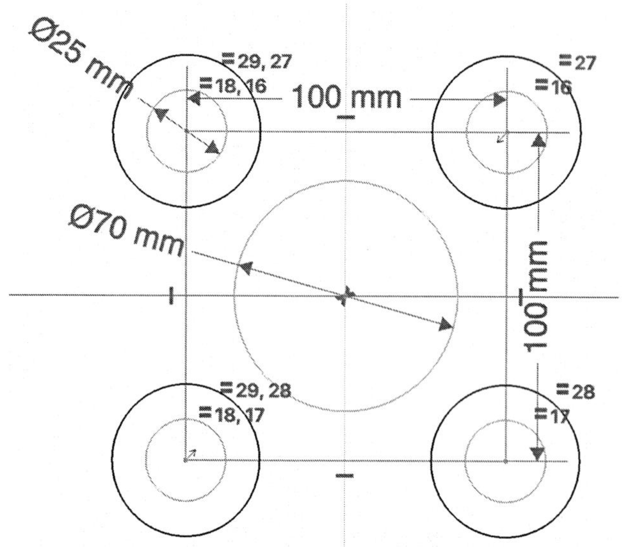

36. Click **Arc** drop-down **>** **Arc From 3 Points** on the **Geometries** toolbar.

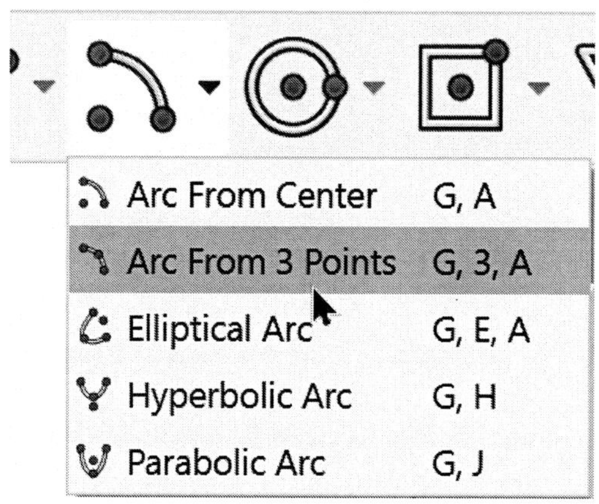

37. Select the outer circle located on the top-left corner.
38. Select the outer circle located on the bottom-left corner.

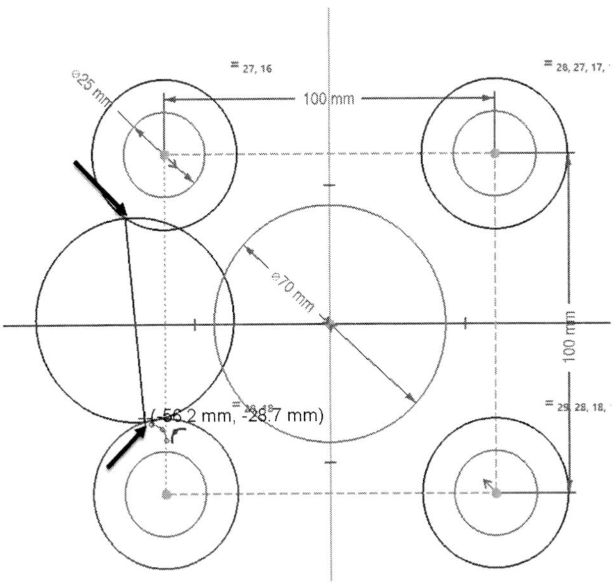

39. Move the pointer toward the right and click to create an arc.

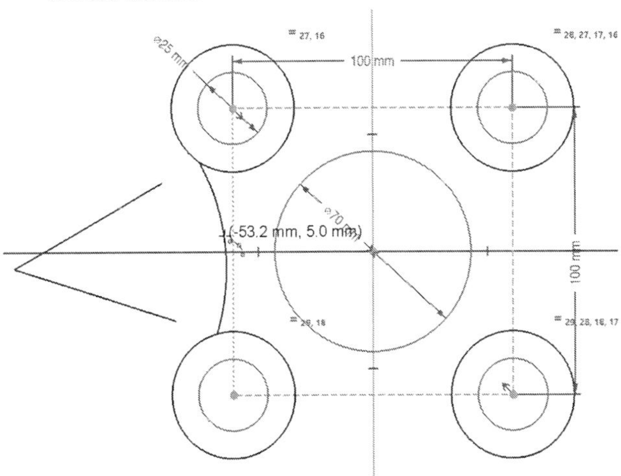

40. Activate the **Arc From 3 Points** tool (**G**, then **3**, then **A**).
41. Move the cursor to the perimeter of the bottom-left circle and click to place the first endpoint.
42. Move the cursor to the perimeter of the bottom-right circle and click to place the second endpoint.
43. Move the cursor upward (inward toward the center axis) to define the curvature, then click to set the third point.

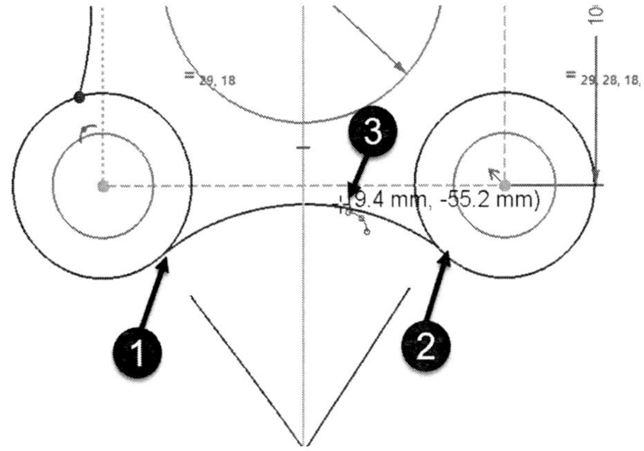

44. Move the cursor to the perimeter of the bottom-right circle and click to place the first endpoint.
45. Move the cursor to the perimeter of the top-right circle and click to place the second endpoint.
46. Move the cursor to the left (inward toward the center axis) to define the curvature, then click to set the third point.

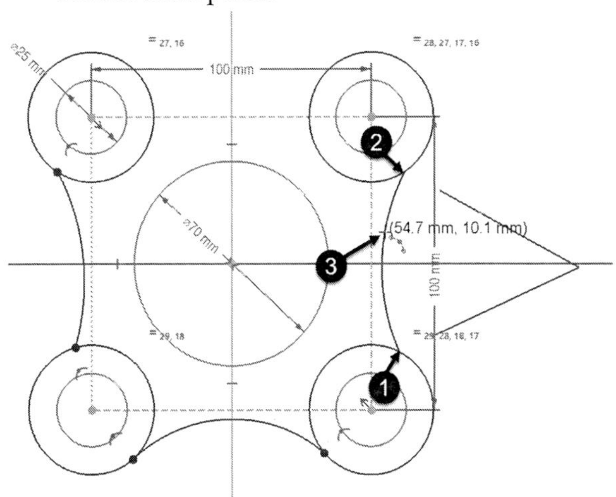

47. Move the cursor to the perimeter of the top-right circle and click to place the first endpoint.
48. Move the cursor to the perimeter of the top-left circle and click to place the second endpoint.
49. Move the cursor downward (inward toward the center axis) to define the curvature, then click to set the third point.

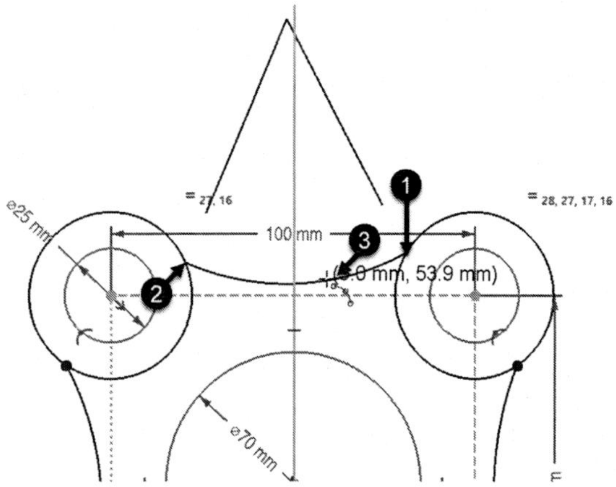

50. Click the **Trim Edge** icon on the **Sketcher Tools** toolbar.
51. Hover your cursor over the inner segment of the top-left circle. The segment that will be removed will highlight, and the trim points (where it intersects the arcs) will be marked.

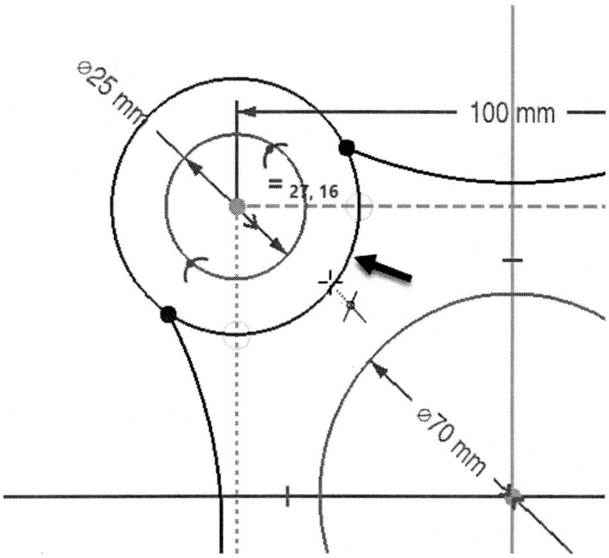

52. Click once to delete that inner segment.

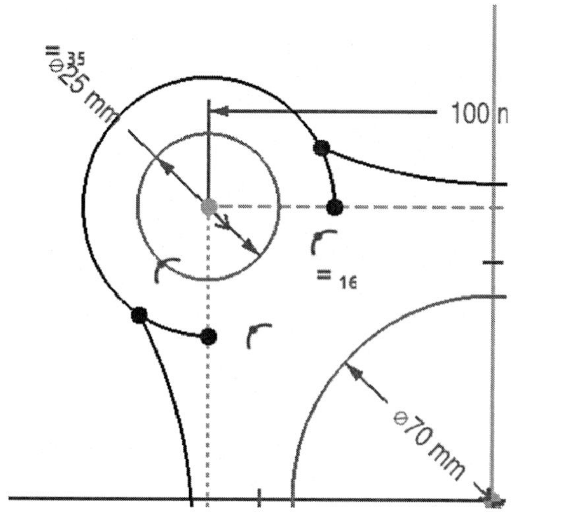

53. Repeat this process for the inner segments of the top-right, bottom-right, and bottom-left circles until only the continuous outer boundary remains.

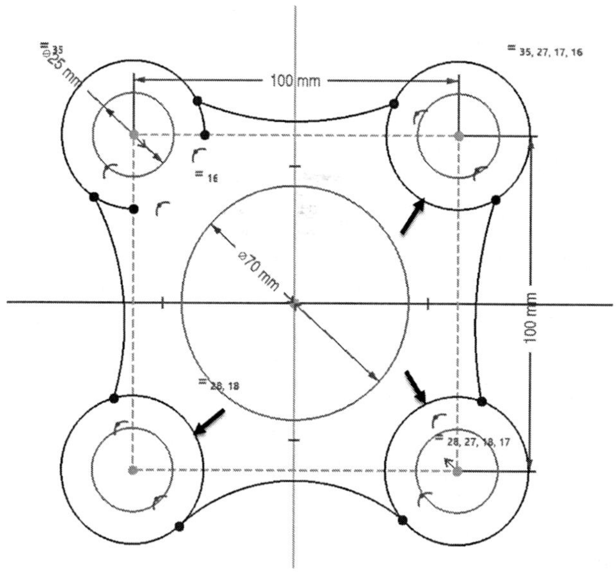

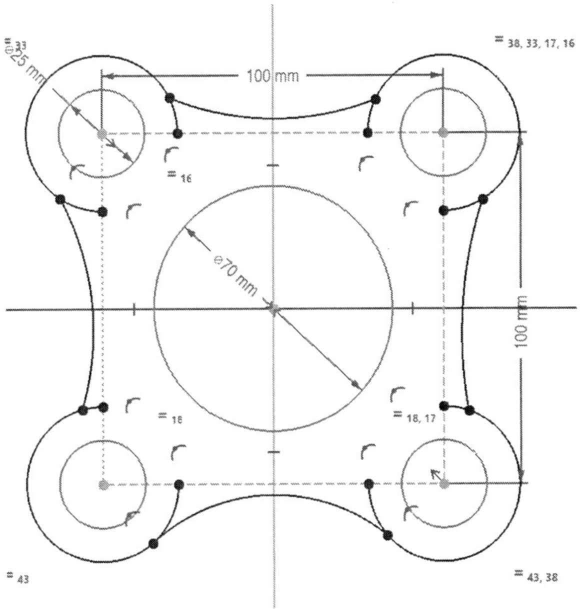

54. Hover your cursor over the small segment of the connecting arc that extends inside the boundary of the top-left circle. The specific segment will highlight.

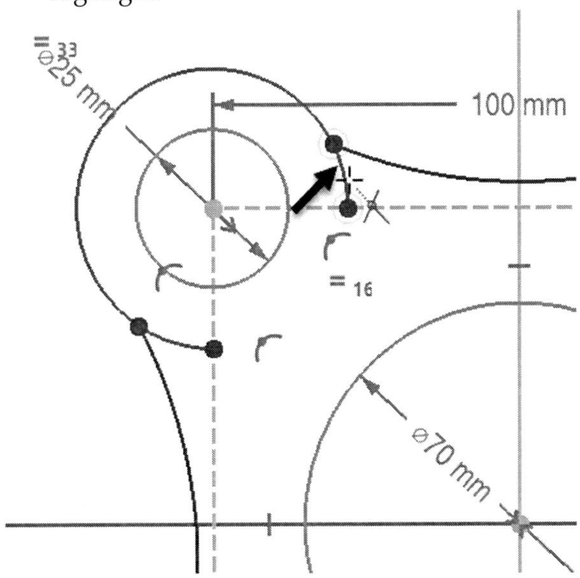

55. Click once to delete that overhanging segment. The arc will now end precisely at the tangency point.

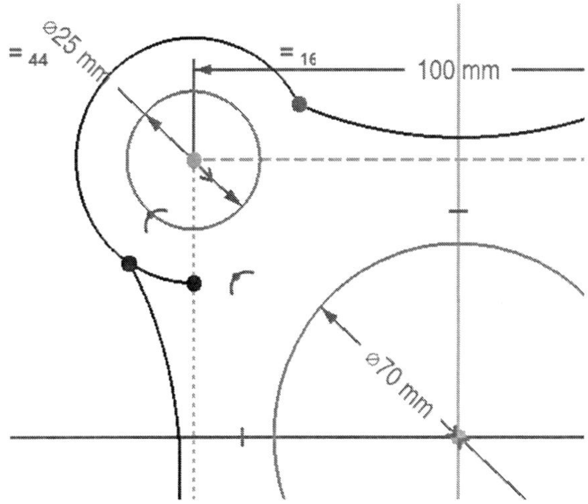

56. Hover over the other overhanging segment of the same arc (where it meets the top-right circle) and click to trim it.

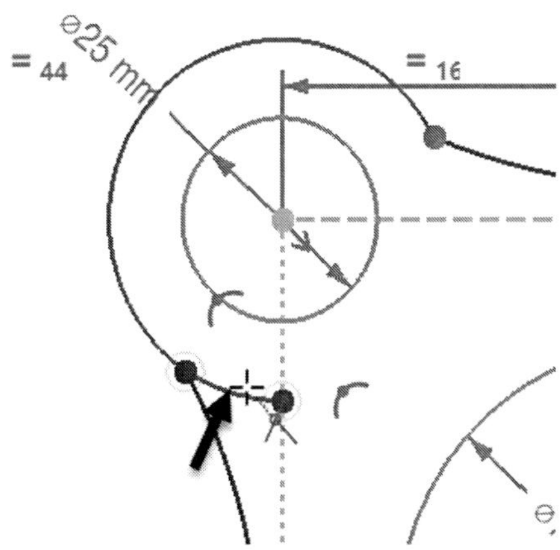

57. Repeat this process for all eight overhanging arc segments around the perimeter of the sketch until all joints are perfectly smooth and no geometry crosses into the interior of the circles.

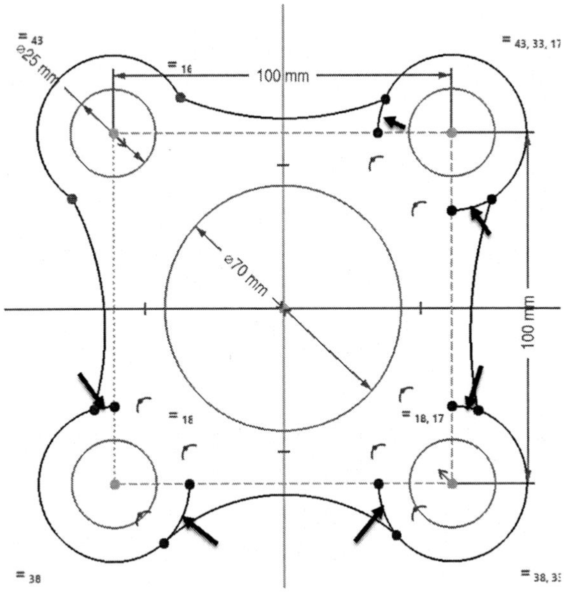

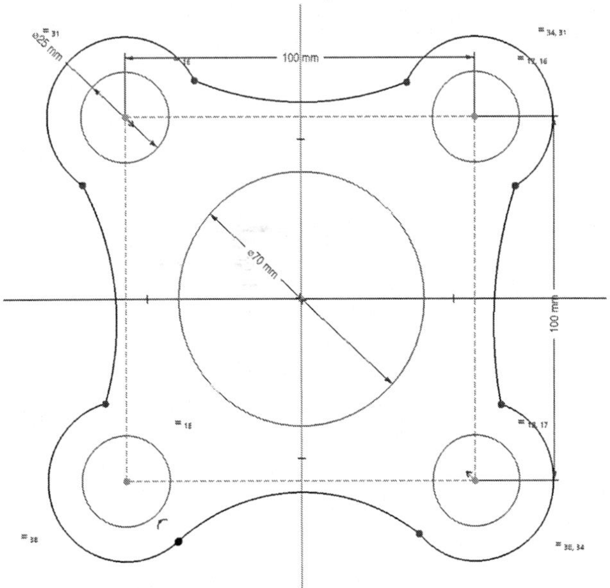

58. Press Esc or right-click to exit the **Trim Edge** tool.
59. Click the **Tangent/Collinear Constraint** icon on the **Constraints** toolbar.
60. Click the left side of the top horizontal arc, then click the perimeter of the top-left base circle.

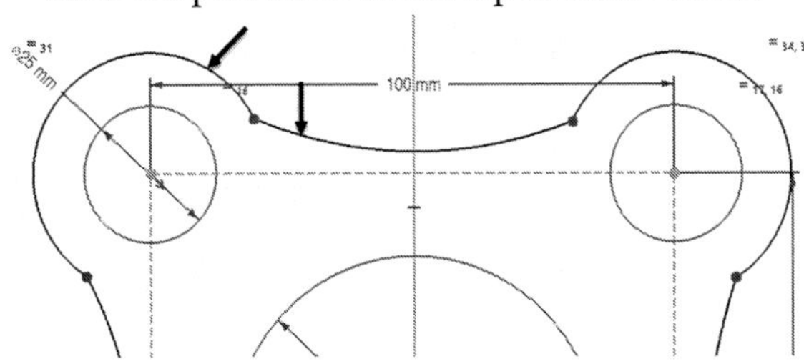

Note: If the endpoint of the arc was already snapped to the circle when you drew it, a "**Sketcher Constraint Substitution**" popup warning will appear (as shown in the image above). This simply informs you that FreeCAD has automatically deleted the basic "Coincident" (touching) constraint and upgraded it to a "Tangent" constraint. You can check the ***Keep notifying*** box if you wish, and click **OK** to dismiss it.

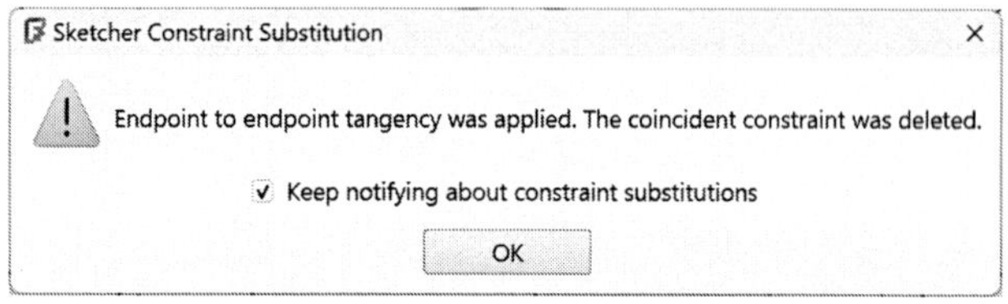

61. Click the right side of the same top horizontal arc, then click the perimeter of the top-right base circle to secure the other end.

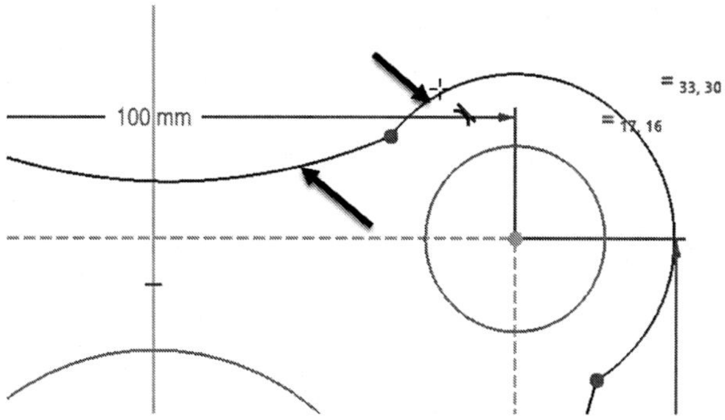

62. Click **OK** on the pop warning message.
63. Apply this exact selection sequence to the remaining three arcs to constrain all eight connection points:

- Constrain the left vertical arc to the top-left and bottom-left circles.

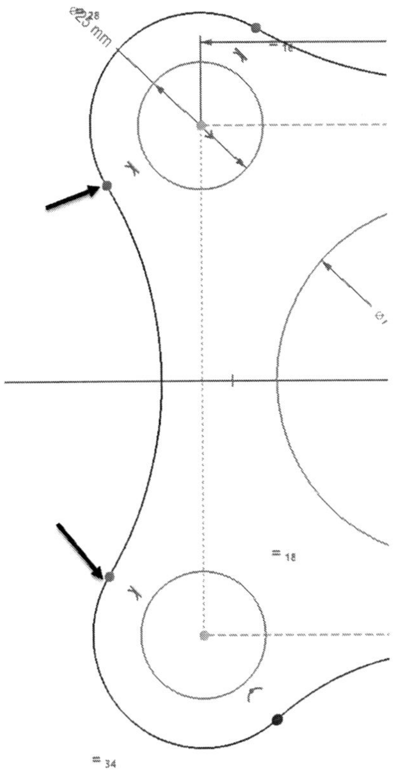

- Constrain the bottom horizontal arc to the bottom-left and bottom-right circles.

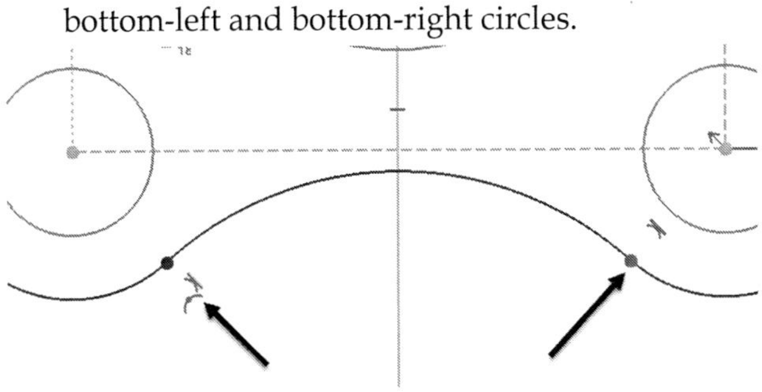

- Constrain the right vertical arc to the top-right and bottom-right circles.

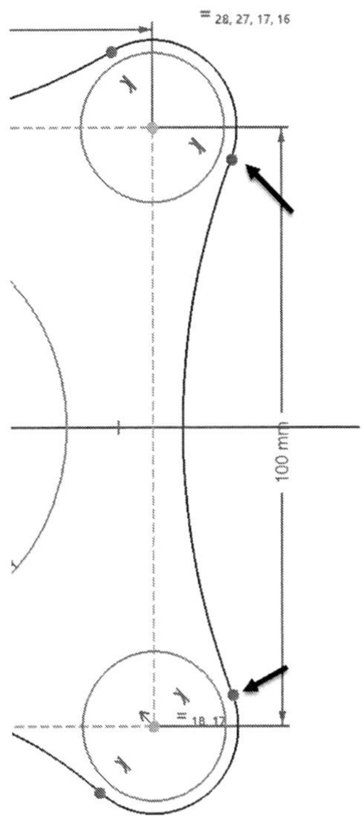

64. Click the **Equal Constraint** icon on the **Constraints** toolbar.
65. Make the arcs equal, as shown.

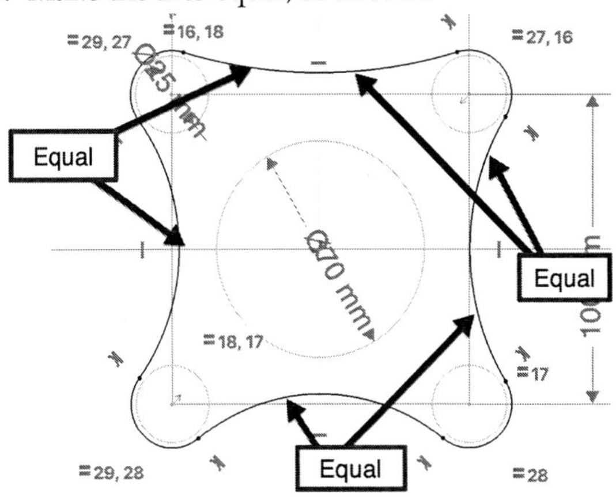

66. Click the **Dimension** drop-down. > **Radius Dimension** icon on the **Constraints** toolbar.

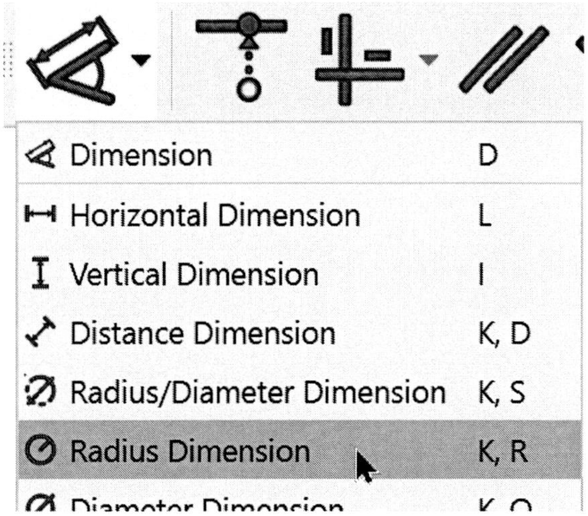

67. Select any one of the arcs concentric to the circles.
68. Type **25** in the **Radius** box and click **OK**.
69. Select any one of the tangent arcs.
70. Type **60** in the **Radius** box and click **OK**.

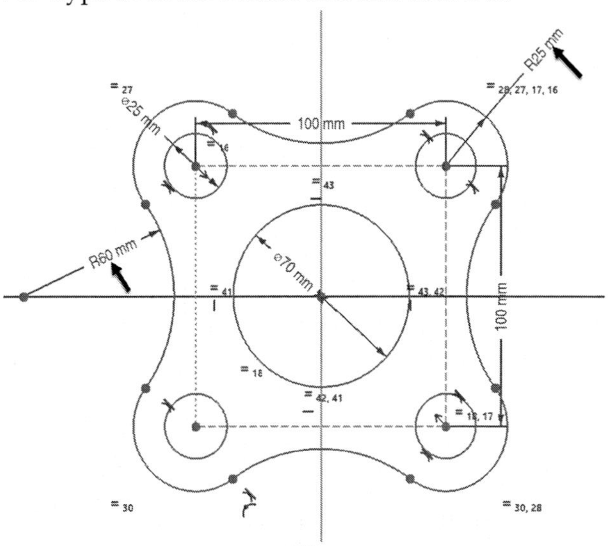

71. Click **Leave Sketch** on the **Edit Mode** toolbar.
72. Save and close the file.
73. Click the **Equal Constraint** icon on the **Constraints** toolbar.
74. Make the arcs equal, as shown.

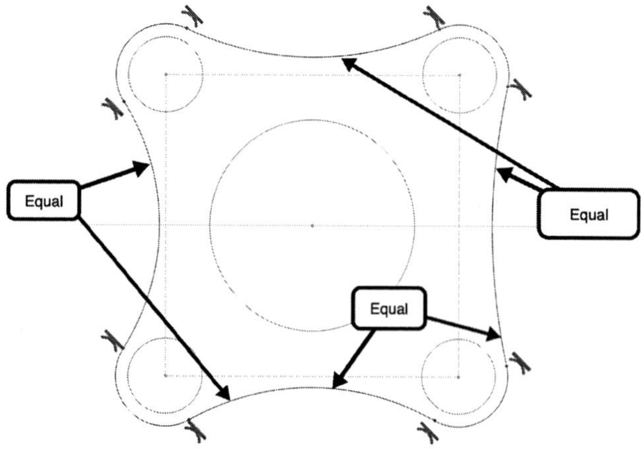

75. Click the **Dimension** drop-down. > **Radius Dimension** icon on the **Constraints** toolbar.
76. Select any one of the arcs concentric to the circles.
77. Type **25** in the **Radius** box and click **OK**.
78. Select any one of the tangent arcs.
79. Type **60** in the **Radius** box and click **OK**.

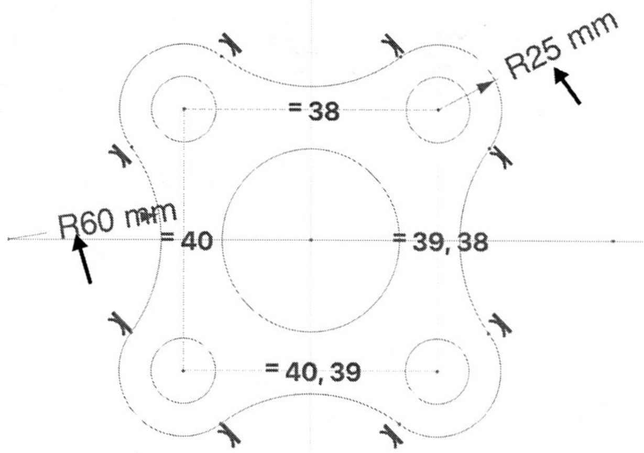

80. Click the **Show/hide all constraints** button on the Constraints section of the **Tasks** panel.
81. Click **Leave Sketch** on the **Sketcher** toolbar.
82. Save and close the file.

Chapter 5: Additional Modeling Tools

In this chapter, you create models using additional modeling tools. You learn to:

- Create slots
- Create circular patterns
- Create holes
- Create chamfers
- Create shells
- Create coils
- Create a loft feature
- Create a sweep feature

TUTORIAL 1

In this tutorial, you create the model shown in the figure:

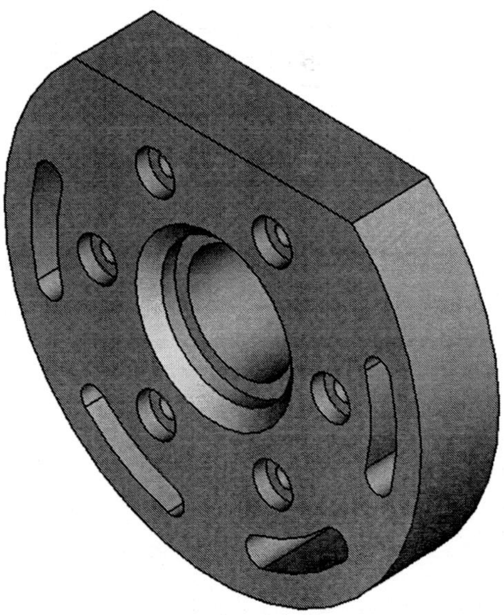

Creating the First Feature

1. Open the FreeCAD application.
2. Click **File > New** on the Menu bar.
3. Select the **Part Design** option from the **Workbenches** drop-down.
4. Click **Edit > Preferences** on the Menu bar.

   The **Preferences** dialog box appears. If you are working on MacOS, then click **FreeCAD > Preferences** on the title bar.
5. Click the **General** > **General** on the left-side of the **Preferences** dialog.
6. Select **Default unit system > Imperial decimal**.
7. Type **3** in the **Number of decimals** box.
8. Check the **Ignore project unit system and use default** option.
9. Click **OK**.
10. Click the **New Sketch** icon on the **Part Design Helper Features** toolbar, and then select the XZ Plane.
11. Deactivate the **Toggle Construction geometry** icon on the **Geometries** toolbar.
12. Click the **Circle From Center** icon on the **Geometries** toolbar.
13. Select the origin point of the sketch.
14. Move the pointer outward and click to create a circle.

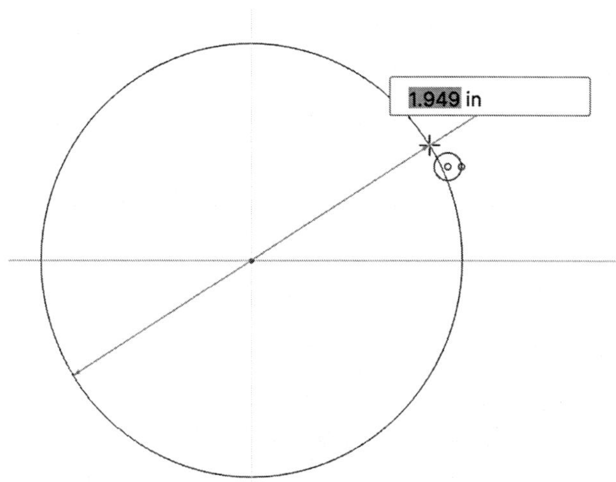

15. Click the **Line** icon on the **Geometries** toolbar.
16. Specify a point at the location outside the circle, as shown.

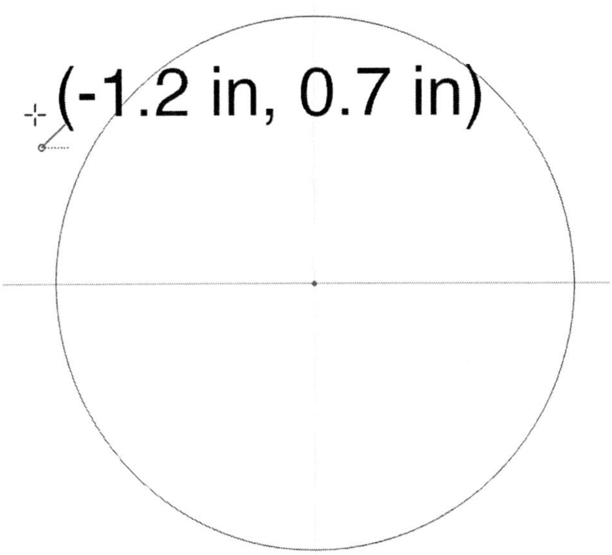

17. Move the pointer horizontally and notice the Horizontal constraint symbol.
18. Click outside the circle – Press Esc to deactivate the **Line** tool.

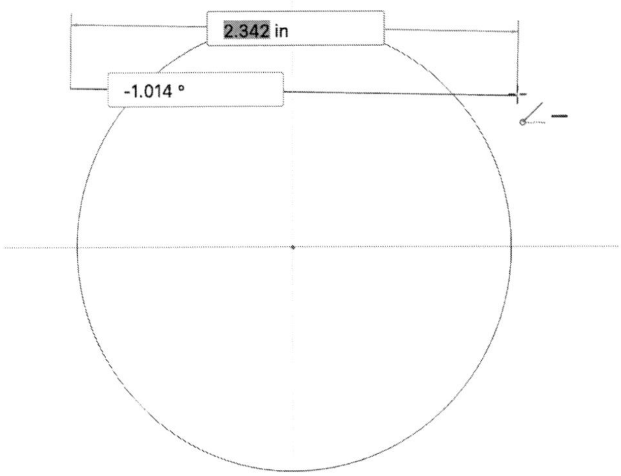

19. Click the **Trim/Extend** drop-down > **Trim Edge** icon on the **Sketcher tools** toolbar.
20. Click on the portions of the sketch to be trimmed, as shown below.

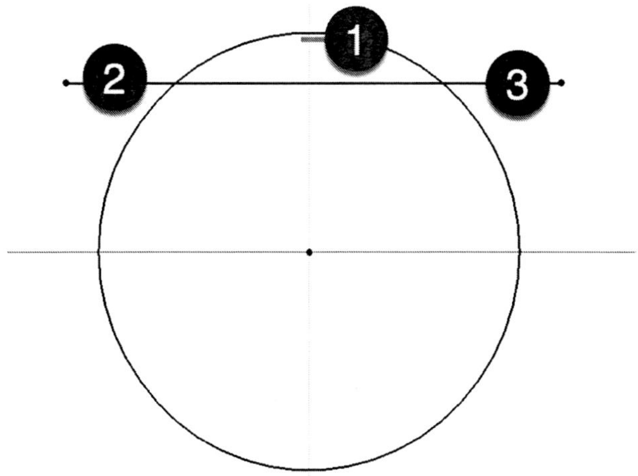

21. Add the **Radius** and **Horizontal Distance** constraints to the sketch.

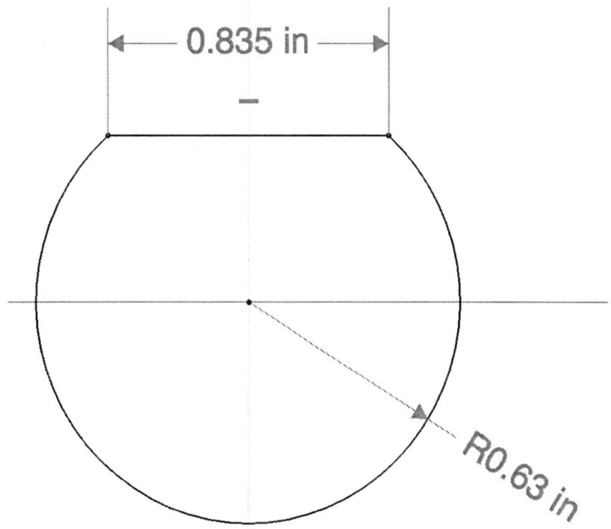

22. Click the **Close** button on the **Tasks** panel.
23. Click the **Pad** icon on the **Part Design Modeling Features** toolbar.
24. Type **0.236** inches in the **Length** box and click **OK**.

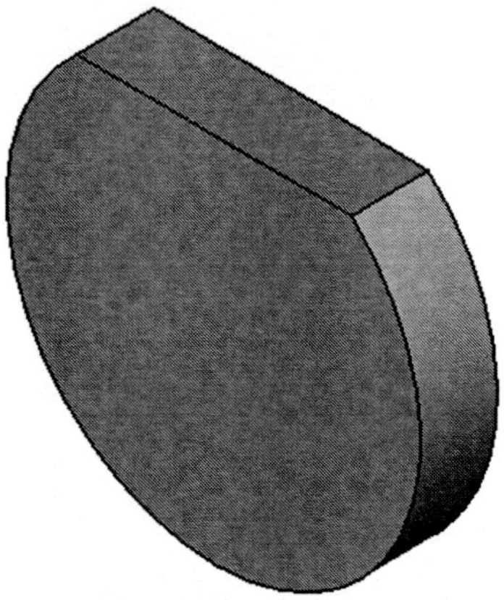

Creating the Pocket feature

1. Click on the front face of the model.

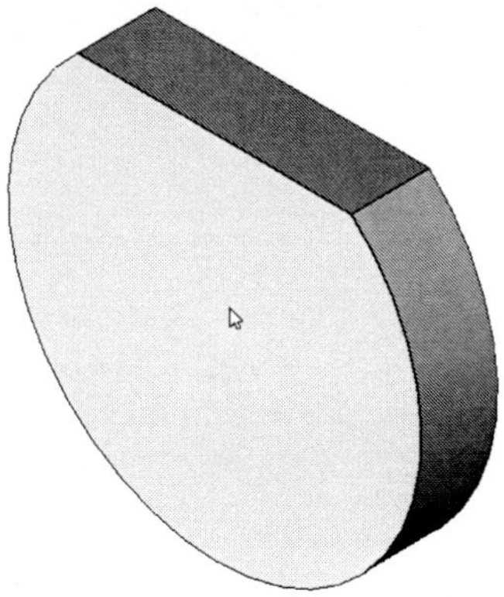

2. Click the **New Sketch** icon on the **Part Design Helper Features** toolbar.
3. On the **Geometries** toolbar, click **Slot drop-down > Create arc slot** .
4. Select the origin as the center point.
5. Move the cursor outside and click in the first quadrant of the circle to specify the start point of the arc slot.
6. Move the cursor and click in the fourth quadrant of the circle to specify the endpoint of the arc slot.

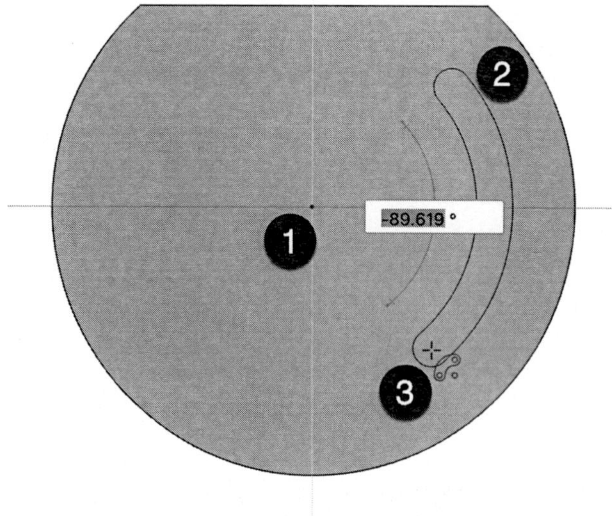

7. Move the pointer and click to specify the slot width.

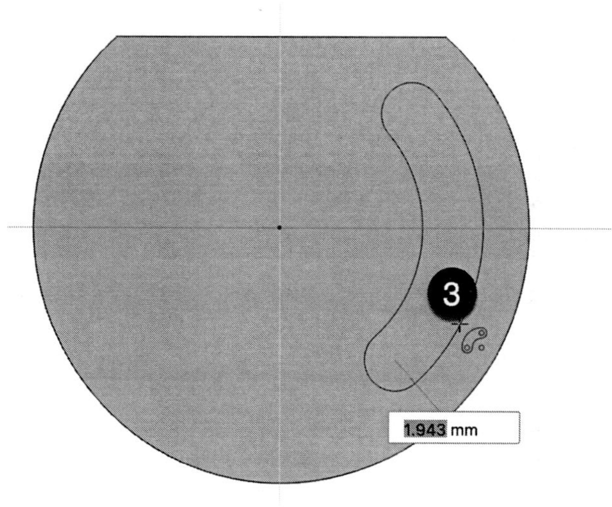

8. Activate the **Toggle Construction geometry** icon on the **Geometries** toolbar; This will turn on construction mode and switch the color of the icons to blue. Any new geometry you make will be in construction mode.
9. Click the **Line** icon on the **Geometries** toolbar.
10. Select the origin point of the sketch.
11. Select the centerpoint of the small arc.

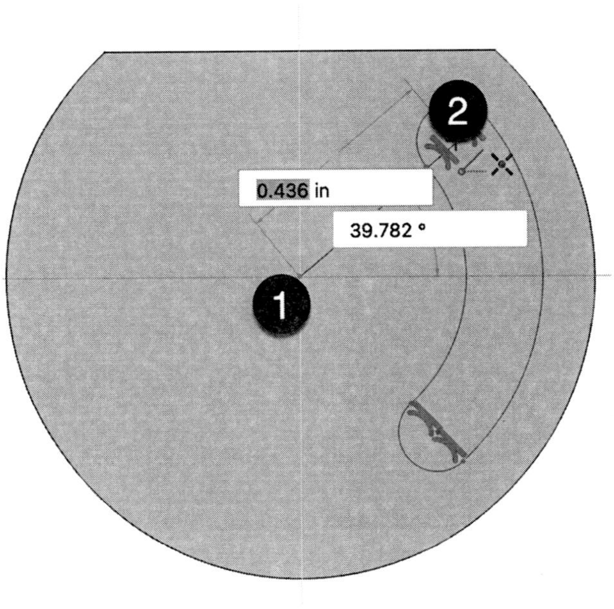

12. Likewise, create a line by selecting the origin and center point of another small arc.

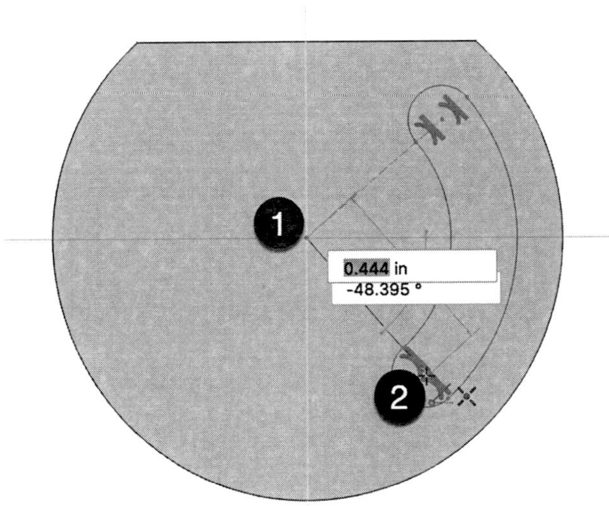

13. Use the **Coincident Constraint**  tool and connect the endpoint of the line and the center point of the small arc, if not correctly connected.

14. Click the **Toggle construction geometry**  icon on the **Geometries** toolbar; the construction mode is turned OFF.

15. Click the **Dimension**  icon on the **Constraints** toolbar.

16. Select any one of the lines.
17. Type 0.512 in the **Length** box and click **OK**.

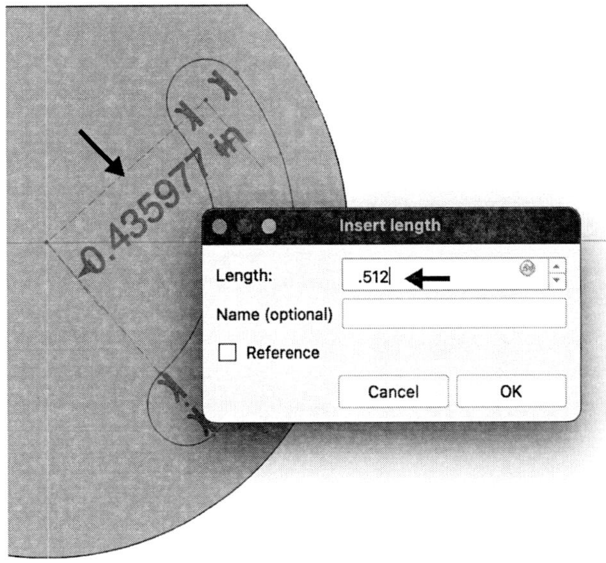

18. Select any one of the small arcs.
19. Type 0.039 in the **Radius** box, and then click **OK**.
20. Select the two construction lines.
21. Type **30** in the **Angle** box, and then click **OK**.
22. Select the horizontal axis of the sketch and anyone of the lines.
23. Type **15** in the **Angle** box, and then click **OK**.

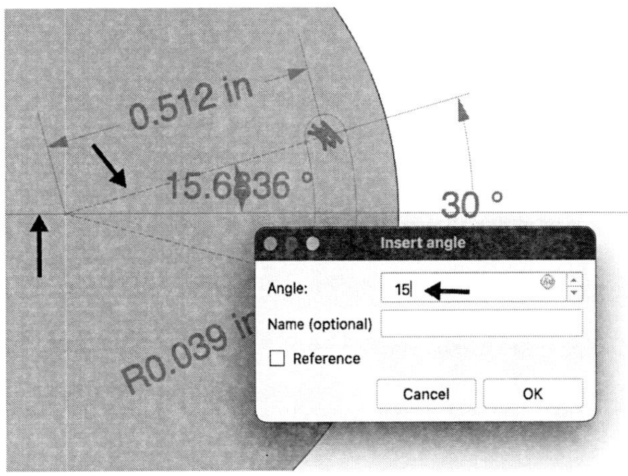

24. Click **Close** on the **Tasks** panel.
25. Click the **Pocket**  icon on the **Part Design Modeling Features** toolbar.
26. Select **Type > Through All** from the **Pocket**

Parameters dialog.

27. Click **OK**.

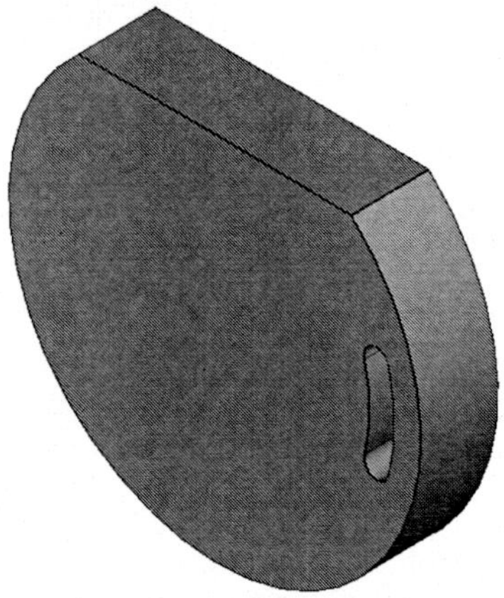

Creating a Polar Pattern

1. Select the Pocket feature from the graphics window.

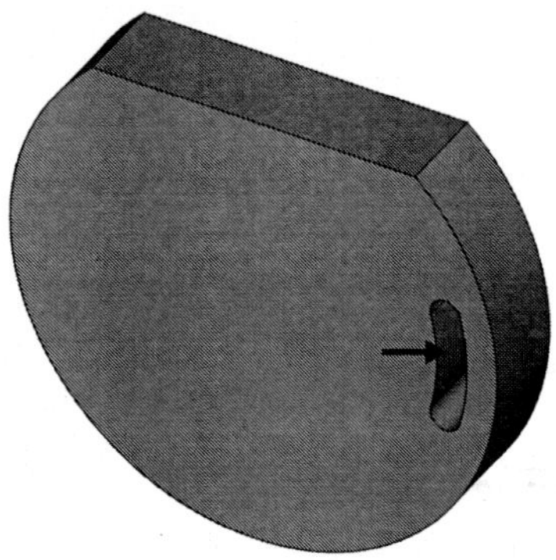

2. Click the **Polar Pattern** icon on the **Part Design Transformations Features** toolbar.
3. Select **Axis > Normal sketch axis**.
4. Select **Mode > Extent**.
5. Type **180** in the **Length** box.
6. Type **4** in the **Occurrences** box.
7. Click the **Reverse the direction of pattern** icon.
8. Click **OK**.

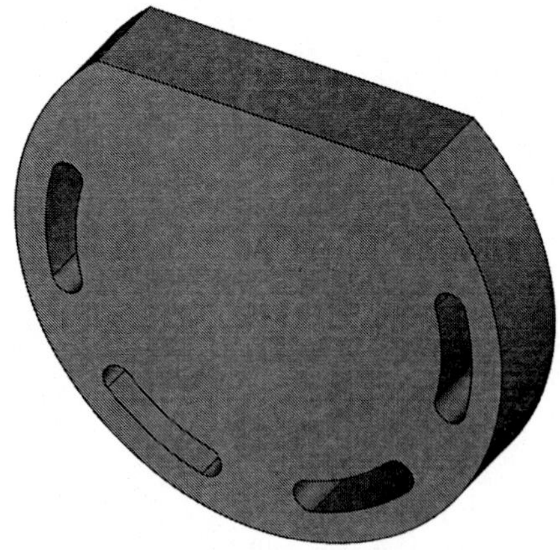

Adding the Pad feature

1. Press and hold the middle and right mouse button.
2. Drag the pointer to rotate the model.
3. Click on the back face of the model.

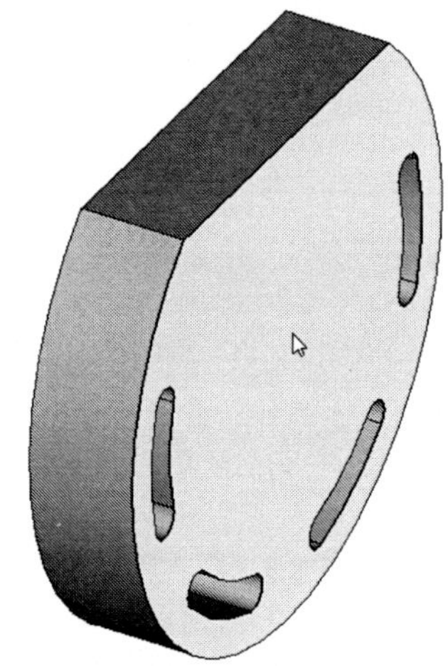

4. Click the **New Sketch** icon on the **Part Design Helper Features** toolbar.
5. Click the **Circle From Center** icon on the **Geometries** toolbar.
6. Select the sketch origin.
7. Move the pointer outward and click to create the circle.
8. Click the **Dimension** icon on the **Constraints** toolbar.
9. Select the circle.
10. Type **0.472** in the **Diameter** box and click **OK**.

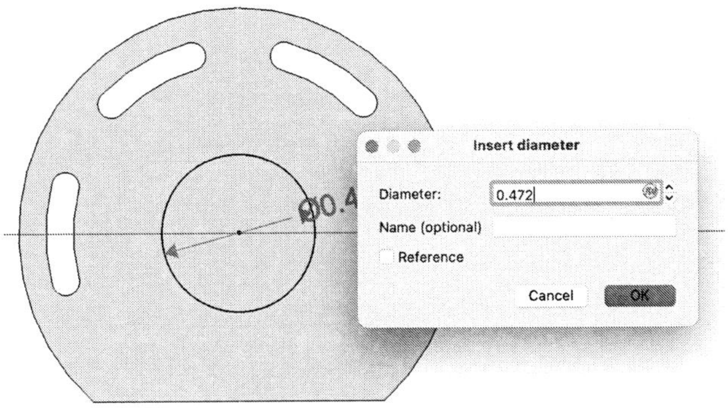

11. Click **Close** on the **Tasks** panel.
12. Click the **Pad** icon on the **Part Design Modeling Features** toolbar.
13. Type **0.078** in the **Length** box.
14. Click **OK**.

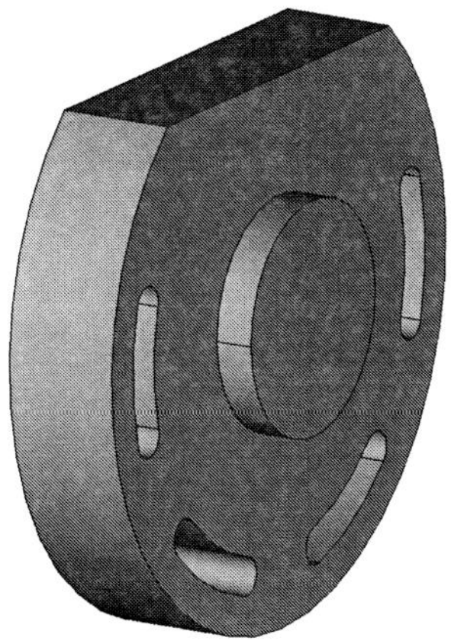

Creating a Counterbore Hole

In this section, you create a counterbore hole concentric to the circular face.

1. Click the small cube located next to the Navigation cube, and then select the **Isometric** option.

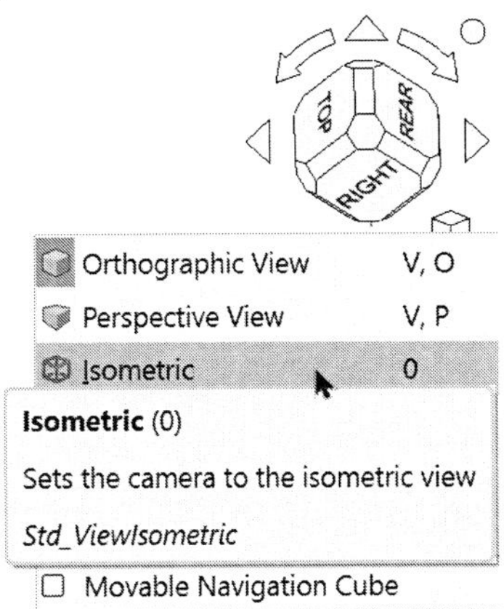

2. Select the front face of the model.

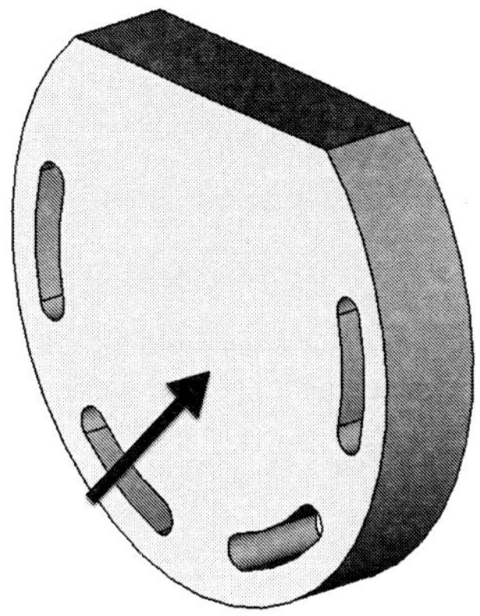

3. Click the **New Sketch** icon on the **Part Design Helper Features** toolbar.
4. Click the **Point** icon on the **Geometries** toolbar.
5. Select the origin point of the sketch.

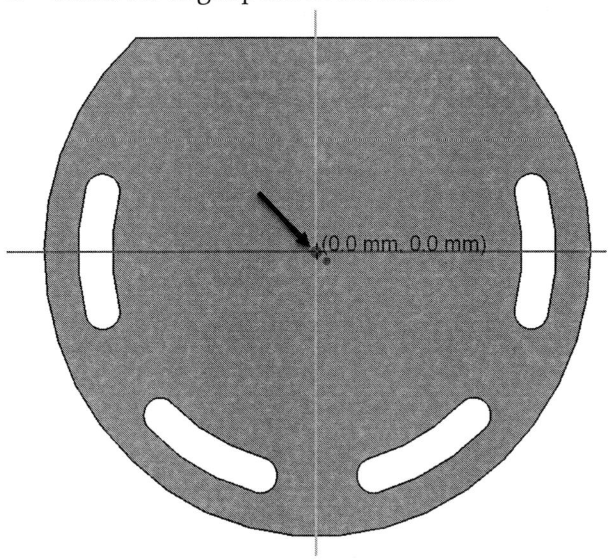

6. Click **Close** on the **Tasks** panel.
7. Click the **Hole** icon on the **Part Design Modeling Features** toolbar.
8. Type **0.314** in the **Diameter** box.
9. Select **Depth > Through All**.
10. On the **Hole Parameters** section, select **Head Type > Counterbore**.
11. Type **0.394** in the **Head diameter** box.
12. Type **0.078** in the **Head depth** box.

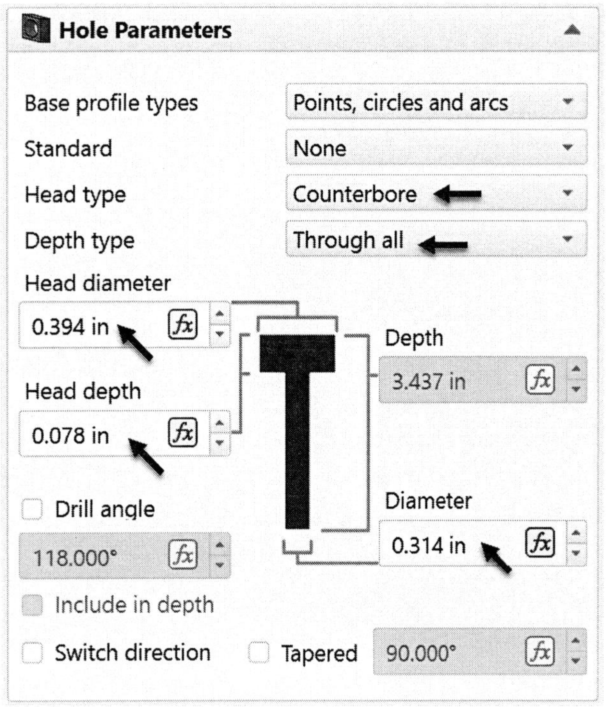

13. Click **OK** on the **Tasks** panel; the counterbore hole is created.

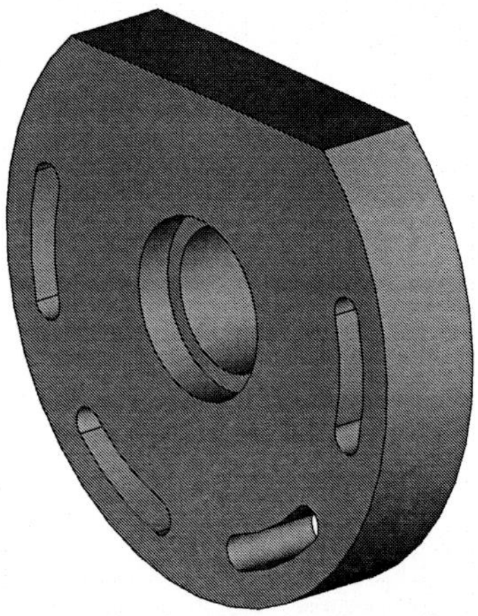

Creating Threaded holes

In this section, you create a threaded hole.

1. Click on the front face of the model.
2. Click the **New Sketch**  icon on the **Part Design Helper Features** toolbar.
3. Click the **Point**  icon on the **Geometries** toolbar.
4. Click on the horizontal axis on the right side.
5. Click the **Dimension**  icon on the **Constraints** toolbar.
6. Selec the origin point and the newly created point.
7. Type 0.351 in the **Length** box and click **OK**.

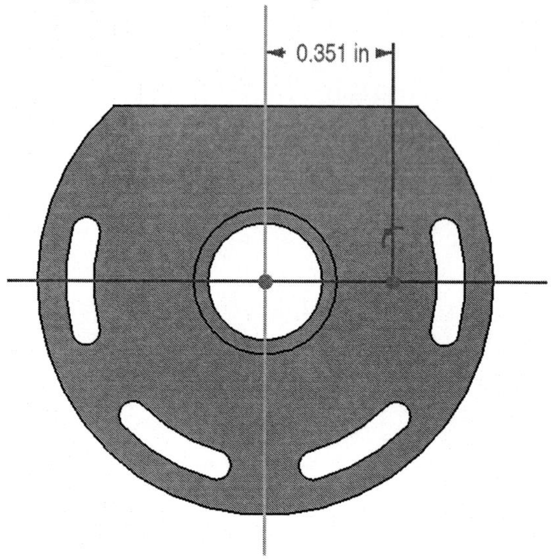

8. Click the **Close** button on the **Tasks** panel.
9. Click the **Hole**  icon on the **Part Design Modeling Features** toolbar; the **Hole Parameters** section appears.
10. In the **Standard** drop-down, select **UTS coarse**.
11. In the **Size** drop-down, select **#1**.
12. In the **Head type** drop-down, select **Counterbore**.
13. In the **Depth type** drop-down, select **Through all**.
14. Set the **Head diameter** to **0.118 in**.
15. Set the **Head depth** to **0.039 in**.
16. Scroll down to the **Threading** section.
17. In the **Hole type** drop-down, select **Modeled thread**.
18. In the **Thread** sub-section, ensure the **Class** drop-down is set to **2B**.
19. Under **Direction**, select the **Right hand** radio button.
20. Ensure the **Thread Depth Type** drop-down is set to **Hole depth**.
21. Click **OK**.

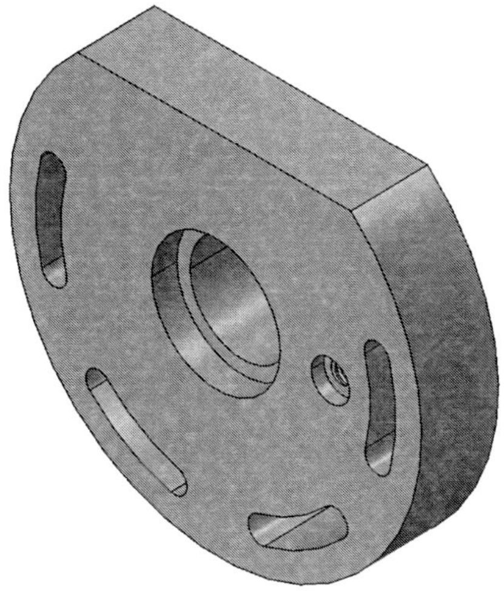

22. Select the Counterbore hole from the graphics window.

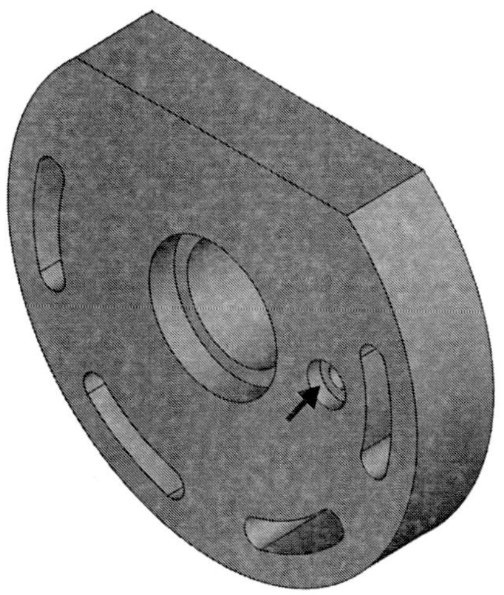

23. Click the **Polar Pattern** icon on the **Part Design Modeling Features** toolbar.
24. Click **OK**.
25. Select **Axis > Normal sketch axis**.
26. Type **360** in the **Length** box.
27. Type **6** in the **Occurrences** box.
28. Click **OK**.

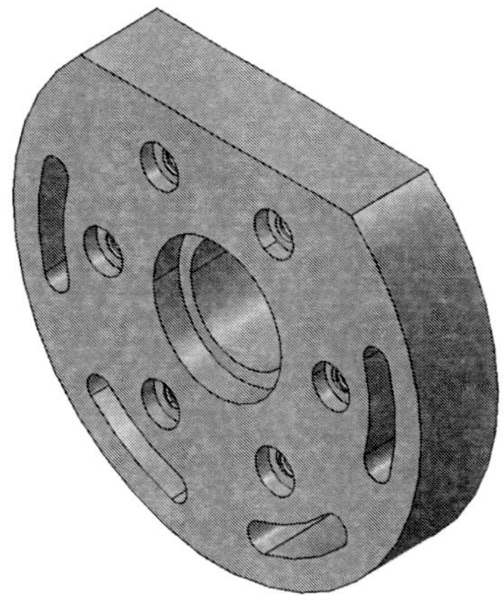

Creating Chamfers

1. Select the circular edge of the counterbore hole.

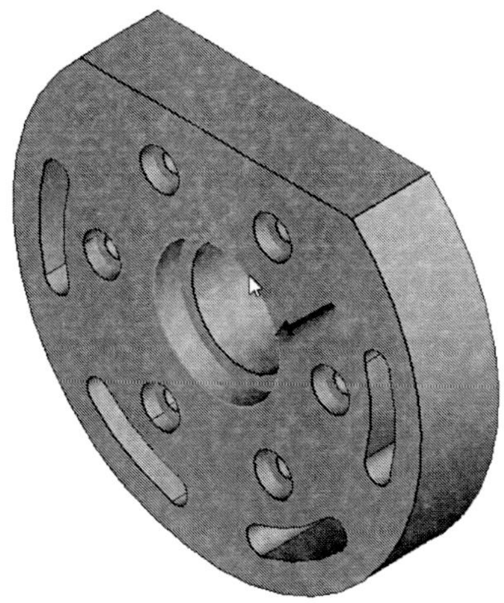

2. Click the **Chamfer** icon on the **Part Design Dressup Features** toolbar.
3. Enter 0.039 in the **Size** box.

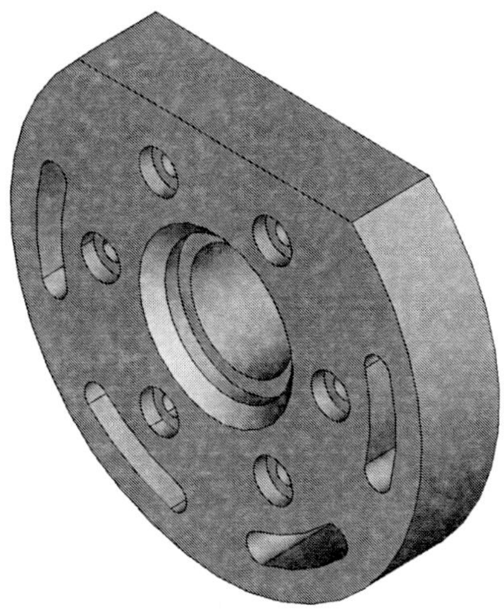

4. Click **OK** to create the chamfer.

5. Save the model and close it.

TUTORIAL 2

In this tutorial, you create the model shown in the figure.

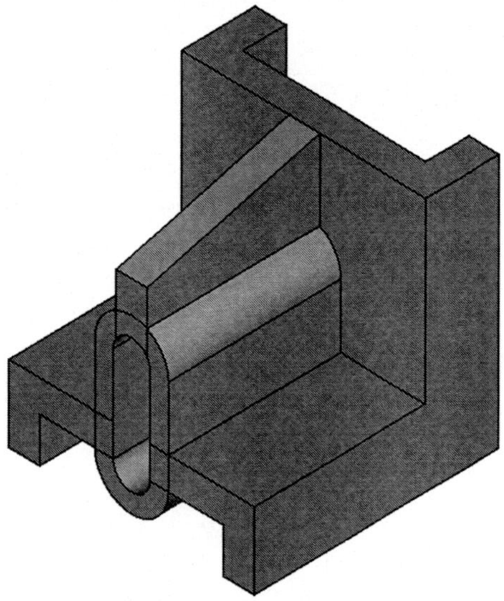

Creating the first feature

1. Open a new FreeCAD file.
2. Select the **Part Design** from the **Workbenches** drop-down.
3. Click the **New Sketch** icon on the **Part Design Helper Features** toolbar, and then Select the YZ-Plane from the **Tasks** panel and click **OK**.
4. On the **Tasks** panel, click the drop-down in the **Constraints** section, and then make sure that the **Auto remove redundants** option is selected.

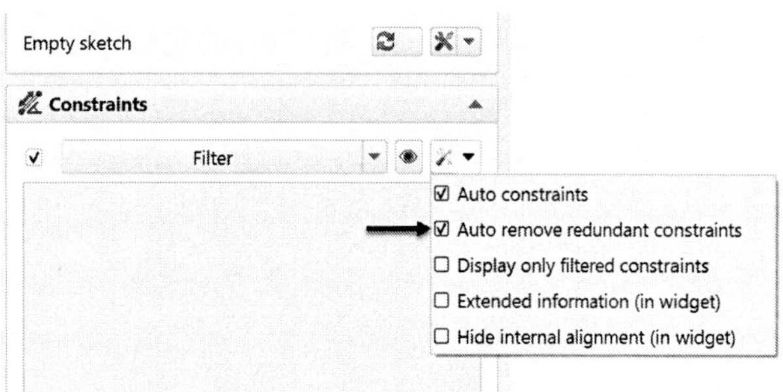

5. Click the **Polyline** tool on the **Geometries** toolbar, or use the keyboard shortcut G then M.
6. Move your cursor to the sketch origin (the intersection of the red and green axes). The cursor will snap to the origin, and a small coincident constraint icon (a red dot in a crescent) will appear next to it.
7. Click once on the origin to set the starting point of the polyline.
8. Move your cursor horizontally to the right along the red axis. A red horizontal constraint line will appear next to the cursor. Click to place the second point, completing the bottom horizontal line.
9. Move your cursor vertically upward. A red vertical constraint line will appear. Click to place the third point, creating the right vertical edge of the "L" shape.
10. Move your cursor horizontally to the left. Ensure the horizontal constraint icon is visible, then click to place the fourth point, creating the top horizontal edge.
11. Move your cursor vertically downward. Ensure the vertical constraint icon is visible, then click to place the fifth point, forming the inner vertical edge of the "L".
12. Move your cursor horizontally to the left again. Ensure the horizontal constraint icon is visible, then click to place the sixth point, creating the inner horizontal edge of the "L".
13. Finally, move your cursor straight down to the origin point where you started. Wait for the coincident constraint icon to appear, indicating the cursor has snapped to the start point, and click to close the profile. Press the Esc key or right-click once.

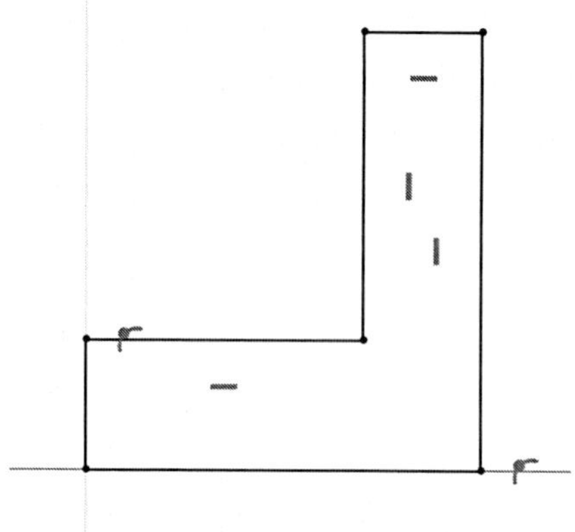

14. Click the **Equal Constraint** icon on the **Constraints** toolbar.
15. Select the vertical and horizontal lines, as

shown.

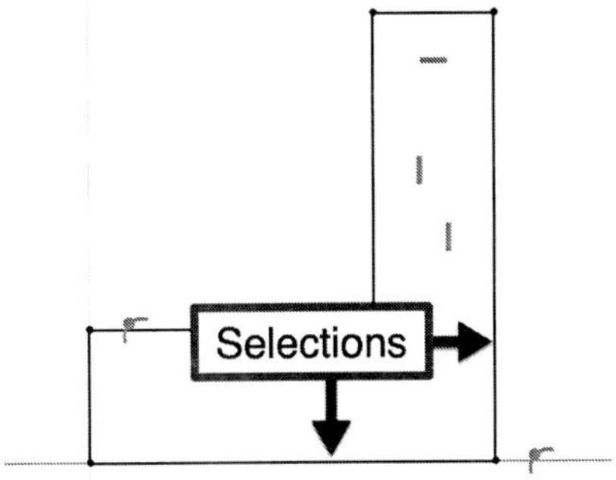

16. Select the two lines to make them equal in length.

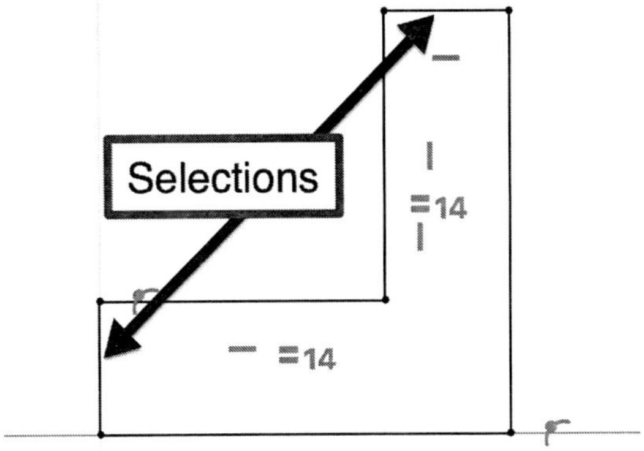

17. Click the **Dimension** icon on the **Constraints** toolbar.
18. Select right vertical line. Next, place the dimension.
19. Type **1.575** in the **Length** box and click **OK**.
20. Select left vertical line. Next, place the dimension.
21. Type **0.472** in the **Length** box and click **OK**.

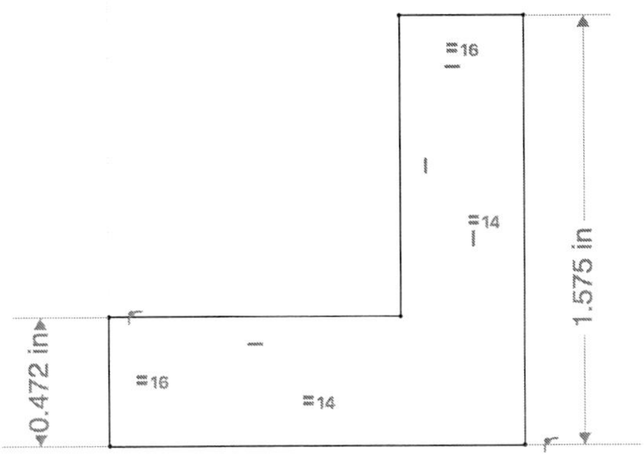

22. Click **Leave Sketch** on the **Edit mode** toolbar.
23. Click the **Pad** icon on the **Part Design Modeling Features** toolbar.
24. Select the **Symmetric** option from the **Mode** drop-down.
25. Set the **Length** to 1.575.
26. Click **OK** to create the first feature.

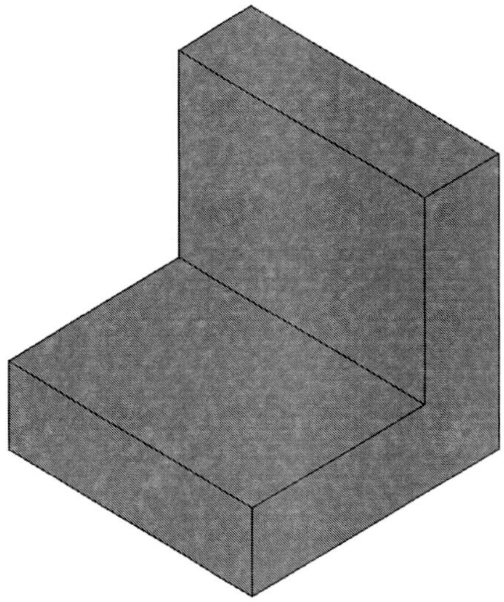

Creating the Shell feature

You can create a shell feature by removing the face of the model and applying thickness to other faces.

1. Press and hold the middle and right mouse button. Next, position the pointer on the model and drag it toward left; the model is rotated such that it back face is visible.
2. Press and hold the Ctrl key.
3. Select the top face and the back face of the model.

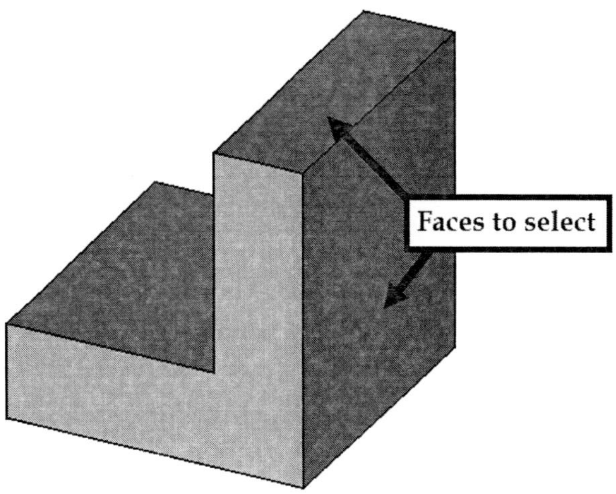

4. Click the **Thickness** icon on the **Part Design Modeling Features** toolbar.
5. Set **Thickness** to 0.197.
6. Select **Join type > Intersection**.
7. Check the **Make thickness inward** option.

Now, you need to select more faces.

8. Click the **Select** button.
9. Select the front face and the bottom face of the model.

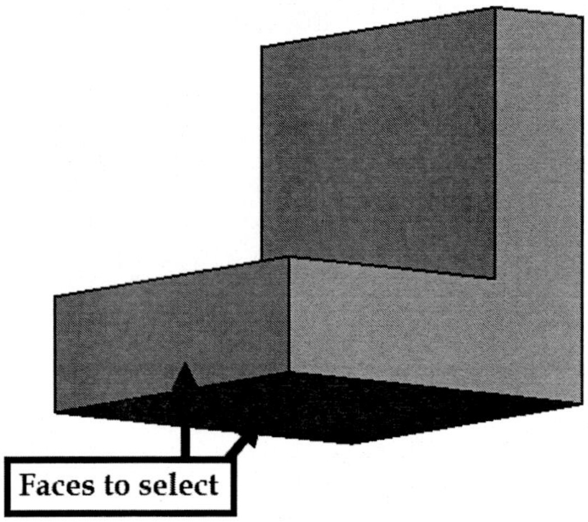

10. Click **OK** to shell the model.

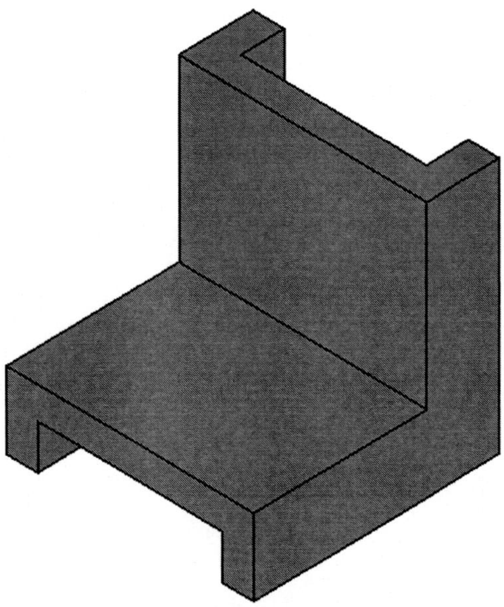

Creating the Third feature

1. Select the front face of the model.

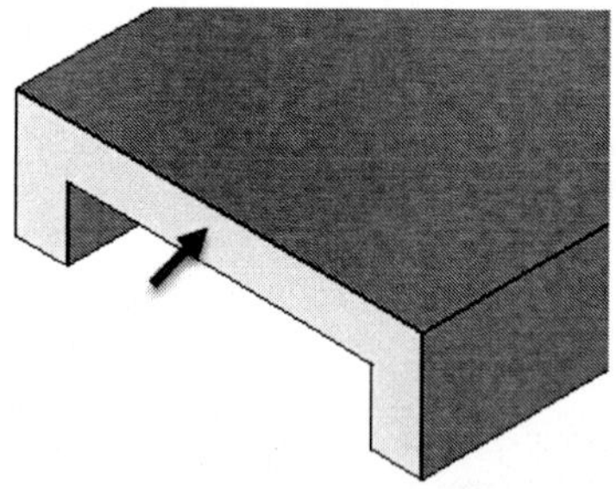

2. Click the **New Sketch** icon on the **Part Design Helper Features** toolbar.
3. Click the **External Projection** icon on the **Sketcher tools** toolbar.
4. Select the edge of the model, as shown.

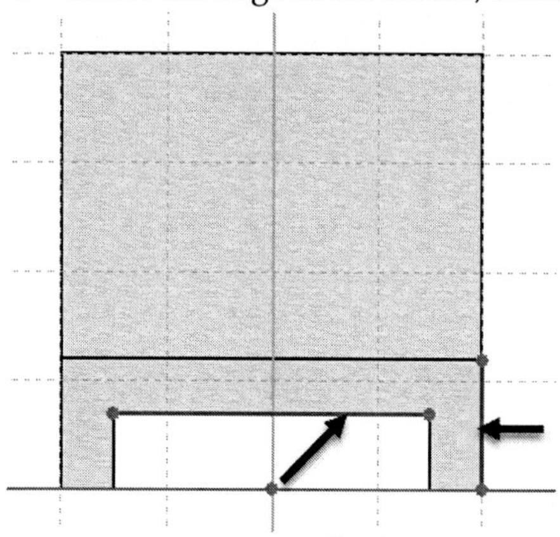

5. Click **Create Slot** on the **Geometries** toolbar.
6. Draw a slot by selecting the first and second points, as shown.

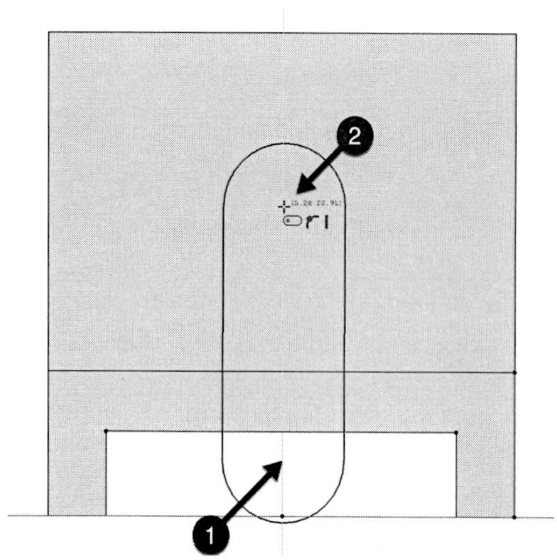

7. Add constraints and dimensions to the slot, as

shown.

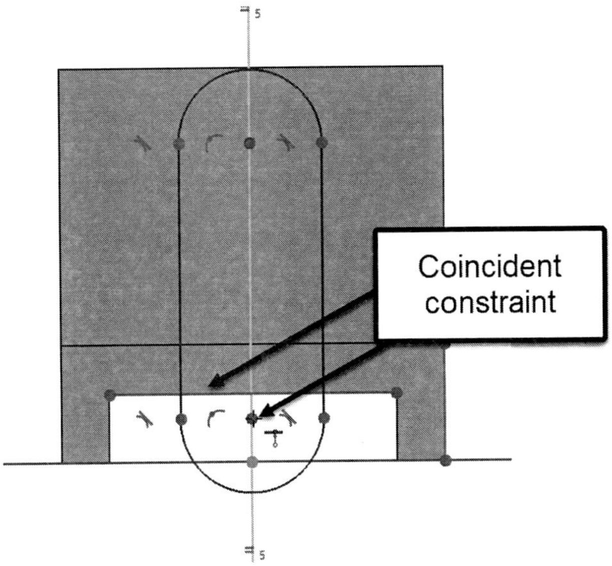

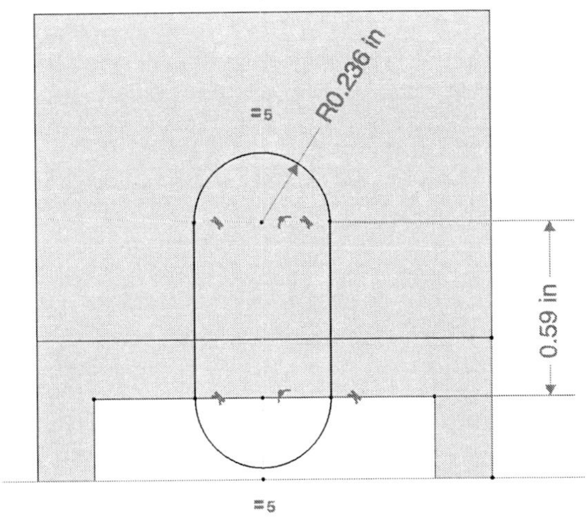

8. Click the right mouse button on the projected geometry and select **Toggle Construction Geometry**.

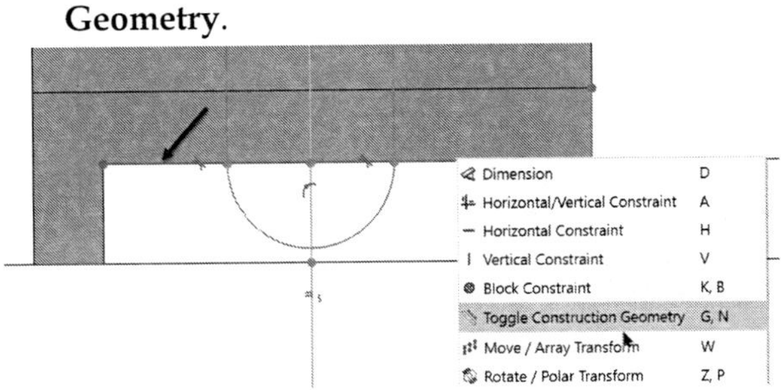

9. Click **Leave Sketch** on the **Edit mode** toolbar.
10. Click the **Pad** icon on the **Part Design Modeling Features** toolbar.
11. Select the **Up to face** option from the **Type** drop-down.
12. Select the back face of the model.

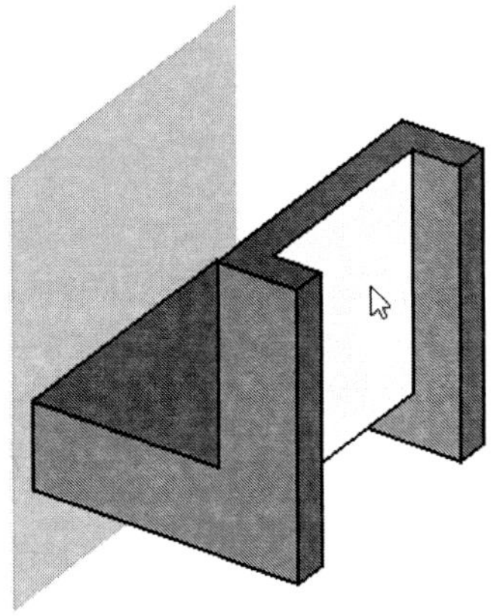

13. Click **OK** to create the feature.

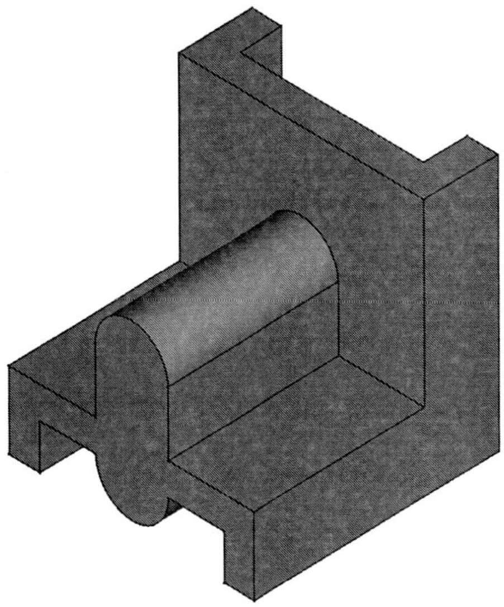

Creating the Rib Feature

In this section, you create a rib feature in the middle of the model. To do this, you must create an offset plane.

1. Click the **New Sketch** icon on the **Part Design Helper Features** toolbar.
2. Select the YZ plane.

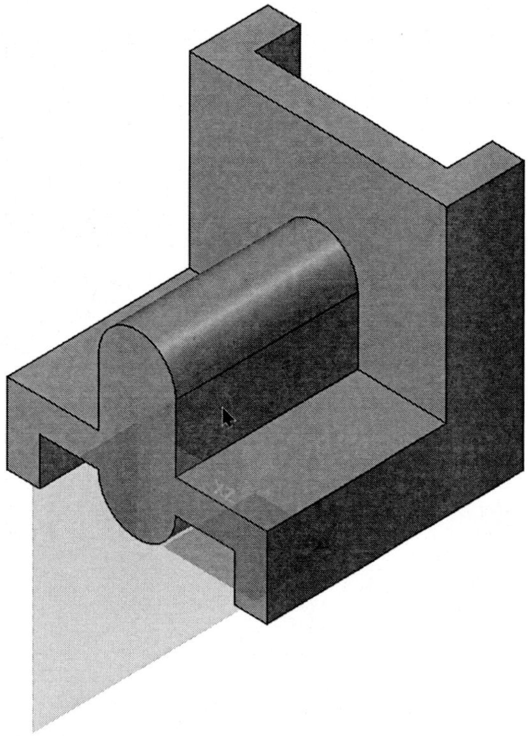

3. On the **View** toolbar, set the **Draw Style** to **Wireframe** .
4. Click the **Toggle Construction Geometry**  icon on the **Geometries** toolbar.
5. Click the **External Projection**  icon on the **Sketcher tools** toolbar.
6. Select the model edges, as shown.

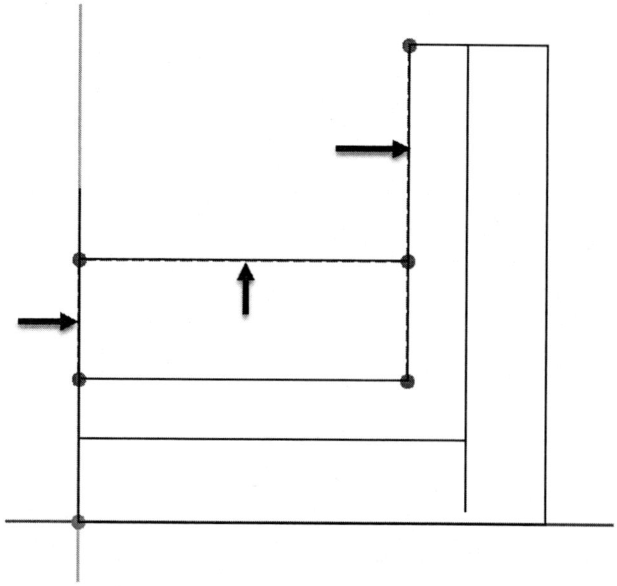

7. Deactivate the **Toggle Construction Geometry** icon on the **Geometries** toolbar.
8. Click the **Polyline** tool icon in the **Geometries** toolbar (G, then M).
9. Click in the empty workspace above the existing geometry to set the start point.
10. Move horizontally to the left to draw the bottom edge. Wait for the horizontal constraint icon to appear and click to place the point.
11. Move vertically upward to draw the right edge. Wait for the vertical constraint icon to appear and click to place the point.
12. Move diagonally up and to the right to draw the slanted top edge. Click to place the point.
13. Move vertically downward back to the starting point. Wait for both the vertical constraint icon and the coincident snap icon to appear, then click to close the profile.
14. Right-click or press Esc to exit the Polyline tool.
15. Select the left vertical line of the newly created profile.
16. Click the **Dimension** icon on the **Constraints** toolbar.
17. Type **0.433 in** into the length dialog box and click **OK**.
18. Click the **Coincident Constraint** icon on the **Constraints** toolbar (or press C).
19. Select the top-right vertex of the new profile.
20. Select the corresponding upper-inner corner

vertex of the existing base sketch.The top-right corner of the profile will snap directly to that point.

21. With the **Coincident Constraint** tool still active, select the bottom-left vertex of the new profile.
22. Select the corresponding inner corner vertex on the left side of the existing base sketch.
23. The profile will snap fully into position, perfectly aligning its left vertical edge and bottom horizontal edge with the existing geometry, matching the final result shown in the bottom half of the reference image.

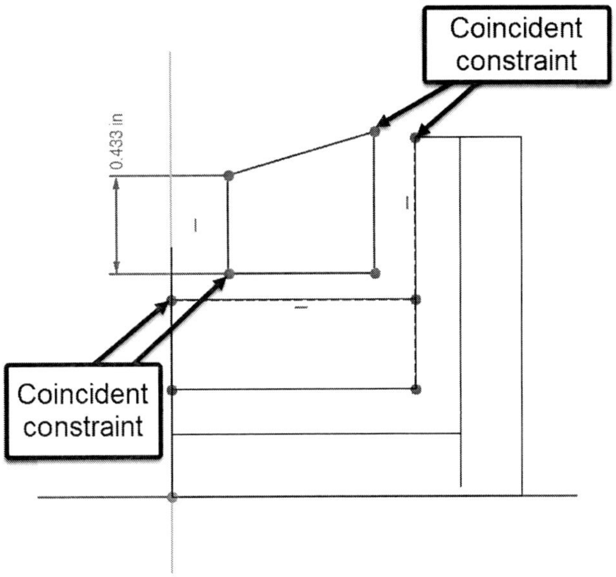

24. Right-click or press Esc to exit the **Coincident Constraint** tool.

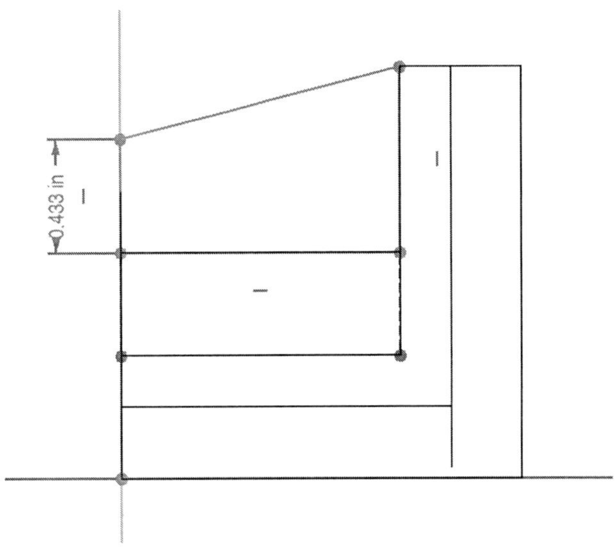

25. Click **Close** on the **Tasks** panel.
26. On the **View** toolbar, set the **Draw Style** to **Flat Lines**.
27. Click the **Pad** icon on the **Part Design Modeling Features** toolbar.
28. Select the **Symmetric** option from the **Mode** drop-down.
29. Type **0.197** in the **Length** box.
30. Click **OK** to create the rib feature.

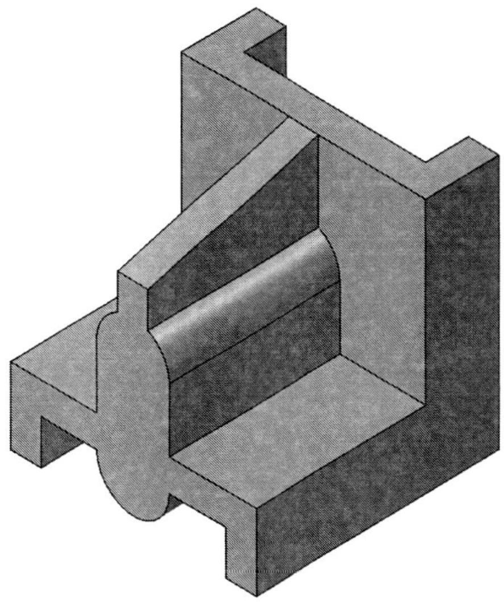

Creating a Pocket Feature

1. Select the front face.
2. Click the **New Sketch** icon on the **Part Design Helper Features** toolbar.
3. Click the **Toggle Construction Geometry** icon on the **Geometries** toolbar.
4. Click the **External Projection** icon on the **Sketcher tools** toolbar.
5. Select the model edges, as shown.

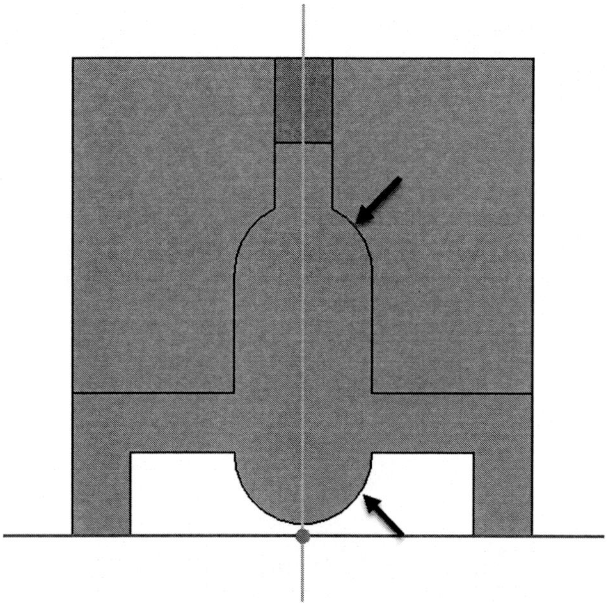

6. Deactivate the **Toggle Construction Geometry** icon on the **Geometries** toolbar.
7. Click the **Slot** icon in the **Geometries** toolbar, or use the keyboard shortcut G then S.
8. Select the center point of the lower circular edge to place the first center point of the slot's arc.
9. Move your cursor straight down vertically.
10. Select the centerpoint of the upper circular edge to place the second center point of the bottom arc.

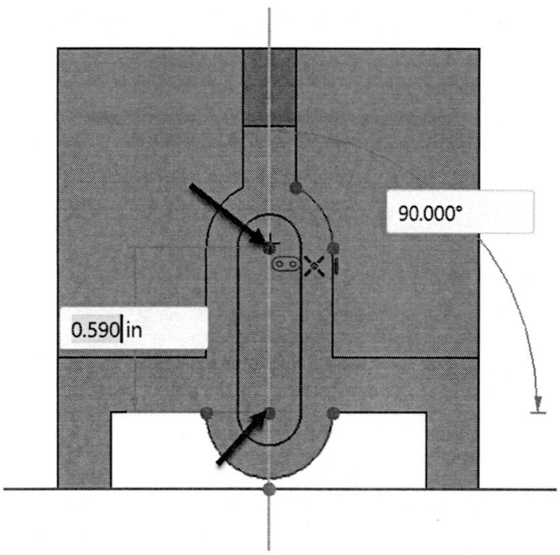

11. Move the cursor outward to define the radius (width) of the slot and click a third time to complete the shape.

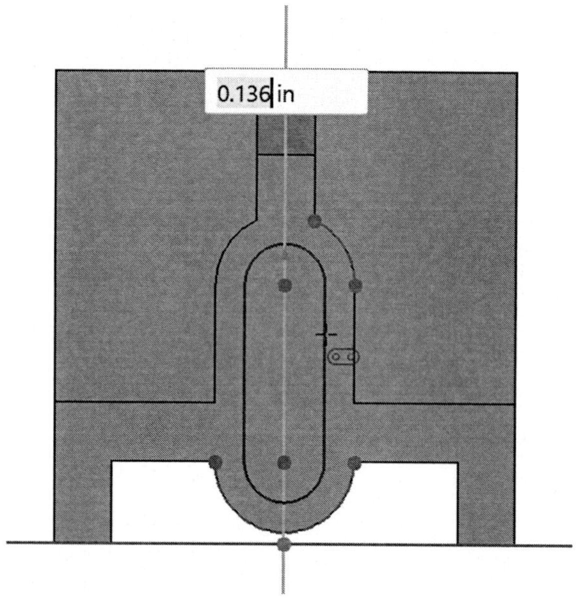

12. Right-click or press Esc to exit the slot tool.
13. Click the **Dimension** icon in the **Constraints** toolbar.
14. Select either the top or bottom curved arc of the slot.
15. Place the dimension.
16. Enter **0.118 in** into the radius box and click **OK**.

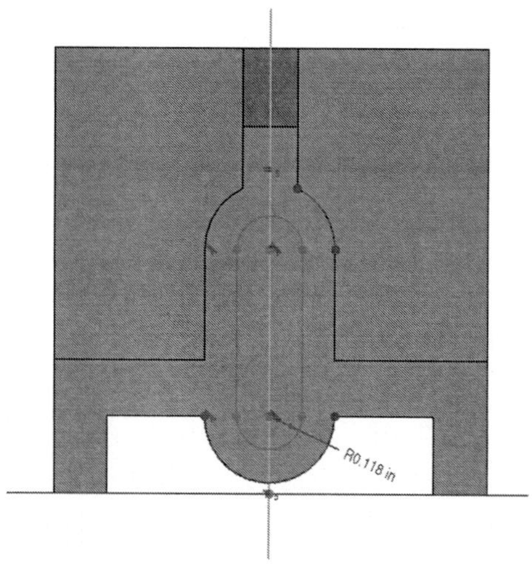

17. Click **Close** on the **Tasks** panel.
18. Click the **Pocket** icon on the **Part Design Modeling Features** toolbar.
19. Select the **Through All** option from the **Type** drop-down.
20. Click **OK** to create the pocket feature.

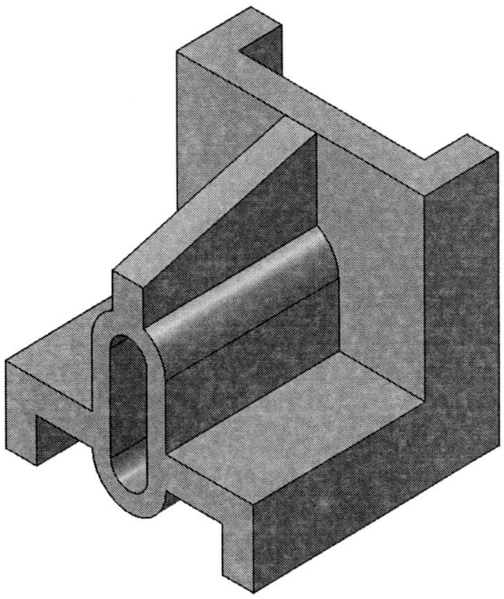

31. Save the model and close it.

TUTORIAL 3

In this tutorial, you create a helical spring.

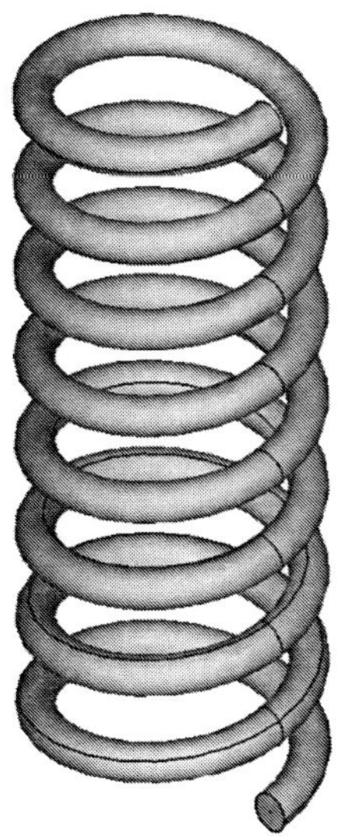

Creating the Profile

1. Open a new FreeCAD file.
2. Select **Part Design** from the **Workbenches** drop-down.
3. Click the **New Sketch**  icon on the **Part Design Helper Features** toolbar.
4. Select the XZ-Plane from the graphics window.
5. Create a circle, as shown.

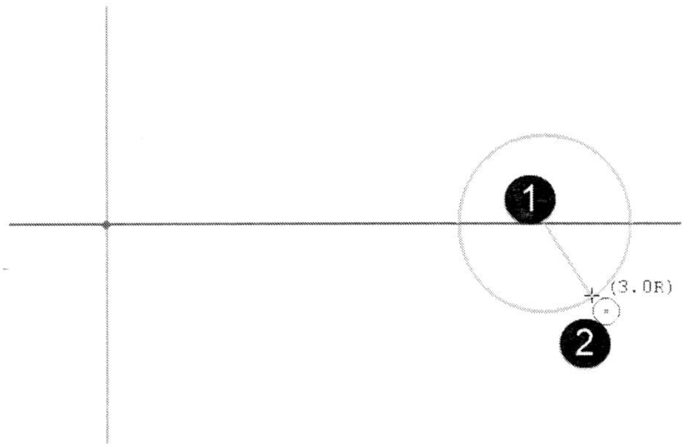

6. Add constraints to it, as shown.

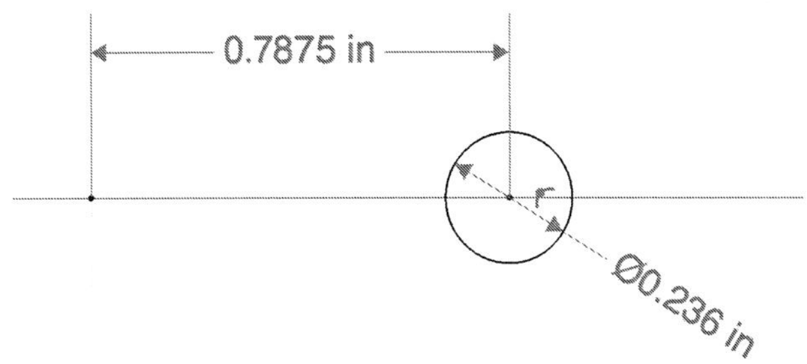

7. Click **Close** on the **Tasks** panel.

Creating the Helix

1. Select **Part** from the **Workbenches** drop-down.
2. Click the **Create primitives**  icon on the **Solids** toolbar.
3. In the **Geometric Primitives** dialog, select **Helix** from the drop-down.
4. Type **0.59** in the **Pitch** box.
5. Type **4.72** in the **Height** box.
6. Type **0.7875** in the **Radius** box.
7. Select **Right-handed** from the **Coordinate system** drop-down.

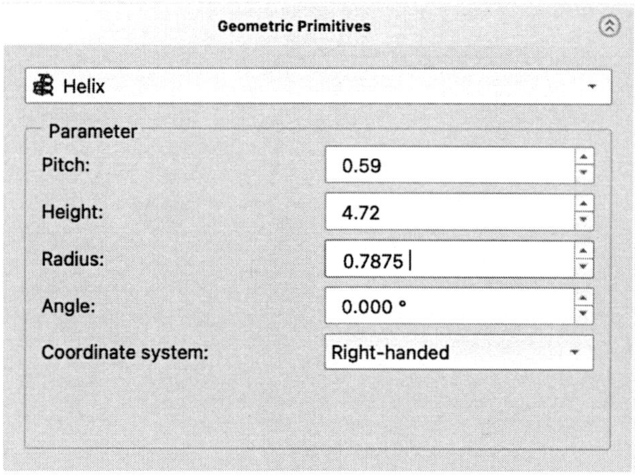

8. Expand the **Location** section.
9. Type **0** in the **X**, **Y**, and **Z** boxes.
10. Click the **Create** button.
11. On the **View** toolbar, click the **Isometric** icon.

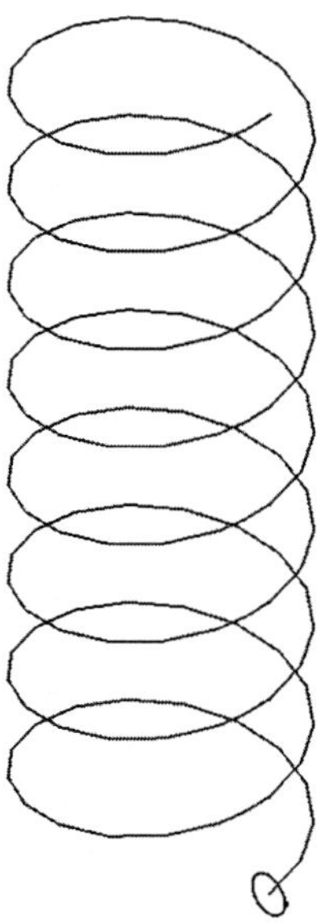

12. Click the **Close** button.

Creating the Sweep

1. Click the **Sweep** icon on the **Part tools** toolbar.
2. Select the **Sketch** from the **Available profiles** section.
3. Click the **Add** button.
4. Check the **Create solid** option.
5. Click the **Sweep Path** button.
6. Select the helix from the graphics window.
7. Click **Done**.
8. Click **OK** to create the sweep.

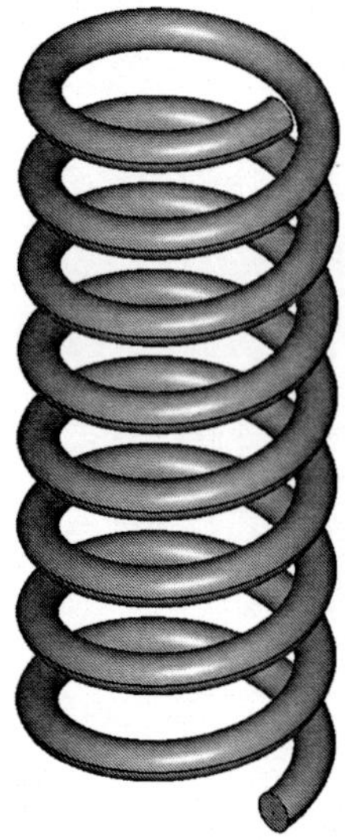

9. Save the model and close the file.

TUTORIAL 4

In this tutorial, you create a shampoo bottle using the **Loft**, **Pad**, and **Sweep** tools.

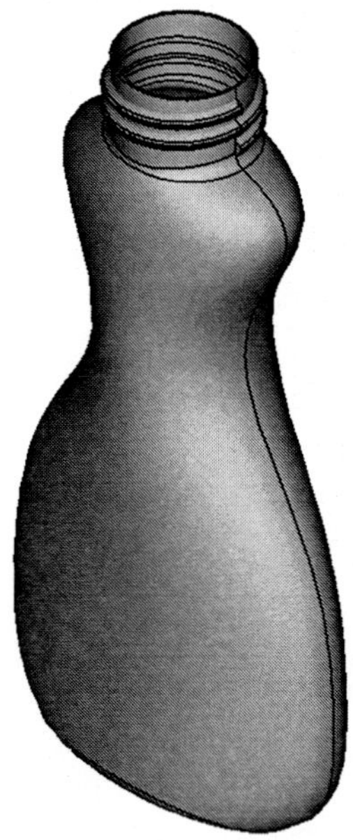

Creating the Loft feature

To create a loft feature, you need to create sections.

1. Start a new FreeCAD file.
2. Select the **Part Design** option from the **Workbenches** drop-down.

3. Click the **New Sketches**  icon on the **Part Design Helper Features** toolbar.
4. Select the **XY-Plane** from the **Tasks** panel and click **OK.**
5. Click the **Circle** drop-down > **Ellipse From Center** on the **Geometries** toolbar.

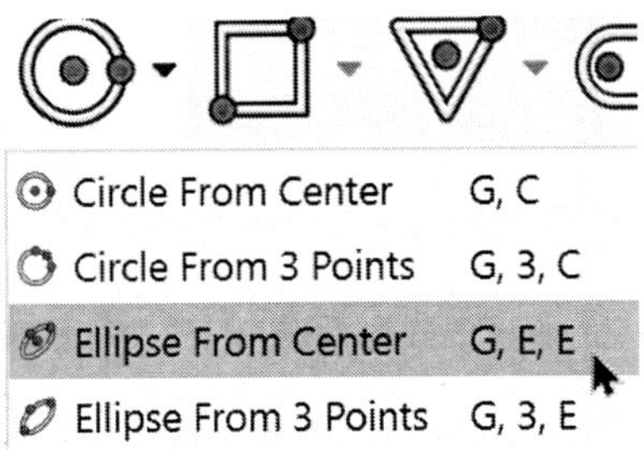

6. Draw the ellipse by selecting the points, as shown.

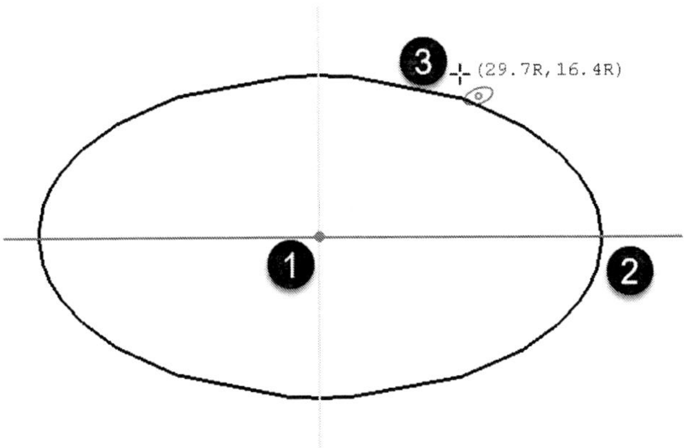

7. On the **Constraints** toolbar, click the **Dimension**  icon.
8. Select the horizontal axis of the ellipse.
9. Place the dimension.
10. Type **3.50** in the **Length** box of the **Insert Length** dialog.
11. Click **OK.**
12. Select the vertical axis of the ellipse.
13. Type **1.968** in the **Length** box of the **Insert Length** dialog.
14. Click **OK.**

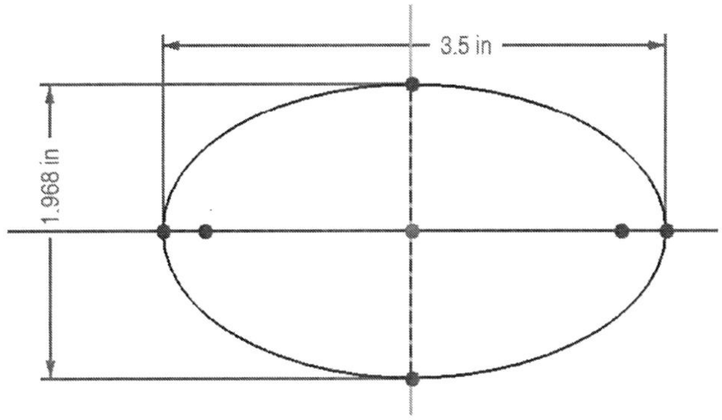

15. Click the **Close** button on the **Tasks** panel.
16. Click the **Coordinate System** drop-down > **Datum Plane** icon on the **Structure** toolbar.

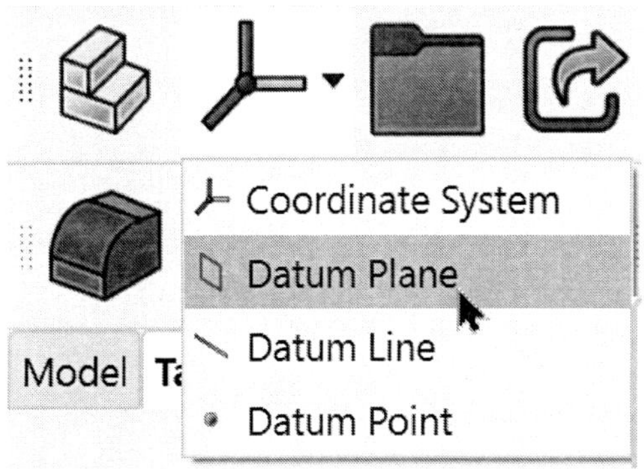

17. Click on the ellipse, if not already selected.
18. Type **1.5** in the **In Z-direction** box.
19. Click **OK.**

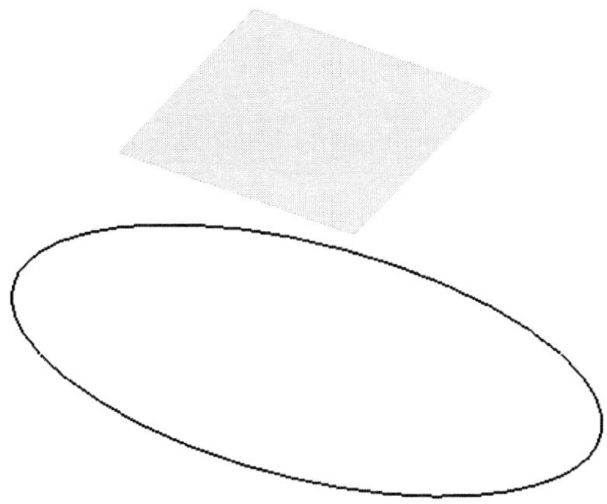

20. Click the **Coordinate System** drop-down > **Datum Plane**  icon on the **Structure** toolbar.
21. Click on the newly created plane.
22. Type **1.5** in the **In Z-direction** box.
23. Click **OK.**

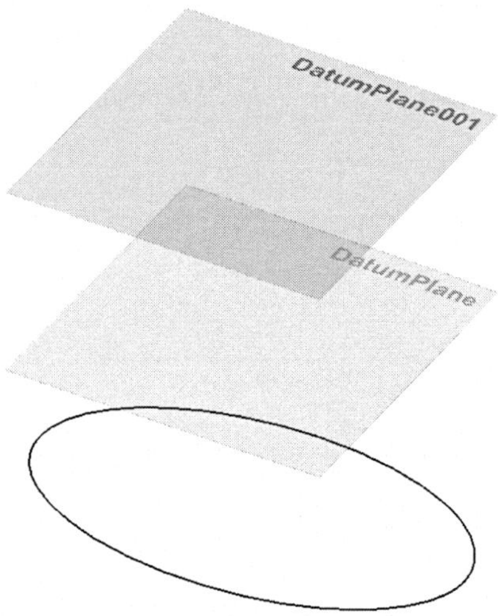

24. Click the **Coordinate System** drop-down > **Datum Plane** icon on the **Structure** toolbar.
25. Click on the newly created plane.
26. Type **1.2** in the **In z-direction** box.
27. Click **OK.**

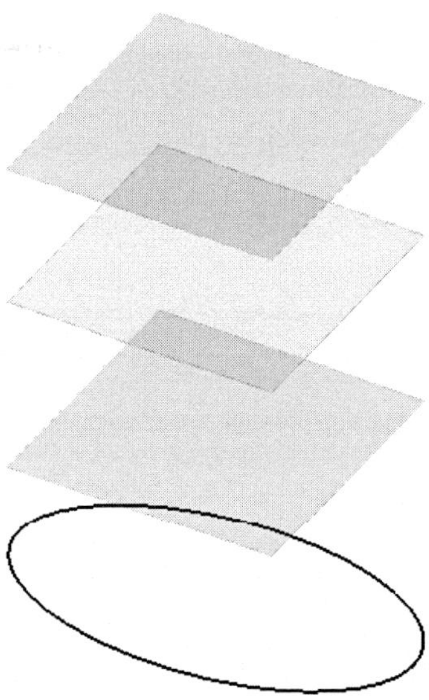

28. Click the **Coordinate System** drop-down > **Datum Plane** icon on the **Structure** toolbar.
29. Click on the newly created plane.
30. Type **1.2** in the **In Z-direction** box.
31. Click **OK.**

32. Click the **Coordinate System** drop-down > **Datum Plane** icon on the **Structure** toolbar.
33. Click on the newly created plane.
34. Type **1.5** in the **In Z-direction** box.
35. Click **OK.**

36. Click the **Coordinate System** drop-down > **Datum Plane** icon on the **Structure** toolbar.
37. Click on the newly created plane.
38. Type **1.2** in the **In Z-direction** box.
39. Click **OK**

40. Click the **New Sketch** icon on the **Part Design Helper Features** toolbar.
41. Select the first datum plane.

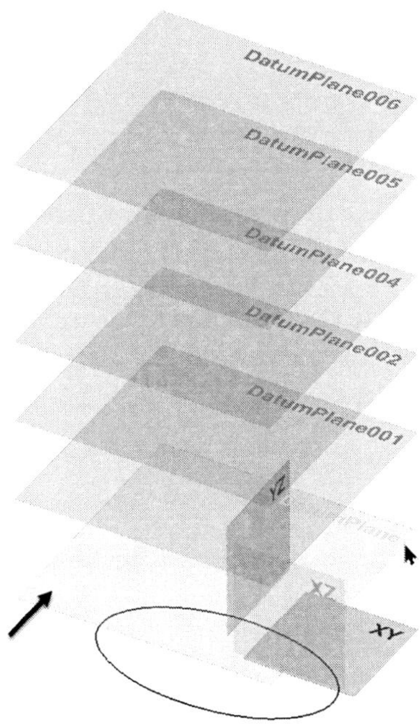

42. Click the **Toggle Section View** icon on the

Edit mode toolbar.

43. Create an ellipse, as shown.

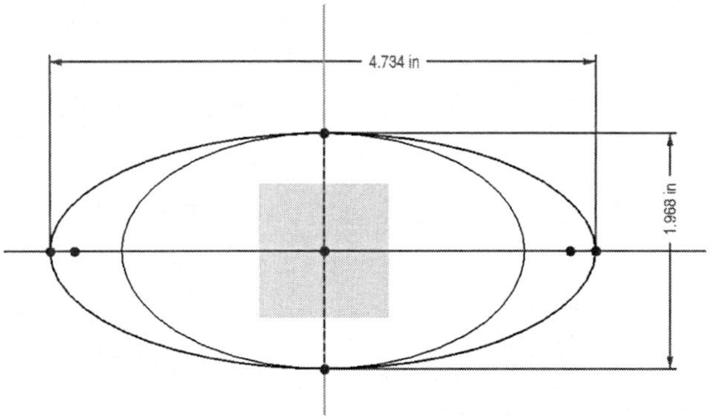

44. Click the **Close** button on the **Tasks** panel.
45. Select the second datum plane.
46. Click the **New Sketch** icon on the **Part Design Helper Features** toolbar.
47. On the Menu bar, click **Sketch > Toggle section View**.
48. Create an ellipse, as shown.

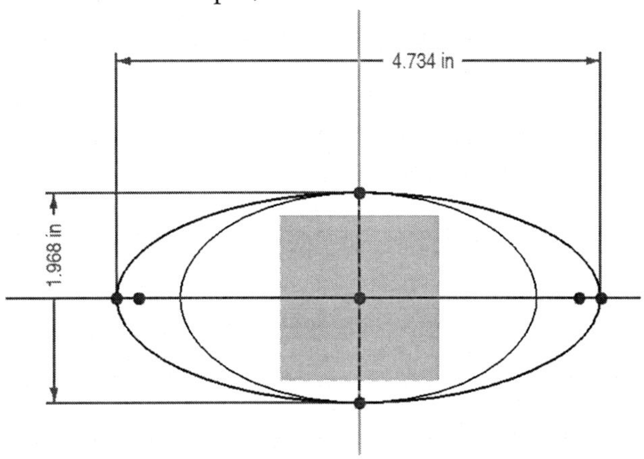

49. Click the **Close** button on the **Tasks** panel.
50. Start a sketch on the third datum plane.
51. Click the **Toggle Section View** icon on the **Edit mode** toolbar.
52. Create an ellipse, as shown.

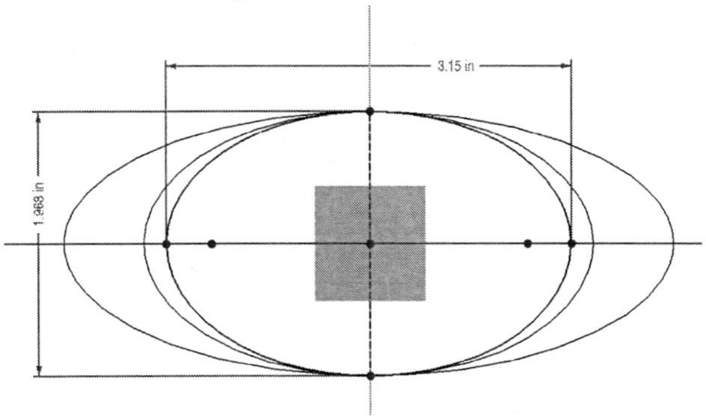

53. Click the **Close** button on the **Tasks** panel.
54. Start a sketch on the fourth datum plane, and then create an ellipse on it.

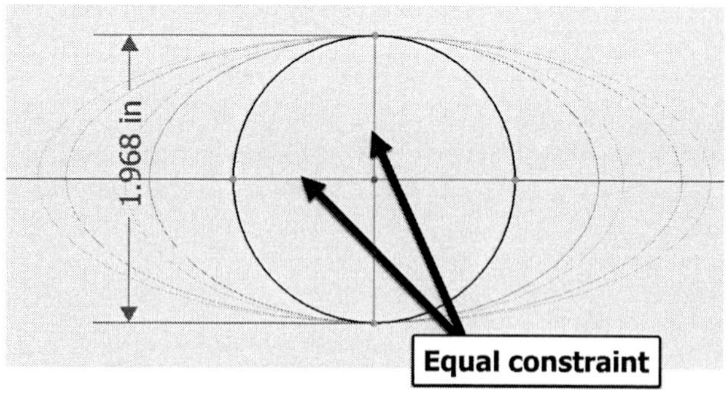

55. Click the **Close** button on the **Tasks** panel.
56. Start a new sketch on the fifth plane.
57. Create an ellipse, as shown.

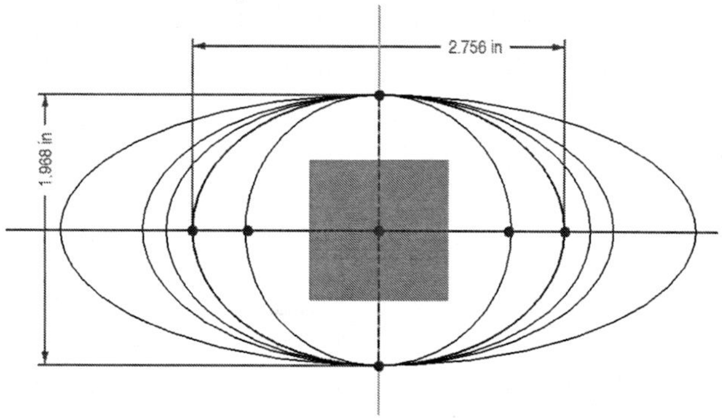

58. Click the **Close** button on the **Tasks** panel.
59. Start a new sketch on the sixth plane.
60. Create a circle, as shown.

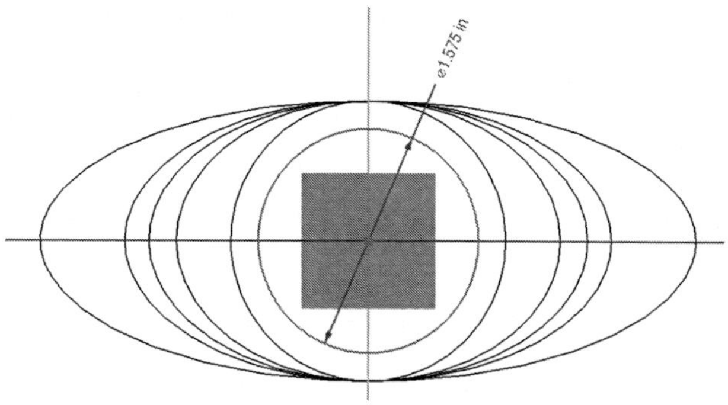

61. Click the **Close** button on the **Tasks** panel.
62. Click in the graphics window to deselect the last sketch.
63. Click the **Additive Loft** icon on the **Part Design Modeling Features** toolbar.
64. Select the ellipse located at the bottom.

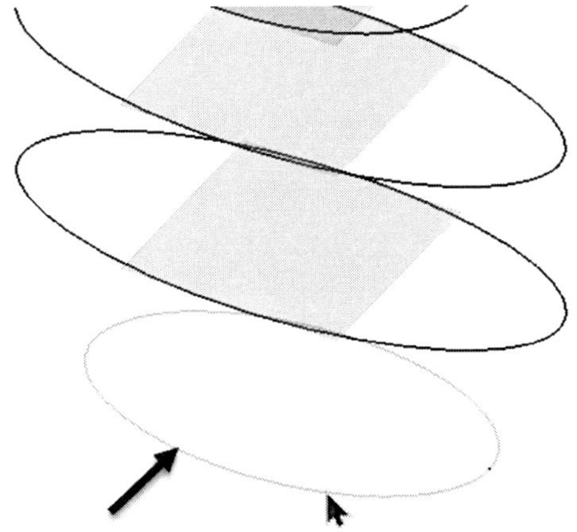

65. Click the **Add section** button and select the next ellipse.

66. Likewise, select the remaining sketches in the order, as shown.

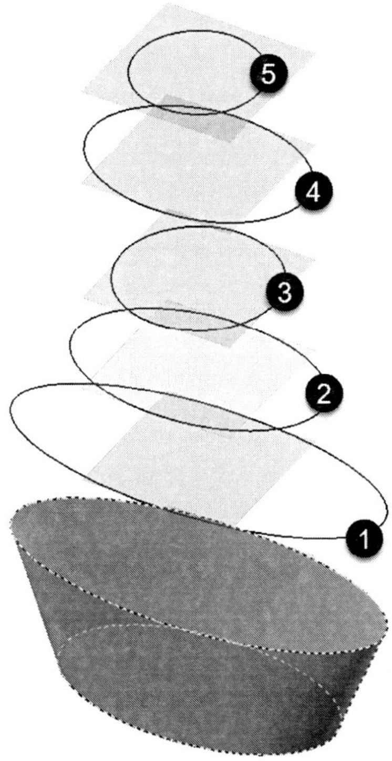

67. Click **OK** to create the loft feature.

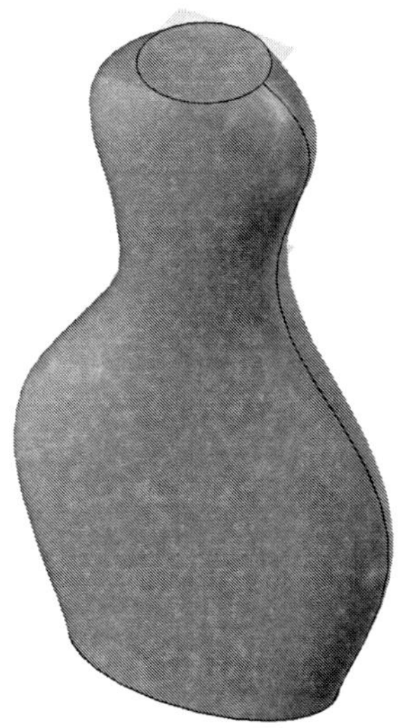

Creating the Extruded feature

1. Click the **Pad**  icon on the **Part Design Modeling Features** toolbar.
2. Check the **Allow used features** option from the **Select Features** dialog.
3. Select the last sketch from the sketch list.

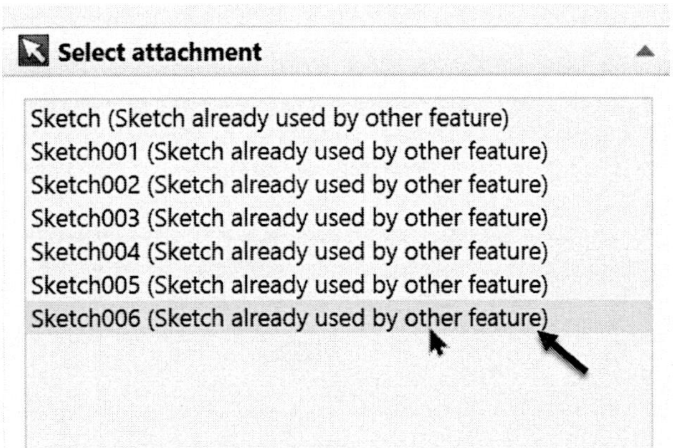

4. Click **OK**.
5. Type **1** in the **Length** box and click **OK**.

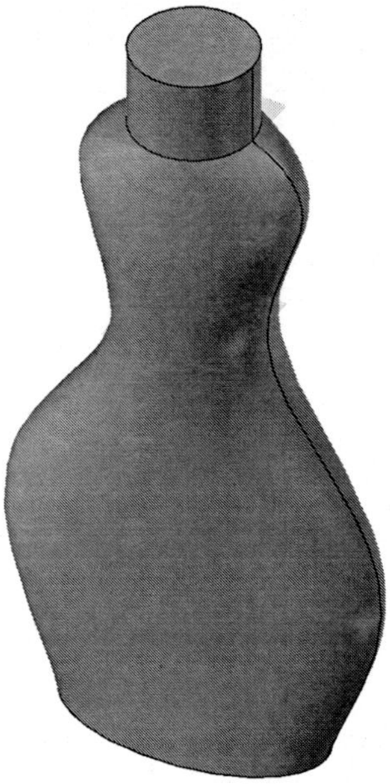

Creating Fillets

1. Press and hold the Ctrl key.
2. Click on the bottom and top edges of the swept feature.

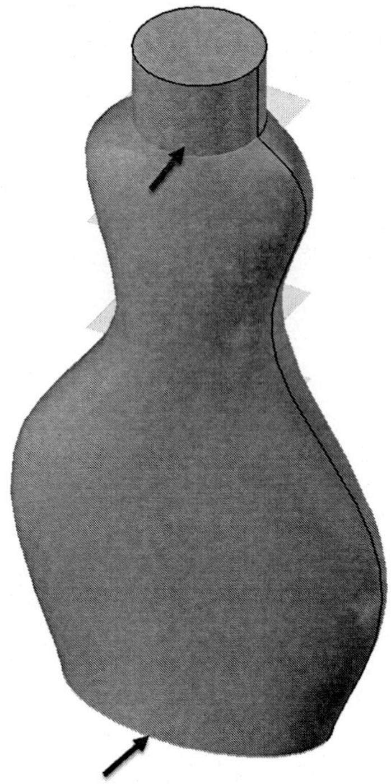

3. Click the **Fillet** icon on the **Part Design Dressup Features** toolbar.
4. Set **Radius** to 0.2.

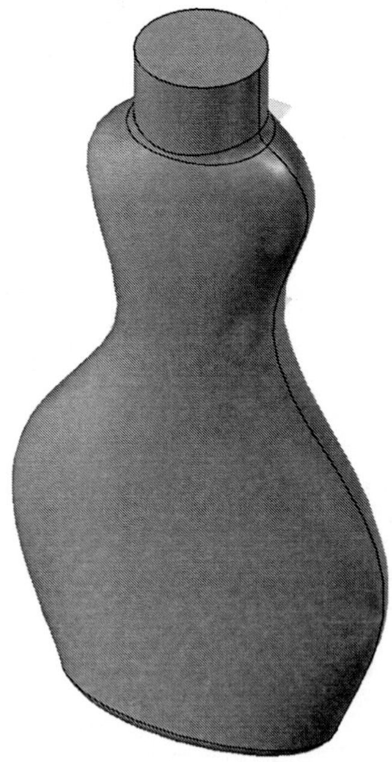

5. Click **OK**.

Shelling the Model

1. Select the top face of the cylindrical feature.

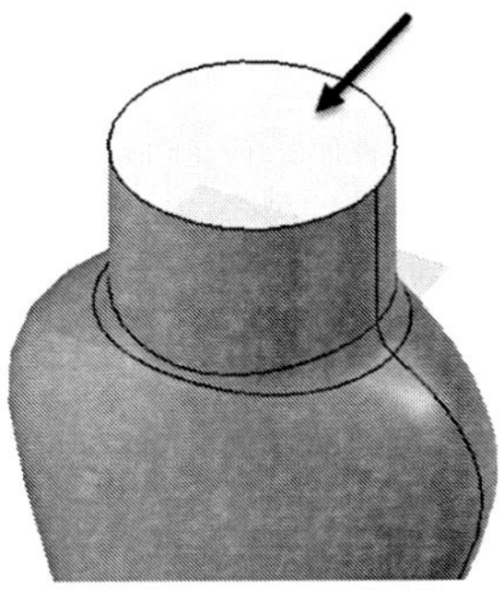

2. Click the **Thickness** icon on the **Part Design Modeling Features** toolbar.
3. Set **Thickness** to 0.03.
4. Click **OK** to create the shell.

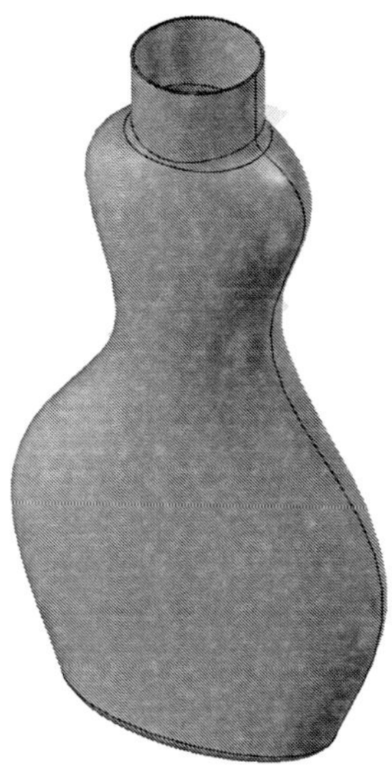

Adding Threads

1. Click the **New Sketch** icon on the **Part Design Helper Features** toolbar.
2. Select the XZ Plane from the **Tasks** panel and click **OK**.
3. Click **Draw Style > Wireframe** on the **View** toolbar.
4. Click the **Toggle Construction geometry** icon on the **Geometries** toolbar.
5. Click the **Line** icon on the **Geometries** toolbar.
6. Select the origin point of the sketch, move the cursor vertically upward and click to create a vertical construction line.

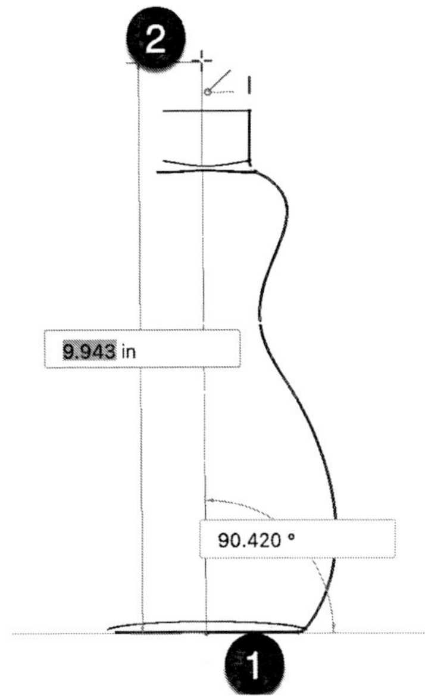

7. Create a horizontal construction line, as shown.

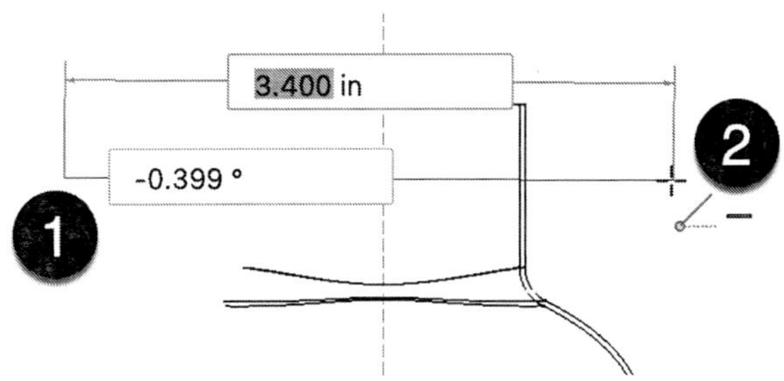

8. Click the **Toggle construction geometry** icon on the **Geometries** toolbar.
9. Click the **Polyline** icon on the **Geometries** toolbar.
10. Create a closed profile, as shown.

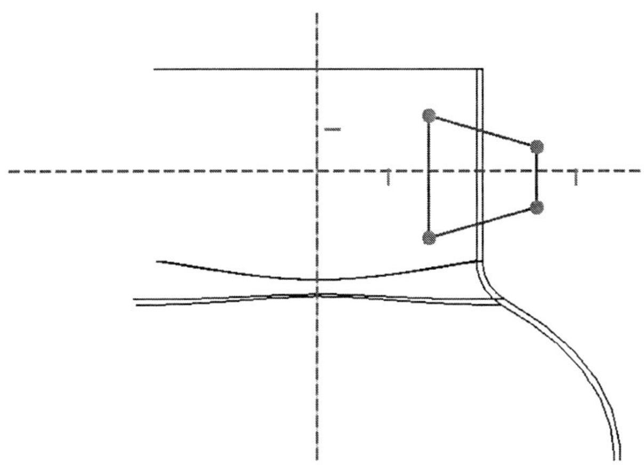

11. Press Esc to deactivate the **Polyline** tool.

12. Add fillets, constraints, and dimensions to the profile.

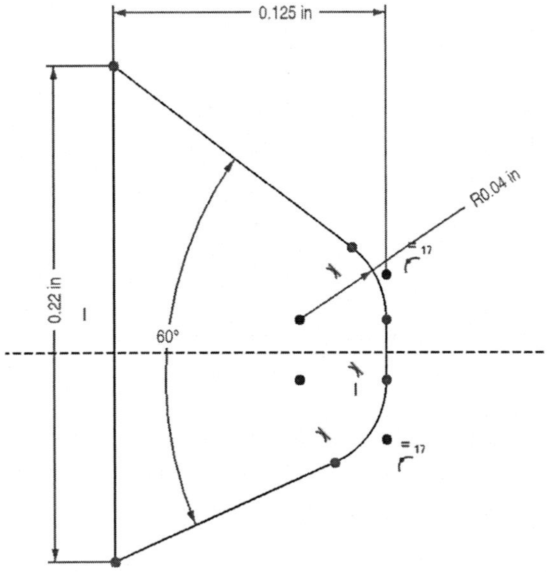

13.

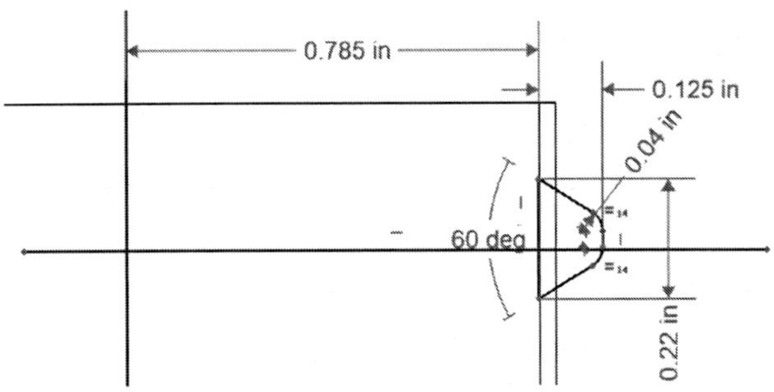

14. Click the **Symmetric Constrain** icon on the **Constraints** toolbar.
15. Select the centerpoints of the arcs.
16. Select the right endpoint of the construction line.

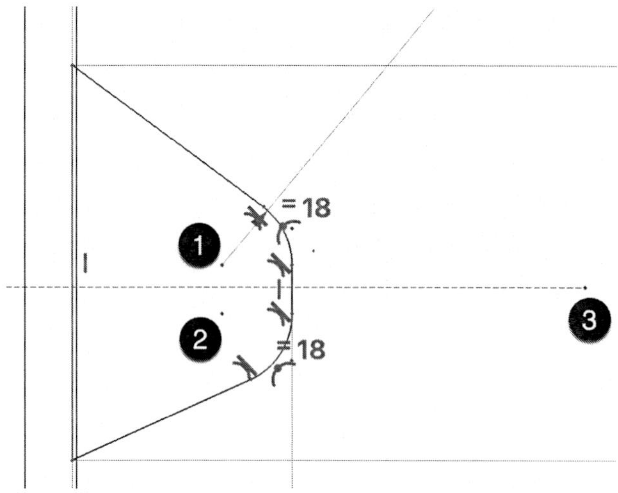

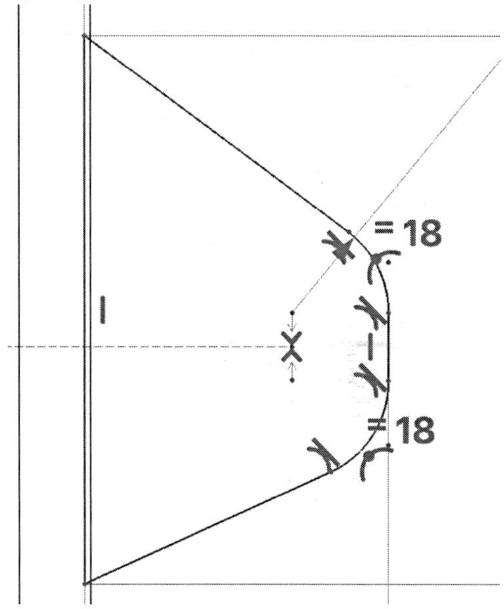

17. Add angular dimension between the inclined line and the horizontal construction line, as shown.

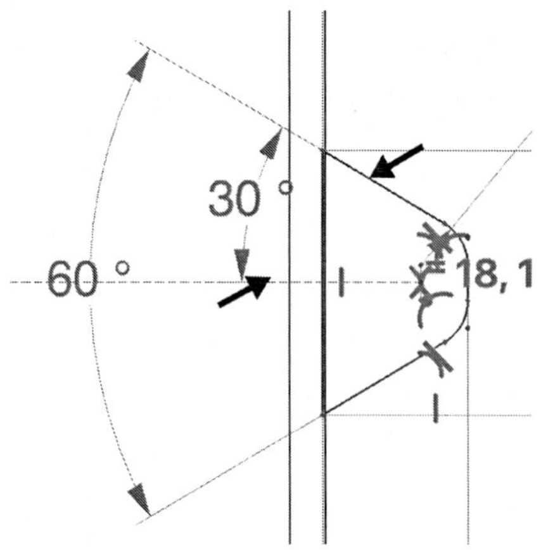

18. Create a **Verical Dimension** between the horizontal construction line and the sketch

origin, as shown.

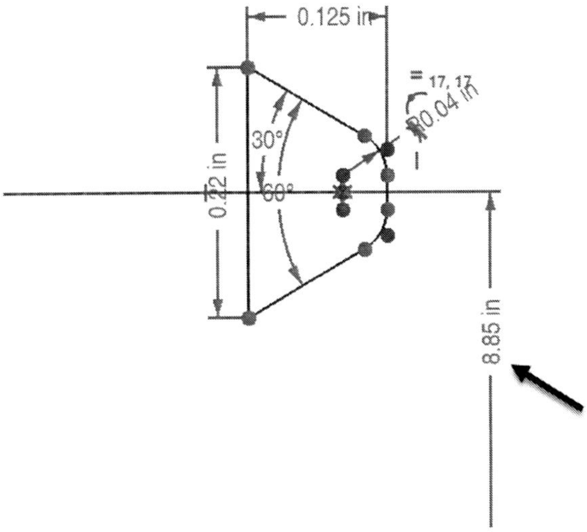

19. Create a **Horizontal Dimension** between the vertical line and the sketch origin, as shown.

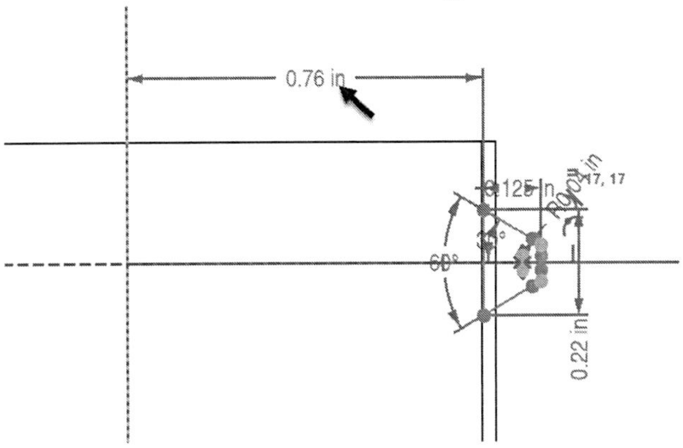

20. Click the **Close** button on the **Tasks** panel.
21. Select **Draw Style > Flat Lines** from the **View** toolbar.
22. Click the **Additive Helix** icon on the **Part Design Modeling Features** toolbar.
23. In the **Helix parameters** dialog, select **Vertical sketch axis** from the **Axis** drop-down.
24. Select **Mode > Pitch-Height-Angle**.
25. Type **0.27** in the **Pitch** box.
26. Type **0.55** in the **Height** box.
27. Check the **Reveresed** option.

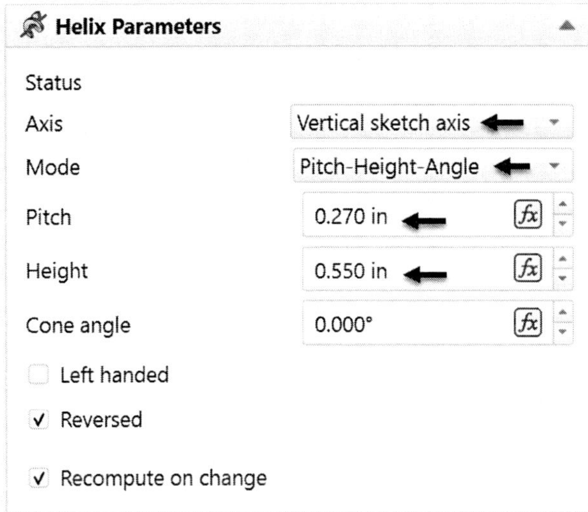

28. Click **OK** to create the additive helix.

29. Save the model.

TUTORIAL 5

In this tutorial, you create the model, as shown.

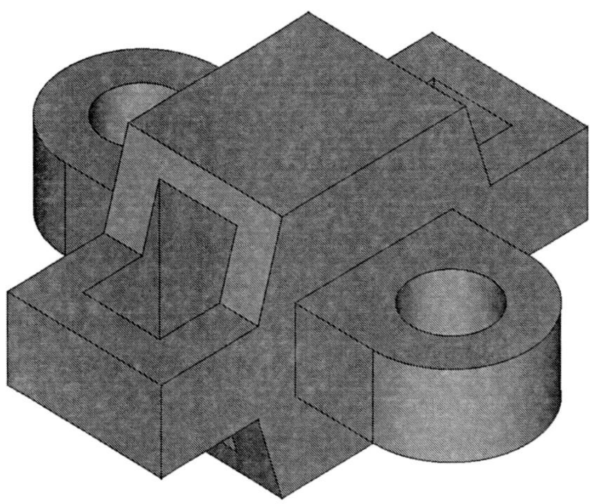

Creating the First feature

1. Open a new FreeCAD file.
2. Select **Part Design** from the **Workbenches** drop-down.
3. Click the **New Sketch**  icon on the **Part Design Helper Features** toolbar.
4. Select the YZ Plane from the **Tasks** panel and click **OK.**
5. On the menu bar, click **Sketch > Geometries > Polyline** .
6. Select the origin point of the sketch.
7. Move the pointer upward and click on the vertical axis of the sketch.
8. Move the pointer horizontally toward left.
9. Move the pointer toward bottom-left corner upto a small distance and click to create the inclined line.
10. Move the pointer horizontally toward left.
11. Move pointer vertically downward and click on the horizontal axis.
12. Move the pointer toward right and select the sketch origin to close the sketch.
13. Add dimensions to the sketch, as shown.

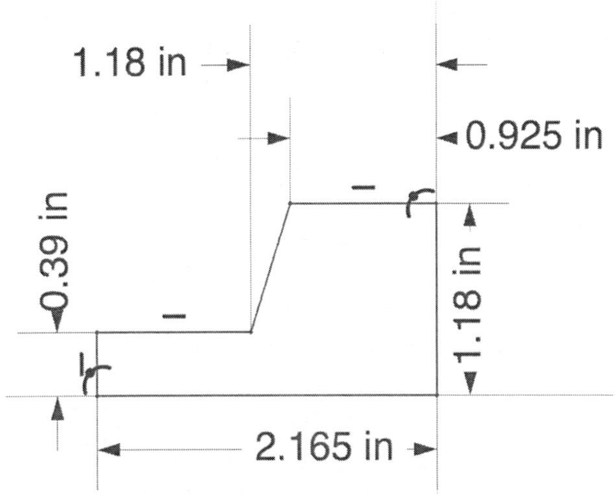

14. Click the **Close** button on the **Tasks** panel.
15. Click the **Pad** icon on the **Part Design Modeling Features** toolbar.
16. Type **1.575** in the **Length** box.
17. Select the **Symmetric** option from the Mode drop-down.
18. Click **OK.**

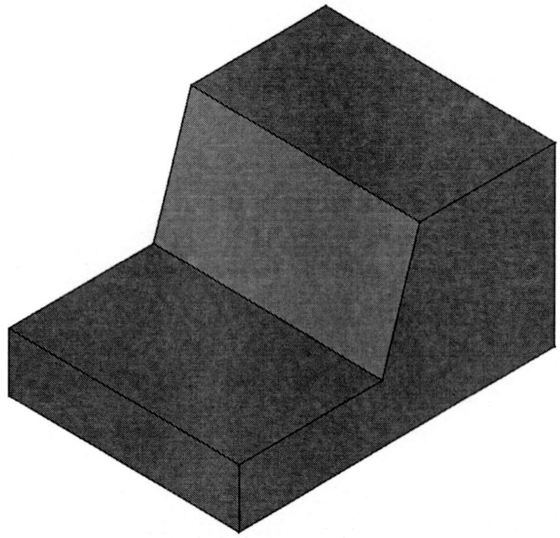

Creating the Pocket Feature

1. Click the **New Sketch** icon on the **Part Design Helper Features** toolbar.
2. Select the XY Plane from the **Tasks** panel and click **OK.**
3. Click the **Toggle Section View**  icon on the **Edit mode** toolbar.
4. Create a rectangle and add constraints to it, as shown.

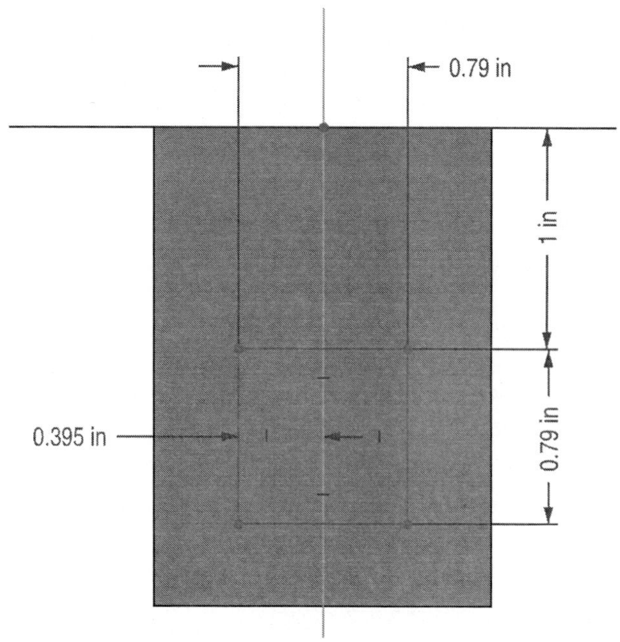

5. Click **Close** on the **Tasks** panel.
6. Click the **Pocket**  icon on the **Part Design**

Modeling Features toolbar.

7. Select **Type > Through All**.
8. Check the **Reversed** option.
9. Click **OK**.
10. Select **Draw Style > Flat Lines** from the **View** toolbar.

11. Click the **Create MultiTransform**  icon on the **Part Design Transformations Features** toolbar.
12. Make sure that the Transform Body option is selected in the MultTransform parameters section.
13. Right-click in the **Transformations** section.
14. Select **Add mirrored transformation**.

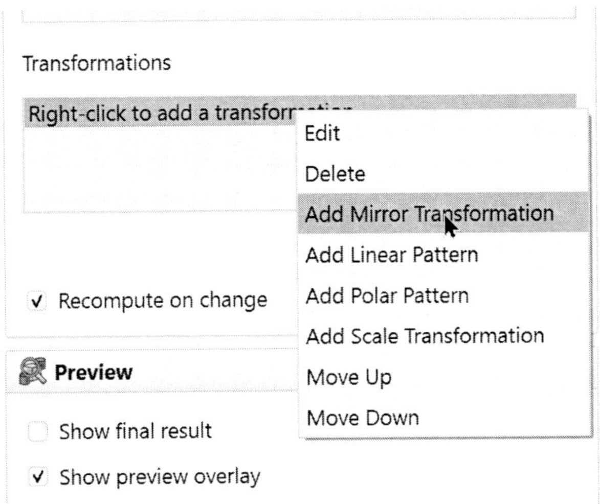

15. Select the **Base XY plane** from the **Plane** drop-down.

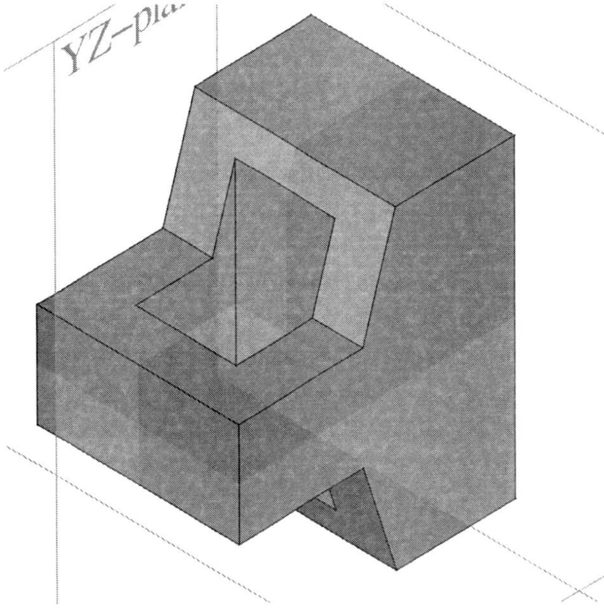

16. Right-click in the **Transformations** section.
17. Select **Add mirrored transformation.**
18. Select the **Base XZ plane** from the **Plane** drop-down.
19. Click **OK** at the bottom of the **Tasks** panel
20. **Click OK** at the top of the **Tasks** panel to mirror the pocket feature.

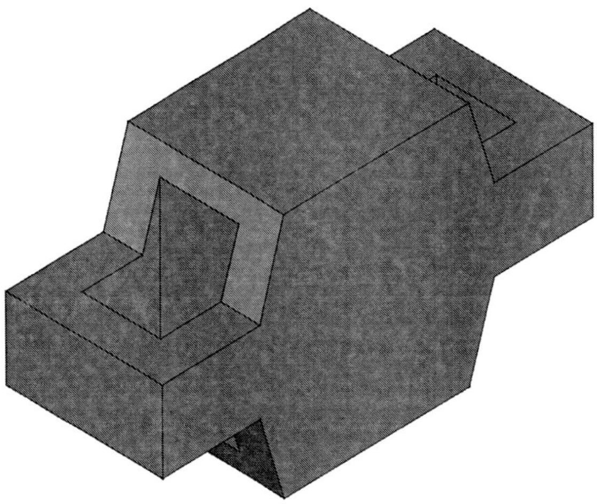

Creating the Second feature

1. Click the **New Sketch** icon on the **Part Design Helper Features** toolbar.
2. Select the XY Plane from the **Tasks** panel and click **OK**.

3. Click the **Toggle Section View**  icon on the **Edit mode** toolbar.
4. Click the **Slot** icon on the **Geometries** toolbar.
5. Click on the horizontal axis on the left side.
6. Move the pointer toward right and click on the horizontal axis.
7. Move the pointer outward and click to specify the slot width.
8. On the menu bar, click **Sketch > Geometries > Circle From Center**.
9. Select the centerpoint of the left arc of the slot.
10. Move the pointer outward and click.
11. Likewise, create a circle concentric to the right arc of the slot.
12. Add dimensions to the sketch, as shown.

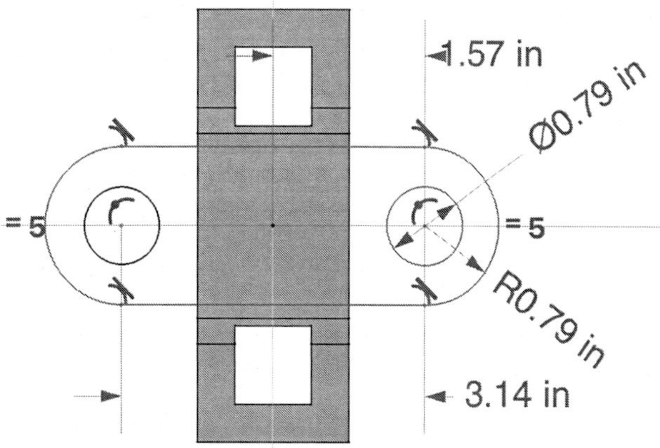

13. Click **Close** on the **Tasks** panel.
14. Click the **Pad** icon on the **Part Design Modeling Features** toolbar.
15. Type **0.78** in the **Length** box.
16. Select the **Symmetric** option ffrom the **Mode** drop-down.
17. Click **OK**.

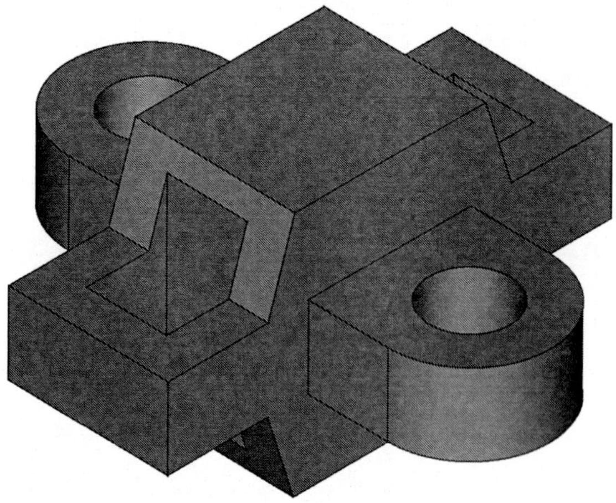

21. Save and close the file.

TUTORIAL 6

In this tutorial, you construct a patterned cylindrical shell.

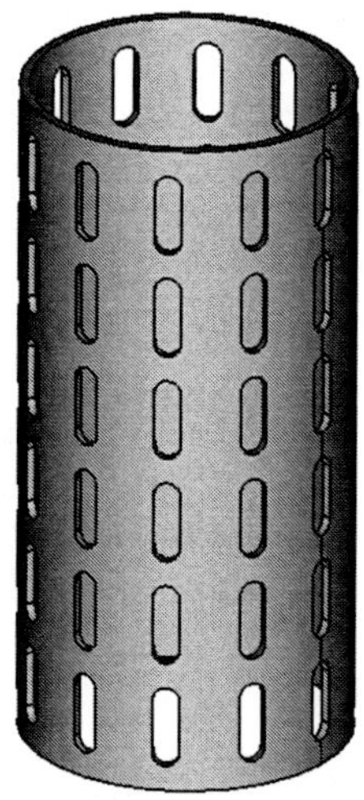

Constructing a cylindrical shell

1. Start a new FreeCAD file.
2. Select **Part Design** from the **Workbenches** drop-down.
3. Create a sketch on the XY plane (add Diameter constraints to the circles).

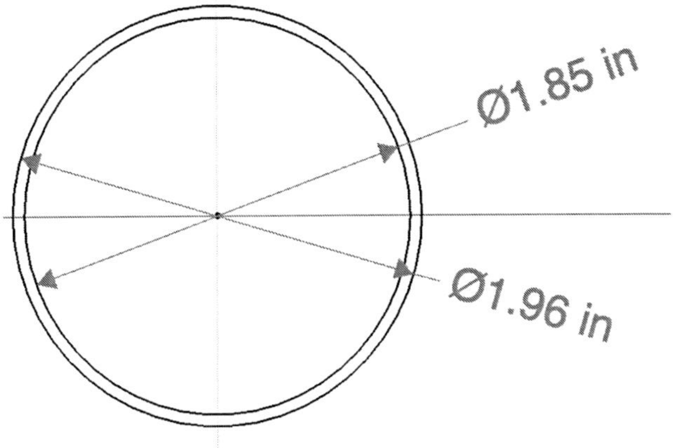

4. Extrude the sketch up to 3.93 depth.

Adding a Slot

1. Activate the **New Sketch** tool.
2. Select the **XZ Plane** from the graphics window.
3. Set the **Draw Style** to **Wireframe**.
4. Click the **Slot** icon on the **Geometries** toolbar.
5. Click on the vertical axis of the sketch to define the first point of the slot.
6. Move the pointer up and click on the vertical axis to define the second point.
7. Move the pointer and click to specify the slot width.

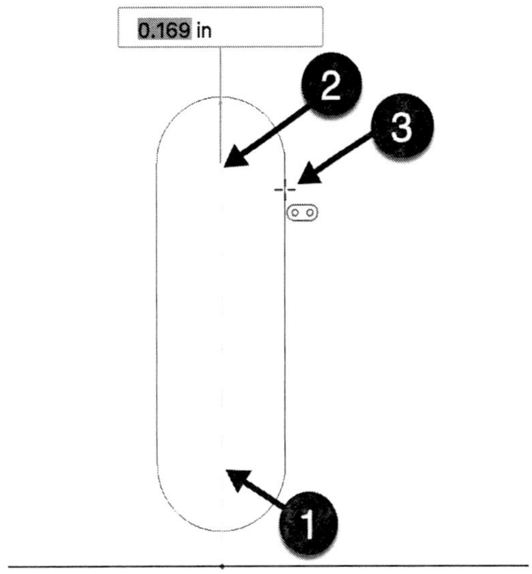

8. Add constraints to the slot.

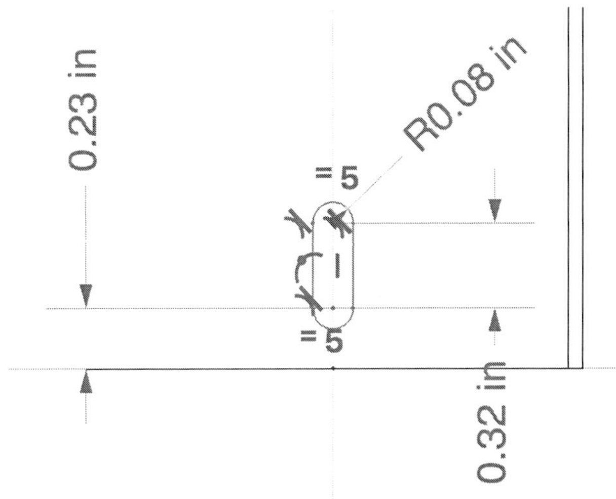

9. Click the **Leave Sketch** icon on the **Edit mode** toolbar.
10. Set the **Draw Style** to **Flat Lines**.
11. Click the **Pocket** icon on the **Part Design Modeling Features** toolbar.
12. On the **Pocket Parameters** section, select **Type > Through All**.
13. Check the **Reversed** option.
14. Click **OK**.

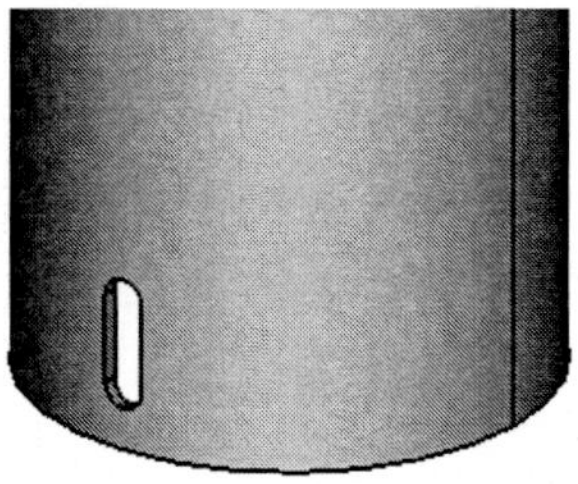

Constructing the Linear and Circular patterns using the MultiTransform tool

1. Click the **MultiTransform**  icon on the **Part Design Transformations Features** toolbar.
2. Select the **Transform tool shapes** option.
3. Click the **Add feature** button and select the pocket feature from the graphics window.
4. Right-click in the **Transformations** section and select **Add linear pattern.**
5. Select **Direction > Base Z axis.**
6. Type **3.145** in the **Length** box.
7. Type **6** in the **Occurrences** box.
8. Right-click in the **Transformations** section and select **Add polar pattern.**
9. Select the **Base Z axis** from the **Axis** drop-down.
10. Select **Mode > Overall Angle.**
11. Type **360** in the **Angle** box.
12. Type-in **12** in the **Occurrences** box.
13. Click **OK** to create the circular pattern.

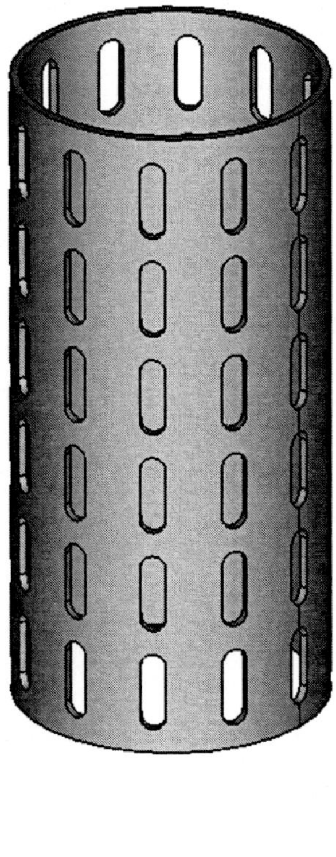

11. Save and close the model.

TUTORIAL 7

In this tutorial, you construct a pulley wheel using the **Revolution** and **Groove** tools.

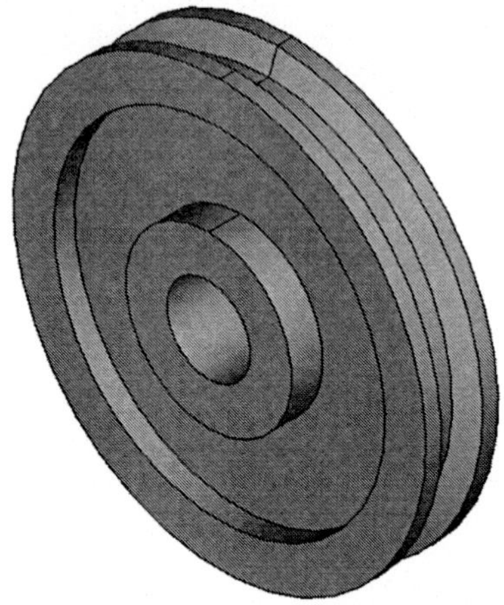

1. Open a new FreeCAD file.
2. Select **Part Design** from the **Workbenches** drop-down.
3. Click the **New Sketch** icon on the **Part Design Helper Features** toolbar.
4. Select the YZ Plane from the **Tasks** panel and click **OK.**
5. Click the **Polyline** icon on the **Geometries** toolbar.
6. Create a closed sketch, as shown.

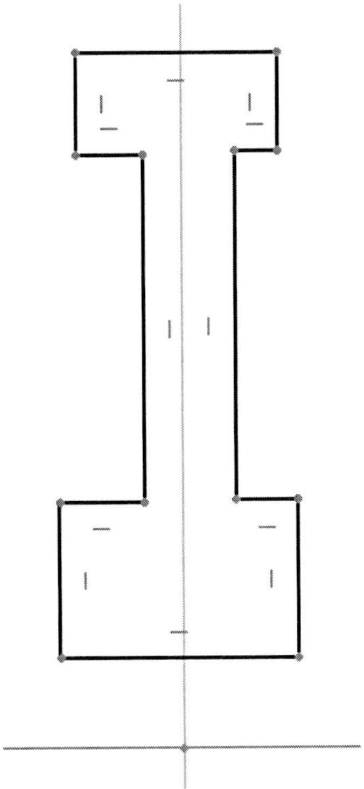

7. Click the **Equal Constraint** icon on the **Constraints** toolbar.
8. Make the entities of the sketch equal in length, as shown.

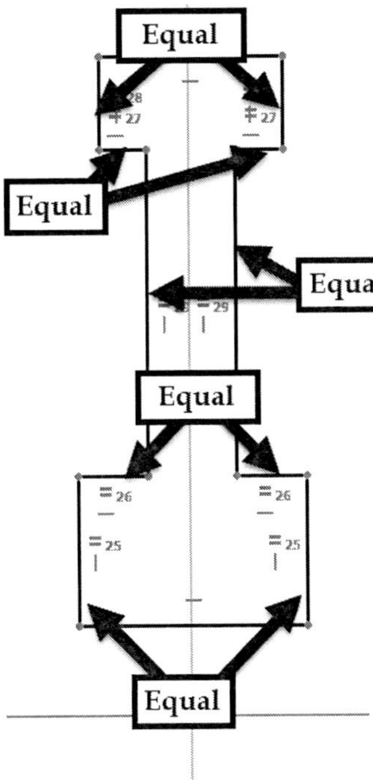

9. Create remaining constraints, as shown.

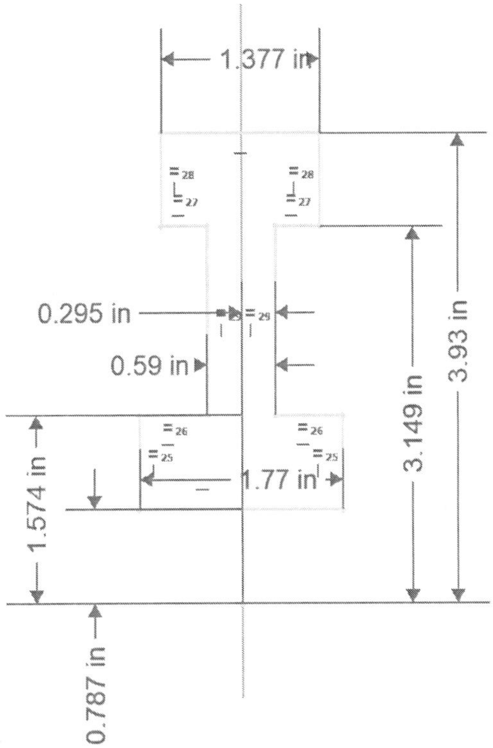

10. Click the **Close** button on the **Tasks** panel.
11. Click the **Revolve** icon on the **Part Design Modeling Features** toolbar; the sketch is selected automatically.
12. Select **Axis > Base Y-axis** from the **Revolution parameters** section.
13. Type **360** in the **Angle** box.
14. Click **OK** to construct the revolved feature.

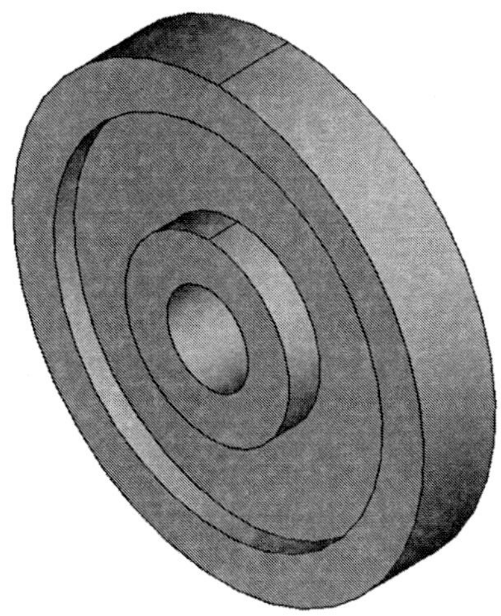

Constructing the Groove feature

1. Click the **New Sketch** icon on the **Part**

Design Helper Features toolbar.

2. Select the YZ Plane.
3. Set the **Draw Style** to **Wireframe**.
4. Create the sketch, as shown.

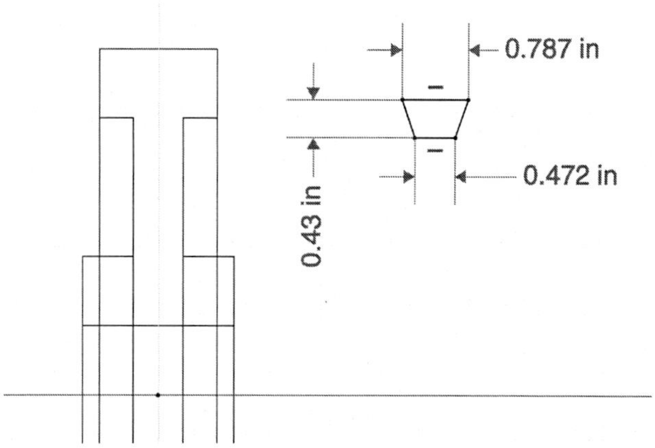

5. Click the **Toggle Construction Geometry** icon on **Geometries** toolbar.
6. On the menu bar, click **Sketch > Sketcher tools > External Projection.**
7. Select the top horizontal edge of the model, as shown.

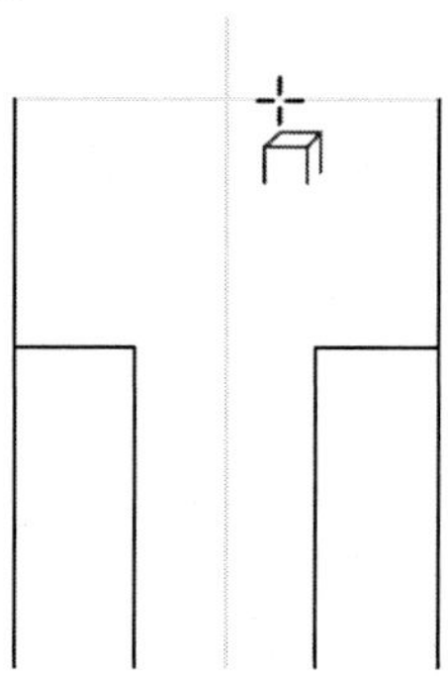

8. On the menu bar, click **Sketch > Constraints > Coincident Constraint.**
9. Select the endpoint of the sketch and the external geometry, as shown.

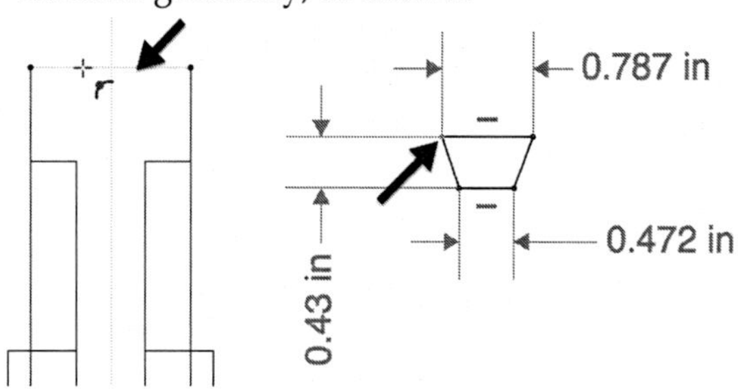

10. On the menu bar, click **Sketch > Geometries > Line.**
11. Select the sketch origin, move the pointer vertically upward and click on the external geometry.

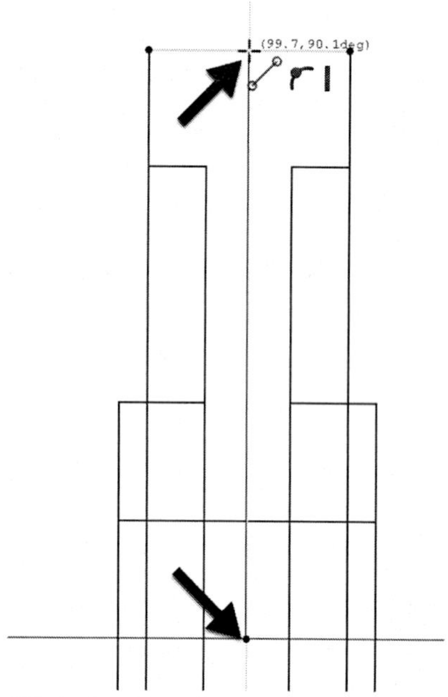

12. Click the **Toggle Construction geometry** icon on the **Geometries** toolbar.
13. Add the Angle constraint between the left inclined line and the bottom horizontal line, as shown.

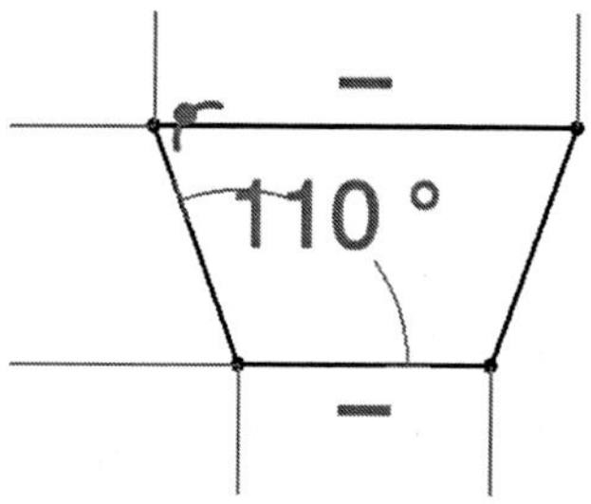

14. Click the **Symmetric Constraint** icon on the **Constraints** toolbar.
15. Select the endpoints of the top horizontal line of the sketch.
16. Select the top endpoint of the vertical line.

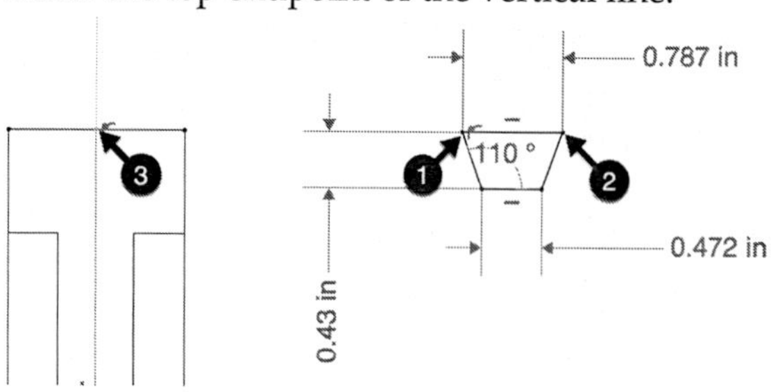

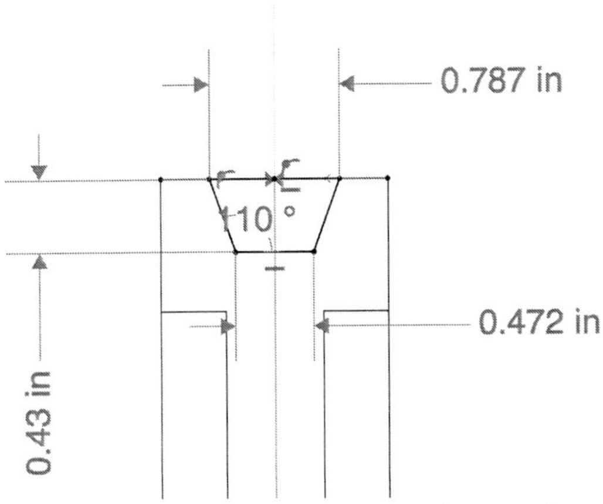

17. Click the **Close** button on the **Tasks** panel.
18. Set the **Draw Style** to **Flat Lines**.
19. Click the **Groove** icon on the **Part Design geometries** toolbar.
20. Select **Axis > Base Yaxis** from the **Revolution parameters** section of the **Model** panel.
21. Type 360 in the **Angle** box.
22. Click **OK**.

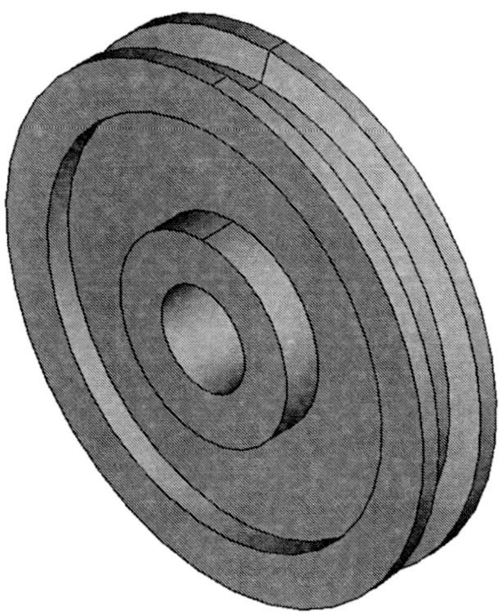

23. Save and close the model.

TUTORIAL 8

In this tutorial, you construct the model shown in the figure.

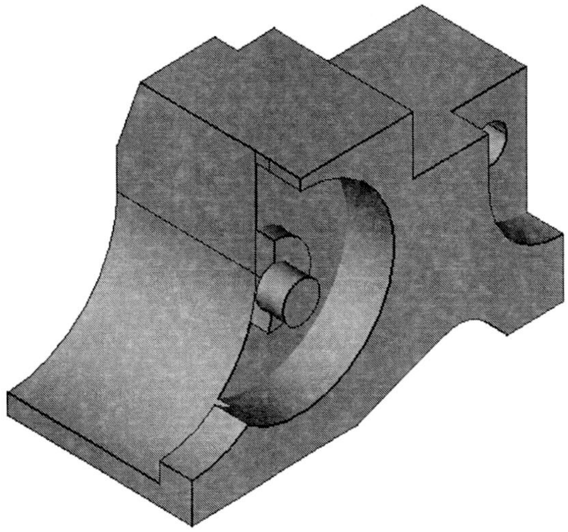

Creating the Base Feature

1. Open a new FreeCAD file.
2. Select **Part Design** from the **Workbenches** drop-down.
3. Click the **New Sketch** icon on the **Part Design Helper Features** toolbar.
4. Select the YZ Plane from the Tasks panel and click OK.
5. Click the **Rectangle** drop-down > **Rectangle** icon on the **Geometries** toolbar.
6. Specify the first and second corners of the rectangle, as shown.

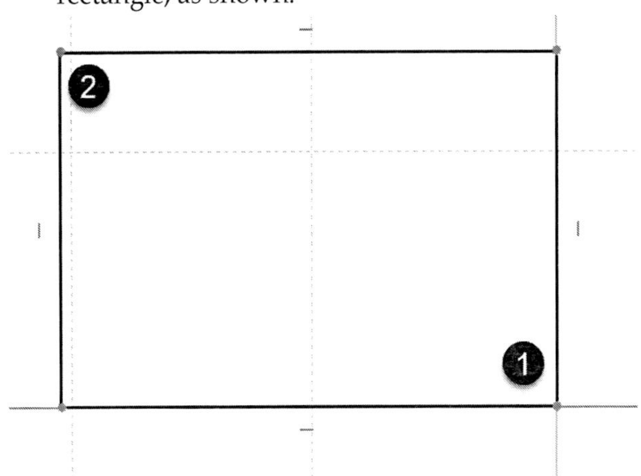

7. Create another rectangle by specifying its first and second corners, as shown.

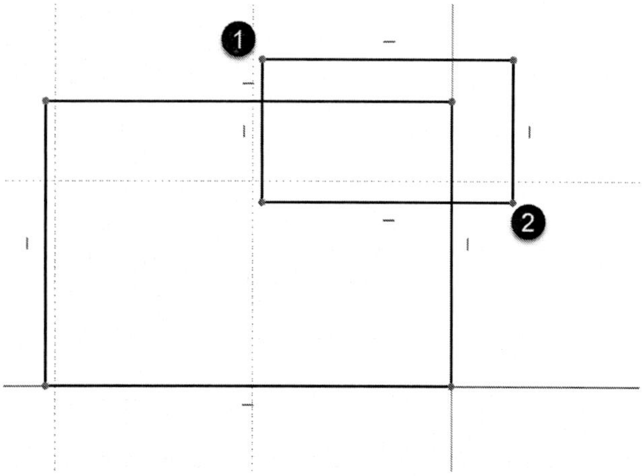

8. Click the **Trim/Extend** drop-down > **Trim Edge** 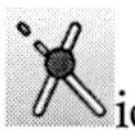 icon on the **Sketcher tools** toolbar.
9. Select the elements of the rectangles to be trimmed, as shown.

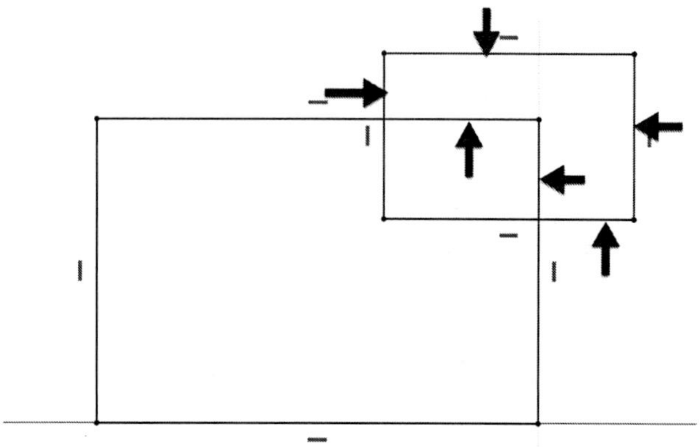

10. Add vertical and horizontal distance constraints to the sketch, as shown.

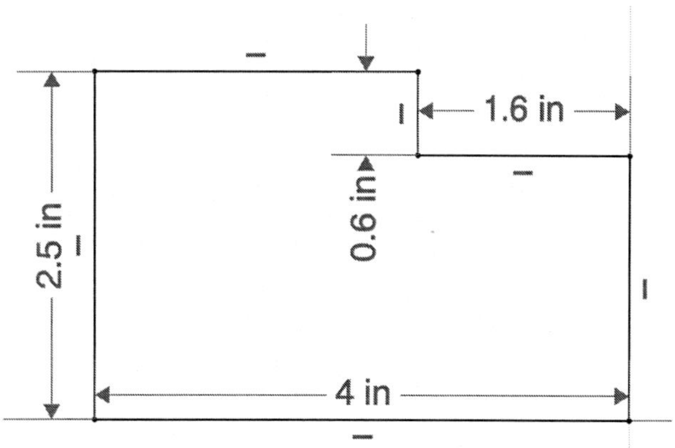

11. Click **Close** on the **Tasks** panel.
12. Click the **Pad** icon on the **Part Design Modeling Features** toolbar; the sketch is selected automatically.
13. Type 2 in the **Length** box.
14. Select **Mode** > **Symmetric** and click **OK**

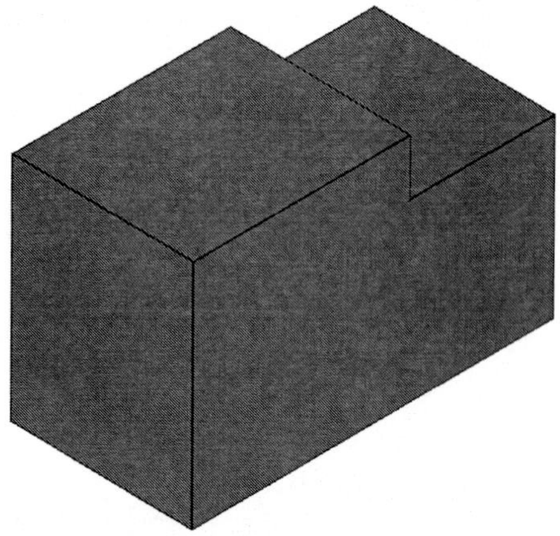

Creating the Pocket Features

1. Click the **New Sketch** icon on the **Part Design Helper Features** toolbar.
2. Select the YZ Plane from the **Tasks** panel and click **OK**.
3. On the menu bar, click **Sketch > Toggle Section View**.
4. Click the **Polyline** 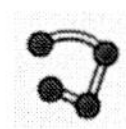 icon on the **Geometries** toolbar.
5. Specify the endpoints of the polyline, as shown.

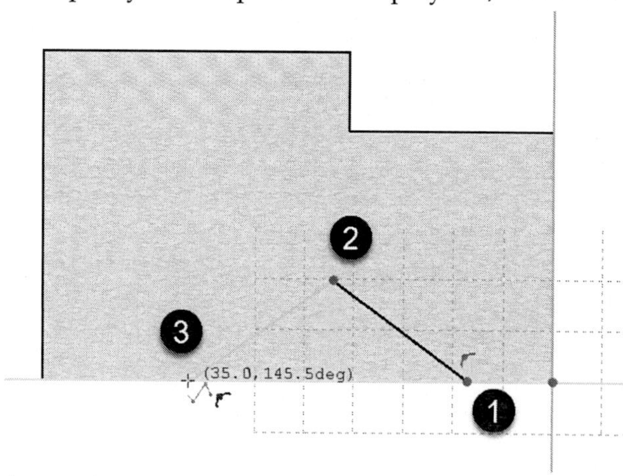

6. Right-click.
7. Click the **Fillet** 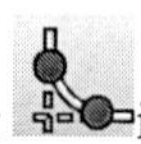 icon on the **Sketcher tools** toolbar.
8. Select the corner point of the sketch, as shown.

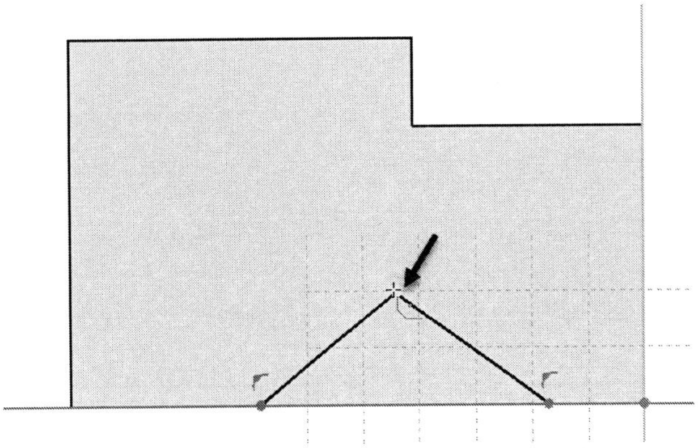

9. Click the **Dimension** drop-down > **Angle Dimension** icon on the **Constraints** toolbar.
10. Select the inclined line and the horizontal axis of the sketch.

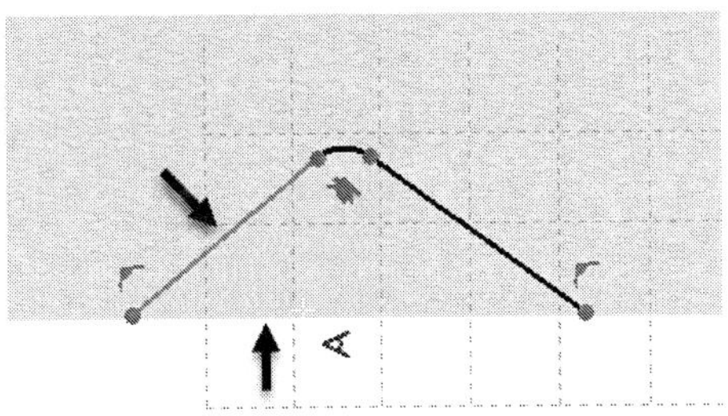

11. Type **20** in the **Angle** box and click **OK.**
12. Select the other inclined line and the horizontal axis of the sketch, as shown.

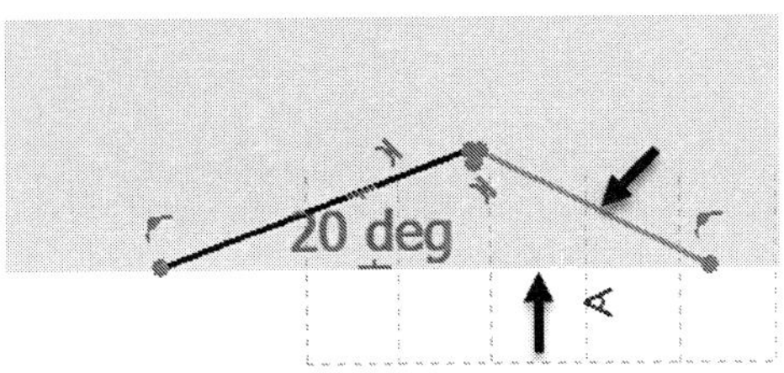

13. Type **135** in the **Angle** box and click **OK.**

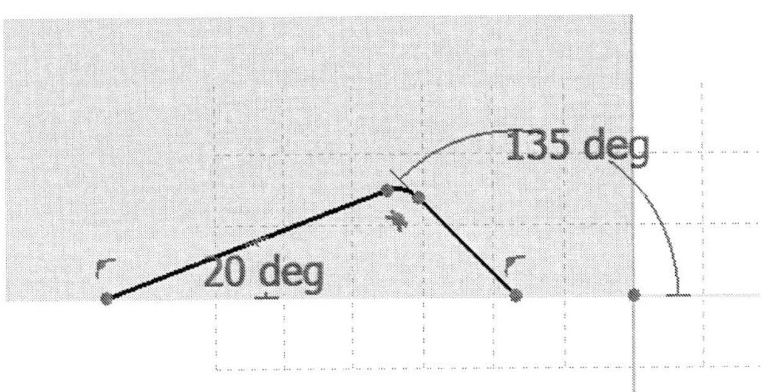

14. Add vertical and horizontal distance constraints to the sketch, as shown.
15. Add the radius constraint to the fillet.

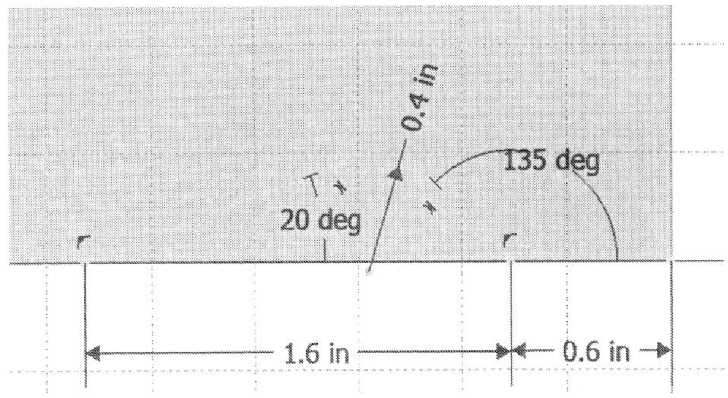

16. Click the **Line** icon on the **Geometries** toolbar.
17. Select the endpoints of the sketch, as shown.

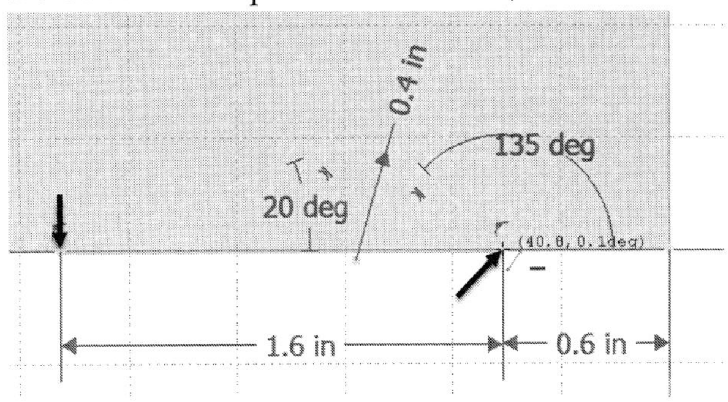

18. Click **Close** on the **Tasks** panel.
19. Click the **Pocket** icon on the **Part Design Modeling Features** toolbar; the sketch is selected automatically.
20. On the **Pocket parameters** dialog, select **Type > Through all.**
21. Select **Mode > Symmetric.**
22. Click **OK** to create the pocket feature.

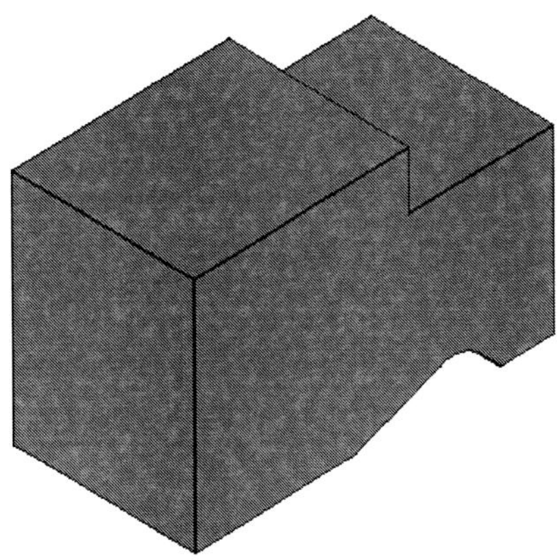

23. Click on the right side face of the model.

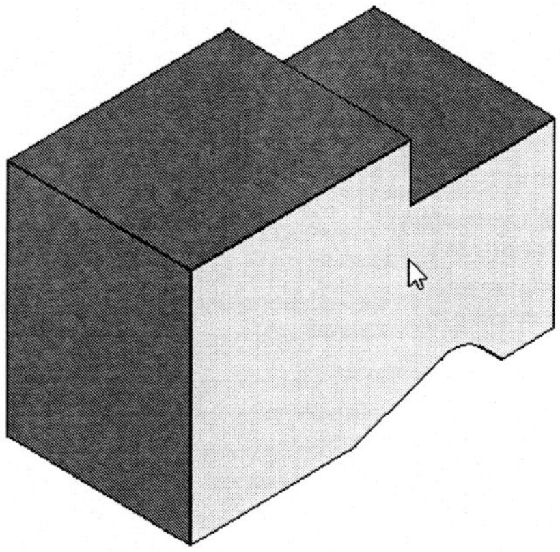

24. Click the **New Sketch** icon on the **Part Design Helper Features** toolbar.
25. Click the **Polyline** icon on the **Geometries** toolbar.
26. Click on the vertical axis of the sketch to define the start point.

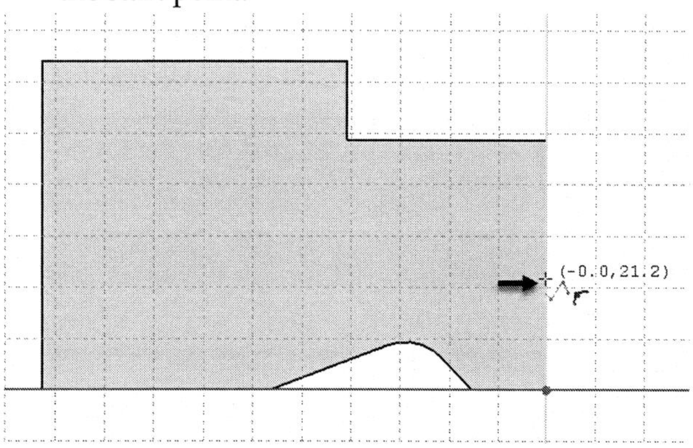

27. Move the pointer vertically upward, and then click to create the vertical line.

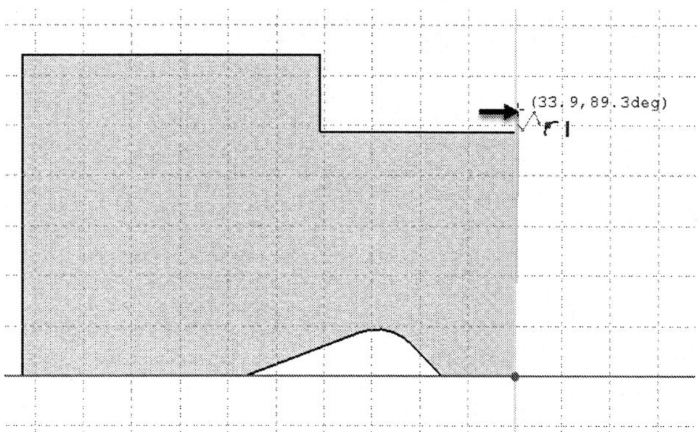

28. Move the pointer horizontally toward left, and then click.

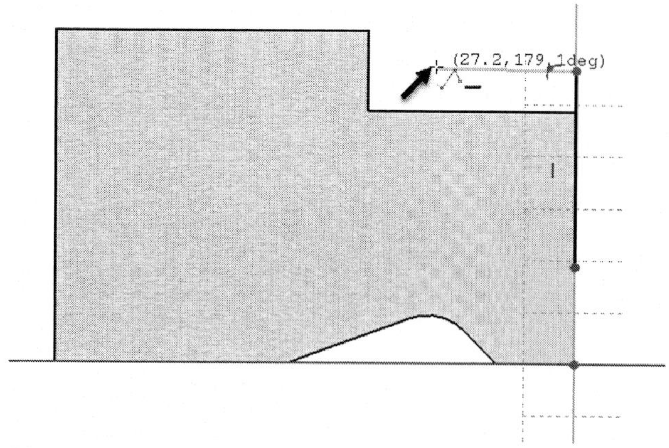

29. Move the vertically downward and click.

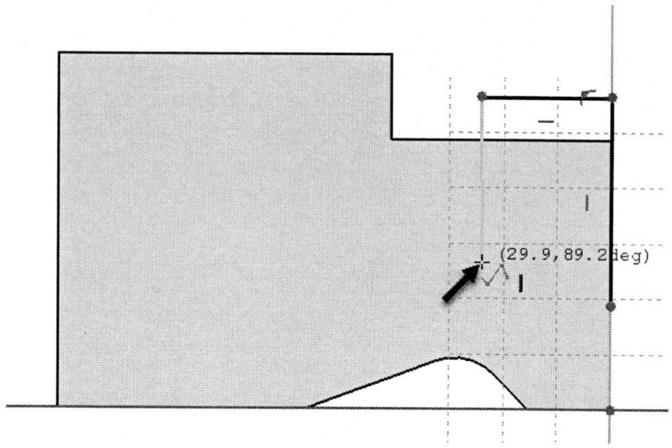

30. Right-click.
31. Click the **Arc** drop-down > **Arc from 3 Points** on the **Geometries** toolbar.
32. Select the endpoints of the two vertical lines.

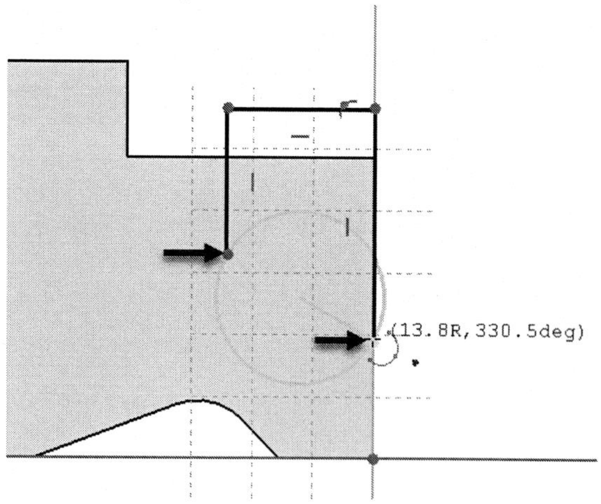

33. Move the pointer outward and click to create the arc.

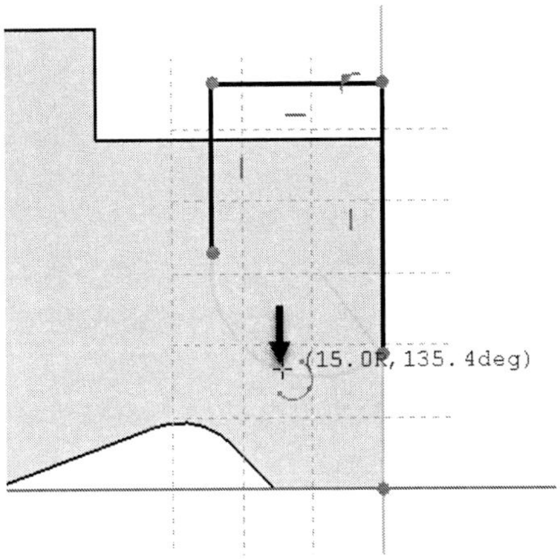

34. Click the **Tangent Constraint** icon on the **Constraints** toolbar.
35. Select the left vertical line and the arc.

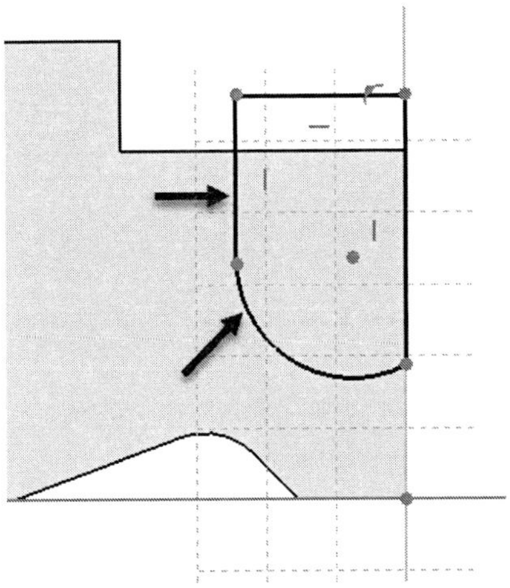

36. Click **OK** on the **Sketcher Constrain Substitution** message box.
37. Click the **Coincident Constraint** icon on the **Constraints** toolbar.
38. Select the center point of the circle and the right vertical line.

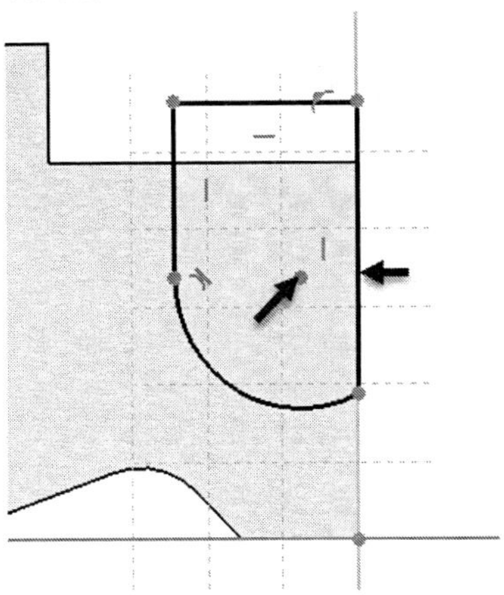

39. Click the **Toggle Construction Geometry** icon on the **Geometries** toolbar.
40. Click the **External Projection** icon on the **Sketcher tools** toolbar.
41. Select the horizontal edge of the model, as shown.

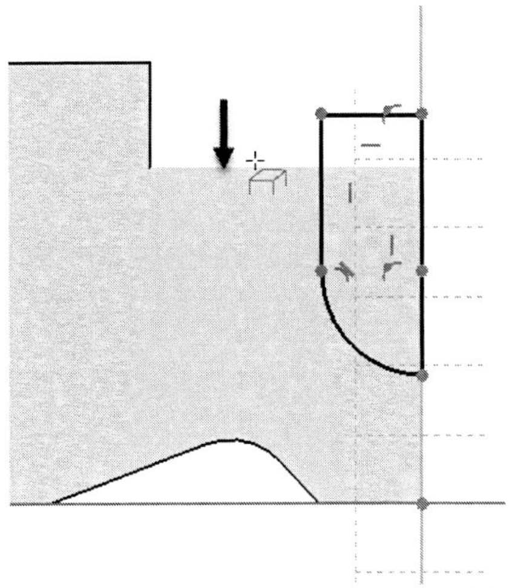

42. Click the **Coincident Constraint** icon on the **Constraints** toolbar.
43. Select the endpoint of the horizontal line and the external geometry.

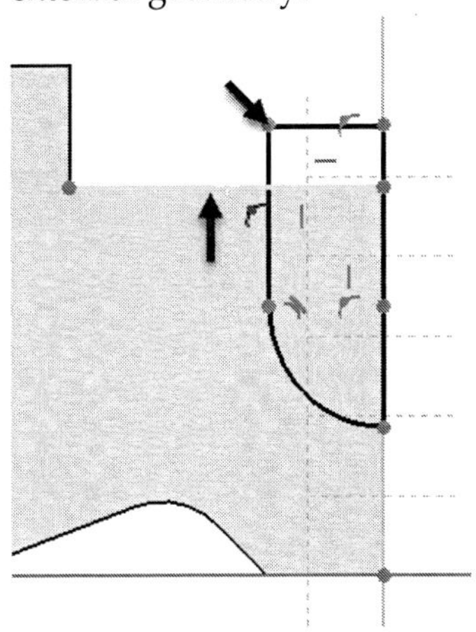

44. Click the **Toggle Construction Geometry** icon on the **Geometries** toolbar.
45. Click the **Dimension** drop-down > **Radius/Diameter Dimension** on the **Constraints** toolbar.
46. Select the arc.
47. Type **0.8** and click **OK**.
48. Click the **Vertical Dimension** icon on the

Constraints toolbar.

49. Select the centerpoint of the arc and the sketch origin.
50. Type 1.4 in the **Length** box and click **OK**.

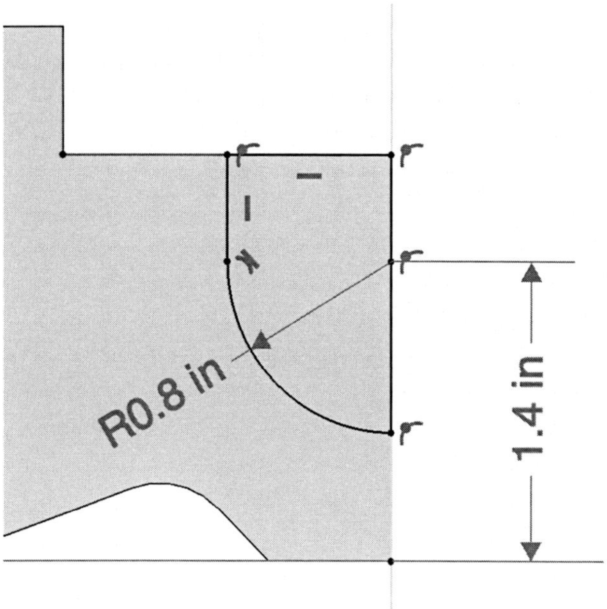

51. Click **Close** on the **Tasks** panel.
52. Click the **Pocket** icon on the **Part Design Modeling Features** toolbar; the sketch is selected automatically.
53. On the **Pocket parameters** dialog, select **Type > Dimension**.
54. Type **0.4** in the **Length** box.
55. Click **OK**.

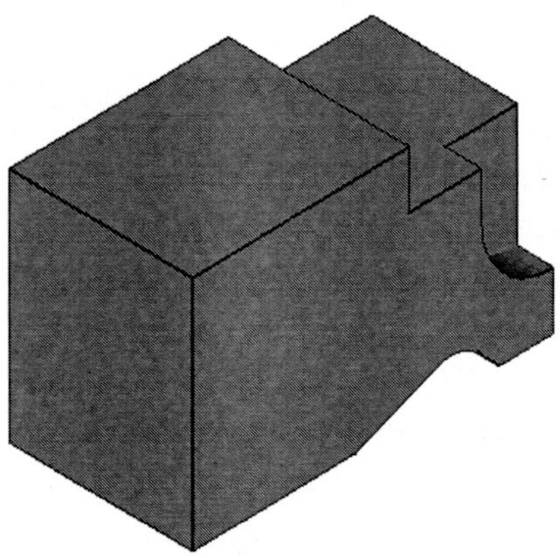

56. Select the flat face of the pocket feature.
57. Click the **New Sketch** icon on the **Part Design Helper Features** toolbar.
58. Create a circle.
59. Click the **Toggle Construction Geometry** icon on the **Geometries** toolbar.
60. Click the **External Projection** icon on the **Sketcher tools** toolbar.
61. Select the curved edge of the model, as shown.

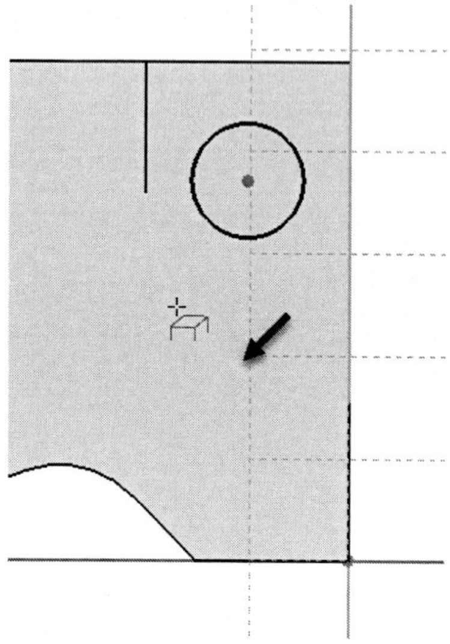

62. Click the **Symmetric Constraint** icon on the **Constraints** toolbar.
63. Select the centerpoint of the curved edge.
64. Select the endpoint of the curved edge.
65. Select the centerpoint of the circle.

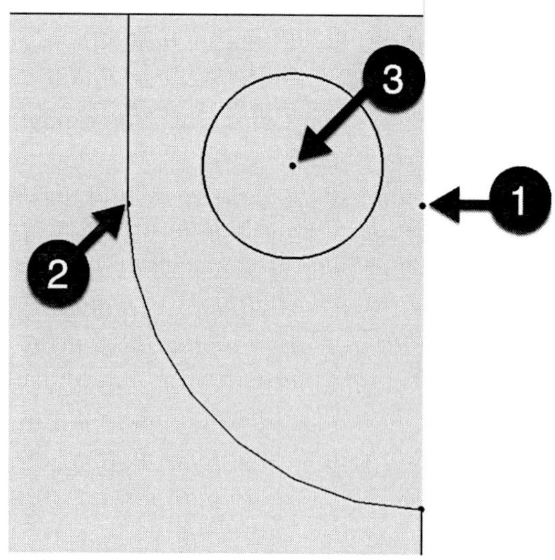

66. Add the diameter constraint to the circle.

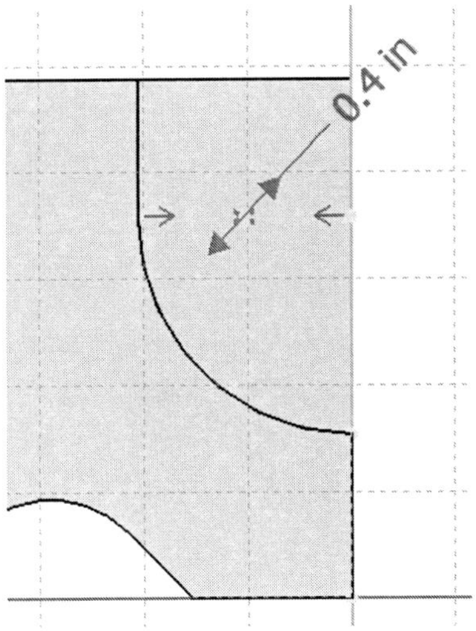

67. Click the **Toggle Construction Geometry** icon on the **Geometries** toolbar.
68. Click **Close** on the **Tasks** panel.
69. Click the **Pocket** icon on the **Part Design Modeling Features** toolbar; the sketch is selected automatically.
70. On the **Pocket parameters** dialog, select **Type > Through all**.
71. Click **OK**.

Creating the Pocket Feature on the left side

1. Click on the top face of the model.

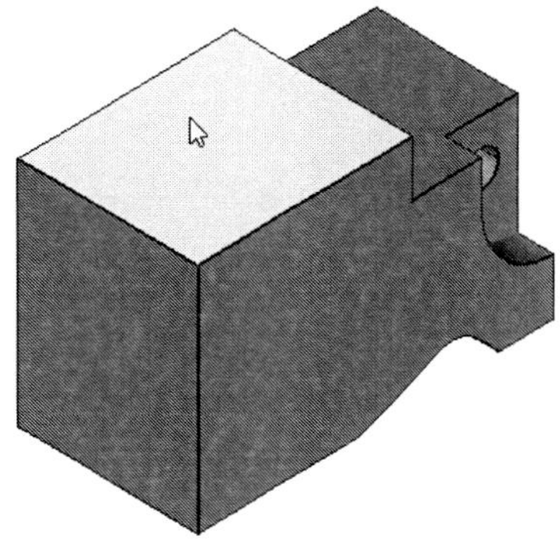

2. Click the **New Sketch** icon on the **Part Design Helper Features** toolbar.
3. Create a rectangle, as shown.

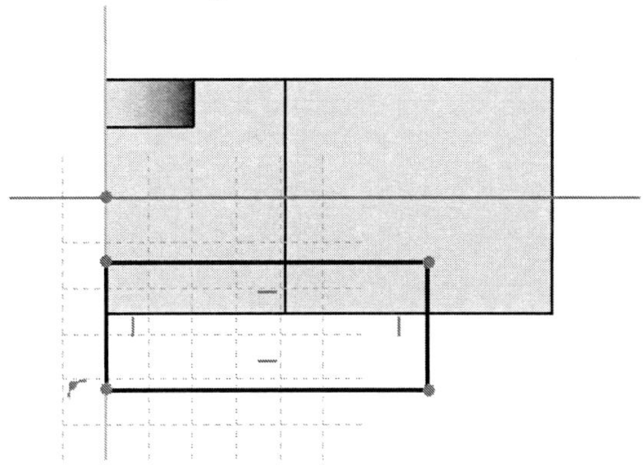

4. Create horizontal and vertical distance constraints, as shown.

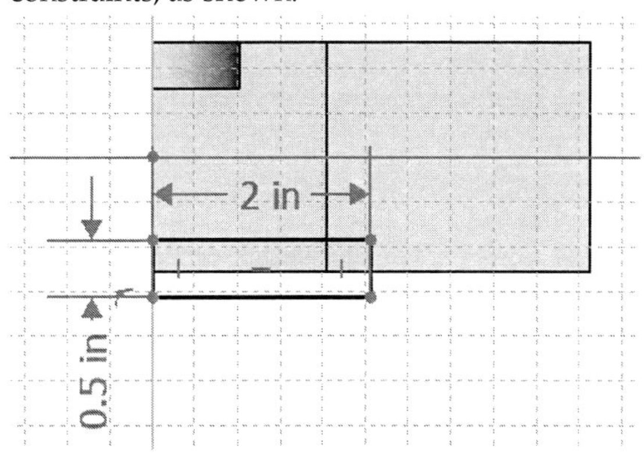

5. Click the **Toggle Construction Geometry** icon on the **Geometries** toolbar.
6. Click the **External Projection** icon on the **Sketcher tools** toolbar.
7. Select the horizontal edge of the model, as shown.

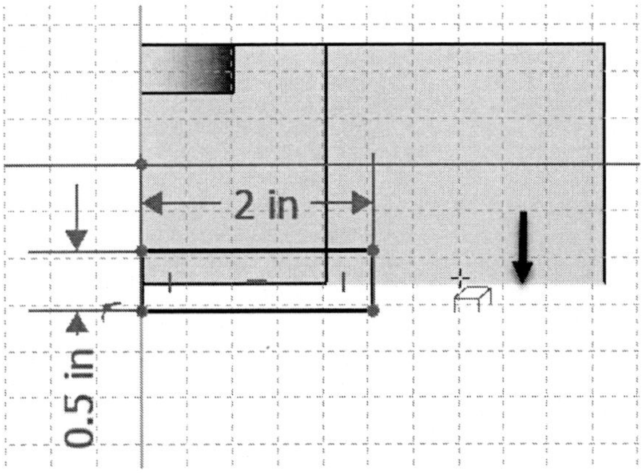

8. Click the **Coincident Constraint** icon on the **Constraints** toolbar.
9. Select the endpoint of the horizontal line and the external geometry.

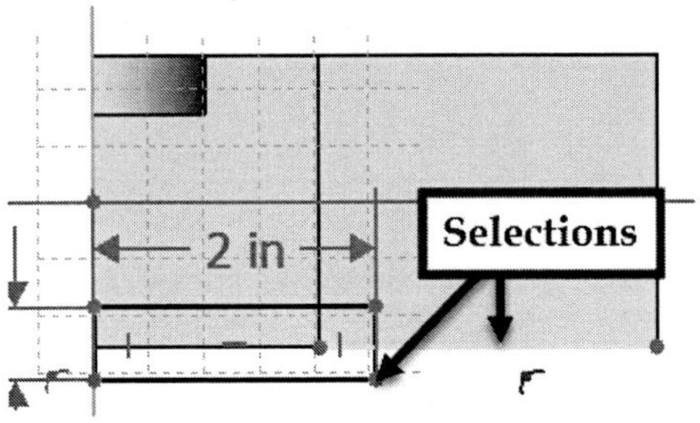

72. Click the **Toggle Construction Geometry** icon on the **Geometries** toolbar.
73. Click **Close** on the **Tasks** panel.
74. Click the **Pocket** icon on the **Part Design Modeling Features** toolbar; the sketch is selected automatically.
75. On the **Pocket parameters** dialog, select **Type > Through all.**
76. Click **OK**.

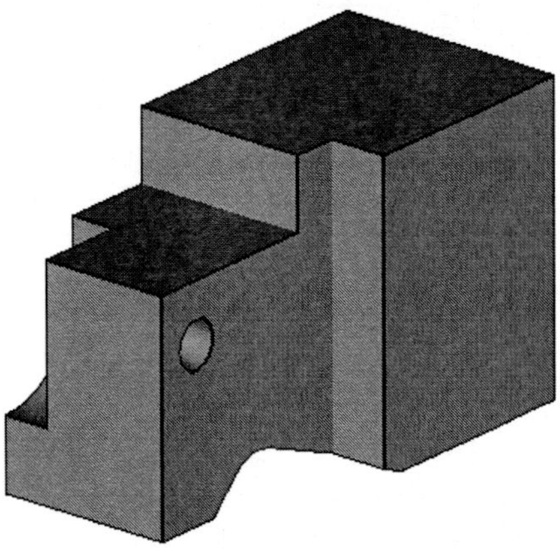

Creating the Angled Cut

1. Click on the front face of the model.

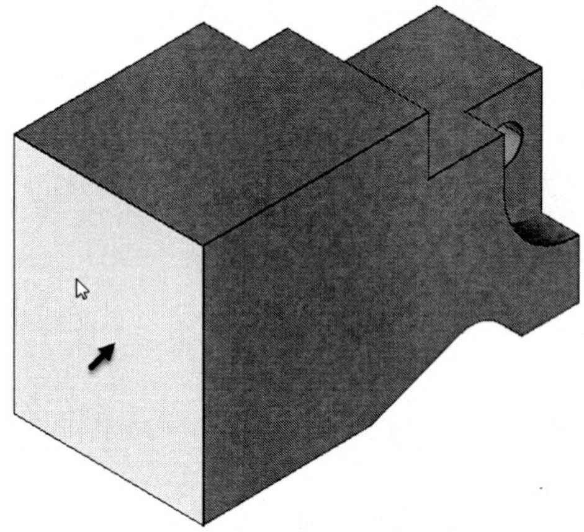

2. Click the **New Sketch** icon on the **Part Design Helper Features** toolbar.
3. Create a line, as shown.

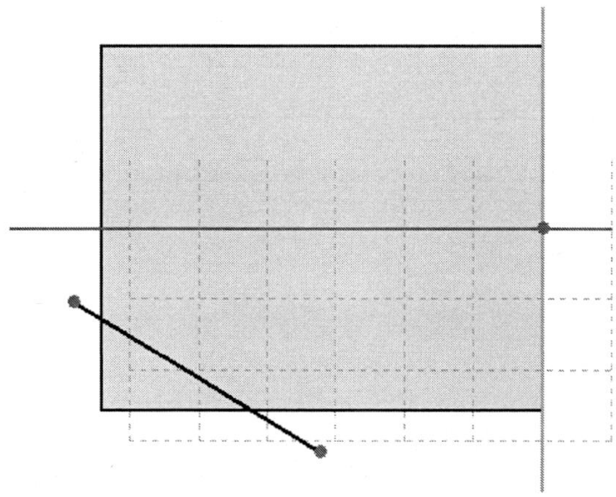

4. Click the **Toggle Construction Geometry** icon on the **Geometries** toolbar.
5. Click the **External Projection** icon on the **Sketcher tools** toolbar.
6. Select the horizontal and vertical edges of the model, as shown.

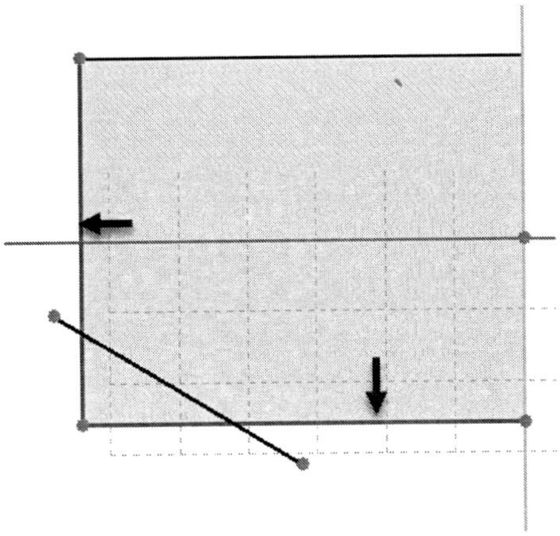

7. Click the **Constraint coincident** icon on the **Constraints** toolbar.
8. Select the endpoint of the line and the vertical edge.
9. Select the endpoint of the line and the horizontal edge.

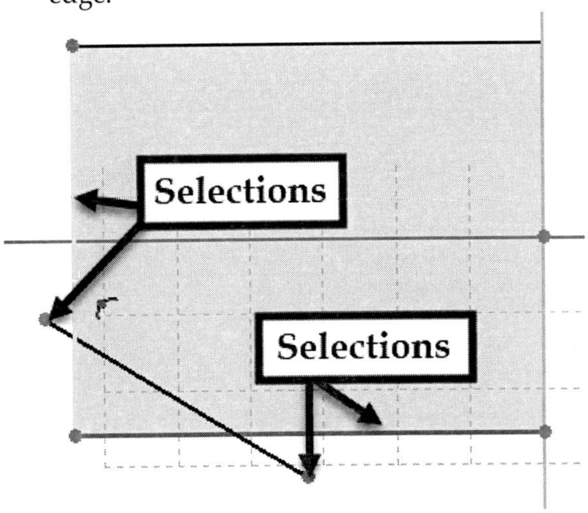

10. Create horizontal distance and angle constraints, as shown.

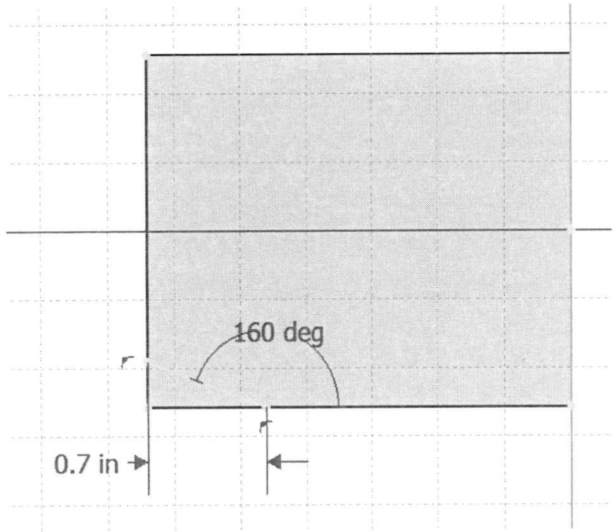

11. Click the **Toggle Construction Geometry** icon on the **Geometries** toolbar.
12. Create vertical and horizontal lines coincident with the extracted edges.

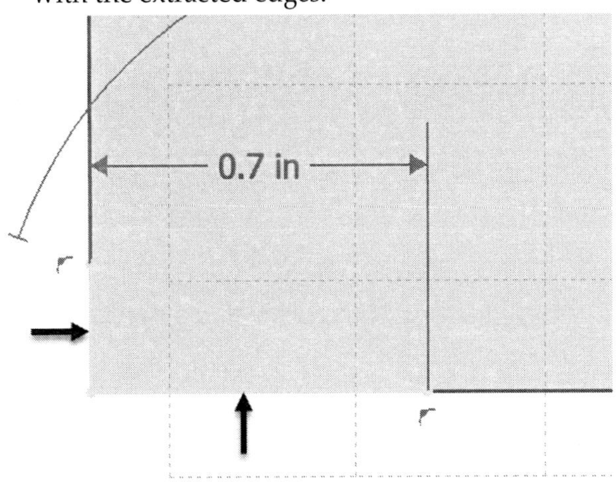

13. Click **Close** on the **Tasks** panel.
14. Click the **Pocket** icon on the **Part Design Modeling Features** toolbar; the sketch is selected automatically.
15. On the **Pocket parameters** dialog, select **Type > Through all**.
16. Click **OK**.

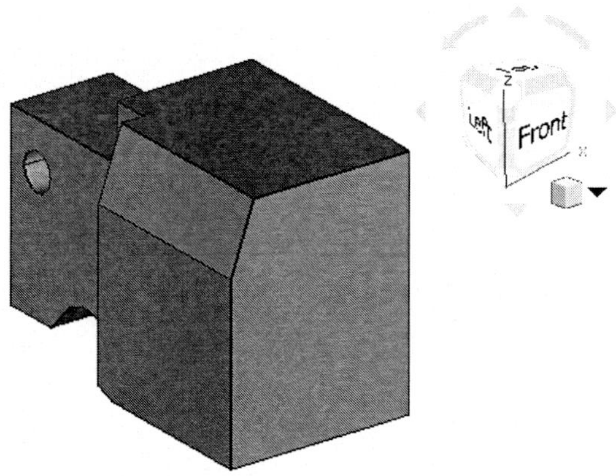

Creating the Pocket feature on the left

1. Click on the left face of the model.

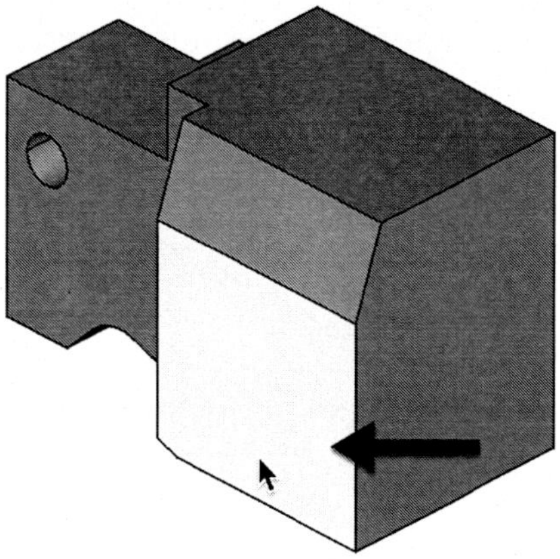

2. Click the **New Sketch** icon on the **Part Design Helper Features** toolbar.
3. Create a line and arc, as shown.

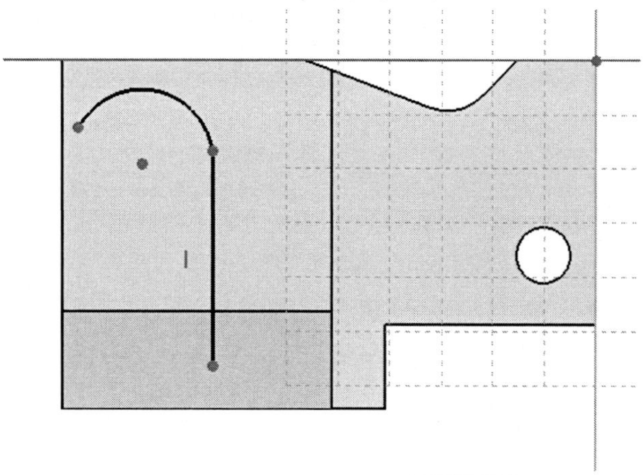

4. Click the **External Projection**  icon on the **Sketcher tools** toolbar.
5. Select the horizontal and vertical edges of the model, as shown.

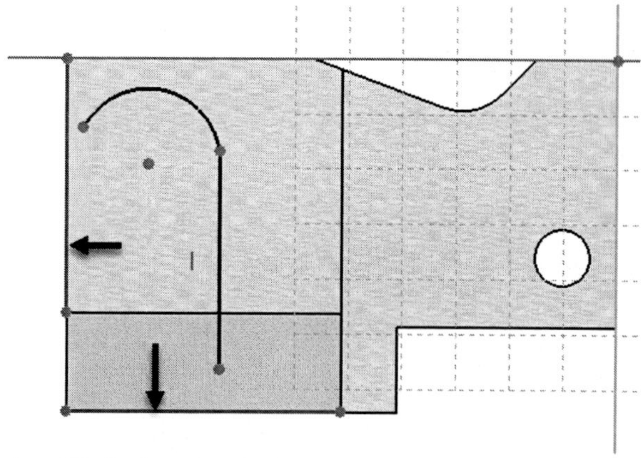

6. Click the **Toggle Construction Geometry** icon on the **Geometries** toolbar.
7. Click the **Coincident Constraint** icon on the **Constraints** toolbar.
8. Select the endpoint of the arc and the vertical edge.
9. Select the endpoint of the line and the horizontal edge.

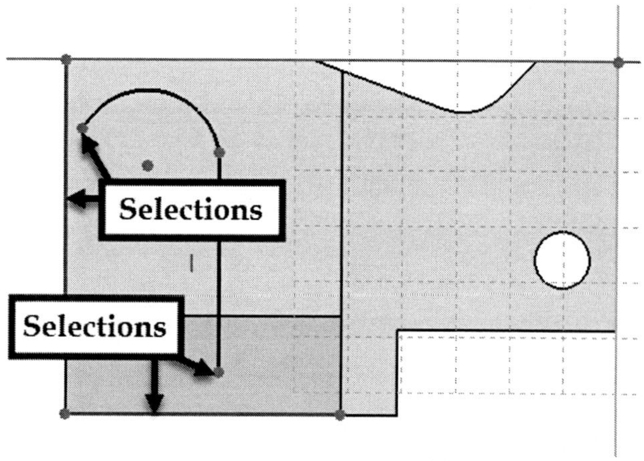

10. Click the **Tangent Constraint**  icon on the **Constraints** toolbar.
11. Select the vertical line and the arc.
12. Create vertical and horizontal lines, as shown.

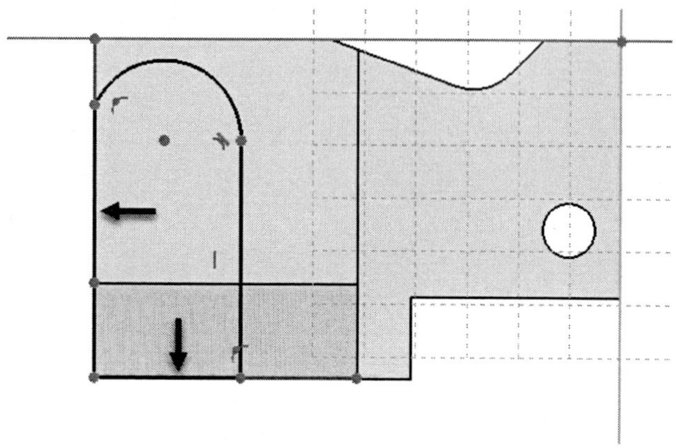

13. Click the **Coincident Constraint** icon on the **Constraints** toolbar.
14. Select the centerpoint of the arc and the vertical edge.

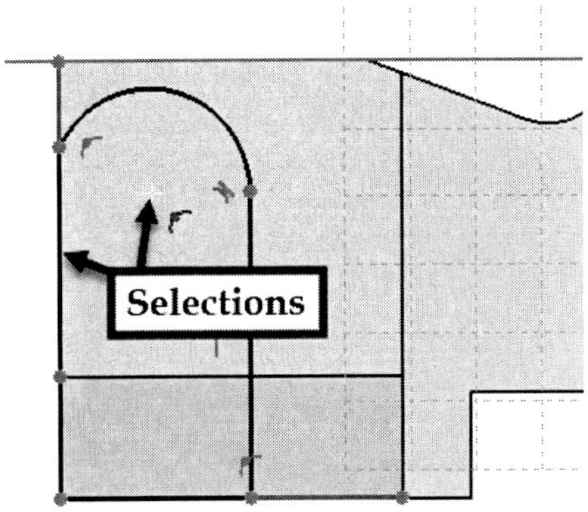

15. Create the radius and vertical distance constraints, as shown.

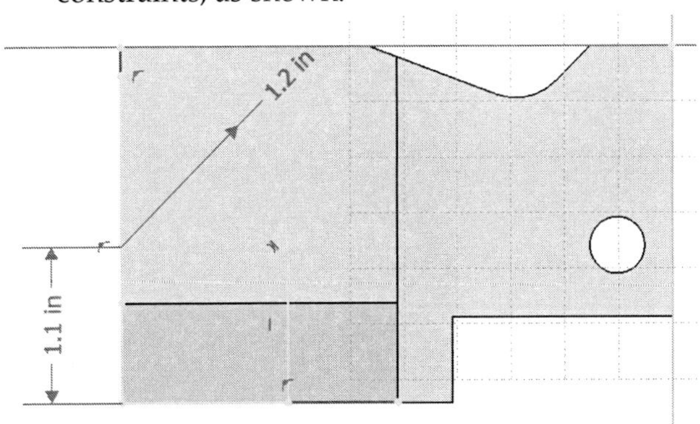

17. Click **Close** on the **Tasks** panel.
18. Click the **Pocket** icon on the **Part Design Modeling Features** toolbar; the sketch is selected automatically.
19. On the **Pocket parameters** dialog, select **Type > Dimension**.
20. Type **1.65** in the **Length** box.

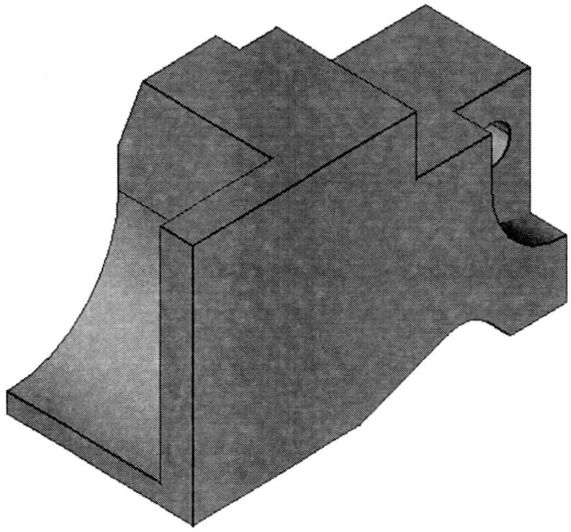

21. Click **OK**.

Creating the Pocket feature on the right

1. Click on the right face of the model.

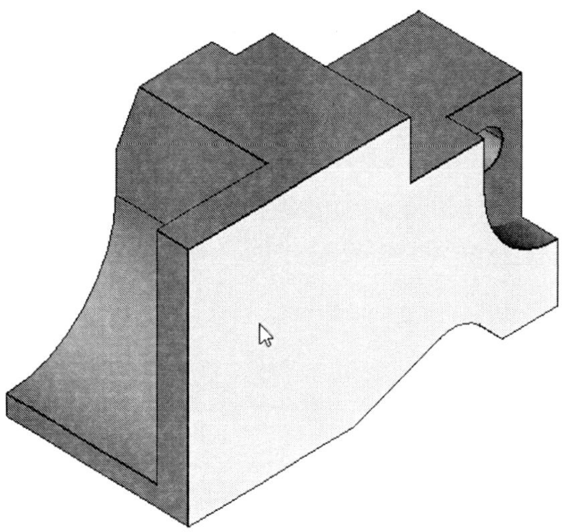

2. Click the **New Sketch** icon on the **Part Design Helper Features** toolbar.
3. Create a circle.
4. Add the diameter and vertical distance constraint, as shown.

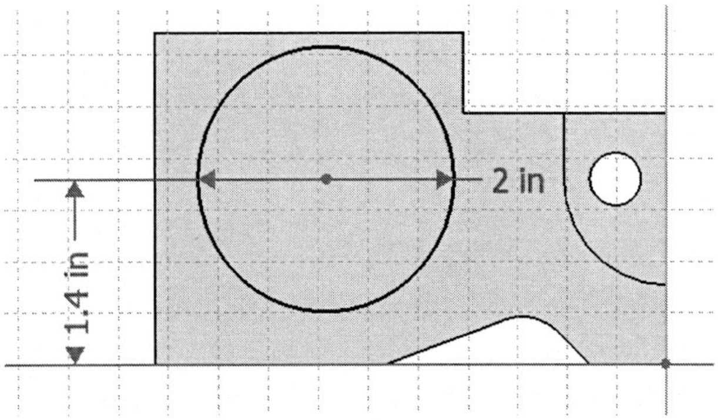

5. Create a vertical line, as shown.

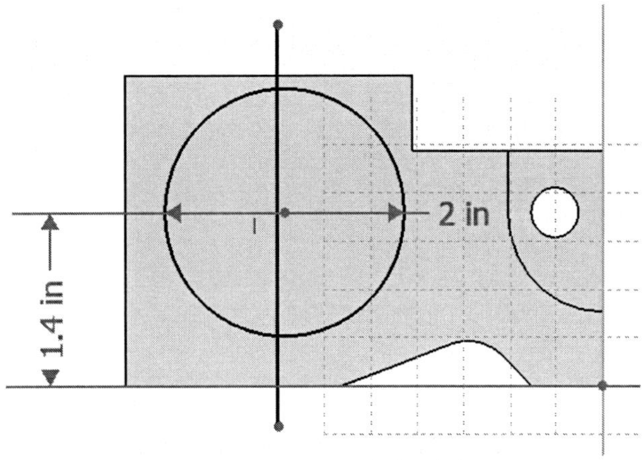

6. Click the **External Projection**  icon on the **Sketcher tools** toolbar.
7. Select the vertical and horizontal edges of the model, as shown.

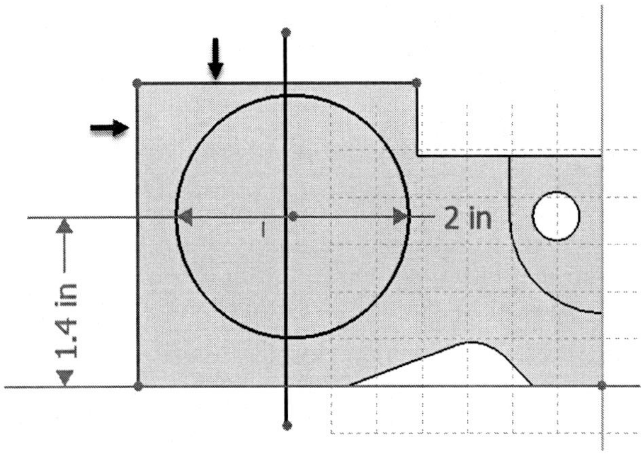

16. Click the **Toggle Construction Geometry** icon on the **Geometries** toolbar.
17. Click the **Trim Edge**  icon on the **Sketcher tools** toolbar.
18. Select the left side portion of the circle.

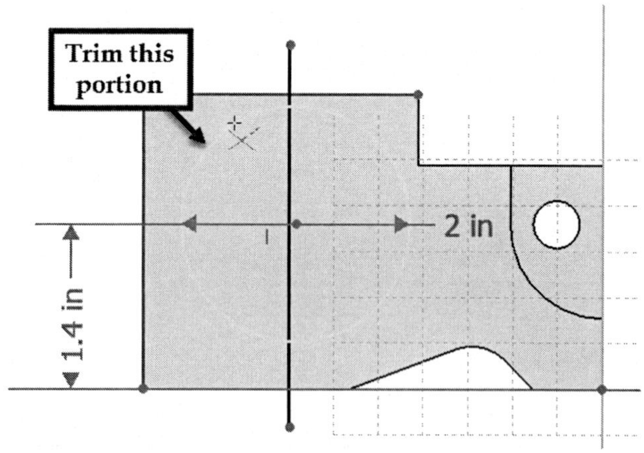

19. Click the **Coincident Constraint** icon on the **Constraints** toolbar.
20. Select endpoint the vertical line and the horizontal edge.

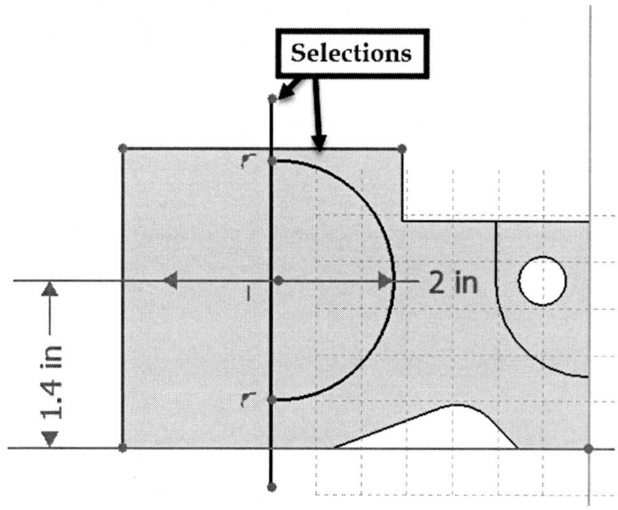

21. Trim the bottom and middle portions of the vertical line.

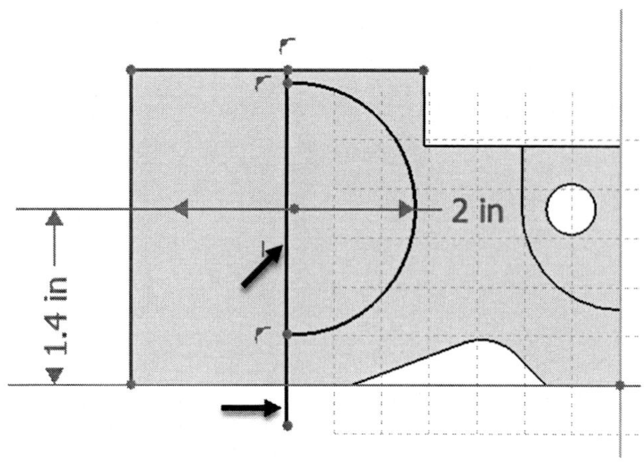

22. Click the **Arc** drop-down > **Arc from 3 Points**  on the **Geometries** toolbar.
23. Select the endpoint of the arc.

24. Move the pointer toward the left and click on the extracted edge.

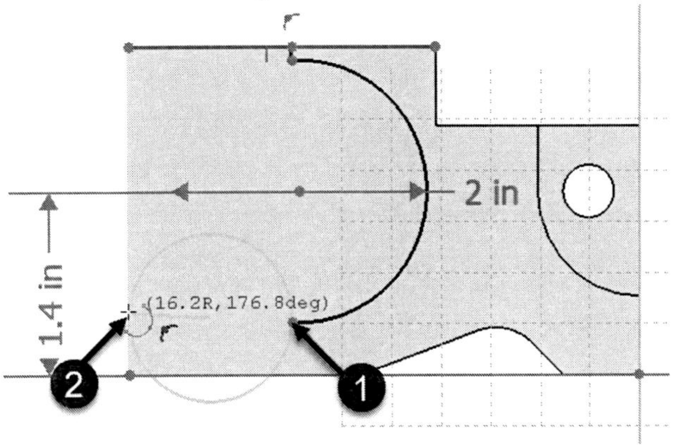

25. Move the pointer downward and click to create the arc.

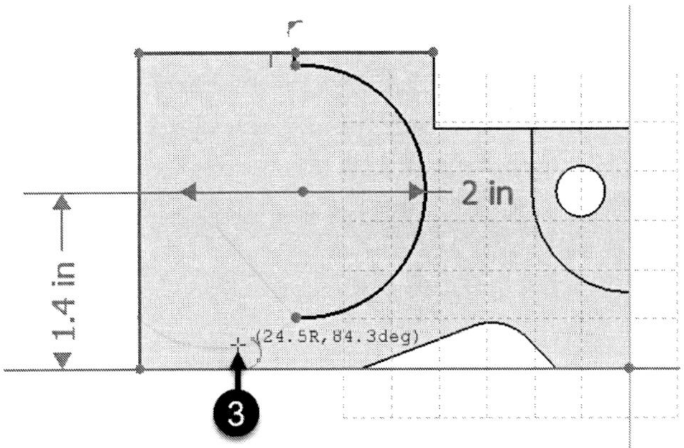

26. Click the **Coincident Constraint** icon on the **Constraints** toolbar.
27. Select the centerpoint of the new arc.
28. Select the extracted vertical edge.

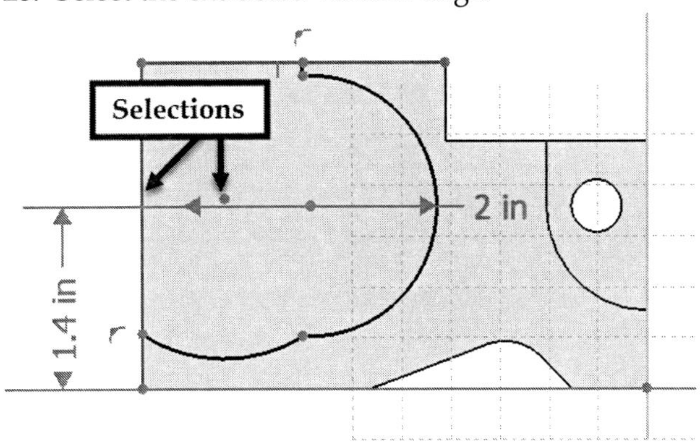

29. Right-click.
30. Select the centerpoints of the two arcs.

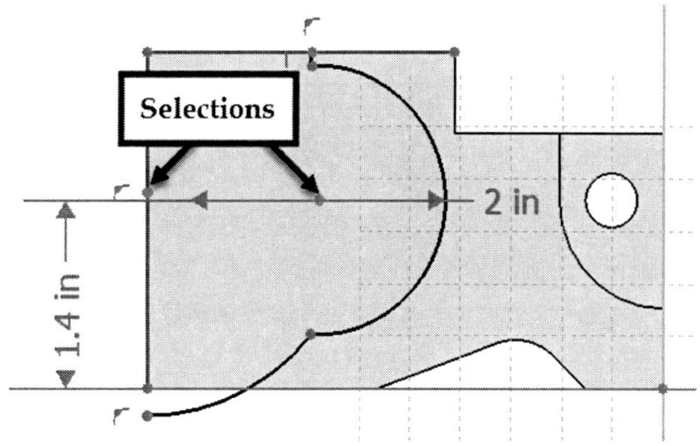

31. Click the **Horizontal Constraint/vertical** drop-down > **Horizontal Constraint** icon on the **Constraints** toolbar.
32. Click the **Equal Constraint** icon on the **Constraints** toolbar.
33. Select the two arcs to make their radius equal.

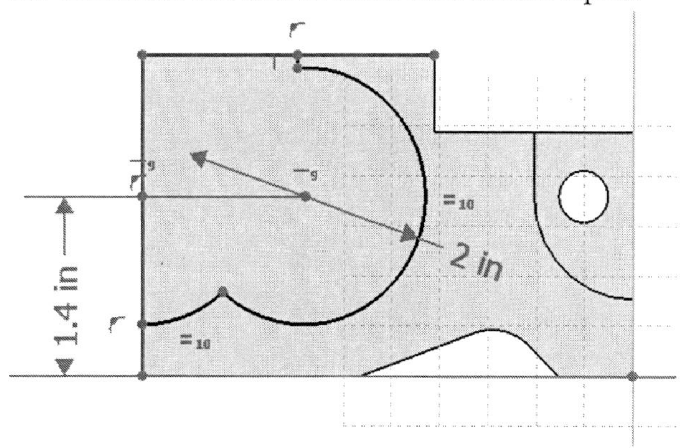

34. Create a horizontal distance constraint, as shown.

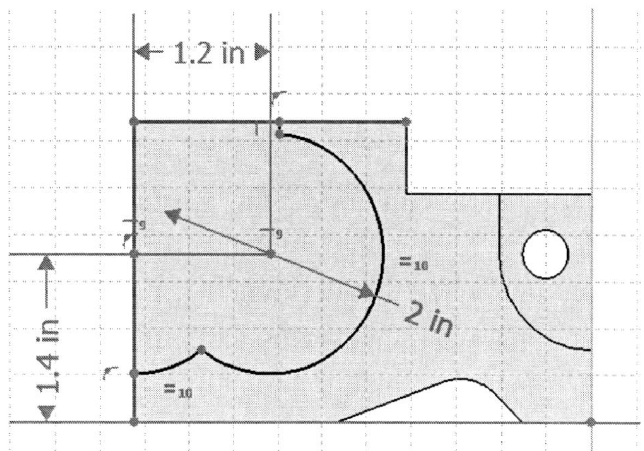

35. Select the center point and endpoint of the arc, as shown.

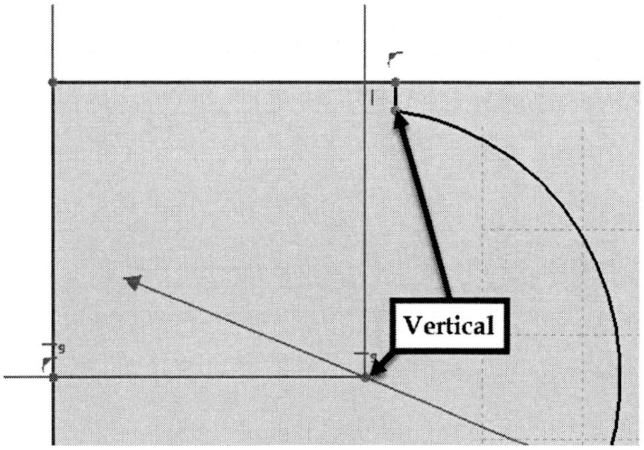

36. Click the **Horizontal Constraint/vertical** drop-down > **Vertical Constraint** icon on the **Constraints** toolbar.
37. Click the **Line** icon on the **Geometries** toolbar.
38. Select the endpoint of the small arc.
39. Move the pointer vertically upward and select the endpoint of the vertical edge.

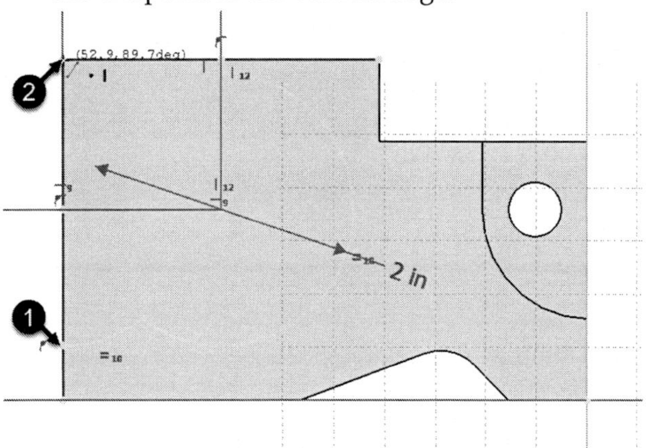

40. Select the endpoint of the vertical edge.
41. Move the pointer toward the right and select the endpoint of the vertical line.

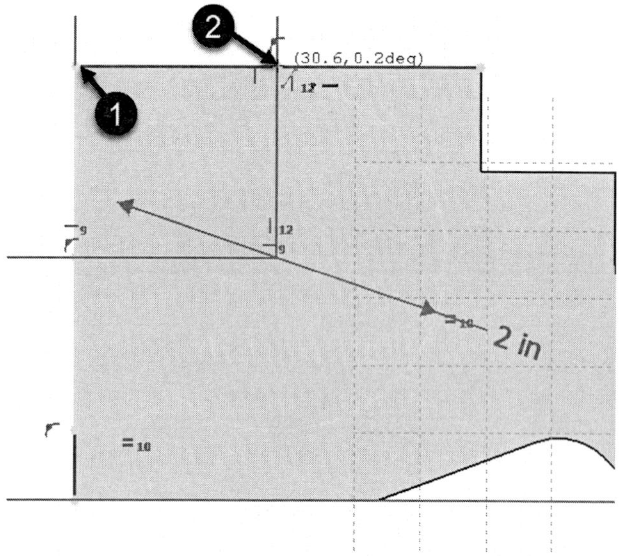

42. Click **Close** on the **Tasks** panel.
43. Click the **Pocket** icon on the **Part Design Modeling Features** toolbar; the sketch is selected automatically.
44. On the **Pocket parameters** dialog, select **Type > Dimension**.
45. Type **0.5** in the **Length** box.
46. Click **OK**.

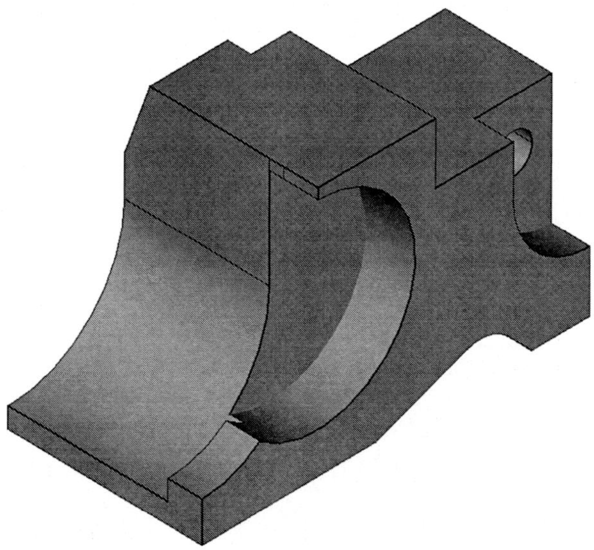

Adding the Pad Features

1. Click on the flat face of the pocket feature.

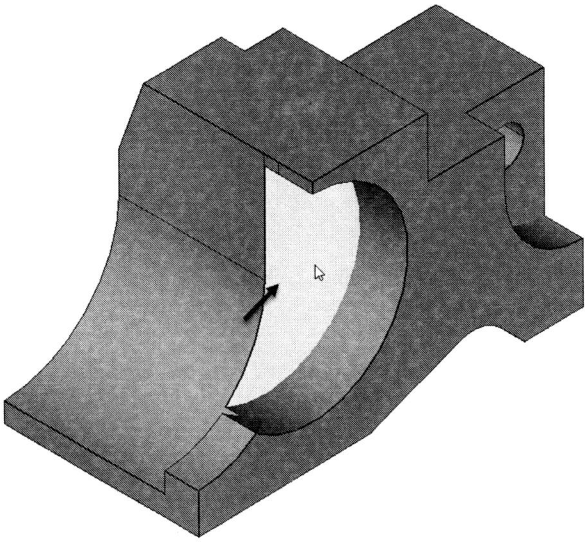

2. Click the **New Sketch** icon on the **Part Design Helper Features** toolbar.
3. Create a circle and add the diameter constraint to it.

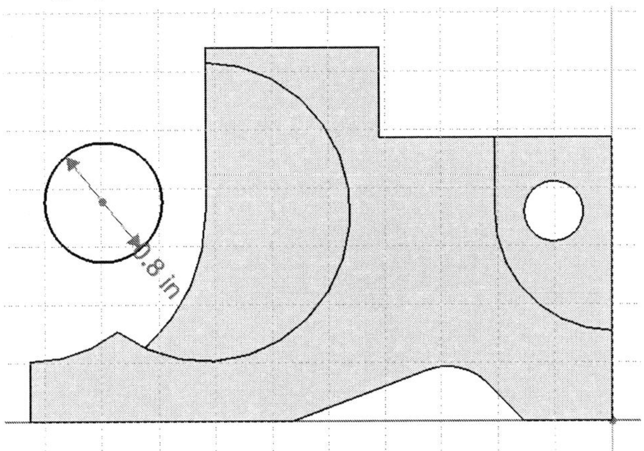

4. Click the **Toggle Construction Geometry** icon on the **Geometries** toolbar.
5. Click the **External Projection**  icon on the **Sketcher tools** toolbar.
6. Select the circular edge of the model.
7. Select the vertical and circular edge, as shown.

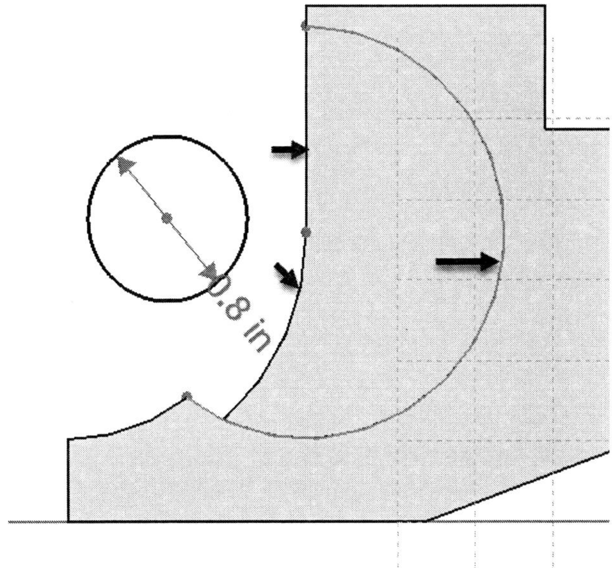

8. Click the **Toggle Construction Geometry** icon on the **Geometries** toolbar.
9. Click the **Coincident Constraint** icon on the **Constraints** toolbar.
10. Select the centerpoint of the circle and the curved edge.

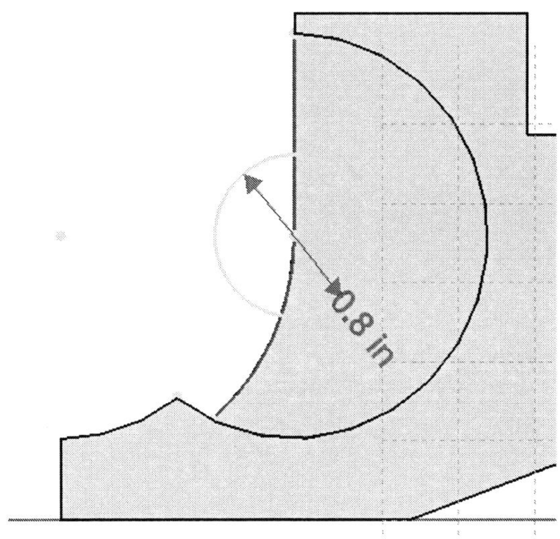

11. Click the **Line**  icon on the **Geometries** toolbar.
12. Specify the start and endpoint of the line, as shown.

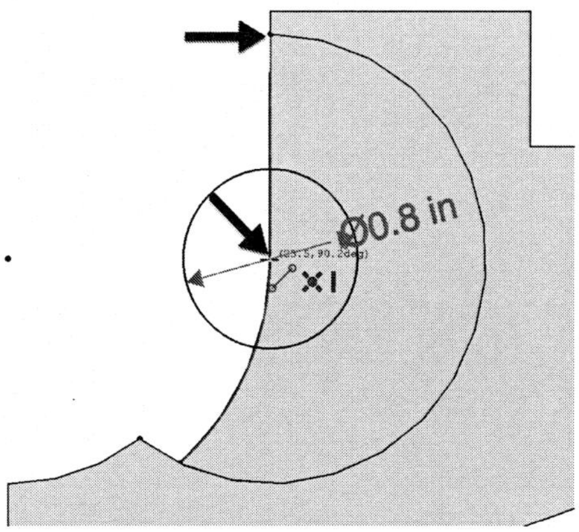

13. Click the **Arc** drop-down > **Arc from Center** on the **Geometries** toolbar.
14. Specify the center, start, and endpoints of the arc, as shown.

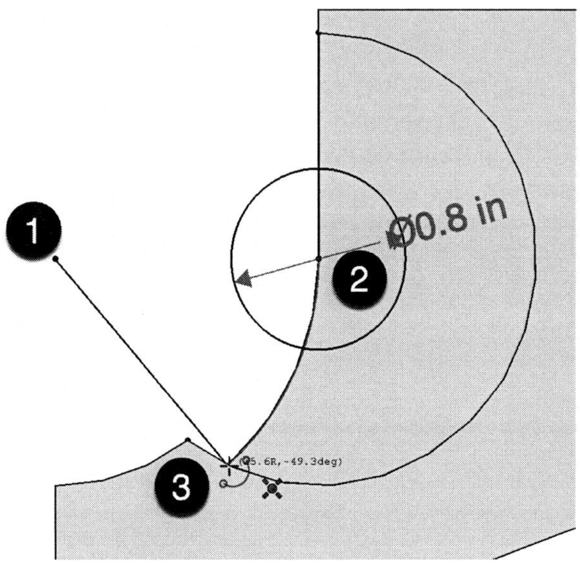

15. Click the **Trim/Extend** drop-down > **Trim Edge** icon on the **Sketcher tools** toolbar.
16. Select the portions of the sketch to be trimmed, as shown.

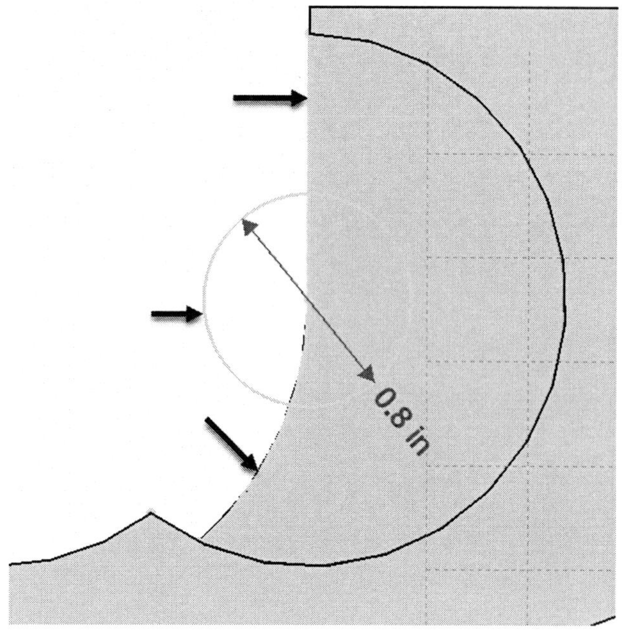

17. Click the **Horizontal Constraint/vertical** drop-down > **Vertical Constraint** icon on the **Constraints** toolbar.
18. Select the line, as shown.

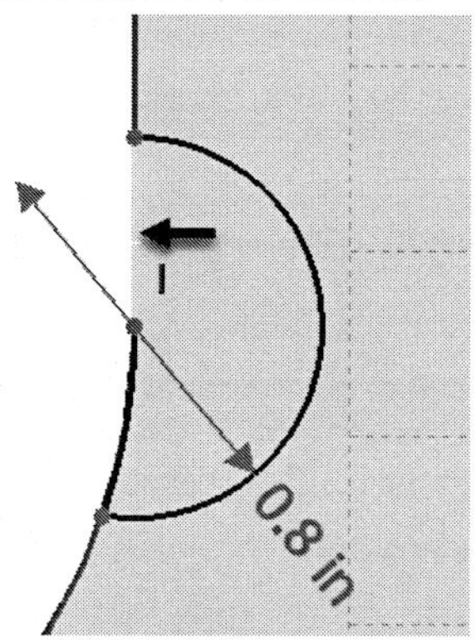

19. Click **Close** on the **Tasks** panel.
20. Click the **Pad** icon on the **Part Design Modeling Features** toolbar; the sketch is selected automatically.
21. Type **0.2** in the **Length** box.
22. Click **OK**.

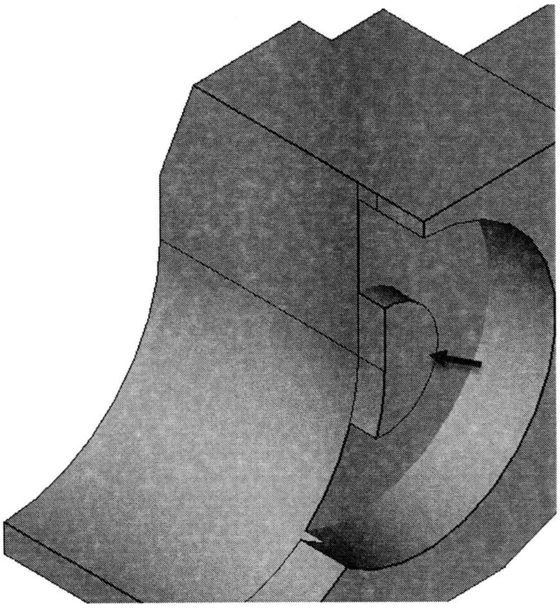

23. Click on the face of the pad feature, as shown.

24. Click the **New Sketch** icon on the **Part Design Helper Features** toolbar.
25. Create a circle and add the diameter constraint to it.
26. Click the **Toggle Construction Geometry** icon on the **Geometries** toolbar.
27. Click the **External Projection**  icon on the **Sketcher tools** toolbar.
28. Select the circular edge of the model, as shown.

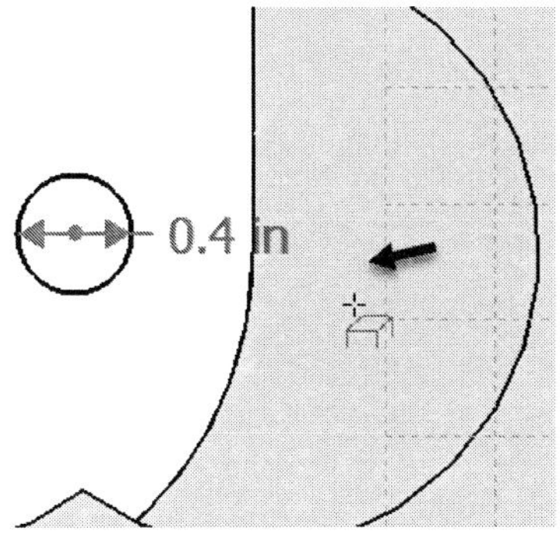

29. Click the **Toggle Construction Geometry** icon on the **Geometries** toolbar.
30. Click the **Coincident Constraint** icon on the **Constraints** toolbar.
31. Select the centerpoint of the circle and the curved edge.
32. Click **Close** on the **Tasks** panel.
33. Click the **Pad** icon on the **Part Design Modeling Features** toolbar; the sketch is selected automatically.
34. On the **Pad parameters** dialog, select **Type > Up To face.**
35. Select the right face of the model, as shown.

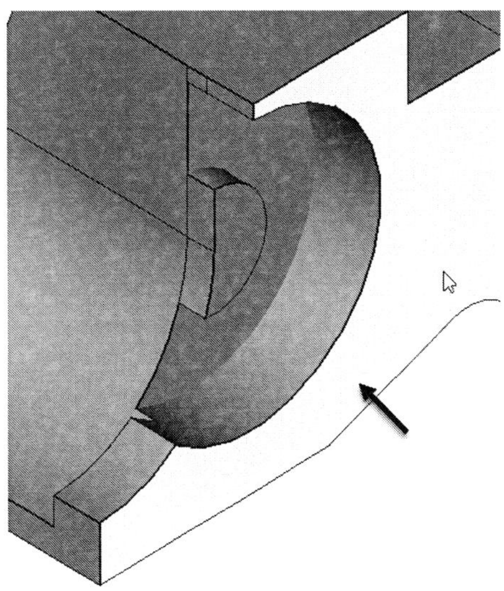

36. Click **OK**.

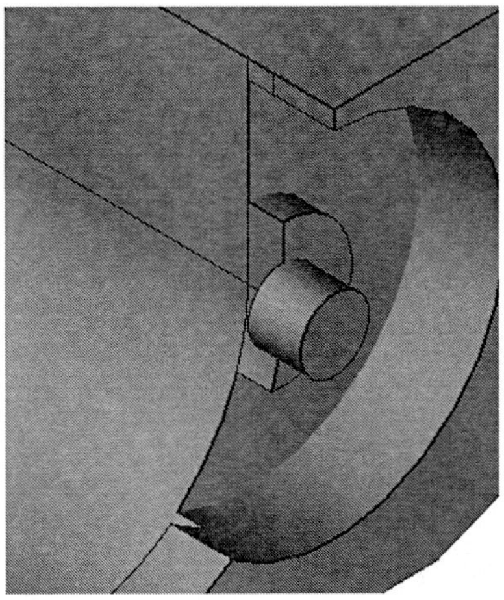

37. Save and close the model.

TUTORIAL 9

In this tutorial, you construct the model shown in the figure.

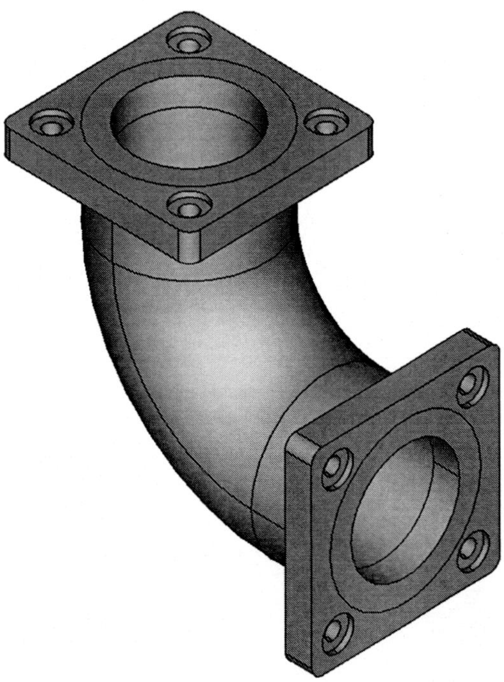

Creating the first feature

1. Open the FreeCAD application.
2. Click **File > New** on the Menu bar.
3. Select the **Part Design** option from the **Workbenches** drop-down.
4. Click the **New Sketch** icon on the **Part Design Helper Features** toolbar, and then select the XZ Plane.
5. Click **OK** to start the sketch.
6. Click the **Polyline** icon on the **Geometries** toolbar.
7. Create a vertical and horizontal lines connected to each other, as shown.

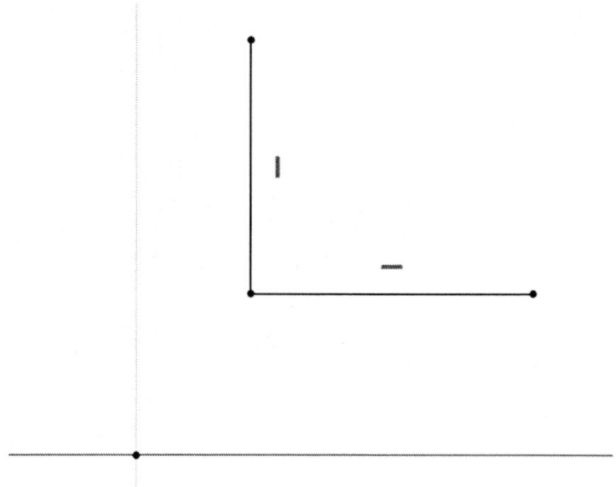

8. Click the **Fillet** drop-down > **Sketch Fillet** on the **Sketcher tools** toolbar.
9. Select the vertical and horizontal lines; a fillet created at the intersection of the two lines.

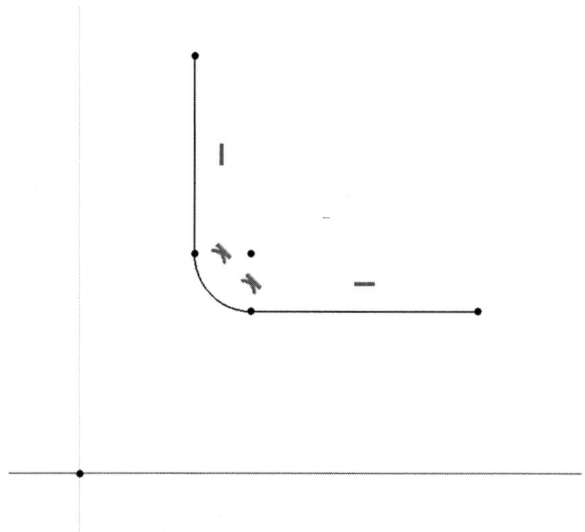

10. Click **Constraints** toolbar > **Vertical Dimension** (or) click **Sketch > Constraints > Vertical Dimension** on the menu bar.
11. Select the vertical line.
12. Enter **5.9** in the **Length** box of the **Insert Length** dialog and click **OK**.
1. On the **Constraints** toolbar, click **Dimension** drop-down > **Radius Dimension** icon.

2. Select the circle and type **10.24** in the **Radius** box of the **Change Radius** dialog.
3. Click **OK**.
4. Click **Constraints** toolbar > **Dimension** drop-down > **Horizontal Dimension** (or) click **Sketch > Constraints > Horizontal Dimension** on the menu bar.
5. Select the horizontal line.
6. Enter **5.9** in the **Length** box of the **Insert Length** dialog and click the **OK** button.
7. Click the **Coincident Constraint** icon on the **Constraints** toolbar.
8. Select the origin point of the sketch
9. Select the center point of the fillet.

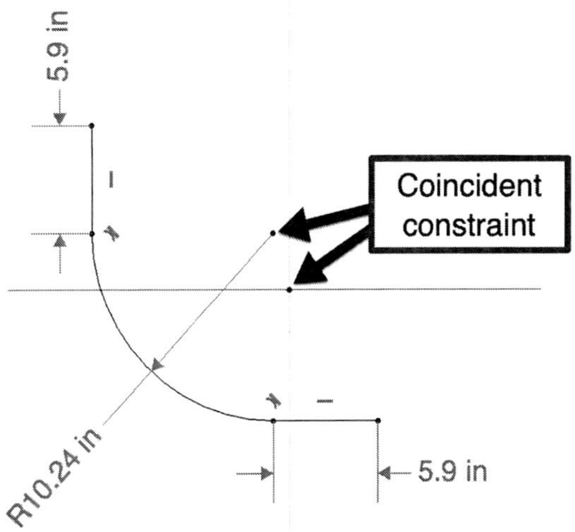

10. Click **Close** on the **Tasks** panel.

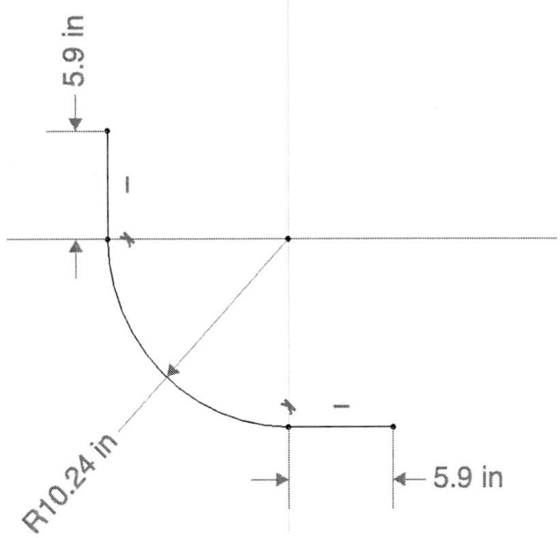

11. On the **Structure** toolbar, click the **Coordinate System** drop-down > **Datum plane** icon.
12. Select the horizontal line of the sketch.
13. Select the endpoint of the horizontal line.
14. Select the **Normal to edge** option from the **Attachment mode** section of the **Tasks** panel.
15. Click **OK**.

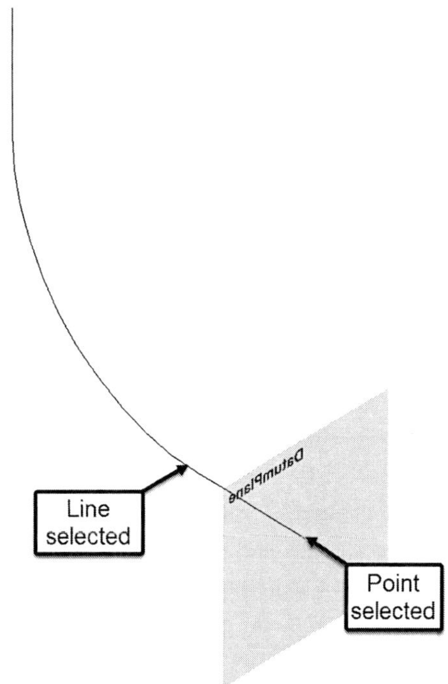

16. Click the **New Sketch** icon the **Part Design Helper Features** toolbar.
17. Select the newly created datum Plane from the graphics window.
18. Click the **Circle From Center** on the **Geometries** toolbar.
19. Click on the origin.
20. Move the pointer outward and click to create a circle.
21. On the **Constraints** toolbar, click the **Dimension** drop-down > **Diameter Dimension** icon.
22. Select the circle and type **11.41** in the **Diameter** box on the **Change diameter** dialog.
23. Make sure that the center of the circle and origin point are coincident.
24. Click **OK**.

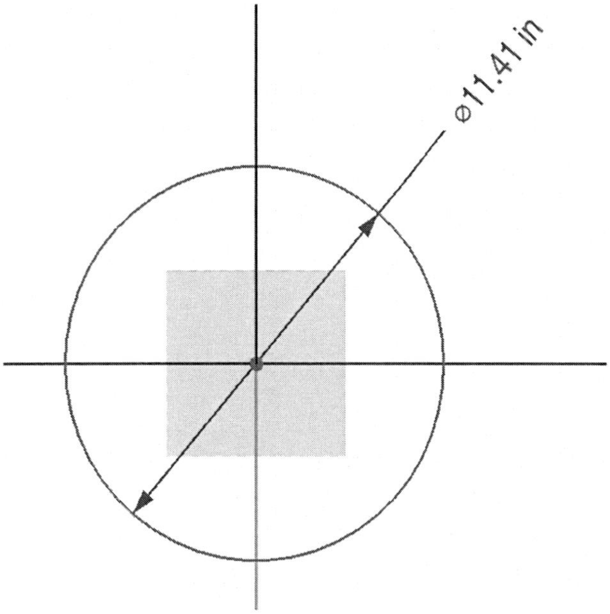

25. Click **Close** on the **Tasks** panel.
26. On the **Part Design Modelling Features** toolbar, click the **Additive pipe**  icon.
27. Click the **Object** button in the **Profile** section and select the circle from the graphics window.
28. Click on the **Object** button under the **Path to sweep along** section and select the first sketch.
29. Click **OK** on the **Tasks** panel.

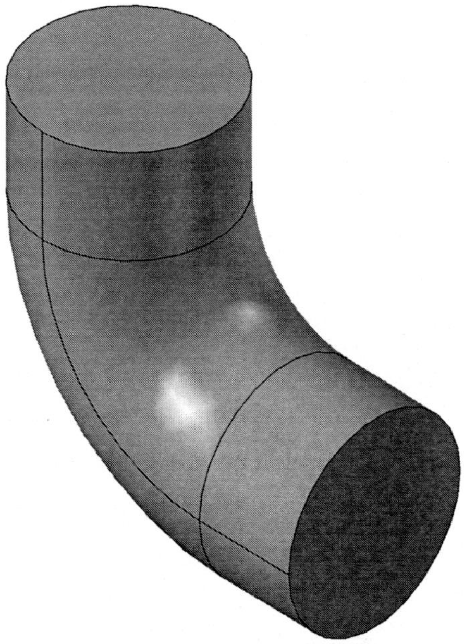

30. Select the datum plane from the graphics window.
31. Click the **Model** panel.
32. Click the Hide icon next to the DatumPlane to hide it.

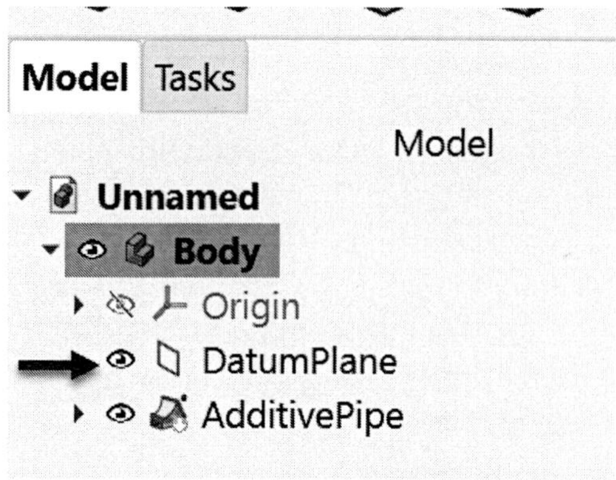

33. Click in the graphics window to deselect the datum plane.

Creating the Shell feature

1. Press **Ctrl** and select the faces, as shown.

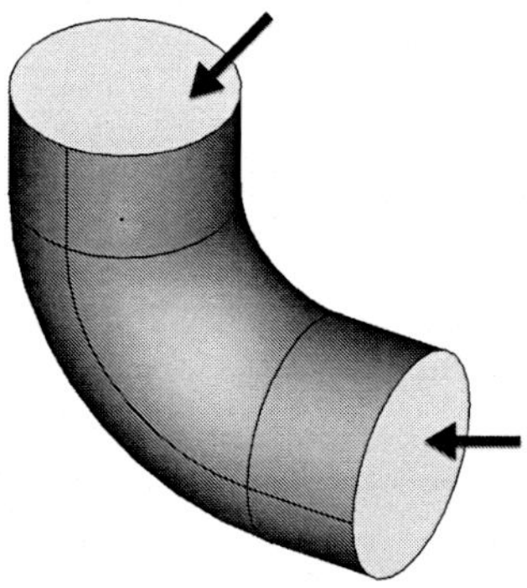

2. Click the **Thickness**  tool on the **Part Design Dressup Features** toolbar.
3. Enter **1.575** in the **Thickness** box under the **Thickness Parameter** section.
4. Check **Make thickness inwards** option.
5. Click **OK** on the **Tasks** panel.
6. Select the flat face of the AdditivePipe, as shown.

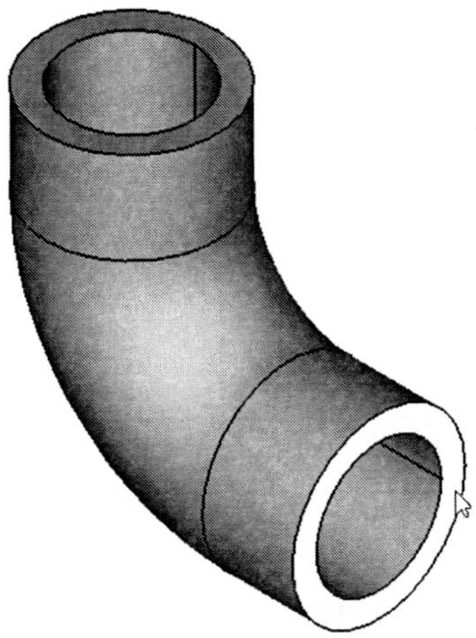

Creating the Flanges

1. Click **New Sketch**  icon on the **Part Design Helper Features** toolbar.
2. Click the **External Projection**  icon on the **Sketcher tools** toolbar.
3. Select the inner circular edge of the model, as shown.

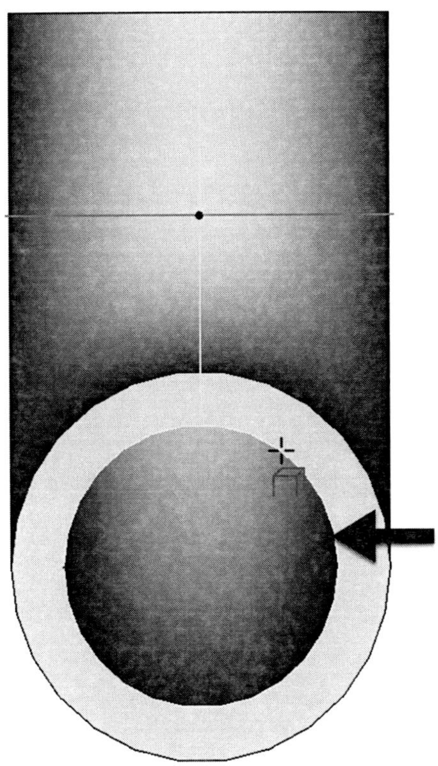

4. Expand the **Geometries** toolbar and click the **Polygon** drop-down > **Square**.

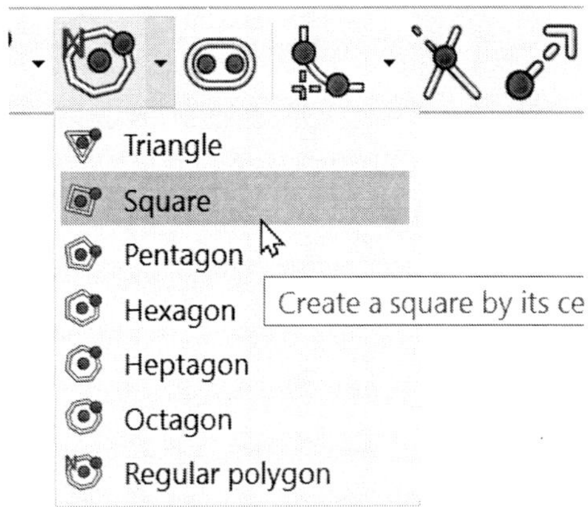

5. Select the centerpoint of the circular edge.
6. Move the pointer outward and click to create a square. Next, Press **Esc**.

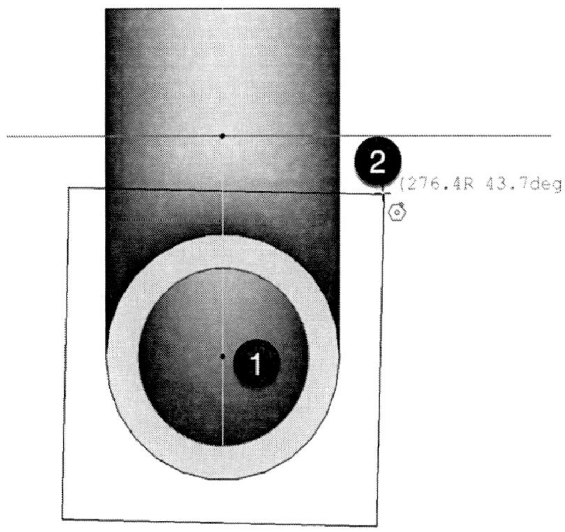

7. On the **Constraints** toolbar, click the **Horizontal constraint** icon.
8. Select the top horizontal line, as shown.

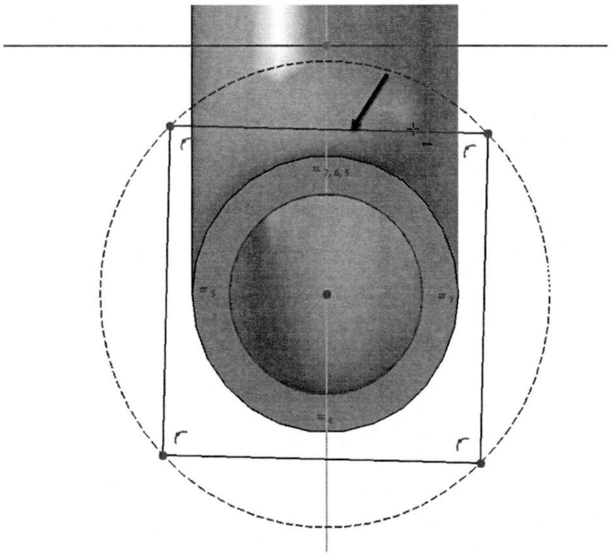

9. Click **Constraints** toolbar > **Dimension** drop-down > **Horizontal Dimension** (or) click **Sketch > Constraints > Horizontal Dimension** on the menu bar.
10. Select the top horizontal line.
11. Enter **14.173** in the **Length** box of the **Insert Length** dialog and click the **OK** button.

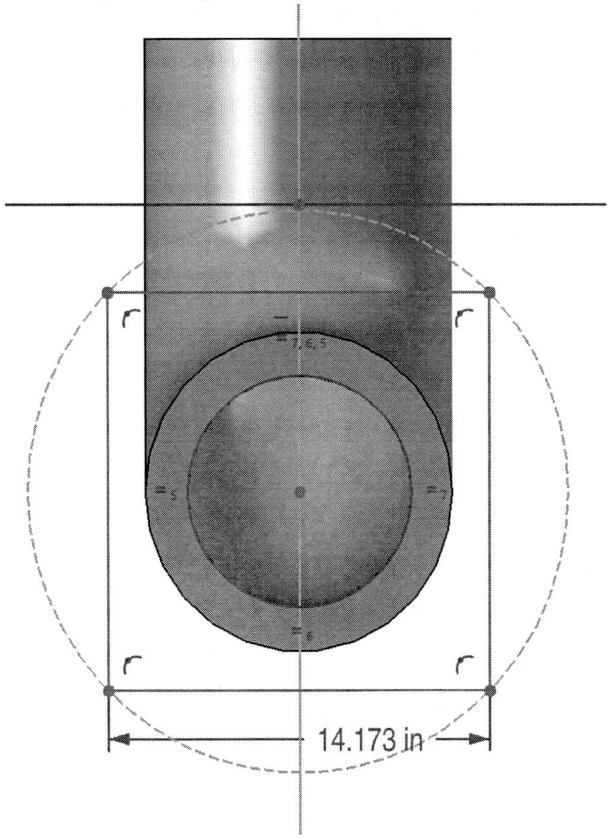

12. Click **Close** on the **Tasks** panel.
13. On the **Part Design Modeling Features** toolbar, click the **Pad** icon.
14. Type **1.969** in the **Length** box of the **Pad Parameters** dialog.
15. Click **OK**.

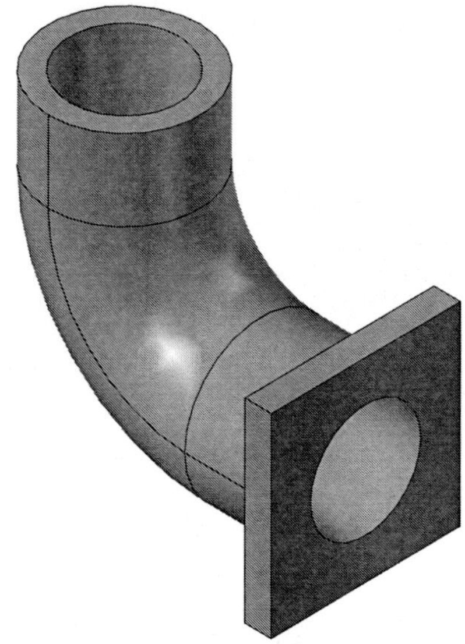

16. On the **Part Design Dressup Features** toolbar, click the **Fillet** icon.

17. Select the edges of the model, as shown.

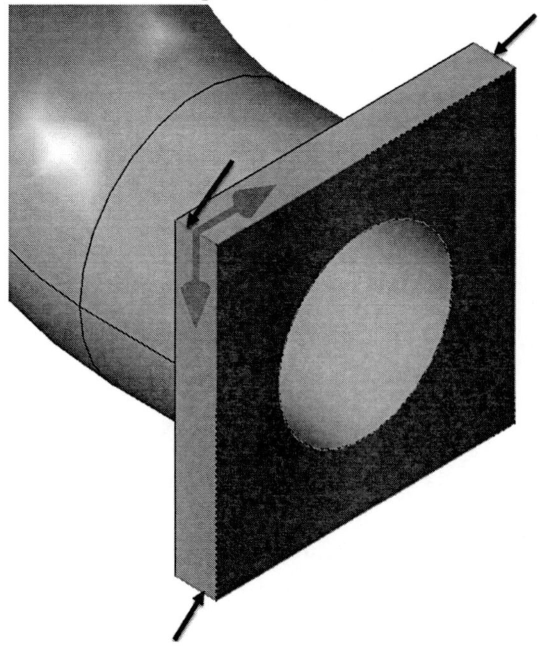

18. Press and hold the middle and right mouse buttons, and then drag the pointer; the model is rotated.
19. Select the edge of the model, as shown.

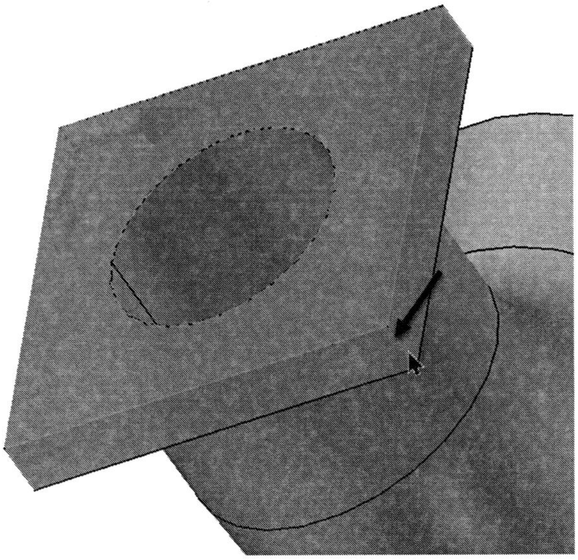

20. Type **0.787** in the **Radius** box.
21. Click **OK**.
22. Click the **ViewCube** drop-down, and then select the **Isometric** option.

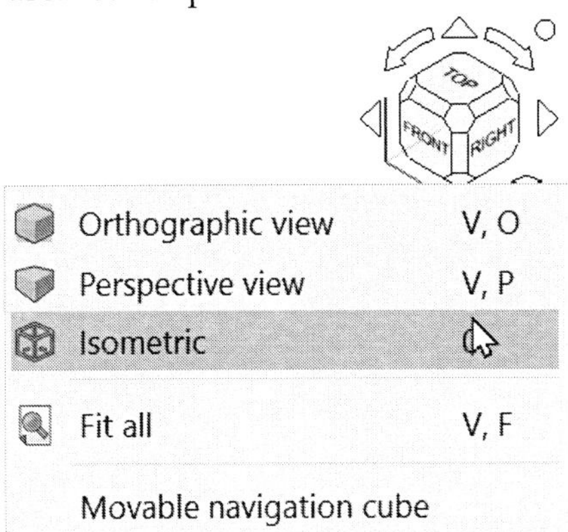

23. Select the flat face of the **Pad** feature, as shown.

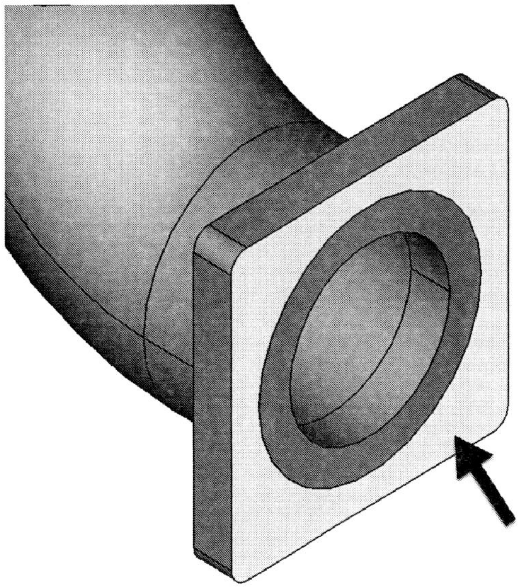

24. Click **New Sketch**  icon on the **Part Design Helper Features** toolbar.
25. Click the **Toggle Construction Geometry** icon on the **Geometries** toolbar.
26. Click the **External Projection**  icon on the **Sketcher tools** toolbar.
27. Select the horizontal and vertical edges, as shown.

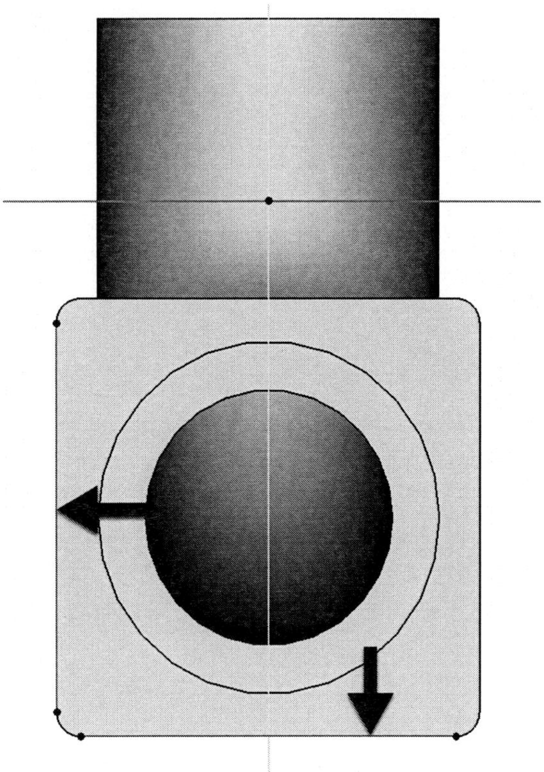

28. Click the **Toggle Construction Geometry** icon on the **Geometries** toolbar.
29. Click the **Circle From Center** on the **Geometries** toolbar.
30. Create a circle, as shown.

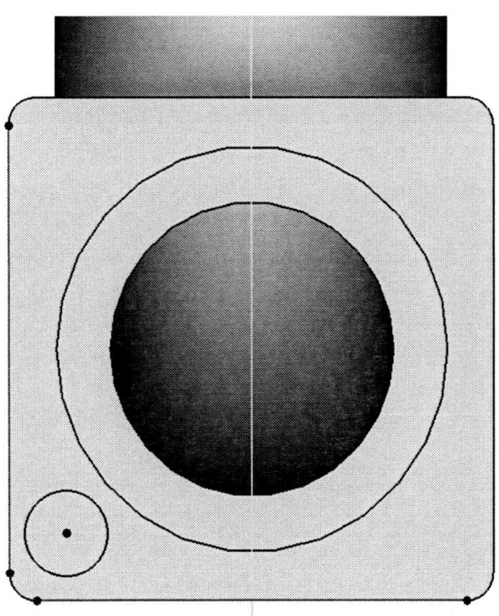

31. Click **Constraints** toolbar **> Vertical Dimension** (or) click **Sketch > Constraints > Vertical Dimension** on the menu bar.
32. Select the centerpoint of the circle.
33. Select the left endpoint of the horizontal edge, as shown.

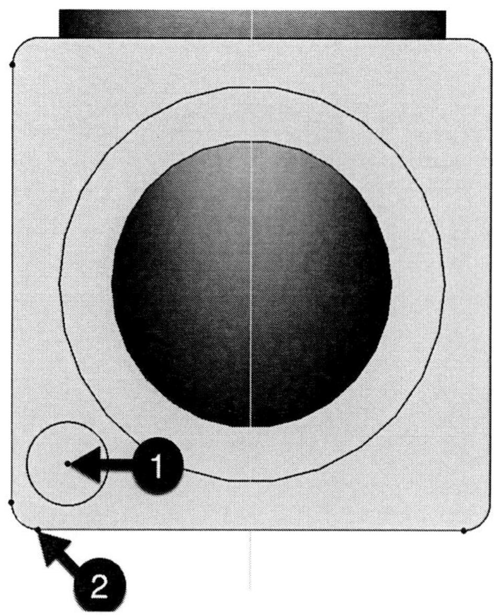

34. Enter **1.969** in the **Length** box of the **Insert Length** dialog and click **OK**.
35. Click **Constraints** toolbar > **Dimension** drop-down > **Horizontal Dimension** (or) click **Sketch > Constraints > Horizontal Dimension** on the menu bar.
36. Select the centerpoint of the circle.
37. Select the lower endpoint of the vertical edge, as shown.
38. Enter **1.969** in the **Length** box of the **Insert Length** dialog and click the **OK** button.

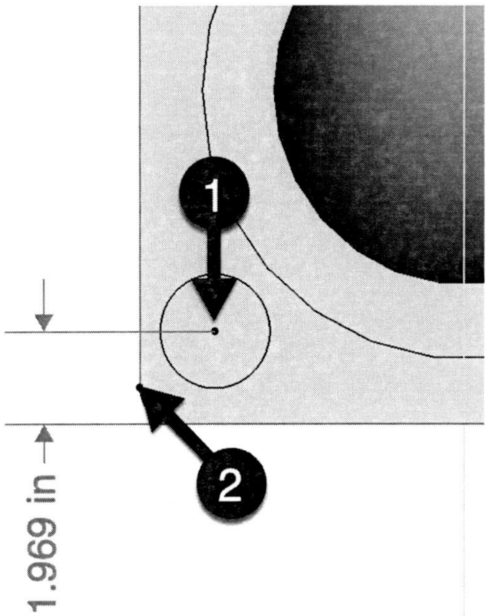

39. Click **Close** on the **Tasks** panel.
40. Click the **Hole**  icon on the **Part Design Modeling Features** toolbar.
41. Type **1.181 in** in the **Diameter** box. This sets the diameter of the initial hole.
42. Select **Depth > Dimension**. This sets the depth of the hole to be a specific dimension rather than a blind hole.
43. Type 1.969 in the **Depth** box located next to the **Depth** drop-down. This sets the depth of the hole.
44. Select **Head Type > Counterbore**. This changes the hole type to a counterbore hole, which has a larger diameter at the top.
45. Type **2.362** in the **Head diameter** box. This sets the diameter of the counterbore hole.
46. Type **0.394** in the **Head depth** box. This sets the depth of the counterbore hole.
47. Uncheck the **Drill Angle** option. This sets the drill point to be flat rather than pointed.

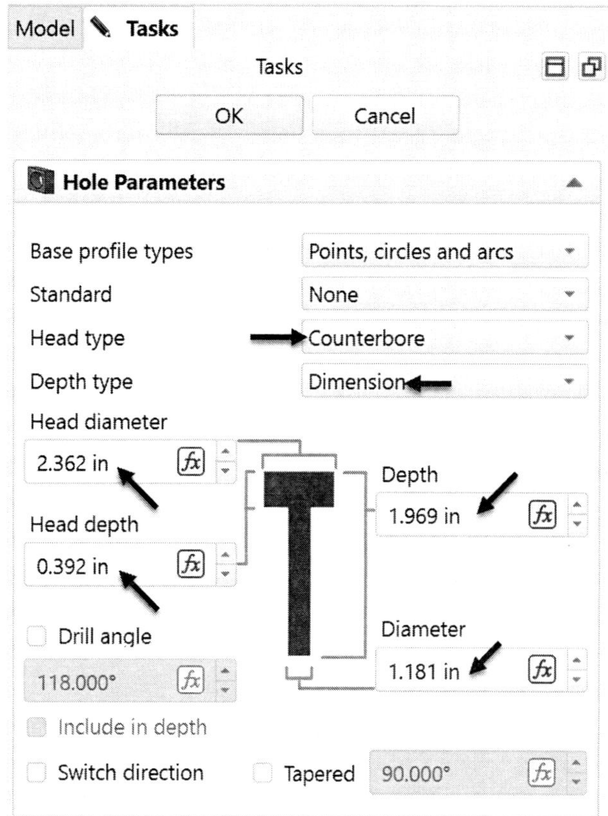

48. Click **OK** on the **Tasks** panel; the counterbore hole is created.

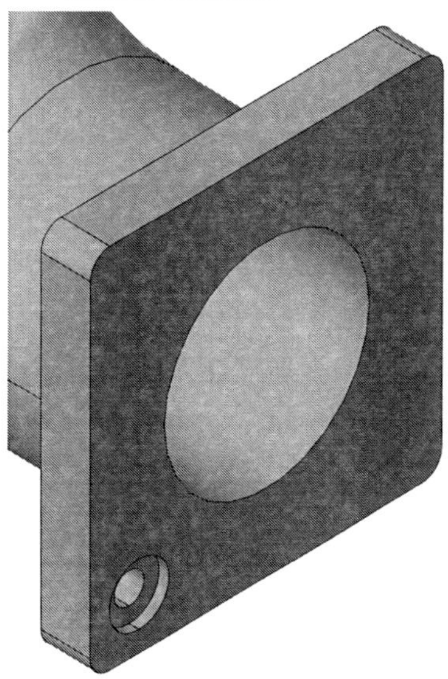

49. Select the **Hole** feature from the **Model** panel.
50. Click the **MultiTransform** 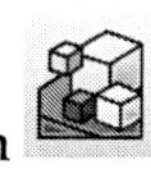 tool on the **Part Design Modeling Features** toolbar. This step is done to apply multiple transformations to the selected feature. In this case, we want to create a

pattern of holes, so we use the **MultiTransform** tool.

51. In the **MultiTransform parameters** section, right click in the **Transformations** section, and then select **Add linear pattern**. This step is done to add a linear pattern transformation to model. A linear pattern is a series of equally spaced objects along a straight line.

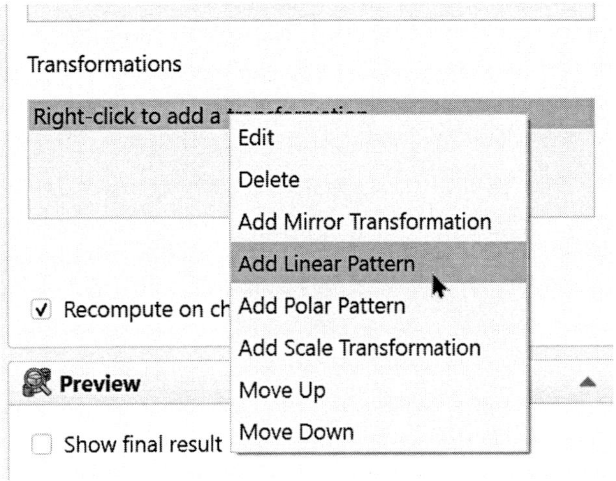

52. Select the **Horizontal sketch axis** from the **Direction** drop-down. This step is done to specify the direction of the linear pattern. In this case, we want the pattern to be horizontal, so we select the Horizontal sketch axis.
53. Type **10.235** in the **Length** box. This step is done to specify the distance between each occurrence of the pattern.
54. Type-in **2** in the **Occurrences** box. This step is done to specify the number of occurrences in the pattern.
55. Right click in the **Transformations** section, and then select **Add linear pattern**. This step is done to add another linear pattern transformation to the MultiTransform tool. We want to create a pattern of holes in both the horizontal and vertical directions.
56. Select the **Vertical sketch axis** from the **Direction** drop-down. This step is done to specify the direction of the second linear pattern. In this case, we want the pattern to be vertical, so we select the Vertical sketch axis.
57. Type **10.235** in the **Length** box. This step is done to specify the distance between each occurrence of the second pattern.
58. Type-in **2** in the **Occurrences** box. This step is done to specify the number of occurrences in the second pattern.
59. Click **OK** to create the multi transformation pattern. After clicking **OK**, you should see the pattern of holes created according to the specified parameters.

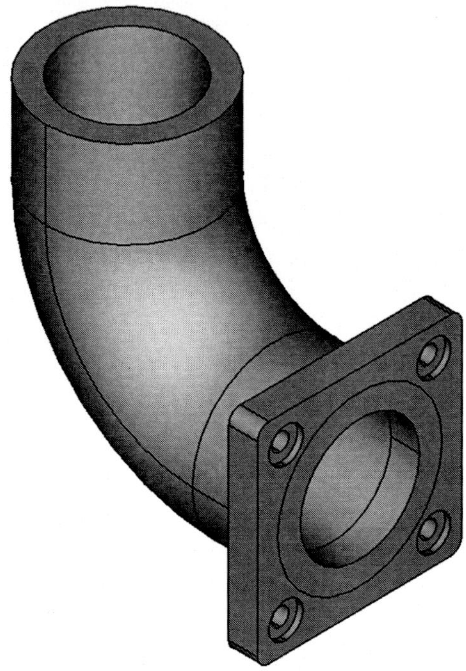

60. Likewise, create another flange on the other end of the AdditivePipe, as shown.

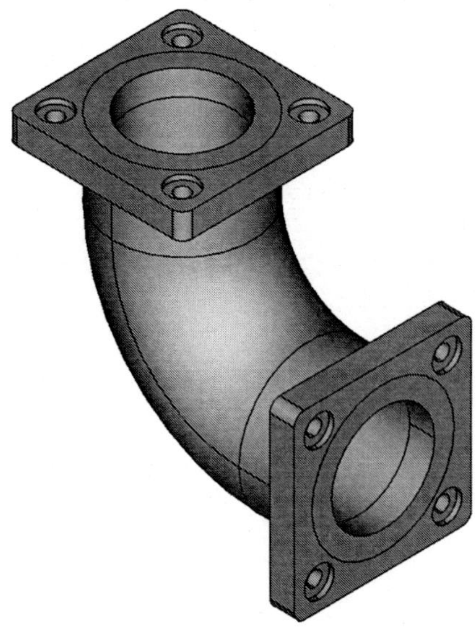

TUTORIAL 10

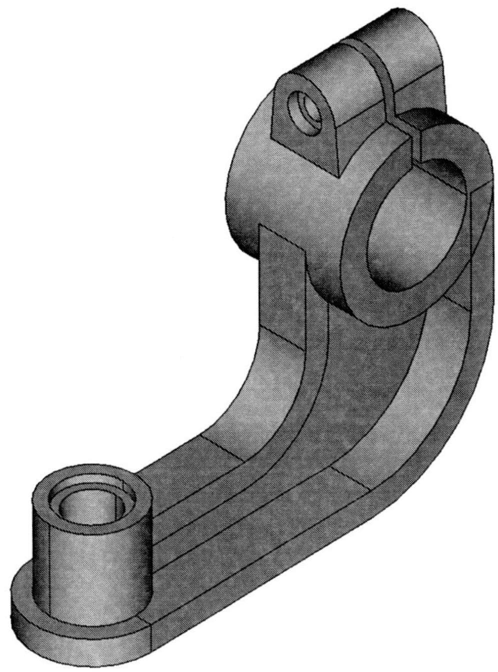

Creating the first feature

1. Open the FreeCAD application.
2. Click **File > New** on the Menu bar.
3. Select the **Part Design** option from the **Workbenches** drop-down.
4. Click the **New Sketch** icon on the **Part Design Helper Features** toolbar, and then Select the YZ Plane from the **Tasks** panel and click **OK**.
5. Click **OK** to start the sketch.
6. Click the **Circle From Center** icon on the **Geometries** toolbar.
7. Select the origin point of the sketch.
8. Move the pointer outward and click to create a circle.
9. On the **Constraints** toolbar, click the **Dimension** drop-down > **Diameter Dimension** ∅.
10. Select the circle and type in **3.937** in the **Diameter** box on the **Change diameter** dialog.
11. Click **OK**.

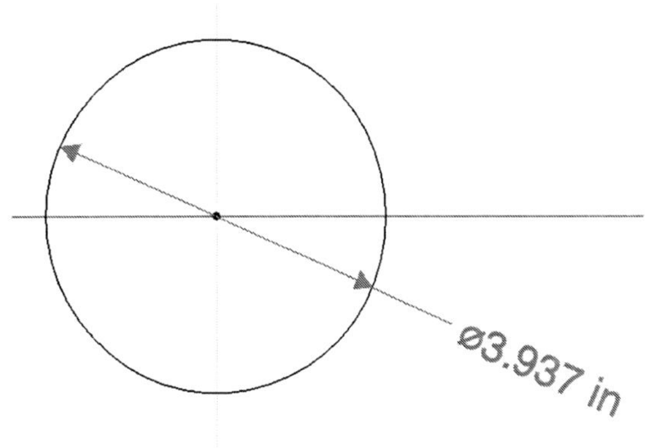

12. Click the **Leave Sketch** icon on the **Edit Mode** toolbar.
13. On the **Part Design Modelling Features** toolbar, click **Pad** icon.
14. Type-in **2.953** in the **Length** box.
15. Select **Mode > Symmetric** and click **OK**.

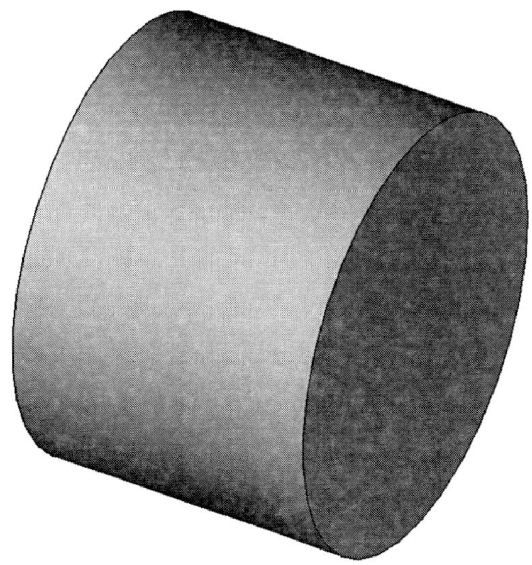

Creating the Second feature

1. Click the **New Sketch** icon on the **Part Design Helper Features** toolbar, and then Select the YZ Plane from the **Tasks** panel.
2. Click **OK** on the **Tasks** panel.
3. Click the **Polyline** tool on the **Geometries** toolbar, and then click on the horizontal axis of the sketch, as shown.
4. Move the pointer vertically downward and click.
5. Likewise, create the other lines, as shown.

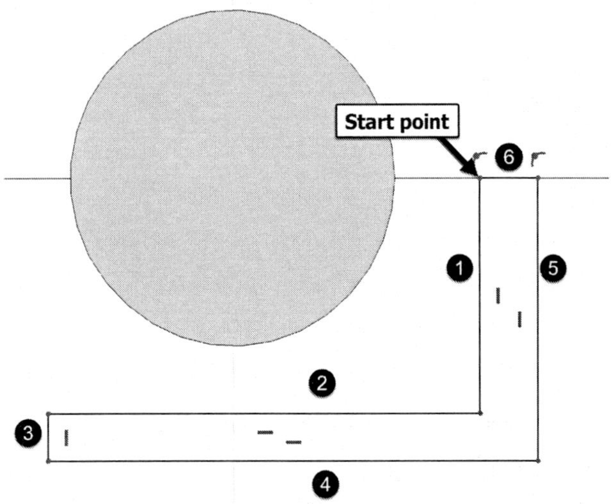

6. Click the **Sketch Fillet** icon on the **Sketcher tools** toolbar and select the corner points of the sketch, as shown.

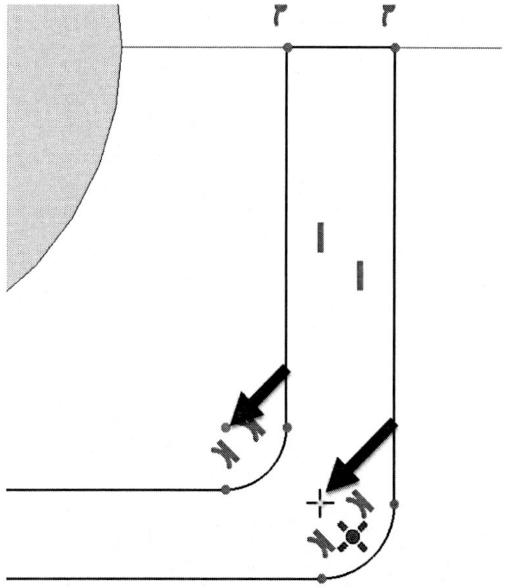

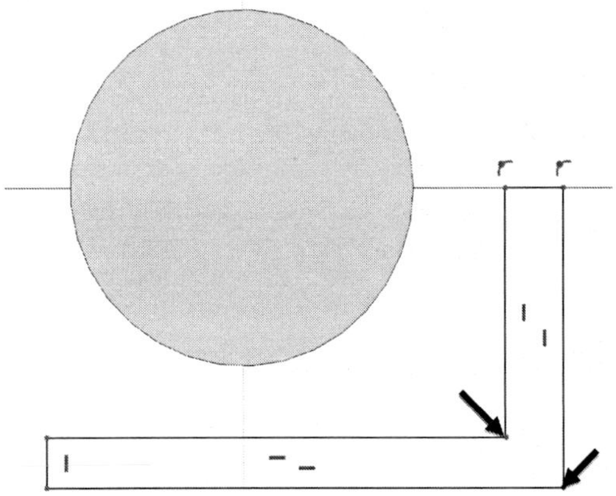

7. Click the **Coincident Constraint**  icon on the **Constraints** toolbar and select the centerpoints of the fillets. The Coincident Constraint is used to affix a point onto (coincident with) one or more other points. In this case, it is used to connect the centerpoints of the fillets. This constraint acts as a concentric constraint if two or more circles are selected. The result of this step is that the centerpoints of the fillets are connected, ensuring that they remain equidistant from each other and that the fillets maintain their shape.

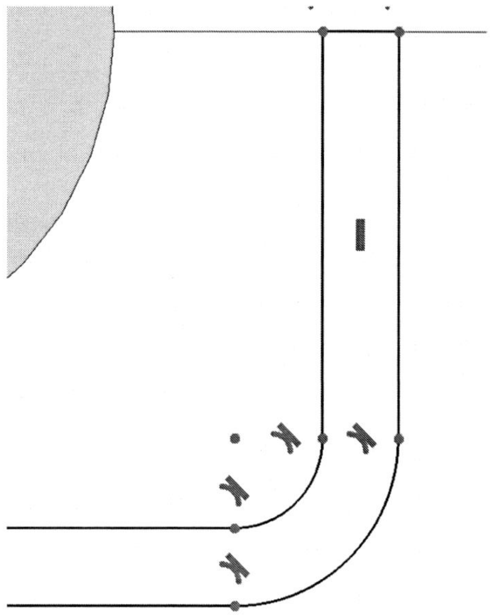

8. Add dimensions to the sketch, as shown.

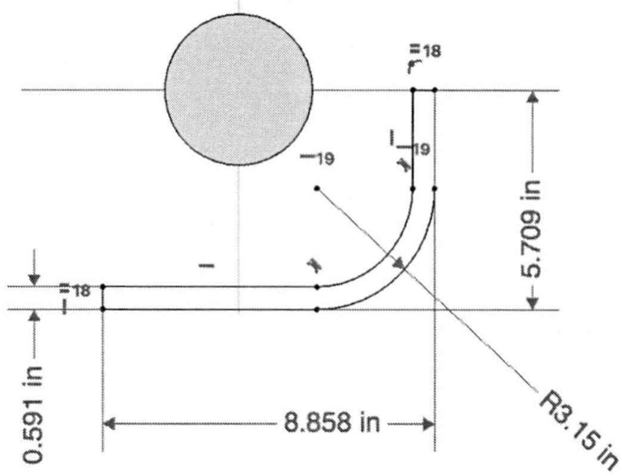

9. Click the **Toggle Construction Geometry** icon

on the **Geometries** toolbar.

10. Click the **External Projection**  icon on the **Sketcher tools** toolbar.
11. Select the circular edge of the model, as shown.

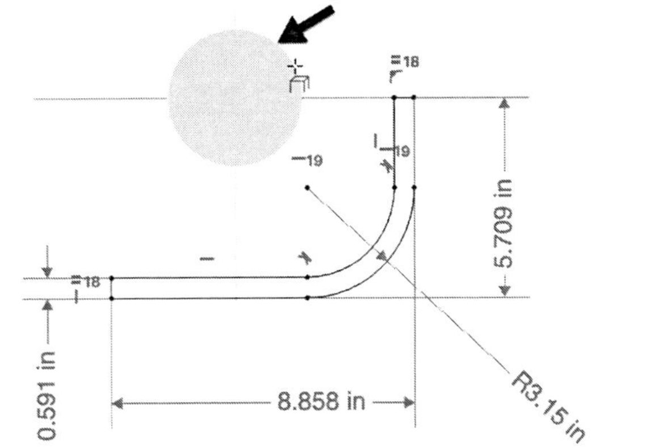

12. On the **Constraints** toolbar, click the **Tangent Constraint**  icon.
13. Select the circular edge and the right vertical line.

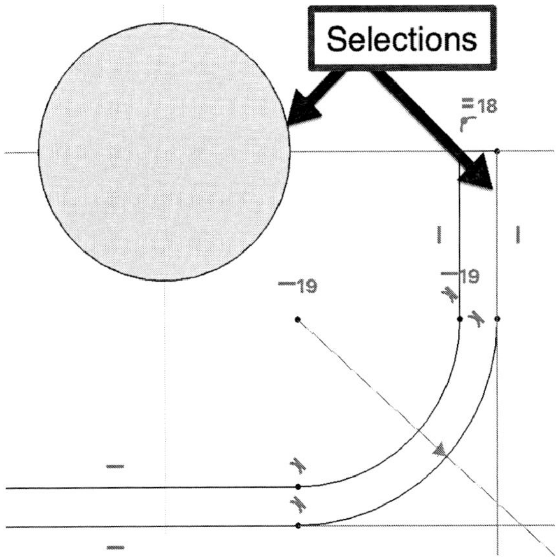

14. Click the **Toggle Construction Geometry** icon on the **Geometries** toolbar.
15. Click **Close** on the **Tasks** panel.

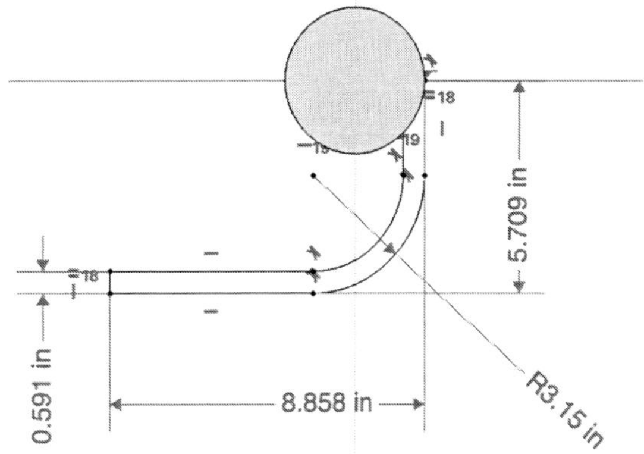

16. Click **Model** panel.
17. On the **Part Design Modelling Features** toolbar, click **Pad**  icon.
18. Type-in **2.953** in the **Length** box.
19. Select **Mode > Symmetric** and click **OK**. This step is done to make the pad symmetric to a plane. When the **Symmetric** option selected, the pad is created symmetrically on both sides of the plane.

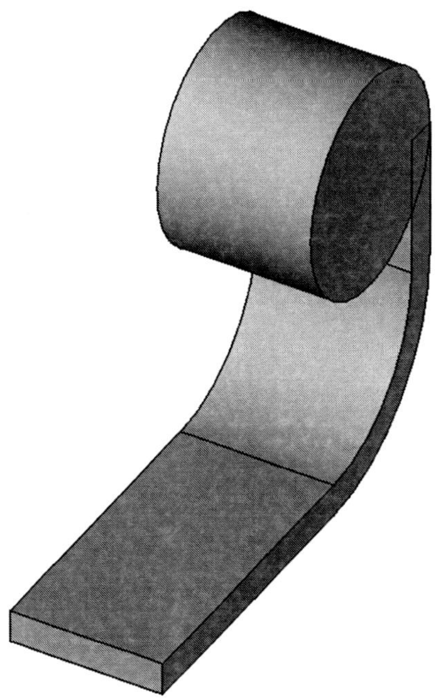

20. Click the **New Sketch**  icon on the **Part Design Helper Features** toolbar, and then select the YZ Plane.
21. Click **OK** on the **Tasks** panel.
22. Create a sketch using the **Polyline** and **Fillet** tools, as shown.

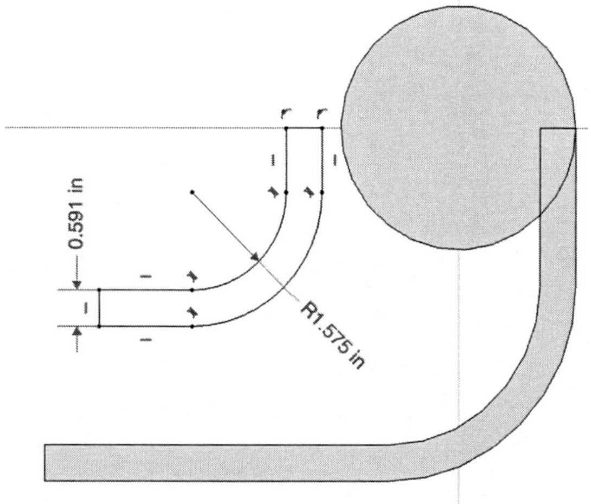

23. Click the **Toggle Construction Geometry** icon on the **Geometries** toolbar.
24. Click the **External Projection** icon on the **Sketcher tools** toolbar.
25. Select the circular, horizontal and vertical edges of the model, as shown.

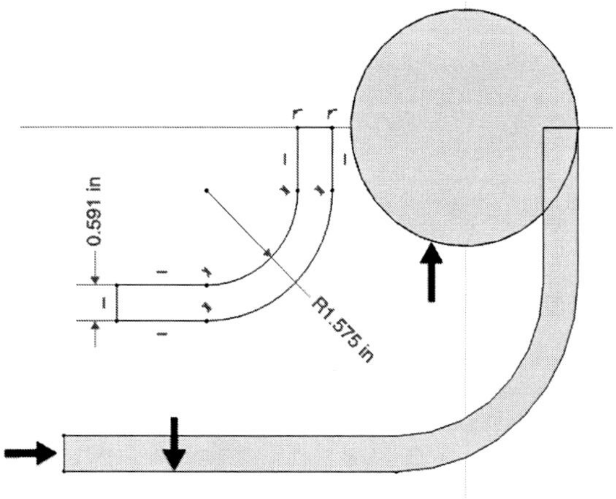

26. Click the **Toggle Construction Geometry** icon on the **Geometries** toolbar.
27. On the **Constraints** toolbar, click the **Tangent Constraint** icon.
28. Select the circular edge and the left vertical line.

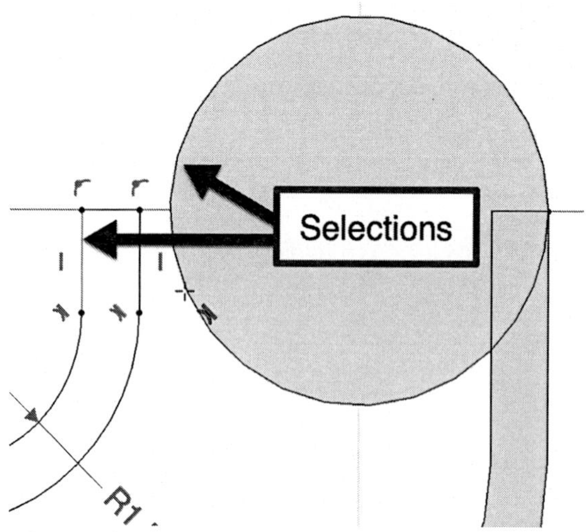

29. On the **Constraints** toolbar, click the **Vertical Constraint** icon.
30. Select the lower end point of the vertical line, as shown.
31. Select anyone of the vertices of the vertical edge, as shown.

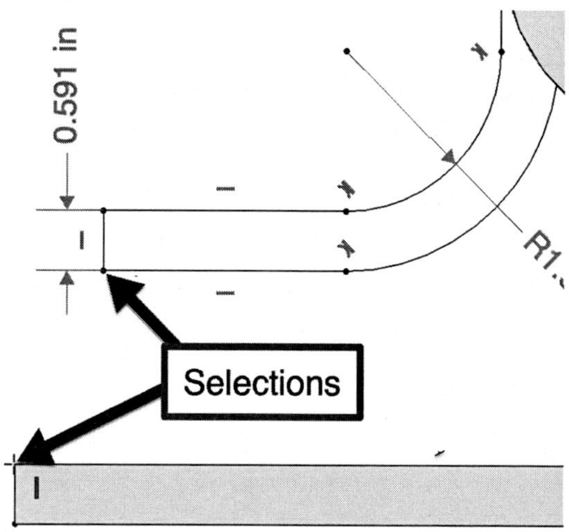

32. Click **Constraints** toolbar **Dimension drop-down > Vertical Dimension** (or) click **Sketch > Constraints > Vertical Dimension** on the menu bar.
33. Select the top endpoint of the vertical line, as shown
34. Select the left endpoint of the horizontal edge, as shown.

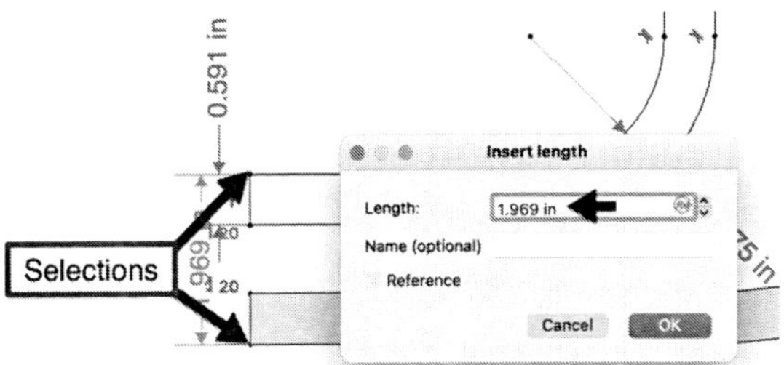

35. Type **1.969** in the **Length** box and click **OK**.
36. Click **Close** on the **Tasks** panel.
37. On the **Part Design Modeling Features** toolbar, click the **Pad**  icon.
38. Type **1.181** in the **Length** box of the **Pad Parameters** dialog.
39. Select **Mode > Symmetric** and click **OK**.

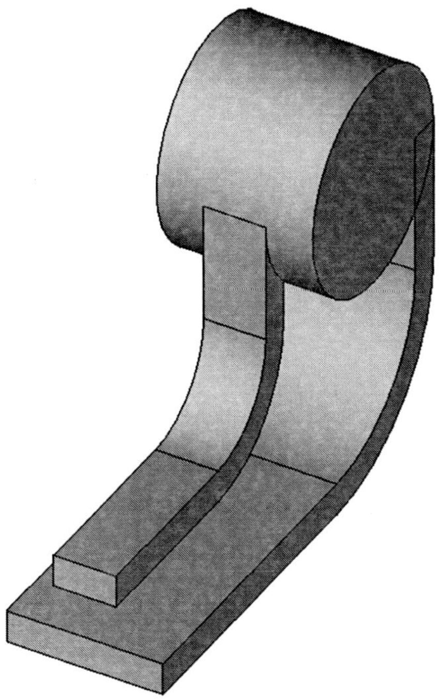

40. Click the **New Sketch**  icon on the **Part Design Helper Features** toolbar, and then select the YZ Plane.
41. Click **OK** on the **Tasks** panel.
42. Click the **Toggle Section View** 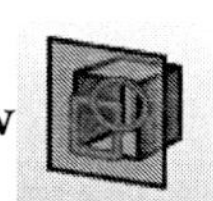 icon on the **Edit Mode** toolbar.
43. Click the **External Projection**  icon on the **Sketcher tools** toolbar.
44. Select the edges of the model, as shown.

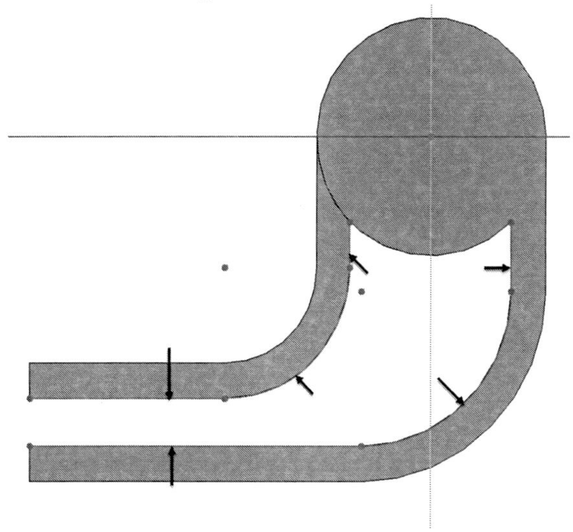

45. Click the **Toggle Construction Geometry** icon on the **Geometries** toolbar.
46. Click the **Arc** drop-down > **Arc from 3 Points** on the **Geometries** toolbar.
47. Select the vertices of the model, as shown.
48. Move the pointer and click.

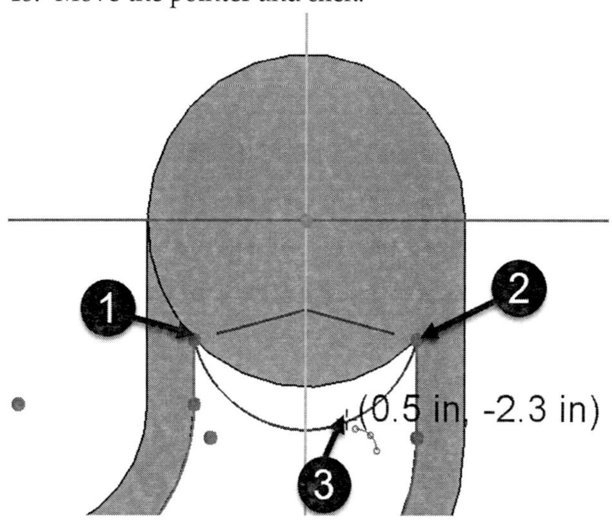

49. Click **Coincident Constraint** icon on the **Constraints** toolbar.
50. Select the centerpoint of the arc and sketch origin.

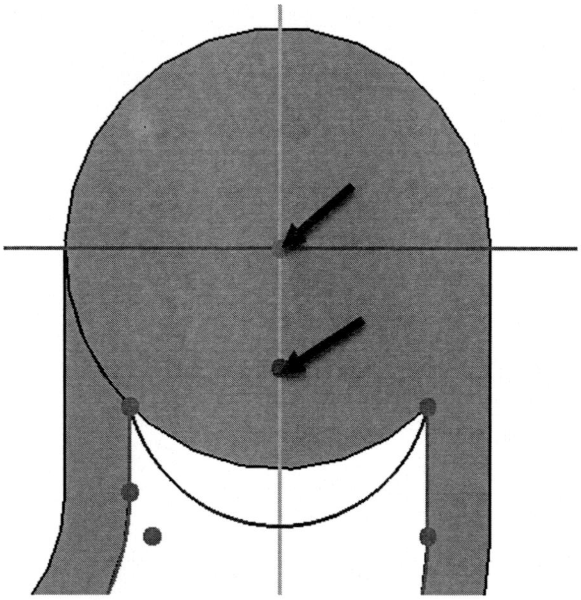

51. Click **Close** on the **Tasks** panel.
52. On the **Part Design Modeling Features** toolbar, click the **Pad** icon.
53. Type **0.787** in the **Length** box of the **Pad Parameters** dialog.
54. Select **Mode > Symmetric** and click **OK**.

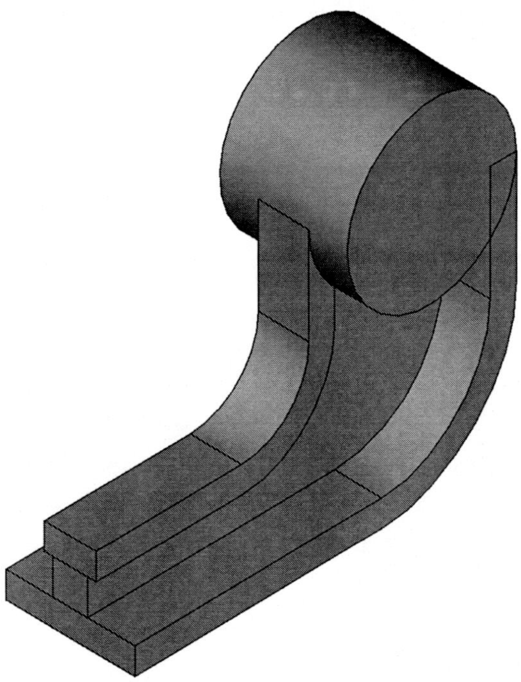

55. Press and hold the right and middle mouse button and drag the pointer upward.
56. Select the bottom flat face.

57. Click **New Sketch** icon on the **Part Design Helper Features** toolbar.
58. Click the **External Projection** icon on the **Sketcher tools** toolbar.
59. Select the edge of the model, as shown.

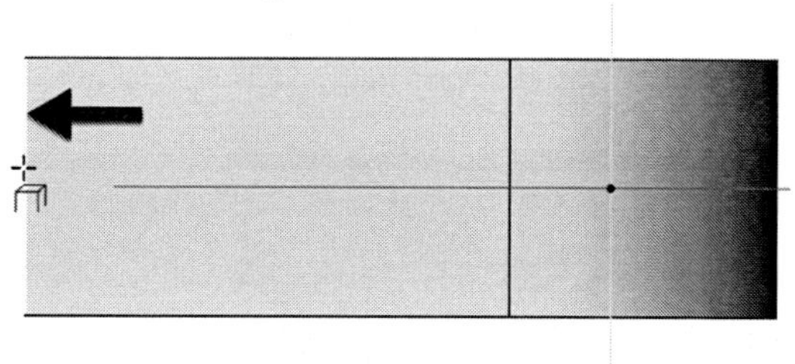

60. Click the **Create arc by three points** icon on the **Geometries** toolbar.
61. Select the two vertices of the edge, as shown.
62. Move the pointer towards left and click.

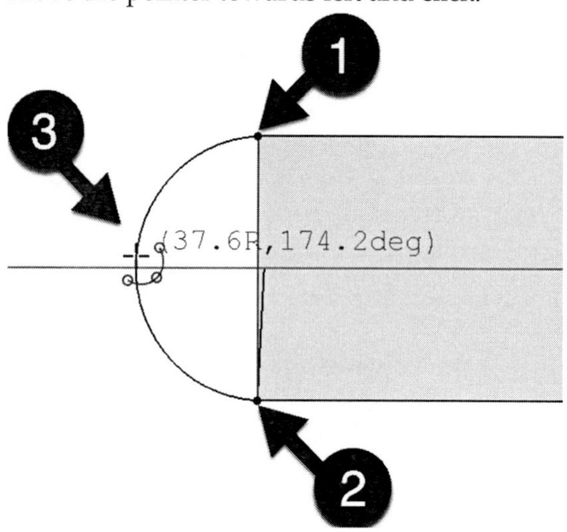

63. On the **Constraints** toolbar, click the **Coincident Constraint** icon.

64. Select the centerpoint of the arc and the vertical edge, as shown.

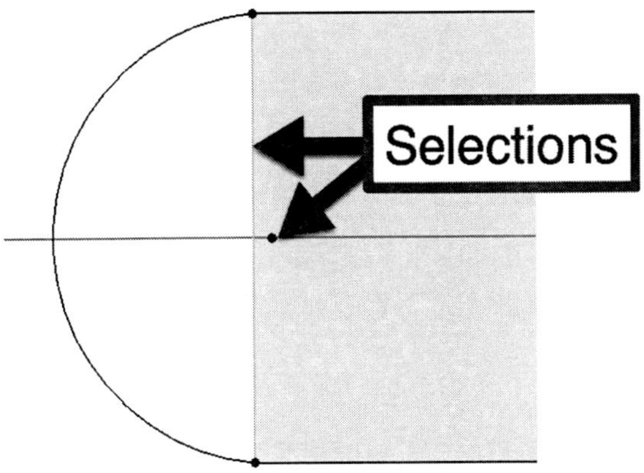

65. Click **Close** on the **Tasks** panel.
66. On the **Part Design Modeling Features** toolbar, click the **Pad** icon.
67. Select **Type > Up to face** on the **Pad Parameters** dialog.
68. Select the horizontal face of the model, as shown.

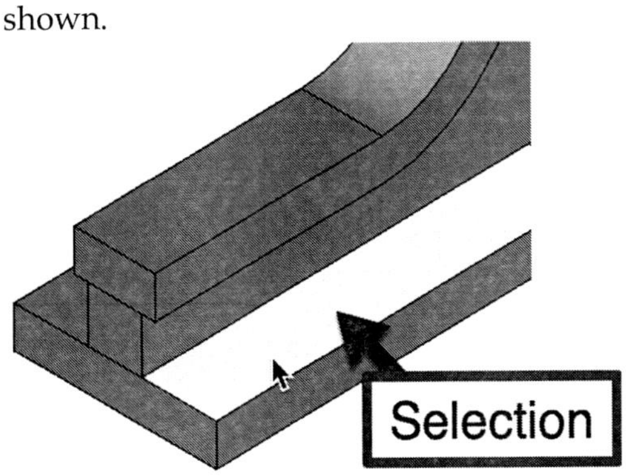

69. Click **OK**.

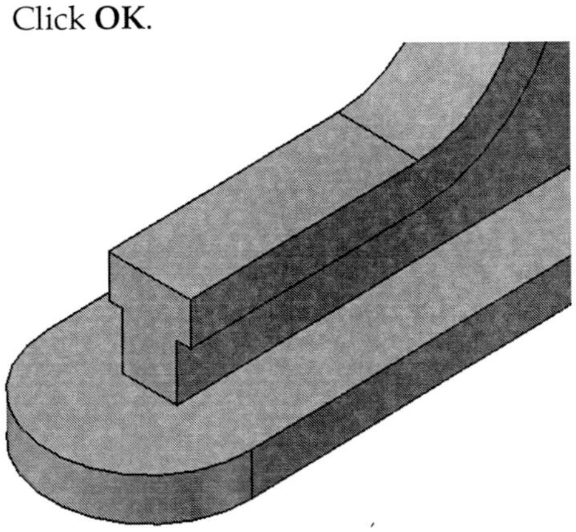

Creating the third feature

1. Select the horizontal face of the model, as shown.

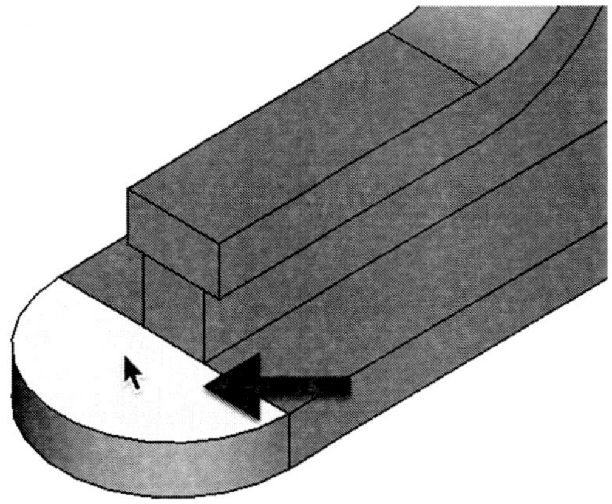

2. Click **New Sketch** icon on the **Part Design Helper Features** toolbar.
3. Click the **External Projection** icon on the **Sketcher tools** toolbar.
4. Select the circular edge of the model, as shown.

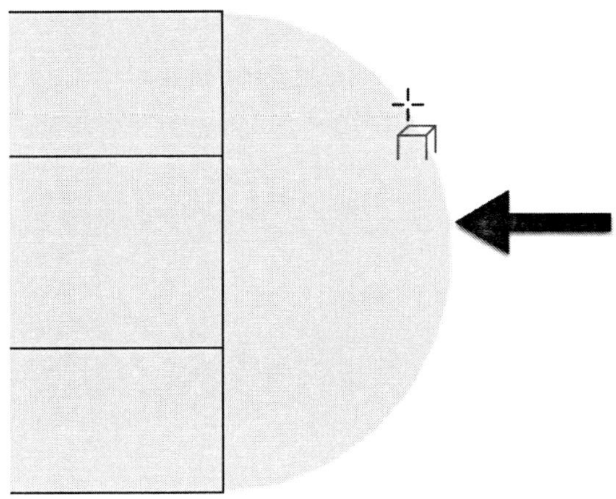

5. Click the **Circle From Center** icon on the **Sketcher geometry** toolbar.
6. Click on the centerpoint of the curved edge.
7. Move the pointer outward and click to create the circle.

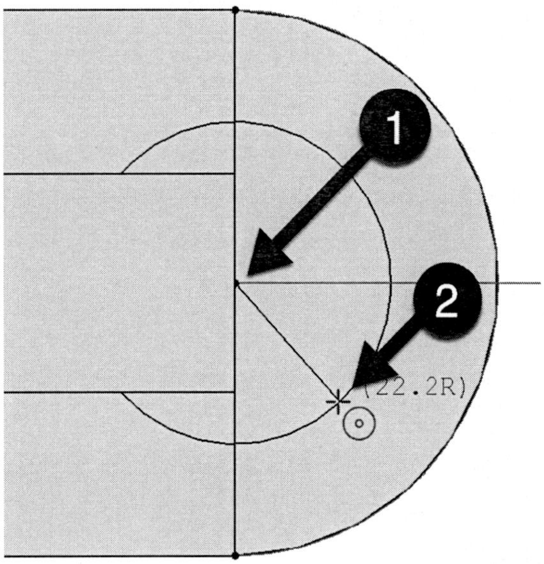

8. On the **Constraints** toolbar, click the **Dimension** drop-down and select **Diameter Dimension** Ø .
9. Select the circle and type-in **2.165** in the **Diameter** box on the **Change Diameter** dialog.
10. Click **OK**.

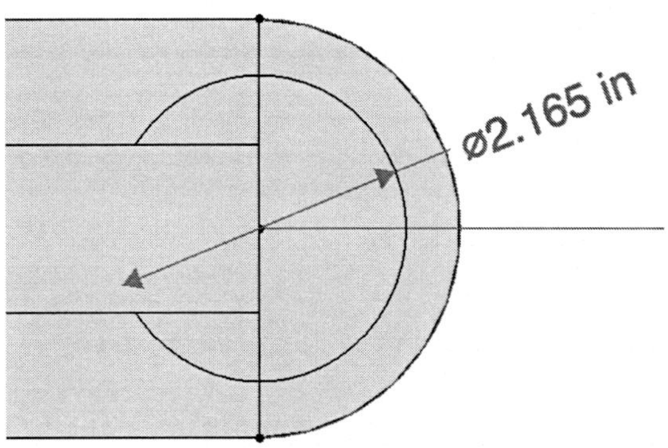

11. Click **Close** on the **Tasks** panel.
12. On the **Part Design Modeling Features** toolbar, click the **Pad** icon.
13. Type **1.969** in the **Length** box of the **Pad Parameters** dialog.

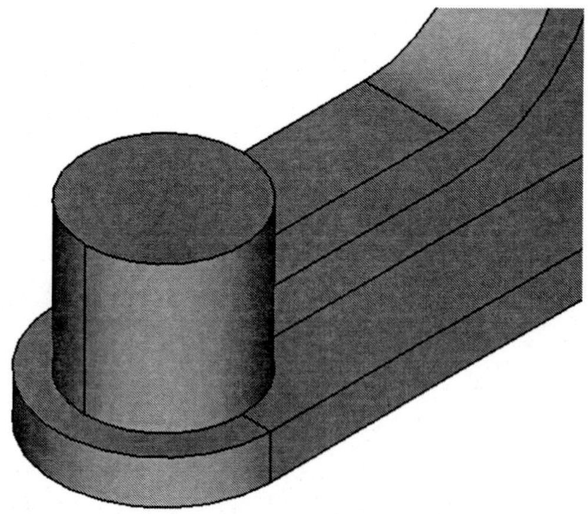

Creating the fourth feature

1. Click the **New Sketch** icon on the **Part Design Helper Features** toolbar, and then select the XZ Plane from the **Tasks** panel.
2. Click **OK** to start the sketch.
3. Click the **Arc From Center** icon on the **Geometries** toolbar.
4. Click on the vertical axis of the sketch.
5. Move the pointer outward and click to specify the first point of the arc.
6. Specify the second point of the arc.

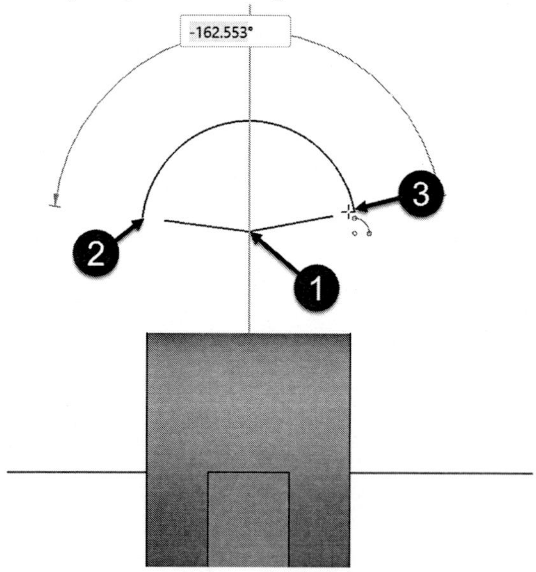

7. Click the **Polyline** tool on the **Geometries** toolbar.
8. Select the startpoint of the arc.
9. Move the pointer downward at the inclined angle and click.

10. Move the pointer horizontally toward right and click.
11. Move the pointer and select the endpoint of the arc.
12. Click the **Equal Constraint** icon on the **Constraints** toolbar.
13. Select the two inclined lines.
14. Click the **Constrain angle** icon on the **Constraints** toolbar.
15. Select the two inclined lines.
16. Type **10** in the **Insert angle** box and click **OK**. The two selected lines will be constrained to be equal in length and have a specific angle between them.
17. Click the **Tangent Constraint** icon on the **Constraints** toolbar and apply the tangent constraint between the lines and the arc.
18. Click the **Dimension** drop-down > **Radius Dimension** icon on the **Constraints** toolbar.
19. Select the arc, type **0.787** in the **Radius** box and click **OK**.

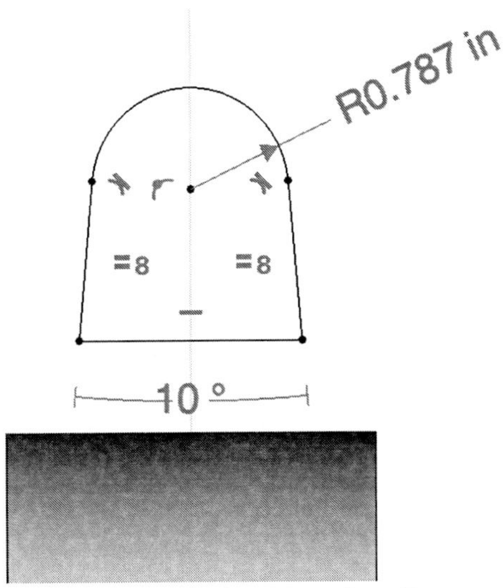

20. Click the **Toggle Construction Geometry** icon on the **Geometries** toolbar.
21. Click the **External Projection** icon on the **Sketcher tools** toolbar.
22. Select the bottom horizontal edge of the model, as shown.

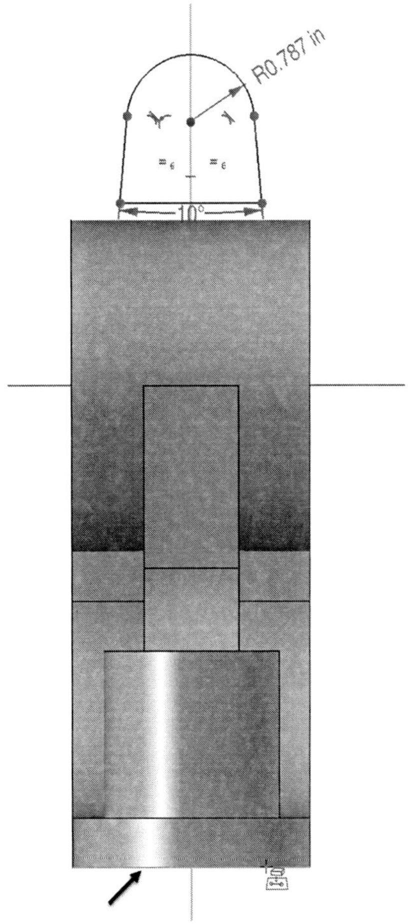

23. Click the **Toggle Construction Geometry** icon on the **Geometries** toolbar.
24. Click the **Toggle Section View** icon on the **Edit Mode** toolbar.
25. On the **Constraints** toolbar, click the **Coincident Constraint** icon.
26. Select the endpoint of the horizontal line, as shown.
27. Select the external geometry, as shown.

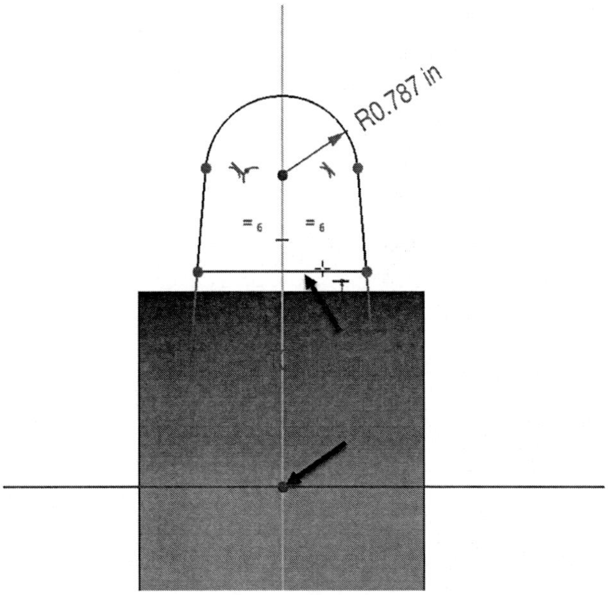

28. On the **Constraints** toolbar, click the **Dimension**  icon.
29. Select the centerpoint of the arc.
30. Select the endpoint of the bottom external geometry.

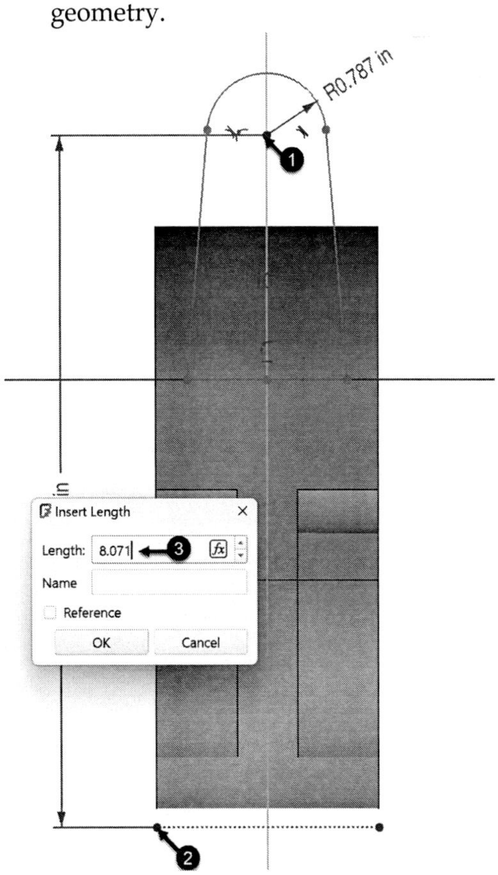

31. Enter **8.071** in the **Length** box of the **Insert Length** dialog and click **OK**.
32. Click **Close** on the **Tasks** panel.
33. On the **Part Design Modeling Features** toolbar, click the **Pad**  icon.
34. Type **2.756** in the **Length** box of the **Pad Parameters** dialog.
35. Select **Mode > Symmetric** and click **OK**.

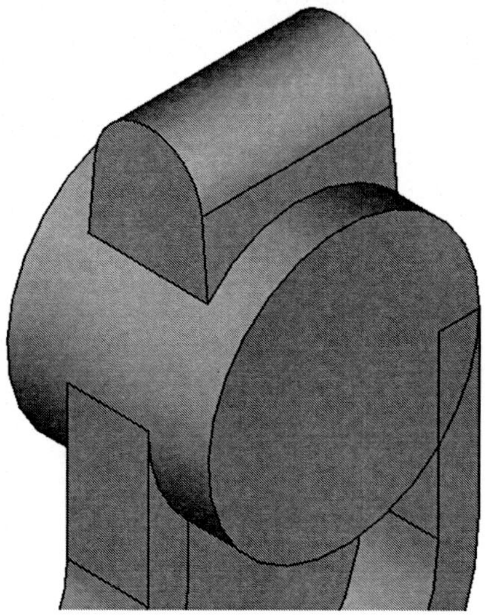

Creating Holes

1. Select the horizontal face of the model, as shown.

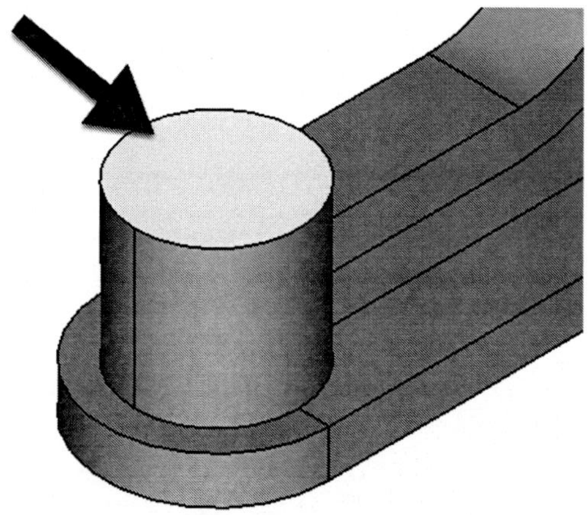

2. Click the **Hole**  icon on the **Part Design Modeling Features** toolbar.
3. Type **1.181** in the **Diameter** box.
4. Select **Depth type > Through All.**
5. On the **Hole Parameters** section, select **Head Type > Counterbore**.
6. Type **1.575** in the **Head diameter** box.
7. Type **0.197** in the **Depth** box.
8. Click **OK** on the **Tasks** panel; the counterbore hole is created.

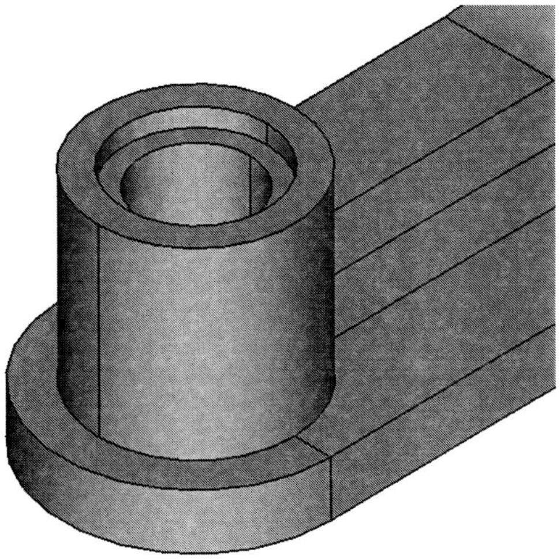

9. Select the circular edge of the model, as shown.

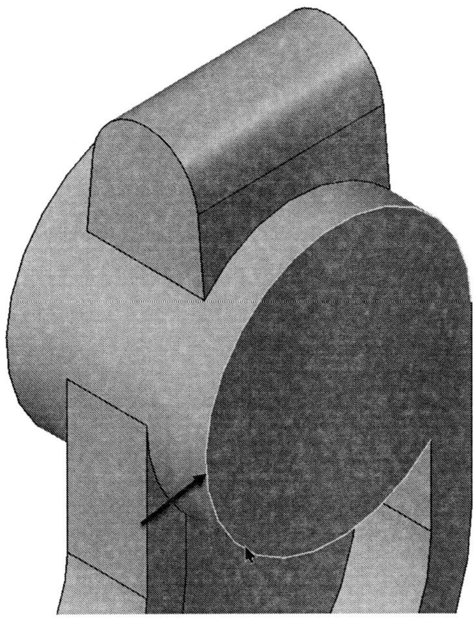

10. Click the **Hole** icon on the **Part Design Modeling Features** toolbar.
11. Type **2.559** in the **Diameter** box.
12. Select **Depth type > Through All**.
13. Click **OK**.

14. Likewise, create a counterbored hole, as shown.

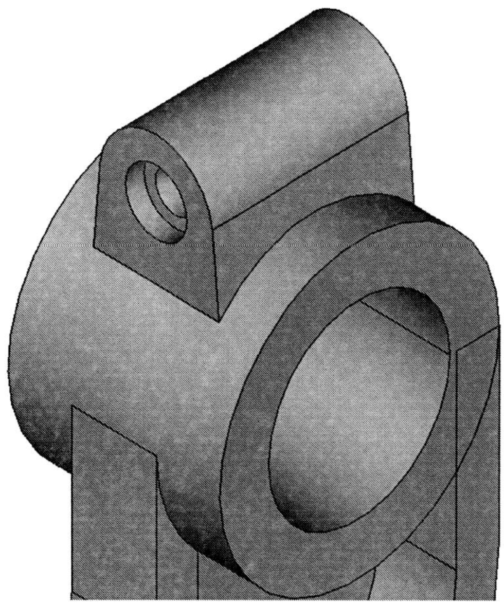

Diameter: 0.551 in
Depth type: Through all
Head type: Counterbore
Counterbore Diameter: 0.866 in
Head Depth: 0.260 in

Creating the Pocket feature

1. Select the flat face of the model, as shown.

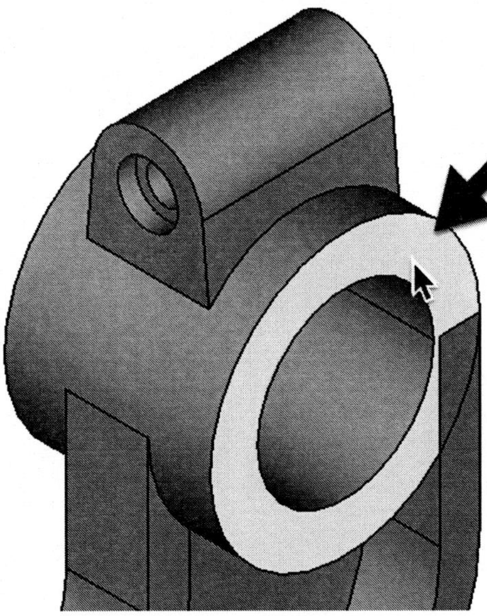

2. Click **New Sketch** icon on the **Part Design Helper** toolbar.
3. Create a rectangle and dimensions to it, as shown.

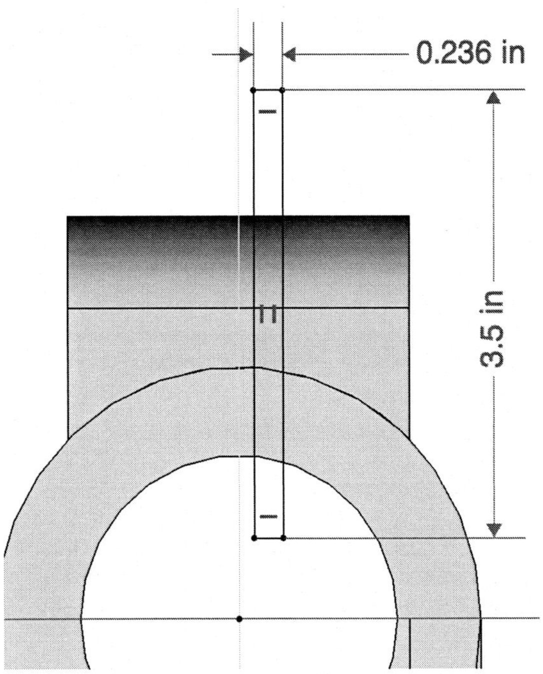

4. On the **Constraints** toolbar, click the **Symmetric Constraint** icon.
5. Select the endpoints of the horizontal line, as shown.
6. Select the sketch origin.

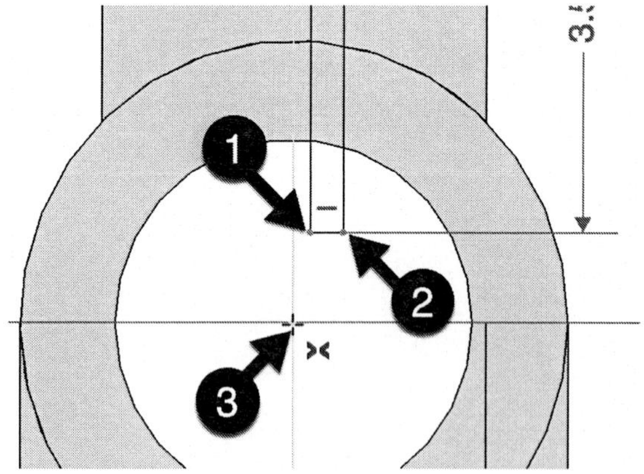

7. Click **Close** on the **Tasks** panel.
8. On the **Part Design Modeling Features** toolbar, click the **Pocket** icon.
9. Select **Type > Through all**, and then click **OK**.

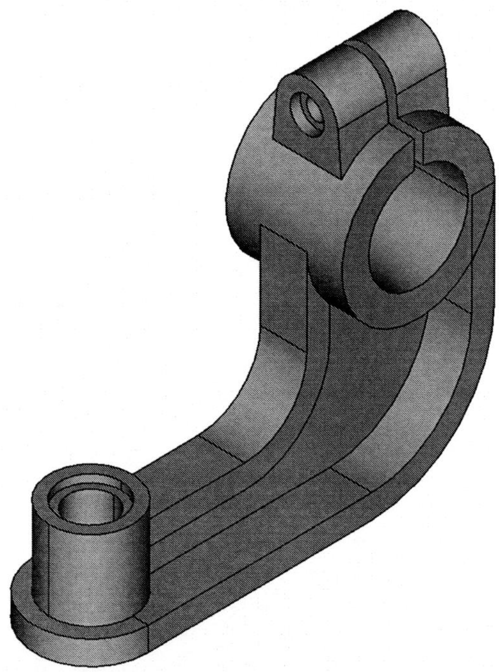

TUTORIAL 11

In this tutorial, you create the model shown in the figure:

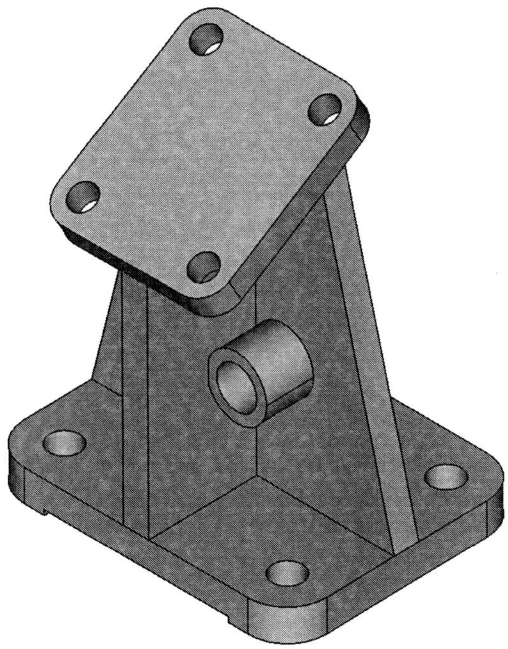

Creating the Base

1. Open the FreeCAD application.
2. Click **File > New** on the Menu bar.
3. Select the **Part Design** option from the **Workbenches** drop-down.
4. On the Menu bar, click **Edit > Preferences**.
5. Click the **General tab** on the **Preferences** dialog.
6. Select **User system > Imperial decimal**.
7. Type **3** in the **Number of decimals** box.
8. Click **OK**.
9. Click the **New Sketch** icon on the **Part Design Helper Features** toolbar, and then Select the XY Plane from the **Tasks** panel and click **OK**.
10. Click the **Rectangle** drop-down > **Centered Rectangle** on the **Geometries** toolbar.
11. Select the sketch origin, move the pointer outward and click. Next, add dimensions to the sketch.

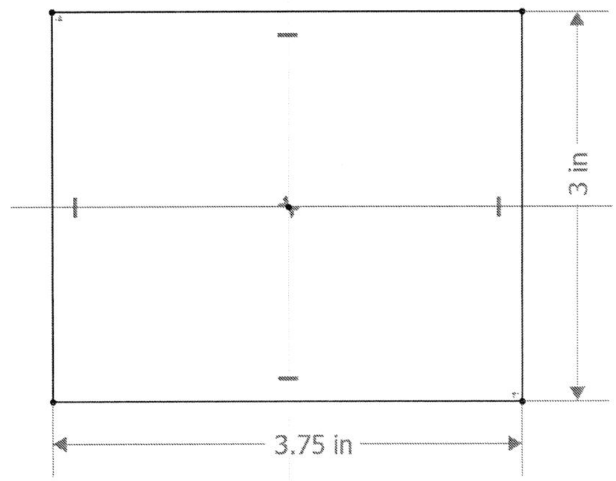

12. Click **Close** on the **Tasks** panel.
13. Click the **Pad** icon on the **Part Design Modelling Features** toolbar.
14. Select **Type > Dimension** on the **Pad parameters** section.
15. Type-in **0.38** in in the **Length** box.
16. Click **OK** on the **Tasks** panel.

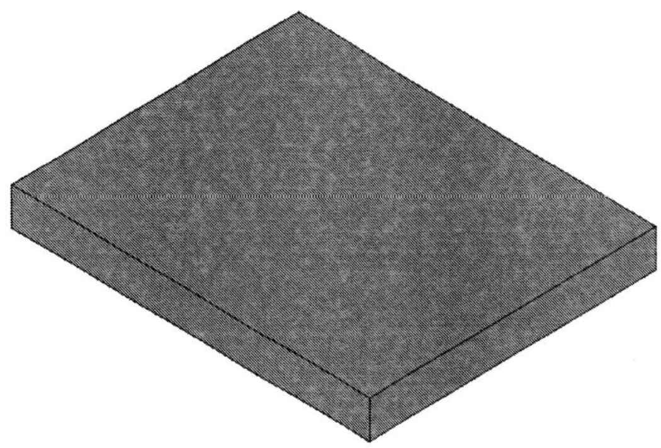

17. Click the **Create fillet** icon on the **Part Design Dressup Features** toolbar.
18. Select the vissible vertical edges of the model, as shown.
19. Press and hold the Middle mouse and Right mouse button, and then drag the cursor. The view is rotated.
20. Select the last visible vertical edge of the model.
21. Type-in **0.50** in in the **Radius** box.
22. Click **OK** on the **Tasks** panel.

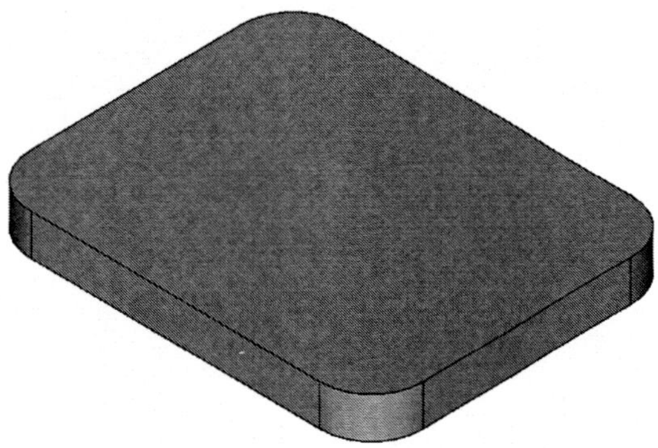

23. Click on the top face of the **Pad** feature and click **New Sketch** on the **Part Design Helper Features** toolbar.

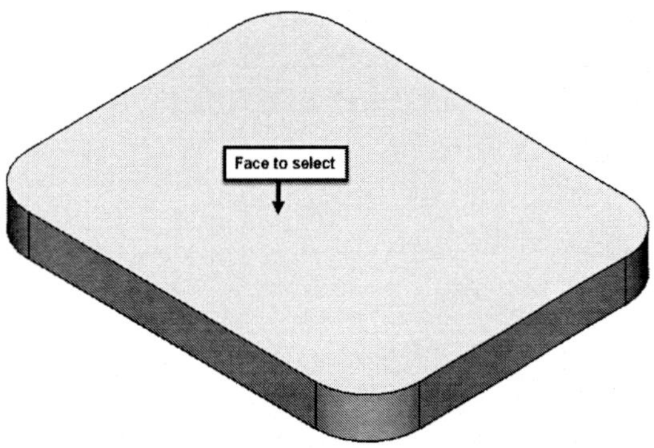

24. On the **Part Design Modelling Features** toolbar, click the **Hole** icon.
25. Select **Depth type > Through all**.
26. Type **0.38** in the **Diameter** box.
27. Click **OK** on the **Tasks** panel.

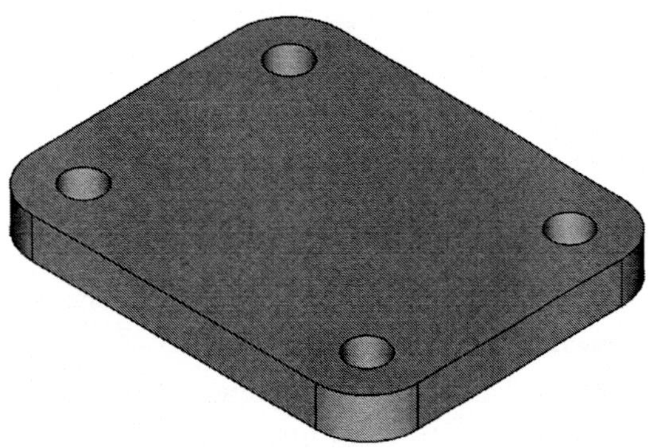

Creating the Rib

1. On the **Part Design Helper Features** toolbar, click the **New Sketch** icon.
2. Select **XZ-Plane** on the **Select feature** and click **OK**.
3. Click the **External Projection** icon on the **Sketcher tools** toolbar.
4. Select the edges of the model, as shown.

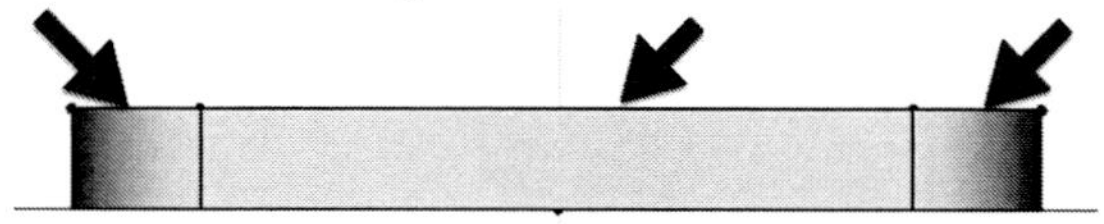

5. On the **Geometries** toolbar, click the **Polyline** icon.
6. Select the right endpoint of the external geometry, as shown.

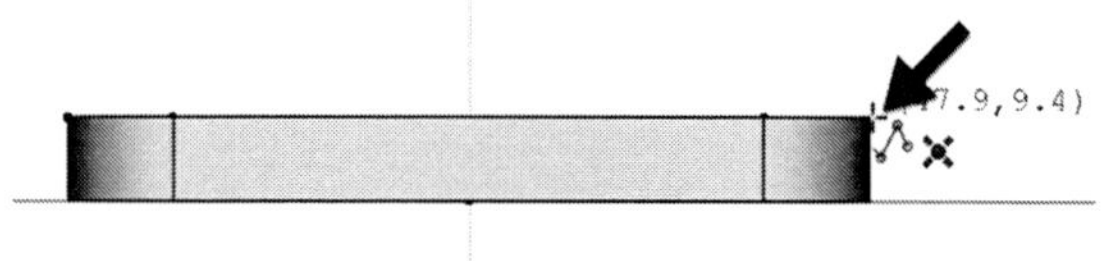

7. Specify the second and third points of the polyline, as shown.
8. Select the left point of the external geometry, as shown.

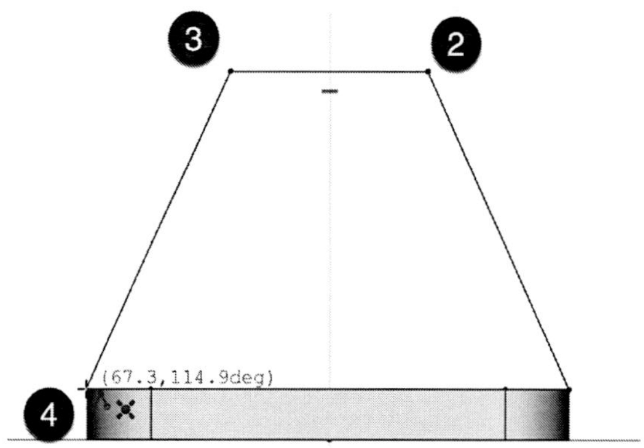

9. Add dimensional constraints to the sketch, and then click **Leave Sketch**.

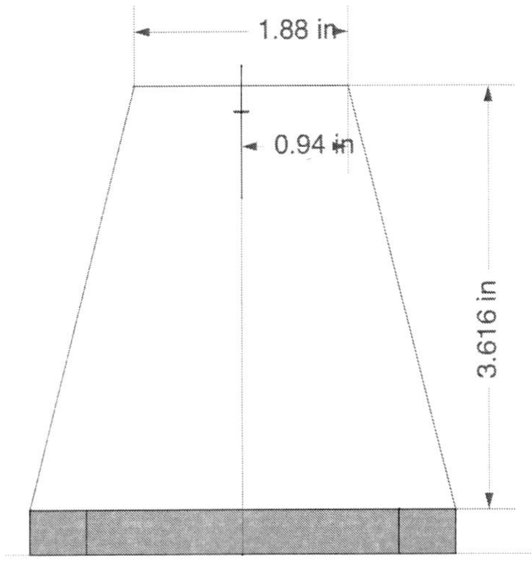

10. On the **Part Design Modeling Features** toolbar, click the **Pad**  icon.
11. Type **0.31** in the **Length** box of the **Pad Parameters** dialog.
12. Select **Mode > Symmetric** and click **OK**.

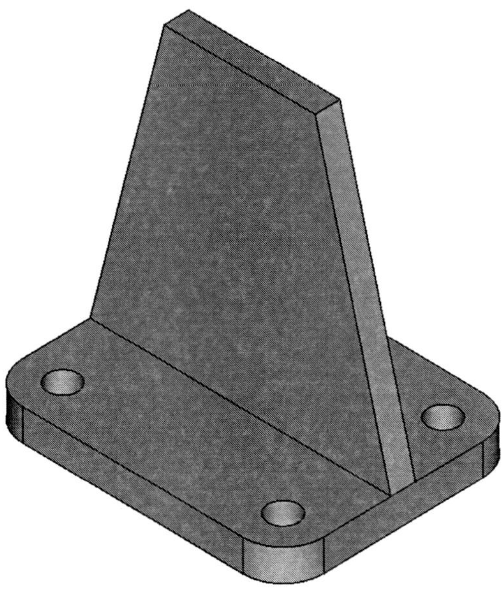

13. Click on the horizontal face of the model, as shown.

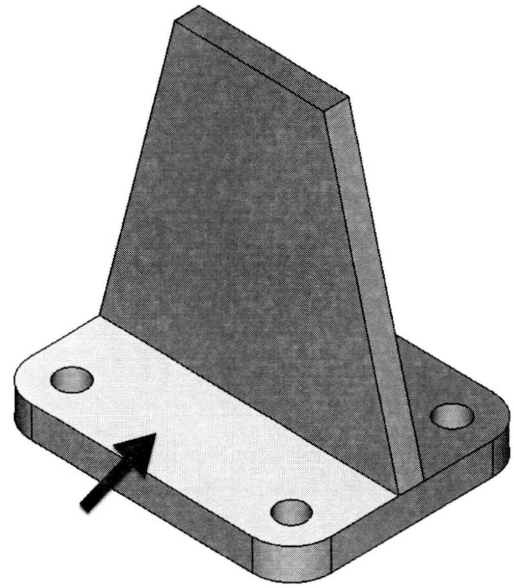

14. Click **New Sketch** on the **Part Design Helper Features** toolbar.
15. Click the **Toggle Construction Geometry** icon on the **Geometries** toolbar.
16. Click the **External Projection**  icon on the **Sketcher tools** toolbar.
17. Select the horizontal edges of the model, as shown.

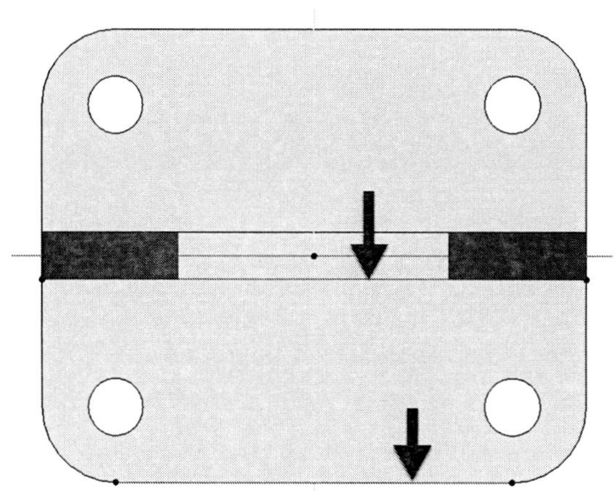

18. Click the **Toggle Construction Geometry** icon on the **Geometries** toolbar.
19. Specify the first and second corners of the rectangle of the two external geometries, as shown.

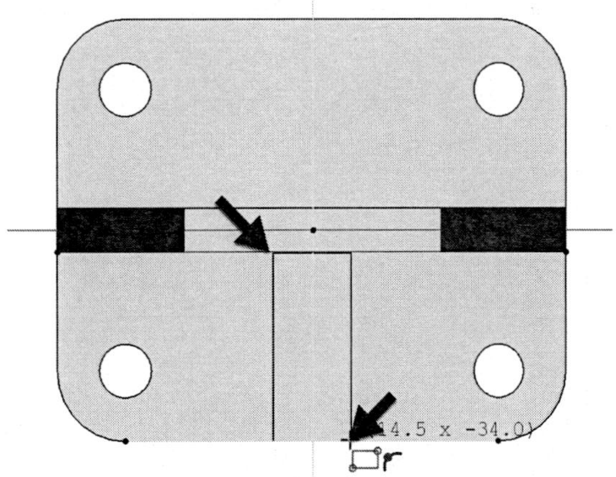

20. Add dimensional constraints to the rectangle, and then click **Leave Sketch**.

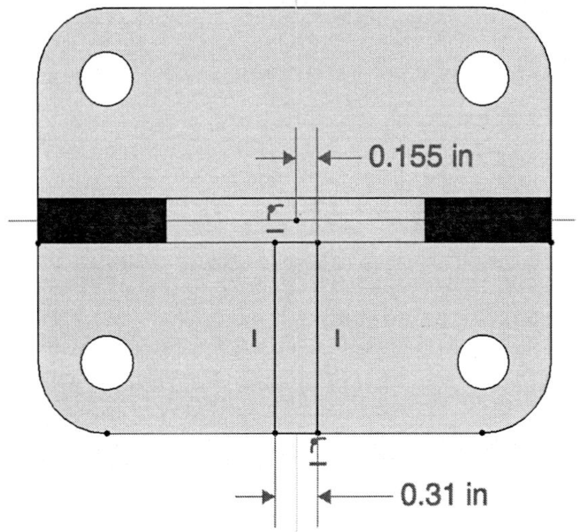

21. On the **Part Design Modeling Features** toolbar, click the **Pad** icon.
22. Select **Type > Up to face** on the **Pad parameters** dialog.
23. Select the horizontal face of the model, as shown.

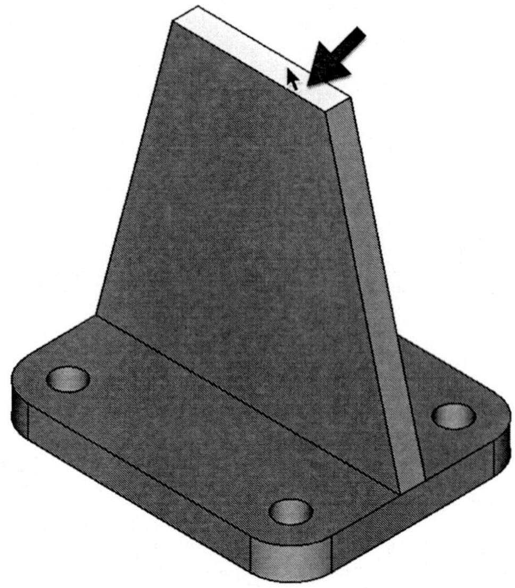

24. Click **OK**.

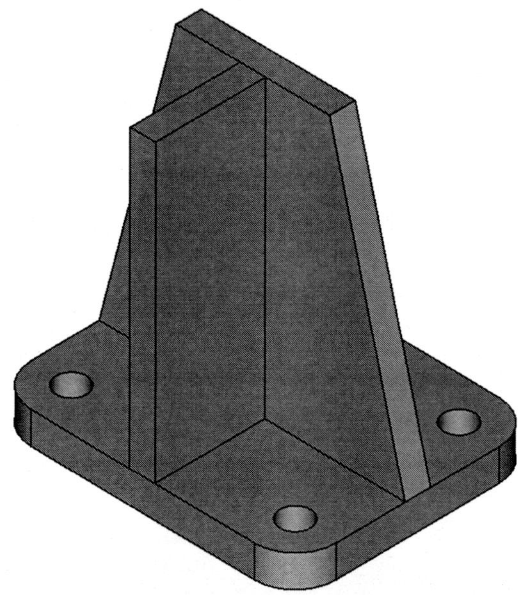

25. On the **Part Design Helper Features** toolbar, click the **New Sketch** icon.
26. Select **YZ-Plane** on the **Select feature** and click **OK**.
27. Click the **Toggle Section View** icon on the **Edit mode** toolbar.
28. On the **Geometries** toolbar, click the **Polyline** icon.
29. Create a closed sketch, as shown.

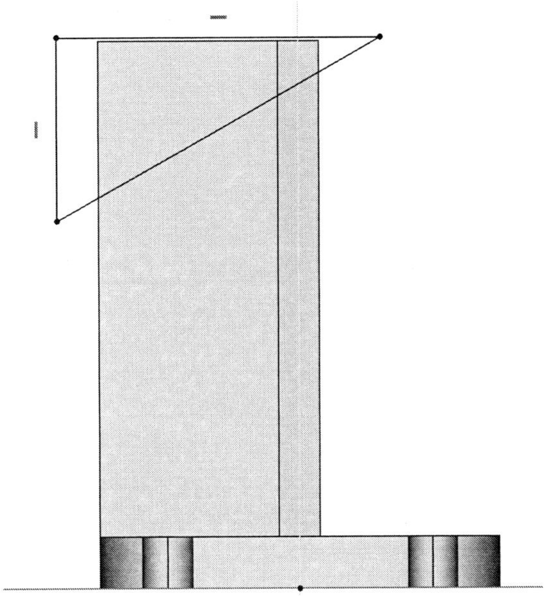

30. Add dimensions to the sketch, as shown.

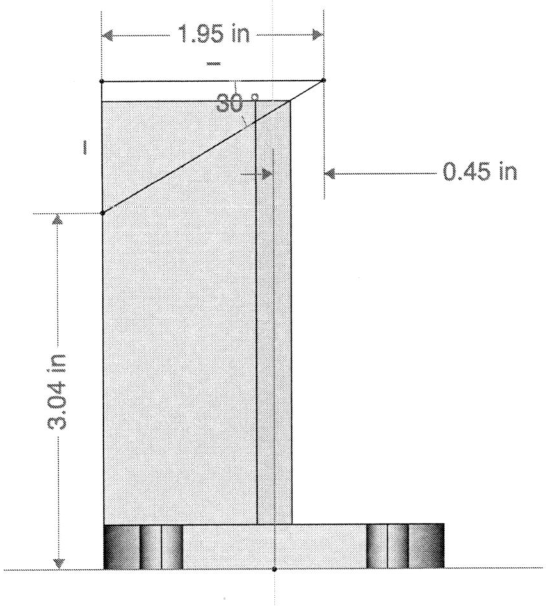

31. Click **Close** on the **Tasks** panel.
32. On the **Part Design Modelling Features** toolbar, click the **Pocket** icon.
33. Select **Type > Through all** under the **Pad parameters** section.
34. Select **Mode** > **Symmetric** and click **OK**.
35. Click **OK** on the **Tasks** panel.

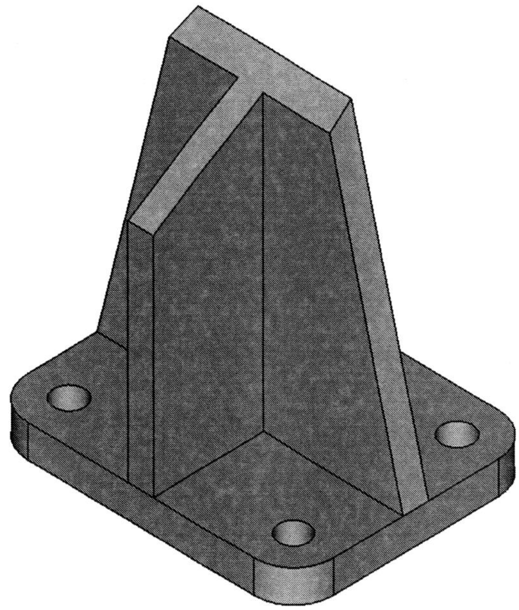

Creating the Third feature

1. Click on the inclined face of the model, as shown.

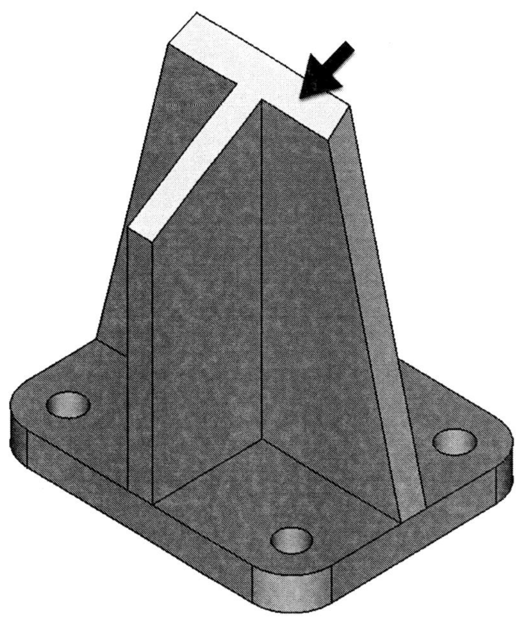

2. On the **Part Design Helper Features** toolbar, click the **New Sketch** icon.
3. Create the rectangle and add dimensions to it, as shown.

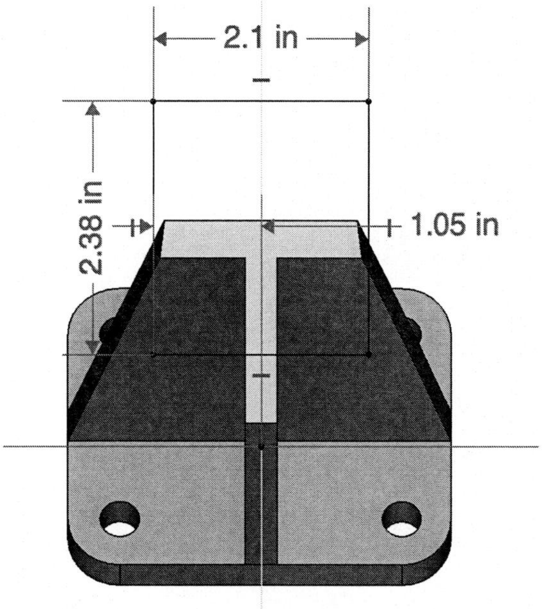

4. Click the **Toggle Construction Geometry** icon on the **Geometries** toolbar.
5. Click the **External Projection**  icon on the **Sketcher tools** toolbar.
6. Select the horizontal edges of the model, as shown.

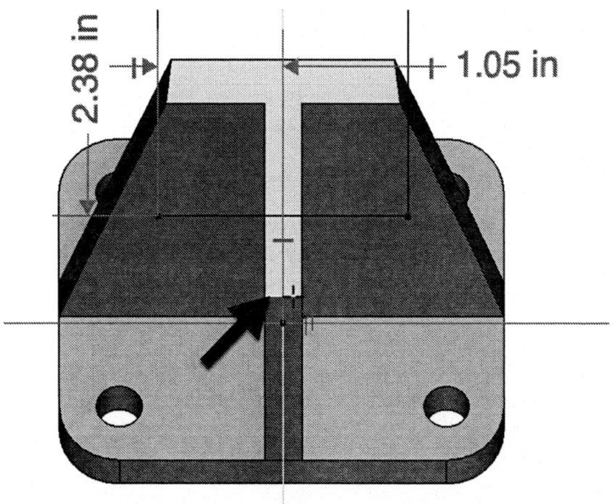

7. On the **Constraints** toolbar, click the **Coincident Constraint** icon.
8. Select the endpoint of the external geometry and the horizontal line, as shown.

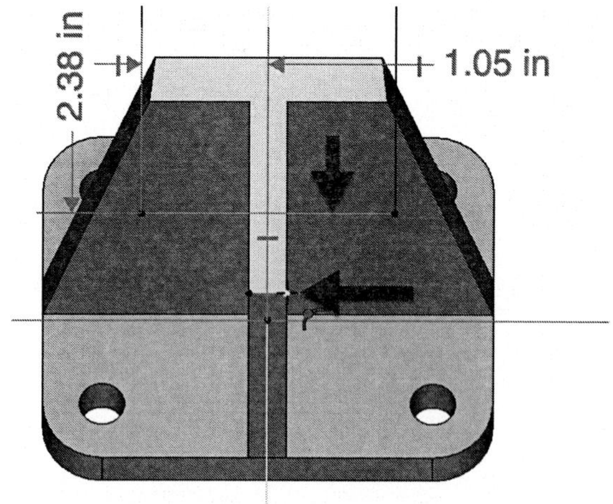

9. Click **Close** on the **Tasks** panel.
10. On the **Part Design Modeling Features** toolbar, click the **Pad** icon.
11. Type **0.31** in the **Length** box of the **Pad Parameters** dialog.
12. Click **OK**.

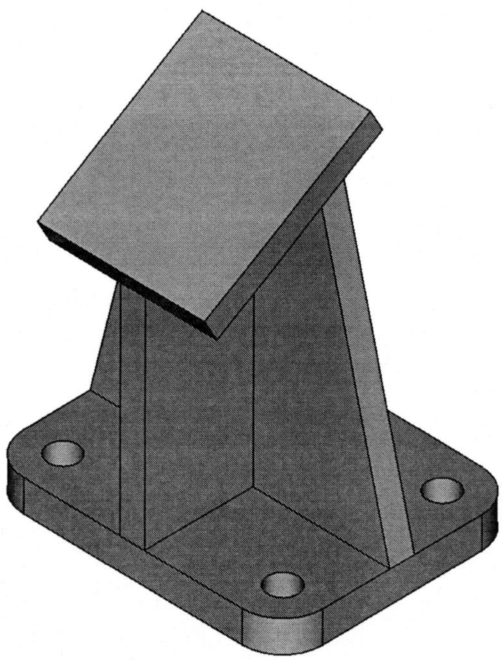

13. Add fillets of 0.31 in radius, as shown.

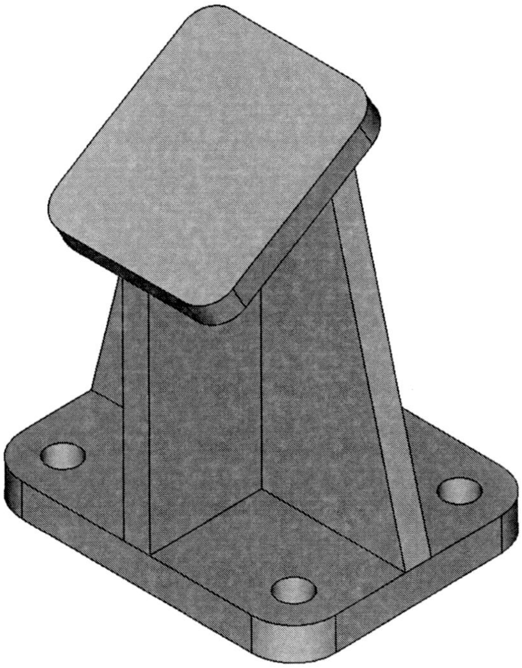

14. Click on the inclined face, as shown.

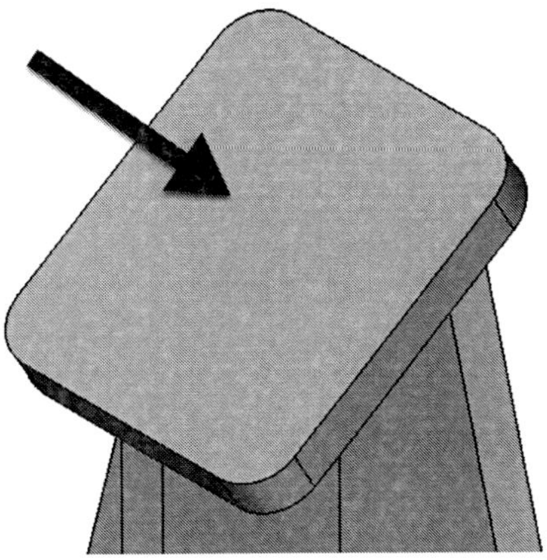

15. Click the **Hole** icon on the **Part Design Modeling Features** toolbar.
16. Type **0.31** in the **Diameter** box.
17. Select **Depth type > Dimension**.
18. Type **0.31** in the **Depth** box.
19. Click **OK** on the **Tasks** panel; the holes are created.

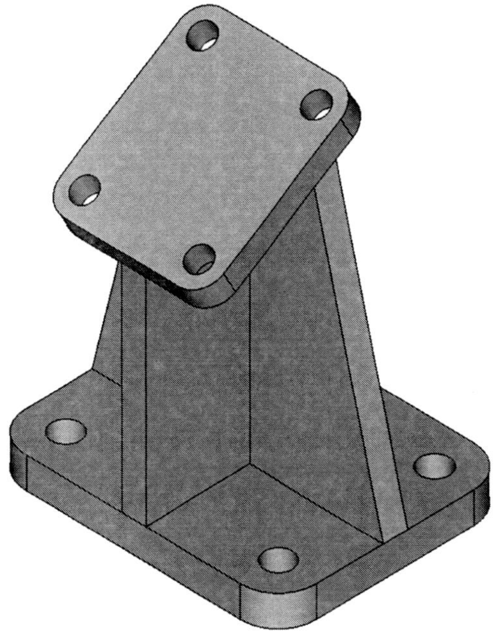

20. Click on the vertical face, as shown.

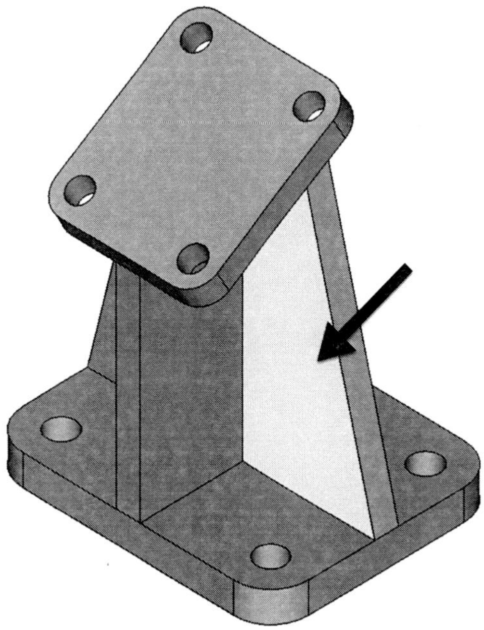

21. On the **Part Design Helper Features** toolbar, click the **New Sketch** icon.
22. Create two circles and add dimensions to it, as shown.

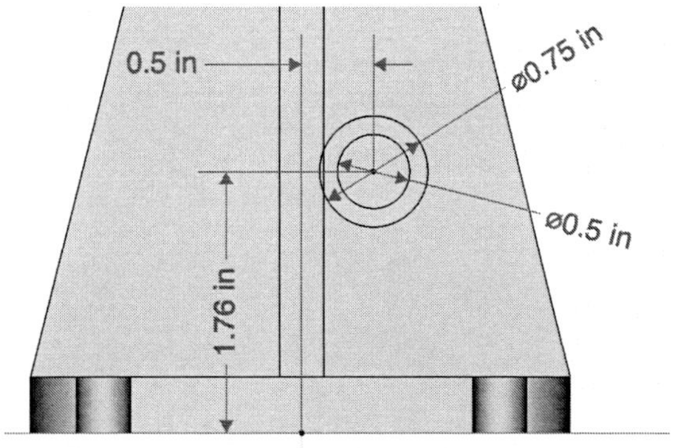

23. Click **Close** on the **Tasks** panel.
24. On the **Part Design Modeling Features** toolbar, click the **Pad** icon.
25. Select **Type > Two sided.**
26. Type **0.59** in the **Length** box under the **Side 1** section of the **Pad Parameters** dialog.
27. Type **0.79** in the **Length** box under the **Side 2** section and click **OK**.

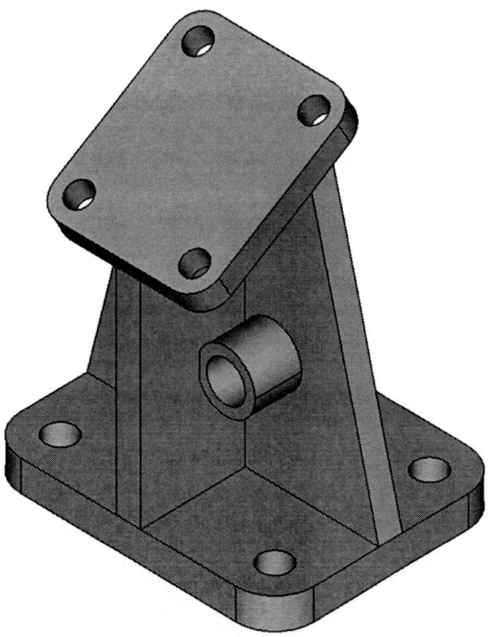

Creating the Pocket Feature

1. Click on the vertical face, as shown.

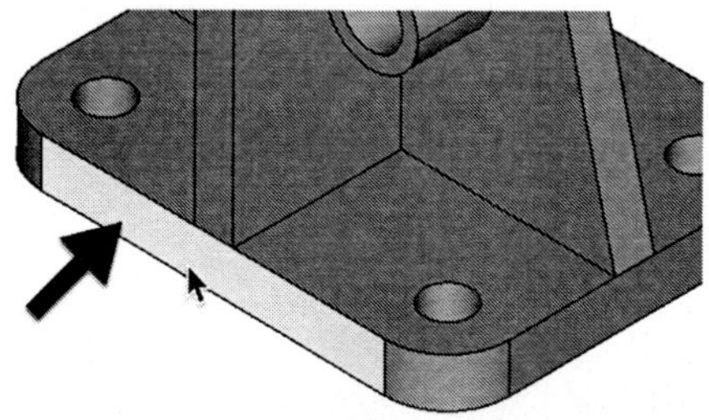

2. On the **Part Design Helper Features** toolbar, click the **New Sketch** icon.
3. Create a rectangle and add dimensions to it.

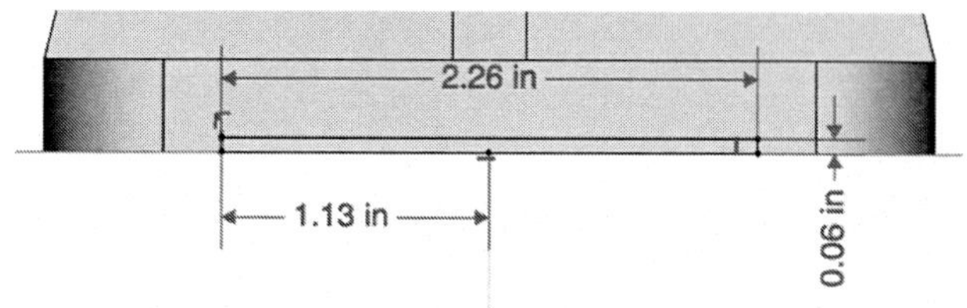

4. Click **Close** on the **Tasks** panel.
5. On the **Part Design Modeling Features** toolbar, click the **Pocket** icon.
6. Select **Type > Through all.**
7. Click **OK**.

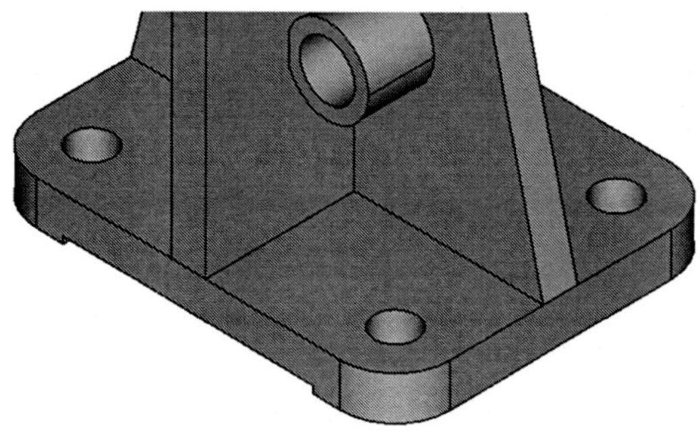

8. Save and close the file.

TUTORIAL 12

In this tutorial, you will create a spreadsheet and use the data in the spreadsheet to control the model.

1. Start a new file and select the **Part Design** option from the **Workbenches** drop-down.
2. On the Menu bar, click **Edit > Preferences.**
3. Click the **General** tab on the **Preferences** dialog.
4. Select **Default unit system > Standard (mm, kg, s degree).**
5. Type **2** in the **Number of decimals** box.
6. Click **Apply** and **OK**.
7. Activate the **New Sketch** command and select

the XY plane. Next, click **OK**,

8. Select the **Circle From Center** tool from the **Geometries** toolbar.
9. Click exactly on the central origin point (where the red and green axes cross) to place the center, then drag outward and click to set the size.
10. Click on the red horizontal axis to the right of the first circle to place its center, then drag outward to set the size.
11. Ensure the left circle's center is locked to the origin. If it isn't, select both points and click the **Coincident Constraint** tool.
12. Ensure the right circle's center stays on the horizontal line. Select the right circle's center point and the red horizontal axis, then click the **Coincident Constraint** tool.
13. Select the **Line** tool on the **Geometries** toolbar.
14. Draw a line roughly above the circles, from left to right. Draw a second line roughly below the circles, from left to right. Don't worry about connecting them perfectly yet.
15. Select the top line and the left circle, then click the **Tangent/Collinear Constraint** tool.
16. Repeat this tangency constraint between the top line and the right circle, the bottom line and the left circle, and the bottom line and the right circle. The lines will automatically snap flush to the outside of both circles.

Your sketch now looks like a belt wrapping around two full pulleys. You need to cut the inner paths to match your image.

17. Select the **Trim an edge** tool (the icon looks like a pair of scissors).
18. Click the inner right half of the large left circle (the part facing the small circle). It will disappear, leaving only the outer arc.
19. Click the inner left half of the small right circle. It will also disappear.

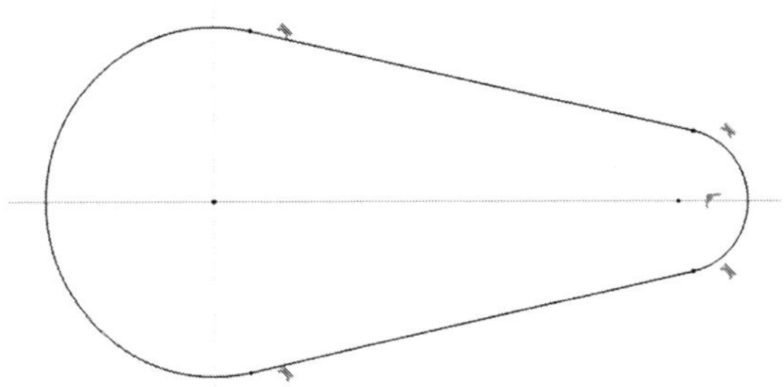

20. Click **Sketch > Constraints > Radius Dimension**  on the menu bar.
21. Select the large arc.
22. Type **30** and press ENTER.
23. Select the small arc.
24. Type **15** and press ENTER.
25. Click the **Horizontal Dimension** icon on the **Constraints** toolbar.
26. Select the sketch origin and the center point of the small arc.
27. Type **60** and press ENTER.

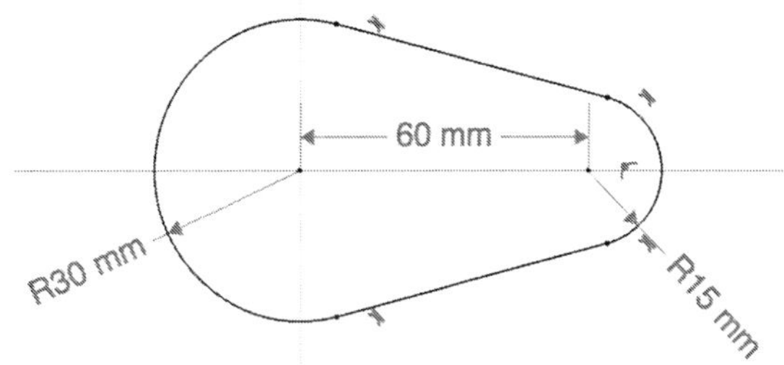

28. Click **Close** on the **Tasks** panel.
29. On the menu bar, click **Part Design > Additive features > Pad**.
30. On the **Pad Parameters** section, type **15** in the **Length** box, and then click **OK**.

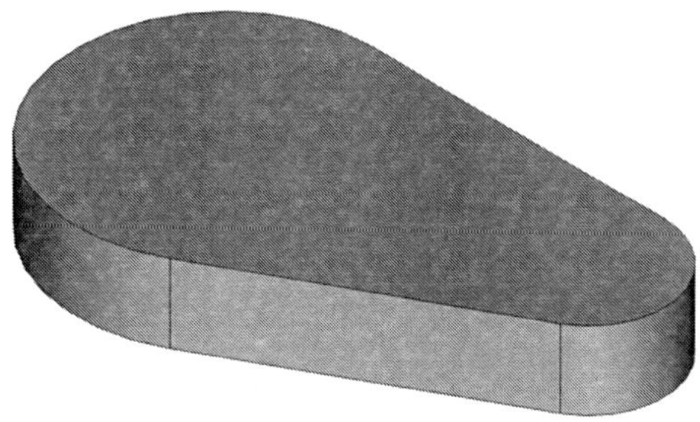

31. Press and hold the CTRL key and select the top and bottom faces of the model.
32. Click the **Thickness**  icon on the **Part Design Dressup Features** toolbar.
33. Type **5** in the **Thickness** box. The value entered here will determine the thickness of the resulting hollow shape.
34. Check the **Make thickness inwards** option and click **OK**. By enabling this option, the thickness will be added to the inside of the object, creating a hollow shape. If this option is not checked, the thickness will be added to the outside of the object, resulting in a larger solid shape.

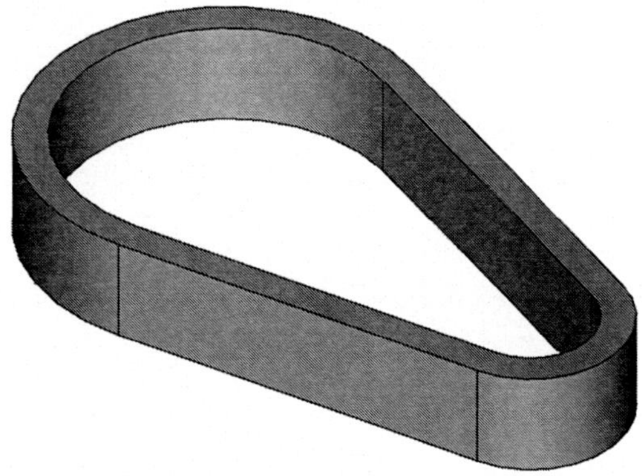

35. Select the **Spreadsheet** option from the **Workbenches** drop-down (or) click **View > Workbench > Spreadsheet** on the menu bar.

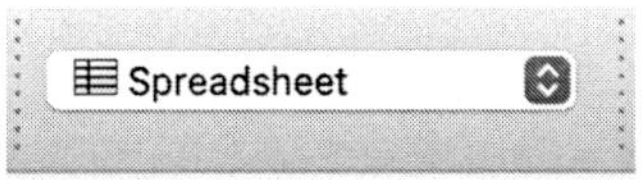

36. Click the **New spreadsheet** icon on the **Spreadsheet** toolbar (or) click the **Spreadsheet > New Spreadsheet** on the menu bar.
37. Click the **Model** panel and double-click on the newly created spreadsheet.

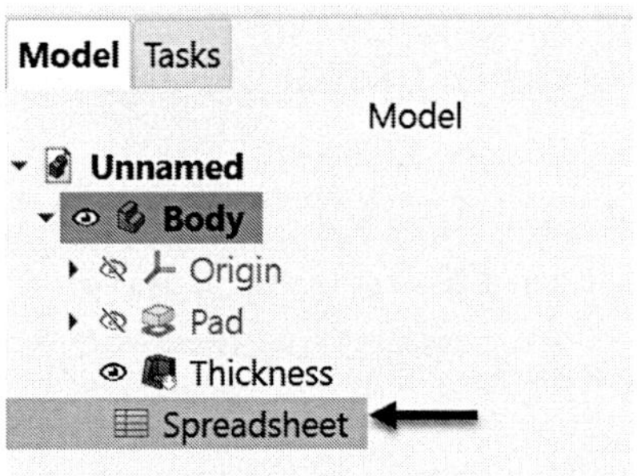

A spreadsheet is displayed in the window.

38. Double-click in the **A1** cell of the spreadsheet and type **Large Radius.**

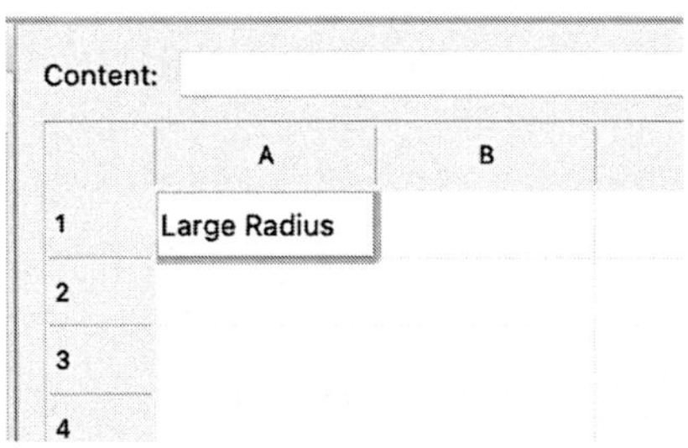

39. Likewise, enter **Small Radius, Horizontal Length**, **Pad Length**, and **Thickness** in the **A2**, **A3**, **A4**, and **A5** cells, respectively.

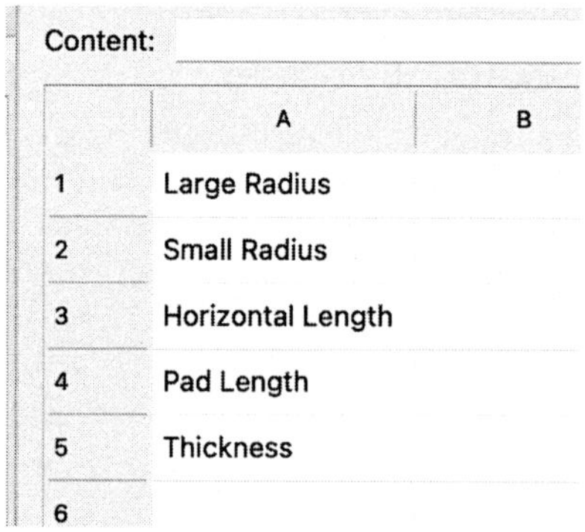

40. Double-click in the **B1** cell and type **30.**

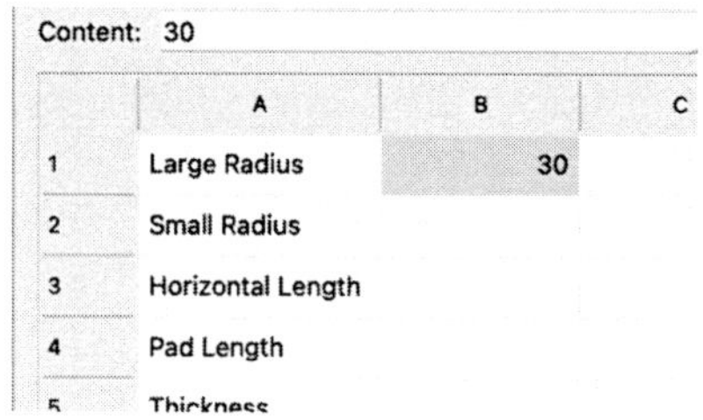

41. Click in the **Alias** box displayed at the top right corner of the spreadsheet and type **Large_radius**. Next, press ENTER.

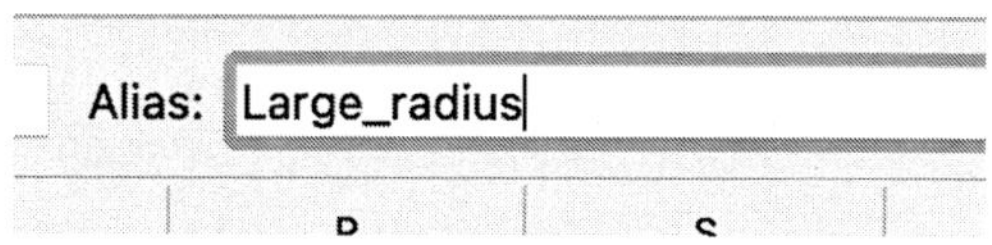

42. Likewise, enter 15, 60, 15, and 5 in the B2, B3, B4, and B5 cells respectively.

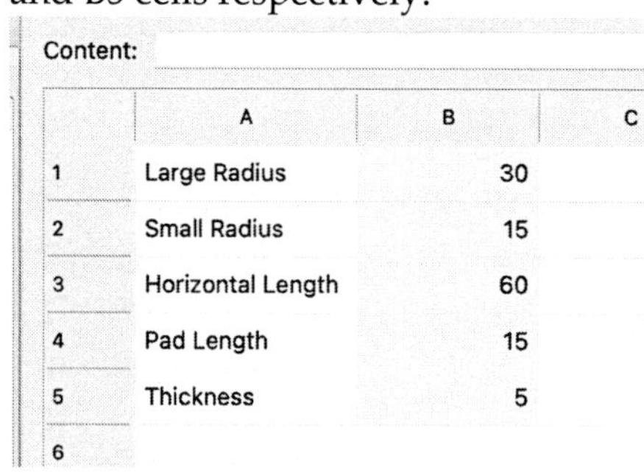

43. Enter **Small_radius, Horizontal_length, Pad_length**, and **Thickness** as the **Aliases** of **B2, B3, B4**, and **B5** cells respectively.
44. Click the **Model** panel and expand the **Pad** feature.
45. Right-click on the **Sketch**, and then select **Edit Sketch.**

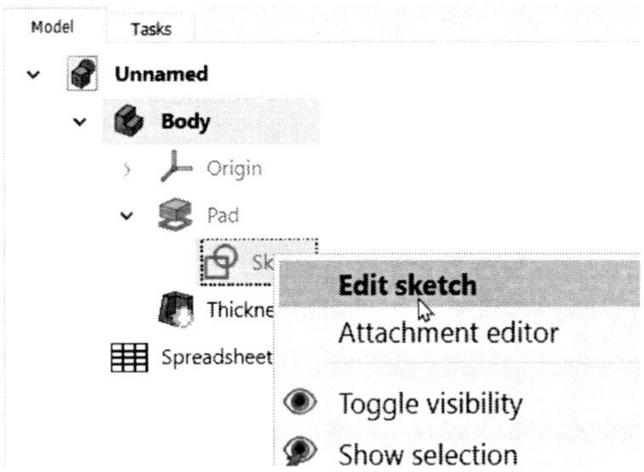

46. Double-click on the 30 mm radius dimension.
47. Click the **Enter expression** icon located in the **Radius** box on the **Insert Radius** dialog.

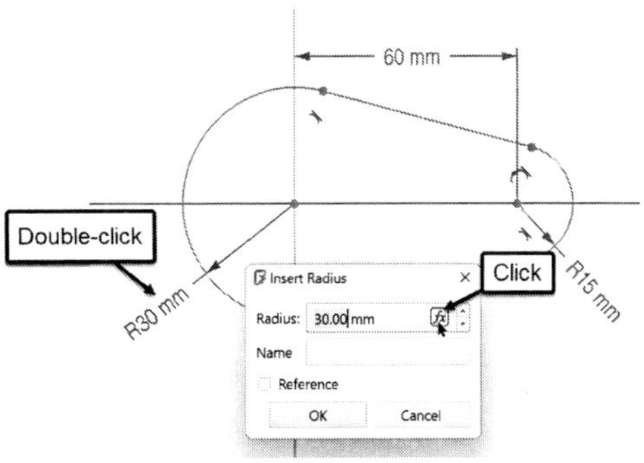

48. On the **Expression editor** dialog, type Spreadsheet, and then select the **Spreadsheet** option.

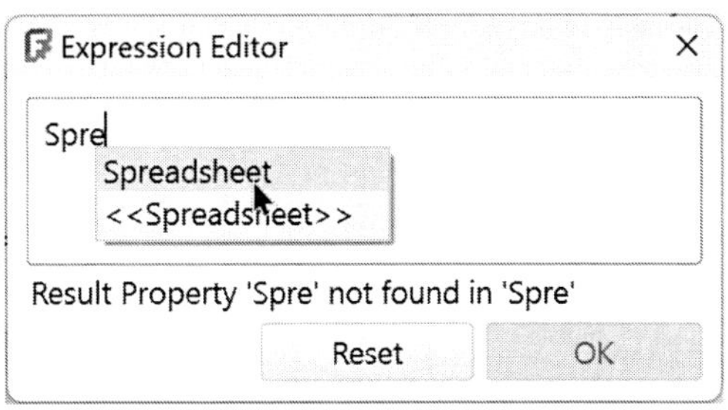

49. Click next to the Spreadsheet. value and type La. Next, select the **Large_radius** value from the listed value.

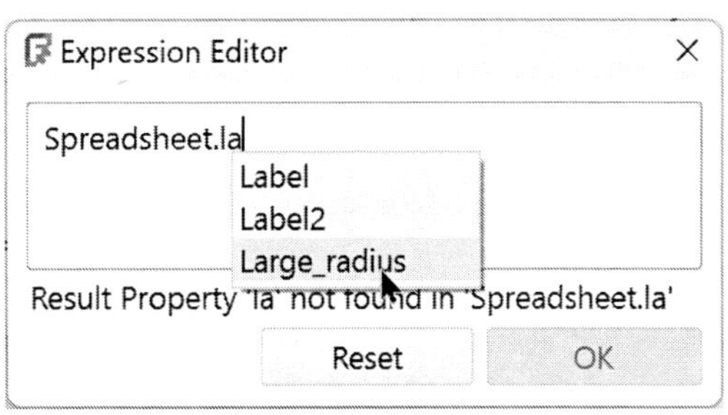

50. Click **OK** on the **Expression editor** dialog.

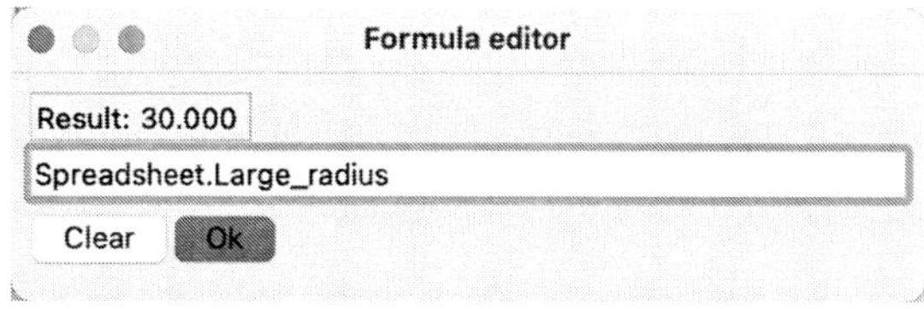

51. Click **OK** on the **Insert Radius** dialog.
52. Double-click on the 15 mm radius value, and then click the **Enter expression** button in the **Radius** box.

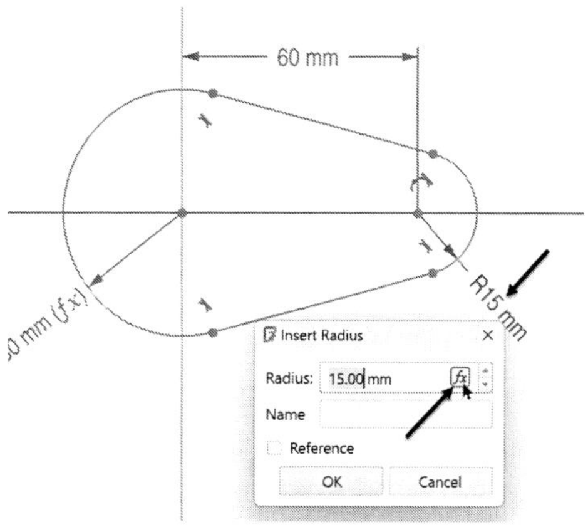

53. Type **Spreadsheet.Small_radius** in the **Expression editor** dialog. Next, click **OK** twice.

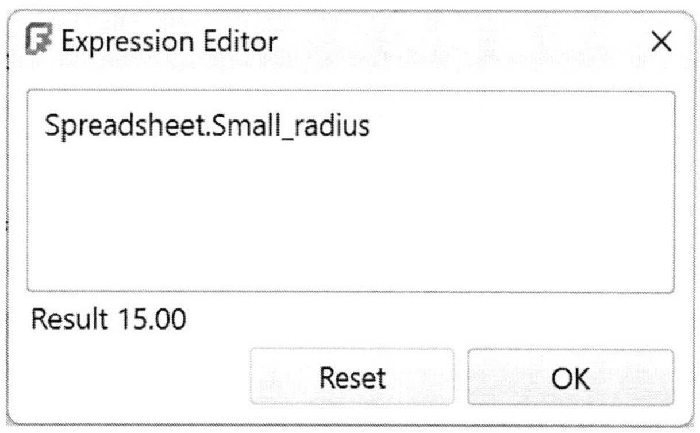

54. Likewise, change the 60 mm dimension value to **Spreadsheet.Horizontal_length** formula using the **Expression editor** dialog.

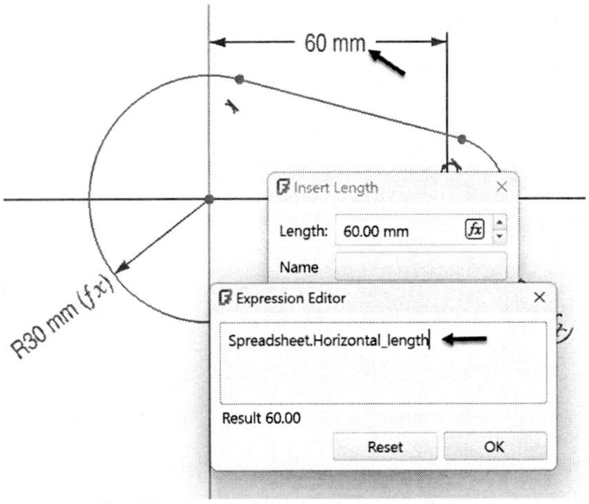

55. Click **Close** on the **Tasks** panel.
56. On the **Model** panel, right-click on the **Pad** feature, and then select **Edit Pad.**
57. Click the **Enter an expression** button in the **Length** box.

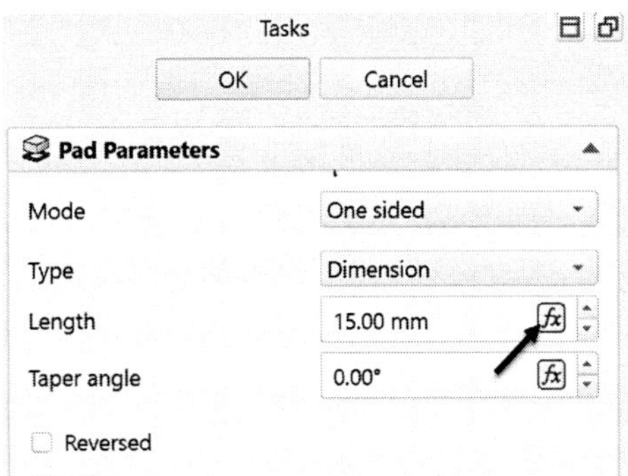

58. Type **Spreadsheet.Pad_length** in the **Expression editor** dialog. Next, click **OK.**

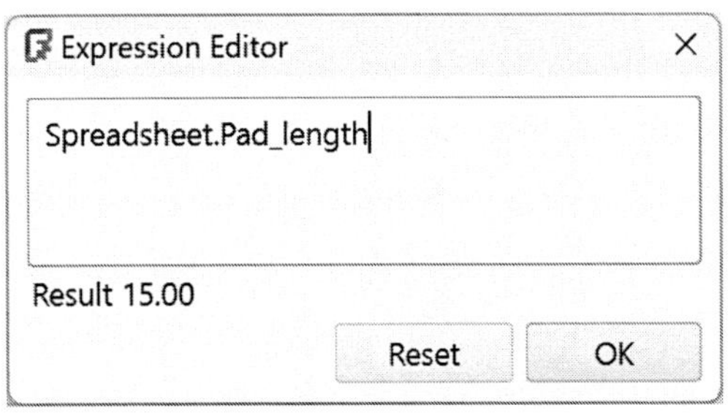

59. Click **OK** on the **Tasks** panel.
60. On the **Model** panel, right-click on the **Thickness** feature, and then select **Edit thickness.**
61. Click the **Enter an expression** fx button in the **Thickness** box.
62. Type **Spreadsheet.Thickness** in the **Expression editor** dialog. Next, click **OK.**
63. Click **OK** on the **Tasks** panel.
64. Double-click on the Spreadsheet feature in the **Model** panel to open the spreadsheet.
65. Click in the B1 cell and change the value to 40.

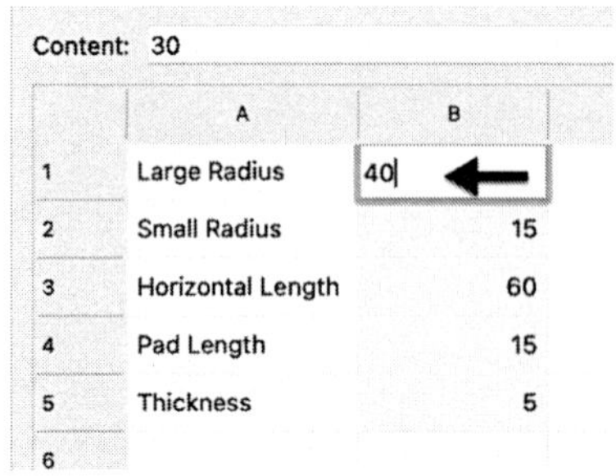

66. Switch to the model window and notice that the model is updated, as shown.

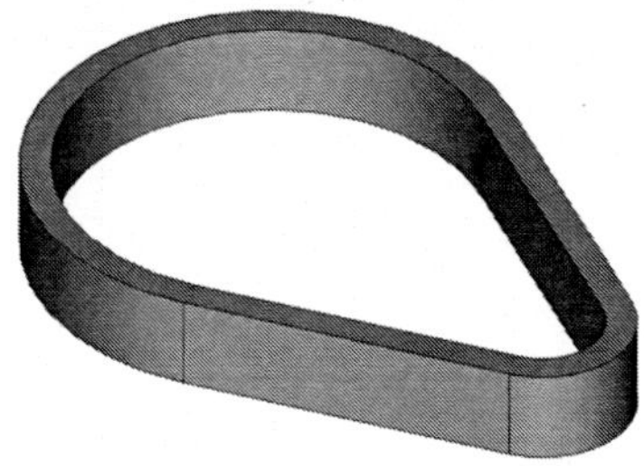

67. Likewise, change the other values in the spreadsheet and notice the updated model.

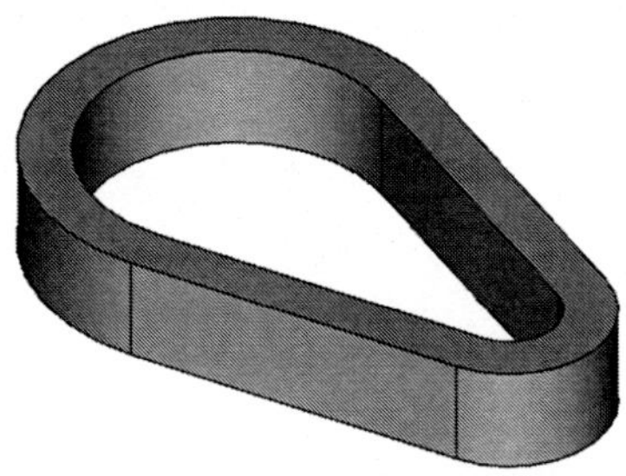

68. Save and close the part file.

TUTORIAL 13

In this tutorial, you will create expressions to drive the parameters of a bolt.

1. Start a new FreeCAD file and activate the Part Design workbench.
2. On the **Part Design Modeling Features** toolbar, click **Additive Primitives** drop-down > **Additive Cylinder.**

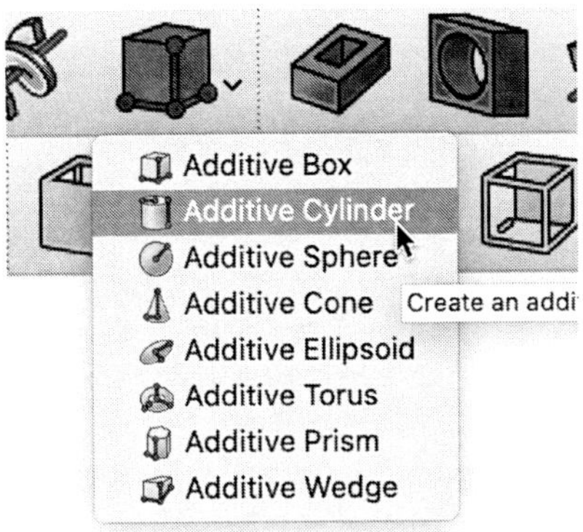

3. Select the YZ_Plane from the graphics window.

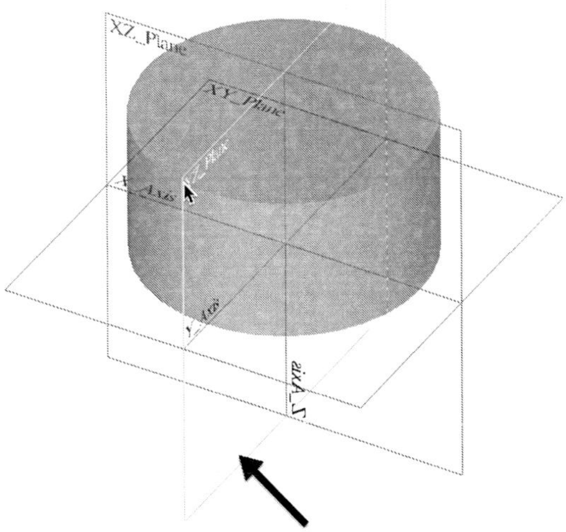

4. Type **10** and **80** in the **Radius** and **Height** boxes, respectively.

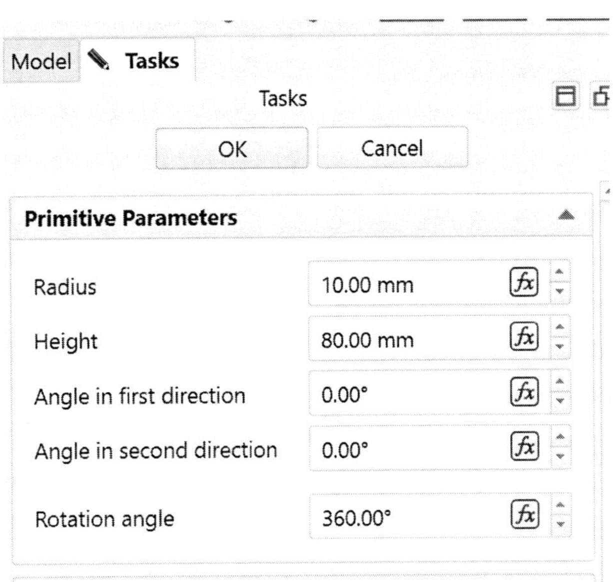

5. Click **OK** to create a cylinder.

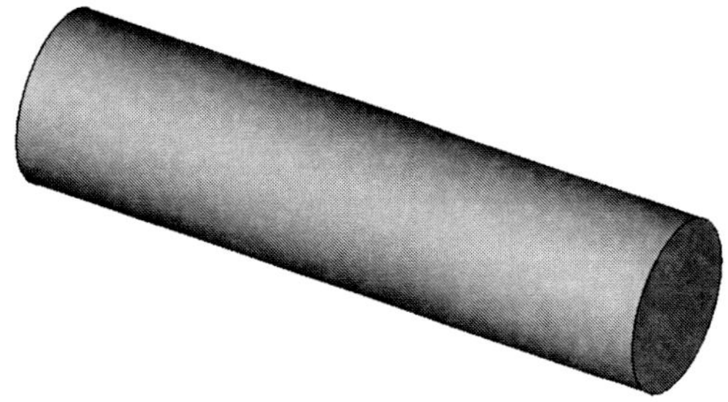

6. Select the right end face of the cylinder.
7. Click the **New Sketch** icon on the **Part Design Helper Features** toolbar.

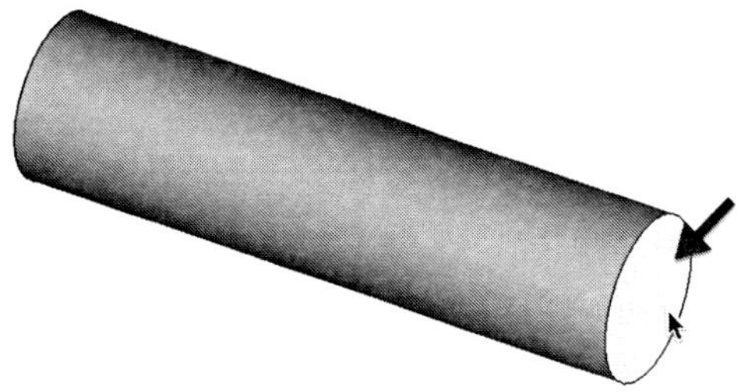

8. Create a hexagon, as shown.
9. Create a dimension between the sketch origin and the right vertex of the hexagon by selecting them.

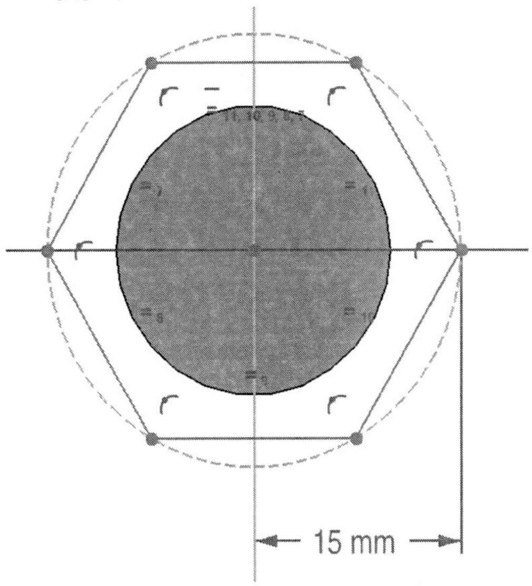

10. Click **Close** on the **Tasks** panel.
11. Click the **Pad** icon on the **Part Design Modeling Features** toolbar.
12. Type **10** in the **Length** box and click **OK**.

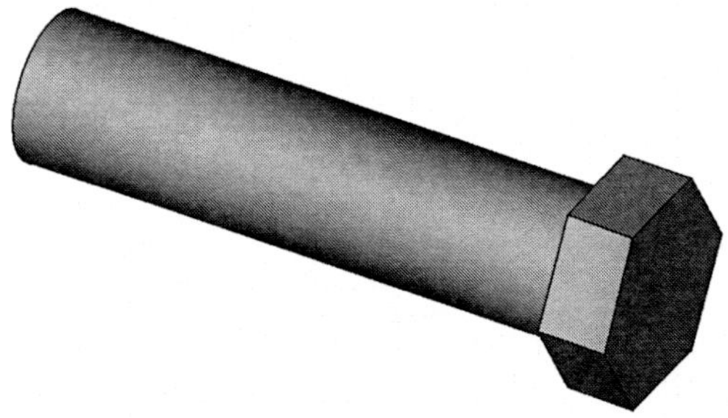

Creating the Spreadsheet

1. Select the **Spreadsheet** option from the **Workbenches** drop-down (or) click **View > Workbench > Spreadsheet** on the menu bar.

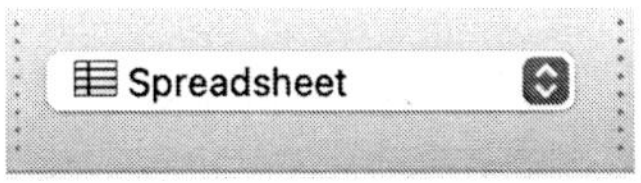

2. Click the **New spreadsheet** icon on the **Spreadsheet** toolbar (or) click the **Spreadsheet > Create Spreadsheet** on the menu bar.
3. Click the **Model** panel and double-click on the newly created spreadsheet.
4. Type-in the values in the **B** and **C** columns in the spreadsheet.
5. Specify the **Aliases** for the values in the **B** and **C** columns, as shown.

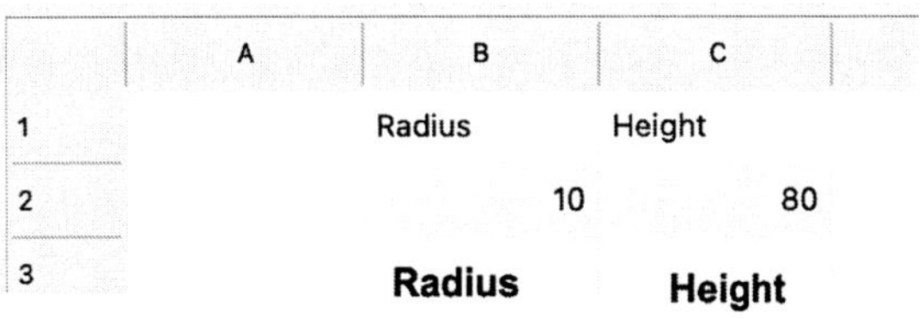

13. On the **Model** panel, click the **Cylinder** feature.
14. Click the **Data** tab at the bottom.
15. Scroll to the **Cylinder** section on the **Data** tab.
16. Click in the **Radius** box and click the **Enter Expression** icon.

17. Type **Spreadsheet.Radius** in the **Expression editor** dialog and click **OK**.

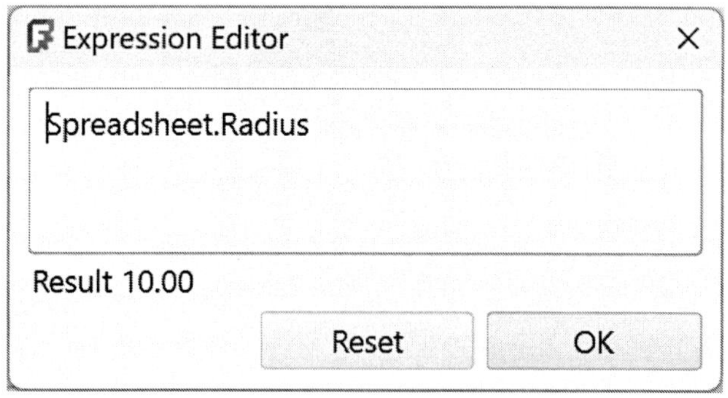

18. Likewise, change the **Height** value to **Spreadsheet.Height**.

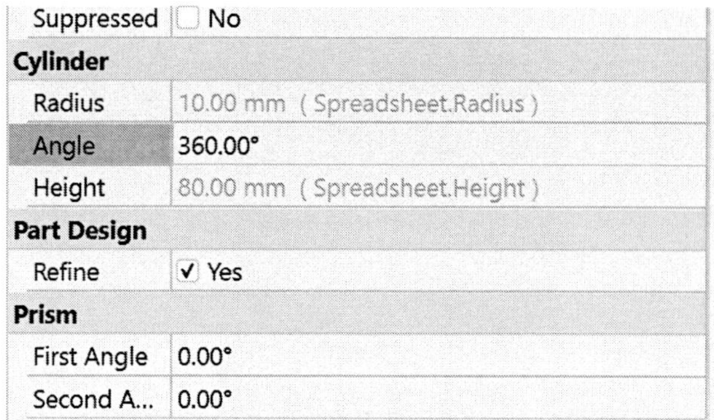

19. Click the **Model** panel and expand the **Pad** feature.
20. Right-click on the **Sketch**, and then select **Edit Sketch**.

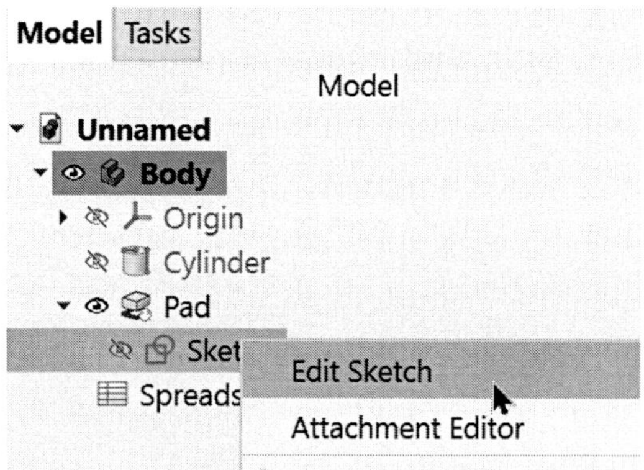

21. Double-click on the 15 mm dimension.
22. Click the **Enter expression** icon located in the **Length** box on the **Insert Length** dialog.
23. On the **Expression editor** dialog, type **2*Spreadsheet.Radius**, and then click **OK**.

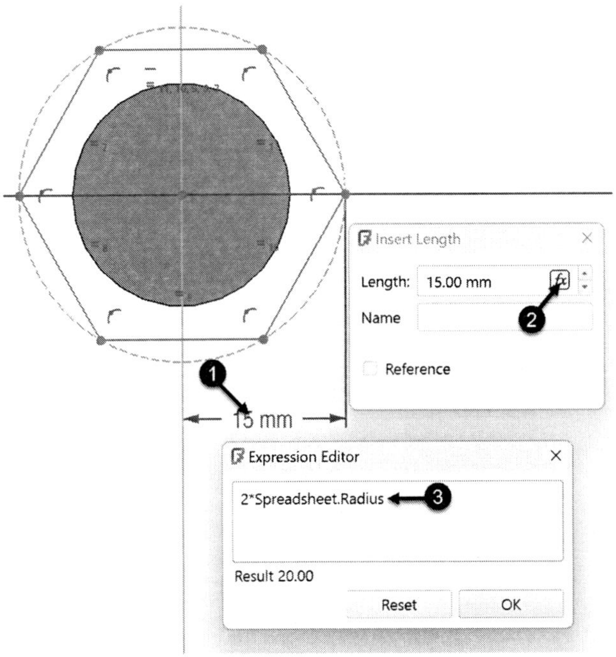

24. Click **OK** on the **Insert Length** dialog.
25. Click **Close** on the **Tasks** panel.
26. On the **Model** panel, click the **Pad** feature.
27. Click the **Data** tab at the bottom.
28. Scroll to the **Side 1** section on the **Data** tab.
29. Click in the **Length** box.
30. Click the **Enter expression**.
31. Type **1.5*Spreadsheet.Radius** in the **Expression editor** dialog.
32. Click **OK**.

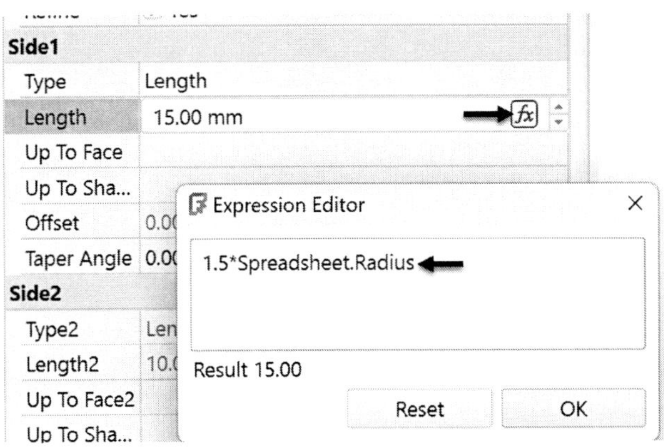

33. Switch to the model window and notice that the model is updated.

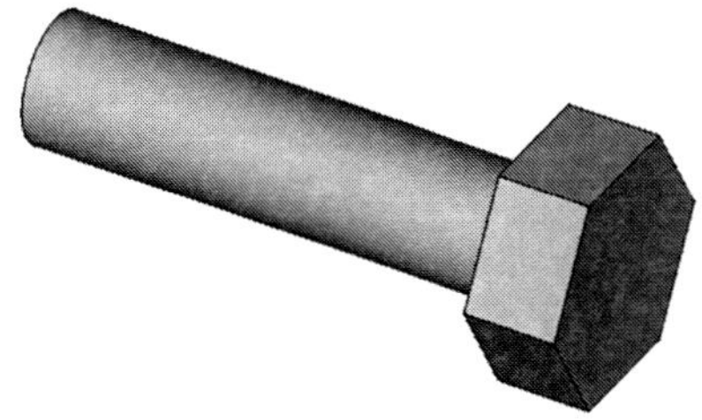

Creating Configuration Table

1. Double-click on the **Spreadsheet** in the **Model** panel.

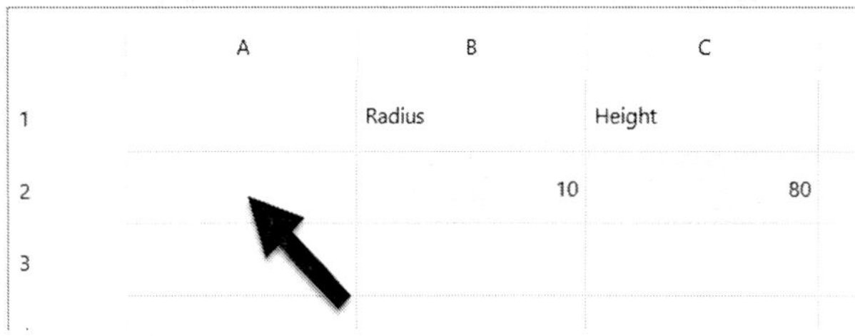

2. Enter **10x80**, **20x60** and **6x20** in the **A3**, **A4**, and **A5** cells.
3. Enter **10**, **20** and **6** in the **B3**, **B4**, and **B5** cells, respectively.
4. Enter **80, 60** and **20** in the **C3, C4**, and **C5** cells, respectively.

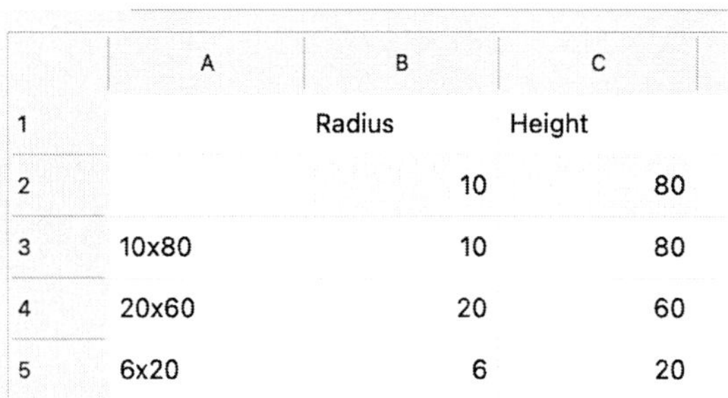

	A	B	C
1		Radius	Height
2		10	80
3	10x80	10	80
4	20x60	20	60
5	6x20	6	20

5. Click the right-mouse button in the **A2** cell and select **Configuration Table** from the shortcut menu.

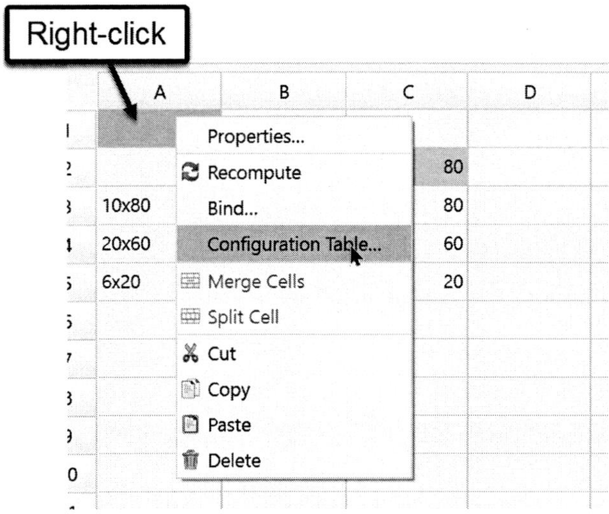

6. On the **Setup Configuration Table** dialog, type **Configuration** (or any name) in the **Property** box.
7. Type **A2** and **ZZ2** in the Cell range boxes, respectively.
8. Type **Parameters** (or any name) in the **Group** box and click **OK**.

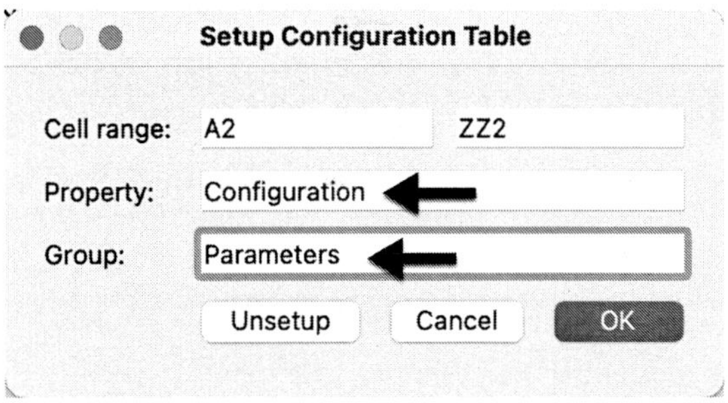

9. On the menu bar, click **Windows > Tile**.

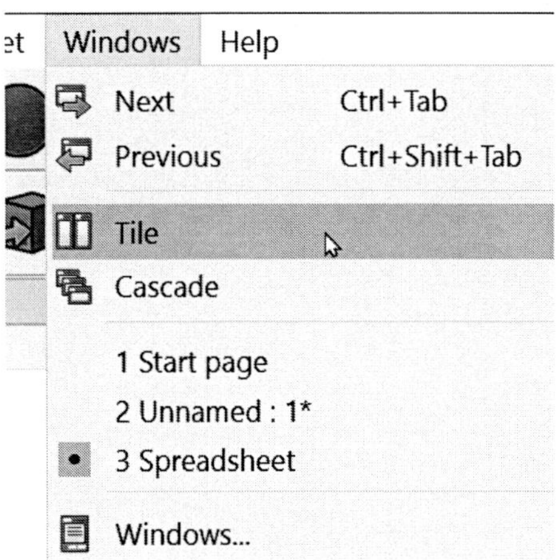

10. Click on the **Spreadsheet** in the **Model** panel.
11. Click the **Data** tab at the bottom.
12. Select **Configurations > 20x60.**

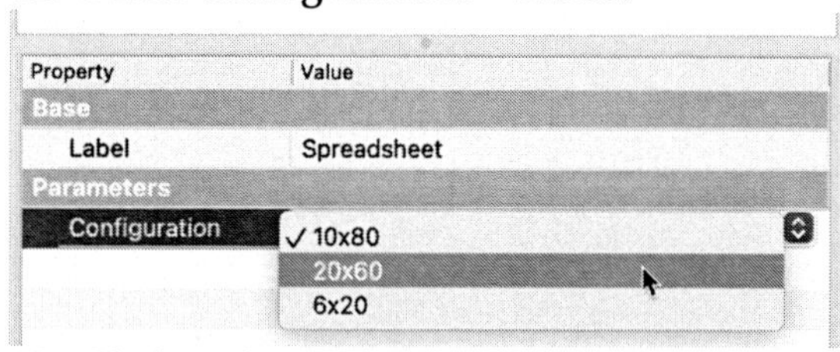

13. Click in the spreadsheet and notice that the model is updated, as shown.

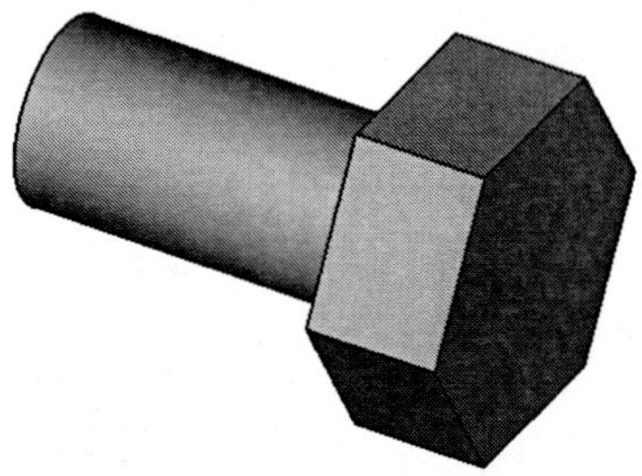

14. Select **Configuration > 6x20** and click in the spreadsheet. The model is updated, as shown.

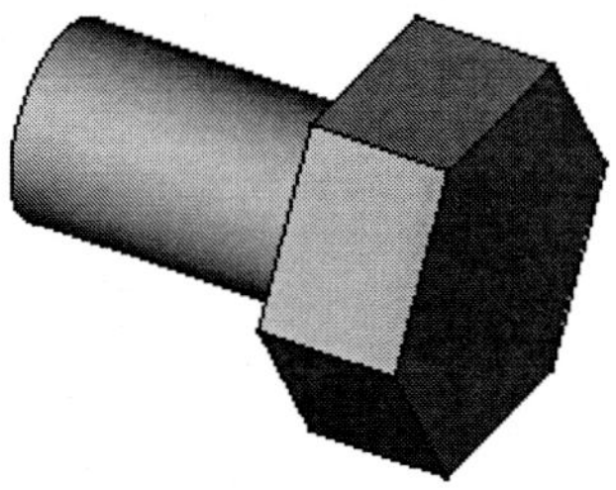

15. Add one more configuration to the table, as shown.

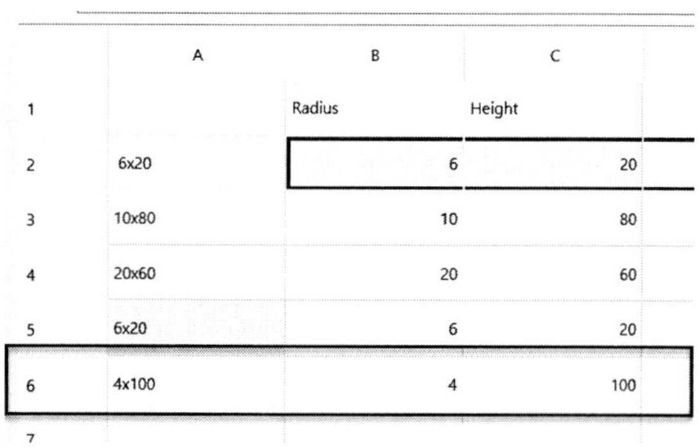

	A	B	C
1		Radius	Height
2	6x20	6	20
3	10x80	10	80
4	20x60	20	60
5	6x20	6	20
6	4x100	4	100
7			

16. Select **Configuration > 4x100** and click in the spreadsheet.

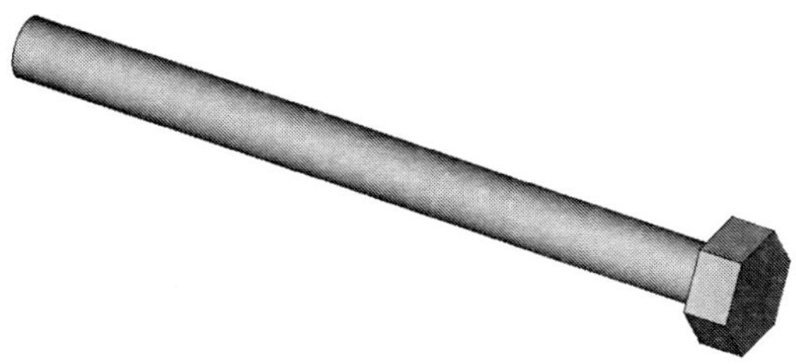

17. Save and close the part file.

Chapter 6: Creating Drawings

In this chapter, you generate 2D drawings of the parts. You learn to:

- Insert standard views of a part model
- Add dimensions

TUTORIAL 1

In this tutorial, you create the drawing of the Tutorial 7 file created in the fourth chapter.

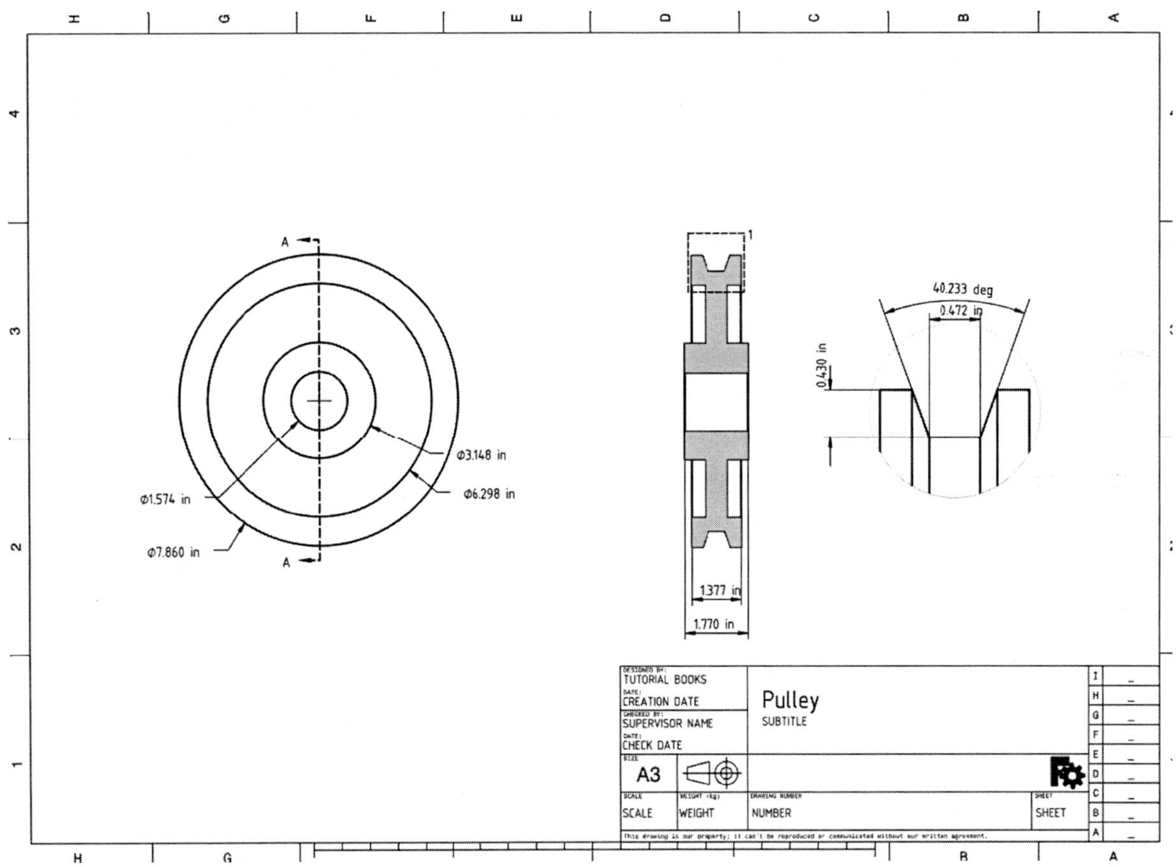

Starting a New Drawing File

1. Click **File > Open** on the Menu bar.
2. Go to the location of the Tutorial 7 file of Chapter 5.
3. Select the Tutorial 7 file and click the **Open** button.
4. Click **Edit > Preferences** on the Menu bar.

   The **Preferences** dialog box appears. If you are working on MacOS, then click **FreeCAD > Preferences** on the title bar.
5. On the **Preferences** dialog box, click the **TechDraw > Dimensions** at the left side.
6. Select **Standard and Style > ASME Referencing**.
7. Click **General > General** at the left side.

8. Select **Default unit system > Imperial decimal (in, lb)**.
9. Check the **Ignore Project unit system and use default** option.
10. Click **OK**.
11. Select **TechDraw** from the **Workbenches** drop-down.
12. Click the **New Page from template**  icon on the **TechDraw Pages** toolbar.
13. Go to the location: *C:\Program Files\FreeCAD 1.1\data\Mod\TechDraw\Templates\ISO*
14. Select the **A3_LandscapeTD** template.
15. Click **Open**.
16. In the **Model** panel, select the **Page**.
17. Click the **Data** tab on the bottom.
18. In the **Properties** section of the **Model** panel, select **Projection Type > Third Angle**.

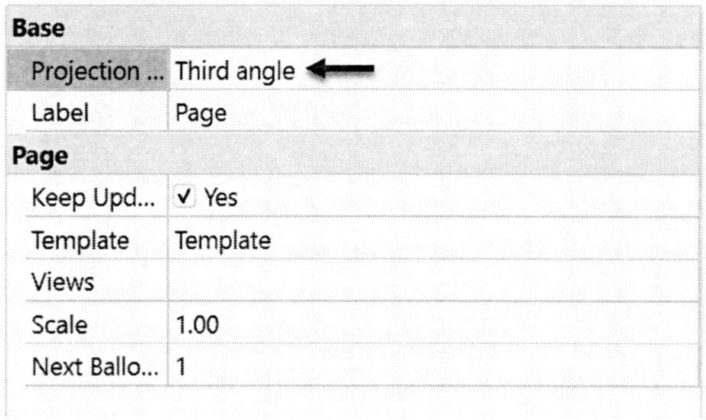

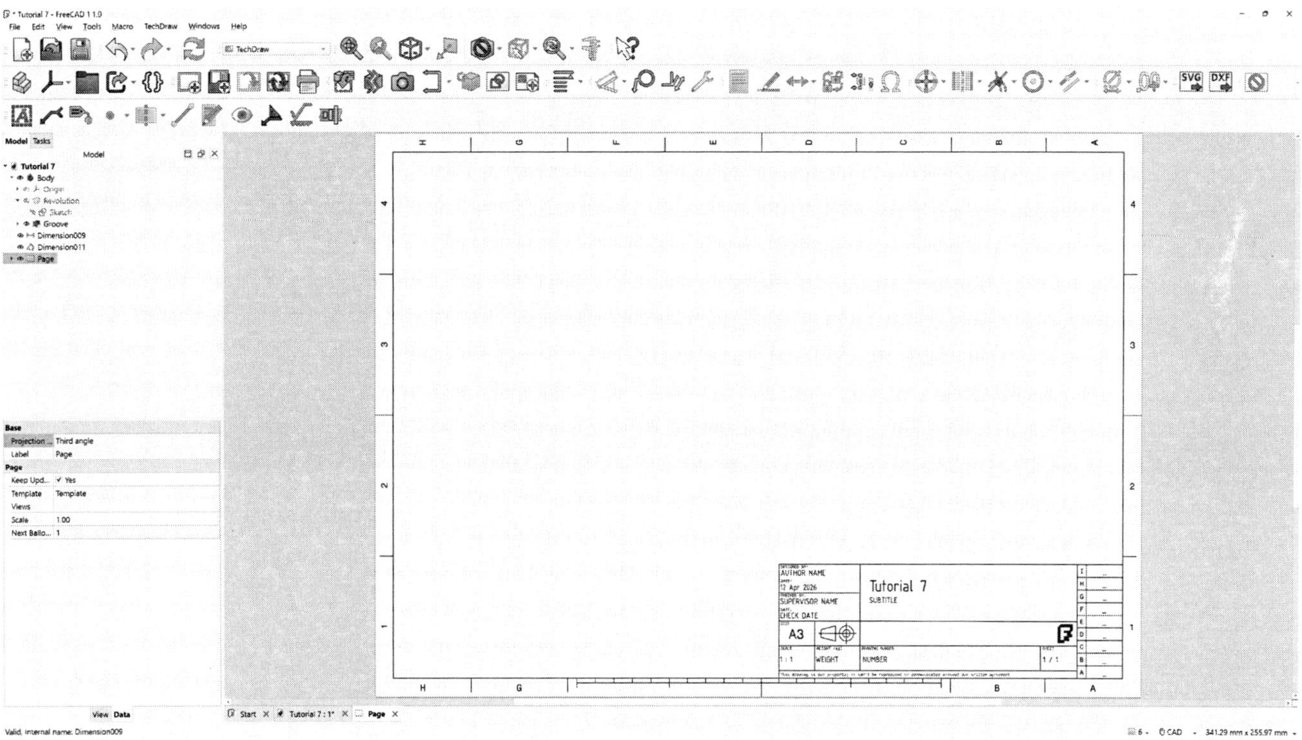

Generating the Base View

1. Click the **Tutorial 7** tab on the bottom of the window.

2. Select the front face of the model.

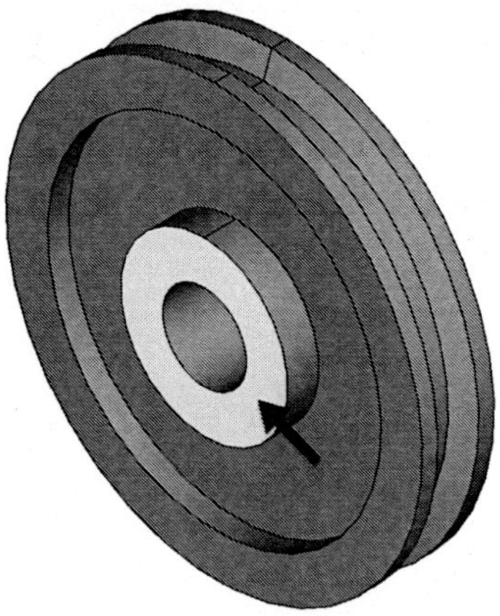

3. Click the **Page** tab on the bottom of the window.

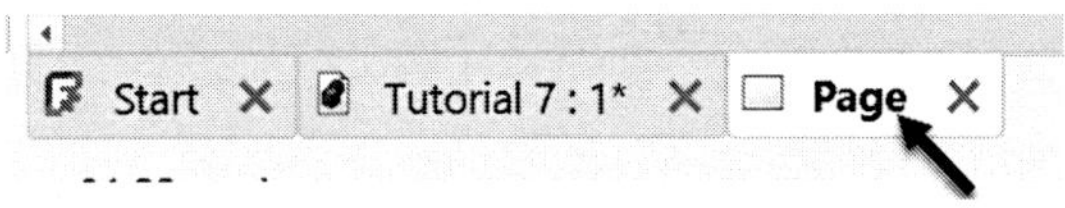

4. To generate the base view, click the **New View**  icon on the **TechDraw Views** toolbar.
5. On the **Projection Group** section, select **Scale > Custom**.
6. Type **1** and **2** in the **Scale Numerator** and **Scale Denominator** boxes located next to **Custom Scale**.
7. Click **OK** on the **Tasks** panel.
8. Click on the dotted borderline of the view.
9. Press and hold the left mouse and drag the view to left.

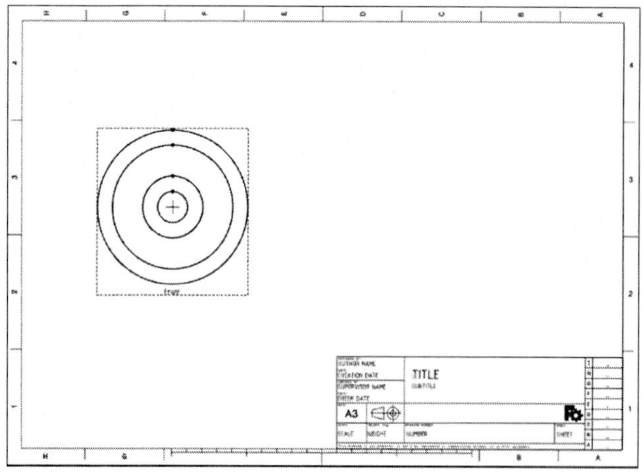

Generating the Section View

1. Select the base view.
2. Click the **Section view** drop-down > **Section View** on the **TechDraw Views** toolbar.

3. Click the **Preset view direction looking left** 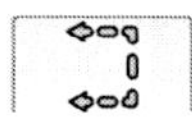 icon on the **Set View Direction** section.
4. Type **0** in the **X**, **Y**, and **Z** boxes, respectively. These values define the location of the section plane.
5. Type **A** in the **Identifier** box.
6. Click **OK** to create the section view.
7. Select the section view from the drawing page.
8. Click the **Position Section View**  icon on the **TechDraw Attributes** toolbar. The section view is horizontally in-line with the base view.

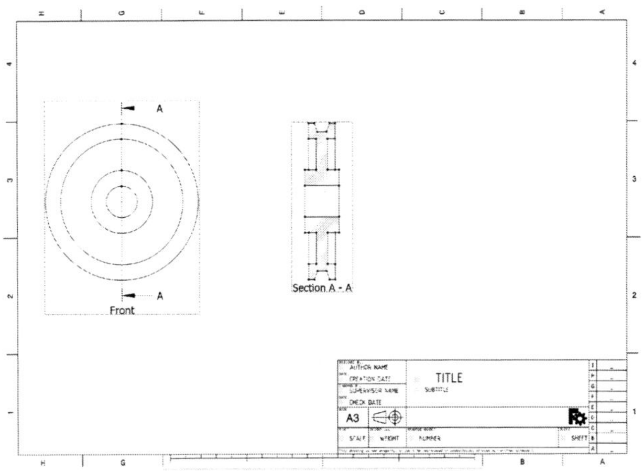

Tip

If the **Position Section View** command does not place the views correctly, align them manually through the **Data** tab. This method is useful for both horizontal placement and vertical placement.

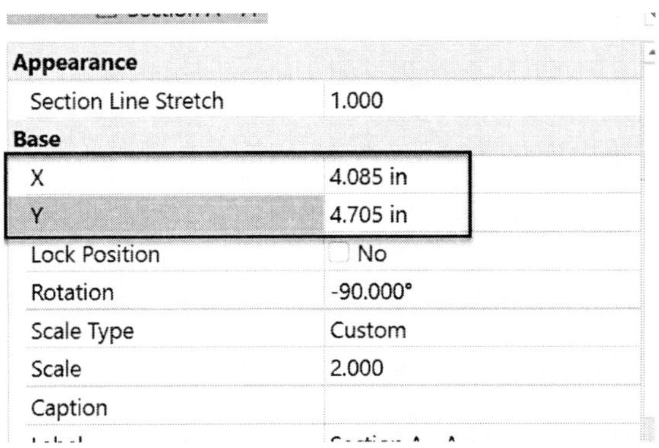

For **horizontal alignment**, when the section view is placed to the left or right of the parent view, select the parent view in the Tree view and note its **Y** value. Then select the section view and enter the same **Y** value. Both views will then lie on the same horizontal level.

For **vertical alignment**, when the section view is placed above or below the parent view, select the parent view and note its **X** value. Then select the section view and enter the same **X** value. Both views will then lie on the same vertical centerline. After editing the value, recompute the page if the view does not update immediately.

Creating the Detailed View

Now, you have to create the detailed view of the groove, which is displayed, in the section view.

1. Select the section view.
2. Click the **Insert detail view in drawing** icon on the **TechDraw Views** toolbar.
3. In the **New Detail Toggle Section View**, type **20** mm in the **Radius** box.
4. Type **1.5** in the **Scale** box. The detailed view is generated.
5. Drag the detailed view to the right side on the drawing sheet.

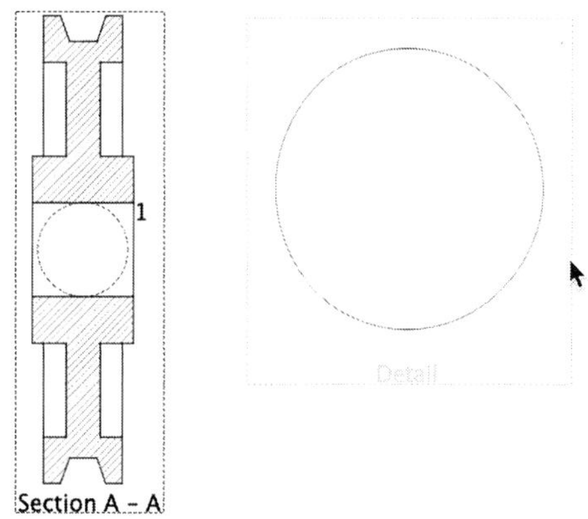

Now, you need to specify the portion of the section view to be displayed in the detailed view.

6. Click the **Drag Highlight** button on the **Tasks** panel.
7. Click on the drag text displayed next to the boundary of the detail view.
8. Drag it upward and place at the location, as shown.

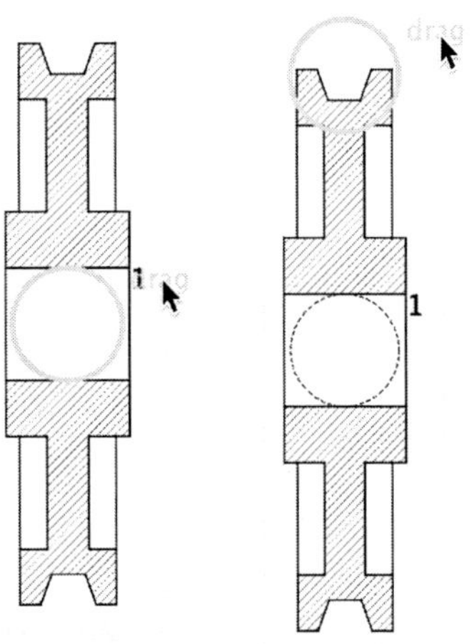

9. Click **OK**.

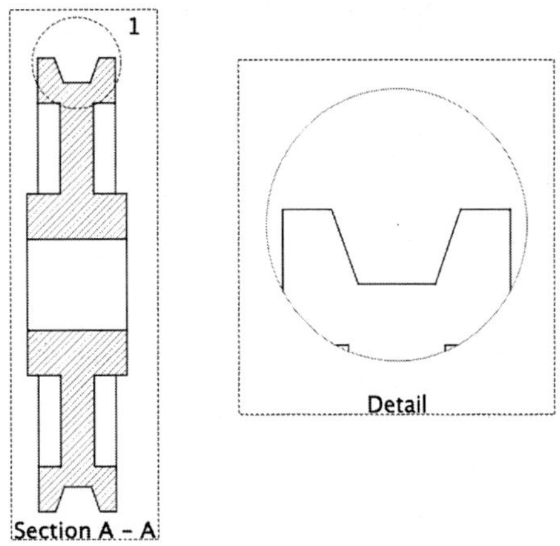

*Note: On the **Edit Preferences** dialog. Go to **TechDraw > General**. Next, navigate to the **Snapping** section and uncheck the **Snap detail highlights** option. This ensures the center point of the detail view boundary can be placed freely without automatically snapping to the vertices of the existing geometry. Next, click **Apply** and **OK**.*

Adding Dimensions

Now, you add dimensions to the drawing.

1. Select the outer circular edge of the base view.
2. Click the **Dimension** drop-down > **Diameter dimension**  icon on the **TechDraw Dimensions** toolbar.
3. Click and drag the dimension outside the view.

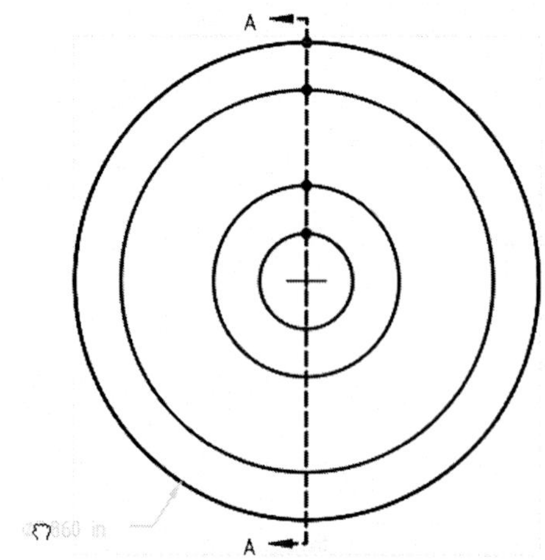

4. Likewise, add remaining dimensions to the base view, as shown.

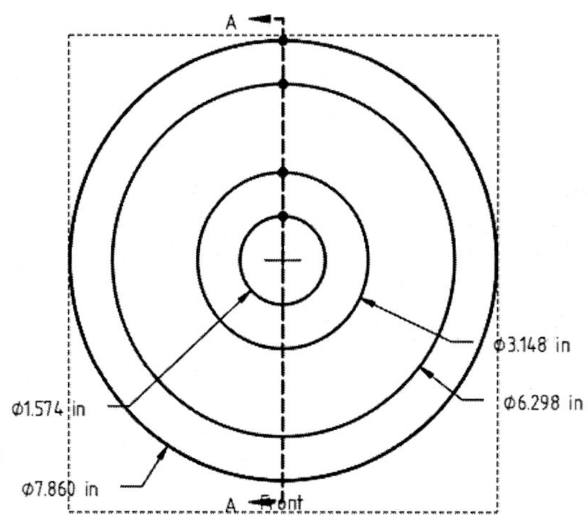

5. Press and hold the CTRL key and select the newly created diameter dimension and click the **View** tab on the **Model** panel.
6. On the **View** tab of the **Model** panel, under the **Dimension Format** section, select **Rendering Extent > Minimal**. The arrow on the other side of the dimension is removed.
7. Press and hold the Ctrl key and select the vertical edges of the section view, as shown.

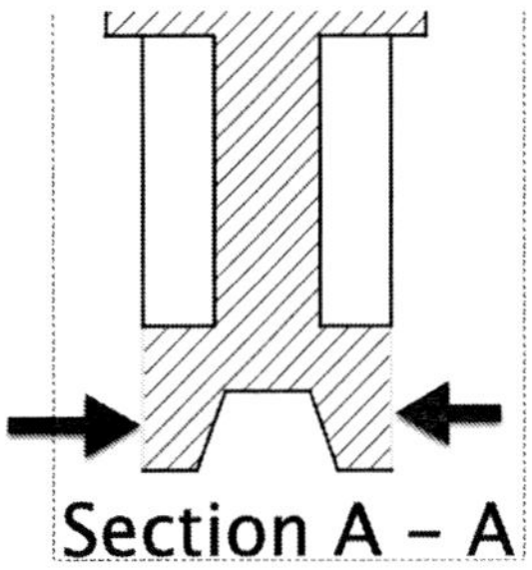

8. Click the **Insert Dimension > Horizontal Length Dimension** icon on the **TechDraw Dimensions** toolbar.
9. Click in the drawing page to deselect the selected edges.
10. Press and hold the Ctrl key and select the vertical edges of the section view, as shown.

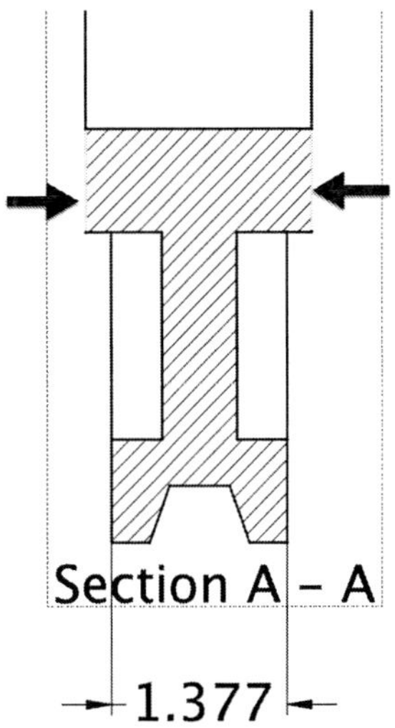

11. Click the **Insert Dimension > Horizontal Length dimension** icon on the **TechDraw Dimensions** toolbar.
12. Press and hold the CTRL key and select the two newly created dimensions.

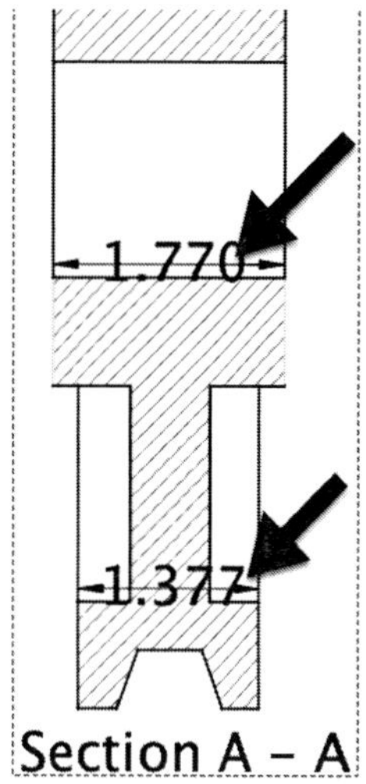

13. On the menu bar, click **TechDraw > Extensions: Attributes/Modifications > Cascade Horizontal Dimensions**. The selected dimensions are arranged.

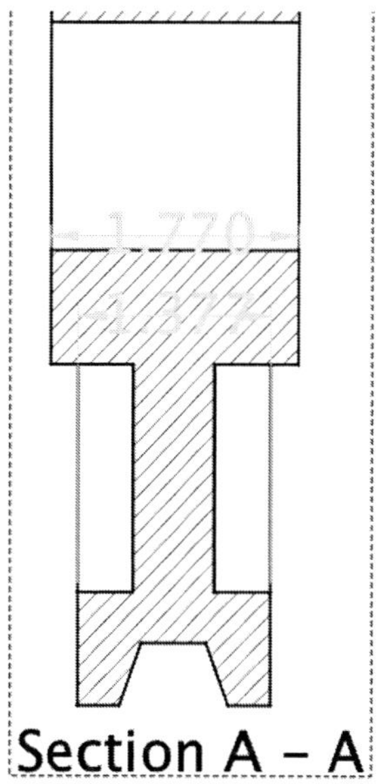

14. Drag the dimension values downward, and then toward right, as shown.

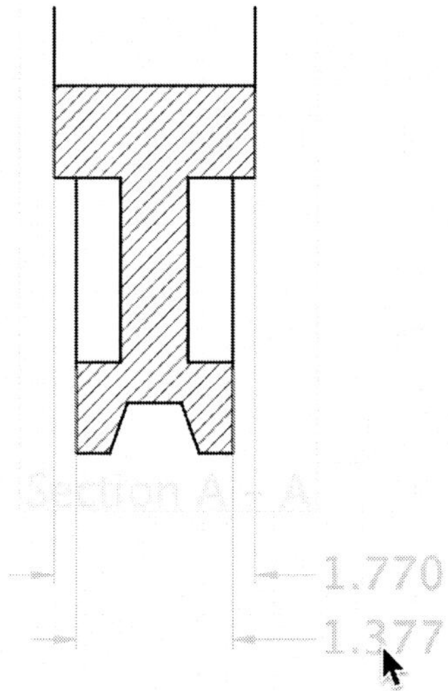

15. Click in the drawing page to deselect the selected dimensions.
16. Press and hold the Ctrl key and select the two inclined lines in the detailed view, as shown.

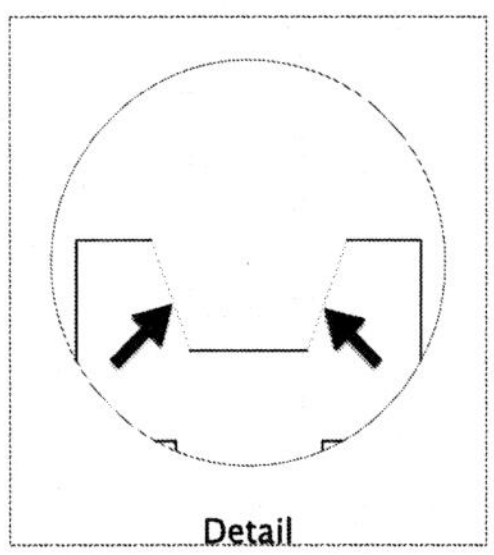

17. Click **Insert Dimension > Angle Dimension** icon on the **TechDraw Dimensions** toolbar.

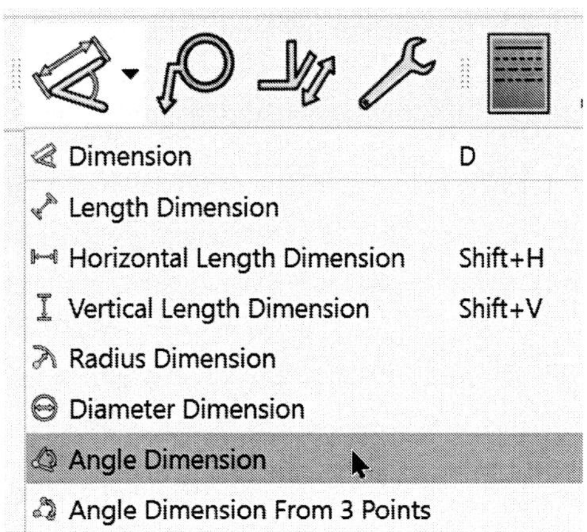

TUTORIAL 2

In this tutorial, you create the drawing shown below.

18. Press and hold the Ctrl key and select the horizontal edges of the detailed view, as shown.

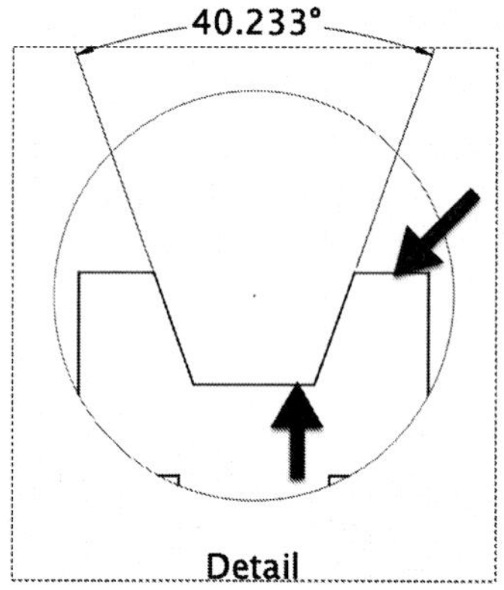

19. Click the **Insert Dimension > Vertical Length dimension** icon on the **TechDraw Dimensions** toolbar.

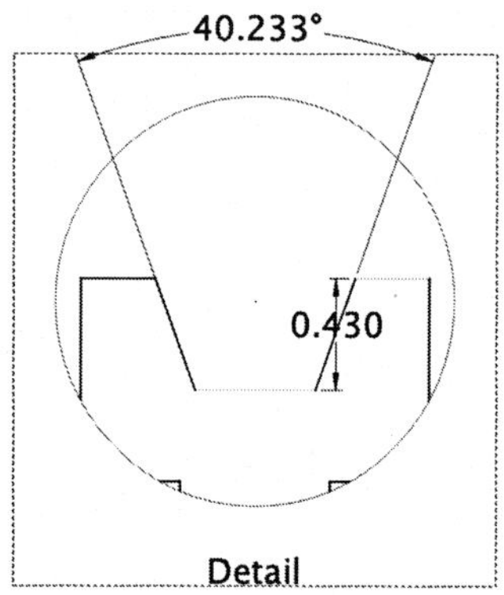

20. Create the remaining dimension, as shown.

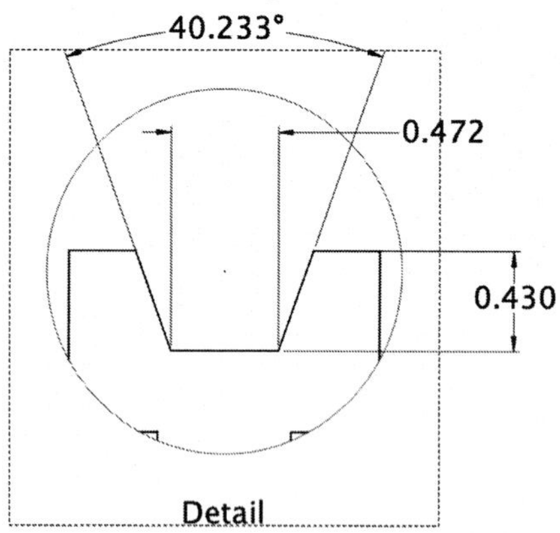

21. Save and close the file.

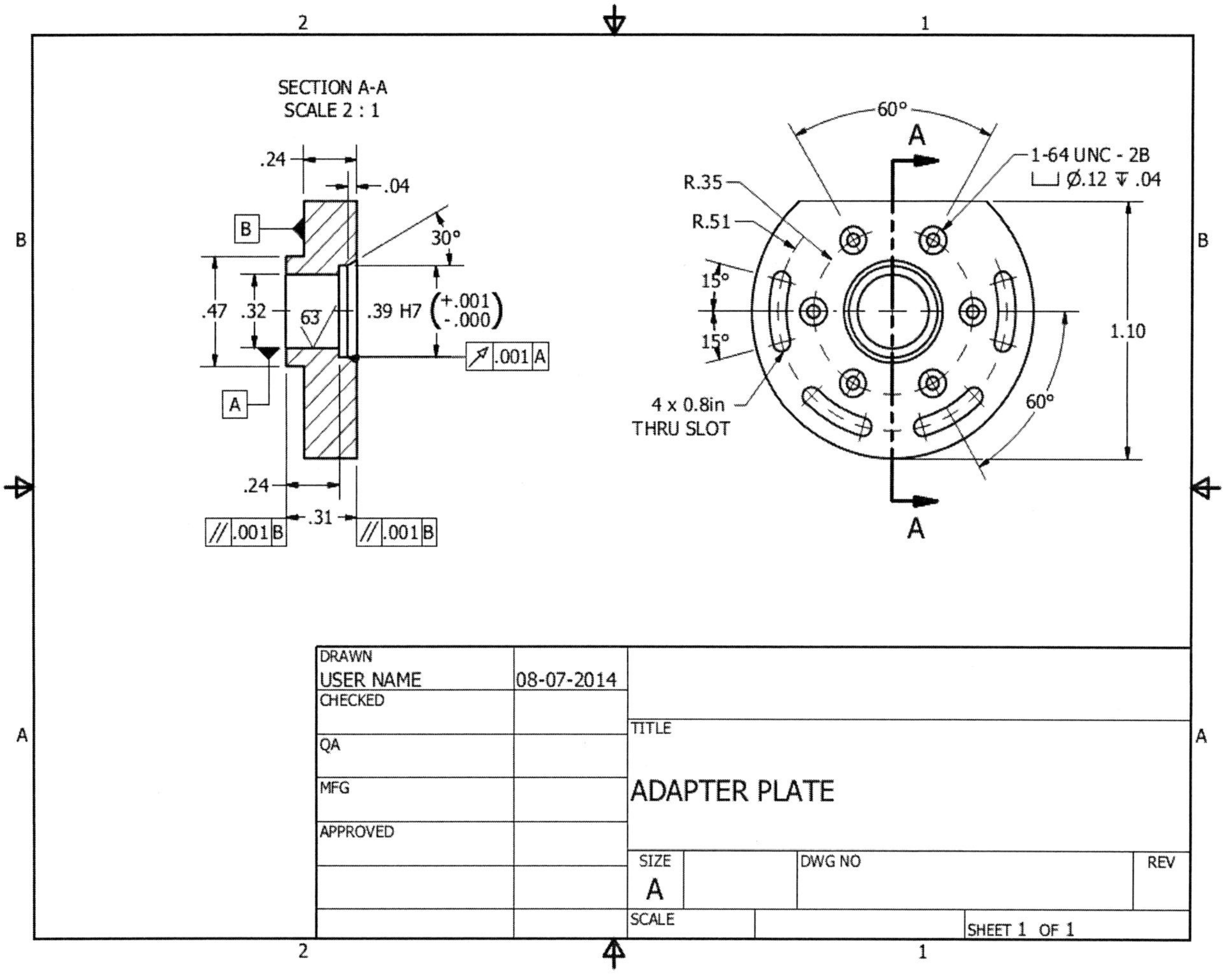
SECTION A-A
SCALE 2 : 1
.24
.04
30°
.47
.32
63
.39 H7 (+.001 / -.000)
.001 A
.24
.31
// .001 B
// .001 B
A
B
60°
1-64 UNC - 2B
⌴ Ø.12 ↧ .04
R.35
R.51
15°
15°
1.10
60°
4 x 0.8in
THRU SLOT
DRAWN
USER NAME
08-07-2014
CHECKED
QA
MFG
APPROVED
TITLE
ADAPTER PLATE
SIZE
A
DWG NO
REV
SCALE
SHEET 1 OF 1

1. Click **File > Open** on the Menu bar.
2. Go to the location of the Tutorial 1 file of Chapter 5.
3. Select the Tutorial 1 file and click the **Open** button.
4. Click **Edit > Preferences** on the Menu bar. The **Preferences** dialog box appears. If you are working on MacOS, then click **FreeCAD > Preferences** on the title bar.
5. On the **Preferences** dialog box, click the **TechDraw > Dimensions** at the left side .
6. Select **Standard ans Style > ASME Referencing**.
7. Uncheck the **Use Global Decimals** option.
8. Type **3** in the **Alternate Decimals** box.
9. Click **OK**.
10. Select **TechDraw** from the **Workbenches** drop-down.
11. Click the **New page** icon on the **TechDraw Pages** toolbar. A new page is added to the TechDraw document.
12. In the **Model** panel, select the **Page**.

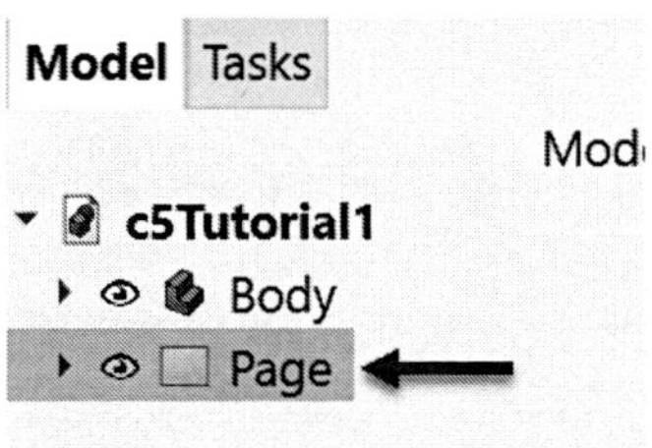

13. Click the **Data** tab on the bottom.
14. In the **Properties** section of the **Model** panel, select **Projection Type > Third Angle**.
10. Click the **Tutorial 1** tab on the bottom of the window.
11. Select the front face of the model. Selecting the front face of the model is the first step to generating a view because it determines which view will be generated.

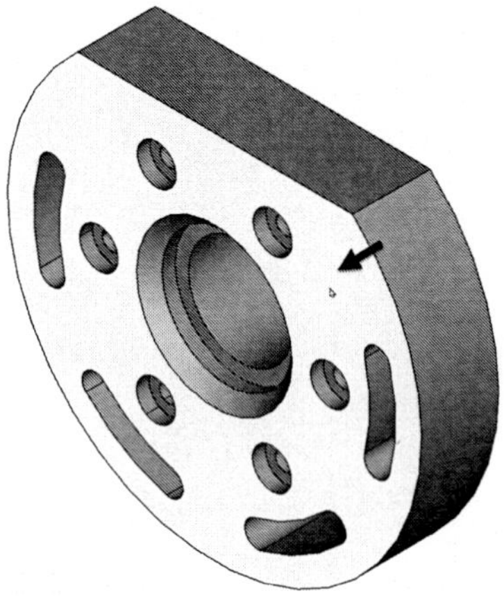

12. Click the **Page** tab on the bottom of the window.
13. To generate the base view, click the **New View** icon on the **TechDraw Views** toolbar.
14. On the **Part Toggle Section View**, select **Scale > Custom**.
15. Type **2** in the **Scale Numerator** box.
16. Click **OK**.
17. Click and drag the base and place it on the right side.
18. Selec the base view and click the **View** tab of the **Model** panel.
19. In the Decoration section, deselect the checkbox next to the **Arc Center Marks** option.

Base	
Keep Label	No
Stack Order	0
Broken View	
Break Line Style	Visible
Break Line Type	Simple
Decoration	
Arc Center Marks	No
Center Scale	0.500
Horiz Center Line	No
Show All Edges	No
Vert Center Line	No
Display Options	
Show In Tree	Yes

20. Select the base view.
21. Click the **Section view** drop-down **> Section View** on the **TechDraw Views** toolbar.

22. Click the **Looking Right** icon on the **Quick Set View Direction** section.
23. Type **0** in the **X**, **Y**, and **Z** boxes, respectively. These values define the location of the section plane.
24. Type **A** in the **Identifier** box.
25. Click **OK** to create the section view.
26. Select the section view from the drawing page.
27. Click the **Position Section View** icon on the **TechDraw Attributes** toolbar.

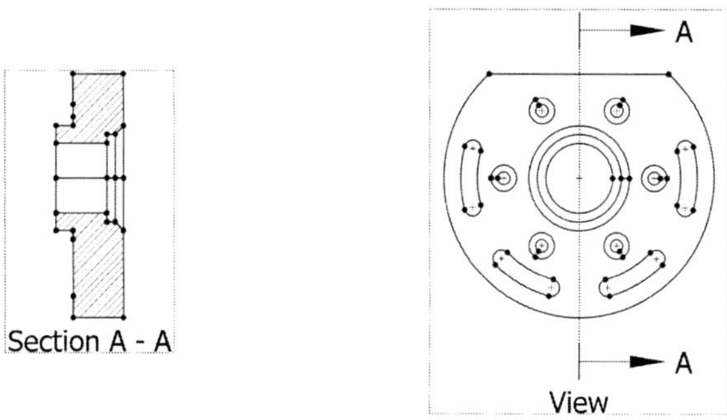

Creating Centerlines and Bolt Circle Centerlines

1. Press and hold the CTRL key and select the parallel lines on the section view, as shown below.

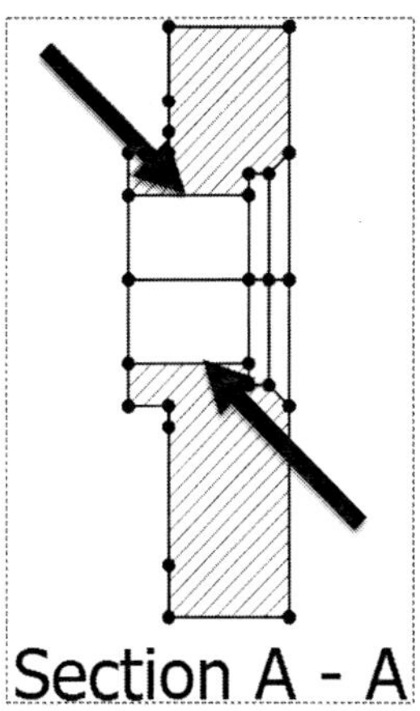

2. Click the **Centerline** drop-down > **Centerline 2 Lines** on the **TechDraw Annotation** toolbar. This step is done to add a centerline between the two selected parallel lines.

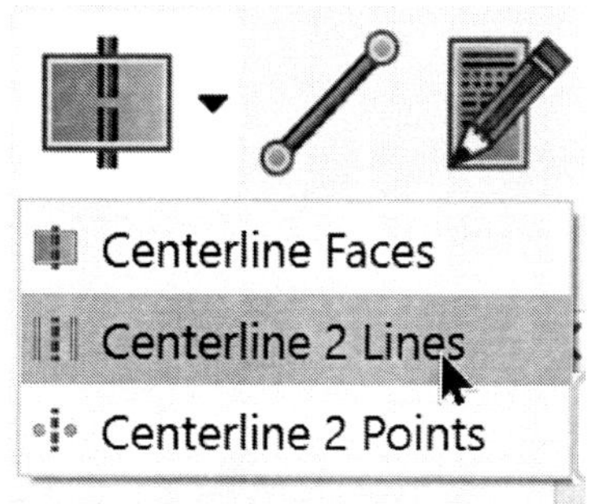

3. On the **Create Center line** section of the **Tasks** panel, select **Style > Center**. This step is done to change the style of the centerline to Center.
4. Type **0.18** in the **Extend By** box.
5. Type **0.3** in the **Extend By** box. This step is done to extend the centerline by a certain distance.

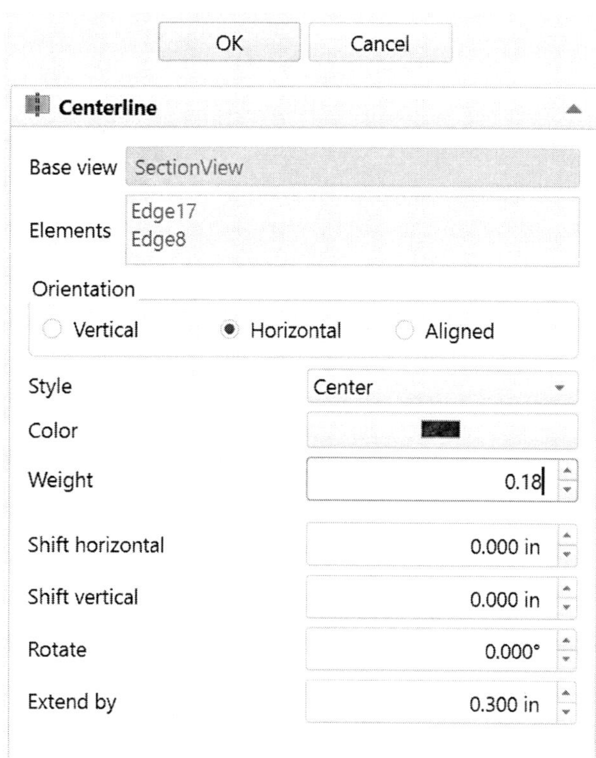

6. Click **OK**. This step is done to finalize the creation of the centerline with the specified style and extension.

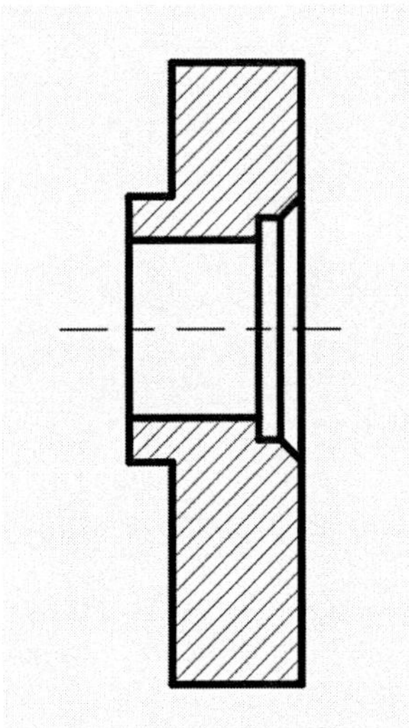

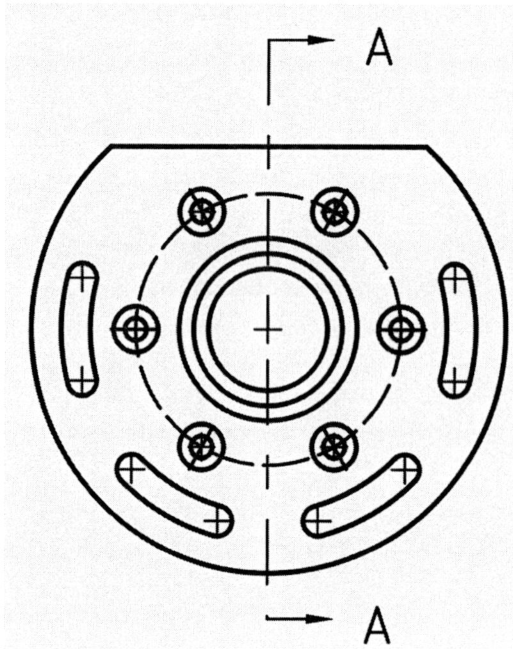

22. Press and hold CTRL key and select the counterbore circles, as shown.

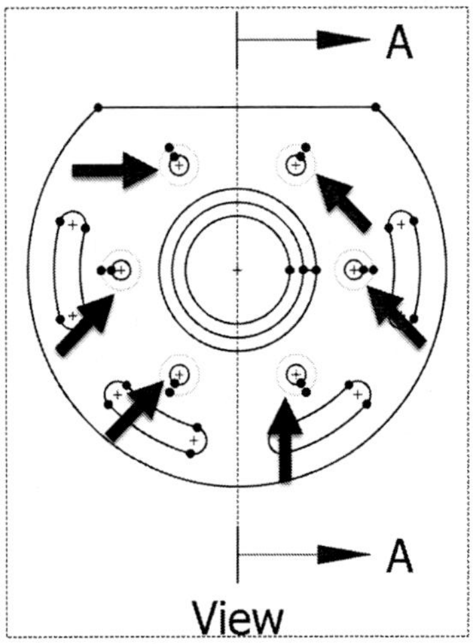

23. Click the **Circle Centerlines drop-down > Bolt Circle Centerlines** on the **TechDraw Centerlines** toolbar.

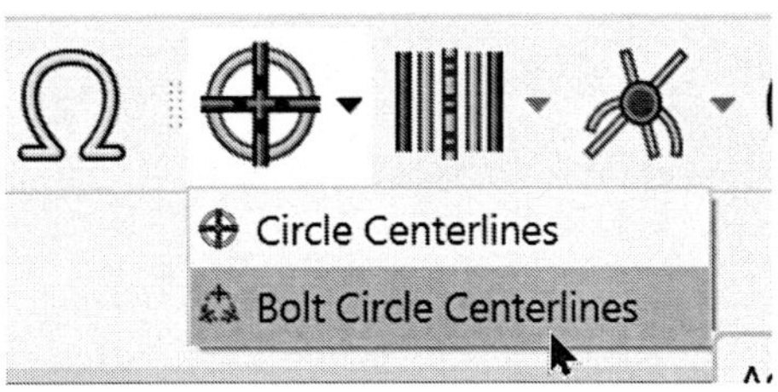

The bolt circle centerlines are created passing through the center points of the selected circles.

24. Press and hold the CTRL key and select the arcs, as shown.

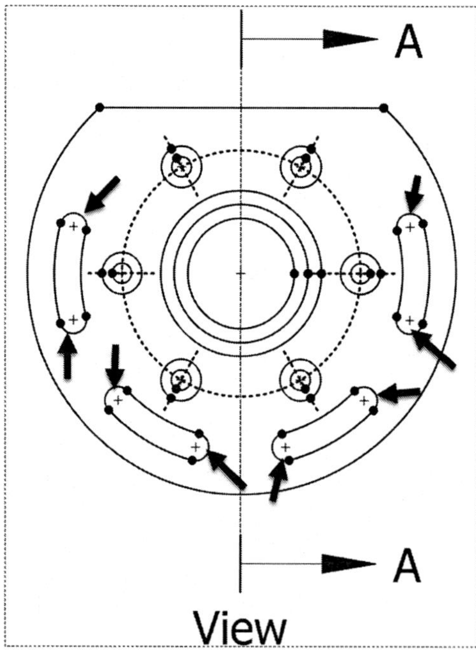

25. Click the **Circle Centerlines drop-down > Add Bolt circle Centerlines** 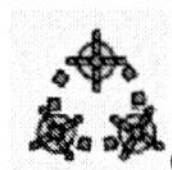 on the **TechDraw Centerlines** toolbar.

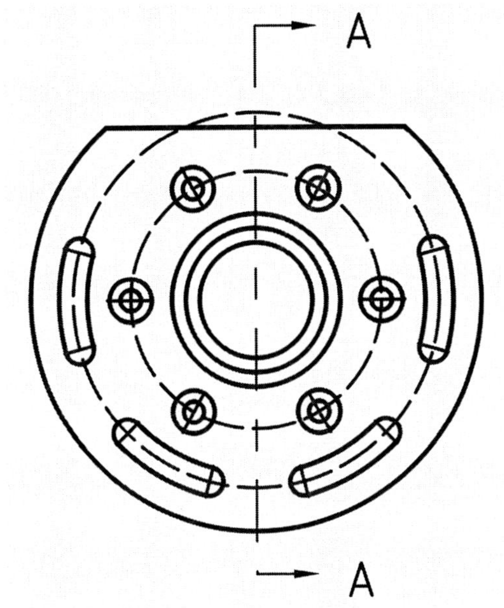

26. Select the circle located at the center.

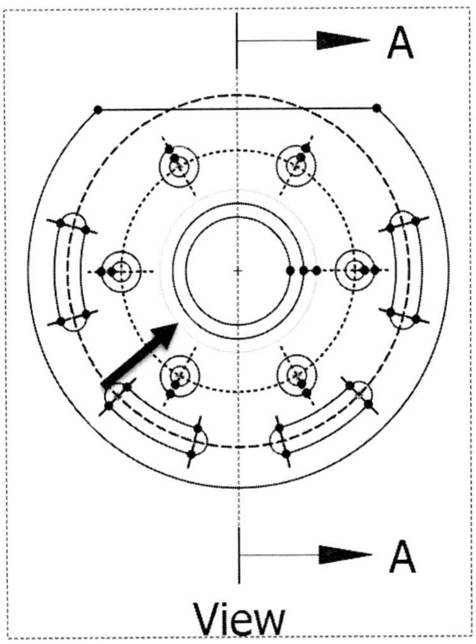

27. Click the **Circle Centerlines** drop-down > **Circle Centerlines** on the **TechDraw Centerlines** toolbar. Centerlines are added to the selected circle.

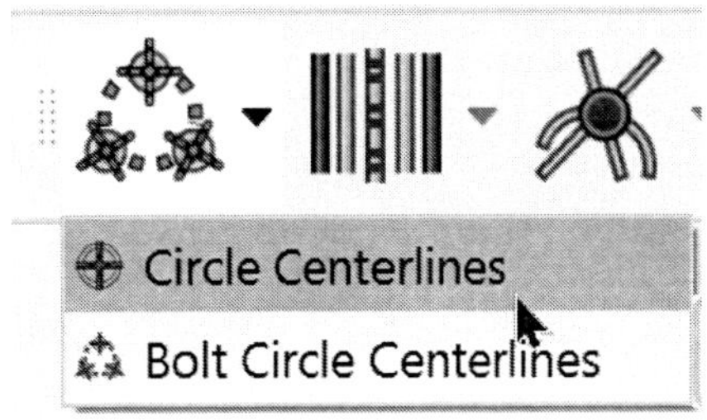

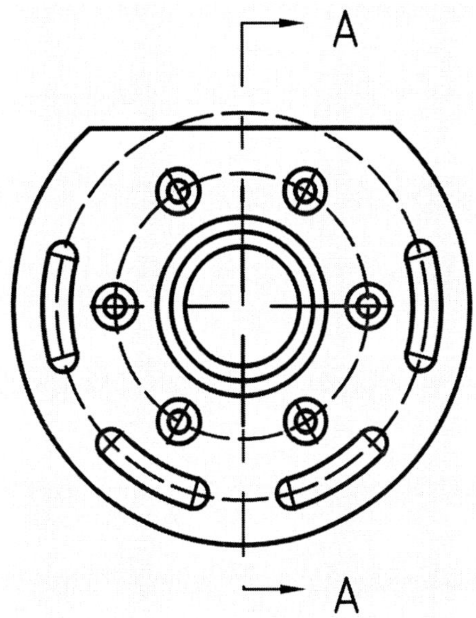

Applying Dimensions

1. Click **Edit > Preferences** on the Menu bar.
2. The Preferences dialog box appears. If you are working on MacOS, then click **FreeCAD > Preferences** on the title bar.
3. On the **Preferences** dialog box, click the **TechDraw** > **Dimensions** at the left side.
4. Select **Standard and Style > ASME Referencing**.
5. Type **0.1** in the **Font Size** box.
6. Type **0.1** in the **Arrow Size** box.
7. Click **OK**.
8. Press and hold the CTRL key and select the centerline on the slot located on the left.
9. Select the centerline of the counterbore hole located at the left.

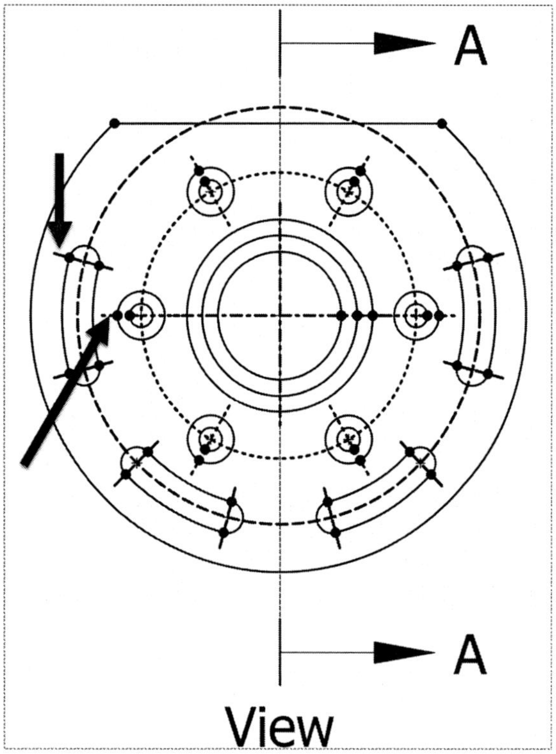

10. Click the **Dimensions > Angle Dimension** icon on the **TechDraw Dimensions** toolbar.
11. Left-click and hold on the angle dimension.
12. Drag the cursor to the left, then release it.

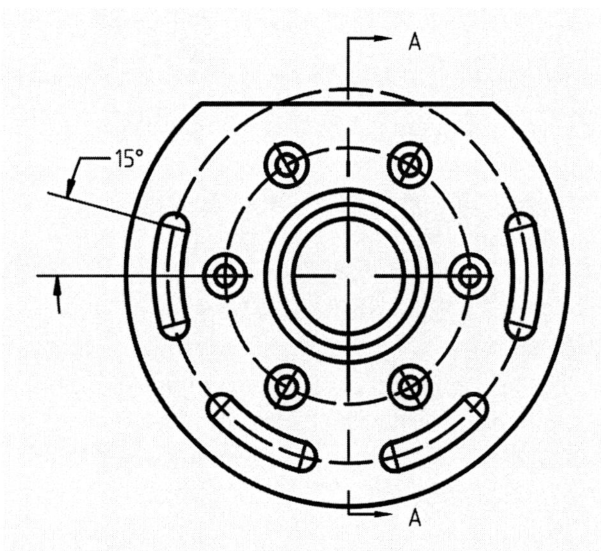

13. Likewise, create another angular dimension, as shown below.

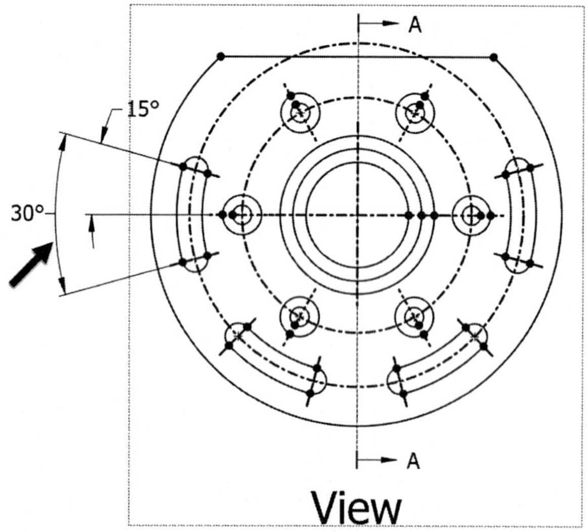

14. Create angular dimensions between the holes, and then between slots. To create the angular dimension between the slot, you need to create the angular dimension between the bolt circles.

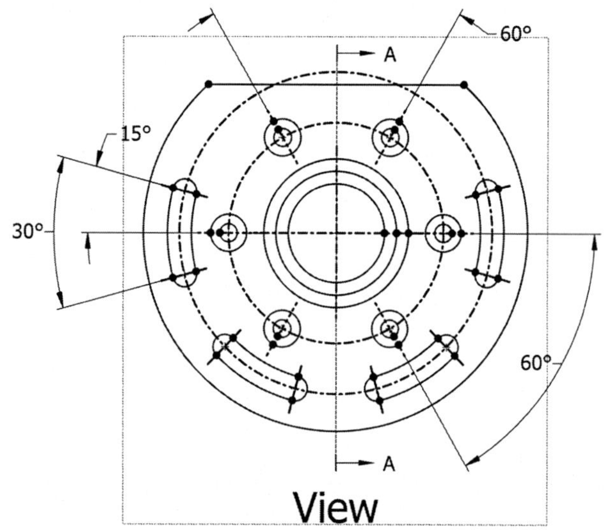

15. Select the pitch circle and click the **Insert Dimension > Diameter Dimension** icon on the **TechDraw Dimensions** toolbar.
16. Left-click and hold on the diameter dimension.
17. Drag the cursor to the left, then release it.

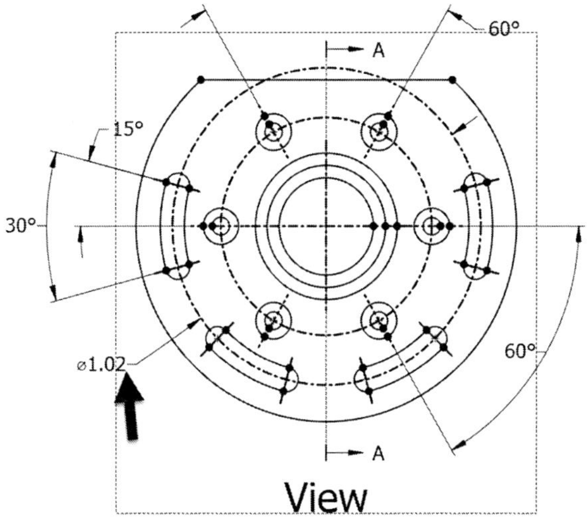

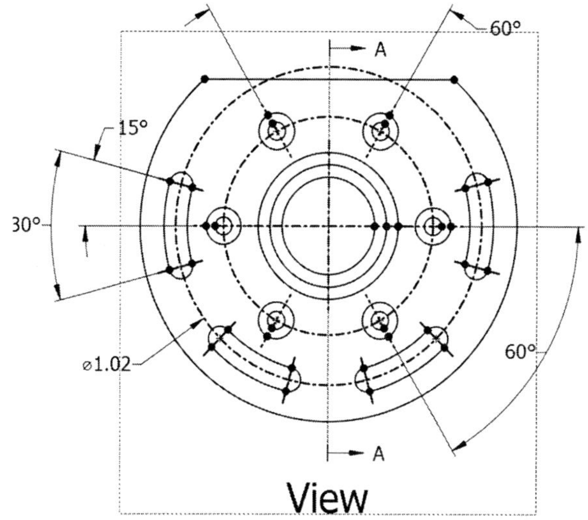

18. Select the newly created diameter dimension and click the **View** tab on the **Model** panel.
19. On the **View** tab of the **Model** panel, under the **Dimension Format** section, select **Rendering Extent > Minimal**. The arrow on the other side of the dimension is removed.

Color	[33, 37, 41]
Flip Arrowhea...	false
Font	osifont
Fontsize	0.100 in
Gap Factor A...	0.000
Gap Factor ISO	0.000
Line Spacing ...	2.000
Line Width	0.005 in
Rendering Ext...	Minimal
Standard And ...	ASME Referencing

View Data

20. Select the counterbore hole and click the **Insert Dimension > Diameter Dimension** icon on the **TechDraw Dimensions** toolbar.
21. Left-click and hold on the diameter dimension.
22. Drag the cursor to the right, then release it.

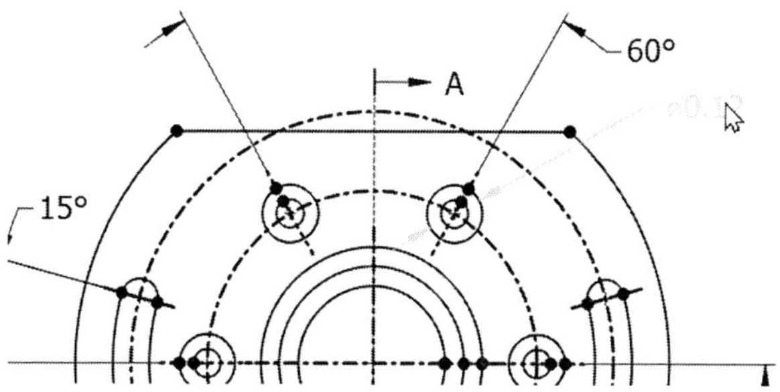

23. Select the diameter dimension of the small hole. Next, click the **Customize Format Label** icon on the **TechDraw Attributes** toolbar.
24. In the **Format** box, click before the diameter value.

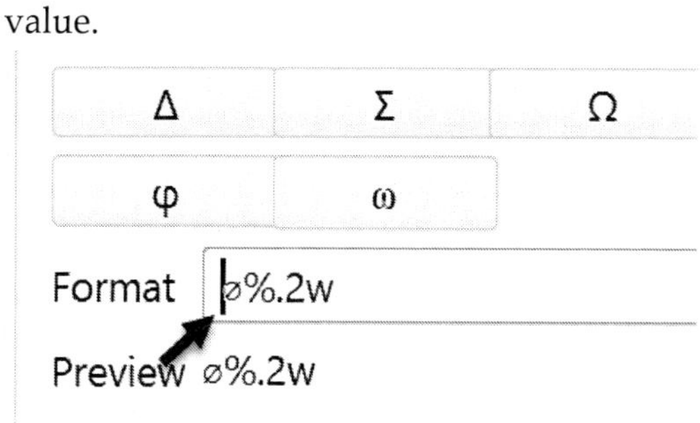

25. Type **1-64 UNC - 2B**. Next, press the SPACEBAR.
26. Click next to **ø%.2w** and press the SPACEBAR.
27. Click the **Downward arrow** button in the **Other** section.

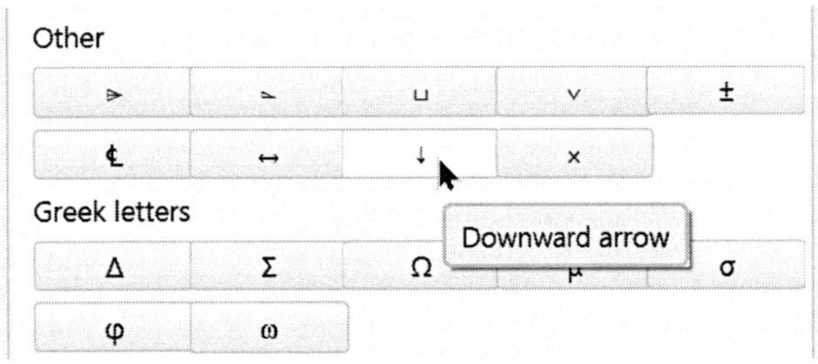

28. Press the SPACEBAR and type 0.4.
29. Click **OK**.
30. On the **View** tab of the **Model** panel, under the **Dimension Format** section, select **Rendering Extent > Minimal**. The arrow on the other side of the dimension is removed.

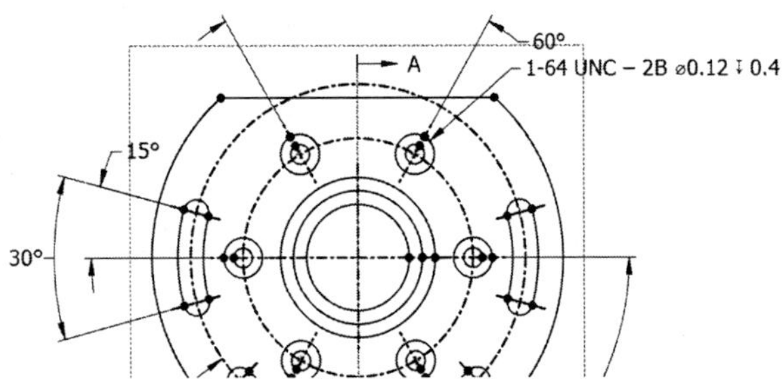

31. Add the pitch circle diameter to counterbore holes.
32. Click the circular edge of the model, click the **Dimension** drop-down > **Radius Dimension**  icon on the **TechDraw Dimensions** toolbar.
33. Click and drag the radius dimension.

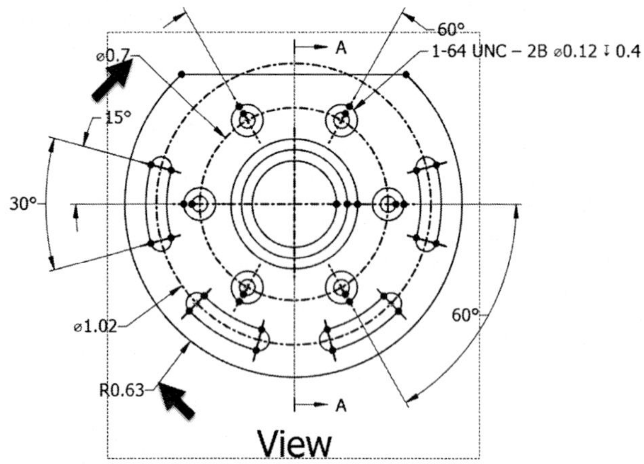

34. Select the slot end, as shown.
35. Click the **Insert Dimension** drop-down > **Insert Radius Dimension**  icon on the **TechDraw Dimensions** toolbar.
36. Click and drag the radius dimension.

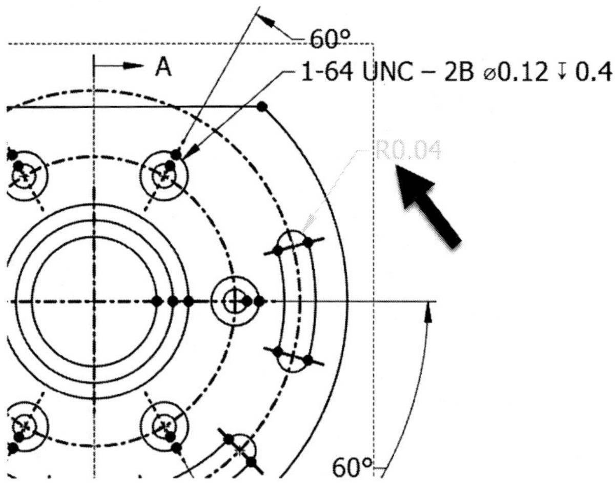

37. Select the radius dimension of the slot. Next, click the **Customize Format Label**  icon on the **TechDraw Attributes** toolbar.
38. In the **Format** box, click next to the radius value.
39. Type **4X**. Next, press the SPACEBAR.
40. Click next to **ø%.2w** and press the SPACEBAR.
41. Type THRU SLOT and click **OK**.

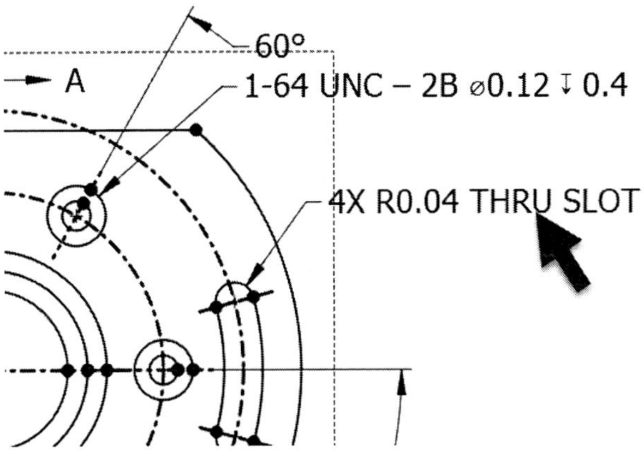

42. Press and hold the CTRL key and select the angular dimensions.
43. Click the **View** tab at the bottom of the **Model** panel.
44. In the **Dimension format** section, select **Standard And Style > ASME Inlined.**

Dimension Format	
Arrow Style	Filled arrow
Arrowsize	0.100 in
Color	[33, 37, 41]
Flip Arrowheads	No
Font	osifont
Fontsize	0.100 in
Gap Factor ASME	0.000
Gap Factor ISO	0.000
Line Spacing Factor ISO	2.000
Line Width	0.014 in
Rendering Extent	Normal
Standard And Style	ASME Inlined

45. Click **Edit > Preferences** on the Menu bar. The **Preferences** dialog box appears. If you are working on MacOS, then click **FreeCAD > Preferences** on the title bar.
46. On the **Preferences** dialog box, click **TechDraw > General** at the left side.
47. Type **0.12** in the **Label Size** box of the **Labels** section and click **OK.**
48. Press and the CTRL key and select the lines, as shown below.

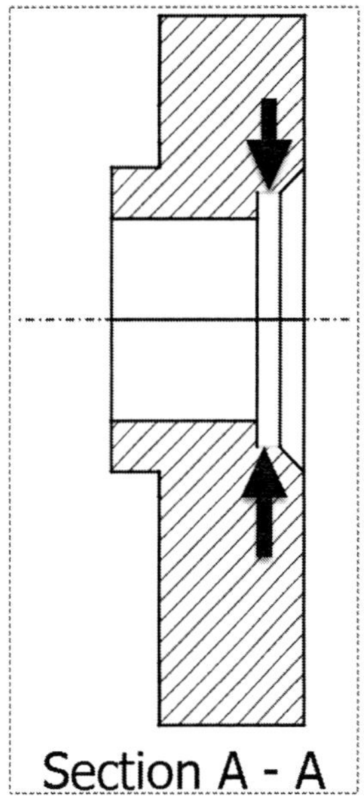

49. Click the **Insert Dimension** drop-down > **Vertical Length Dimension** icon on the **TechDraw Dimensions** toolbar.
50. Left-click and hold on the dimension Move the pointer toward the right and click to place the dimension.

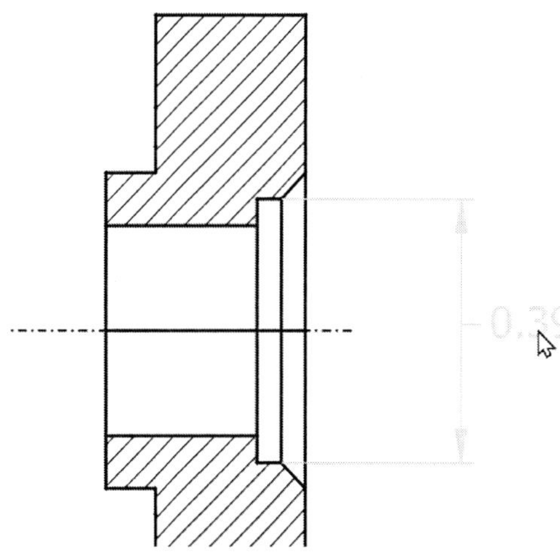

51. Double-click on the newly created dimension.
52. On the **Dimension** section of the **Tasks** panel, uncheck the the **Equal Tolerance** option.
53. Type 0.001 in the **Overtolerance** and **Undertolerance** boxes, respectively.
54. Type **%+.3w** in the **OverTolerance Format Specifier** and **UnderTolerance Format Specifier**

boxes, respectively.

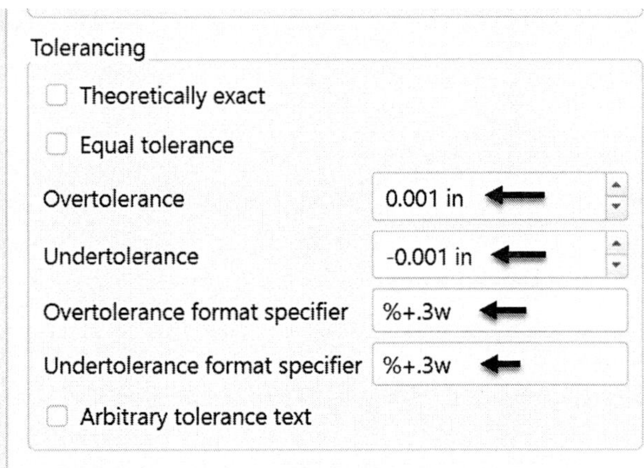

55. Select the newly created dimension and click **Increase decimal Places**  icon on the **TechDraw Attributes** toolbar.
56. Select the newly created dimension and click the **View** tab on the **Model** panel.
57. Select the **Standard and Style > ASME Inlined** under the **Dimension Format** section.

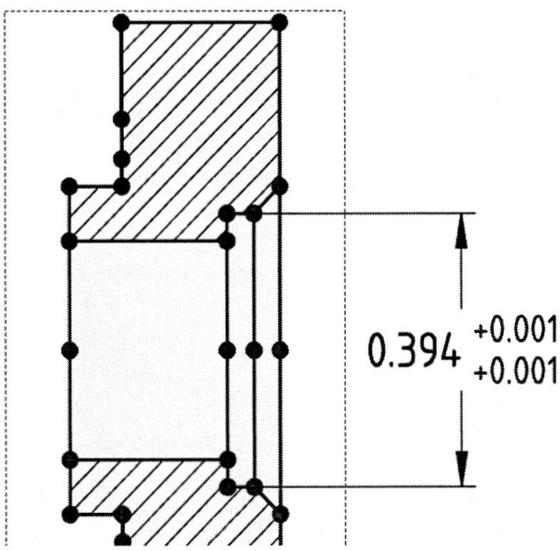

58. Press and hold the CTRL key and select the vertices of the section view, as shown.

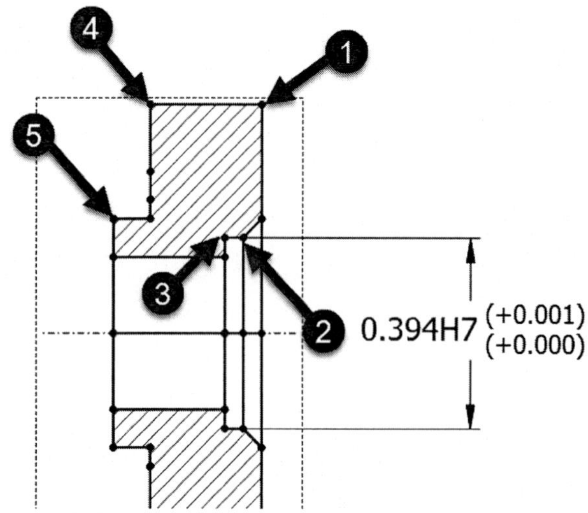

59. Click **Dimension** drop-down **> Horizontal Coordinate Dimensions** on the **TechDraw Dimensions** toolbar.

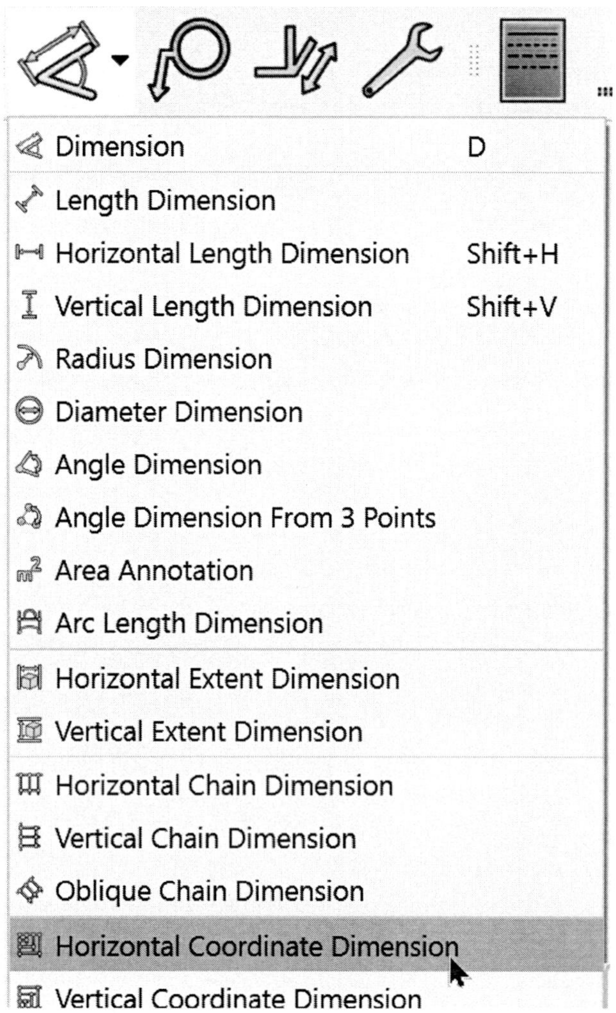

60. Click and drag the dimensions to arrange them

properly, as shown.

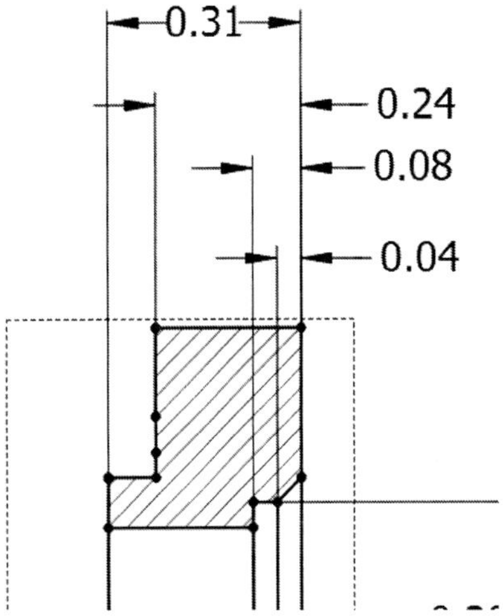

61. Press and hold the CTRL key and select the vertices of the section view, as shown.

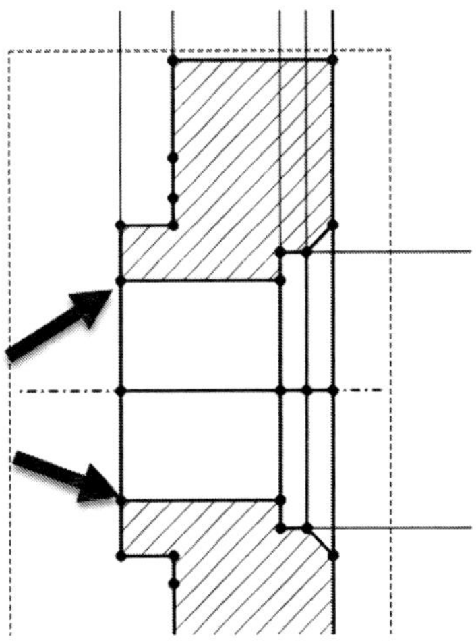

62. Click the **Dimension** drop-down > **Insert Vertical Dimension** icon on the **TechDraw Dimensions** toolbar.

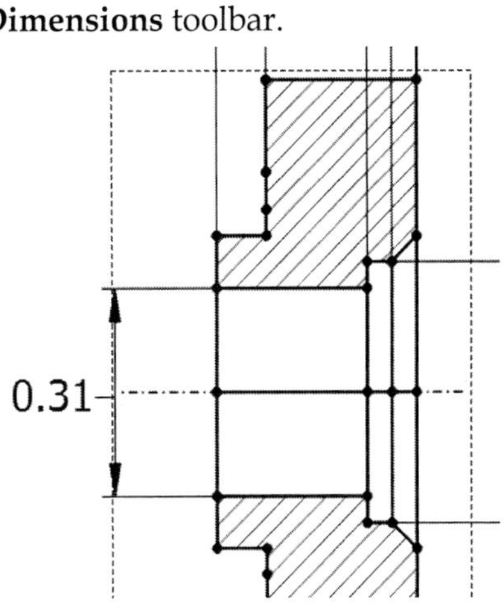

63. Likewise, apply the other dimensions, as shown below.

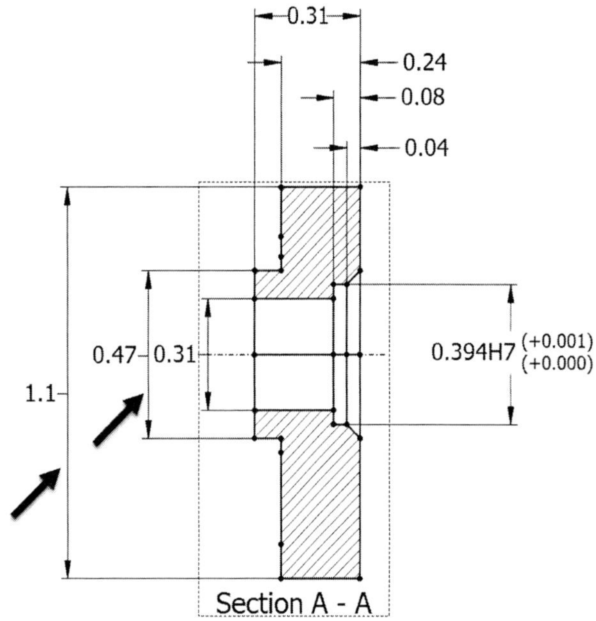

64. Press and hold CTRL key and select the newly created dimensions and click the **View** tab on the **Model** panel.
65. Select the **Standard and Style > ASME Inlined** under the **Dimension Format** section.

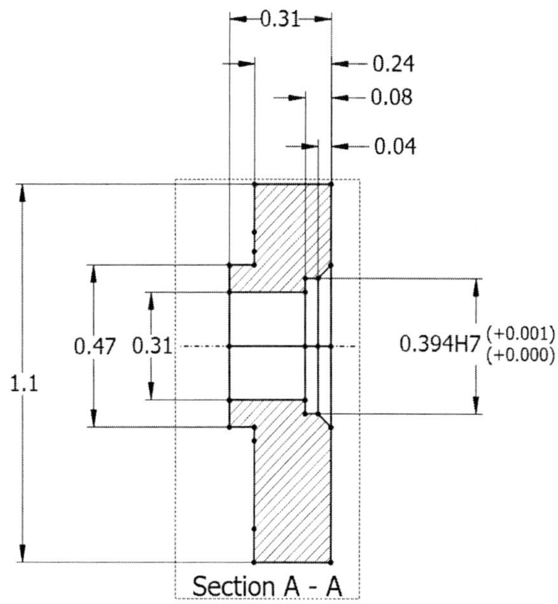

Placing the Balloon Annotation

1. Click on the inner horizontal edge of the section

view, as shown.

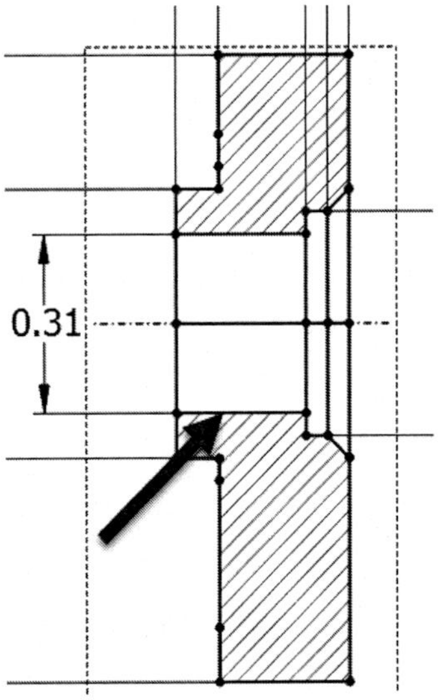

2. Click **Balloon Annotation** on the **TechDraw Dimensions** toolbar.

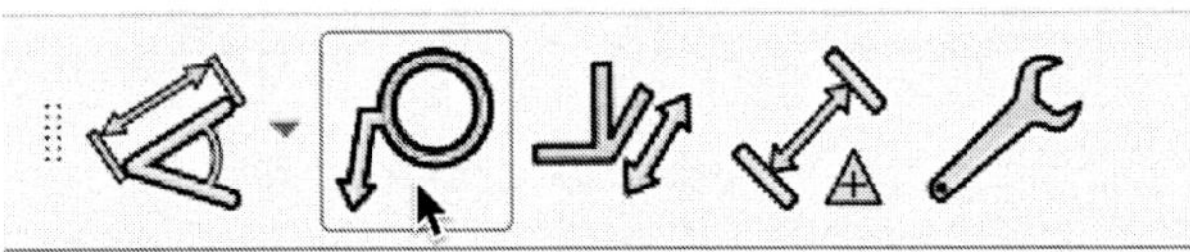

3. Select the vertical edge of the section view, as shown.

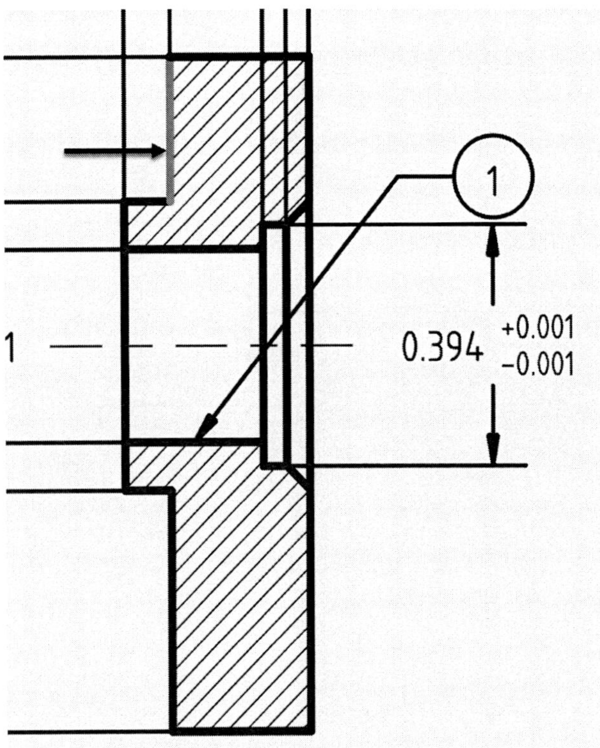

4. Click **Balloon Annotation** on the **TechDraw Dimensions** toolbar.
5. Left-click and hold on the first balloon annotation. Move the pointer toward the bottom left and click to place the balloon.

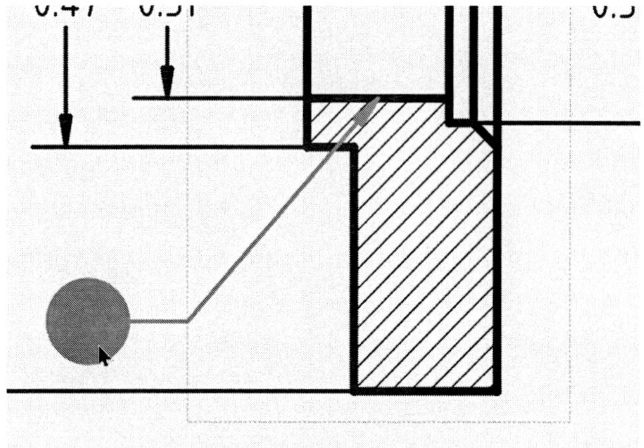

6. Select the first balloon annotation and click the **Data** tab on the **Model** panel.
7. Select the **End Type > Filled Arrow** under the **Base** section.
8. Select **Bubble Shape > Square**.
9. Type **A** in the **Text** box.

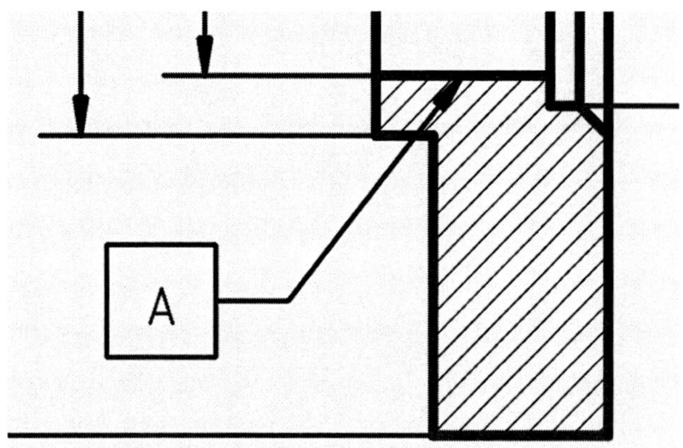

10. Select the second balloon annotation, and drag it toward left. Place it such that the leader is

horizontal.

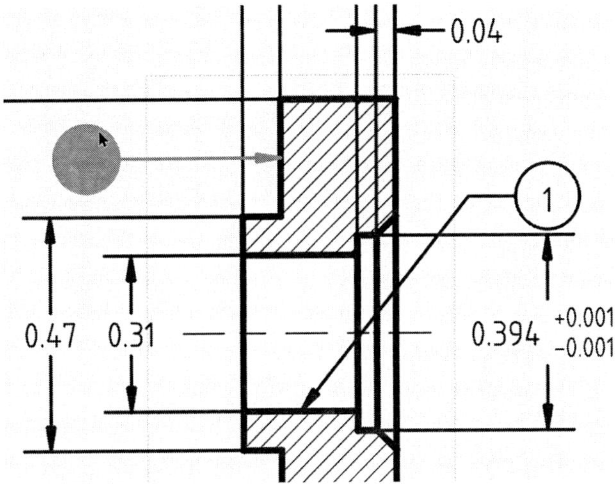

11. Select the **End Type > Filled Triangle** under the **Base** section.
12. Select **Bubble Shape > Square.**
13. Type **B** in the **Text** box.

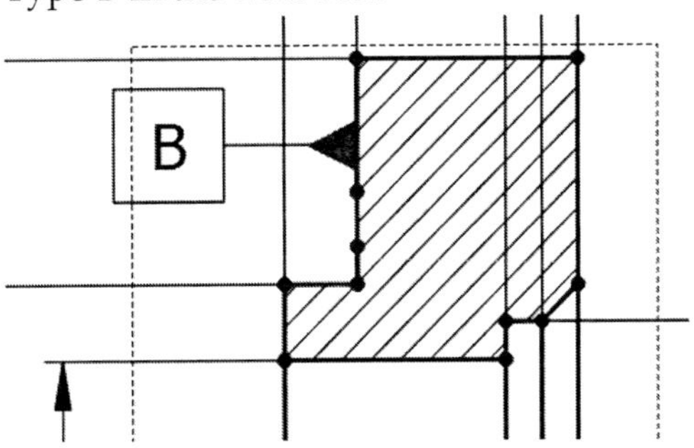

Placing the Feature Control Frame

1. Click the inner horizontal edge section view, as shown.

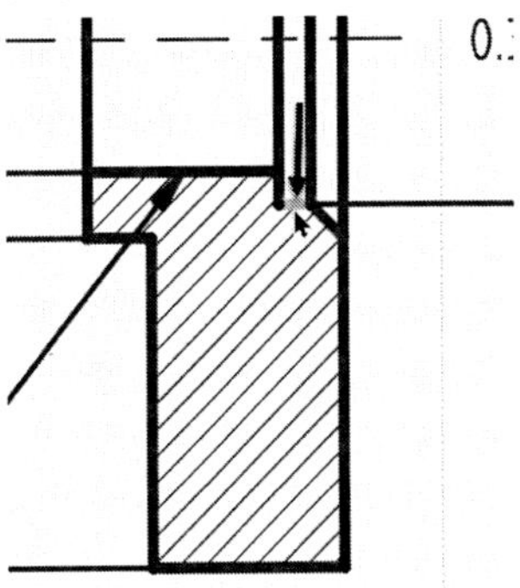

2. Click **Balloon Annotation**  on the **TechDraw Dimensions** toolbar.
3. Click on the vertical edge of the section view, as shown.

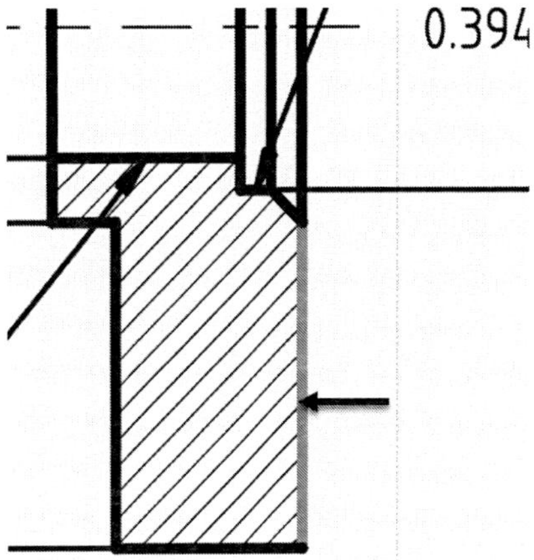

4. Select the first balloon annotation and click the click the **Data** tab on the **Model** panel.
5. Select **Bubble Shape > Rectangle.**
6. Select the first balloon annotation. Next, click the **Customize Format Label**  icon on the **TechDraw Attributes** toolbar.
7. Select the text in the **Format** box, and press DELETE.
8. Click the **Circular runout** button under the **GD&T** section of the **Customize Format** dialog.

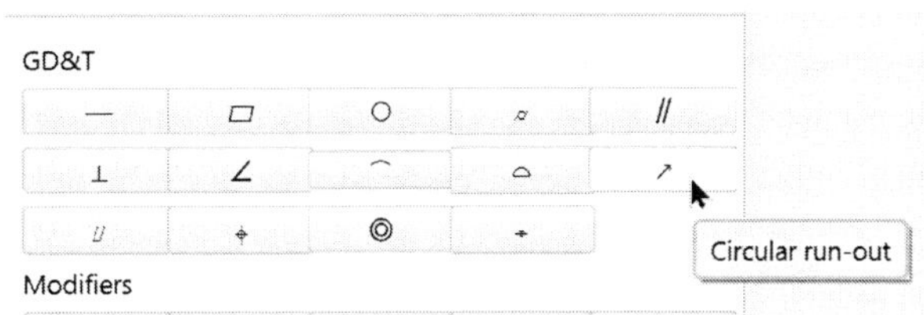

9. Type " | " on your keyoboard in the **Format** box. A new indicator field is initiated
10. Type **.001**.
11. Type " | " on your keyoboard in the **Format** box. A new indicator field is initiated
12. Type **A** and click **OK.**
13. Click and drag the balloon annotation to the location, as shown.

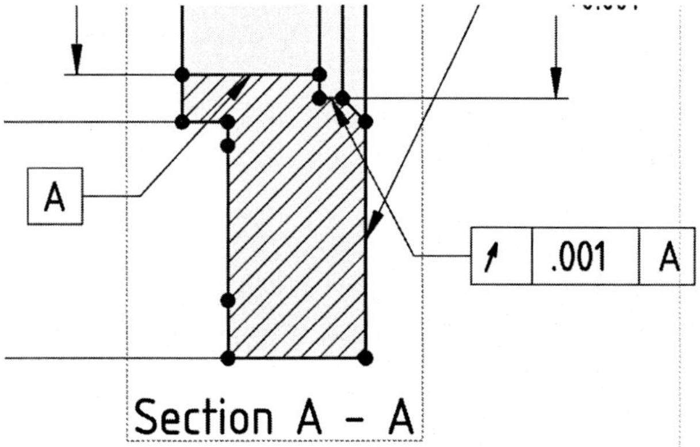

14. Likewise, modify the second balloon annotation and adjust its location, as shown.

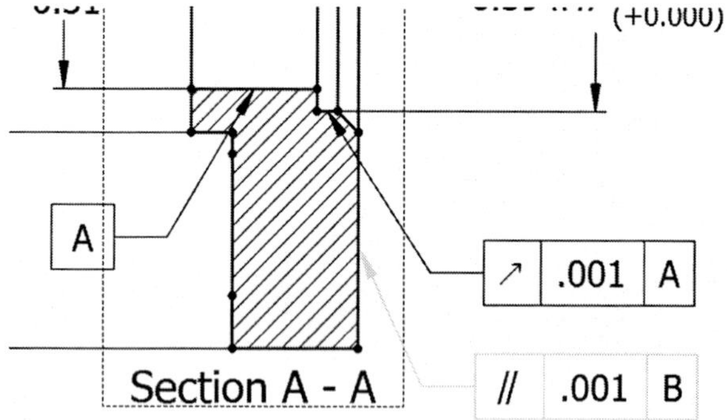

15. Click **Save**.
16. Close the file.

Chapter 7: Sheet Metal Modeling

TUTORIAL 1

In this tutorial, you create the sheet metal model shown in the figure.

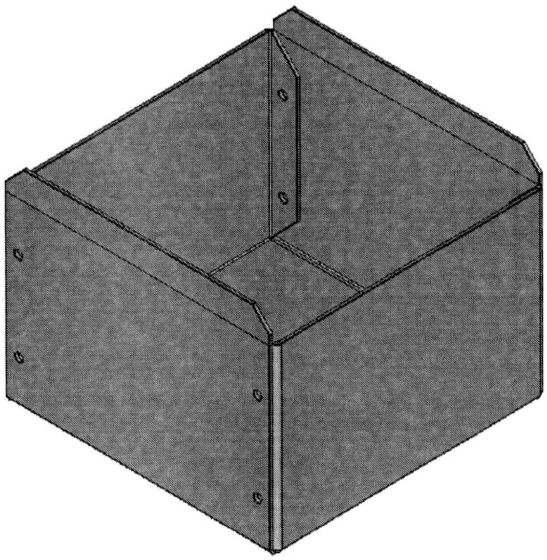

Creating the Base Feature

1. Open a new FreeCAD file.
2. Select **Sheet Metal** from the **Workbenches** drop-down.
3. Click **Edit > Preferences** on the Menu bar. The **Preferences** dialog box appears. If you are working on MacOS, then click **FreeCAD > Preferences** on the title bar.
4. Click the **General** > **General** on the left-side of the **Preferences** dialog.
5. Select **Default unit system > Standard.**
6. Type **2** in the **Number of decimals** box.
7. Check the **Ignore Project unit system and use default** option.
8. Click the **Apply** button located at the bottom.
9. Click **OK.**
10. Click the **Add base shape** icon on the SheetMetal toolbar. The **Sheet metal base shape properties** section appears on the **Tasks** panel.
11. Select **Flat** from the **Base shape type** drop-down.
12. Set the **Thickness** to 1.50 mm.
13. Set the **Width** to 152.00.
14. Set the **Length** to 152.00.
15. Click the center point in the Location of part origin graphic.
16. Check the **Fill gaps** option.
17. Check the **Embed in new Body** option.
18. Click **OK** on the **Tasks** panel. A flat base shape is created.

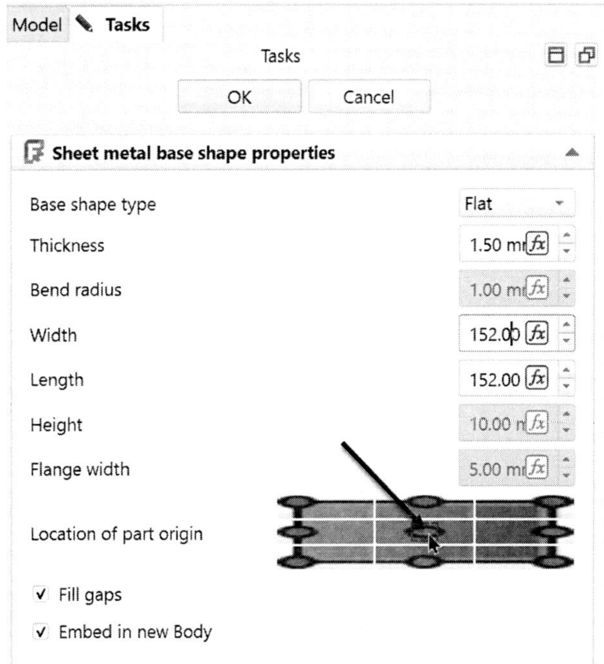

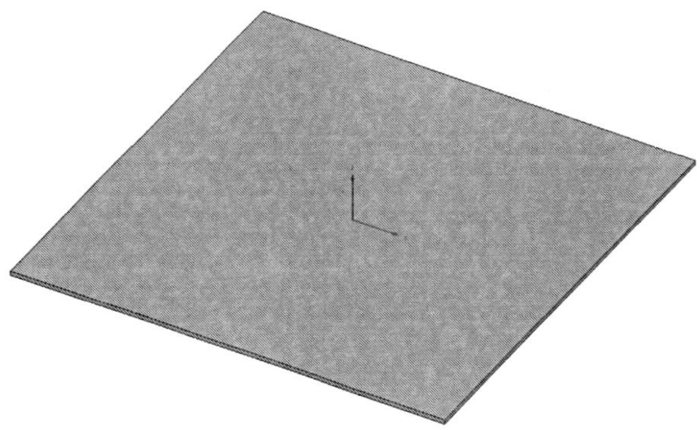

Creating the flange

1. Press and hold the CTRL key and select the edges on the top face, as shown.

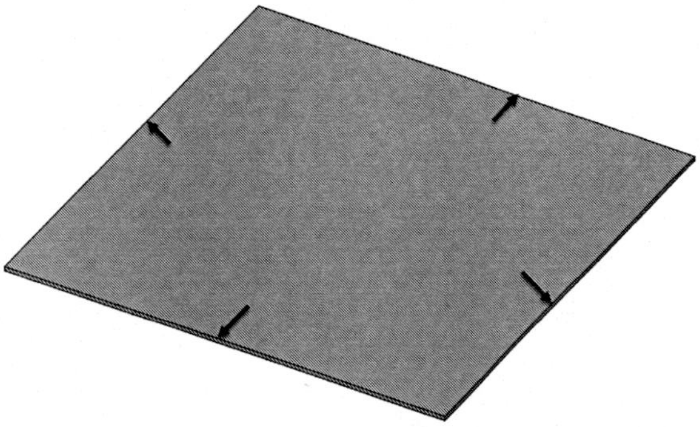

2. Click the **Make Wall**  icon on the **Sheet Metal** toolbar.
3. On the **Flange Properties** panel, under the **General** tab, enter **100.00** mm and **1.00** mm in the **Length** and **Bend radius** boxes, respectively. The length and radius of the bend are changed.
4. Select **Material Outside** from the **Wall position** drop-down.

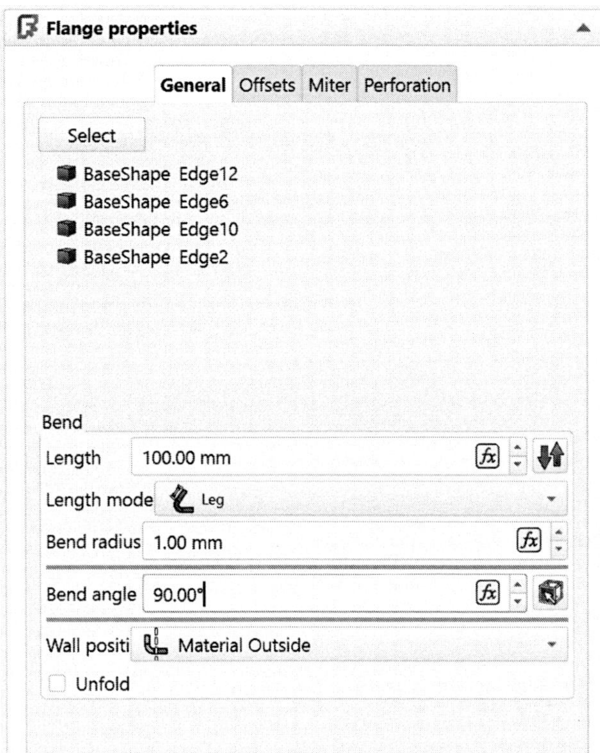

5. Click the **Miter** tab and uncheck the **Auto Miter** option.

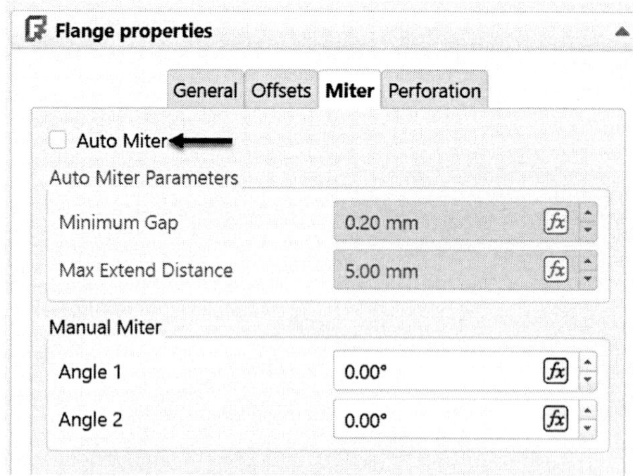

6. Click **OK**.

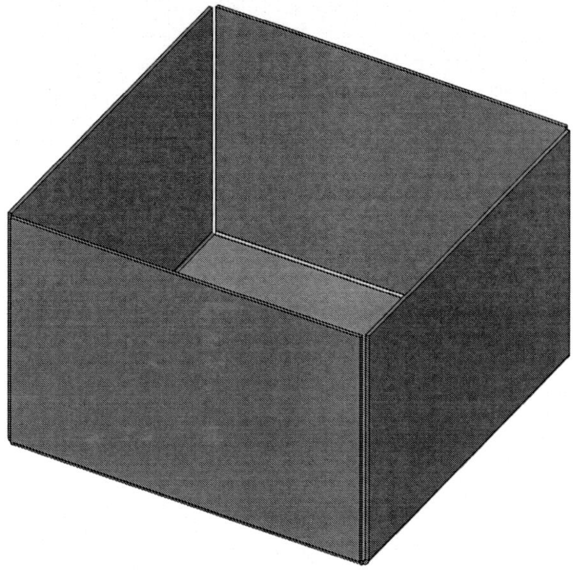

7. Select the inner edge of the flange, as shown.

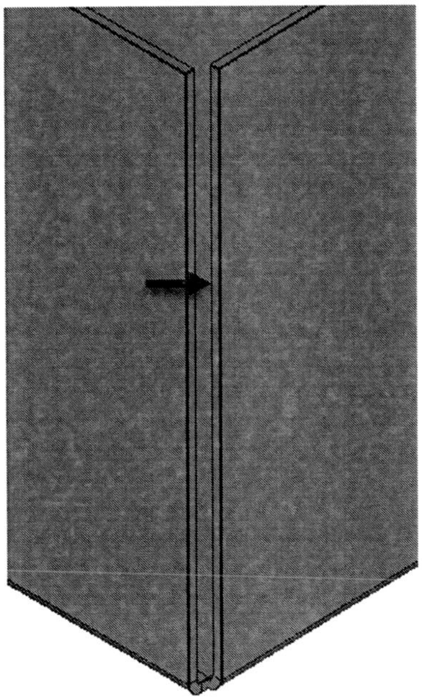

8. Click the **Make Wall**  icon on the **Sheetmetal** toolbar.
9. Select **Wall position > Material Inside**.
10. Type **15** in the **Length** box.

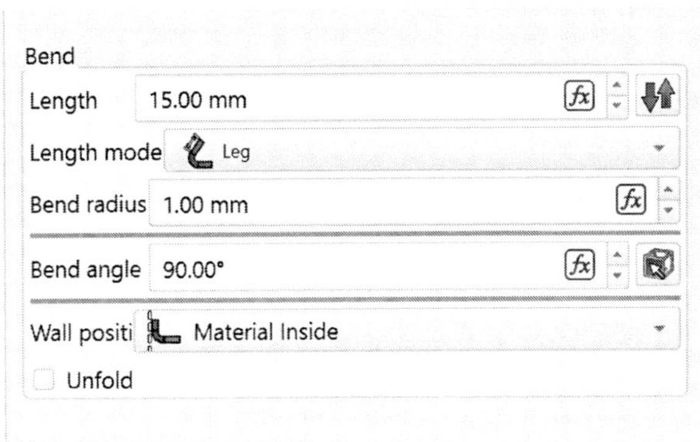

11. Click the **Miter** tab and uncheck the **Auto Miter** option.
12. Type **45** in the **Angle1** and **Angle2** boxes, respectively.

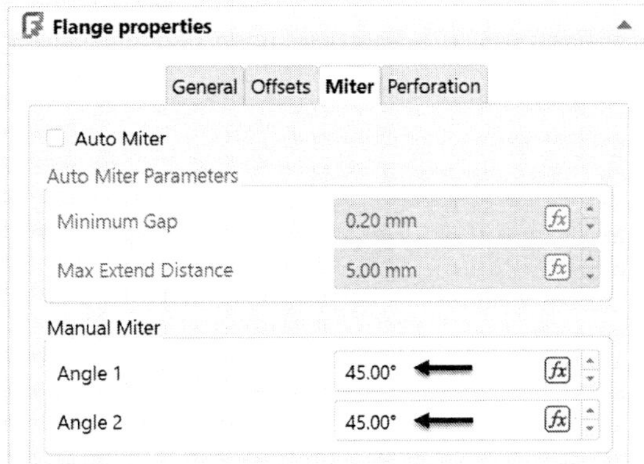

13. Press and hold the middle mouse button and the right mouse button.
14. Drag the pointer toward left such that the other end of the flange is displayed.

The flange is displayed.

15. Likewise, create three more miter flanges, as shown.

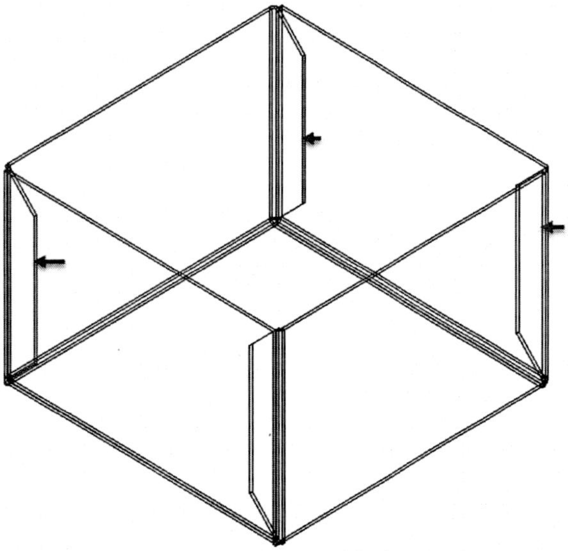

Extending a face

1. Press and hold the CTRL key and select the outer edges of the flanges, as shown.

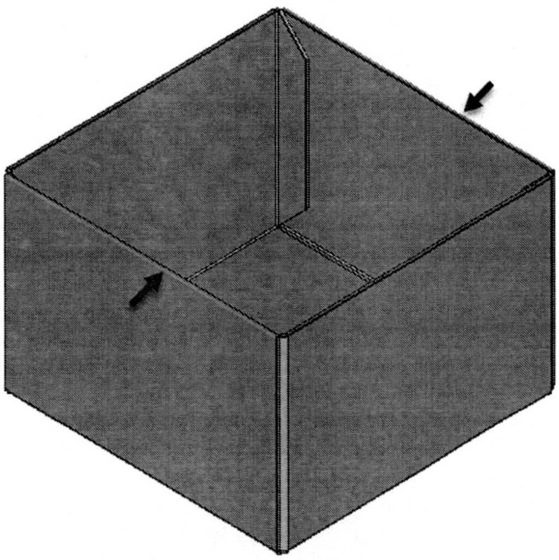

2. Click the **Extend face**  icon on the **Sheetmetal** toolbar.
3. Select **Extend** from the **Model** panel.
4. Type **15** in the **Length** box of the **Extend Properties** panel.
5. Click **OK**.

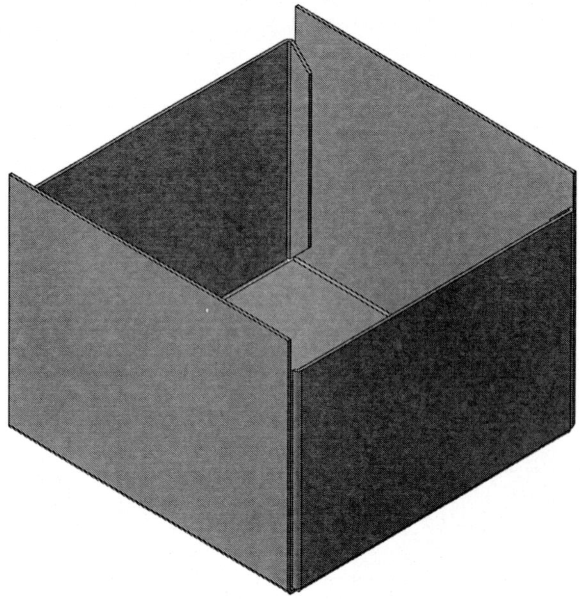

6. Select **Part Design** from the **Workbenches** drop-down.
7. Select the edge of the extended face, as shown.

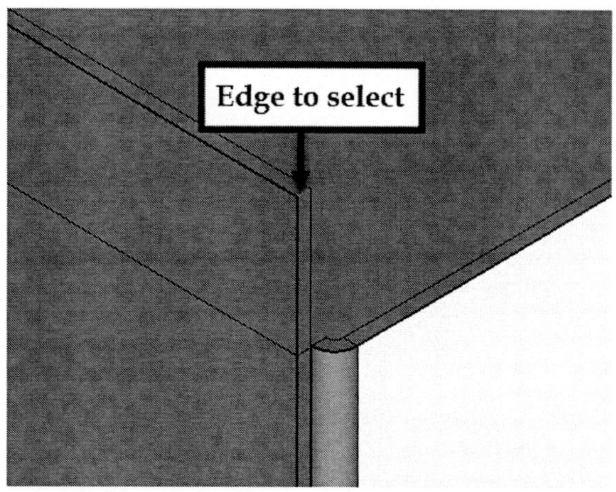

8. On the **Part Design Dressup Features** toolbar, click the **Chamfer**  icon.
9. On the **Chamfer parameters** dialog, click the **Select** button.
10. Select the corner edge of the extended face, as shown.

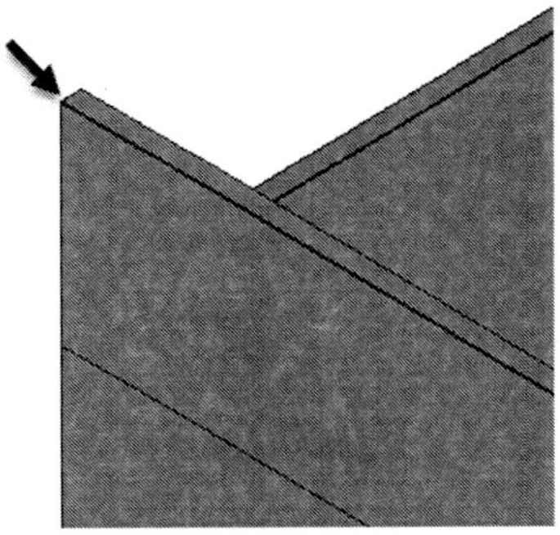

11. Select the corner edges of another extended face.

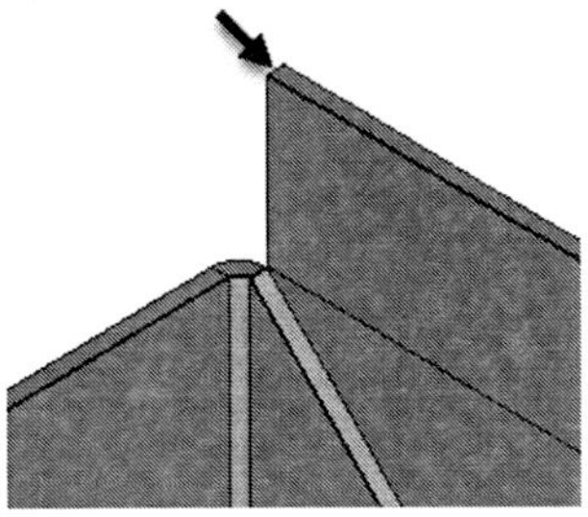

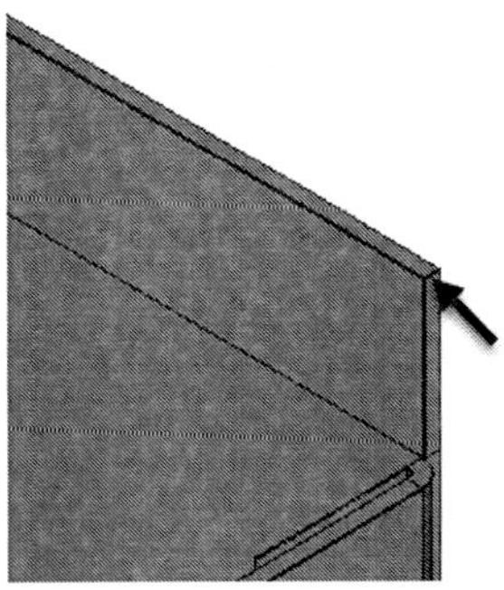

12. Select **Type > Equal distance.**
13. Type **10** in the **Size** box and click **OK**.

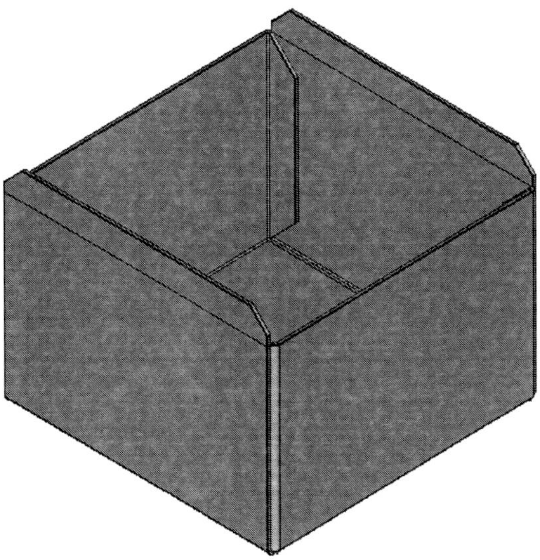

Creating the Pockets

1. Select the flat face of the flange.

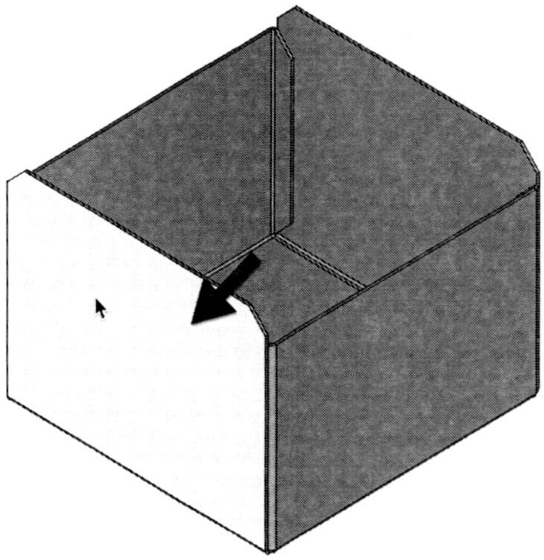

2. Click the **New Sketch** icon on the **Part Design Helper Features** toolbar.
3. On the **View** toolbar, click **Draw Style** drop-down > **Wireframe.**

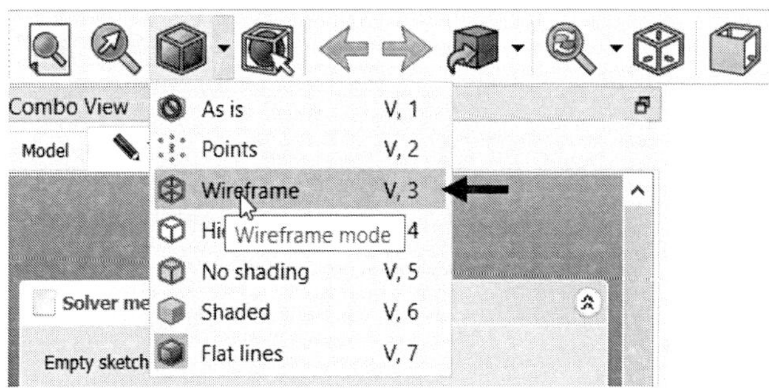

4. Create four circles, as shown.

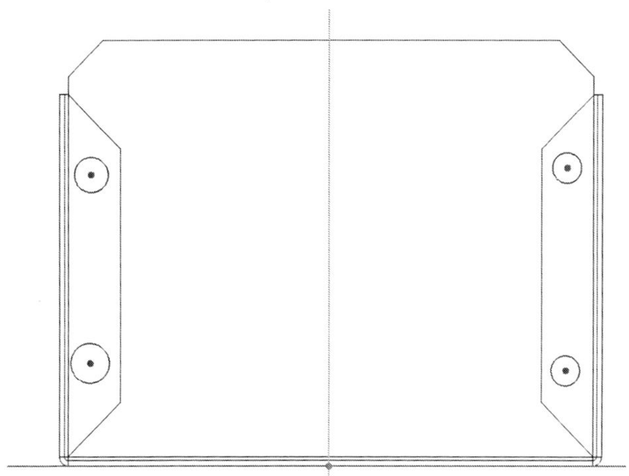

5. Click the **Equal Constraint** icon on the **Constraints** toolbar.

6. Select all the circles one-by-one in the clockwise direction.
7. Select the first and last circle; all the circles are made equal in diameter.
8. On the menu bar, click **Sketch > Geometries > Toggle construction geometry**.
9. Click **Rectangle** drop-down > **Centered rectangle** on the **Geometries** toolbar.
10. Click the vertical axis. Next, move the pointer outward and select anyone of the centerpoints of the circles.

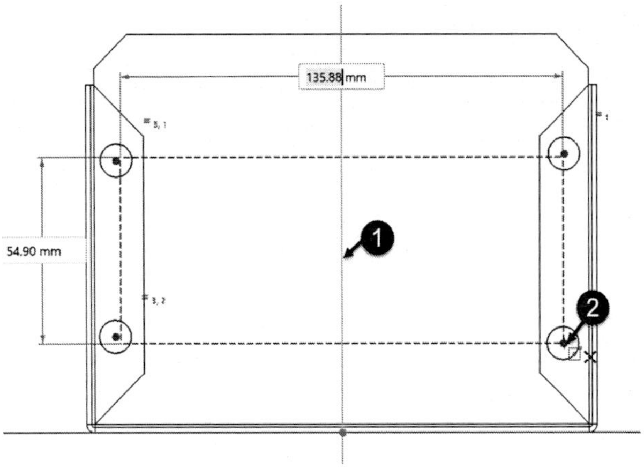

11. Click the **Toggle construction geometry** icon on the **Geometries** toolbar.
12. Create horizontal and vertical distance constraints, as shown.
13. Create the diameter dimension, as shown.

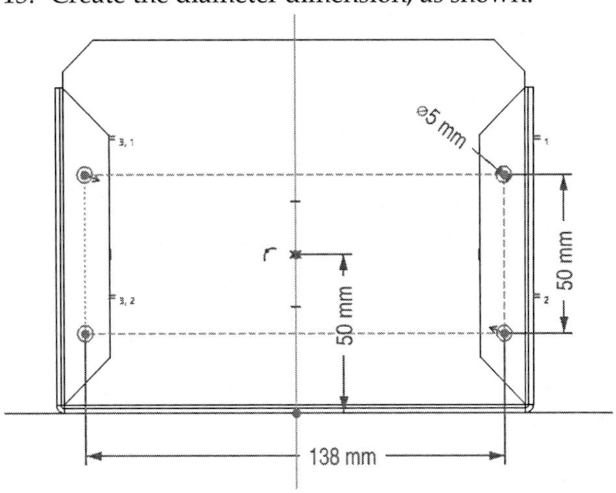

14. Click **Leave Sketch** on the **Edit mode** toolbar.
15. On the **Part Design Modeling Features** toolbar, click the **Pocket** icon.
16. On the **Pocket Parameters** dialog, select **Type > Through All.**
17. Click **OK.**
18. On the **View** toolbar, click **Draw Style** drop-down > **Flat Lines.**

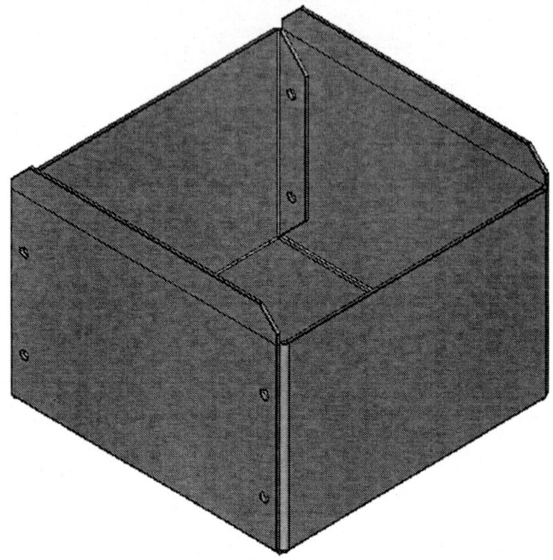

Creating the Flat Pattern

1. Select **Sheet Metal** from the **Workbenches** drop-down.
2. Click on the flat face of the sheet metal model.

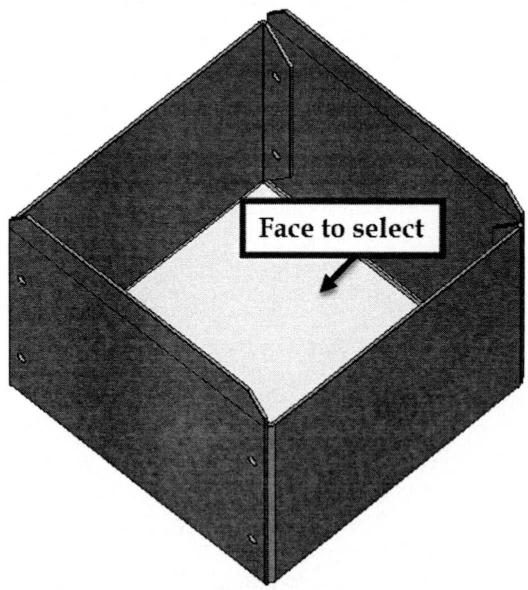

3. Click the **Unfold** icon on the **Sheetmetal** toolbar.
4. Select the **Standard > ANSI** option.

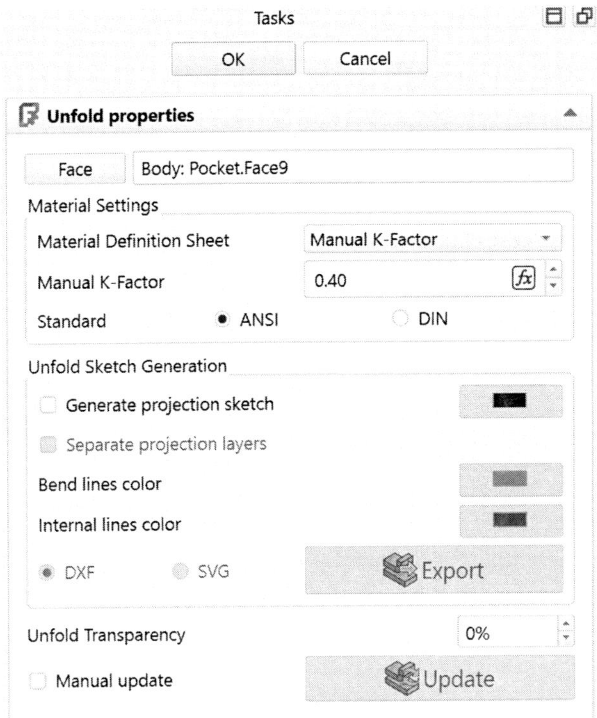

5. Click **OK**.

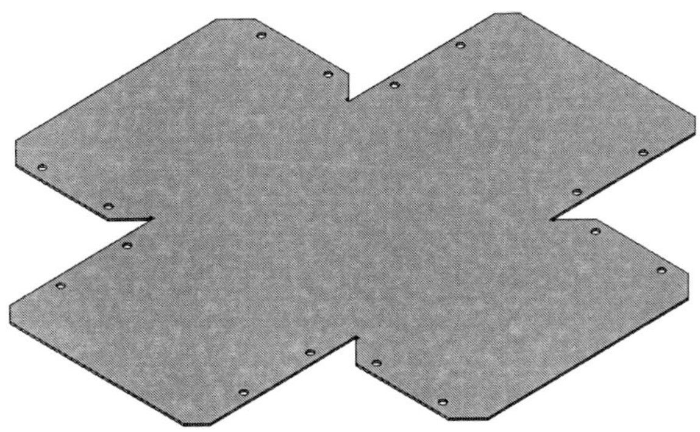

6. Save the sheet metal part.

Creating 2D Drawing of the sheet metal part

1. Select **TechDraw** from the **Workbenches** drop-down.

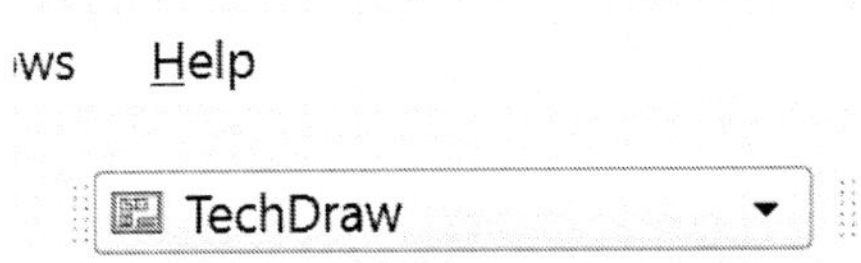

2. Click the **Insert new Page using Template** icon on the **TechDraw pages** toolbar.

3. Browse to the location: *C:\Program Files\FreeCAD 1.1\data\Mod\TechDraw\Templates\ISO*
4. Double-click on the **A2_Landscape_ISO5457_minimal** template.
5. Select **Body** from the **Model** tab.

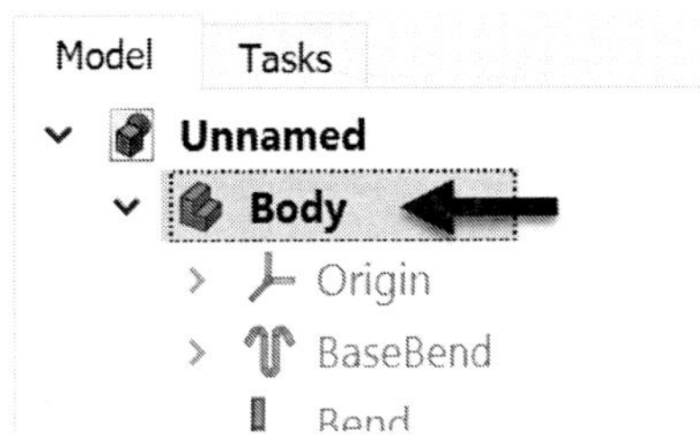

6. Click the **Insert View**  icon on the **Techdraw Views** toolbar.
7. On the **Part View** dialog, select **Scale > Custom**.
8. Type **1** and **2** in the **Custom Scale** boxes, respectively.
9. Click the **Set direction of the camera, or selected face if any, as primary direction** button.

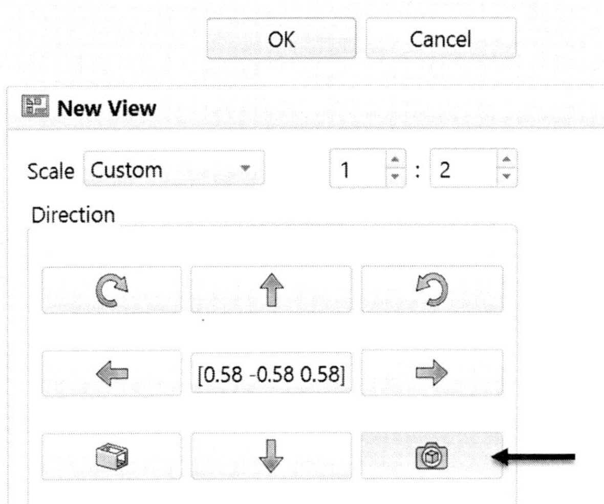

10. Click **OK** on the **Part View** dialog.

11. Click **Edit** > **Recompute** on the menu bar.
12. Switch to the drawing sheet tab.
13. Click and drag the view to the bottom right corner, as shown.

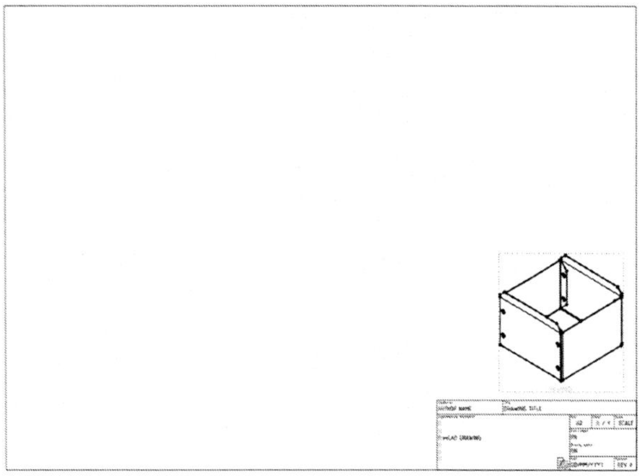

14. Switch to the sheet metal model file.
15. On the **View** toolbar, click the **View orientation** drop-down > **Top**.

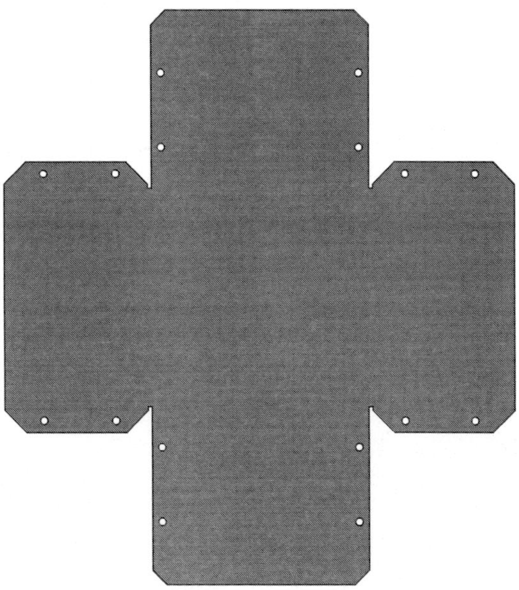

16. Select **Body_unfold** from the **Model** tab.

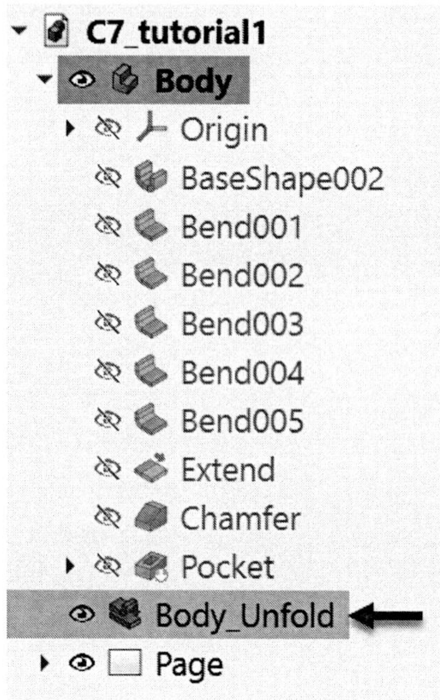

17. Switch to the **Page** tab.
18. Click the **New View**  icon on the **Techdraw Views** toolbar.
19. On the **New View** dialog, select **Scale > Custom**.
20. Type **3** and **4** in the **Custom Scale** boxes, respectively.
21. Click the **Rotate up** 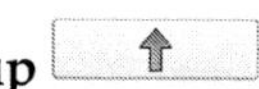 button on the **Tasks** panel.
22. Click **OK** on the **New View** dialog.

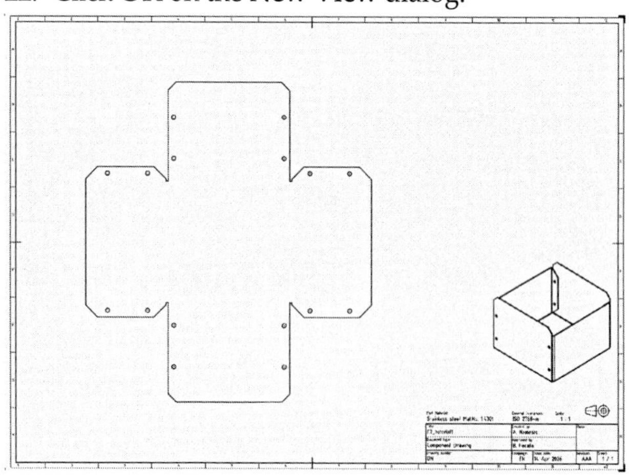

23. Add dimensions to the unfolded view.

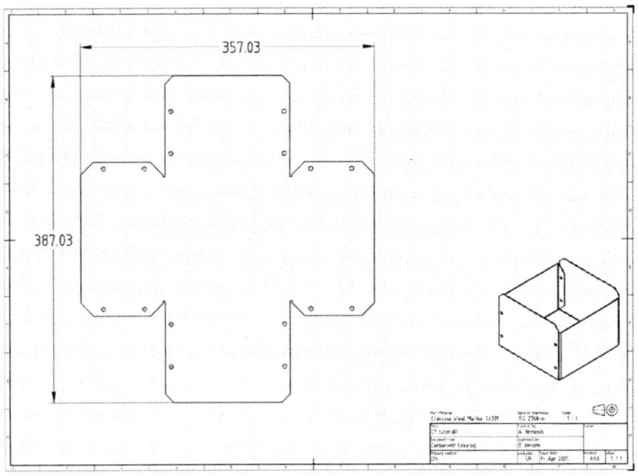

24. Save and close the sheet metal files.

TUTORIAL 2

In this tutorial, you create the model shown in the figure.

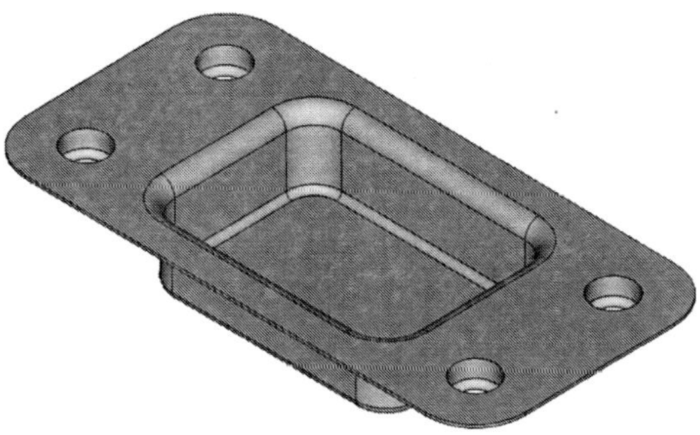

Creating the Base Feature

1. Open a new FreeCAD file.
2. Select **Part Design** from the **Workbenches** drop-down.
3. Click the **New Sketch** icon on the **Part Design Helper Features** toolbar.
4. Select the XY Plane from the **Tasks** panel and click **OK**.
5. Click the **Rectangle** drop-down > **Centered Rectangle** 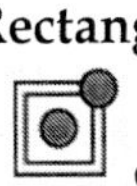 on the **Geometries** toolbar.
6. Create a rectangle and add dimensions to it, as shown.

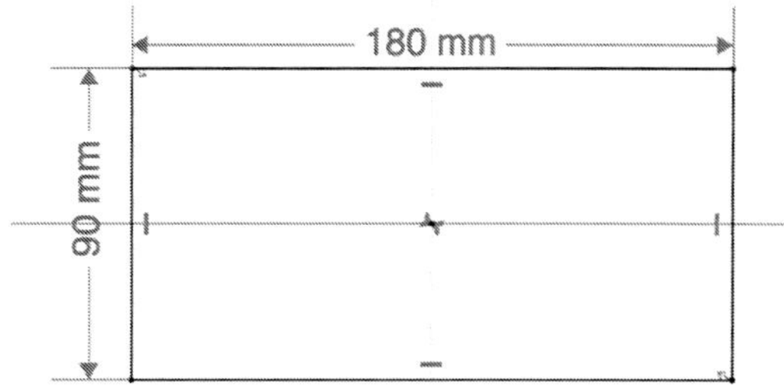

7. Click the **Close** button on the **Tasks** panel.
8. Click **Part Design > Additive Features > Pad** on the menu bar.
9. Type **15** in the **Length** box and click **OK**.

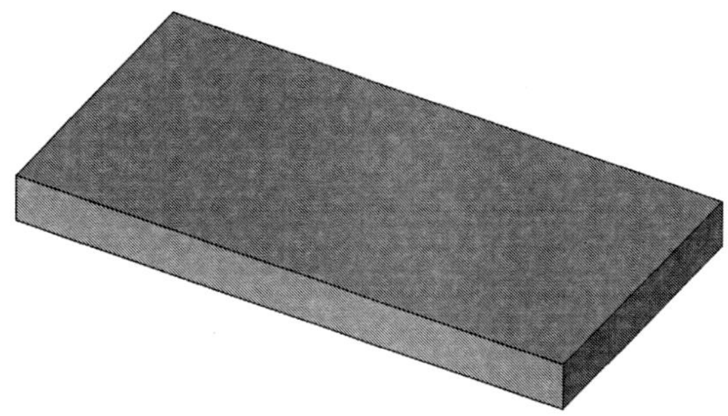

10. Press and hold the middle and right mouse buttons. Next, drag the pointer to rotate the model.
11. Click on the bottom face of the model.
12. Click **New Sketch** on the **Part Design Helper Features** toolbar.
13. On the menu bar, click **Sketch > Geometries > Toggle construction geometry** .
14. Click **Rectangle** drop-down > **Centered rectangle**  on the **Geometries** toolbar.
15. Select the sketch origin, move the pointer outward and click.
16. Click the **Toggle construction geometry** icon on the **Geometries** toolbar.
17. Create four circles on the vertices of the rectangle.
18. Add constraints and dimensions to the sketch.
19. Click **Close** on the **Tasks** panel.

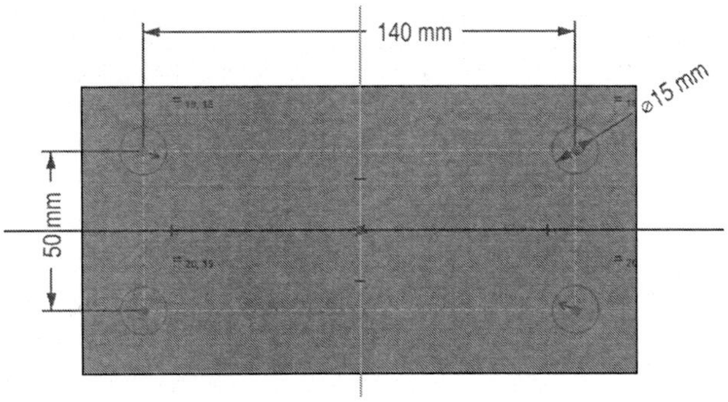

20. Click the **Pad** icon on the **Part Design Modeling Features** toolbar.
21. Type **8** in the **Length** box and click **OK.**
22. Press and hold the CTRL key and click on the bottom faces of the second Pad feature.

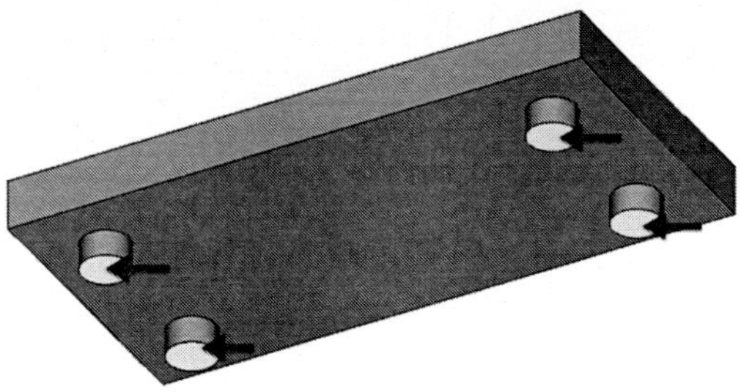

23. Click the **Fillet** icon on the **Part Design Dressup Features** toolbar.
24. Type 2 in the **Radius** box and click **OK.**

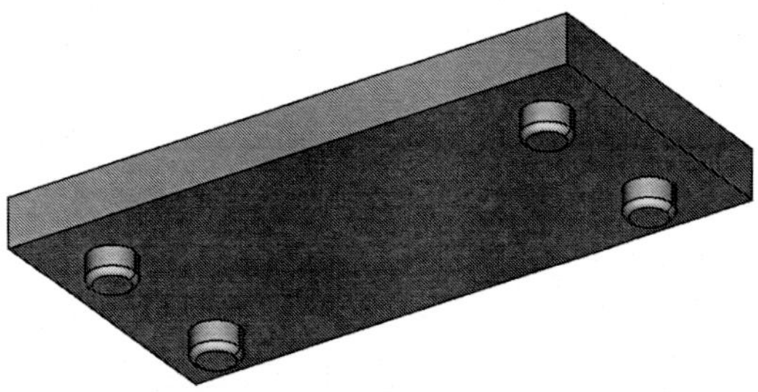

25. Click on the bottom face of the first Pad feature.
26. Click the **New Sketch** icon on the **Part Design Helper Features** toolbar.
27. Create a centered rectangle and add dimensions to it, as shown.

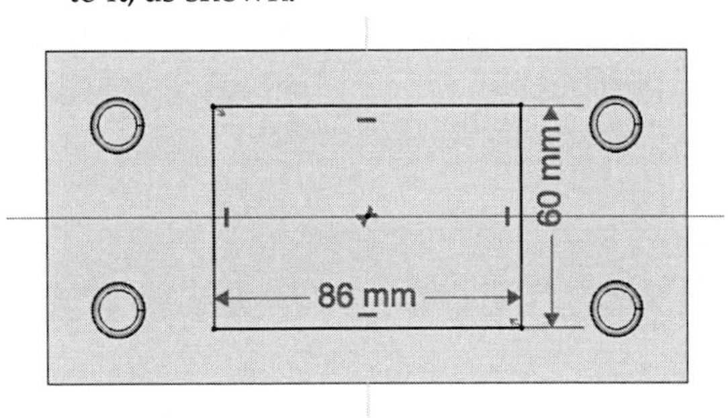

28. Click the **Close** button on the **Tasks** panel.
29. Click **Part Design > Additive features > Pad** on the menu bar.
30. Type **25** in the **Length** box and click **OK.**

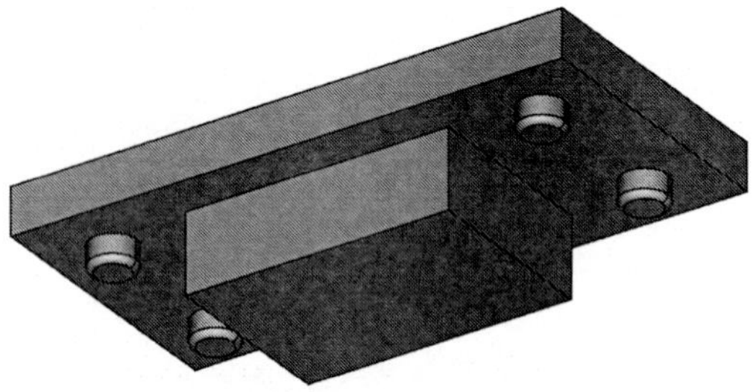

31. Press and hold the CTRL key and select the vertical edges of the newly created Pad feature.
32. Click the **Fillet** icon on the **Part Design Dressup Features** toolbar.
33. Type **10** in the **Radius** box and click **OK.**

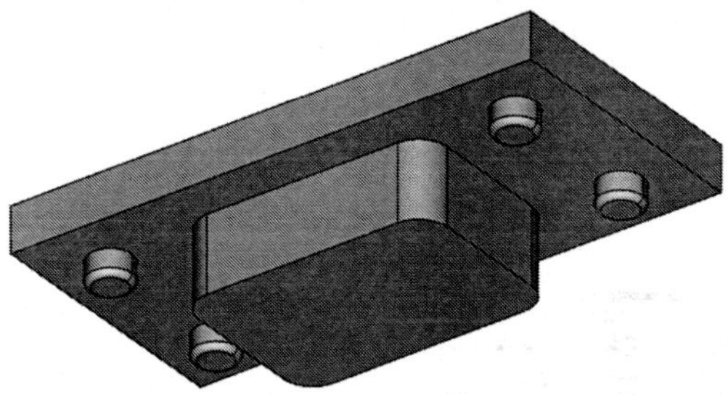

34. Click on the bottom face of the newly created Pad feature.

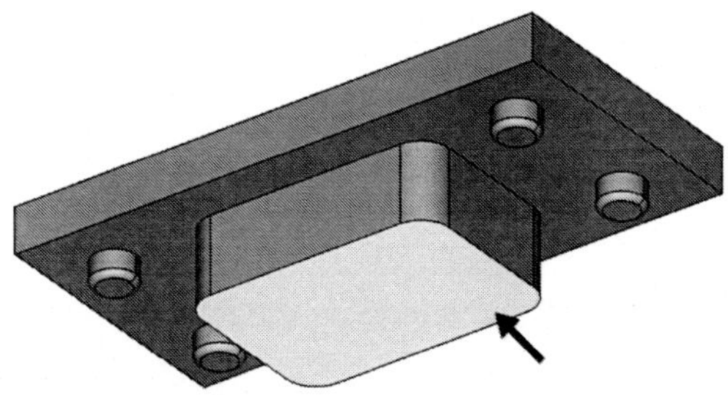

35. Type **2** in the **Radius** box and click **OK.**
36. Click on the edge of the model, as shown.

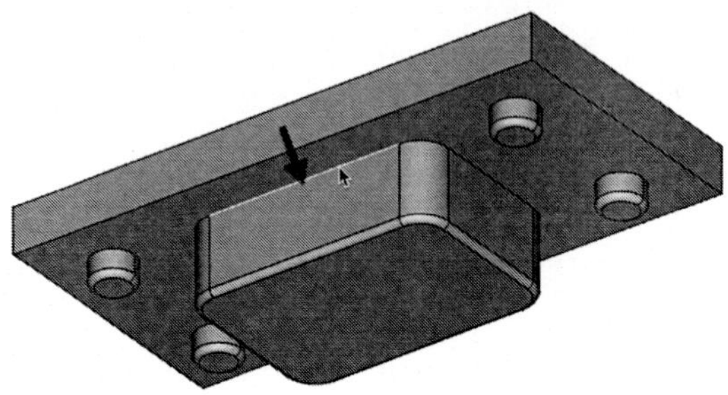

37. Click the **Fillet** icon on the **Part Design Dressup Features** toolbar.

38. Type **5** in the **Radius** box and click **OK**.

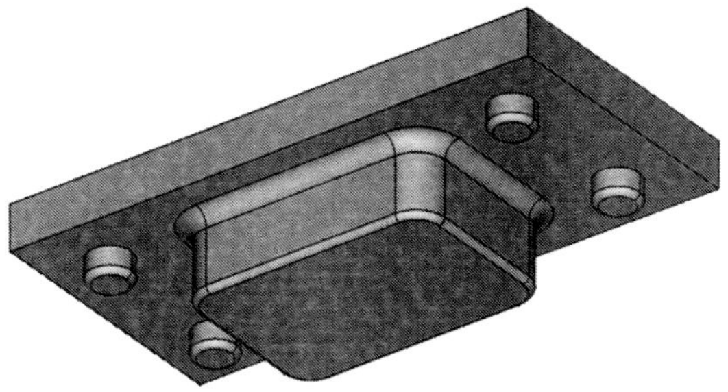

39. Press and hold the CTRL key and click on the vertical edges of the model, as shown.

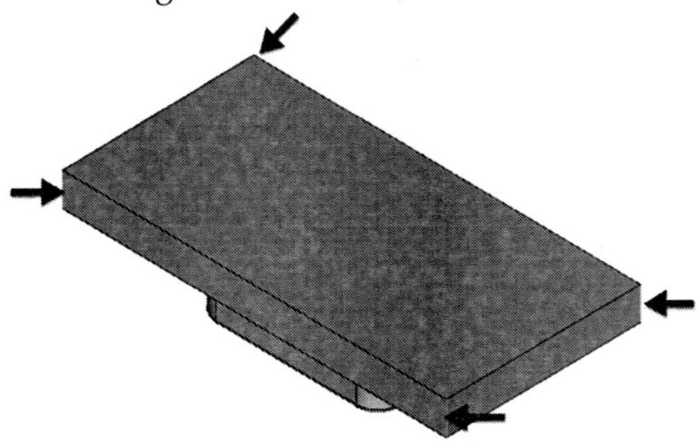

40. Click the **Fillet** icon on the **Part Design Dressup Features** toolbar.
41. Type **18** in the **Radius** box and click **OK**.

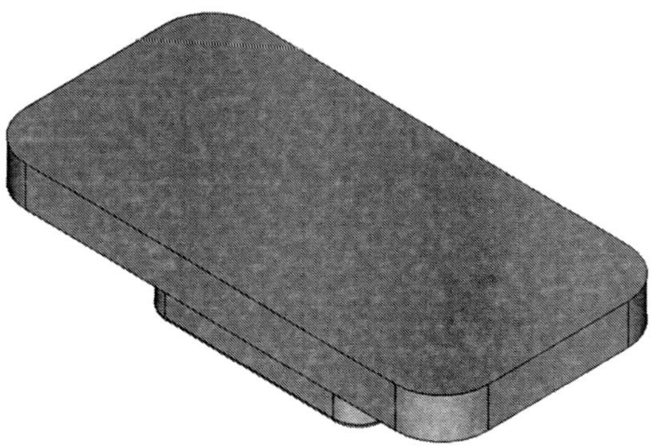

Creating Thickness feature

1. Press and hold the CTRL key and select top face and the side faces attached to it, as shown.

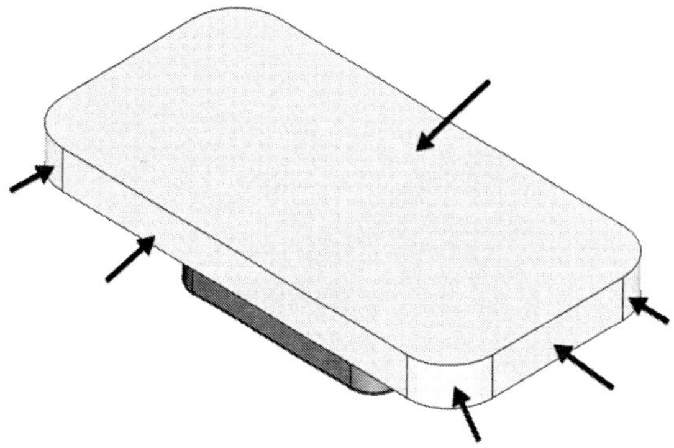

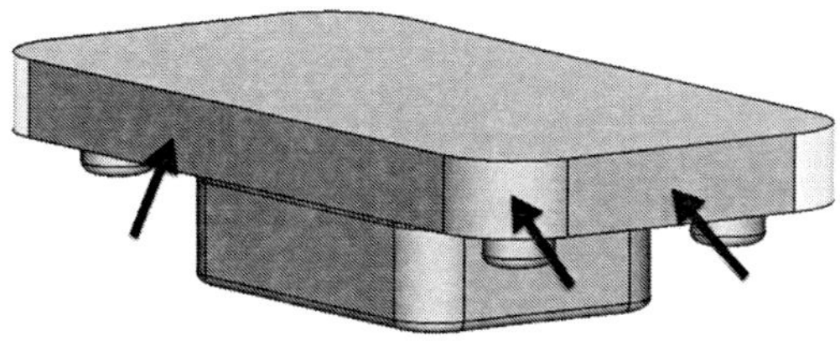

2. Click the **Thickness** icon on the **Part Design Modeling Features** toolbar.
3. Click the **Select** button on the **Tasks** panel.
4. Rotate the model and select the bottom faces of the Pad features.

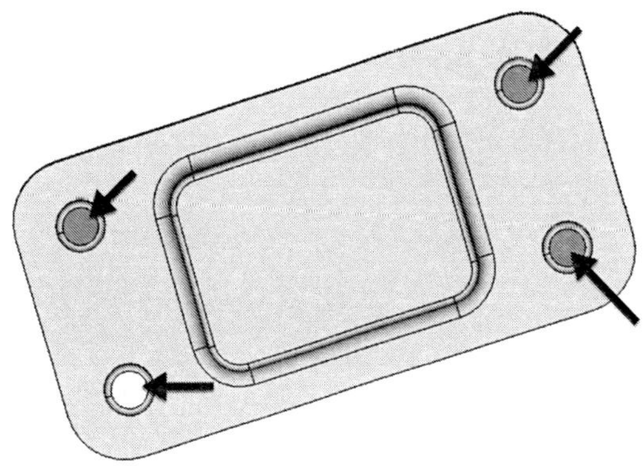

5. Type **1** in the **Thickness** box.
6. Click **OK**.

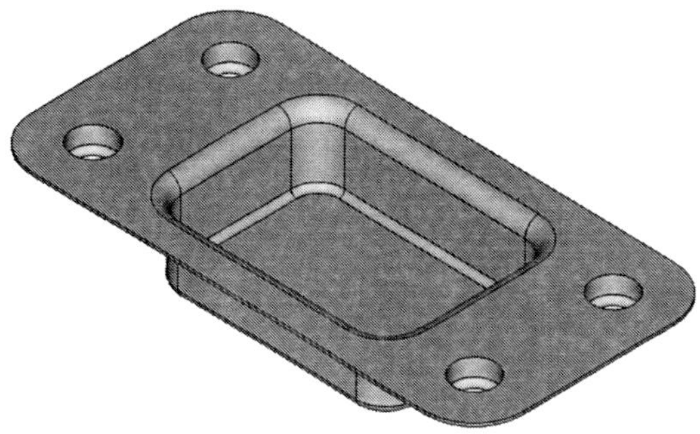

7. Save and close the file.

TUTORIAL 3

In this tutorial, you create the sheet metal model shown in the figure.

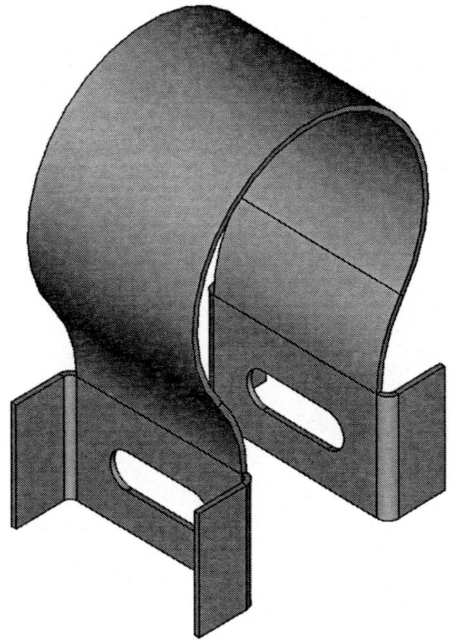

Creating the Base Feature

1. Open a new FreeCAD file.
2. Select **Part Design** from the **Workbenches** drop-down.
3. Click the **New Sketch** icon on the **Sketcher** toolbar.
4. Select the **YZ-Plane** option and click **OK.**
5. Select the **Arc** drop-down > **Arc from Center**  from the **Geometries** toolbar.
6. Select the sketch origin to define the center of the arc.
7. Specify the start and end points of the arc, as shown.

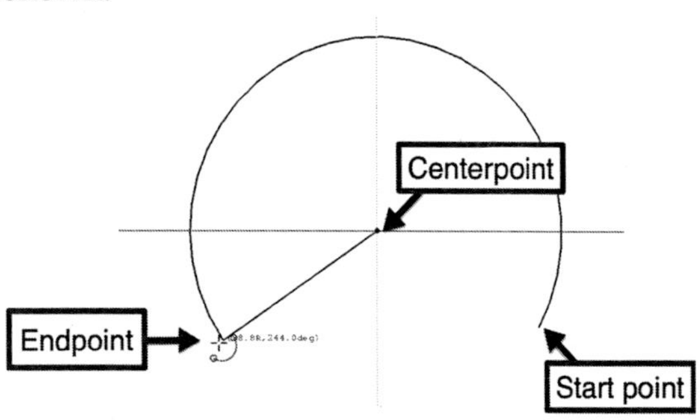

8. Select the **Arc** drop-down > **Arc from 3 Points** from the **Geometries** toolbar.
9. Select the endpoint of the arc.
10. Move the pointer downward and click.
11. Move the pointer toward right and click to create the arc.

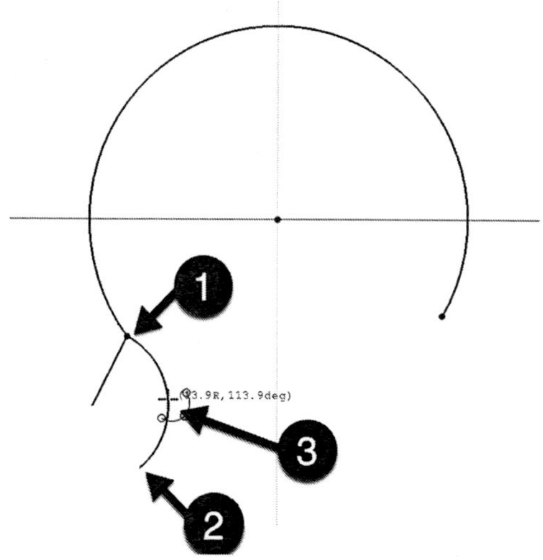

12. Likewise, create another arc, as shown.

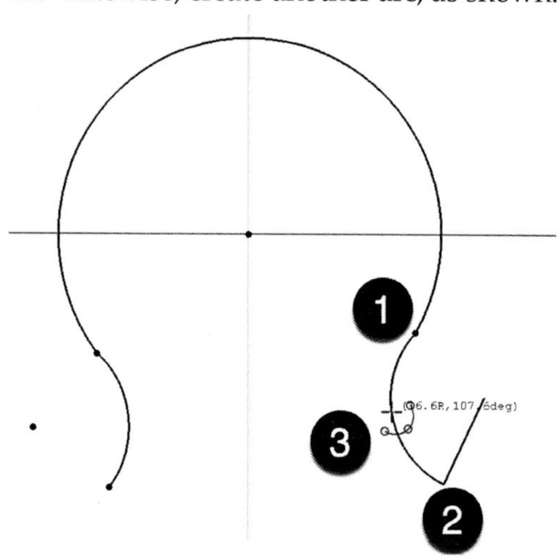

13. Create two vertical lines from the endpoints of the arcs, as shown.

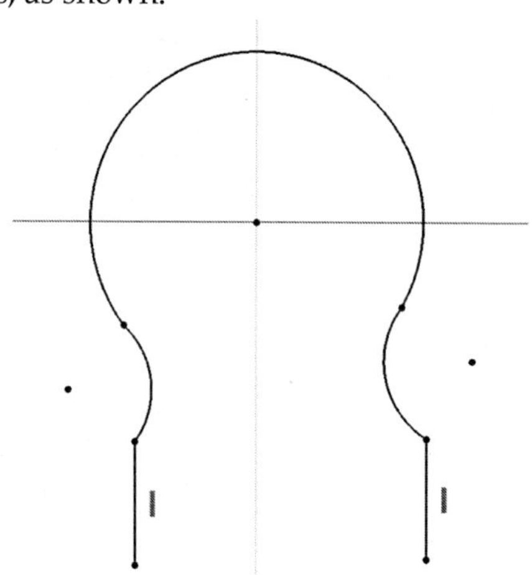

14. Add dimensions to the sketch, as shown.

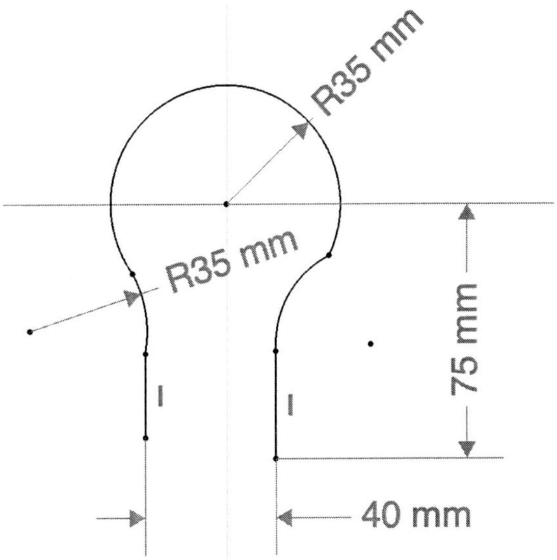

15. Add constraints to the sketch, as shown.

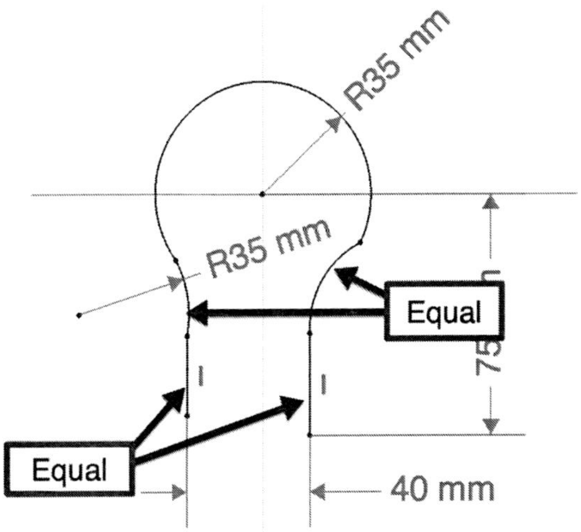

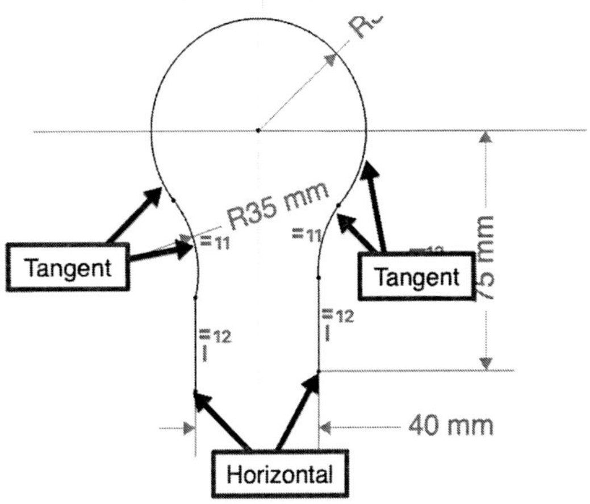

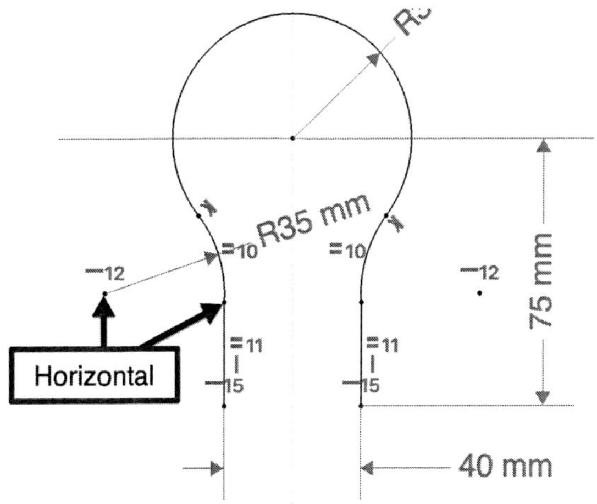

16. Click the **Close** button on the **Tasks** panel.
17. Select **Sheet Metal** from the **Workbenches** drop-down.
18. Select the sketch, if not already selected.
19. Click the **Make Base Wall**  icon on the **Sheetmetal** toolbar.
20. Type **1.5** in the **Thickness** box.
21. Type **50** in the **Length** box.
22. Check the **Symmetric** option.

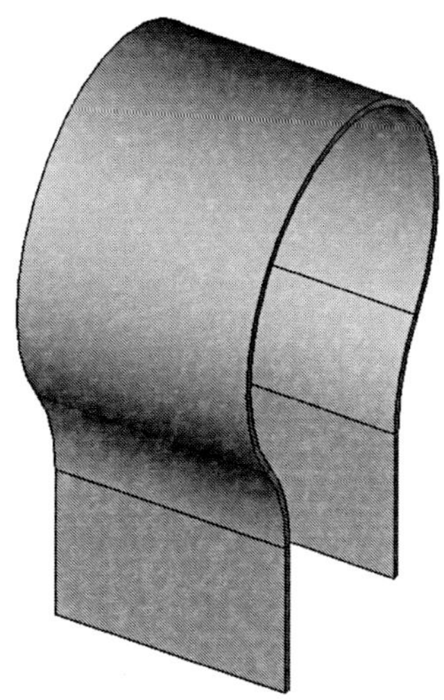

Creating the flange

1. Press and hold the CTRL key and select the edges, as shown.

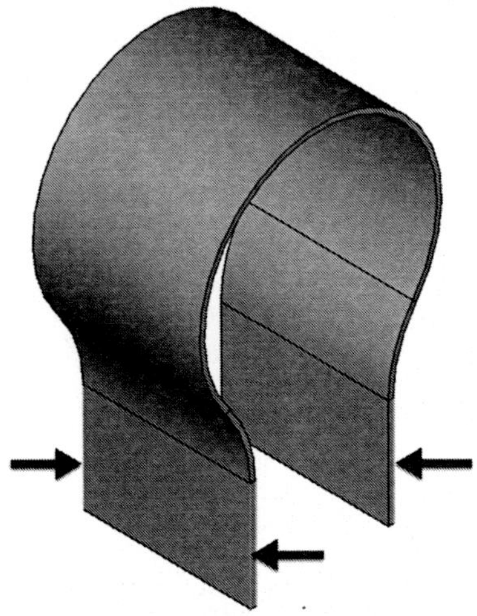

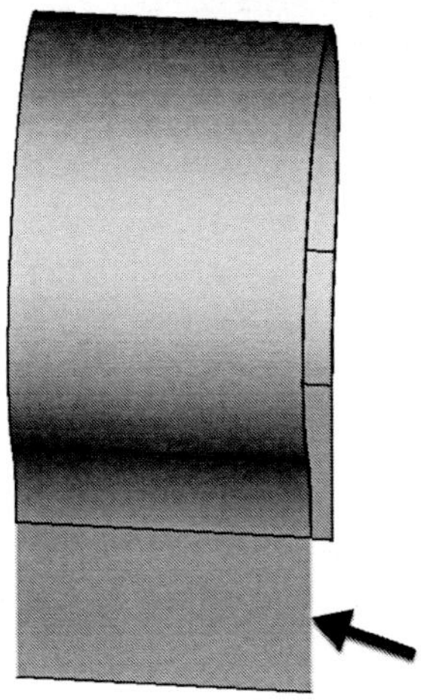

2. Click the **Make Wall**  icon on the **Sheetmetal** toolbar.
3. Enter **18** and **2** in the **Length** and **Bend radius** boxes, respectively.
4. Select **Length Mode > Outer Sharp.**
5. Select **Bend Type > Material Outside.**
6. Select **invert > true.**

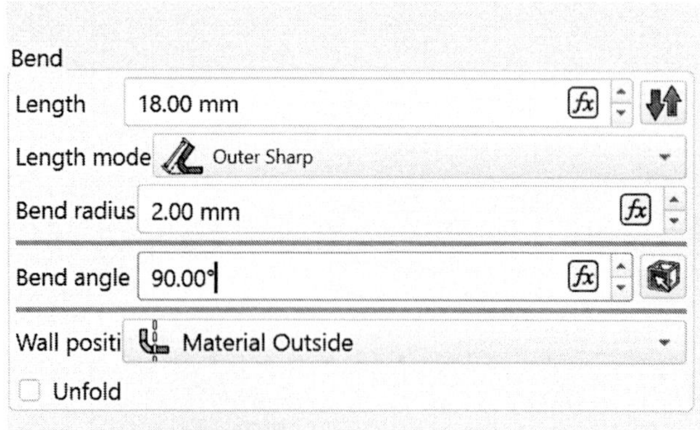

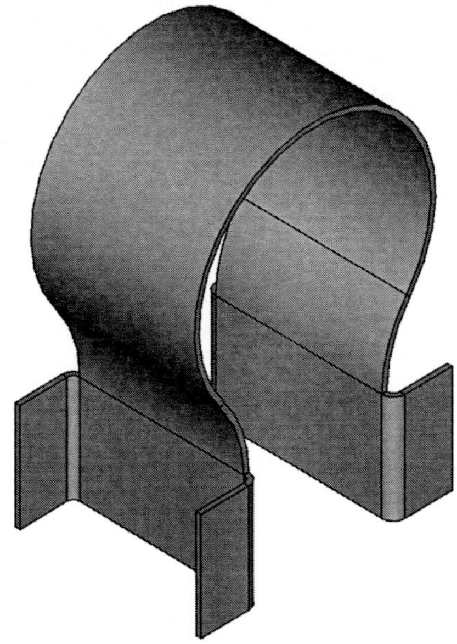

Creating Extruded Cuts

1. Select **Part Design** from the **Workbenches** drop-down.
2. Click on the flat face of the flange, as shown.

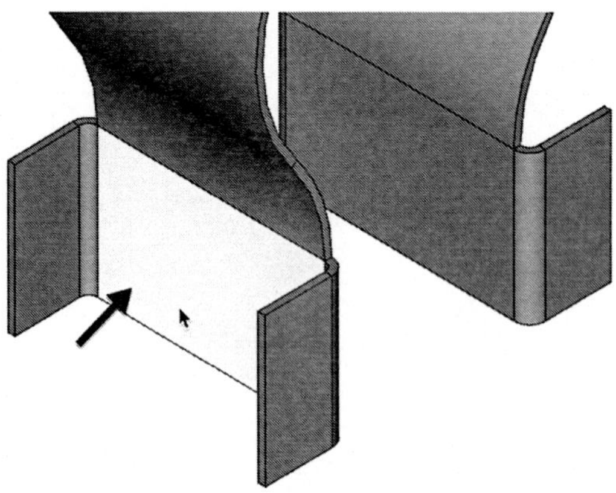

3. Click the **New Sketch** icon on the **Sketcher** toolbar.
4. Select the **Create slot** icon from the **Geometries** toolbar.

5. Create a slot and add dimensions to it, as shown.

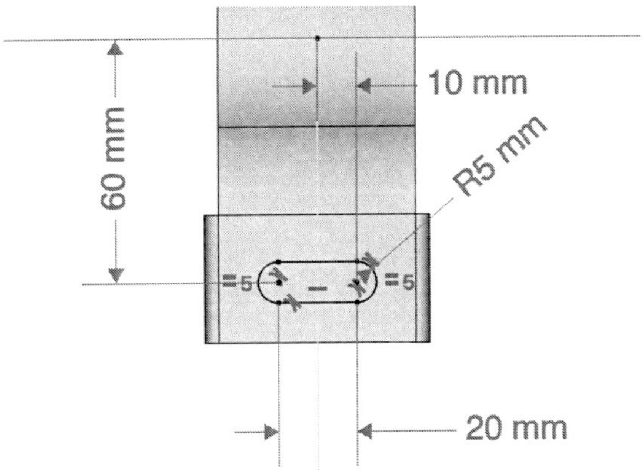

6. Click **Close** on the **Tasks** panel.
7. Select **Sheetmetal** from the **Workbenches** drop-down.
8. Select the flat face of the sheet metal model, as shown.

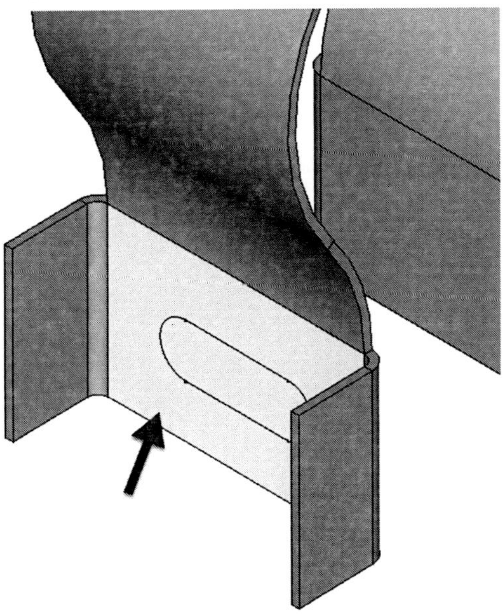

9. Press and hold the CTRL key and select the newly created sketch from the **Model** panel.

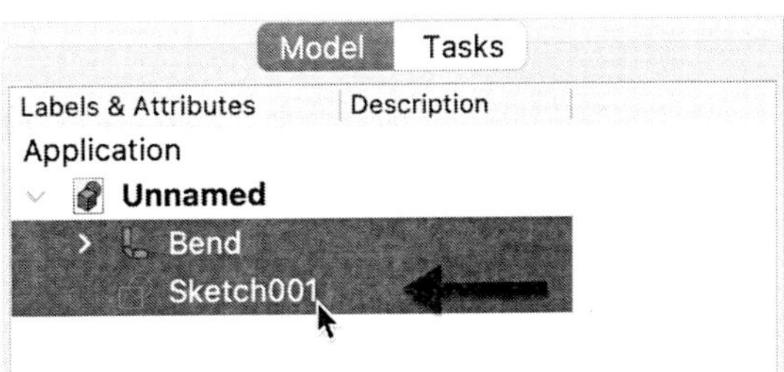

10. Click the **Sketch on Sheet Metal**  icon on the **Sheetmetal** toolbar. An extruded cut is created on the flat face using the sketch.
11. Click **OK**.

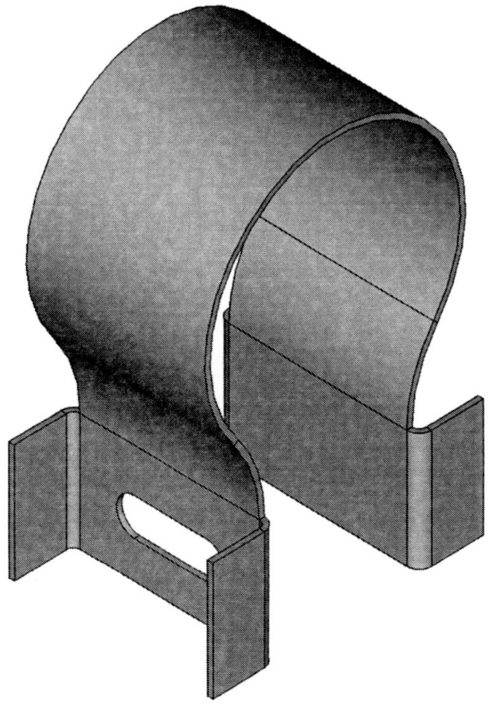

12. Likewise, create another extruded cut on the right vertical face of the sheet metal body.

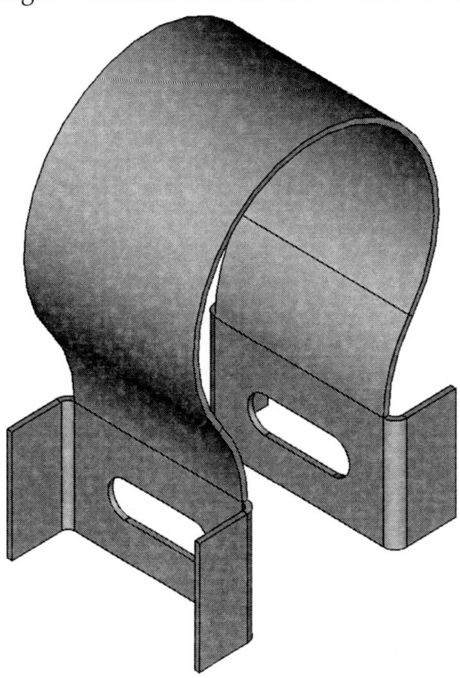

13. Save and close the sheet metal file.

TUTORIAL 4

In this tutorial, you create the sheet metal model shown in the figure.

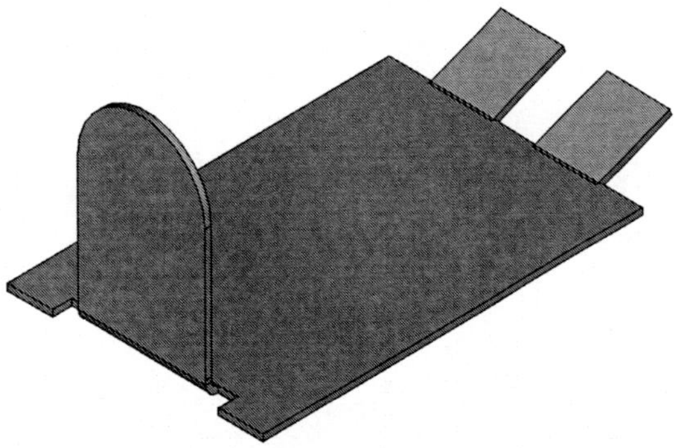

Adding Corner Reliefs

1. Start a new FreeCAD file.
2. Select **Part Design** from the **Workbenches** drop-down.
3. Click the **New Sketch** icon on the **Sketcher** toolbar.
4. Select the XY Plane.
5. Create the sketch, as shown. Next, click **Close** on the **Tasks** panel.

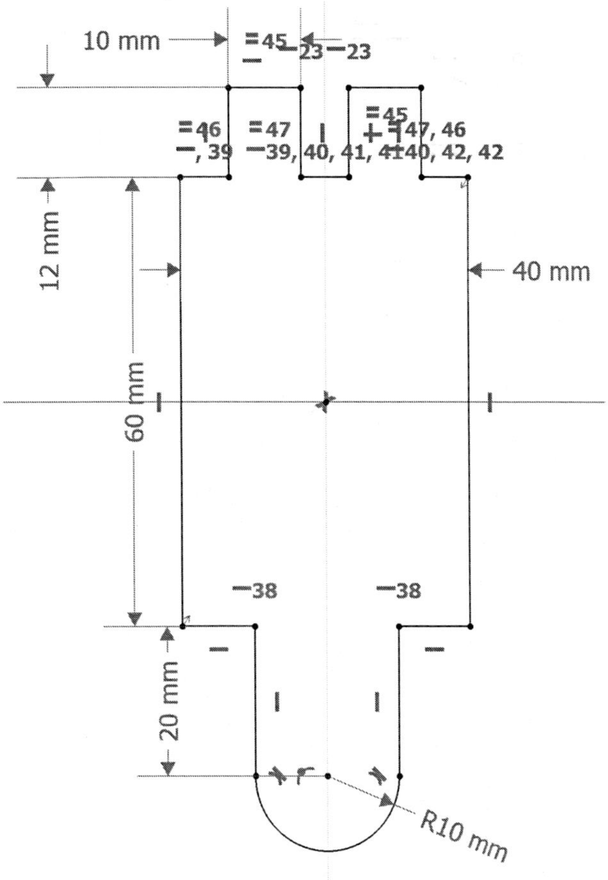

6. Select **Sheet Metal** from the **Workbenches** drop-down.
7. Click the **Make Base Wall**  icon on the **Sheetmetal** toolbar.
8. Type **1** in the **Thickness** box and click **OK**.

9. Click on the lower endpoint of the vertical edge, as shown.

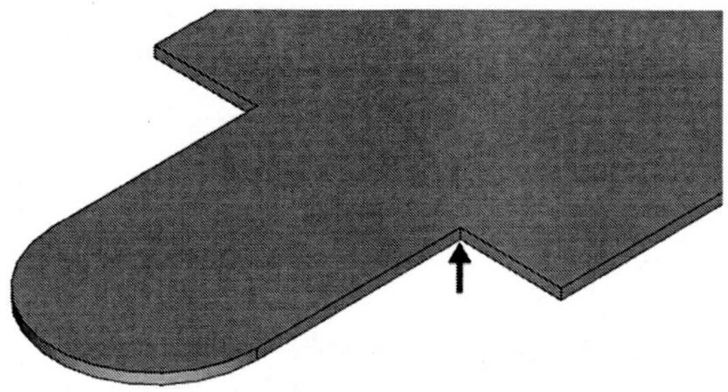

10. Press and hold the CTRL key and select the upper endpoint of the vertical edge, as shown.

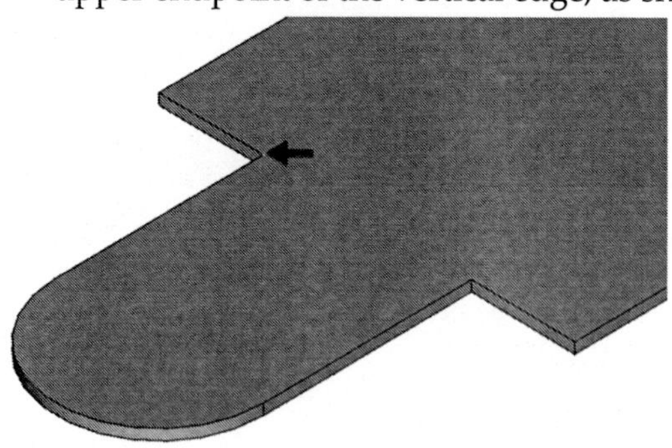

11. Click the **Make Relief**  icon on the **Sheet Metal** toolbar.

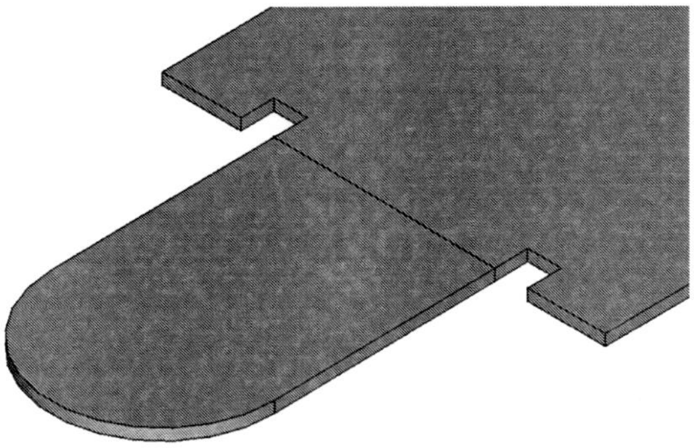

12. Type **3** in the **Size** box.

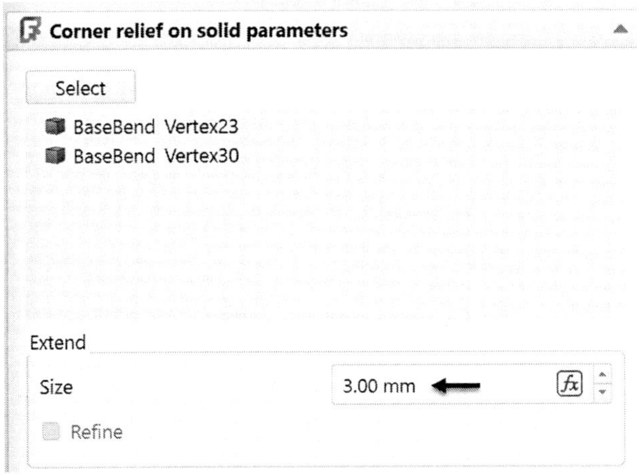

13. Click in the graphics window to update the relief size.

Fold a wall using a Sketch

1. Select **Part Design** from the **Workbenches** drop-down.
2. Click on the top face of the sheet metal part.
3. Click the **New Sketch** icon on the **Part Design Helper Features** toolbar.
4. On the menu bar, click **Sketch > Geometries > Toggle construction geometry**.
5. Click the **External Projection**  icon on the **Sketcher tools** toolbar.
6. Select the horizontal edges of the sheet metal part, as shown.

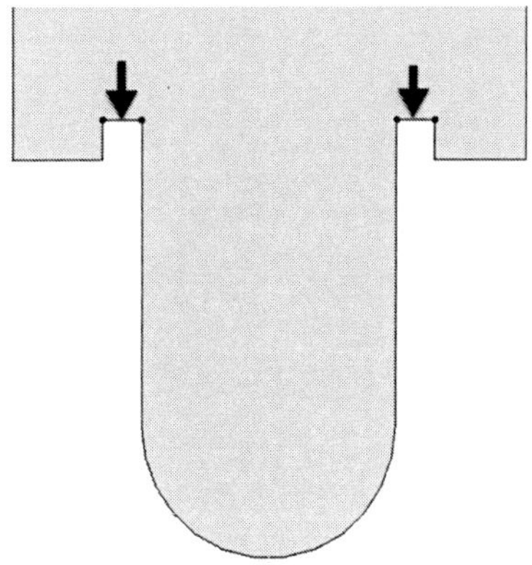

7. On the menu bar, click **Sketch > Geometries > Toggle construction geometry**.
8. Click the **Line**  icon on the **Geometries** toolbar.
9. Select the inner endpoint of the external geometry, as shown.

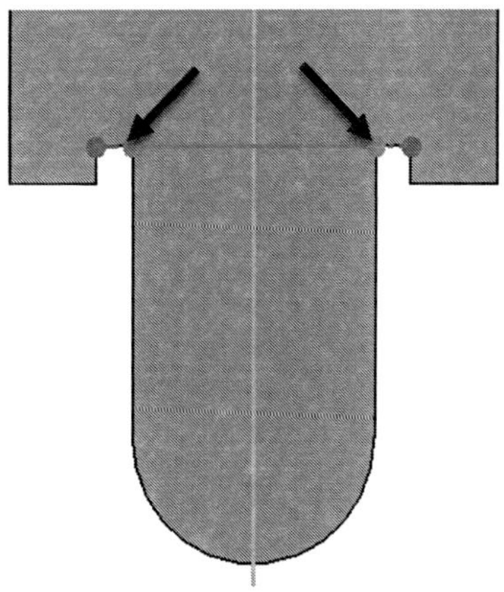

10. Click the **Close** button on the **Tasks** panel.
11. Click on the top face of the sheet metal part.
12. Click the **New Sketch** icon on the **Part Design Helper Features** toolbar.
13. On the menu bar, click **Sketch > Geometries > Toggle construction geometry**.
14. Click the **External Projection** icon on the **Sketcher tools** toolbar.
15. On the menu bar, click **Sketch > Geometries > Toggle construction geometry**.
16. Select the horizontal edges of the sheet metal part, as shown.

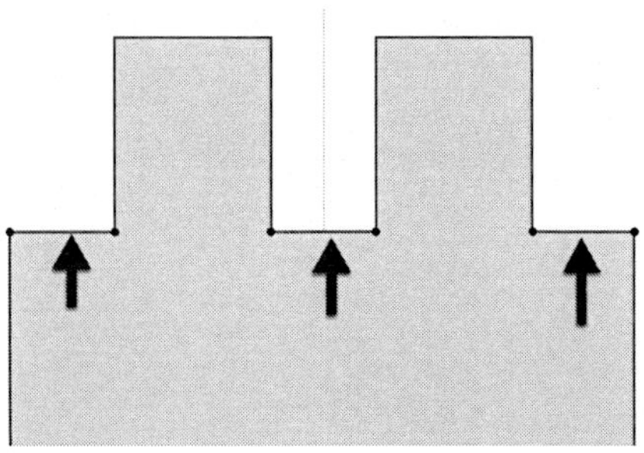

17. Click the **Line** icon on the **Geometries** toolbar.
18. Select the endpoints of the external geometry, as shown.

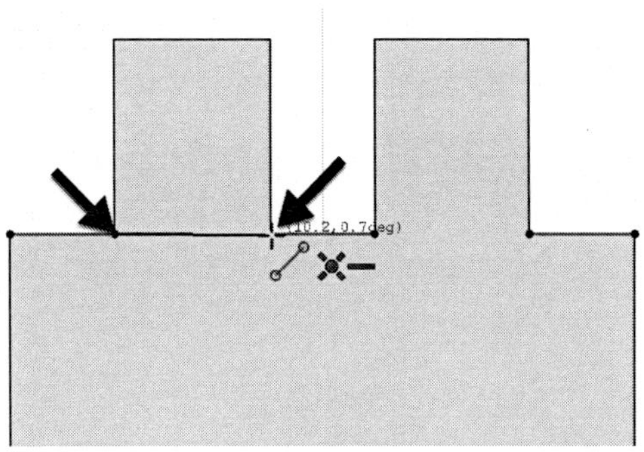

19. Likewise, create another horizontal line, as shown.

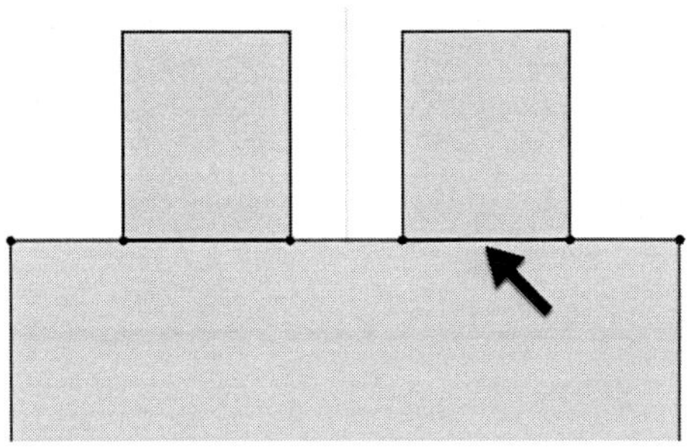

20. Click **Close** on the **Tasks** panel.
21. Select **Sheet Metal** from the **Workbenches** drop-down.
22. Press and hold the CTRL key and select the top face of the sheetmetal part and the line, as shown.

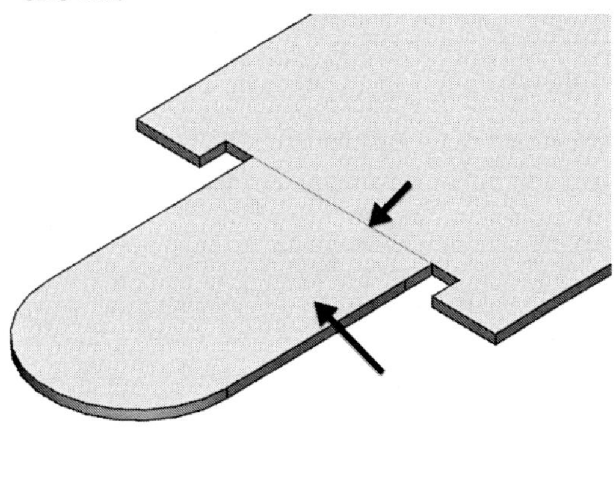

23. Click the **Fold a Wall**  icon on the **Sheet Metal** toolbar.
24. Selec **Position > Forward**. The wall is folded, as shown.

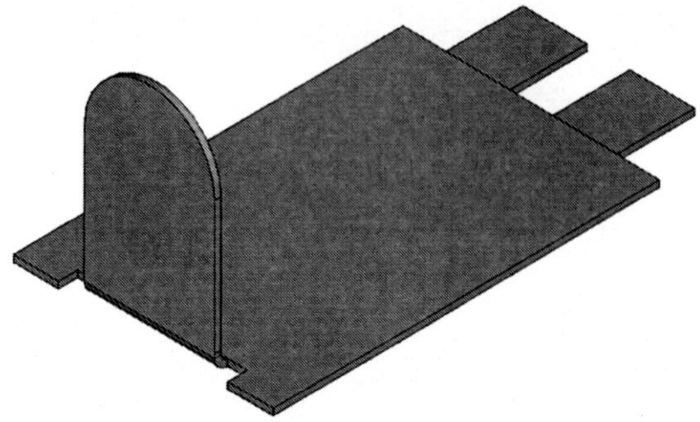

25. Click **OK**.
26. Press and hold the CTRL key and select the top face of the sheetmetal part and the lines, as shown.

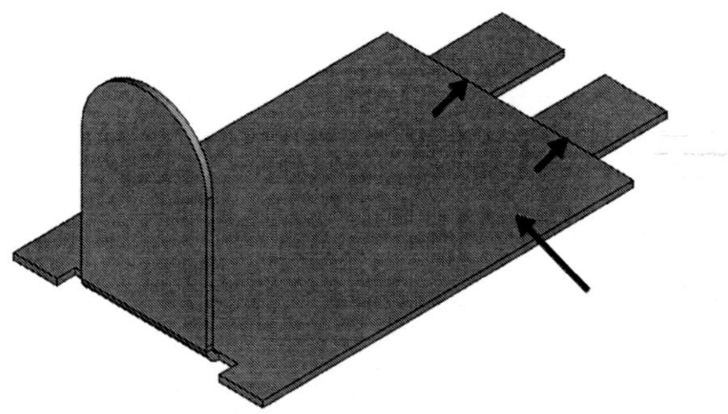

27. Click the **Fold a Wall**  icon on the **Sheet Metal** toolbar

The wall is folded, as shown.

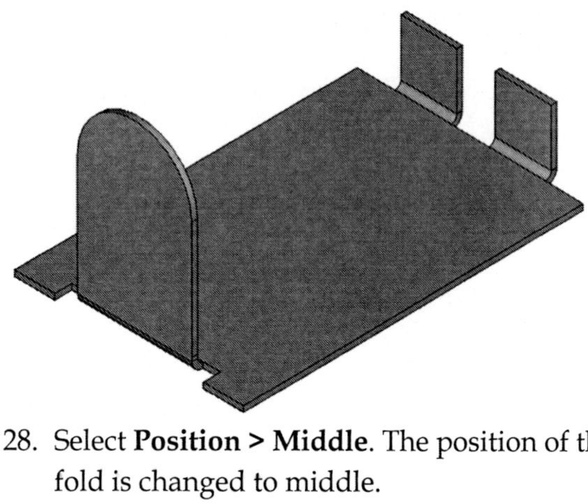

28. Select **Position > Middle**. The position of the fold is changed to middle.

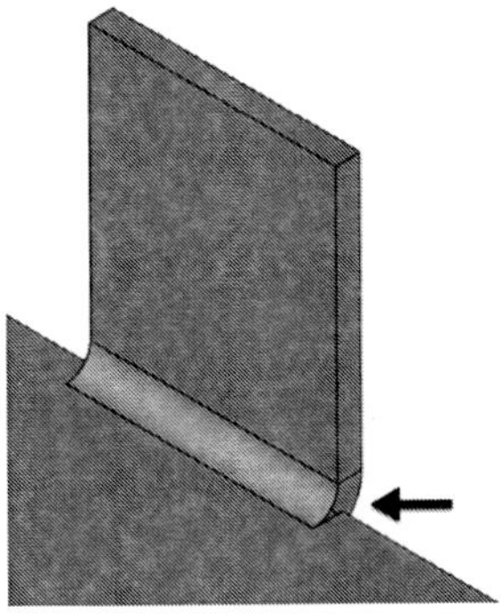

29. Select the **Position > Backward** to change the fold position to backward.

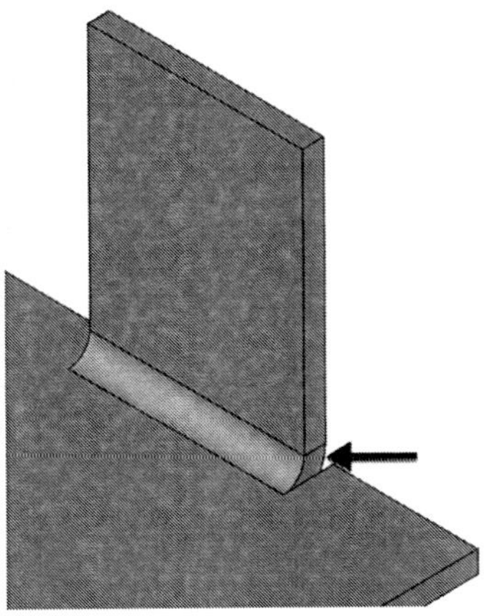

30. Type **20** in the **Bend Angle** box, and then click in the graphics window.

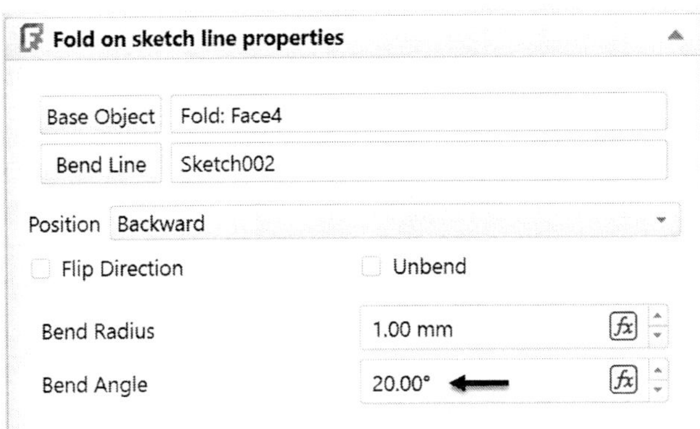

14. Save and close the file.

TUTORIAL 5

In this tutorial, you create the sheet metal model shown in the figure.

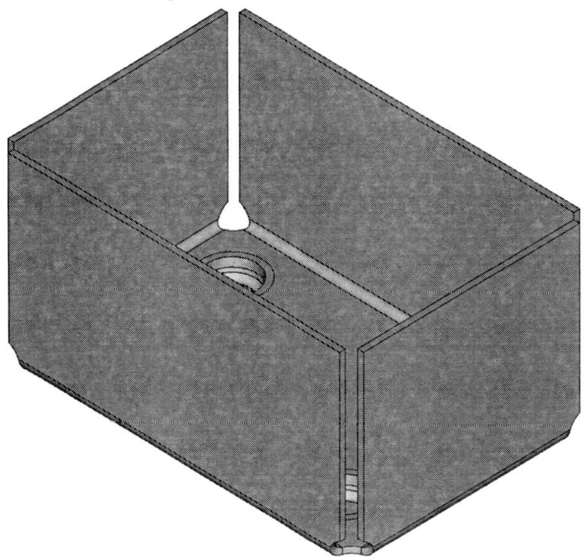

Ripping the Edges of the Model

1. Close the FreeCAD application, and then restart it.
2. Open a new FreeCAD file.
3. Select **Part Design** from the **Workbenches** drop-down.
4. Click the **New Sketch** icon on the **Part Design Helper Features** toolbar.
5. Select the XY Plane from the **Tasks** panel and click **OK**.
6. Click the **Rectangle** drop-down > **Centered Rectangle** on the **Geometries** toolbar.
7. Create a closed sketch, as shown.

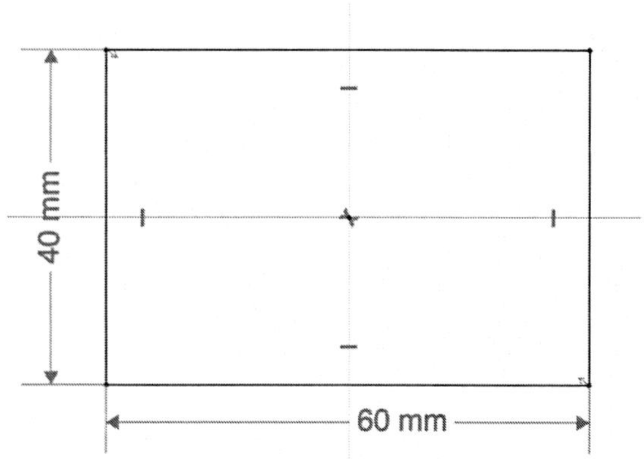

8. Click the **Close** button on the **Tasks** panel.
9. Click the **Pad**  icon on the **Part Design Modeling Features** toolbar.
10. Type **30** in the **Length** box.
11. Click **OK**.

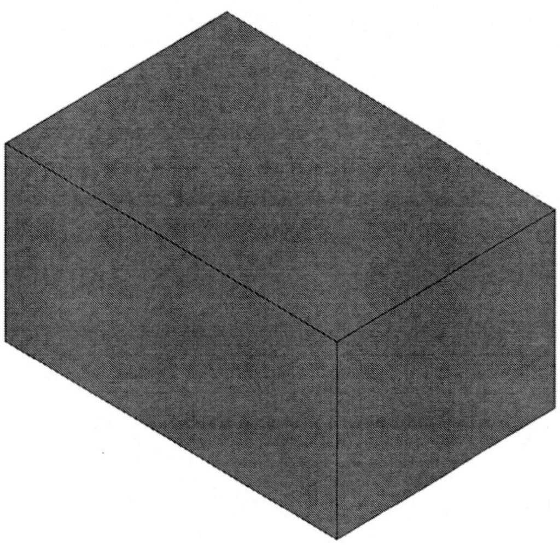

12. Select the top face of the model.
13. Click the **Thickness** icon on the **Part Design Dressup Features** toolbar.
14. Type **1** in the **Thickness** box.
15. Select **Joint Type > Intersection**.
16. Check the **Make thickness inwards** option.
17. Click **OK**.

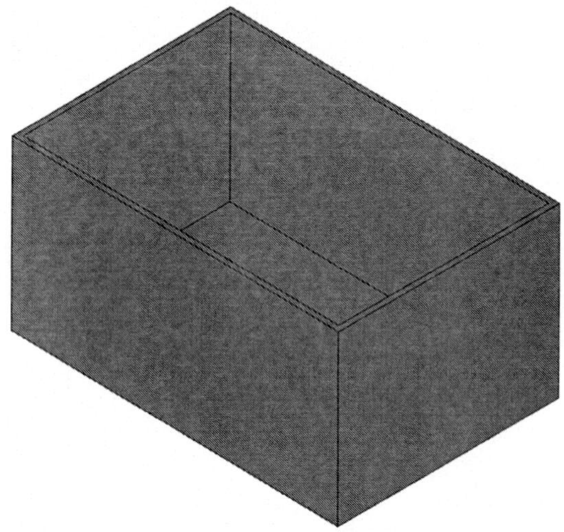

18. Select **Sheet Metal** from the **Workbenches** drop-down.
19. Press and hold the CTRL key and select the vertical edges of the model, as shown.

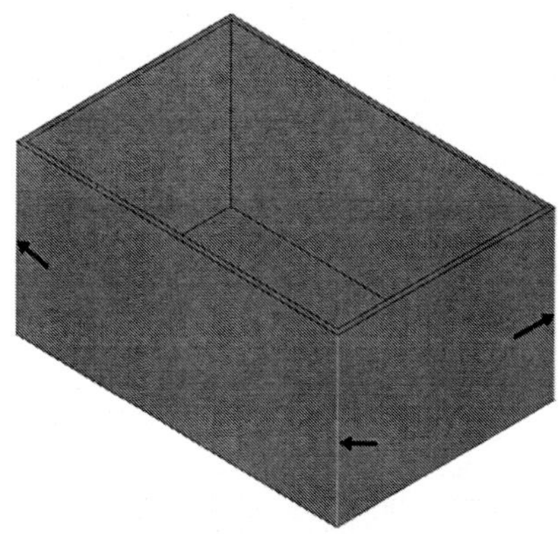

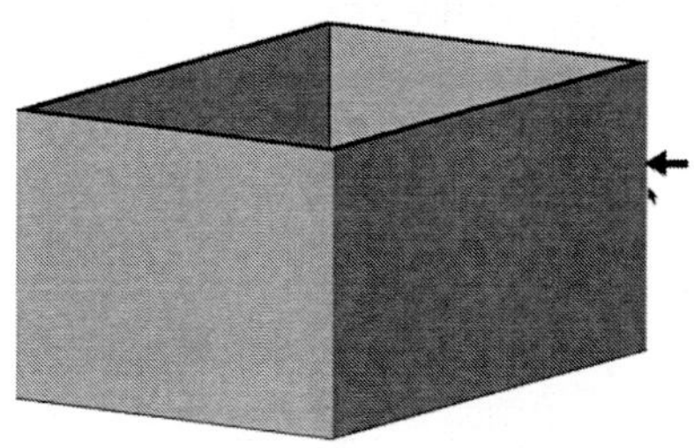

20. Click the **Make Junction**  icon on the **Sheetmetal** toolbar.
21. Type **2** in the **Width** box.
22. Click **OK**. The selected edges are ripped opened.

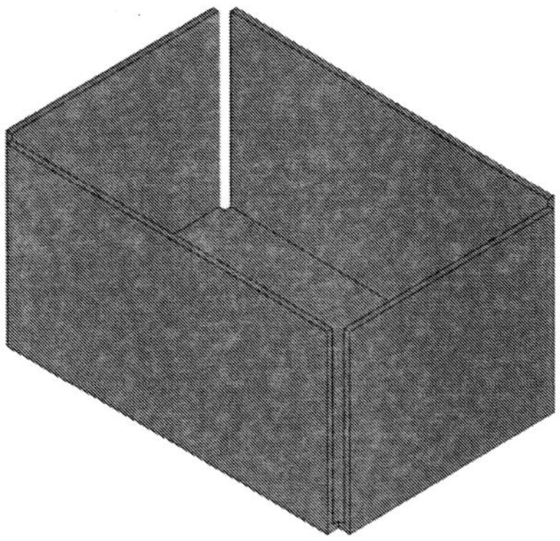

Making Bends

In this section, you will convert an edge into a bend using the **Make Bend** command.

1. Press and hold the CTRL key and select the edges on the bottom face, as shown.

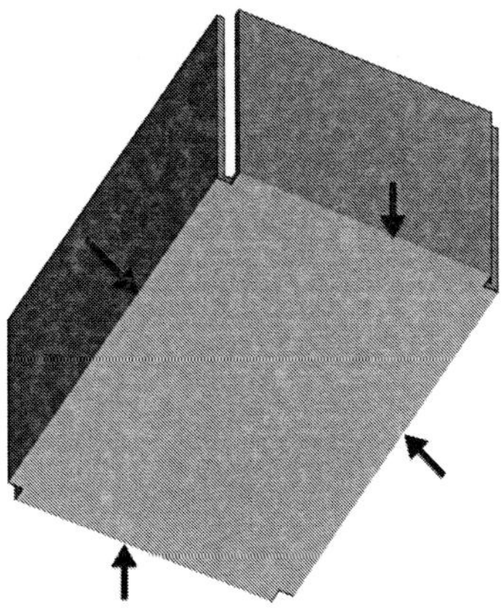

2. Click the **Make Bend**  icon on the **Sheetmetal** toolbar.
3. On the **Bend sharp corner properties** panel, enter **1** in the **Radius** box.

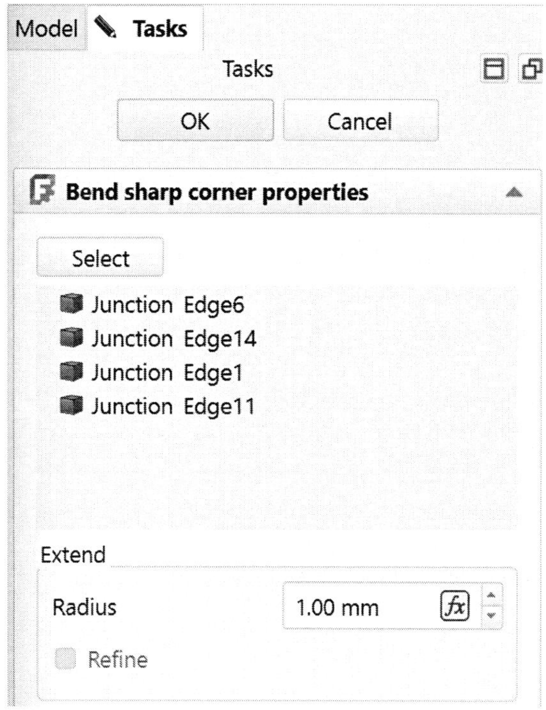

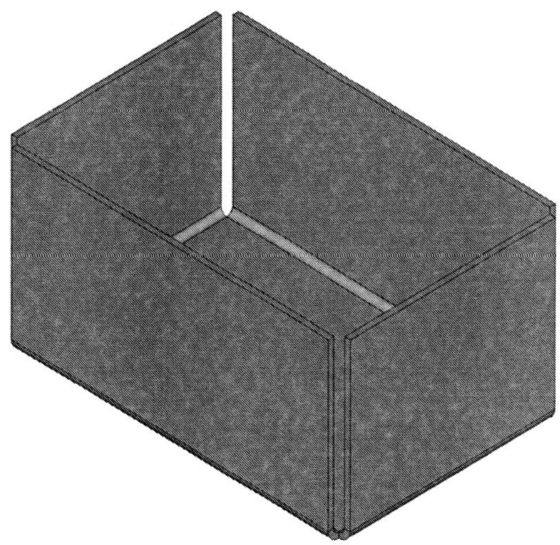

Adding Corner Relief

In this section, you will add corner reliefs to the bends. You add corner reliefs to the model to prevent deformation when the sheetmetal model is folded or unfolded.

1. Press and hold the CTRL key and select the intersecting edges of the bends, as shown.

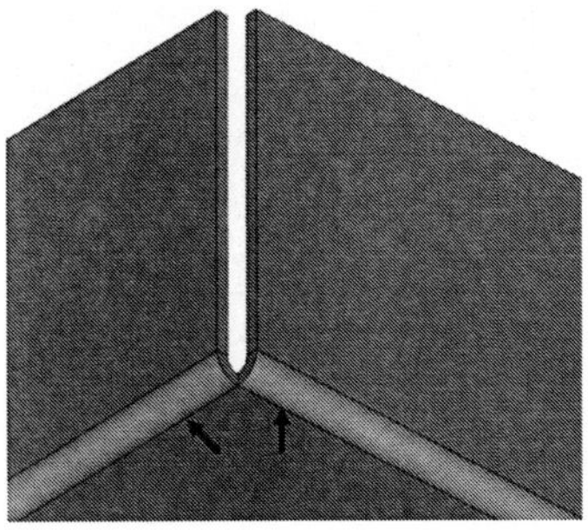

2. Click the **Add Corner relief** icon on the **Sheetmetal** toolbar.
3. Select **Relief Type > Circular**.

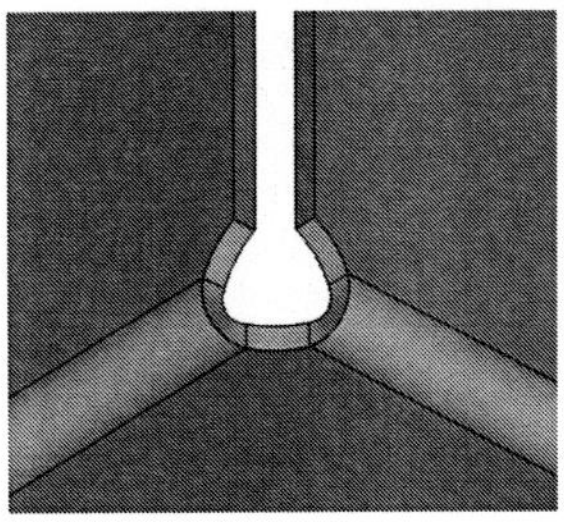

You can also select the **Square**, or **Sketch** from the **Relief Type** section.

Square

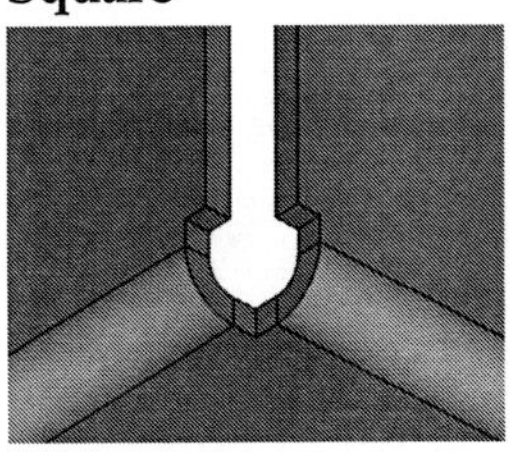

4. Type **3** in the **Relief Size** box.
5. Click **OK**.
6. Likewise, add reliefs to other corners, as shown.

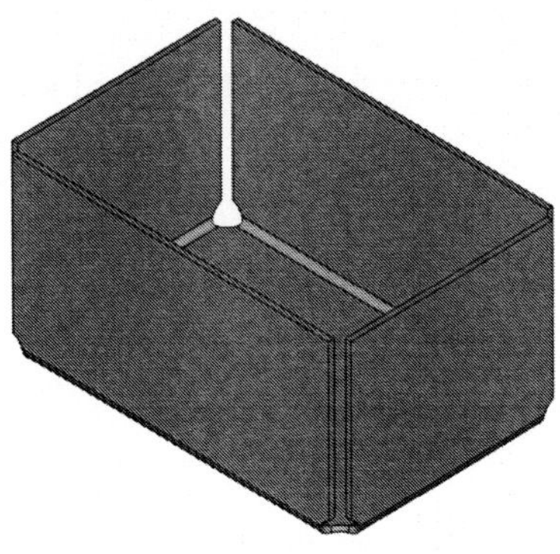

Making a Forming in Wall

1. Select the **Part Design** option from the **Workbenches** drop-down.
2. Click the **New Body** icon on the **Part Design Helper Features** toolbar.
3. Click the **New Sketch** icon on the **Part Design Helper Features** toolbar.
4. Select the **XY-Plane** and click **OK**.
5. Click **Sketch > Toggle Section View** on the menu bar.
6. Create a sketch, as shown.

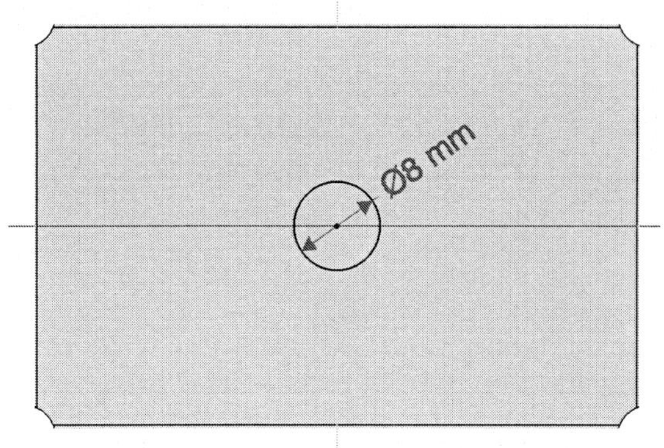

7. Click **Close** on the **Tasks** panel.
8. Click the **Pad** icon on the **Part Design Modeling Features** toolbar.
9. Select **Mode > Two sided**.
10. In the **Side 1** section, type **1.5** and **0** in the **Length** and **Taper angle** boxes, respectively.
11. in the **Side 2** section, type **1.5** an **-8** in the **Length** and **Taper angle** boxes, respectively. Click **OK**.

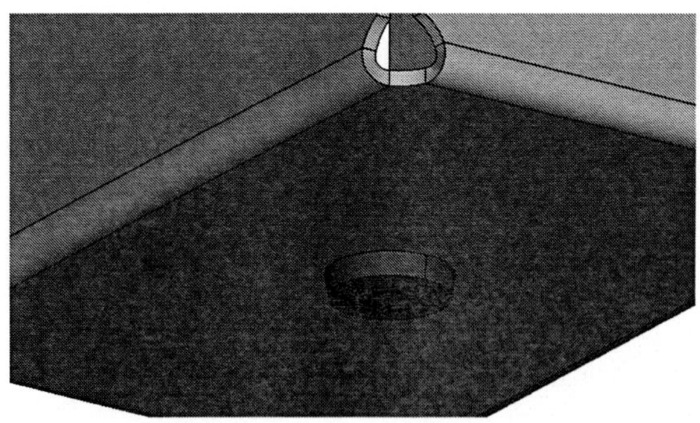

12. Click on the circular edge of the pad feature, as shown.

13. Click the **Fillet** icon on the **Part Design Dressup Features** toolbar.
14. Type **1** in the **Radius** box and click **OK**.

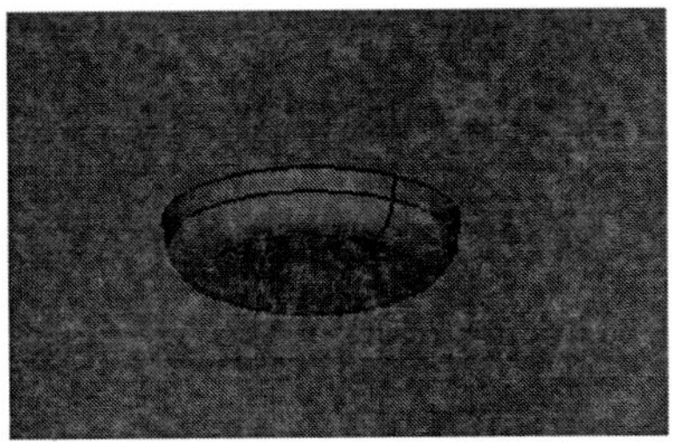

15. In the **Model** panel, right-click on the first **Body** and select **Active body**.

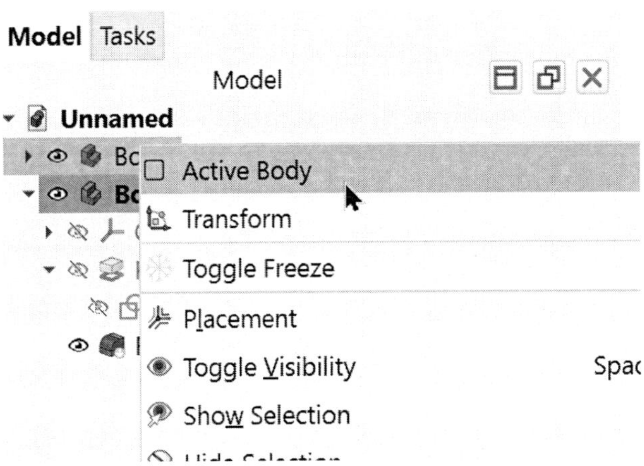

16. Select the **Sheet Metal** option from the **Workbenches** drop-down.
17. Press and hold the CTRL key and select the inner horizontal face and the top face of the newly created body.

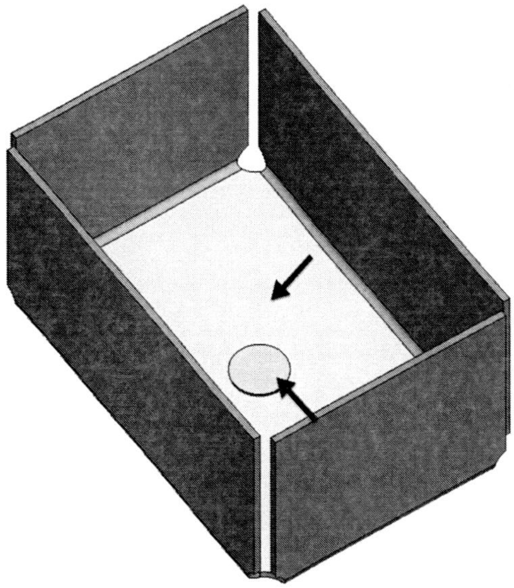

18. Click the **Make Forming in Wall** icon on the **Sheet Metal** toolbar. The forming is created in the wall.

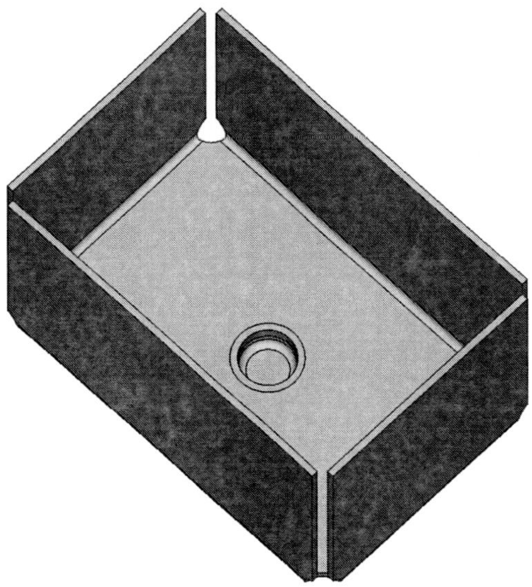

19. In the **Model** panel, select the **WallForming** feature.
20. In the **Data** tab, type **20** and **10** in the **Offset X** and **Offset Y** boxes.

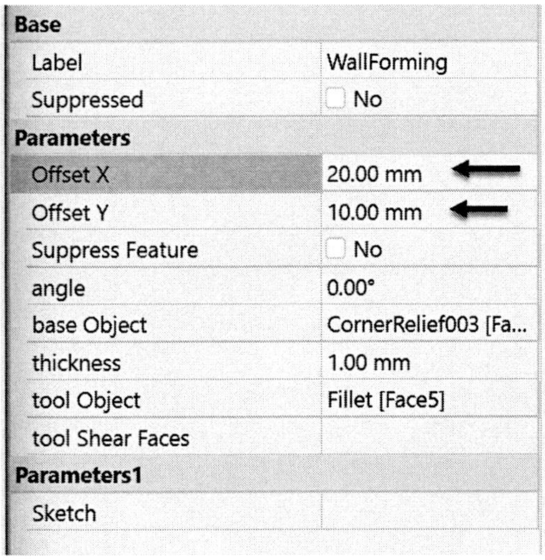

Base	
Label	WallForming
Suppressed	No
Parameters	
Offset X	20.00 mm
Offset Y	10.00 mm
Suppress Feature	No
angle	0.00°
base Object	CornerRelief003 [Fa...
thickness	1.00 mm
tool Object	Fillet [Face5]
tool Shear Faces	
Parameters1	
Sketch	

The wallforming feature is offset along the x and y coordinates, as shown.

21. In the **Model** panel, expand the **Body001** node, and then select the **Fillet** feature.

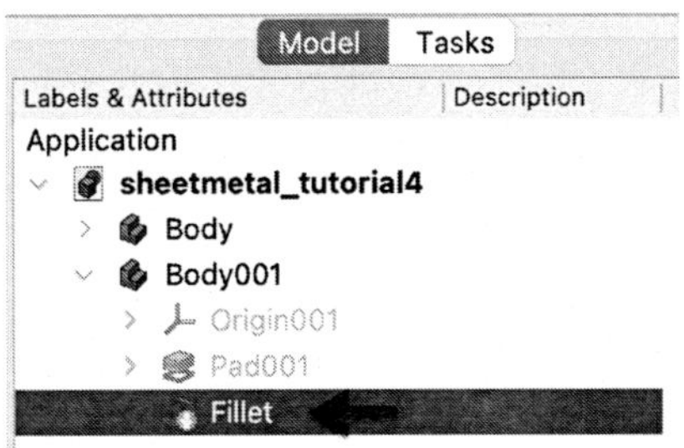

22. Click the **View** tab and select checkbox next to the **Visibility**.

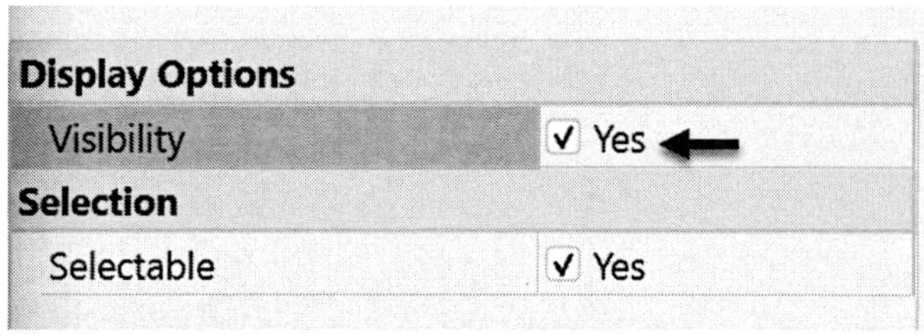

Display Options	
Visibility	Yes
Selection	
Selectable	Yes

23. Select the **Sheet Metal** option from the **Workbenches** drop-down.
24. Press and hold the CTRL key and select the inner horizontal face and the top face of **Body001**.

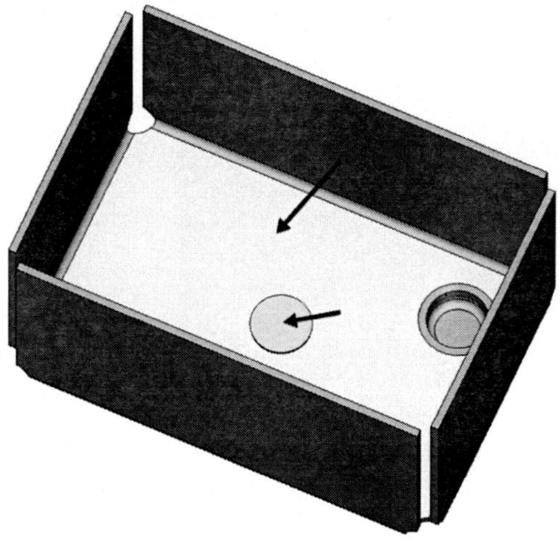

25. Click the **Make Forming in Wall**  icon on the **Part Design Modeling Features** toolbar. The forming is created in the wall.
26. In the **Model** panel, select the **WallForming001** feature.
27. Click the **Data** tab.
28. Expand the **Offset** option.
29. Type **20** and **-10** in the **Offset X** and **Offset Y** boxes. The wall forming is offset to the new location.

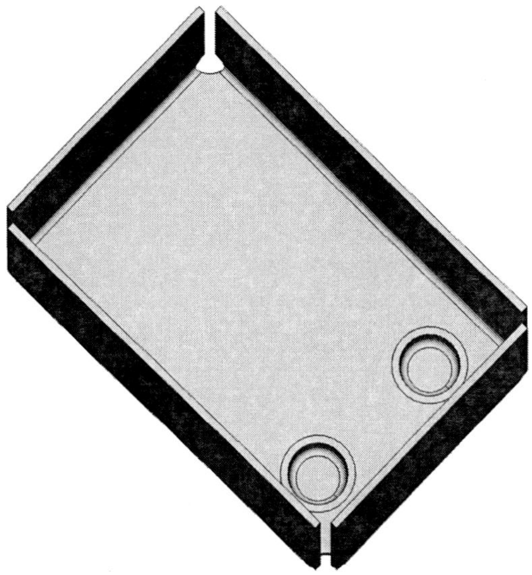

30. Likewise, create two more wall formings and offset them to new locations.

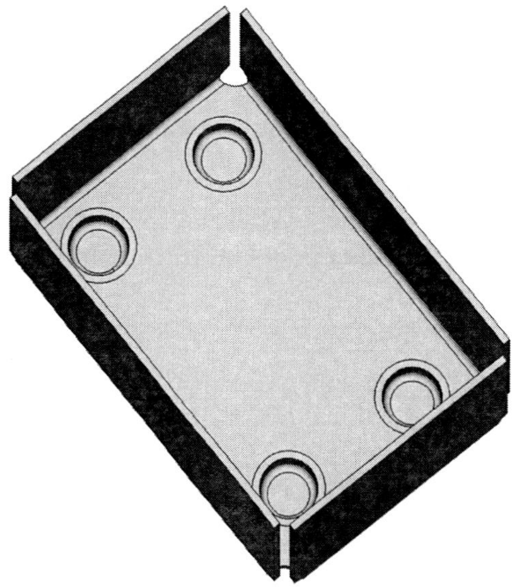

15. Save and close the file.

Chapter 8: CAM Overview

TUTORIAL 1

In this tutorial, you generate paths for the machining operations of the part shown in the figure below.

1. Start the FreeCAD 1.1 application.
2. Download the Tutorial 1-part file of Chapter 12, and open it.
3. Select **CAM** from the **Workbenches** drop-down.

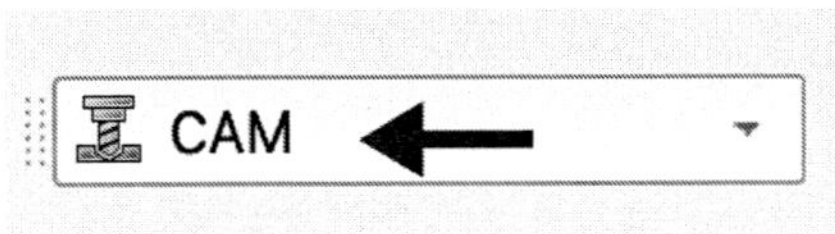

4. Click **Edit > Preferences** on the menu bar. If you are working on MacOS, then click **FreeCAD > Preferences** on the title bar. This will open the **Preferences** dialog box, where you can customize various settings for your FreeCAD workspace.
5. Click the **General** > **General** on the left side of the **Preferences** dialog.
6. Select **Default Unit system > Metric small parts and CNC (mm, mm/min).**
7. Check the **Ignore project unit system and use default** option.
8. Click **OK.**

Creating the Job

1. Click the **New Job** icon on the **Project Setup** toolbar.

2. On the **New Job** dialog, select the checkbox next to the Body.

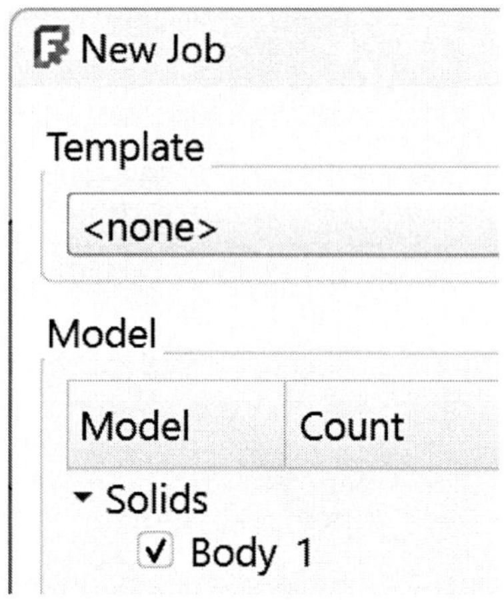

3. Click **OK.**
4. On the **Job Edit** dialog, click the **Setup** tab.
5. Select **Extend Model's Bound Box** from the drop-down located at the top.
6. Type **5** in the **Ext. X** and **Ext. Y** boxes.
7. Type **50** and **2** in the first and second **Ext. Z** boxes, respectively.

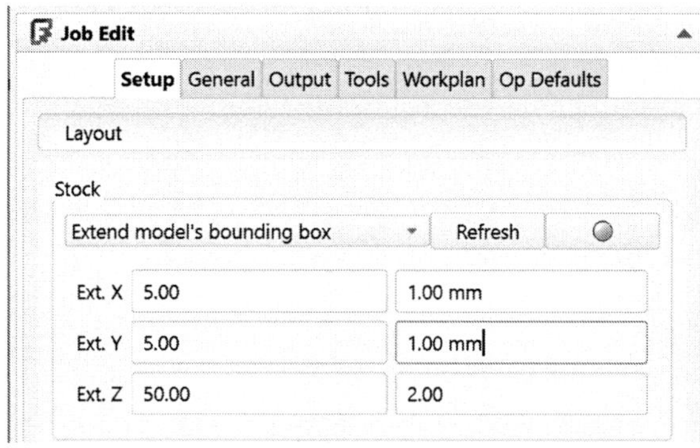

8. Click on the top-left corner of the bounding box.

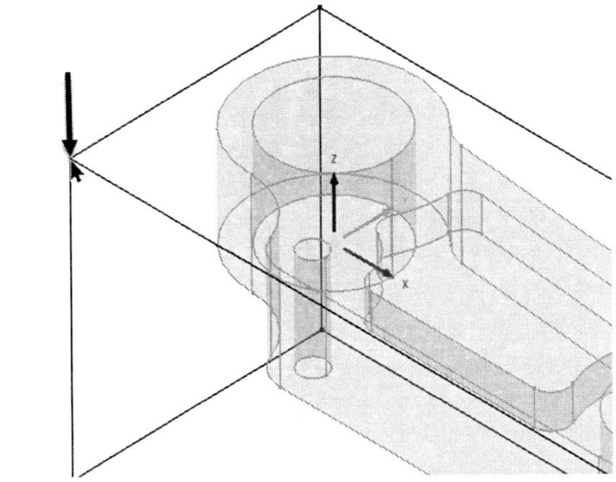

9. Click the **Set Origin** button in the **Alignment** section of the **Setup** tab of the **Job Edit** dialog.

The origin is moved to the selected location, as shown.

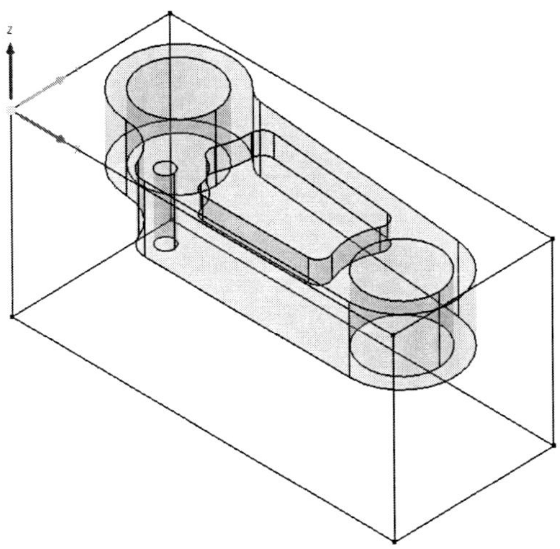

10. Click the **Output** tab on the **Job Edit** dialog.
11. Select **linuxcnc** from the **Processor** drop-down.
12. Type **Tutorial1.ngc** in the **Output file** box.
13. Click **OK**.

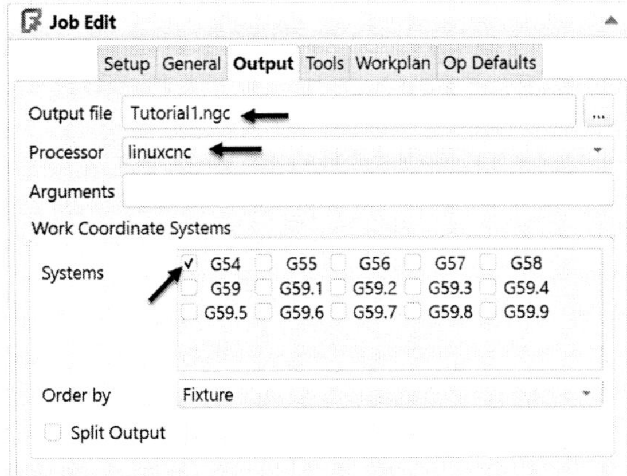

14. In the **Model** panel, go to **Job001 > Model**.
15. Press and hold the Ctrl key and select **Stock** and **Model-Body**.
16. Right-click and select **Show selection**.

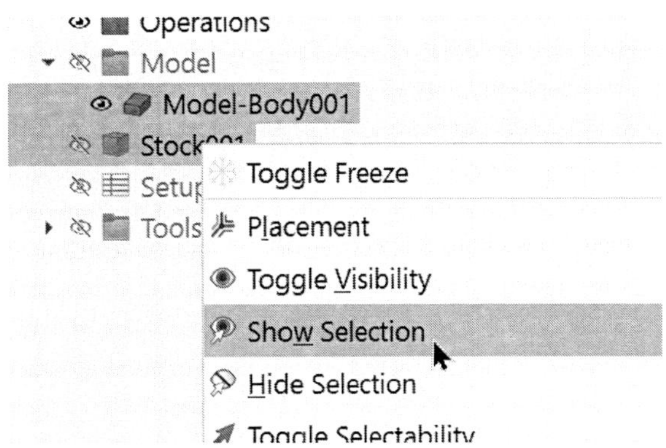

17. Right click on **Body**, and then select **Hide selection**.

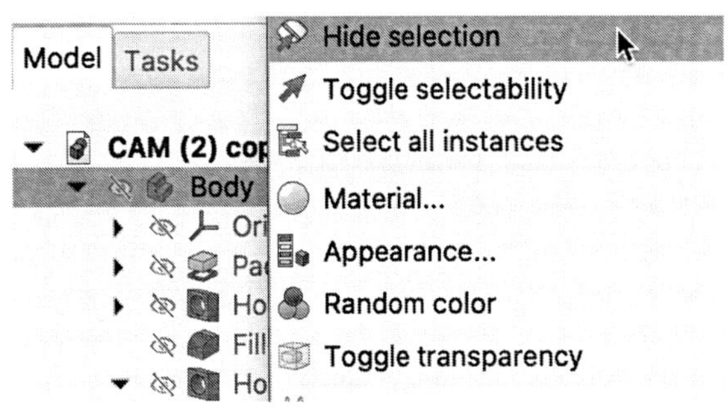

Adding Tools to the Job

Follow the steps given next to add tools in Windows version of FreeCAD 1.1.

1. Click the **Add toolBit** icon on the **Tool Commands** toolbar.

2. Click the **Open Library editor** button on the Tool Selector.

3. Click **Adds a new library** on the **Library Manager** dialog.

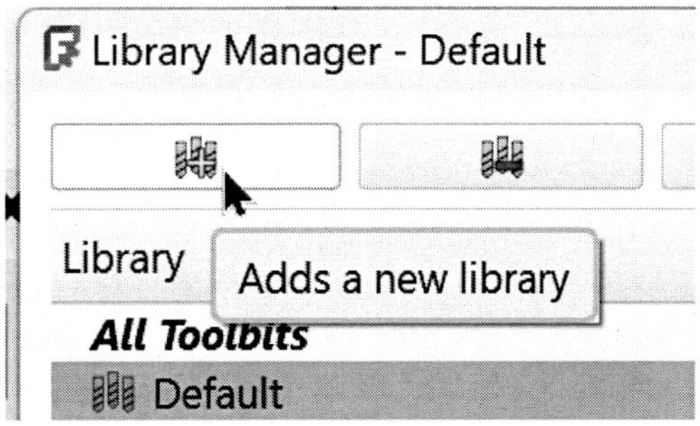

4. Type **Tutorial_Library** in the **Name** box and click **OK**.

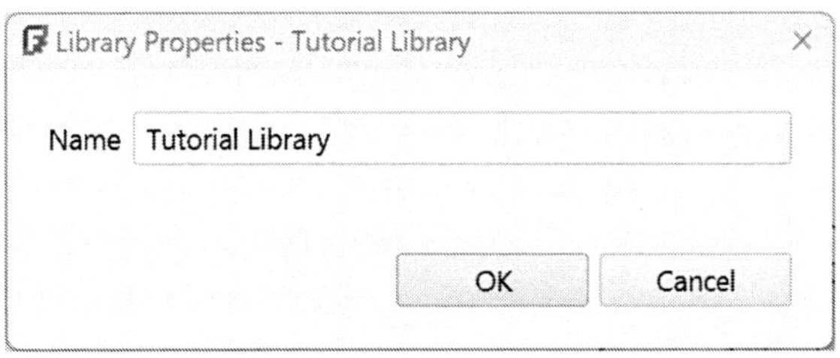

5. Select the **Tutorial_Library** from the **All Toolbits** list.
6. Click **Adds a toolbit** on the **Library Manager** dialog.

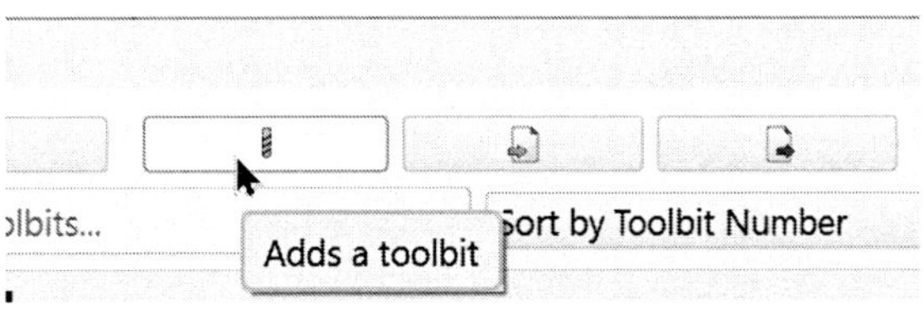

7. Click the **Endmill** button on the **Toolbit Shape Selection** dialog.

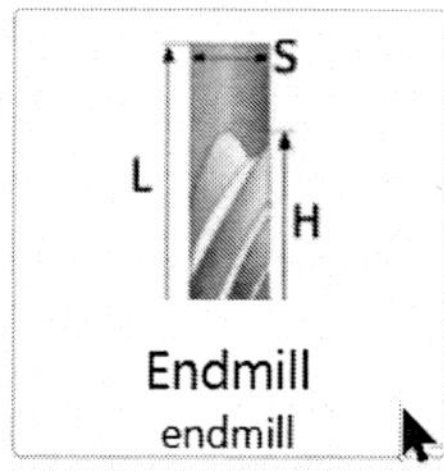

8. Right-click on the newly created toolbit, and then select **Edit**.

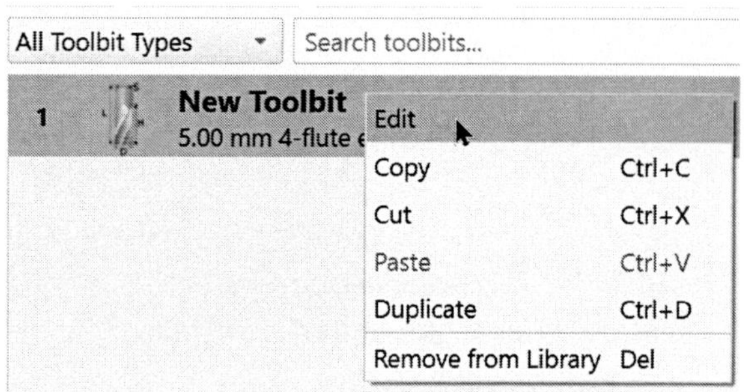

9. On the **Toolbit Parameter Editor** dialog, type **End Mill 5 mm** in the **Label** box.
10. Select **Material > Carbide**.
11. Type **4** in the **Flutes** box.
12. Type **5** and **30** in the **Diameter** and **Cutting edge height** boxes, respectively.
13. Type **6** in the **Shank diameter** box.
14. Type **55** in the **Length** box.
15. Click **OK**.

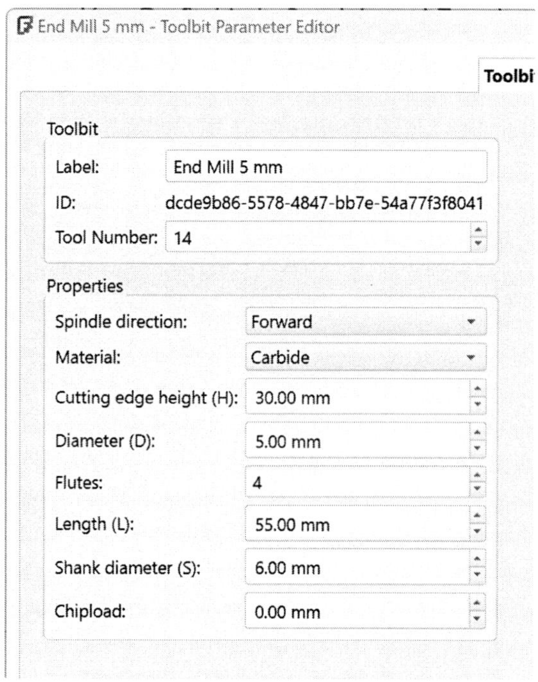

16. Click **Adds a toolbit** 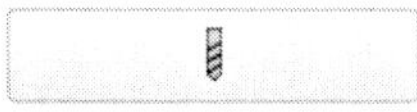 on the **Library Manager** dialog.
17. Click the **Drill** button on the **Toolbit Shape Selection** dialog.

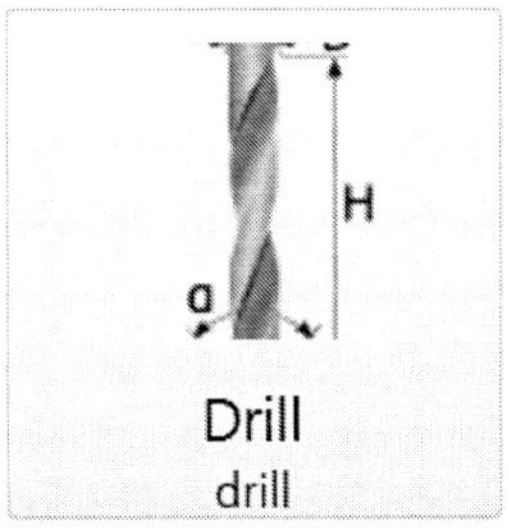

18. Right-click on the newly created toolbit, and then select **Edit**.

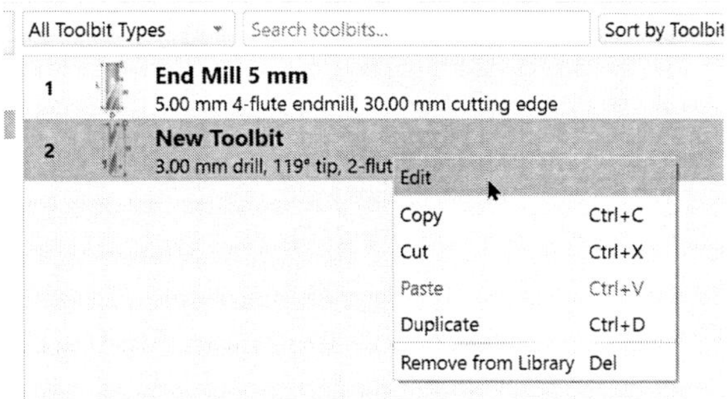

19. On the **Toolbit Parameter Editor** dialog, type **Drill 5 mm** in the **Label** box.
20. Select the **Material > Carbide**.
21. Type **2** in the **Flutes** box.
22. Type **5**, **15**, and **118** in the **Diameter**, **Length**, and **Tip Angle** boxes, respectively.
23. Click **OK**.

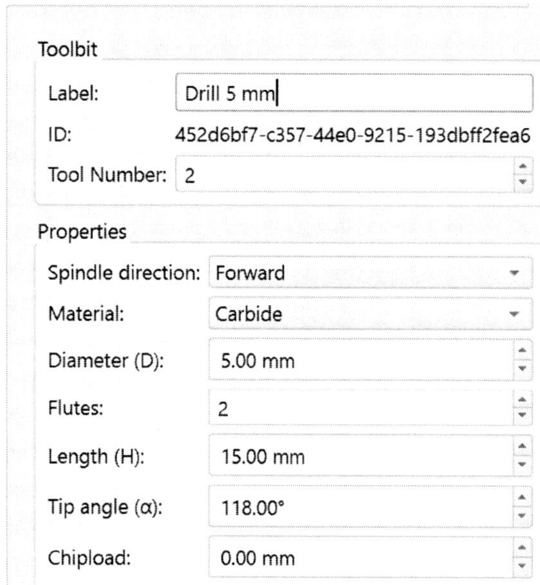

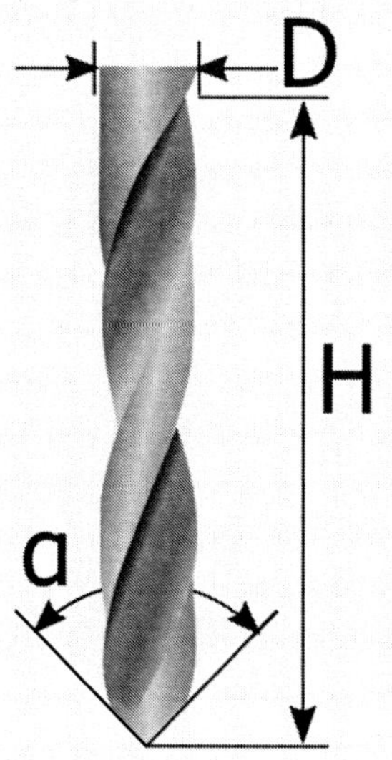

24. Close the **Library Manager** dialog.
25. On the **Toolbit Selector** dialog, select the **Tutorial Library** table from the drop-down.
26. Select the two newly created tools and click the **Add to Job** button to add the tools to the job.
27. Click **Close** on the **Toolbit Selector** dialog.

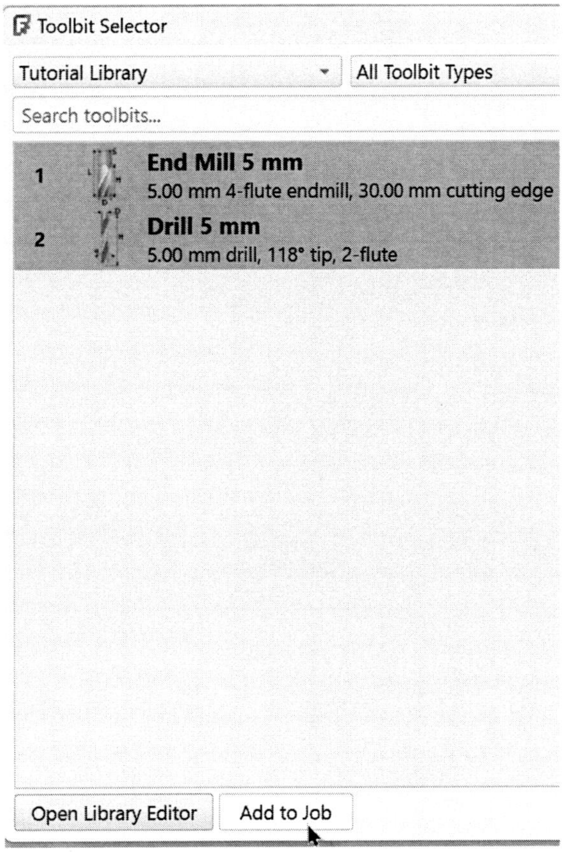

Follow the steps given next to add tools to the Job in the Mac version of the FreeCAD 1.1.

1. Click the **ToolBit Dock**  icon on the **Tool Commands** toolbar.
2. Select **Default** from the drop-down located on the **Tool Selector**.
3. Press and hold the CTRL key and select the End Mill 5 mm and 5 mm Drill tools from the Tool Selector.

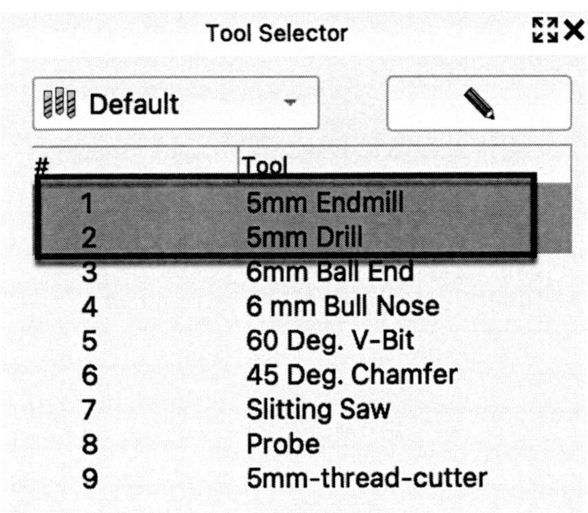

4. Click the **Add to Job** button located at the bottom of the Tool Selector.

5. Expand the **Tools** folder on the **Model** panel; the tool controllers are listed.

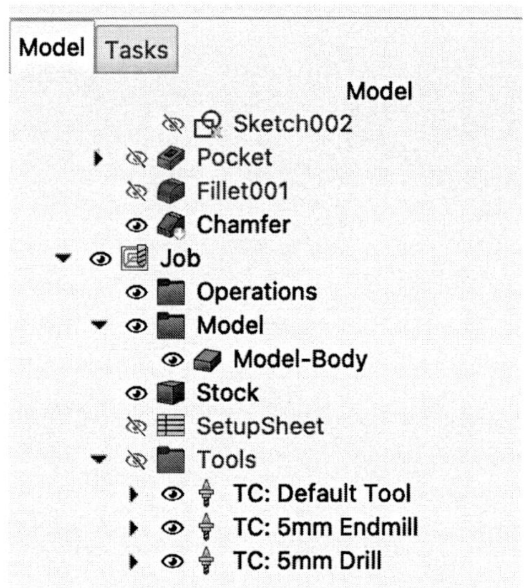

Creating the Facing Operation

1. Click the **Face** icon on the **New Operations** toolbar.

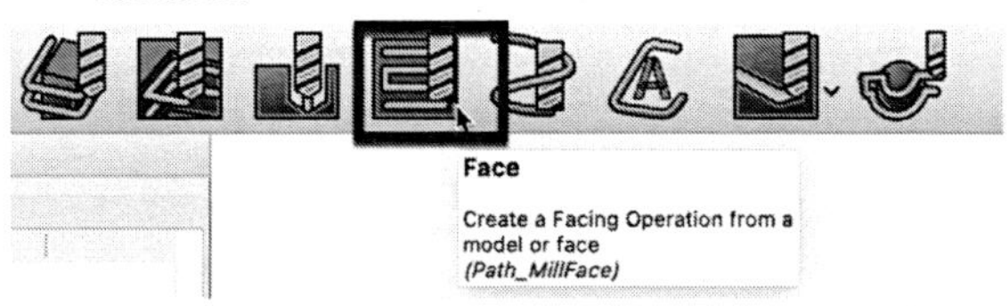

2. Select the **Endmill 5mm** tool controller from the **Tool controller** drop-down. Click **OK**.

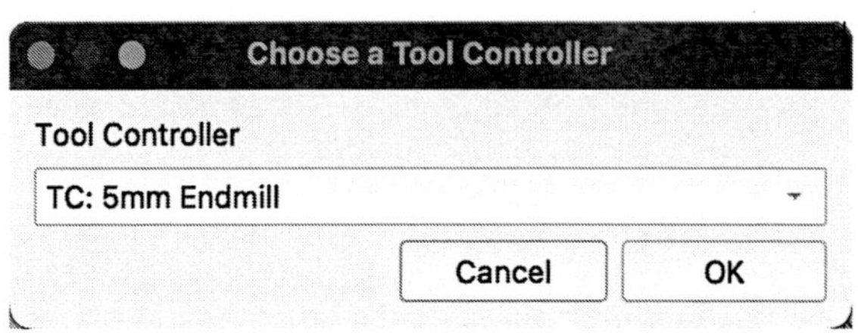

3. Expand the **Base Geometry** section on the

MillFace dialog.

4. Select the top face of the model.

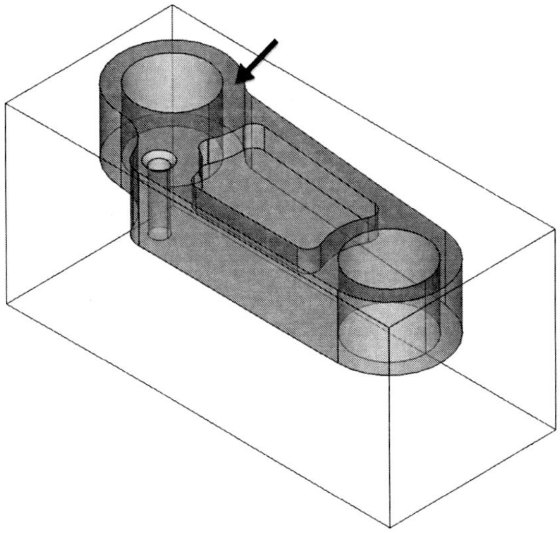

5. Click the **Add** button in the **Base Geometry** section.
6. Expand the **Depths** section on the **MillFace** dialog. Notice that the **Final Depth** value is calculated automatically.
7. Click the **Expression** icon next to the **Step Down** box.

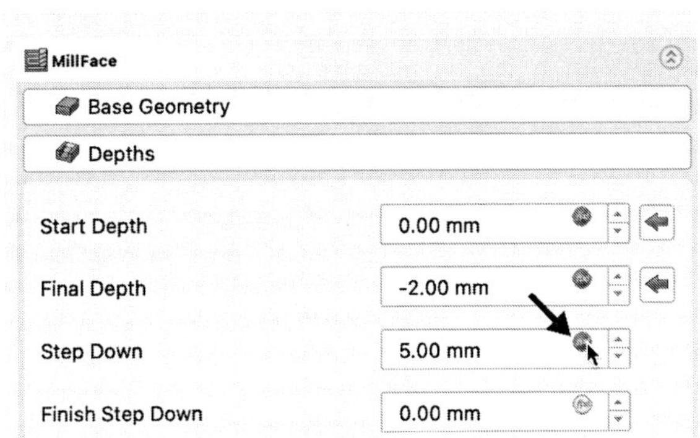

8. Type **1** in the **Expression editor** dialog.

9. Click **OK**.
10. Expand the **Operation** section on the **MillFace** dialog.
11. Select **Boundary Shape > Stock**.
12. Select **Cut Mode > Conventional**.
13. Select **Pattern > Zig Zag**.
14. Leave the default values in the **Angle**, **Step Over Percent**, and **Material Allowance** boxes.

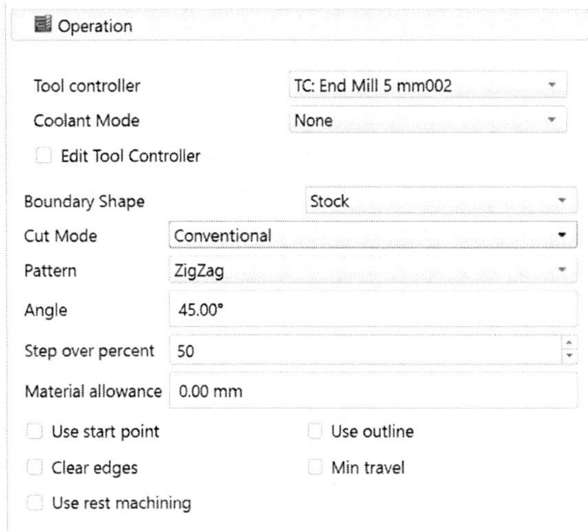

15. Click the **Apply** button located at the top of the **Tasks** tab; the preview of the toolpath appears.

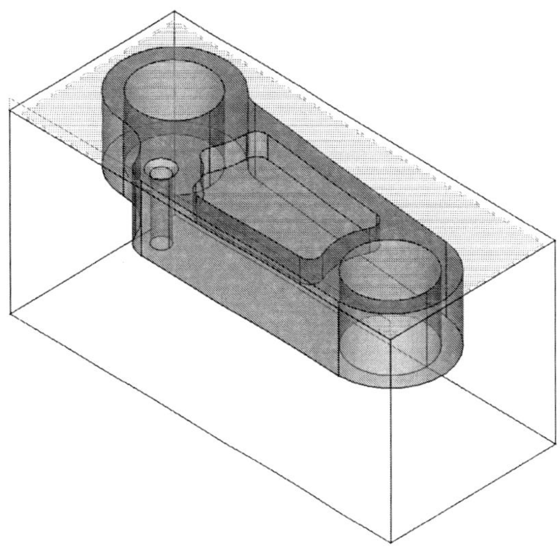

16. Click **OK** to accept the toolpath. You can also change the values on the **MillFace** dialog and click **Apply** to see the result.
17. Expand the **Operations** node in the **Model**

tab of the **Model** panel; the **MillFace** operation is listed.

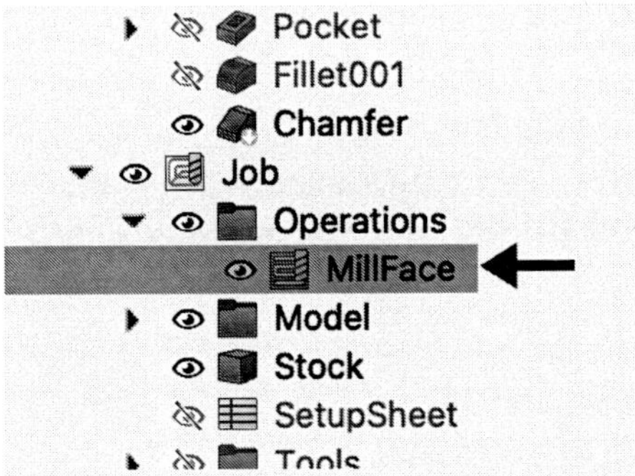

18. Place the pointer on the path and notice that arrow. It displays the direction of the path.

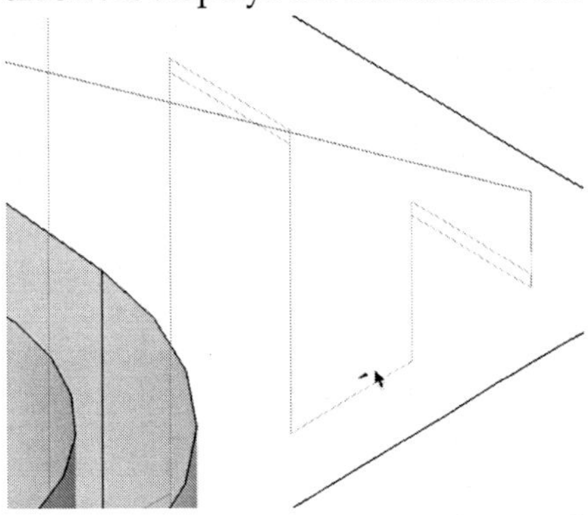

Notice the safety path. You can change the safe height and clearance using the **SetupSheet**.

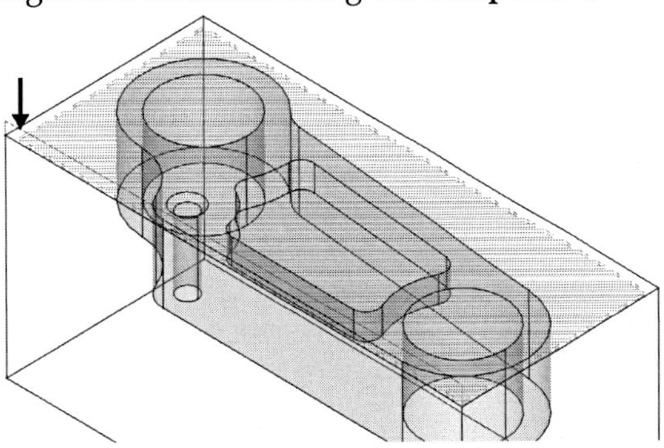

19. Select **SetupSheet** under the Job node in the **Model** tab.

You can change the **Clearance Height Offset** and **Safe Height Offset** values in the **Properties** panel.

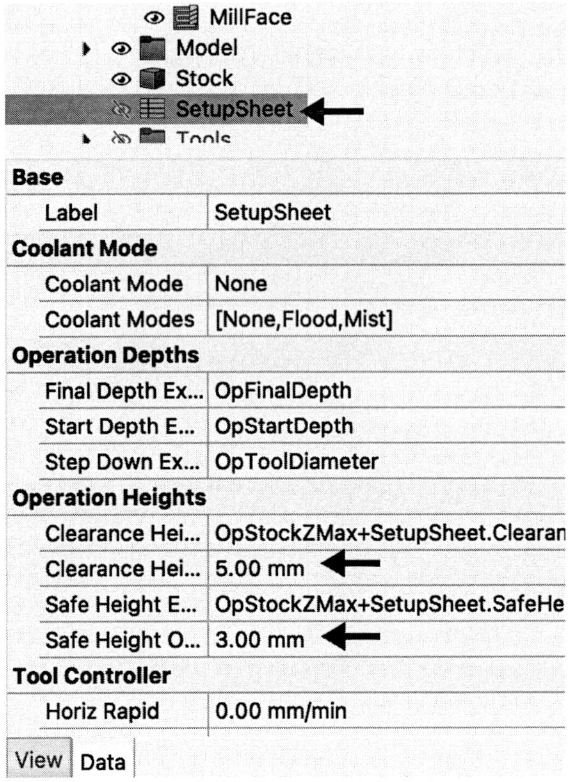

You can also define the feed of the tool.

20. Double-click on **Endmill 5mm** tool controller under the **Job** node.

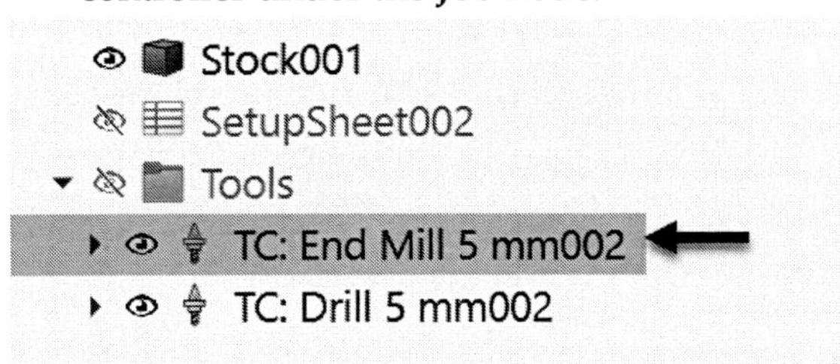

21. Type **200**, **60**, and **10000** in the **Horizontal Feed**, **Vertical Feed** and **Spindle** boxes, respectively.

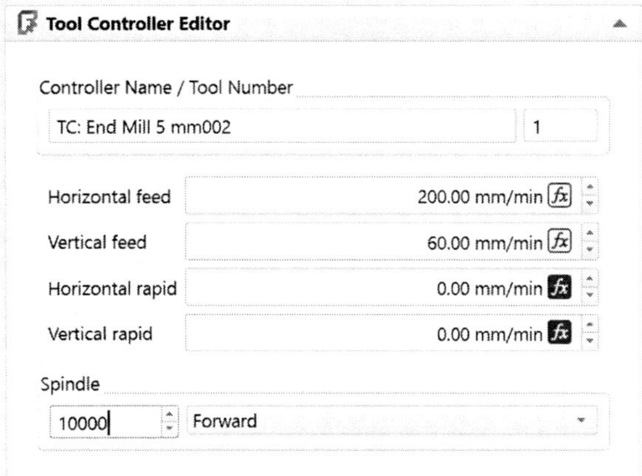

22. Click **OK**.
23. Select the **MillFace** operation from the **Model** tab.

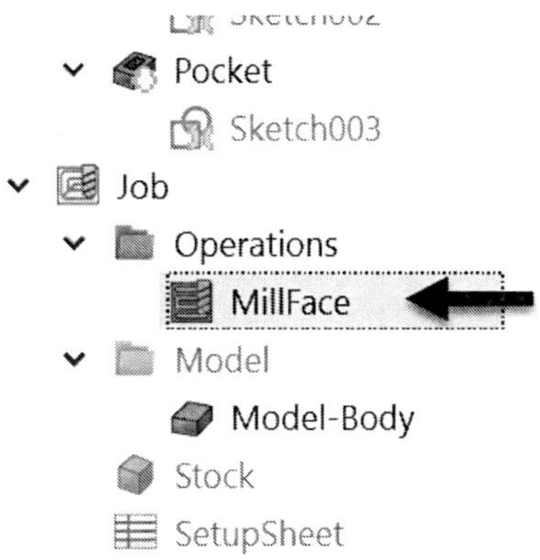

24. Click the **Toggle Operation** icon on the **Tool Commands** toolbar.

The MillFace path is hidden.

Creating the Pocket Operation

1. Select the flat face of the pocket, as shown.

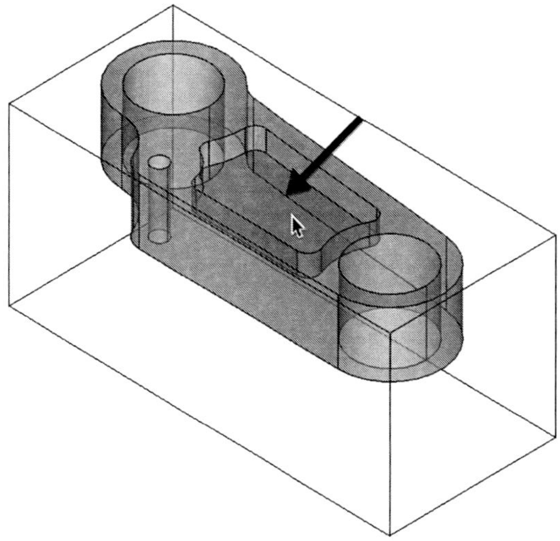

2. Click the **Pocket Shape** icon on the **New Operations** toolbar.

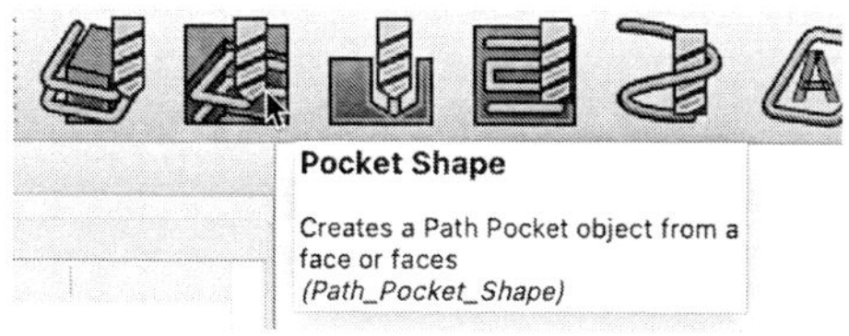

3. Expand the **Depths** section.
4. Click the **Expression** icon next to the **Step Down** box.
5. Type **1** in the **Expression editor** dialog, and then click **OK**.
6. Expand the **Operation** section.
7. Select **5mm Endmill** from the **Tool Controller** drop-down.
8. Select **Cut Mode > Conventional**.
9. Select **Pattern > ZigZagOffset**.
10. Click **Apply** to view the path.

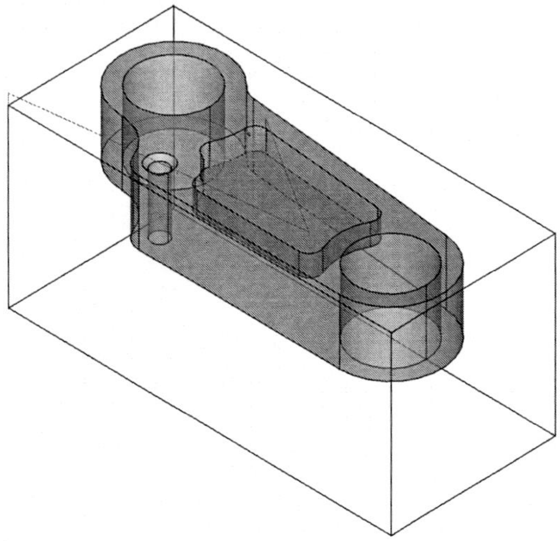

11. Click **OK.**

Creating the Drill Operation

1. Click the **Drilling** icon on the **New Operations** toolbar.

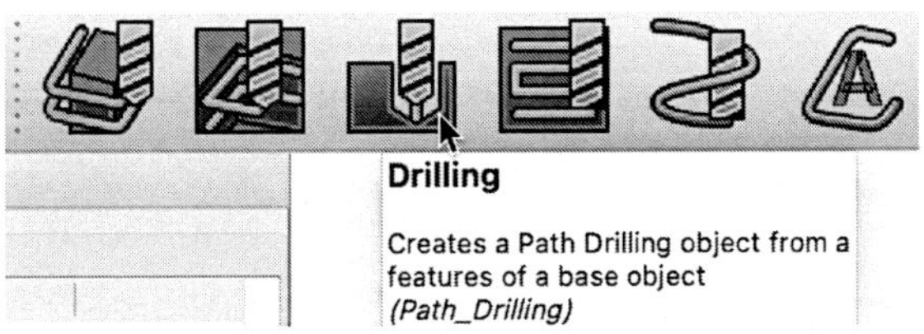

2. On the **Drilling** dialog, expand the **Base Geometry** section and notice that the all the holes are selected automatically.
3. Expand the **Depths** section and click the **Expression** icon next to the **Final Depth** box.
4. Make sure that the **Result** value is -32 on the **Expression editor** dialog.
5. Click **OK.**

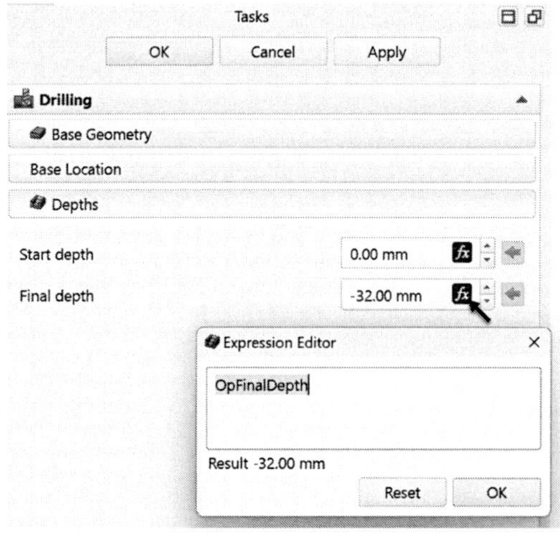

6. Expand the **Operation** section and select **5mm Drill** from the **Tool Controller** drop-down.
7. Click **Apply** and **OK**. The drill operation is created on three holes, as shown.

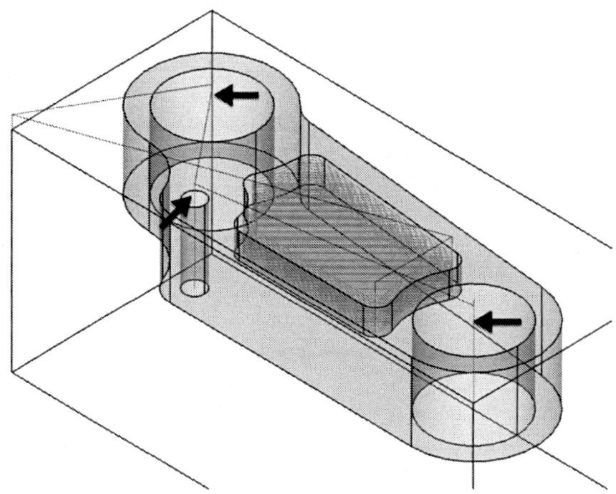

Drilling Holes using the Helix Operation

1. Click the **Helix** icon on the **New Operations** toolbar.

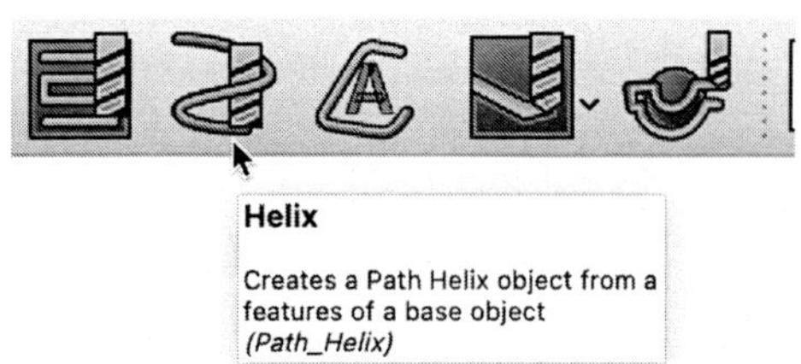

2. Select **5mm Endmill** from the **Tool Controller** drop-down in the **Operations** section.
3. Expand the **Base Geometry** section and click the **Reset** button; all the holes available on

the model are selected.

4. Expand the **Depths** section and click the **Expression** icon next to the **Step Down** box.
5. Type **2** in the **Expression editor** dialog.

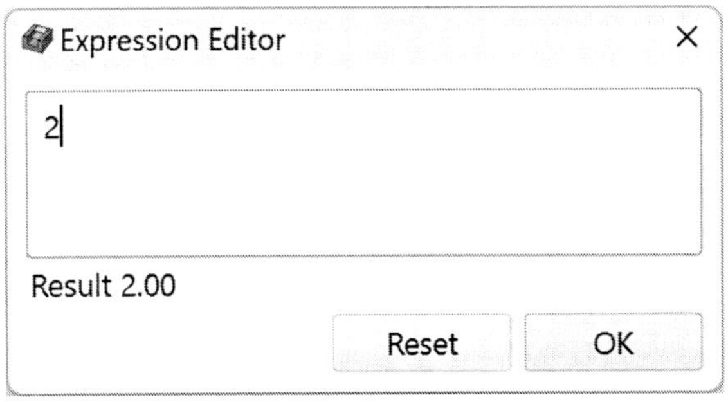

6. Click **OK**.
7. Click **Apply** and **OK**.

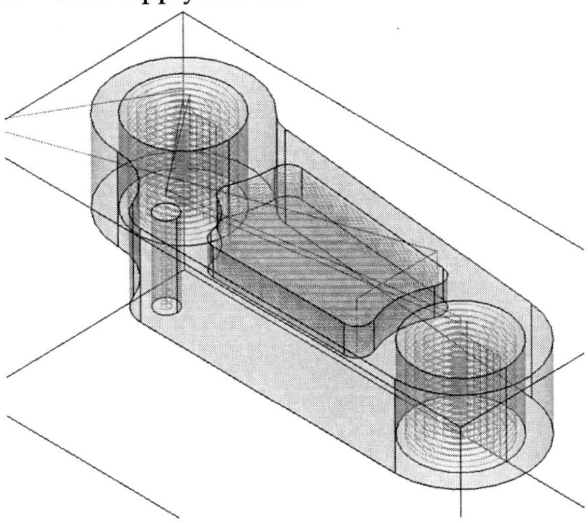

Creating the Contour Operation

1. Click the **Profile** icon on the **New Operations** toolbar.

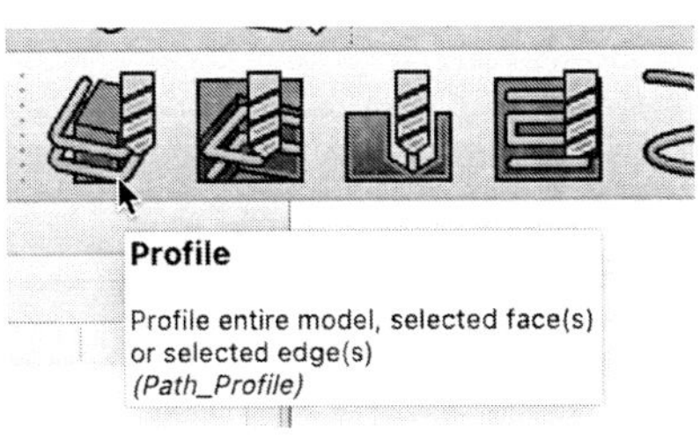

2. Select **Endmill 5mm** from the **Tool Controller** drop-down in the **Operations** section.
3. Check the **Use Compensation** option.
4. Expand the **Depths** section.
5. Click the **Expression** icon next to the **Step Down** box.
6. Type **2** in the **Expression editor** dialog.
7. Click **OK**.
8. Click the **Expression** icon next to the **Final Depth** box.
9. Type **-32** in the **Expression editor** dialog.
10. Click **OK**.
11. Click **Apply** and **OK**.

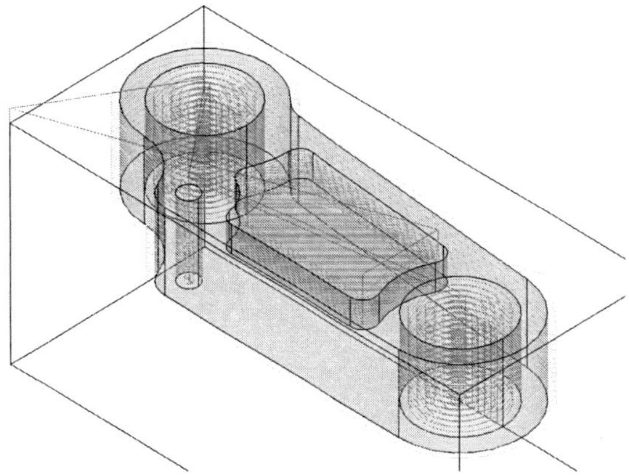

12. Select the **MillFace** operation from the **Model** tab.
13. Click the **Toggle Operation** icon on the **Tool Commands** toolbar.

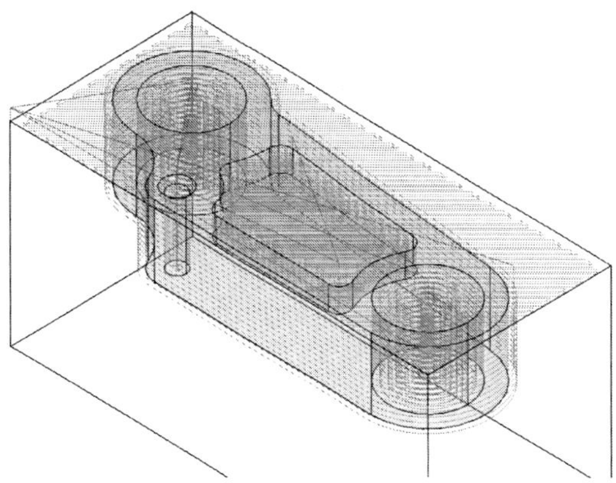

Simulating the Operations

1. Click the **CAM Simulator** icon on the **Tool Commands** toolbar.

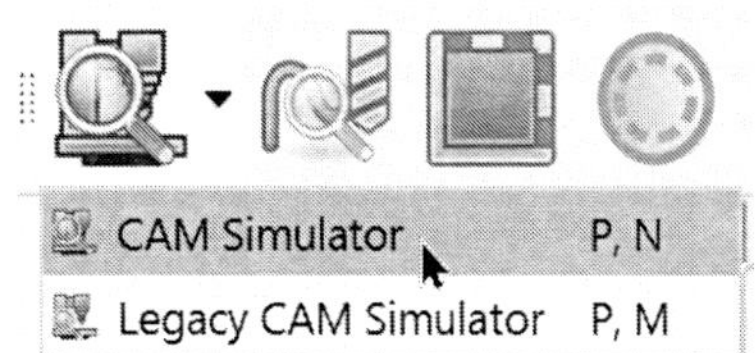

2. Make sure that all the operations are selected on the **Path Simulator** dialog.
3. Click the **Activate/resume simulation** icon.

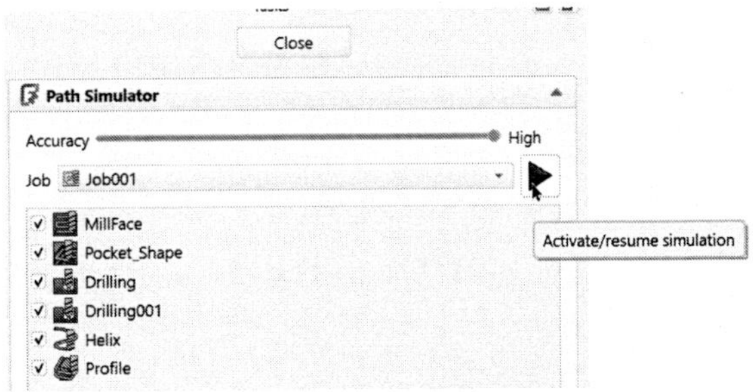

The **New CAM Simulator** window displays a 3D animation of the cutting tool removing material from the stock. The bottom of the window contains controls to manage the playback and view settings.

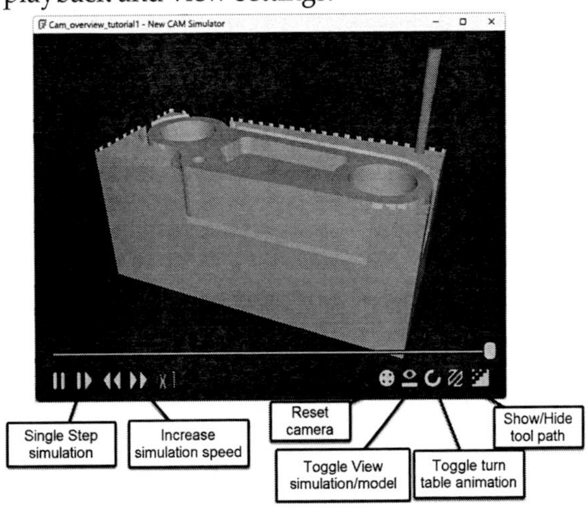

Playback Controls

- **Play Simulation:** This icon helps you to play/pause simulation
- **Single Step simulation:** Advances the simulation one tool movement at a time.
- **Increase simulation speed:** Accelerates the playback of the cutting operations.
- **Timeline slider:** Allows you to manually drag forward or backward through the entire machining sequence.

View Controls

- **Reset camera:** Restores the default 3D view orientation.
- **Toggle View simulation/model:** Switches the display between the simulated cut material and the original target model.
- **Toggle turn table animation:** Rotates the workspace automatically to inspect the part from multiple angles.
- **Show/Hide tool path:** Displays or hides the lines representing the tool trajectory.

Review the simulation to confirm the toolpaths cut the material as expected. Close the simulator window to return to the main FreeCAD interface.

4. Click **Close** on the **Tasks** panel.

Post Processing

1. On the **Model** panel, expand the **Job > Operations** node.
2. Select the **MillFace** operation.

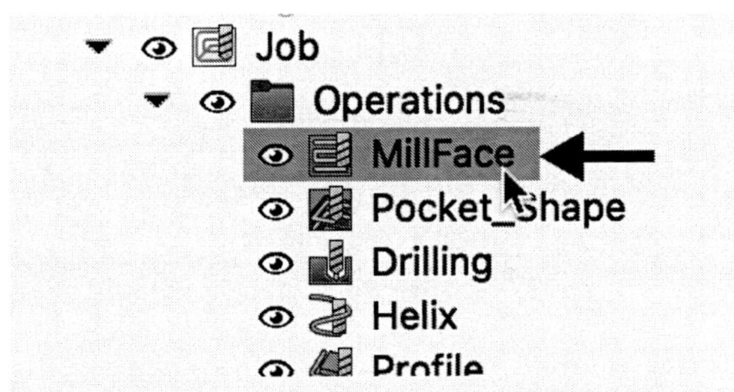

3. Click the **Inspect Toolpath** icon on the **Tool Commands** toolbar.

The G-Code is displayed on the FreeCAD dialog. If you want to learn about the G-code, please visit:

https://linuxcnc.org/docs/html/gcode/g-code.html

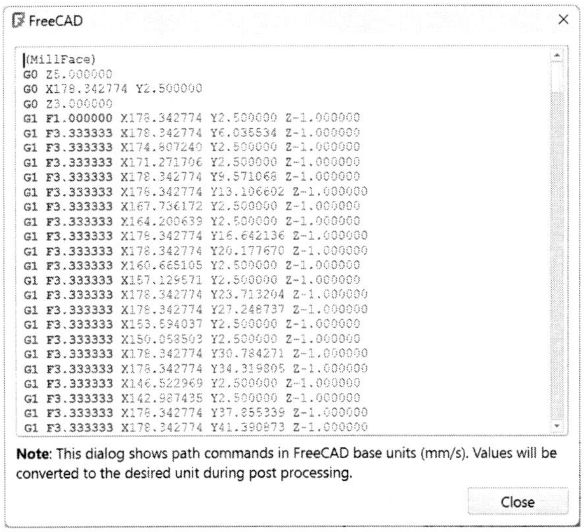

4. Inspect the G-Code and click **Close**.
5. Likewise, inspect the G-Code of other operations.
6. Select the **Job** node from the **Model** tab.
7. Click the **Post Process** icon on the **Project Setup** toolbar.

8. Specify the location of the post-processor file and click **Save**.
9. Save and close the FreeCAD file.

Chapter 9: Assembly Joints

In this chapter, you will learn to

- Create assembly joints

TUTORIAL 1

In this tutorial, you create a slider-crank mechanism by applying Joints.

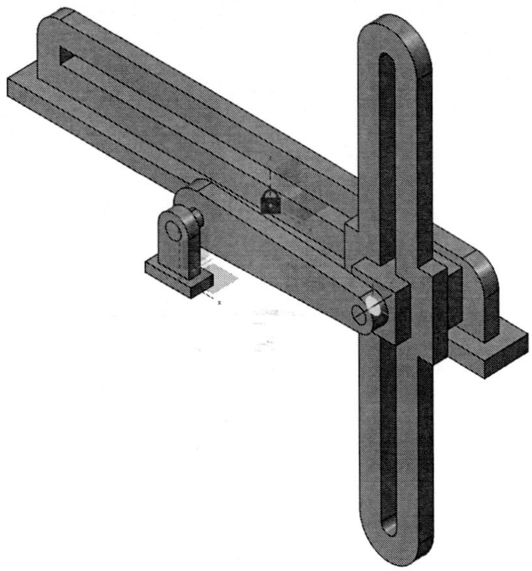

1. Create the Slider Crank Assembly folder on your local drive.
2. Download or prepare the part files for the mechanism (Base, Slider1, Slider2, Arm, Pin, Pivot).
3. Start FreeCAD and create a new document.
4. Select **Assembly** from the **Workbenches** drop-down.
5. Click the **New Assembly**  icon on the **Assembly** toolbar to initialize the assembly container.
6. Save the file as Slider Crank Assembly.FCStd.

Inserting the Components into the Assembly

1. Click the **Insert Component**  icon on the **Assembly** toolbar.
2. Click the **Open file** button on the **Tasks** panel.
3. Browse to your **Slider Crank Assembly** folder and select the **Base** file.
4. Click **Open** to insert it.
5. Select the Body under the Base component in the Tasks panel.

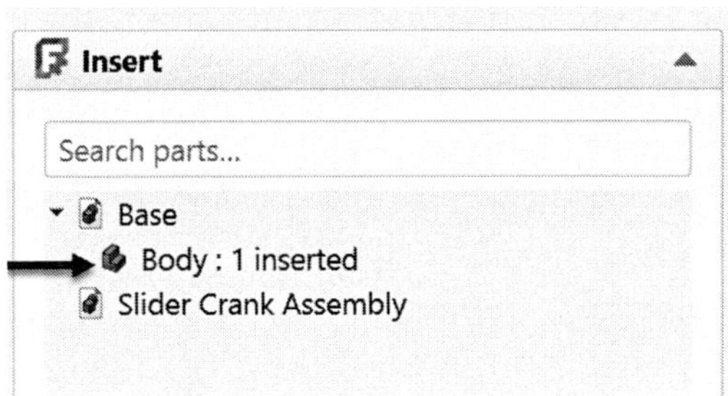

6. Ensure the Base component is oriented correctly in the 3D view.

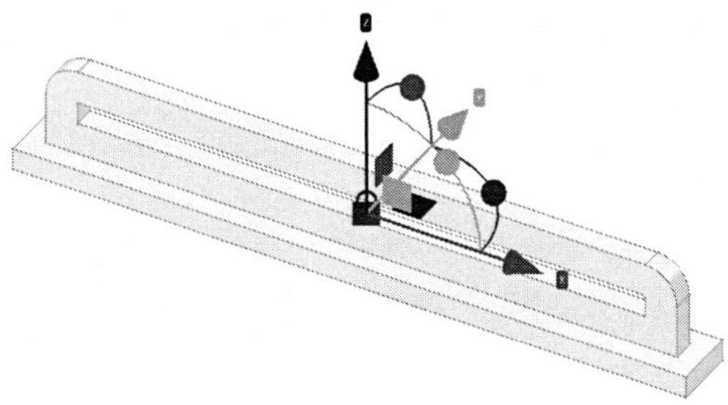

7. Click **Yes** on the **Ground Part** message box to lock the Base at the origin.
8. On the **Insert** section of the **Tasks** panel, click the **Open file** button.
9. Browse to your **Slider Crank Assembly** folder and select the Slider1, Slider2, Crank, Pin, Pivot files holding the CTRL key.

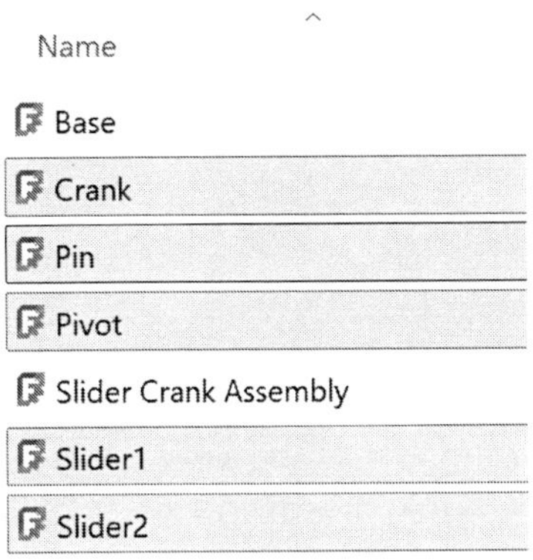

10. Click **Open**.
11. Select Bodies under the **Slider1**, **Slider2**, **Crank**, **Pin**, **Pivot** files in the **Tasks** panel to insert them into the graphics window.

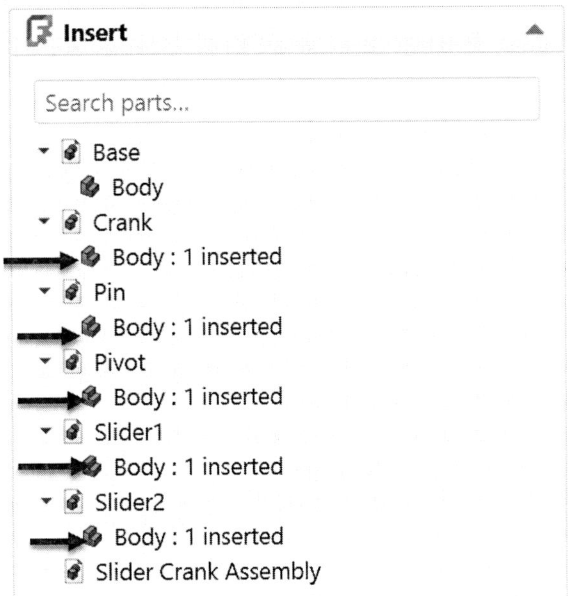

12. Click and drag the components to arrange them properly.

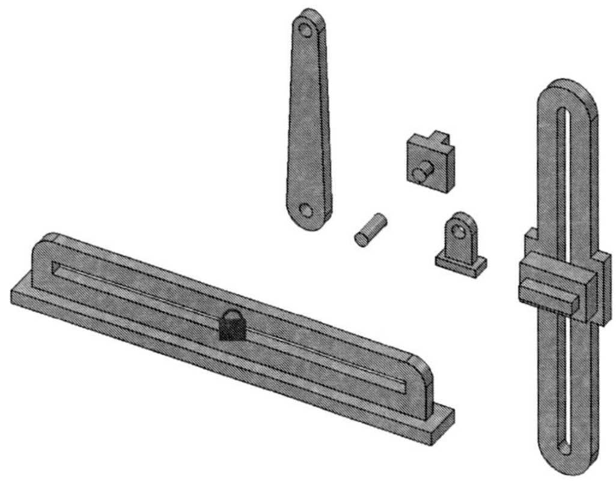

Creating the Slider Joint

1. Click **Slider Joint**  icon on the **Assembly Joints** toolbar.
2. Place the pointer on the midpoint of the inner horizontal edge of the Base component.
3. Make sure that the axes of the joint origin are oriented in the direction, as shown.

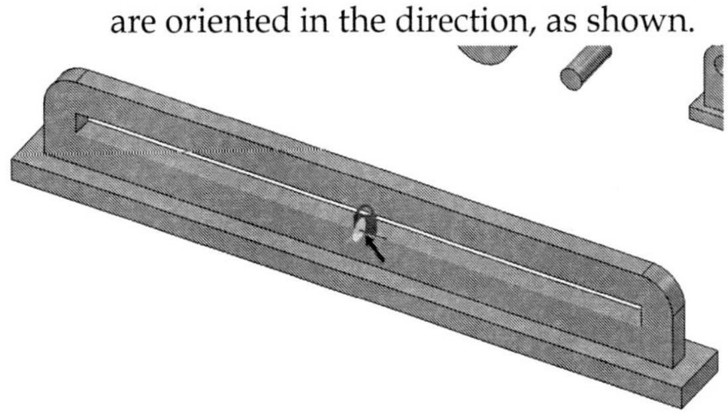

4. Click to define the joint origin.
5. Place the pointer on the midpoint of the horizontal edge of the Slider2 component.
6. Make sure that the axes on the joint origin are oriented in the direction, as shown.

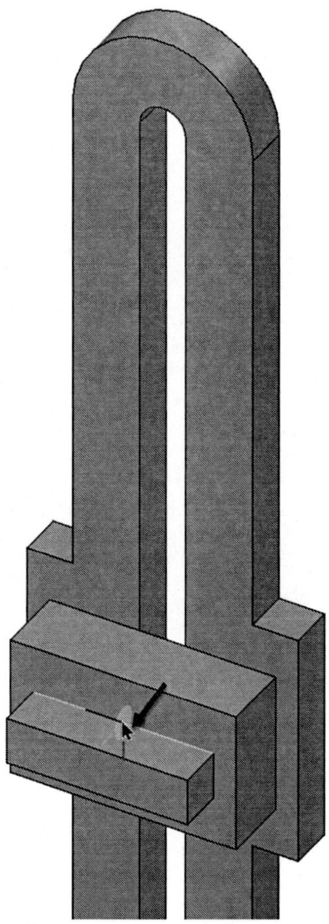

7. If necessary, use the **Reverse** button in the **Tasks** panel to correct the orientation.
8. Click **OK**.

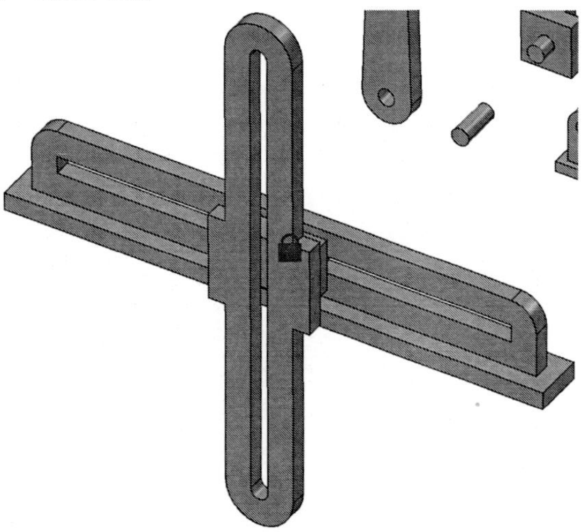

Editing the Joint Limits

You have noticed that the slider slides beyond the base component. You need to restrict the motion of the slider between the two faces, as shown.

Before defining the joint limits, you need to know the distance between the center of the Slider 1 and anyone of the limiting faces

1. On the **View** toolbar, click **Measure** .
2. Press and hold the CTRL key and select the flat face and the curve face, as shown.

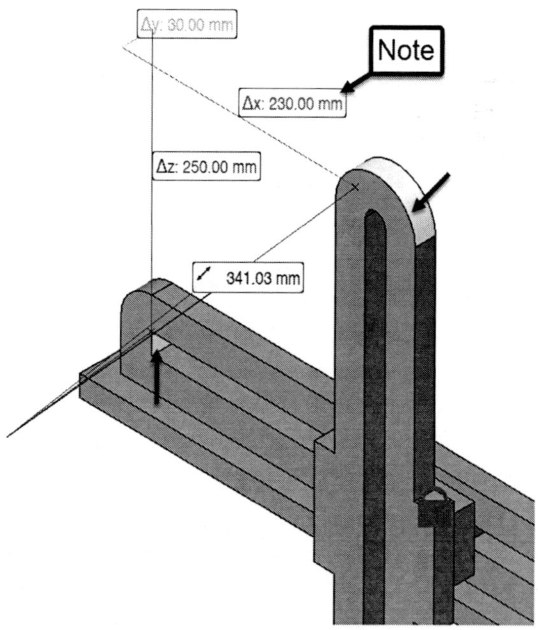

3. Nore the distance along the X direction between the two selected faces.
4. Press ESC.
5. In the Tree view, expand the **Joints** group and double-click the **Slider** joint to edit it.
6. In the Task panel for the Slider joint, locate the **Limits** section.
7. Check the **Min length** option.
8. Type **230** (or your measured minimum) in

the box.

9. Check the **Max length** option.
10. Type the **-230** in the box.
11. Click **OK**.

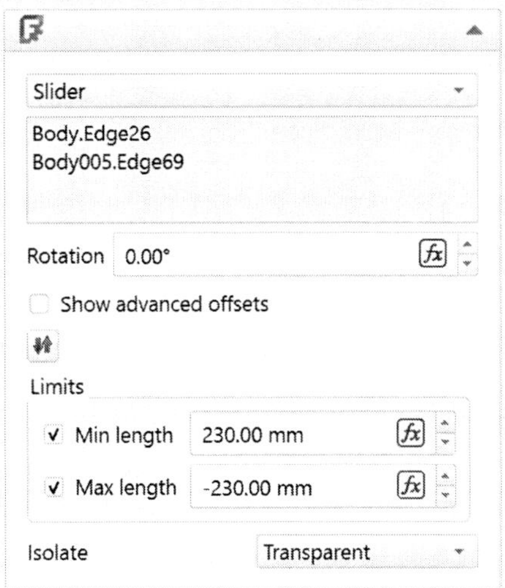

12. Drag the slider manually in the 3D view to verify it stops at the defined limits.

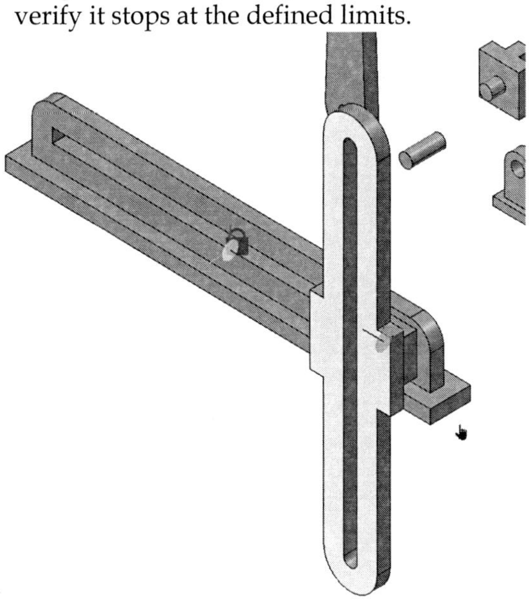

Creating Second Slider Joint

1. Click **Slider Joint** icon on the **Assembly Joints** toolbar.
2. Place the pointer on the midpoint of the inner vertical edge of the Slider2 component.
3. Make sure that the axes of the joint origin are oriented in the direction, as shown.

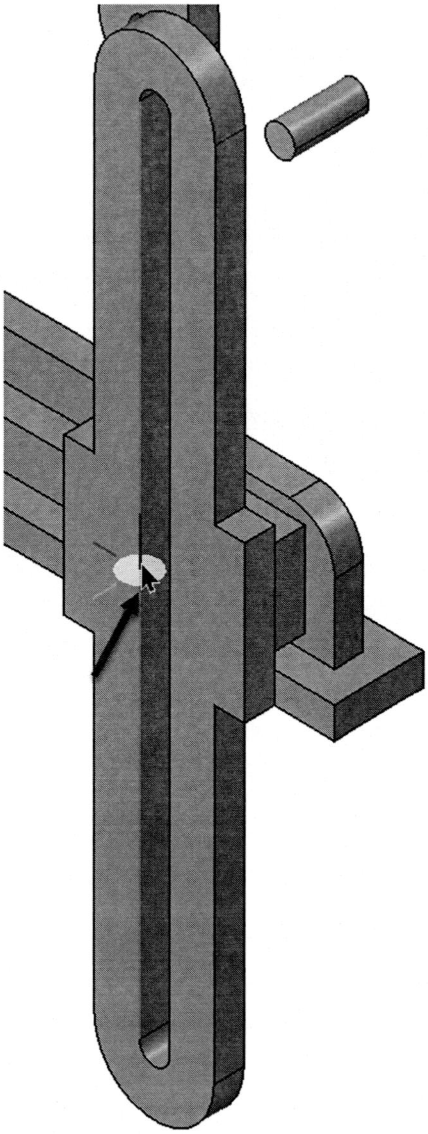

4. Click to define the joint origin.
5. Press and hold the middle mouse button and the right mouse button. Next, drag the cursor to rotate the view.
6. Place the pointer on the midpoint of the vertical edge of the Slider1 component.
7. Make sure that the axes on the joint origin are oriented in the direction, as shown.

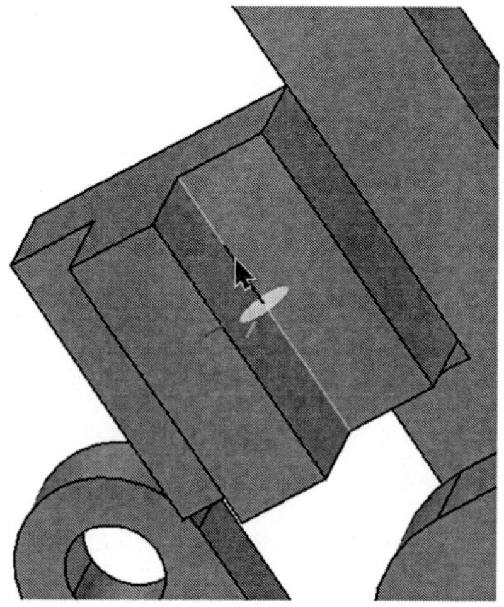

8. Click to define the joint origin.
9. Click the small cube located next to the Navigation cube, and then select the **Isometric** option.

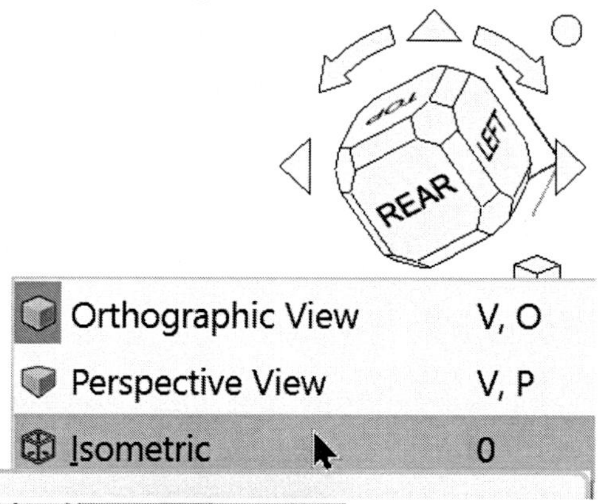

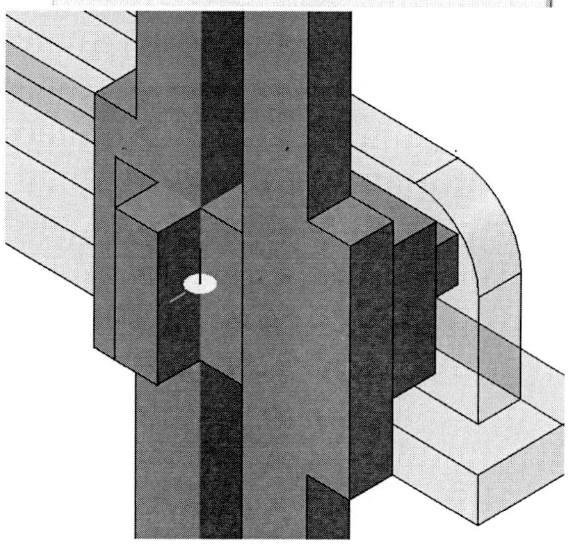

10. Type 180 in the **Rotation** box; the Slider1 is rotated by 180 degrees.

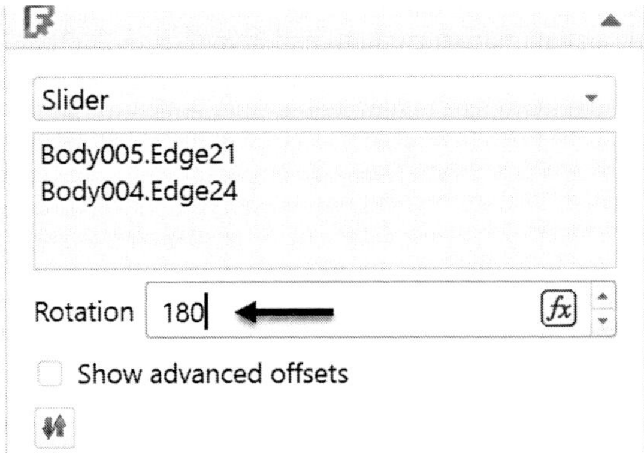

11. Click **OK**.

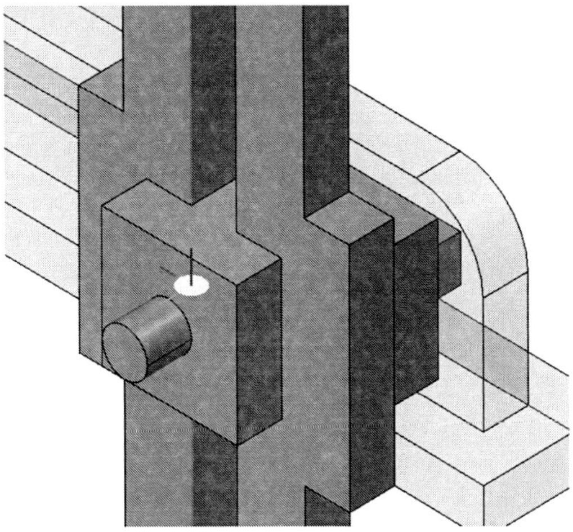

Creating the Revolute Joint

1. Click **Revolute Joint** icon on the **Assembly Joints** toolbar.
2. Select the circular edge of the Slider1.

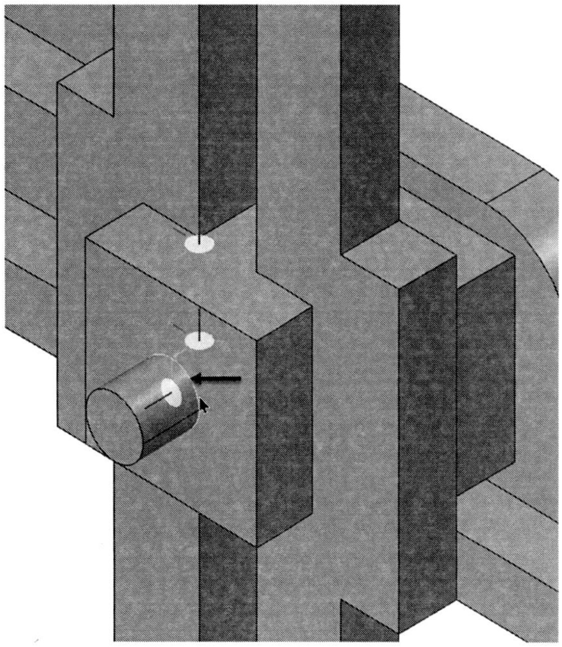

3. Select the circular edge of the crank, as shown below.

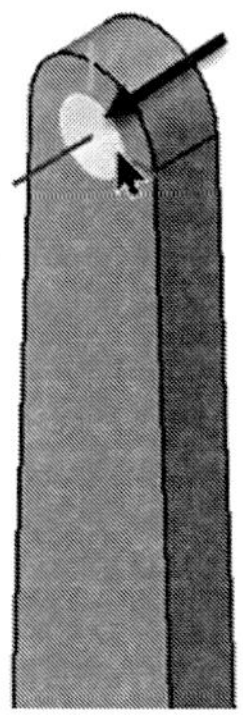

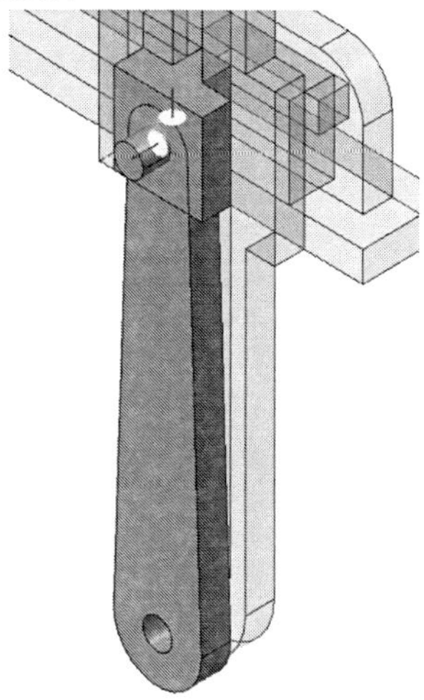

4. Click the **Reverse** icon to reverse the orientation of the crank.

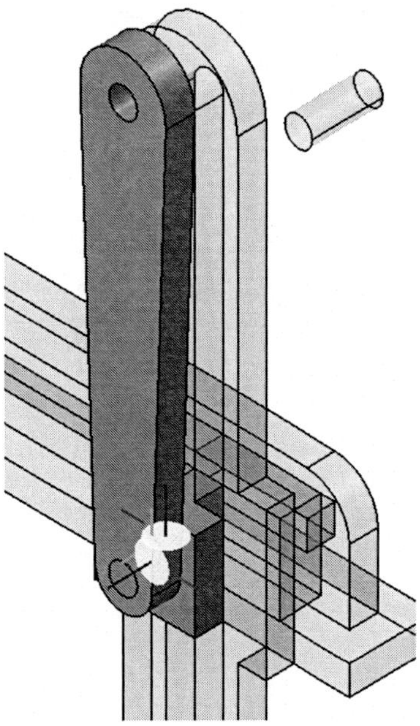

5. Click **OK.**
6. Click and drag the crank to check the revolute joint.

Creating the Rigid Joint

1. Click **Rigid Joint** icon on the **Assembly Joints** toolbar.
2. Rotate the model view and select the circular edge of the Crank, as shown.

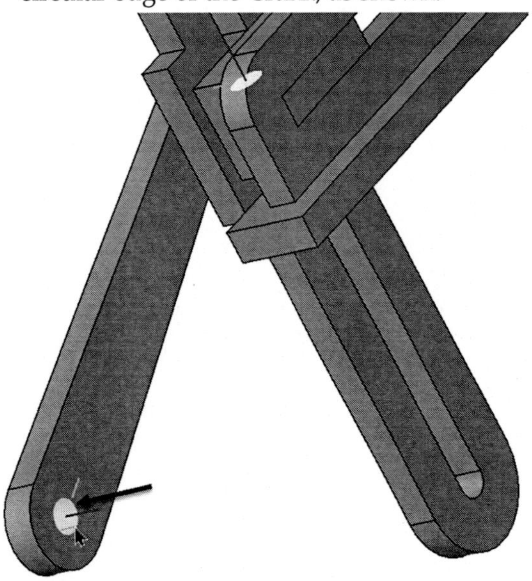

3. Select the circular edge of the pin, as shown.

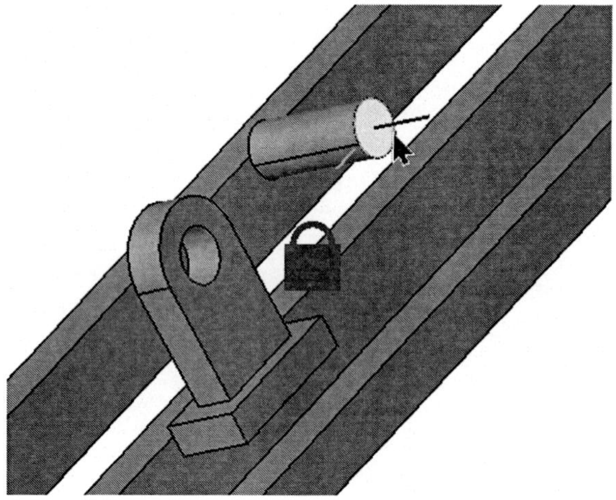

4. Click **OK**.

Adding more assembly joints

1. Click **Revolute Joint** icon on the **Assembly Joints** toolbar.
2. Select the circular edge of the Pin.

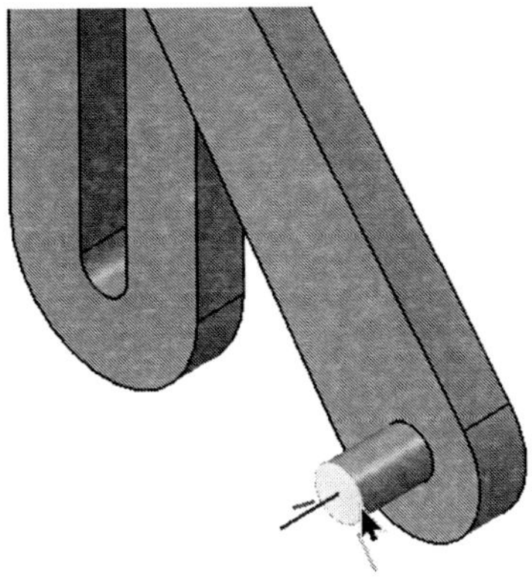

3. Select the circular edge of the Pivot.

4. Click **OK**.

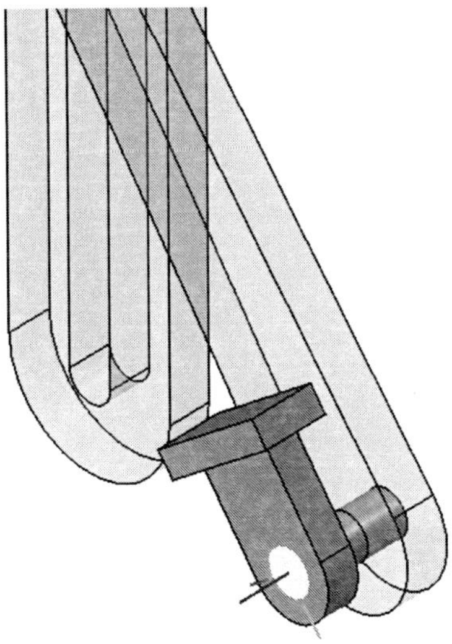

5. Click and drag the Pivot to the location, as shown.

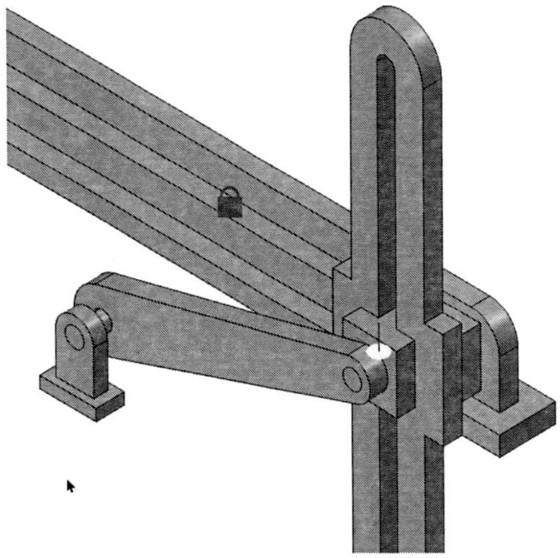

6. Click **Distance Joint** icon on the **Assembly Joints** toolbar.
7. Rotate the model view and select the bottom face of the Base component, as shown.

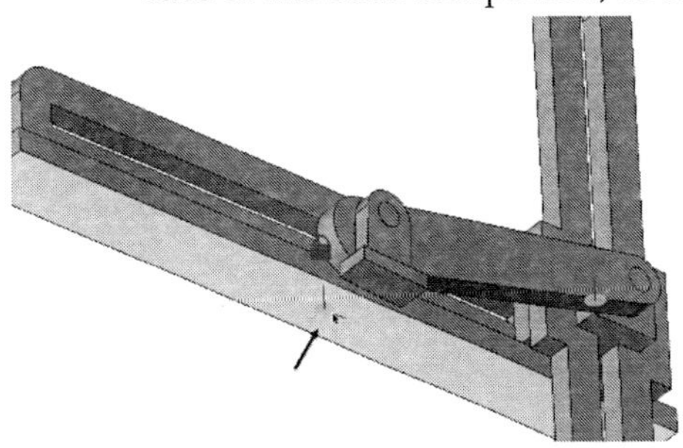

8. Select the bottom face of the Pivot, as shown.

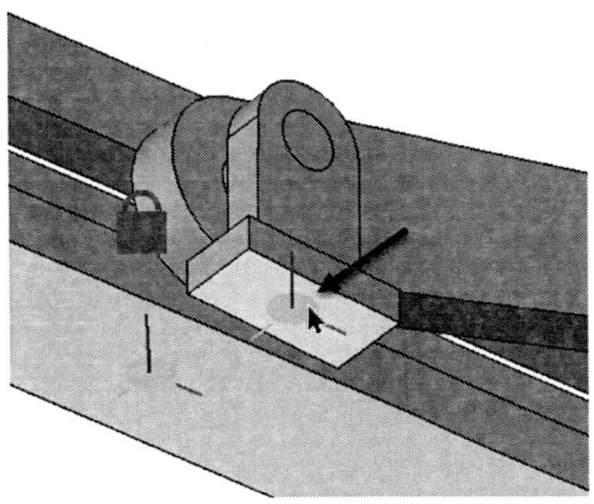

9. Type **0** in the **Distance** box and click **OK**.

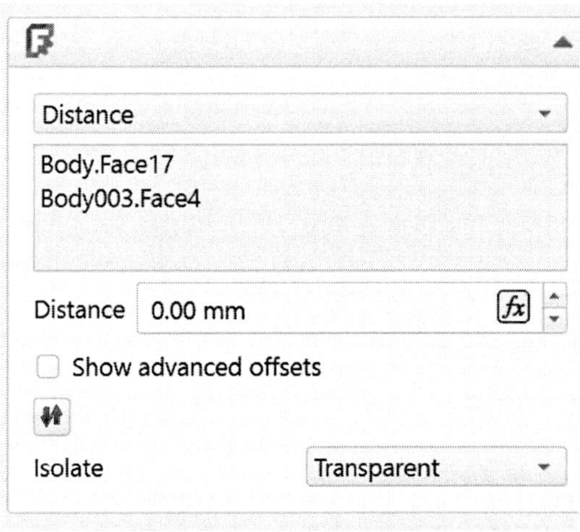

10. Click the **Model** tab and expand the Body and Body003 nodes.
11. Turn ON the origins of the Body and Body003 by clicking the eye icons located next to them.

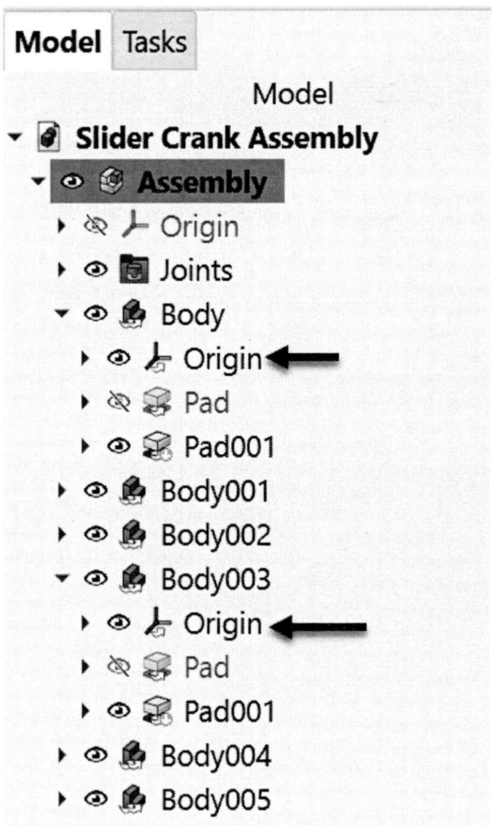

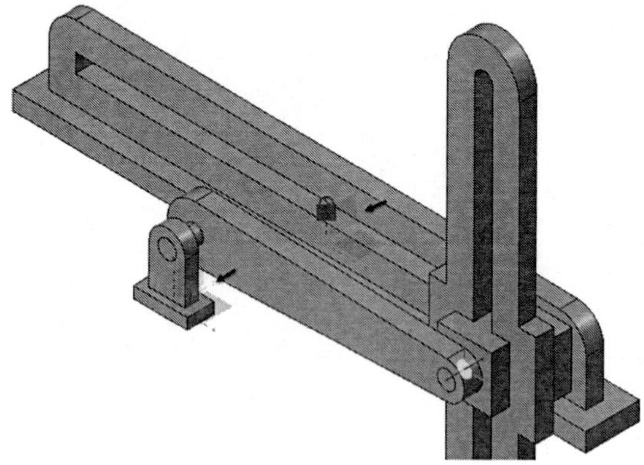

12. Click **Distance Joint** icon on the **Assembly Joints** toolbar.
13. Select the YZ-Plane of the Base component.
14. Select the YZ-Plane of the Pivot.

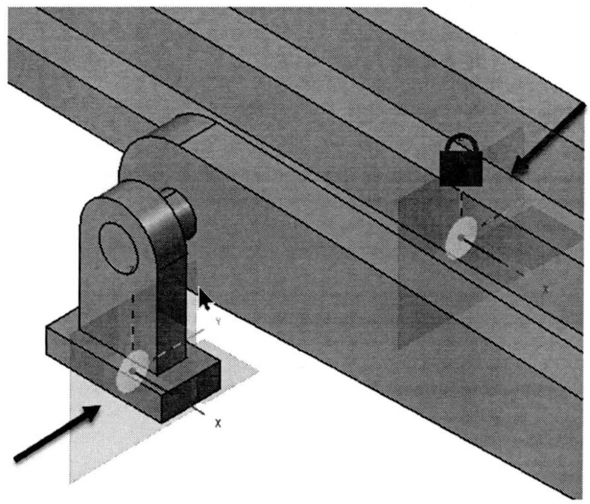

15. Type **0** in the **Distance** box and click **OK**.

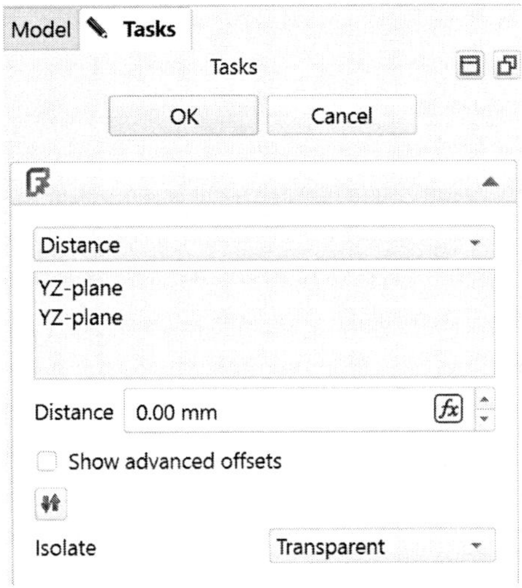

16. Click and drag the crank and notice that the slider moves along the slot.
17. Save and close the assembly and its parts.

Index

9 788199 428980

Printed at Repro India Ltd.